LESSONS FROM THE FINANCIAL CRISIS

The *Robert W. Kolb Series in Finance* series provides a comprehensive view of the field of finance in all of its variety and complexity. The series is projected to include approximately 65 volumes covering all major topics and specializations in finance, ranging from investments, to corporate finance, to financial institutions. Each volume in the *Kolb Series in Finance* consists of new articles especially written for the volume.

Each *Kolb Series* volume is edited by a specialist in a particular area of finance, who develops the volume outline and commissions articles by the world's experts in that particular field of finance. Each volume includes an editor's introduction and approximately thirty articles to fully describe the current state of financial research and practice in a particular area of finance.

The essays in each volume are intended for practicing finance professionals, graduate students, and advanced undergraduate students. The goal of each volume is to encapsulate the current state of knowledge in a particular area of finance so that the reader can quickly achieve a mastery of that special area of finance.

LESSONS FROM THE FINANCIAL CRISIS

Causes, Consequences, and Our Economic Future

Robert W. Kolb

The Robert W. Kolb Series in Finance

WILEY

John Wiley & Sons, Inc.

For general information on our other products and services or for technical support,
please contact our Customer Care Department within the United States at (800) 762-2974,
outside the United States at (317) 572-3993 or fax (317) 572-4002.

Wiley also publishes its books in a variety of electronic formats. Some content that
appears in print may not be available in electronic formats. For more information about
Wiley products, visit our Web site at www.wiley.com.

Library of Congress Cataloging-in-Publication Data:
Lessons from the financial crisis : causes, consequences, and our economic future /
Robert W. Kolb, editor.
     p.   cm. — (The Robert W. Kolb series in finance)
  Includes bibliographical references and index.
  ISBN 978-0-470-56177-5 (cloth)
  1. Financial crises.   2. Global Financial Crisis, 2008-2009.
3. Financial crises—United States.   I. Kolb, Robert W., 1949–
  HB3722.L476 2010
  330.9—dc22   2009050964

Printed in the United States of America.

10 9 8 7 6 5 4 3 2 1

For Lori, as always.

Contents

Acknowledgments

M y first appreciation extends to the authors who contributed to this volume. Their work is what makes the volume possible. I would also like to thank Pamela Van Giessen, Jennifer MacDonald, and Melissa Lopez at John Wiley & Sons for their editorial expertise and their support and encouragement of the idea behind this volume. I also wish to thank Sarah Schaffer for her expert editing work.

Editor's Note

Taken together, the articles in this volume present a deep understanding of the financial crisis we have all endured. But it must be acknowledged that even this volume is only an initial view. The financial crisis has been an economic event that ranks second only to the Great Depression. Like the Great Depression, the financial crisis will be studied for decades to come, and yet greater understanding of these recent events is sure to emerge with further study. Much of that understanding will come from the further researches of those represented in this volume.

Introduction

Many efforts to understand the historical origins, the present meaning, and the future trajectory of the present financial crisis rely on the Great Depression as a touchstone. For some, the Great Depression serves merely as a metaphor, while others try to use that great historical event as a reliable guide to our future. While the current financial crisis differs greatly from the Great Depression, there is at least one important similarity—those who are enduring the crisis struggle to understand the event even as it evolves, and many will continue to study the crisis for decades to come.

Already many popular and journalistic books on the crisis have appeared and gained considerable attention. Some are quite good and make fascinating reading. Yet the broad scope of these books and their focus on drama and personalities implies that they cannot provide the definitive word on the crisis. Far from the limelight of the best-seller list and television interview shows, an entirely alternative literature continues to develop, a literature that will ultimately be of more value in understanding the crisis than the rapidly produced and impressionistic accounts that already sit on bookstore shelves.

Lessons from the Financial Crisis: Causes, Consequences, and Our Economic Future aims to bring to the attention of the general public an understanding of the conceptual underpinnings of the issues that lie at the heart of the crisis. Objective conceptual studies of the crisis are being produced mainly by academics and economists at government agencies, and this research is directed toward policy makers and academic economists. Not surprisingly, much of this thought and study is not accessible to a wider public because the work is often highly mathematical, uses complex econometric techniques, and appears in academic journals. The core idea of *Lessons from the Financial Crisis* is to bring the broader meaning of this contemporary research to a wider audience, and to achieve this now, rather than at the leisurely academic pace of the usual publication outlets.

This book consists of 78 articles written specifically for this volume. Almost all of them present the conclusions of more formal studies that are in preparation by professional economists. In the writing of these articles, every care has been taken to reduce academic jargon and superfluous technology and thus to focus on the broader meaning of the specific discoveries of the underlying research. As such, this book is really about understanding the financial crisis, why it began, how it developed, its effects on people, its implication for our economy, and its broader ramifications for our society.

The articles are arranged into eleven broad sections:

1. Overview of the Crisis
2. Causes and Consequences of the Financial Crisis
3. Borrowers
4. The Process of Securitization
5. Risk Management and Mismanagement
6. The Problem of Regulation
7. Institutional Failures
8. The Federal Reserve, Monetary Policy, and the Financial Crisis
9. Implications of the Crisis for our Economic System
10. International Dimensions of the Financial Crisis
11. Financial Solutions and Our Economic Future

OVERVIEW OF THE CRISIS

The discussion in this first section takes the broadest overview of the crisis. For example, most analysts believe that leverage played a pivotal role in causing the crisis. But do perhaps the roots of the crisis lie in the very nature of our society? One paper in this section considers whether the tendency toward excessive leverage lies in the very nature of liberal democracy. Another article focuses on the important role of subprime mortgages in the crisis, but argues that the problems that arose in the mortgage market are but a symptom of deeper structural and politico-economic problems of present-day globalized capitalism, rather than the primary cause of the crisis. Another contribution asks: "Should we have seen it coming?" and argues that the present crisis is a rerun of previous crises from which we have failed to learn our lessons.

CAUSES AND CONSEQUENCES OF THE FINANCIAL CRISIS

The second section moves to consider more proximate causes of the crisis and to evaluate the emerging consequences of the crisis for our economy and our lives. In retrospect, it does seem clear that housing prices in the United States rose to unsustainable extremes, and one article in this section argues that this "asset bubble" interacted with financial innovation to create a disaster of a proportion beyond that which could have been created by either factor alone. In the rush to understand the causes of the crisis, it is not surprising that many initial analyses were faulty. One paper debunks various "myths of the subprime crisis" and concludes: "The subprime crisis was building for years before showing any signs and was fed by lending, securitization, leveraging, and housing booms."

To some extent, the cause of the crisis can be traced to good intentions of government policy: the urge to extend the perceived benefits of homeownership to a portion of society for which owning a home has always been out of reach. One of the consequences of this well-intentioned effort was the inflicting of financial harm on exactly those families that were supposed to benefit. But beyond that effect, the crisis has had great societal effects with a tremendous socialization of risk and the saddling of our society with a debt burden of enormous proportions.

BORROWERS

Beyond controversy, problems in the housing market lie at the heart of the broader financial crisis, and at the heart of the housing market lie those who borrowed to buy homes. This section considers the role of borrowers, and most specifically subprime borrowers, in fomenting the crisis. Of course, one cannot speak of millions of borrowers in a meaningful way without taking into account their individual differences. Furthermore, some of the borrowers contributed to causing the crisis, while many others were simply victims. Without doubt, still others of these subprime borrowers unwittingly contributed to causing the crisis and yet fell victim to the crisis as well.

One simple development appears to have had a profound effect on borrowers and the generation of the crisis. As one article in this section shows, automated underwriting systems greatly accelerated the loan approval process and reduced the cost of making loans. The cost savings of this automated process made it profitable to lend to borrowers that were previously not attractive. As a result, loan origination expanded considerably.

Predation in subprime lending has garnered considerable emotional attention. As some articles in this section explain, many subprime borrowers were the victims of *predatory lending,* in which mortgage brokers and lending institutions profited by putting naïve borrowers into homes and mortgages that they could not afford. Yet at the same time, other borrowers engaged in *predatory borrowing,* or mortgage fraud, in which they acquired homes by misrepresenting their financial capabilities and their intentions for the property.

THE PROCESS OF SECURITIZATION

The securitization of mortgages consists essentially in purchasing mortgages, collecting them into a pool, and then selling securities that give ownership to portions of the cash flows from that pool of mortgage. The first mortgage securities were merely *pass-through certificates* that gave each holder a fractional ownership of all of the payments from the pool of mortgages, and this simple method of securitization worked quite well for decades.

In recent years, financial innovation in mortgage securitization proceeded to create many more types of securities based on pools of mortgages. It is not too much to say that the payments from mortgage pools were "sliced and diced" into ever more complicated and obscure packages called a *collateralized debt obligation,* or a CDO. The actual valuation of these securities quickly becomes extremely difficult as the securities become more complex. Yet this entire process of securitization played a tremendous role in the mortgage market and in the broader financial crisis.

Partially due to the obscurity of these instruments and the difficulties in assessing their true value, it appears in retrospect that there was a tremendous underpricing of risk. Because these convoluted securities were overpriced, given the true risks they have proven to embody, losses were tremendous when defaults on the underlying mortgages started to bloom and markets eventually began to realize just how risky these securities actually were.

Beyond the complexity of the securities, the movement from the old simple *originate-to-hold* model of mortgage production to the *originate-to-distribute* model had a tremendous effect. In the originate-to-hold model, a lender, typically a local bank or savings and loan, would lend to a home buyer and hold the mortgage for the life of the loan. By contrast, in the originate-to-distribute model, the lender makes the loan with no intention of holding the mortgage, but rather with the plan of selling the mortgage into the securitization process. As articles in this section explain, this new way of originating mortgages involved a change in incentives for various participants in the mortgage origination process that has proven to be extremely perverse. For example, a lender planning to hold a mortgage among its own assets will ensure that the borrower can pay as promised, but if the mortgage is to be originated and sold immediately, the borrower's capacity to pay becomes a matter of limited importance if not indifference.

RISK MANAGEMENT AND MISMANAGEMENT

Before its humbling in the subprime and broader financial crisis, contemporary finance prided itself on its sophistication in evaluating and managing risk. The failures of those methods of risk analysis and management are now painfully apparent. The articles in this section appraise the errors in risk management and look to ways to improve the process.

In recent years, financial analysis has become increasingly sophisticated and much more mathematical. These complicated techniques, it now seems, failed to capture the true risk of mortgage-backed securities. There is now a painful reassessment of those techniques, and the immediate future is sure to witness less reliance on these more sophisticated techniques. In spite of stunning failure, it also seems clear that these mathematical techniques can be very useful, so the question becomes how to harness the benefits of greater analytical power without becoming the mere captive of these sophisticated models.

One risk management flaw that is now apparent can be characterized as an *outsourcing* of risk management to credit rating agencies, such as Standard & Poor's, Moody's, and Fitch. Due to analytical errors and perverse incentives, it now seems clear that these agencies wildly overstated the safety of many mortgage-backed securities. Yet while these credit agencies deserve much criticism, so do those investors who failed to take responsibility for their own risk assessment. Again in retrospect, it now seems clear that many investors were foolish and irresponsible in taking a triple-A rating from the credit agencies as a green light for investing without any further inquiry.

THE PROBLEM OF REGULATION

Perhaps the most frequently hailed cause of and presumed remedy for the financial crisis turns on regulation. According to one facile analysis, deregulation caused the entire problem, and what is needed is more regulation. The truth is more complicated, of course. The articles in this section consider the role of regulation, its absence, and the failure of regulators to enforce existing regulations.

Some analysts regard the structure of housing regulation as a prime cause of the crisis, as the United States has had a policy that goes back to the Great Depression of encouraging ever more widespread home ownership. Furthermore, if one looks at the institutions that took the largest and most foolish risks, many of them are the most particular creatures of government, such as large commercial banks and government-sponsored entities such as Fannie Mae and Freddie Mac.

But it must also be acknowledged that beyond poorly designed regulation, relaxation of regulation and weak regulatory enforcement also played a role. For example, the SEC loosened its capital requirements for investment banking firms in 2004, and the firms responded by increasing their leverage and risk. Similarly, in 2000 the government abjured the regulation of credit default swaps, a locus of enormous losses in the crisis that threatened profound systemic risk.

INSTITUTIONAL FAILURES

Beyond the debacle in regulation, other social and economic institutions failed to perform and thereby contributed to the economic crisis. In a disaster of the proportions that we are experiencing, there is plenty of blame to share, and the articles in this section analyze some of the particular institutional problems that were revealed in the crisis.

For example, the last 20 years have seen the rise of financial firms of enormous power and scope. We might call them financial conglomerates. Citicorp, for example, gave a signal of its size on November 18, 2008, when it announced that it would lay off 50,000 employees worldwide. (A firm that can suddenly discover it has 50,000 extra people on the payroll must be a very large firm indeed!) As one article in this section indicates, a very large proportion of the losses in the crisis were concentrated in these financial conglomerates.

Economists and finance academics come in for a share of the blame as well for emphasizing elegant models divorced from real-world markets. In addition, the financial crisis has revealed serious problems in corporate governance, including management conflicts within firms that arise between senior and mid-level managers. Also, government-sponsored entities, a peculiar kind of firm that is private, yet government-created and government-controlled, have failed their social function as well.

THE FEDERAL RESERVE, MONETARY POLICY, AND THE FINANCIAL CRISIS

By mid-2009, the financial crisis seemed to be waning, and there was talk of "green shoots" in an economy on the mend. Virtually every day the Federal Reserve System was in the news taking action in one way or another to help end the crisis. But the Federal Reserve, according to many analysts, helped to foment the crisis, then played a critical role during the crisis in limiting its effect, and presently may be laying the foundation for more financial problems in the future by the very actions that it has taken to avert disaster.

Some charge that a Federal Reserve policy of easy money and artificially low interest rates before the crisis helped to fuel a mortgage borrowing binge that led directly to the housing crisis and its subsequent systemic effects. On that analysis, the Fed receives a share of the blame for actually causing the crisis.

While the Fed may have played a role in starting the crisis, it has been a major actor in efforts to preserve the financial system from ruin as well. Ben Bernanke, chairman of the Federal Reserve Board, has, in effect, been training his whole professional life for this crisis, as he made his academic reputation by his work on the Great Depression. Now as things seem to be more stable and it looks like a total financial collapse has been averted, the Fed has received considerable credit for its decisive action in response to the crisis as it deepened. Yet new worries arise from the Fed's apparently successful actions in saving the financial system. The very actions that helped avert disaster during the crisis may be laying the foundation for serious inflation in the months and years to come.

IMPLICATIONS OF THE CRISIS FOR OUR ECONOMIC SYSTEM

The financial crisis has certainly revealed that our financial and economic system is not as robust as we may have thought previously. Externally imposed stresses often reveal the weaknesses in all kinds of structures, from bridges to marriages, and that has certainly been the case as the financial crisis has tested our entire economic system.

The articles in this section consider some of the specific weaknesses revealed by our financial crisis. Perhaps foremost among these is the exposure of our complex and worldwide financial system to systemic weaknesses in which a challenge to one part of the structure is transmitted quickly to other parts that were previously thought to be well-insulated from the original source of trouble. The Asian financial crisis and the collapse of Long-Term Capital Management in the 1990s provided early signals of the systemic linkages in our era of financial globalization, but that point has been driven home with tremendous force by our present crisis.

New linkages have been revealed as well, perhaps most strongly in two areas: credit contagion and counterparty risk. For example, the rumors that swirled around Bear Stearns brought the creditworthiness of its obligations into doubt, but the uncertainty attached to Bear quickly brought suspicion upon the other firms with which it dealt, for if Bear failed to honor its obligations, what would be the effect on the financial soundness of its creditors? Closely related to this issue of credit contagion is the idea of counterparty risk, a problem that emerged as particularly acute with credit default swaps. When AIG was revealed to have written insurance against the failure of many firms that were suddenly defaulting, what was the implication for the counterparties to those swaps, and what was the likely effect on them if AIG defaulted on its own promises? As the financial crisis revealed with amazing suddenness, fear of insolvency traveled as fast as rumor itself.

INTERNATIONAL DIMENSIONS OF THE FINANCIAL CRISIS

According to some, the navel of the world lies somewhere between New York City and Washington, D.C. While such an idea may be false in general, it does seem that the United States played a special role in the crisis with its huge subprime mortgage market and its insatiable demand for investment from abroad. Even if the financial crisis illustrates the idea of American *exceptionalism*, the crisis spread far beyond its shores, as the articles in this section demonstrate.

While the subprime crisis and mortgage problems may have been most acute in the United States, other countries clearly experience similar problems. Furthermore, the flight from risk experienced in the United States was a phenomenon shared around the world.

Perhaps the experience of Iceland was the most acute among all nations. Improbably, the financial crisis that may have been centered in the United States eventually spread to overwhelm the entire banking system of Iceland and to lead to a virtually complete, if temporary, economic collapse.

FINANCIAL SOLUTIONS AND OUR ECONOMIC FUTURE

The articles in this section provide a summing up along with some signposts toward an improved future. After any disaster, one of the first tasks is a damage assessment, and articles in this section analyze the long-term economic implications of the crisis. But beyond that evaluation, other articles point the way forward to responses and possible solutions.

So often, efforts to respond to one problem lay the foundations for the next, so there is a great incentive to respond to the present crisis in a way that will not create future harm. The process of securitization of home mortgages has been revealed to contain disastrous flaws. Yet, securitization offers the promise of a financial system that can stimulate the flow of credit in a socially beneficial manner. This raises the question of how the process of securitization might be restructured to avoid the pitfalls of the previous system while preserving the benefits of heightened credit availability.

There can be no doubt that more financial regulation is on the way, but how should that be structured? Credit default swaps have been virtually unregulated to date, but potential default on these agreements was shown to have very serious systemic implications. It is now virtually certain that those instruments will be regulated. Some have called for the banning of naked credit default swaps—a naked swap being one in which one of the contracting parties has no underlying financial risk or exposure. But such a proposal may merely reveal a lack of understanding of how such derivatives markets operate and the valuable role that market makers perform in bearing risk for those who wish to transfer it away.

Fannie Mae and Freddie Mac are government creatures in at least two important senses. First, before the crisis, they were regulated by the federal government, and the president appointed a plurality of their board members. Second, during the crisis, they were taken into conservatorship, and their obligations were guaranteed by the federal government. The government presumably does not want to operate these firms forever. As a consequence, it will need to create a new regulatory structure for these firms that will be more successful than the previous failed system.

LESSONS FROM THE FINANCIAL CRISIS

PART I

Overview of the Crisis

CHAPTER 1

Leverage and Liberal Democracy

GEORGE BRAGUES
University of Guelph-Humber, Toronto, Canada

Whenever something out of the ordinary happens that is destructive and menacing, the search for causes is almost always intense and prolific. That has certainly been the case with respect to the financial crisis of 2007–2009. Whether on CNBC, the pages of the *Wall Street Journal* and the *Financial Times*, the economic blogs, or even explanatory videos on YouTube, plenty of culprits have been put forward.

One reads and hears about greedy mortgage brokers and bankers whose pay structure encouraged them to cut ethical corners and undertake huge risks. Some point the finger at conflicted rating agencies that assigned Triple-A ratings to financially engineered junk. Free market skeptics cite an ideologically driven policy of laissez faire on the part of regulatory bodies. Defenders of free markets counter with the government's push to increase home ownership among the middle classes and the poor through Fannie Mae, Freddie Mac, and the Community Reinvestment Act. Economists speak of informational asymmetries arising from the enhanced opportunities for mortgage originators to unload credit risk onto the investing community as a result of securitization. Others note the dramatic expansion of complex securities like credit default swaps. Many have singled out the excessively low interest rates maintained by the U.S. Federal Reserve (Fed) between 2002 and 2005. But those who think the American central bank has been made a scapegoat refer instead to the Asian savings glut that kept long-term interest rates low even as the Fed subsequently endeavored to tighten monetary policy.

No doubt, whenever the definitive account of the crisis is written by future historians, it will have to integrate several of these factors. Yet it will need to go beyond these, if only because the story would otherwise be restricted to proximate causes. We would overlook the ultimate source of our difficulties, the larger historical forces that laid the foundation for the proximate causes that mainstream commentators have emphasized. Interestingly enough, it is the heterodox traditions of economics that have most acutely sensed the need to probe deeper. Marxists, for example, interpret the crisis as the culmination of the financialization of capitalism, a phenomenon manifest in the growth of debt that has been gathering force since the 1970s in response to the systemic dearth of investment opportunities.[1] Austrian economists, by contrast, blame that financialization, with all of its attendant ills, on the political monopolization of money and credit creation rendered possible by the institution of central banking.[2]

Though these explanations rightly focus on the prevalence of debt—and more precisely the leverage that it reflects—they still do not get to the root of the matter. To reach that, we have to go back and familiarize ourselves with the original principles of the liberal democratic order within which our financial markets operate. That regime was founded on the recognition of leverage as a morally legitimate tool of economic life. Precisely because of tendencies inherent in liberal democracy, however, leverage was progressively freed from virtually all traditional moral limits. This has left present-day capitalist economies all too prone to financial calamities of the sort in which we now find ourselves.

By *liberal democracy*, what is meant here is not simply a particular form of government in which the ultimate authority for public decisions rests with a majority of the populace. Liberal democracy is more comprehensively understood as a mode of social organization that first arose in the seventeenth and eighteenth centuries in northern Europe—the very place and time, not uncoincidentally, when historians typically date the first great financial crises. Over the succeeding centuries, it spread globally such that its principal representatives now include the United States, Canada, much of Europe, Japan, Israel, Australia, and New Zealand, though it has also made significant inroads into Asia, Africa, and Latin America. The defining feature of the regime is its neutral stance about the meaning and purpose of human life. Accordingly, the state's role in a liberal democracy is limited to enabling individuals to pursue their fulfillment as they each see fit in an environment of freedom and equality, subject to the proviso that no harm is done to others in the process.

The early philosophic exponents of liberal democracy, such as John Locke and Adam Smith, well understood that this political vision implied freedom of commerce. They also realized that most people, once given the liberty to pursue whatever their hearts desired, would end up defining their happiness in terms of material affluence. Consequently, they saw that the chief occupation of governments in liberal democracies would become, as indeed it has, the promotion of economic growth, best accomplished through the establishment of a market society.

Among the biggest obstacles to this, however, was the long-standing moral inhibition against the lending of money with interest—originally known as usury. If the financial crisis has taught us anything, it has reminded us of the overwhelming importance of credit in market societies. Without loans—which few would obviously make without the provision of interest—individuals could not readily make large purchases to obtain appliances, cars, and houses. Firms would find it hard to manage the operational challenges posed by the level of receipts and outlays not being perfectly synchronized at each and every point in time. When those outlays happen to be for capital goods, firms must wait for a substantial period before generating a return on their investment. Of course, equity finance would still be an option, but it would be cumbersome to acquire shares in a person's future income stream. Though companies do issue stock to fund their activities, the rate of return that must be offered to investors has to be higher, given the risks entailed in being placed last in line to claim the firm's cash flows. Many with savings to deploy will shy away from such risks, while numerous capital projects with lower prospective rates of return, yet still above what a debt financing would cost, will go unfunded.

While denounced in biblical texts, the moral case against lending had its authoritative philosophic articulation in the writings of Aristotle and St. Thomas Aquinas. Aristotle, the Greek philosopher of the fourth century B.C. whose opinions on a wide variety of subjects were considered truth well into the seventeenth century A.D., insisted that money is naturally intended to be used in exchange for goods. But earning interest on loans is against nature precisely because it involves producing money from money.[3] In the thirteenth century, Aquinas elaborated and refined this argument by distinguishing between goods whose use consists in their own consumption and those in which the employment does not destroy the thing. Food is an example of the first, a house of the second. No moral problem is entailed in selling the use of the house for a period of time, as opposed to the house itself, as there would be a distinct item of value being exchanged. It would be unjust, though, to charge for both a hamburger and the use of the hamburger. These not being separable; one would be selling a good that literally does not exist. Aquinas held that money is more analogous to food than a house, in that its defining feature is for it to be used up in purchases of goods. Consequently, a lender that trades money now in return for anything more than that same amount of money later is essentially fleecing the borrower.[4]

By the time the architects of liberal democracy addressed the issue of usury, the Aristotelian-Thomist picture of money as a consumption item essentially incapable of reproducing itself had already been ruptured. In the sixteenth and seventeenth centuries, a few of the late scholastic thinkers noticed that money could be deployed so as to become productive of more money.[5] The budding of commerce in the Renaissance, with merchants and bankers adopting various stratagems to evade the usury laws, gave practical confirmation of money's generative aspects. Thus, in 1691, John Locke could almost take it as a given that money, by furnishing the means to engage in profitable trade, has productive uses and that interest is the price for securing this benefit.[6] Adam Smith would subsequently reiterate this point in *The Wealth of Nations* (1776), as well as observing that legal prohibitions on loaning at interest merely force borrowers to pay higher rates to compensate the additional risks to the lender of being prosecuted and not having the courts available to enforce their debt contracts. It was left to Smith's admirer, Jeremy Bentham, to give the coup de grâce to the traditional teaching on interest in his *Defense of Usury* (1787). His chief argument was that individuals, being the best judges of their interest, should be free to contract for loans at any rate they deem appropriate. Finance had finally found a home in liberal democracy.

With this, the use of leverage gained a decisive encouragement, insofar as individuals and firms could now take on higher debt-equity ratios without moral qualms. Initially, though, this acceptance of leverage was qualified. In coming to the moral defense of interest lending, Smith set the condition that rates not be permitted to go much above the market level for low-risk debt. Were it to go above that, Smith feared, a sizable portion of the credit available would end up in the hands of profligate consumers and Pollyannaish entrepreneurs. Much of the capital stock built up by society over generations would go to waste. Not only that, Smith promoted the virtues of prudence and frugality in his moral and economic writings, as did Benjamin Franklin, the eighteenth-century American statesman and inventor, whose counsel remained an influential part of the self-help literature well into the nineteenth century.

But the individual freedom that liberal democracy extols would ultimately act as an acid on these caveats. To a people attached to the ideals of personal autonomy and self-expression, deferred gratification will inevitably be felt as a harsh restraint. Plato presciently set down this feature of democracy two and a half millennia ago.[7] Time preferences thus changed, with present goods becoming more preferred to future ones. People saved less and willingly assumed more debt in pursuit of their life goals.

This additional debt had to come from somewhere. Critical in enabling this was the consolidation of fractional reserve banking in the nineteenth century. This institution arose out of the money warehouses run by goldsmiths, where people could deposit their gold and silver in return for warehouse receipts, which in turn functioned as currency in the marketplace. Within these depository establishments, it was soon noticed that there was no need to continually have every ounce of gold and silver available for potential redemption, since relatively few receipt holders demanded their metal on any given day. Even when they did, there were often others making new deposits to balance the outflow. Profits could be increased, it was figured out, by issuing more warehouse receipts than the stockpile of metals would cover.[8] The excess receipts could be lent and interest charged. To this day, this same operation continues, except that banks now extend loans on the basis of deposits of government-issued notes rather than precious metals. But the essence of fractional reserve banking remains in that deposits are only a proportion, and a slight one at that, of the loans outstanding.

That the morality of this practice elicits so little discussion is arguably the most astounding fact of modern finance. With the bulk of the money lent out having virtually no underpinning except for the creative powers of the banking system, the people exchanging actual goods and services for this currency are, for all intents and purposes, receiving nothing intrinsic in return. A profound injustice seems to be at work here. Then again, this would be to assume Aquinas's premise that money is to be understood in terms of its substance.

Bentham's critique of Aquinas' usury teaching provides the foundation upon which liberal democracy is built and tells us, instead, that money is to be viewed solely as a utility. If the economic success of liberal democratic economies since the nineteenth century is any indication, this utility must be acknowledged. What the currency manufactured out of the fractional reserve system effectively does is allow society to raise the level of investment beyond what its members, through the sacrifice of present consumption, have managed to save. For the borrower, it is less a matter of being entrusted with the stewardship of some portion of the capital stock and more about receiving some paper and electronic tokens. The borrower is then ordered to perform the following command: go out and harness the natural and human resources at your disposal so as to produce goods and services for which other people will be willing to trade at least enough paper and electronic tokens to pay off your loan. Finance has evolved to the point that it does not merely grease the wheels of trade and bring savers and investors together; it actually drives those wheels, its chief business having become to create a vast chain of obligations to generate more value out of the world.

The problem with this arrangement, of course, is that it places a lot more stress on getting the allocation of credit right. With all the leverage involved, all it takes is a slice of the loan portfolio to go bad for depositors to lose confidence and threaten runs on the banks. When that prospect beckons, banks are forced to call in loans and restrict credit even to borrowers in good standing, wreaking havoc on the economy. As everyone knows, this is pretty much what has just happened as a result of the bad bet the financial system made on subprime mortgages.

Despite this risk, no growth-addicted liberal democracy could have ever been expected to morally question the extra economic torque that fractional reserve banking provides through its pyramiding of savings. As demonstrated time and time again, whenever the viability of the system was threatened in crises past, a fix has always been preferred, whether in the form of government-backed deposit insurance, the extensive regulation of financial institutions, or the formation of a central bank to serve as a lender of last resort to troubled banks. Needless to say, these are far from perfect solutions, since they encourage banks to be more audacious, secure in the knowledge that the government will extend them a lifeline should they run into difficulties.

What also explains the maintenance of fractional reserve banking is the power it confers on governing classes to manage the money supply, particularly when all of the commercial banks are overseen by a central bank. By changing the short-term rate of interest, adding or subtracting from commercial bank reserves, or modifying the required ratio of loans to deposits, governments can try to smooth the vicissitudes of the economy and hinder recessions. There was a time when this was not expected of governments, when the franchise was limited to a male, property-owning elite that could withstand downturns in the economic cycle. That changed in the twentieth century when the franchise was extended to every adult person. The upshot of all this is that a significant part of the responsibility of ensuring the optimal allocation of credit is shifted to the central bank. And no matter how much independence the latter might theoretically have, democratic political pressures will influence the central bank to err on the side of preventing recessions and, in the process, potentially setting up the next leverage-induced boom—precisely what the Fed did in keeping interest rates low for so long after the bust of the dot-com bubble.

None of this is to say that liberal democracy is fatally flawed. The political alternatives are surely worse on balance. What the financial crisis does help clarify, though, are the full terms of the bargain that liberal democracy made in originally according its moral stamp of approval to leverage.

NOTES

1. John Bellamy Foster and Fred Magdoff, *The Great Financial Crisis: Causes and Consequences* (New York: Monthly Review Press, 2009).

2. Thomas E. Woods, Jr., *Meltdown* (Washington: Regnery Publishing, 2009).

3. Aristotle, *The Politics*, trans. T. A. Sinclair (New York: Penguin, 1981), Bk. I. x.

4. Thomas Aquinas, *On Law, Morality, and Politics*, 2nd ed., trans. Richard J. Regan (Indianapolis: Hackett Publishing, 2002), 148–151.

5. Alejandro A. Chafuen, *Faith and Liberty: The Economic Thought of the Late Scholastics* (Lanham, MD: Lexington Books, 2003), 122–125.

6. John Locke, *Some Considerations on the Consequences of the Lowering of Interest and Raising the Value of Money*, http://socserv.mcmaster.ca/econ/ugcm/3ll3/locke/consid.txt.

7. Plato, *The Republic*, trans. Allan Bloom (New York: Basic Books, 1968), 561c–561e.

8. See Murray Rothbard, *The Mystery of Banking* 2nd ed. (Auburn, AL: Ludwig Von Mises Institute, 2008), 85–94, and George Cooper, *The Origin of Financial Crises* (New York: Random House, 2008), 47–50.

ABOUT THE AUTHOR

George Bragues is program head of business at the University of Guelph-Humber in Toronto, where he teaches economics, philosophy, and politics. His research interests include business ethics as well as the sociopolitical aspects of finance. He is an occasional contributor to the op-ed pages of the *Financial Post* in Canada. His articles have been published in such venues as the *Journal of Business Ethics, The Independent Review, History of Philosophy Quarterly, Episteme,* and *Business Ethics Quarterly.*

CHAPTER 2

A Property Economics Explanation of the Global Financial Crisis

GUNNAR HEINSOHN
University of Bremen

FRANK DECKER
Sydney, and University of Bremen*

THE BREACH OF BAGEHOT'S FIRST PRINCIPLE OF CENTRAL BANKING SPARKED THE CRISIS

Neither bare greed nor market failure are at the bottom of the global financial crisis, but the altruistic belief by the world's two largest central banks that interest rates close to zero would benefit businesses and workers struggling after a crisis. In 1994, the Bank of Japan cut its discount rate below 2 percent. It reached 0.1 percent in September 2001, and it has remained at under 1 percent ever since. In November 2002, the Federal Reserve Bank (Fed) dropped its target rate to 0.75 percent and in December 2008 operated near 0.25 percent. Those who malign bankers as predators may as well punish their dog for eating the prime steak left outside on the BBQ plate. Who would pass up such a bargain?

But what is interest, and why must the interest rate not equal zero? This can best be illustrated using the nineteenth-century example of a private and note-issuing commercial bank. Here, the bank issues money in the form of promissory notes when it advances credit, often in secured loan contracts. The borrower receives the bank notes, which represent claims over the property of the bank. The bank receives a loan asset secured by the borrower's property and an interest payment.

Property is involved on both sides. The bank has to reserve a certain amount of property, the bank capital, to serve as a buffer for unforeseen losses and to ensure the redeemability of its notes on demand. This capital is now burdened because it must not be activated a second time, sold, or encumbered. Similarly, the borrower's

---

*The authors would like to thank Ulf Heinsohn for his support on an earlier version of this work.

property is now encumbered as security for the loan. Both bank capital and loan collateral back the note issue.

Property economics[1] argues that interest arises because the bank must be compensated for the burdening of its capital in this process. In other words, interest is demanded for losing *property premium,* an immaterial yield that accrues from an asset that is unencumbered and free. This is so because unencumbered property allows owners to raise funds against it when needed to protect their solvency.

Both the property of the bank and the property of the borrower remain in the possession and use of the parties during the loan contract. Only the immaterial property side, represented by legal rights over the bank property and the borrower's collateral, are relevant for this transaction. If the bank property was farmland, the bank would continue to till the soil and to harvest the crop. The bank money is derived from the fence around the field and not the soil. There is no sacrifice from the postponement of consumption involved.

As long as private banks issue their own money, of course, nobody must remind them to demand interest, because as proprietors liable for their note issue, they need to protect their capital and solvency. The proprietor's property premium and associated interest rates represent market rates.

The underlying principles are the same for a modern central banking system. They include:

- Central banks create money in repurchase agreements and loans with commercial banks secured by eligible collateral or by purchasing assets outright. Like commercial banks, they have balance sheets with assets, liabilities, and equity, and require capital (equity) to back the note issue against unforeseen losses.
- Commercial banks provide bank funds to businesses[2] through loans and need bank capital to protect their solvency.
- Businesses provide property as collateral for loans or to ensure that their property remains unencumbered through loan covenants. Even *fiat* money, if sound, is always backed by valuable property titles. Any departure from this principle, for example, by simply monetizing government debt, will destroy a currency.

The central bank, like the private note-issuing bank, must be compensated for the burdening of its capital by interest. This holds even in a crisis, when a central bank acts as the lender of last resort providing funds to illiquid but otherwise solvent borrowers, which was first shown by the originator of central banking theory, Walter Bagehot. He formulated the first principle of central banking: "First: That these loans [by the central bank] should only be made at a very high rate of interest. This [...] will prevent the greatest number of applications by persons who do not require it."[3]

Unlike private note-issuing banks driven by market forces, modern central banks have the power to violate Bagehot's principle. As a government organization seemingly protected from insolvency risks, and as the monopoly provider of funds for interbank settlement, a central bank can force interest rates below market rates or even waive interest payments altogether. That this power creates a moral dilemma was most clearly demonstrated in the 2008 global financial crisis. While near-zero rates were a short-term reprieve for many, they not only deprived the bank owners (taxpayers) of the compensation due to them, but also produced a severe financial crisis.

FROM CHEAP MONEY TO THE SUBPRIME FIASCO

A normal bank transaction begins with an innovative business well endowed with collateral. Businesses are compelled to borrow so they can invest and stay in competition. They don't borrow a second time for the mere reason that the interest rate suddenly dropped. In this respect, variations in the interest level can largely be neglected as determinants of investments. If, however, the starting point is central bank money offered at ultra-low rates, commercial banks have to track down alternative investment opportunities to remain competitive.

Banks invest the unexpected plum credits by buying every title yielding a higher profit than the mini-interest charged by the central bank. The resulting credit boom creates extra demand, and the price of all investment classes will suddenly rise. This was reflected in the strong growth of outstanding U.S. private sector debt, which between 2002 and 2007 increased by 59 percent, reaching 294 percent of GDP.[4]

But what are these appreciations, really? If breakfast eggs were an asset class, a farmer would thank the Lord for the doubling of the price of his hens, but his wife would understand that only their price has been inflated. After all, she isn't collecting a single egg more than before from the coop.

The U.S. financial system created a special masterpiece so it could profit from cheap central bank money. It discovered asset classes that never existed before. Subprime and "Alt-A" borrowers, customers with impaired credit or limited income or asset verification, could now take out mortgages. By 2006, subprime and Alt-A mortgages, largely originated by nonbanking institutions like mortgage brokers, made up 40 percent of all U.S.-issued mortgage-backed securities.[5]

Using the tried-and-tested techniques of securitization, high-risk subprime mortgages were turned into low-risk AAA-rated debt. Structuring a pool of mortgages into tranches allows typically 90 percent of the underlying total debt to be rated AAA/AA (by rating agencies who receive their fees from this service), with other tranches exposed to the initial losses. Subprime assets rated AAA/AA became, in turn, attractive assets for pension funds, commercial banks, and special vehicles like conduits and structured investment vehicles (SIVs) all over the world. The latter engage in credit arbitrage by issuing short-term asset-backed commercial paper (ABCP) to fund high-yielding long-term assets.[6]

The rest is now known. The Fed let its interest rate move up to 6 percent (May 2006), and mortgage interest rates had to follow suit. The new asset-free class of debtors defaulted on their nonrecourse loans, and the growing number of foreclosures depressed house prices. In 2008, senior tranches of securitized subprime claims had lost most of their value, and global markets for these securities collapsed. Credit enhancement through securitization proved to be illusory as defaults in the underlying subprime mortgages were highly correlated.

When money market funds became concerned about the underlying quality of the assets, the market for ABCP collapsed, and conduits and SIVs could no longer roll over their paper. Some sponsoring banks were forced to provide liquidity to these vehicles by taking subprime assets back on their balance sheets. Other banks were caught warehousing out mortgages as part of the securitization process or had made direct investments in mortgage and asset-backed securities.[7] Banks, in turn, were forced to write down their assets and were teetering toward insolvency, with liabilities at risk of exceeding assets because their equity capital, their property, could not balance asset writedowns any further. Banks hoarded liquidity to maintain their ongoing business. Funds in the interbank market other than overnight maturities became very difficult to obtain.

THE BREACH OF BAGEHOT'S SECOND PRINCIPLE OF CENTRAL BANKING THROUGH LOWERING COLLATERAL STANDARDS AND AGGRESSIVE BALANCE SHEET EXPANSION

Bagehot's second principle states that central banks must accept all good banking collateral in a crisis. This seeks to distinguish illiquid but solvent from insolvent borrowers and has become central bank doctrine ever since. Bagehot was drawing on the lessons from the English crisis of 1825–1826 when the Bank of England had successfully stayed the panic by widening eligible collateral from commercial bills to first Exchequer bills and later to goods.

However, more than good collateral is required. Bagehot also noted that the "*amount* of the advance" was the "the main consideration" for a central bank. Bagehot's objective was the "efficient use" of the bank reserve against all good securities consistent with the safety of the bank.[8] A central bank should not make advances "by which the Bank will ultimately lose."[9] His second principle therefore implies that neither a commercial bank nor a public institution should supply cash to insolvent borrowers or take risks out of proportion to its capital.

While initially following central bank doctrine and providing easier access to loans secured by a wider range of eligible collateral, the Fed during 2008 relaxed its collateral standards in ways not followed by other major central banks. Eligible collateral could now include problem assets like nonagency securities backed by subprime mortgages,[10] investment grade securities,[11] and shares and debt below investment grade (junk).[12] Since October 2008, the Fed has suspended the need for collateral altogether by purchasing unsecured commercial paper outright.[13]

In parallel with relaxing its collateral standards, the Fed expanded its balance sheet in ways not seen before. Federal Reserve System assets[14] increased from $906 billion on July 2, 2008, to $2,250 billion on November 12, 2008, now including a large amount of riskier nongovernment assets, while the holding of Treasury bills decreased dramatically. This balance sheet expansion coincided with the Fed finding it increasingly difficult to influence the federal funds rate. For the period of November 2008, the effective rate averaged around 0.25 percent, a whopping 0.75 percent below the 1 percent target rate. Monetary policy through interest rate targeting had come to an end.

The ballooning balance sheet also resulted in a decline of the total Federal Reserve System capital, which dropped from 3.8 percent of total assets (August 8, 2007) to 1.9 percent (November 12, 2008). In comparison, a commercial bank under the old Basel I accord would have required a capital of about 8 percent of its nongovernment guaranteed asset holdings. This means that a mere 1.9 percent loss on the Fed's assets would wipe out all capital. In such a situation, losses will have to be balanced with proceeds from selling portions of the Fed's equity capital. Once this property is exhausted, the central bank is technically bankrupt and has to be recapitalized by the taxpayer.

The popular belief that the Fed has the unlimited ability to print money and cannot go bankrupt, reinforced by the Fed chairman Ben Bernanke, who noted that "the balance sheet of the central bank should be of marginal relevance,"[15] overlooks the often-hidden capital requirements of the recently created Fed facilities. At least for the Term Asset-Backed Securities Loan Facility (TALF),[16] the need for additional bank capital is now officially acknowledged. The $200 billion facility will receive a $20 billion investment from the U.S. Treasury.[17]

One could argue that while quick in their response, the Fed's strategy has also increased the risk of providing insolvent institutions with credit without requiring them to fix the structural problems that created the need for liquidity in the first place. Thus, central bank action is at the risk of prolonging a crisis and wasting public funds that would have been better used to wind up, nationalize, or recapitalize troubled institutions at the outset. This is precisely the moral hazard Bagehot sought to avoid.

But the missing capital is only one dimension of the problem. A central bank expanding its balance sheet by accepting risky collateral or engaging in unsecured lending also puts the country's currency at risk. An excess supply of money not backed by sound central bank assets cannot be withdrawn by asset sales, competes to buy supplies, and bids up prices. Inflation is the inevitable long-term consequence.

THE STATE AS PROPRIETOR OF LAST RESORT

A central bank can provide illiquid but solvent commercial banks, still in the disposition of unencumbered property, with liquid funds. But the central bank cannot help insolvent banks because it cannot provide them with new property to serve as bank capital or compensate losses. Neither can the central bank provide the missing collateral for bank loans to near-insolvent businesses.[18] This limits the ability of a central bank to influence the duration and severity of a crisis. Japan's experience showed that even a massive increase in the money supply does not necessarily reach companies because banks will foremost seek to refinance themselves in a crisis, reducing capital requirements by replacing private sector loan assets with risk-free central bank balances and government securities. This makes clear that there is no real economy operating in its own right that only needs money to facilitate its barter operations, even if all the Nobel prize–winning economists say so. There are only businesses tied to credit contracts. *Real economy* just means fulfilling countless credit contracts between bank and business proprietors. If one side is missing, the system collapses. This network of millions of creditor-debtor contracts forms the hand outlined by Adam Smith, but which he could only conceptualize as being something enigmatic and invisible.

Once there are too many property-denuded banks, an institution is required that does not provide money but fresh property, against which bank funds can be created. This institution is the State. It has to step in as the proprietor or co-proprietor of last resort so that it can at least re-enable banks to lend to companies that are still capable of pledging collateral. After the fall of Lehman Brothers, the panic was stayed only after European countries announced programs to recapitalize or part-nationalize their banks, and many governments guaranteed bank liabilities. The United States has eventually had to follow this agenda.

A functioning system thus requires sufficient property in the form of bank capital to absorb losses (banks and central banks), collateral to secure loans (companies), and adequate levels of interest rates to compensate for the burdening of property in this process. The 2008 crisis has always been beyond the reach of a lender of last resort.

NOTES

1. See Gunnar Heinsohn, *Privateigentum, Patriarchat, Geldwirtschaft* (1984); Gunnar Heinsohn and Otto Steiger, *Eigentum, Zins und Geld* (1996); Gunnar Heinsohn and Otto Steiger, *Eigentumsökonomik* (2006); Gunnar Heinsohn and Otto Steiger, "Interest and Money: The Property Explanation," in *Handbook of Alternative Monetary Theory*, eds. Philip Arestis and Malcolm C. Sawyer (2006); and Otto Steiger, "Property Economics versus New Institutional Economics," *Journal of Economic Issues* 40(1): 183–208 (2006).

2. Nonfinancial.

3. Walter Bagehot, *Lombard Street* ([1873], 1962) 97.

4. Federal Reserve statistical releases.

5. Office of Federal Housing Enterprise Oversight, Mortgage Market Note 07-1, September 6, 2007.

6. See, for example, Susan Black and Chay Fisher, "The Asset-backed Commercial Paper Market," *Reserve Bank of Australia Bulletin*, January 2008.

7. See, for example, Adrian Blundell-Wignall and Paul Atkinson, "The Subprime Crisis: Causal Distortions and Regulatory Reform," *Reserve Bank of Australia*, Conference 2008.

8. Bagehot, preceding n. 3, 101.

9. Ibid., 97.

10. For example, in the Term Action Facility (TAF), see Federal Reserve Discount Window, Frequently Asked Question No. 5. www.frbdiscountwindow.org/ (accessed June 7, 2009).

11. Through the Term Securities Lending Facility (TSLF).

12. A certain proportion is permitted in triparty repo system collateral. See Edmund L. Andrews, "Fed Loosens Standards on Emergency Loans," *New York Times*, September 15, 2008.

13. Through the Commercial Paper Funding Facility (CPFF).

14. See Federal Reserve statistical releases.

15. Remarks by Governor Ben S. Bernanke before the Japan Society of Monetary Economics, Tokyo, Japan, May 31, 2003.

16. Providing loans secured by auto loans, student loans, credit card loans, small business loans, and commercial mortgage-backed securities.

17. See Federal Reserve Bank, TALF White Paper, March 3, 2009.

18. Heinsohn and Steiger, *Interest and Money*, preceding n. 1, 505. The severe New South Wales 1843 depression provides an interesting example in which the missing collateral was created by legal enactment. This resolved the crisis. See Frank Decker, "The Legal and Economic History of the Lien on Wool and Stock Mortgage Act 1843 (NSW)," *Legal History* 12(2): 151–175 (2008).

ABOUT THE AUTHORS

Gunnar Heinsohn is professor emeritus of social sciences at the University of Bremen (Germany). E-mail: gheins@uni-bremen.de. He holds summa cum laude doctorates in sociology (1974) and economics (1982). The second dissertation tried to replace the barter paradigm of economics by the property paradigm. In the *Encyclopedia of Economic Works*, covering the most inspiring 650 economic treatises of altogether 460 authors worldwide from antiquity to the twentieth century, the author is the only living scholar of the German-language area represented with four different studies (cf. D. Herz and V. Weinberger, eds., *Lexikon ökonomischer Werke*, Düsseldorf, 2006, 186–190). The money explanation of *Eigentum, Zins und Geld* [Property, Interest, and Money, Reinbek, 1996, 4th ed., 2006; with Otto Steiger (1938–2008)] is, since 2000, represented by the Geldmuseum der Deutschen Bundesbank (Money Museum of the Bundesbank, Frankfurt am Main) in juxtaposition with the money views of Aristotle, Adam Smith, Bernard Laum, and John Maynard Keynes.

Frank Decker holds a Ph.D. in physics from the Free University of Berlin, a master's of applied finance from Macquarie University, Sydney, and is currently completing a Ph.D. in economics from the University of Bremen. He continues to work internationally as a management consultant. Decker's academic work has focused on monetary theory and the interaction between property law and economics. Specific work includes the *2008 Global Financial Crisis*, the study of Australia's early monetary history, the New South Wales 1843 depression, the legal history of the Lien on Wool and Stock Mortgage Act of 1843 (NSW), and the role of security rights for economic development.

CHAPTER 3

Of Subprimes and Sundry Symptoms: The Political Economy of the Financial Crisis

ASHOK BARDHAN
Haas School of Business, UC Berkeley

The U.S. economy is in the grip of what looks to be the worst financial and economic crisis since the Great Depression. Starting with the downturn in the housing market and rising foreclosures, the crisis spread to Fannie Mae and Freddie Mac, the government-sponsored enterprises, and to investment banks and other financial entities holding dodgy assets backed by collapsing real estate. Once the entire financial system was infected with the subprime virus, the health of the real economy took a turn for the worse. At present, unemployment is higher than at any time in a quarter century, and there is no silver lining on the economic horizon. A number of other, related issues of concern, while in abeyance right now, also keep surfacing. They include the ever-present disruptive impact of globalization, in the more recent avatar of sustained global imbalances, and the ongoing churning in the labor market brought about by offshoring. Is it a coincidence that so many concerns and issues have erupted simultaneously, and is there a connection, however tenuous, between them?

A key contention of this short piece is that subprimes are a symptom of deeper structural and politico-economic problems of present-day globalized capitalism, rather than the primary cause of the crisis. These problems include the incentive-institutional structure of the financial system, the nature of distributed globalization (finance centers and entrepots in the West, production centers in the East; savings generation in the East and debt accumulation in the West), the ideological environment of not just laissez faire but laissez financier, and the governance contradictions facing the political management of global economic development.

THE EVOLUTION OF THE CURRENT CRISIS

The genesis of the current crisis lies, as is so often the case, in developments related to the real estate sector, more specifically the housing segment. In any country, the health of the housing sector is a critical indicator of the health of the economy at large. This is due to a number of factors, including the size of the sector, its linkages to other sectors in the economy, and the social and political implications of an industry that is interwoven into the fabric of the family, the community, and the economy. Housing and home ownership have long constituted one of the bedrocks of the U.S. social and economic system. Starting with the Depression era, the housing finance system has evolved into a host of agencies designed ultimately to keep the cost of home ownership low, stable, and secure. From a sociological point of view, home ownership is believed to promote community-based values, nurture respect for law and order, and provide a stake in the stability and prosperity of the system; from an economic point of view, the hopefully steady appreciation of home values, the main asset held by a household, would provide the basis for a continuous increase in consumption, the driving force, or engine, of the U.S. economy.

The past decade saw an unprecedented run-up in house prices. Historically low interest rates created a conducive financial environment for borrowing, while lax lending standards set up an accommodating institutional setting for subprime and dodgy loans. In 2006, the last year of the housing boom, the share of subprime mortgages in total mortgage originations reached 20 percent, compared to only 6 percent in 2002. Over 80 percent of these loans were promptly pooled and securitized by private financial institutions, a higher proportion than the relatively more creditworthy mortgages securitized and backed by Fannie and Freddie. This process of securitization, while doing an admirable job of generating liquidity for lumpy, nonliquid assets, did not just disperse risk but also succeeded in distancing mortgage originators from the ultimate investors in mortgage securities. The risk-attenuating benefits of securitization failed to offset the new informational costs generated. Ultimately, it led to risk doubly compounded—the most inexperienced and risky borrowers were sought out and offered mortgages on sometimes disingenuous and deceptively easy terms; these mortgages were precisely the ones that were securitized, leaving investors in far-off lands holding securities they knew little about, and whose funds now generated more mortgages and higher house prices.

By the second half of 2006, prices had peaked in most U.S. urban housing markets. Over 14 million new mortgage loans were originated, and the total amount of home mortgages outstanding crossed $10 trillion by the end of 2006, having doubled in a little over five years. By the end of 2006, prices started declining, and sales weakened. Early 2007 witnessed significant increases in defaults and foreclosures, and a number of financial companies started filing for bankruptcy. By summer, the crisis had spread to the larger financial system with the emergence of a general credit and liquidity crunch, widening spreads of interest rates in the private markets above U.S. government bond yields, collapsing transactions in derivatives, and a disappearing market for loans of all kinds. Mounting losses in the financial sector continued in 2008, with Bear Stearns an early victim. The first apogee of the crisis was reached with the stocks of Fannie Mae and Freddie Mac plummeting over several days in July and ultimately losing over 80 percent of their value. The months of September and October saw hectic activity in financial markets and in corridors of power, with the failure of Lehman Brothers turning out to be a rude wake-up call. Ever since then, the policy establishment has lurched from one initiative to another, with monetary easing, a fiscal stimulus, and financial bailout being the linchpins. The economy has not budged much. At the same time, through all this maelstrom of activity, the plight of homeowners and the burgeoning problem of foreclosures has yet to receive the same level of policy intensity directed at it.

SUBPRIMING THE FINANCIAL PUMP

The collapse of the subprime mortgage market heralded the unraveling of the seamy aspects of the entire financial system. While subprime loans have been the focus of attention and denunciation, we should be clear that not the entire universe of subprime loans is necessarily socially harmful. Leniency in the strict rationing of bank credit, as well as institutional arrangements that lower mortgage costs give people who would otherwise find it difficult to get a mortgage the opportunity to own a home. Neither is a bump up in home ownership rates necessarily an adverse economic or social event. Indeed, U.S. housing policy shows that subsidies work; wealth inequality in the United States would be even higher were it not for the significant level of home ownership. The point, however, is that the recent uptick in ownership rates was not a result of a deliberate, constructive social policy but a phenomenon born of other structural motivations embedded in the system.

Among economic and financial causes one can also cite the savings glut in emerging economies channeled to the United States through the medium of international capital flows, and leading to excessive liquidity and low interest rates. The phenomenon of global imbalances is partly due to a global shortage of creditworthy debt instruments, in contrast to the abundance of U.S. Treasuries. Intricately intertwined with all this is the role of the United States as the guarantor of last resort and as a financial entrepot, and of the dollar as the numeraire par excellence.

The cheap money environment fostered a frantic search for higher returns, leading to higher risk taking and high leverage (huge debts on the buying side), as well as corner cutting (on the selling side). Securitization, the influx of new investors, and an incentive structure that rewarded new deals meant that dealmaking, debt dispersal through sequential transfers of investments, and derivatives of derivatives proliferated. The velocity of turnover of these instruments and their opaqueness were exemplified by the attitude: "Let someone else be left holding this toxic stuff when the ceiling comes crashing down." The bandwagon effect led to a swift and prolonged bubble in housing, as well as in other asset classes. The sustaining fuel for this towering house of cards was the steady and robust growth in house prices, and at the first sign of weakness in the housing market, the entire structure began to unravel.

The complex character of some of the financial instruments served to hide the feeling that a subtle subversion of the financial system was under way. The fundamental objectives of finance—allocation of savings to investors, risk mitigation, and hedging and insurance activity—were being undermined not just by routine speculation but by naked gambling. For example, trades in credit default swaps between parties with no insurable interest is tantamount to a gamble; any separation of the economically relevant party—the one with an insurable interest—from the transaction deprives the act of larger economic purpose and value.

OVERGLOBALIZATION

It may be easier to appreciate the virulence and speed with which the crisis has spread if we recognize that in addition to domestic overfinancialization, there was perhaps international overglobalization. While overfinancialization could be seen in the increase in the size of financial assets relative to the real economy (GDP), overglobalization was evident in ever-larger trade and capital flows.

A large part of the new trade volumes generated were a result of diversion from potential consumption by domestic consumers to consumption by consumers halfway across the world. There is an ongoing debate in China, for example, whether the economic wisdom of having nearly a 40 percent share of exports in GDP has served the developmental goals of the country well. At least some of the blame for income inequality, lopsided development, and consumption stagnation in that country can be laid at the feet of the overgrown external sector. Global financial flows also exploded over the last decade. Massive U.S. current account deficits were financed by China, Japan, and oil-exporting countries. The U.S.-China globalization axis may have been critical but by no means was it the only game in town. Reckless lending by Western banks to Eastern European clients drove much of the importing frenzy in those countries. In addition to trade generated by underlying patterns of global specialization and competitiveness, it seemed as if it was finance that drove and propelled international trade. A bubble in the financial sector was accompanied by a bubble in globalization. Indeed, double-digit declines in real national variables are so rare that declines in 2009 projected export volumes of more than 30 percent, as in the case of Japan, Korea, and Taiwan, make one wonder about the bubble-like nature of the underlying demand.

STRUCTURAL FACTORS

Over the years, preference for an economic ideology that stresses an asset-ownership-based model of compensation and standard of living, rather than one based primarily on salary or wage-based earnings has been promoted as a pillar of the ownership form of a market economy. The heightened notion of a stake-in-the-system leads to the daily obsession with stock markets, housing prices, and other assets, regardless of the often-minuscule share of equity owned by most people, and is stoked by some economists who extol the virtues of an ownership society to the detriment of fair, living wages, which is the foundation of any sustainable economic order. The credit-fed boom in housing created illusory wealth to the tune of trillions of dollars. While an asset price bubble can impart a transient feel-good glow, it seems that the financial sector has now transitioned to fulfilling a systemwide need for sequential bubbles as a key avenue to generate windfall profits in the absence of any dramatic innovations or productive investments taking place in the economy. The excessive risk-taking and the proliferation of speculative instruments belies the traditional role of the financial sector and reflects a mismatch between fund availability and productive and profitable investments in the developed world. At the macro-level of the economy, the bubbles are justified as long as they are in an inflating mode, since they boost consumption driven by borrowings against the paper wealth created.

Following the money trail is yet another way of uncovering the motivating factors underlying the political economy of the crisis. Alan Greenspan, the former Fed chairman, kept interest rates low for a considerable length of time, thus mispricing risk across the whole economy, but enabling Wall Street to operate at low cost. One of the key prices in the economy—the price of money itself—was subsidized for the benefit of private equity funds (which rely heavily on borrowed money to fund acquisitions), hedge fund operators (who also take on enormous leverage, that is, operate on borrowed money), and sundry other investors. In effect, the financial system evolved from providing subsidies to the home-owning class to showering subsidies on the investor class. While the cost side was subsidized, there was a mad stampede on the revenue side to find short-term, and in the prevailing gold rush atmosphere, not just high but windfall profit opportunities with the previous highs being the benchmark to be bested, all lubricated by lax regulatory oversight. And, of course, in the case of massive failure and mismanagement, there was to be, as a final gift from the powers that be, a guaranteed taxpayer-financed bailout.

The financial system has long had the peculiar status of being both the dynamic core as well as the Achilles heel of a modern market economy. The weakness springs from the contradiction between the financial system's regulatory needs, and the capacity and propensity for subtle government intervention on behalf of big investors; from the nature of linkages between the nominal variables of the financial system and the ones in the real economy; from the opacity and complexity of money creation and financial structures; and from the potential for recurring asset bubbles. One can confidently conclude that there will be a greater role by the state and government institutions in the future, not just because of the structural likelihood of the recurrence of crises, but also because of the dramatic increase in financial complexity and its regulatory requirements, the increasing range of conflicting interests, and issues of inequality and fairness. In the future, comparative advantage in governance may matter more than that in specific industrial sectors.

In the case of developed economies, the pressure for creation of well-paying jobs because of the phenomenon of offshoring and globalization, and productivity problems associated with increasingly service-oriented economies with their winner-take-all occupations portend serious political problems for governments. The two connecting threads that run through this entire smorgasbord of crises can be simply described as the transformative impact of the rapid growth of emerging economies (India and China in particular) on the one hand, and the weakening role of the U.S. dollar as the fulcrum in the global financial system, on the other (see Exhibit 3.1 for a schematic view of global dollar-denominated capital flows).

The flux in the global financial environment reflects the tectonic restructuring taking place in the global economy. The birth pangs of a new alignment of economic powers are being felt with each hiccup and tremor in financial and currency markets. In this sense, the spreading financial crisis and the global recession can be termed the first major crisis of the era of modern globalization. The need for sound global political management of the crisis will be felt soon enough, since common as well as conflicting interests have to be addressed; giving free market space to emerging economies and their continued growth has to be reconciled with lowered expectations in the advanced countries, and with the end of the bubble-and-currency-based propping up of living standards.

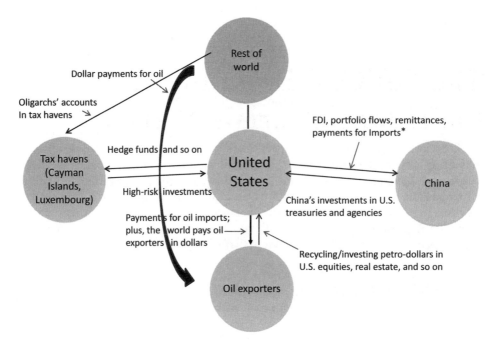

Exhibit 3.1   Global Dollar Flows
*Offshoring involves both FDI (for captive offshoring units) as well as imports.

REFERENCE

Bardhan, A. 2008. "Of subprimes andsubsidies: The political economy of the financial crisis."
    Available at SSRN: http://ssrn.com/abstract=1270196.

ABOUT THE AUTHOR

Ashok Bardhan is a senior research associate at the Fisher Center for Real
Estate and Urban Economics, Haas School of Business, UC Berkeley. He has an
MS in physics and mathematics from Moscow, Russia, an M.Phil. in international
relations from New Delhi, India, and a Ph.D. in economics from UC Berkeley. His
research includes papers on the impact of global economic and financial integration
on real estate; on mortgage insurance, housing finance, and real estate in emerging economies; business process outsourcing and offshoring of R&D and innovative activity; and on the Internet, e-commerce, and real estate. He is a co-author
of a book, *Globalization and a High-Tech Economy: California, the United States and
Beyond* (Springer 2004). His current research projects include the linkages between
the higher education sector and the labor market, globalization and urban ag-
glomerations, and a cross-country study of the determinants of sustainable urban
development.

CHAPTER 4

The Political Economy of the Financial Crisis of 2008

ROGER D. CONGLETON
Professor of Economics and Senior Research Associate in the Center for Public Choice
at George Mason University

GOVERNMENT SUPPORT FOR MORTGAGE MARKETS

In the good old days, mortgages were held by the banks that made loans; so if there were any problems with mortgages, they tended to be concentrated in the banks located in regions with declining housing prices, unemployment, and net out-migration. This changed in 1932 and 1938, when Hoover founded, respectively, the Federal Home Loan Banks (FHLBs) and Roosevelt founded the Federal National Mortgage Association (FNMA or "Fannie Mae"). Their purpose was to add liquidity to the home mortgage market to facilitate home sales. The FHLBs initially provided short-term loans to savings and loan (S&L) banks, whose liquidity was reduced by bank runs and mortgage defaults at the beginning of the Great Depression. Fannie Mae purchased and held mortgages from banks and also insured mortgages, which allowed banks to create more mortgages at lower prices, because the risks associated with mortgage defaults were shifted to Fannie Mae.

Between the various housing policies of the federal and state governments and the rising incomes associated with renewed economic growth after World War II, home ownership rates increased from 43.6 percent in 1940 to 61.9 percent in 1960.

Fannie and Freddie and Mortgage-Backed Securities

The 61.9 percent ownership rate of 1960 was evidently not enough, and the federal government took additional steps to encourage more home ownership. Fannie Mae was privatized in 1968, which meant that a private management company was created to manage the great portfolios of mortgages that Fannie Mae had already purchased. In 1970, the Federal Home Loan Mortgage Corporation (FHLMC, also known as Freddie Mac) was established to make loans and loan guarantees and to create a market for mortgage-backed securities (MBS). Freddie Mac pooled the mortgages that it purchased and sold MBS to investors on the open market. The guarantees and pooling of mortgages by Freddie reduced the risks associated with the purchase of MBS and induced more investors to hold them. This created a new financial market in MBS and further increased the supply of mortgages by introducing a new method of mortgage finance.

The new (private) government-sponsored enterprises (GSEs) no longer had formal backing from the U.S. government, although they were managed partly through government appointees and subject to different forms of government oversight from other firms in financial markets. Most investors nonetheless believed that U.S. taxpayers would back up the GSEs after they were privatized, if need be, which proved to be correct in September 2008.

The implicit backing of taxpayers allowed the FHLB, Fannie Mae, and Freddie Mac to borrow money at lower rates than other banks (about 0.4 percent less, according to Congressional Budget Office estimates). GSEs also faced somewhat different regulatory constraints from ordinary investment banks. They were, for example, exempt from most state taxes and regulations, which also provided an implicit subsidy of approximately a billion dollars. These implicit subsidies to housing (the implicit insurance risk) were not on the federal government's balance sheets, nor were the risks associated with the implicit guarantees of the federal government. No fees were charged for this insurance, and no insurance reserves were accumulated. All these implicit subsidies increased Fannie's and Freddie's advantage over ordinary financial firms, which helped them remain major players in the mortgage market.

Regulations Induced Riskier Mortgage-Backed Securities

After 1992, Fannie Mae and Freddie Mac were required to purchase affordable mortgages from banks, which essentially meant mortgages that did not pass the usual creditworthiness requirement for loans. With affordable housing in mind, the U.S. Department of Housing and Urban Development (HUD) established annual targets for extending loans to underserved areas and for low- and moderate-income housing. These goals for Fannie Mae and Freddie Mac were gradually increased, from 30 percent in 1993 to 55 percent in 2007.

Both Fannie Mae and Freddie Mac met or exceeded their targets, which helped to create a new market in subprime (e.g., substandard) mortgages and mortgage-backed securities. Encouragement to extend such subprime loans continued to be received from HUD administrators under Presidents Clinton and Bush, in part because this allowed housing to be subsidized without the need for additional Congressional approval or funds. The same 1992 act assigned oversight responsibility for the GSEs to an agency of HUD.

OTHER REGULATORY-INDUCED SUPPLIES OF MORTGAGES AND CREDIT

The supply of funds for credit was further increased by a series of regulatory reforms that facilitated the formation of large national and international banking-insurance conglomerates. For example, the Riegle-Neal Interstate Banking Act of 1994 allowed bank holding companies to own banks in several states and allowed the merger of banks from different states. The Gramm-Leach-Bliley Act of 1999 effectively repealed the Glass-Steagall Act of 1935 by allowing bank holding companies to hold insurance and security companies as well as banks. In 2004, a special ruling of the U.S. Securities and Exchange Commission (SEC) allowed the five largest investment banks in the United States to reduce their capital reserves. The SEC allowed these already less regulated banks to become far more highly leveraged enterprises, which allowed them to increase the pool of assets under their control. Within a few years, they jointly controlled $4 trillion in financial assets, but with relatively little net equity.

Another change that initially increased the supply of loanable funds was the use of mark-to-market accounting rules. Revised accounting guidelines (adopted after the Sarbanes-Oxley Act of 2002) required more assets to be valued at current market prices, just as ordinary stock portfolios are. A firm's capital base increases under such mark-to-market rules during times of rising financial asset prices (i.e., during housing and stock market bubbles). This new capital could be sold to others or used as collateral for new loans. Leverage increases rates of return, as long as asset values continue to appreciate, and competition among firms (and employees) tends to favor those earning the highest returns. Expanded use of mark-to-market valuation was broadly supported by financial firms—until the asset bubbles burst.

Delinquencies on residential mortgages were relatively low in the period after the 1992 recession and, if anything, exhibited a slight downward trend through 2005. As long as housing prices rose, the asset values of the houses supporting the subprime mortgages were sufficient (indeed, more than sufficient) to support such relatively risky loans, which together with easy refinancing, allowed relatively high profits for mortgage bundlers and insurers, such as Fannie Mae and Freddie Mac, and also for homeowner speculators. Competition favored firms with optimistic assessments of risk and the growth of loanable funds, because they could loan at lower rates than firms with more prudent assessments.

This allowed a bubble in mortgage-backed securities to be built on top of the bubble in housing prices. Investors around the world were encouraged to hold these relatively safe assets, rather than government securities. Pension funds, mutual fund managers, hedge funds, insurance companies, and state, local, and national governments all held MBS as safe alternatives to U.S. government securities.

Bundling and insuring mortgages can be highly profitable when home prices are rising and default rates are low. Because of the risk-premium effect, bundling subprime mortgages can be much more profitable than bundling prime mortgages—because there is more room for reducing risks through diversification and insurance. New wealth is created by producing less risky assets (MBS), which can be sold to other investors or used as collateral for other loans, which may be used to purchase other securities. Indeed, MBS were often used to purchase mortgages from banks, which held them as capital, instead of their own mortgages.

The demand for safe assets was high and rising during the late 1990s and early 2000s, as the baby-boom generation saved for retirement with 401(k) accounts and foreign holders of dollars generated by high and rising U.S. trade deficits sought profitable places to invest their dollars. The pool of mortgages and MBS thus increased rapidly and became significant elements in investment portfolios and capital reserves of investors and firms worldwide.

Fannie Mae and Freddie Mac continued to be major players in mortgage finance markets, even as private firms of various kinds entered those markets. Together,

Fannie Mae and Freddie Mac issued more than 70 percent of mortgage-backed securities in 2000 and 60 percent of MBS in 2002. The GSEs purchased or guaranteed 84 percent of new mortgages. Indeed, the combined debt and MBS obligations of these GSEs exceeded the total publicly held debt of the U.S. government by $1.3 trillion. Fannie and Freddie remained major players in the mortgage market even as they approached bankruptcy in 2007 and 2008.

POLITICS AND THE SIZE OF THE MORTGAGE MARKET

The politics of government interventions in the mortgage market differs from interventions in many other markets, because of the size of the market and its relative importance to ordinary voters and investors throughout the world. For example, the president of the United States selects about a third of Fannie's and Freddie's boards of directors (5 of 17 and 5 of 18, respectively). Their size and importance have also produced an unusual amount of political and news attention. The archives of the *New York Times* include nearly 10,000 pieces reporting on the regulation and finances of Fannie Mae. Nonetheless, government intervention in the supply side of the mortgage market has never risen to the point of being a central issue in national election campaigns.

The regulatory details are worked out within Congress and HUD, with the assistance of various lobbying groups. Among the most prominent lobbyists are the GSEs themselves and organizations representing commercial banks and realtor groups.

Majority Support

Before the housing bubble burst in 2006 and 2007, it could be argued that the various housing policies of the federal government had broadly advanced the interests of the median voter (who is a homeowner) at the same time that it balanced the interests of an assortment of economic interest groups. The mortgage resale market had become more complex, as more and more sophisticated methods were used to pool revenues from mortgages and create mortgage-backed securities. Many experts believed that the new securities markets increased liquidity and reduced, rather than increased, systemwide risks—although such considerations were of no more concern for the typical voter than the manner in which steel was produced and fabricated for automobiles.

Median house prices rose steadily, with only minor downturns, during the entire postwar period. And after 2000, median house prices rose at a much faster rate than usual: nearly 10 percent a year. In 2004, home ownership rates peaked at 69.2 percent. As long as "it worked," why should voters worry about the details?

Minority Warnings

A variety of congressional hearings were held regarding subprime mortgages, and new regulations were adopted by Congress, although many believed that such regulations had not gone far enough. Concerns were also expressed about the viability and oversight of Fannie Mae and Freddie Mac. Several proposals were made to strengthen and depoliticize their regulation and to increase capital requirements, but none were able to secure majorities in Congress, in part, because of successful lobbying efforts by Fannie Mae and Freddie Mac and, in part, because promoting home ownership was a popular cause.

The HUD mandates to purchase more and more loans from low- and middle-income groups, together with competition from other unregulated mortgage purchasers, induced the GSEs to purchase mortgages from less-and-less creditworthy persons (and mortgage originators) with term structures that were less and less likely to be viable. The risks associated with mortgage-backed securities and their derivatives appeared to be underpriced. There were warnings about a bubble in home prices from a broad cross-section of newspapers and economists, as with Case and Shiller (2003) and Yellen (2005).

Nonetheless, majorities in Congress and two presidents supported the various housing and credit-market policies as cost-effective (and largely off-budget) methods for expanding home ownership and financial markets.

THE END OF THE BUBBLES

The bubble warnings finally proved correct in 2006 and 2007, and housing prices began to fall for the first time in more than a decade. This was the first significant U.S.-wide housing price decline in the postwar period. The decline was much greater and faster than in recent recessions. According to the Case-Shiller index, average U.S. home prices peaked in 2006 and fell by about 18 percent over the next two years. The U.S. Census series on median home prices peaked in 2007 and showed a similar broad decline during 2007 and 2008. Diversifying across regions of the country could not reduce this risk, as average house values fell throughout the United States. (Indeed a few real estate bubbles also burst in other countries at about the same time.)

Although explanations for the existence and bursting of asset bubbles vary, there is little disagreement among economists that the end of major asset bubbles can have real effects on other markets. For example, Case, Quigley, and Shiller (2001) demonstrate that stock market and real estate price fluctuations have significant effects on household consumption levels and that the effect of housing price declines tends to be larger than those of stocks. The 18 percent decline in U.S. home values between 2006 and 2008 was the sharpest in the postwar period and reduced homeowner wealth by more than $3 trillion. The end of the housing bubble had direct wealth effects on private consumption, which produced modest increases in unemployment and increased mortgage defaults in much of the United States.

The reduction in house values and reduced economic growth after the 2006–2007 period made subprime and prime mortgages riskier than in previous years, because the asset value of the house supporting the mortgage was in many cases less than the value of the outstanding mortgage. This, together with the beginning of a modest recession, caused delinquencies to rise, and subprime mortgages were disproportionately represented among those delinquencies. Nearly 25 percent of subprime mortgages were 90 days or more delinquent or in foreclosure in 2008 (Bernanke 2008). As the new subprime loan practices became more widely known, the assumption that residential mortgages were safer than most other loans was replaced with the assumption that they were far riskier than many other assets.

Most mortgages and mortgage-backed securities initially remained relatively low-risk assets as delinquency rates began to climb in 2005, because most were insured by Fannie Mae, Freddie Mac, and other mortgage and MBS insurers. About half of all mortgages and MBS were insured by Fannie Mae and Freddie Mac. Many others were insured by other large private financial firms. As delinquency rates began to exceed the normal range of the post-1992 period in 2007, insurance claims began to increase.

Unfortunately, but perhaps predictably, insufficient reserves had been maintained by those insuring mortgages and mortgage-backed securities, because insurers had evidently assumed that the benevolent national trends between 1995 and 2005 were the new market norm. As the risk of default mortgages more than doubled, the risk of default by insurers also rose. This further increased the risk associated with credit-backed securities, and their value fell rapidly as potential buyers demanded higher and higher risk premiums. This was not simply a cash flow problem that could be solved with a bit of temporary borrowing. As insurer losses accumulated, the stock prices of insurers naturally fell, which meant that they could not raise new money to make their guaranteed payments to MBS holders by selling stock or borrowing supported by the value of equity capital.

The mortgage insurers saw their credit ratings rapidly decline as the credit-rating agencies revised their estimates of expected insurance losses. Several major insurers went bankrupt as their insurance obligations exceeded their assets (Bear Stearns, Fannie Mae, Freddie Mac, and so on).

GOVERNMENT POLICIES AND THE GREAT EVAPORATION OF WEALTH AND CAPITAL

There were $10.4 trillion in outstanding mortgages on one- to four-family homes in 2006, of which $7 trillion worth were held in mortgage pools and trusts supporting mortgage-backed securities (*Statistical Supplement to the Federal Reserve Bulletin,* October 2008, 33). The value of the MBS supported by those mortgage pools would have initially exceeded the value of the mortgage pools themselves, because of the lower-risk premiums paid for securitized mortgages than for the mortgages themselves. The reassessment of risks associated with MBS and their derivatives caused approximately 60 to 90 percent of their value to evaporate, which implied that on the order of $5 trillion of financial wealth (and potential credit) disappeared from the world's financial system. The mortgage market losses were about the same magnitude as the reduction in homeowner equity, but they had larger effects on the real economy because they were concentrated in one very important sector of the economy rather than spread out among households. That concentration also had political consequences (i.e., the various bailouts of 2008 and 2009).

In the end, the proximate cause of the great collapse of the securitized credit market was the end of the housing bubble, which induced an initially mild recession, and the subsequent flight to relatively safe and transparent assets.

Government policies did not cause these adjustments, although the housing, mortgage, and MBS markets were all much larger and more fragile because of programs and regulations adopted by the federal government in previous decades.

REFERENCES

Bernanke, B. S. 2008. Mortgage delinquencies and foreclosures. Speech at Columbia Business School (May 5).

Case, K. E., J. M. Quigley, and R. J. Shiller 2001. Comparing wealth effects: The stock market versus the housing market. *Cowles Foundation Discussion Paper 1335*. New Haven, CT: Yale University.

Case, K. E., and R. J. Shiller. 2003. Is there a bubble in the housing market? *Cowles Foundation Paper* 1089. New Haven, CT: Yale University.

Congleton, R. D. 2009. "On the political economy of the financial crisis and bailout of 2008–2009," *Public Choice* 140: 287–317.

Jenkinson, N. 2008. Ratings in structured finance: What went wrong and what can be done to address shortcomings? *CGFS Papers* 32. Basel, Switzerland: Committee on the Global Financial System.

Yellen, J. 2005. Housing bubbles and monetary policy. Speech at the Federal Reserve Bank of San Francisco (October 21).

ABOUT THE AUTHOR

Roger D. Congleton is a professor of economics and a senior research associate in the Center for Public Choice at George Mason University. Congleton has written and lectured widely on the political economy of public policy. His most recent books are edited volumes: *Democratic Constitutional Design and Public Policy* (MIT Press, 2006) and *40 Years of Research on Rent Seeking* (two volumes, Springer 2009, co-edited with A. Hillman and K. Konrad). Congleton has also served as the Fulbright Distinguished Professor of American studies in Denmark, as the Adam Smith Professor of economics and philosophy at Bayreuth University, and as director of the Center for Study of Public Choice.

CHAPTER 5

The Global Financial Crisis of 2008: What Went Wrong?

HERSHEY H. FRIEDMAN
Professor of Business and Marketing, Department of Economics, Brooklyn College of the City University of New York

LINDA WEISER FRIEDMAN
Professor of Statistics & Computer Information Systems, Baruch College Zicklin School of Business and the Graduate Center, City University of New York

T he current financial crisis, the worst debacle we have experienced since the Great Depression, with millions of jobs lost and trillions of dollars in market value evaporated, did not suddenly appear out of nowhere. An early warning was the savings and loan disaster (1986–1995) in which 1,043 banks failed with a cost to U.S. taxpayers of about $124 billion; it was ignored. A few years later, in several colossal corporate scandals—Enron, Tyco International, Adelphia, WorldCom, and many others—companies used dubious accounting practices or outright accounting fraud to deceive the public and enrich executives. The Sarbanes-Oxley Act of 2002 was enacted to prevent future financial disasters of this nature.

The dot-com bubble of 1995 to 2001 was a different kind of crisis, fueled by irrational spending on Internet stocks without considering traditional business models. Investors did not seem to care about earnings per share or other more traditional measures. Moreover, there were too many companies trying to create online businesses. This bubble was not based on fraud as much as overvaluation of stocks (especially the IPOs) and excessive speculation. The recent housing bubble, on the other hand, which was very much a part of the current financial meltdown, was fueled to a large degree by the ready availability of deceitful mortgages. What was apparent from the dot-com bubble was that prices cannot go up forever—a lesson not learned by the mortgage industry.

In 1998, Long-Term Capital Management (LTCM), borrowed over $125 billion, but had equity of just $5 billion. The financial crisis started by LTCM at that time demonstrated how the entire financial system could be put at risk by a single fund. The Federal Reserve Bank crafted a $3.5 billion rescue package in 1998 to protect the financial markets from a total collapse because of the actions of the hedge fund. LTCM's sophisticated mathematical models were developed by two Nobel laureates—Myron Scholes and Robert C. Merton—who were both members of the board of the hedge fund.

It is time we started to learn from our past mistakes. In a general way, these crises demonstrate what can happen when organizations do not behave in an ethical, socially responsible manner. Here, we examine some specific considerations.

IS THE PURSUIT OF SELF-INTEREST ALWAYS GOOD?

One pillar of mainstream economics is based on the famous saying of Adam Smith in his classic work, *The Wealth of Nations:* "It is not from the benevolence of the butcher, the brewer or the baker that we expect our dinner, but from their regard to their own interest." Smith demonstrated how self-interest and the "invisible hand" of the marketplace allocate scarce resources efficiently.

Today, students are taught that "economic man" (*homo economicus*) acts with perfect rationality and is interested only in maximizing self-interest, resulting in an economic system (capitalism) that is both efficient and productive. For the corporation, self-interest has become synonymous with unconstrained maximization of profits and maximization of shareholder wealth. The famous speech by Gordon Gekko in the movie *Wall Street* is based on the idea that the pursuit of self-interest is good for all of us—"Greed, for lack of a better word, is good. Greed is right."

We often forget that Adam Smith, in his first book, *The Theory of Moral Sentiments,* made it clear that he believed that economic growth depended on morality. In 1937, at his second inaugural address, President Franklin D. Roosevelt stated: "We have always known that heedless self-interest was bad morals; we know now that it is bad economics." Lawrence H. Summers, in a 2003 speech to the Chicago Economic Club said: "For it is the irony of the market system that while its very success depends on harnessing the power of self-interest, its very sustainability depends upon people's willingness to engage in acts that are not self-interested." The financial meltdown of 2008 shows quite clearly what happens when everyone is solely concerned with self-interest.

Closely tied to the pursuit of self-interest is the belief that free markets do not need regulation. Even our so-called watchmen and gatekeepers—corporate directors, investment bankers, regulators, mutual funds, accountants, auditors, and so on—have fallen into the self-interest trap and disregarded the needs of the public.

FREE MARKETS AND THE ROLE OF REGULATION

The federal government did not do a good job monitoring Wall Street. Arthur Levitt, former chairman of the Securities and Exchange Commission (SEC), said: "As an overheated market needed a strong referee to rein in dangerously risky behavior, the commission too often remained on the sidelines." Not only was there a relaxation of enforcement, there was also a reduction in SEC staff. Senator Charles E. Schumer, as well as other members of Congress, believed that the rules had to be changed to encourage free markets and deregulation if the United States were to remain competitive.

The problems began at a 2004 meeting between the SEC and five major investment banks, which wanted an exemption from a regulation that limited the amount of debt they could have on their balance sheets. This would enable them to invest in mortgage-backed securities and credit default swaps (CDS). The SEC agreed to loosen the capital rules and also decided to allow the investment banks to monitor their own riskiness by using computer models to analyze the riskiness of various securities, that is, switch to a voluntary regulatory program. The firms did act on the new requirements and took on huge amounts of debt. The leverage ratio at Bear Stearns rose to 33:1; this made the firm's business very risky since it held only $1 of equity for every $33 of debt.

The Fed could have put a stop to highly risky and fraudulent mortgages by using its power under a 1994 law (Home Owner Equity Protection Act) to prevent fraudulent lending practices. It was obvious that the mortgage industry was out of control and was allowing individuals with very little money to borrow huge sums of money. Washington Mutual, for example, approved almost every mortgage request. Loan officers were encouraged to approve mortgages with virtually no checking of income. The term NINJA loan was used to describe mortgage loans made to people with "No Income, No Job or Assets." Fed chairman Alan Greenspan could also have used the monetary powers of the Fed to raise interest rates and end the housing bubble. Various states did try to do something about predatory lending but were blocked by the federal government. Freddie Mac and Fannie Mae purchased $400 billion of the most risky subprime mortgages. In September 2008, the federal government had to take over both Fannie and Freddie.

Greenspan has admitted that he allowed the markets for derivatives and CDS to go out of control. Warren E. Buffett has called derivatives "financial weapons of mass destruction." Greenspan, on the other hand, felt that "derivatives have been an extraordinarily useful vehicle to transfer risk from those who shouldn't be taking it to those who are willing to and capable of doing so."[1] Greenspan finally admitted at a congressional hearing in October 2008 that he had relied too much on the "self-correcting power of free markets."

CDS were originally developed to insure bond investors against default risk, but they took on a life of their own and were used for speculation purposes. A CDS encourages speculation since the owner of the CDS does not actually have to own the underlying security. This is equivalent to buying fire insurance on someone else's house. The markets for derivatives and CDS became unregulated thanks to the Commodity Futures Modernization Act of 2000. This law was pushed by the financial industry in the name of free markets and deregulation. It also made it virtually impossible for states to use their own laws to prevent Wall Street from doing anything about these financial instruments. No one even knows the exact size of the CDS market; estimates range from $35 trillion to $55 trillion. When American International Group (AIG) was bailed out by the federal government it held almost half a trillion dollars worth of CDS. Insurance companies (supposedly) understand the concept of risk diversification. Thus, the demise of one insured individual has no correlation to the others who are insured by the same firm. Here, the default of one bond was highly correlated to the default of others. Once bonds started defaulting, AIG was in big trouble.

EXECUTIVE COMPENSATION

Richard Fuld, the CEO of Lehman Brothers, earned approximately half a billion dollars between 1993 and 2007; that's quite a bit of money to destroy a solid,

158-year old firm. AIG Financial Products, a 377-person office based in London, nearly destroyed its mother company, a trillion-dollar firm with approximately 116,000 employees. This small office found a way to make money selling CDS to financial institutions holding very risky collateralized debt obligations, making billions in bonuses selling this super-risky garbage security.

One big problem is how compensation was determined at many Wall Street firms. Bonuses made up a huge part of how people were compensated. One individual at Merrill Lynch received $350,000 as salary but $35,000,000 as bonus pay. Bonuses, based on short-term profits, distorted the way incentives work and encouraged individuals to take huge risks. For example, billions in bonuses were handed out by Merrill Lynch in 2006 when recorded profits—an illusion, as they were based on toxic mortgages—hit $7.5 billion. These bonuses were not rescinded after the company lost billions. E. Stanley O'Neal, former CEO of Merrill Lynch, not only collected millions of dollars in bonuses but was given a severance package worth about $161 million when he left the firm.

Some firms are now changing the way bonuses work: the money will be kept in escrow accounts and are returned if profits turn out to be illusory.

CONFLICTS OF INTEREST

Could we have avoided the global financial crisis if executives had been truly ethical? No question.

A large number of people knew that the mortgages they were dealing with were toxic. It does not take a great financial expert to see that mortgages with no down payments given to people with no income were extremely foolhardy. The rationale that they believed that housing prices would continue to keep going up is not credible—and, indeed, it is not even a legitimate justification for this behavior. Conflict of interest—for example, make an obscene amount of money in bonuses by encouraging toxic mortgages or make considerably less money in salary by giving mortgages only to people who can afford them—is difficult for most people. The bankers failed the test. They encouraged mortgage brokers to do everything possible to get people to take out mortgages.

Executives at Fannie Mae also purchased highly risky mortgages—mortgages that were so new the computer models could not analyze them properly—and their compensation increased dramatically. One consequence was that subprime mortgages that in the past would have been avoided by lenders, became more acceptable to banks all over the country.

All three major credit rating agencies—Moody's, Standard & Poor's, and Fitch Ratings—have been accused of being overly generous in how they rated the securities that consisted of bundled, low quality mortgages. The big question that has arisen is whether these firms assigned very good ratings (AAA) because of stupidity or to make more money. By ingratiating themselves with clients, they were able to steer more business to themselves. There is no question that the firms were able to make considerably more by providing ratings for complex financial securities than for simple bonds. Rating a complex $1 billion mortgage pool could generate approximately five times more in fees than rating $1 billion of municipal bonds.

There was a time when the credit rating agencies would not be compensated by the issuer of the security because of a conflict of interest. Revenues came from investors who purchased their publications. Given the conflict of interest, it is not surprising that numerous high-risk collaterized debt obligations (made up of thousands of subprime mortgages) were receiving AAA ratings. Is it possible that no one wanted to kill the goose that was producing so many golden eggs for the credit rating agencies?

Also, when the major investment banks such as Lehman Brothers and Bear Stearns were partnerships, they were much more conservative because they were risking their own money. Once they became public companies, they did not mind taking on huge amounts of risk, because they were no longer risking their own wealth. They were, in effect, using other people's money to become super wealthy.

MODELS HAVE ONLY LIMITED VALUE

Models are representations of reality. They will not work if conditions change dramatically. Back in 2004, when the investment banks wanted the SEC to give them an exemption from the regulation that limited the amount of debt they could have on their balance sheets, one individual who was opposed to the changes said the computer models would not work in periods of "severe market turbulence." He pointed out that computer models did not protect Long-Term Capital Management from collapse.[2] Of course, no one listened to him.

Models rely on interpretation by people. If those interpreting the model are afraid of losing their jobs, they will construe the models in a way that pleases top management. As noted, executives were doing everything possible to show stellar performance—even if it meant taking on huge amounts of risk—for those fat yearly bonuses. Whenever there are conflicts of interest, poor decisions are likely to be made.

When Fannie Mae decided to expand into riskier mortgages in the year 2000, they believed that their sophisticated models would allow them to purchase riskier mortgages and that these computer models would protect them from the increased risk. Not incidentally, Fannie Mae would charge higher fees for risky mortgages. These mortgages became super-risky because of very low down payments and unverified income on the part of the borrower. It is doubtful that any model could anticipate that millions of homeowners would find it easy to walk away from their mortgage. In the past, relatively few people defaulted on a mortgage because they had had to make a substantial down payment.

CONCLUSION

Free markets do not work well unless there is accountability, responsibility, ethics, and transparency. Predatory capitalism that disregards the concern for others and is based purely on self-interest may even be more dangerous than communism. We must recognize that what we have experienced is not the breakdown of an economic system. It is a values meltdown more than anything else.

NOTES

1. Peter S. Goodman, "Taking Hard New Look at a Greenspan Legacy," *New York Times*, October 9, 2008.
2. Stephen Labaton, "Agency's '04 Rule Let Banks Pile Up New Debt and Risk," *New York Times*, October 3, 2008.

ABOUT THE AUTHORS

Hershey Harry Friedman is a professor of business and director of business programs at Brooklyn College of the City University of New York. He earned a Ph.D. in business from the Graduate Center of the City University of New York in 1977. He has published more than 200 scholarly papers. His work has appeared such journals as *Business Horizons, Journal of Advertising Research, Journal of Applied Psychology, Journal of Macromarketing, Decision Sciences, Journal of Statistical Computation and Simulation, Simulation, Journal of the Market Research Society, Journal of Systems and Software, Journal of Leadership Studies, Management Online Review,* and the *Journal of Business Ethics.*

Linda Weiser Friedman is professor of statistics and computer information systems at the Baruch College Zicklin School of Business and the Graduate Center of the City University of New York. She received her Ph.D. degree in operations research in 1983 from the Polytechnic Institute of New York. Her scholarly articles have appeared in such journals as *Behavioral Science, Communications of the AIS, Journal of Systems and Software, Simulation, Journal of Statistics Education,* and *Journal of Internet Commerce.* She has published two professional books, *Comparative Programming Languages* (Prentice-Hall) and *The Simulation Metamodel* (Kluwer).

CHAPTER 6

The Roots of the Crisis and How to Bring It to a Close

JAMES K. GALBRAITH
University of Texas Economist

W hat caused the crisis? How long will it last? And—what should be done? First, let me give you a brief intellectual and economic history of the past 80 years because the roots of this crisis are in the realm of ideas. And the ideas of economists are notoriously particularly dangerous in this respect. At the broadest level, we could simply say that the roots of the crisis lie in the instability of capitalism itself. And then we would be done. But it's not quite adequate to leave matters there. At a second level, we might say that the roots of the crisis lie in our failure to recognize the instability of the capitalist system—not in the system itself but in our misapprehension of it. That's a step forward, but it doesn't quite get you where we need to go. At the third level, the message is appropriate, particularly for an audience of risk managers, that the roots of the crisis lie in a failure to act in prudent recognition of the fact that the system might be unstable. And therefore, a failure to keep in place a system of regulation, which had its flaws to be sure, but that had been created for a reason in the cauldron of the last great crisis—the Great Depression—and the New Deal.

That's why we need to go back 80 years to the Great Crash. Then, as now, the dominant view in economics was market equilibrium. A relatively new idea presented by Alfred Marshall was that the opposing forces of supply and demand provided balance and resulted in a stable economic system. In the summer of 1929, that view was upheld by the balmy prediction of Irving Fisher, the great monetary economist, that stocks had reached a permanently high plateau.

There were dissenting views. Thorstein Veblen offered an evolutionary perspective, which emphasized cumulative causation, the very simple idea that one thing leads to another and that there is no ultimate direction to the system. And in England, John Maynard Keynes was working on monetary production—the idea that credit and the real economy might have something to do with each other. He was also considering unemployment equilibrium, the idea that an imbalance in employment might not be self-correcting. At that time, these economic views were not dominant, but more like an embryo, and then the Great Depression happened.

As a result of the Great Depression, both government and economics changed. The prevailing view in government now favored a comprehensive regulation of economic activity and the reduction of risk, or more properly, the confinement of risk to that part of the population that could reasonably bear it. As a result, we got FDIC deposit insurance, Social Security, and the Glass-Steagall Act, which defined different roles for commercial and investment banks in an effort to prevent future collapses and failures of U.S. banks. We also got Fannie Mae and the creation of a 30-year fixed rate mortgage, and even the much-lambasted National Industrial Recovery Act, whose objective was to stabilize the prices of major industrial markets.

A regulated private financial sector does not produce booms, and it therefore also avoids busts and the speculative euphoria that precedes them. The New Deal had to generate economic activity on its own, which it did up to a point by completely rebuilding America's schools, putting in place a thousand airfields that didn't previously exist, paving 700,000 miles of roads, building two aircraft carriers, and among many other things the Marine Air Terminal and the Triborough Bridge.[1]

World War II and the Cold War changed the game again by creating a financially stable middle class—something that had never before existed in a growing economy that was near full employment. Veblen's successor in this period was actually my father, who wrote about the role of the industrial corporation as a stable force in this environment. Keynes's successor was Hyman Minsky, who taught that stability, however apparent and however apparently stable, breeds instability. Confidence induces the taking of risk. This was true not only in financial markets, but also in academic fashion as the memories of the Crash and the Depression faded, economists grew increasingly bolder and increasingly inclined to take intellectual risks, that is to say, to rewrite theory and to forget history. By the time I finished graduate school in 1981, the world of stochastic normality with rational agents in the competitive environment—general equilibrium—was thoroughly back in control.

There were also dissenters in finance. Benoit Mandelbrot challenged Eugene Fama with the new mathematics of fractal geometry and fat tail distributions (events that can go very, very bad very fast). In macroeconomics, Robert Eisner challenged the idea of a natural rate of unemployment. As with Keynes and Veblen before them, few listened to their warnings, and as a result, we were just as unprepared for the new crisis as we had been for the old one.

As the dot-com bubble exhausted itself, the new deal in finance was dismantled with the repeal of Glass-Steagall in 1999, and this paved the way for what I've called the rise of the predator state: a national government that in the first decade of the new century systematically turned regulation over to the industries to be regulated, and not just to them, but to their lobbies, which tended to represent the most aggressively antigovernment, antiregulation, and antistabilization aspects of each industry. And we forgot what the New Dealers knew, which is that a regulatory system exists to preserve honesty and stability in a functioning market and therefore to preserve the integrity, and the reliability, and the faith of participants in the market itself, while also forcing the pace of productivity improvement by making it hard to be one of the more regressive or reactionary players.

Instead, clear signals were sent. How clear? Well, during a press conference, the first director of the Office of Thrift Supervision in the Bush administration took a chainsaw to a stack of copies of the Federal Register containing the underwriting rules. That's a very clear signal about what would be supervised and what would not be. Thus began the mortgage debacle.

THE NATURE OF RISK ASSESSMENT

The nature of assessment of risk is the calculation of probabilities of adverse events. And with mortgages, these events include death, disability, interest rates, shocks, recessions, and refinancing. Some of these risks can be reduced by pooling, others less so.

Consider this description of a 2007 mortgage borrower that had appeared in Richard Cohen's *Washington Post* column on January 13, 2009: Marvene Halterman of Avondale, Arizona, age 61, after 13 years of uninterrupted unemployment, and at least as many of living on welfare, got a mortgage. She got it even though at one time she had 23 people living in the 576 square-foot house with one bath and some ramshackle outbuilding. She paid $103,000 for it, an amount that far exceeded the value of the house, which has since been condemned. Halterman's house was never exactly a showcase. The city had once cited her for all the junk, clothes, and tires on her lawn. Nevertheless, *a local financial institution*, Integrity Funding LLC, *gave her a mortgage valuing the house at about twice what a nearby and comparable property sold for. Integrity Funding then sold the loan to Wells Fargo and Company, which sold it to HSBC Holdings PLC, which then packaged it with thousands of other risky mortgages and offered this indigestible porridge to investors.* Standard & Poor's and Moody's Investor Service took a look at it all—as they are supposed to do—and pronounced it—you got it—Triple-A.

THE UNRAVELING

The unraveling began in August 2007 when banks began to realize that other banks had portfolios that were at least as bad as their own. A gradual recognition that institutions were at risk followed. Bear Stearns came down; Northern Rock in England experienced a run. There was an effort to hold the line after Merrill Lynch's downfall led to Lehman Brothers' demise. Fear of a spreading of collapse produced the rush to Congress to enact the Troubled Asset Relief Program (TARP).

On the day before the first vote on the TARP legislation, I was one of just three people to meet with a group of worried and desperate members of Congress who were unsure how they should vote. Our advice was the only bit of outside advice they were able to get in the very short time that was permitted them between the presentation of the legislation and the demand that they approve it.

And so we got a temporary resolution of the immediate problem. A resolution that was not along the lines that Treasury Secretary Henry Paulson originally envisaged, a repurchase of the assets, but rather along lines that became dictated by necessity—an increase in deposit insurance, a backstopping of the commercial paper market, and the purchasing of preferred equity in banking institutions, which is leading to the second phase of the asset repurchasing program.

These efforts have led us to characterize this problem as a financial crisis, but it's not. It's an economic crisis. And an economic crisis cannot be solved by purely financial means. Injecting money into financial institutions will not solve the crisis.

HOW DEEP? HOW LONG?

People ask how deep and how long this economic crisis will be. There is an ongoing effort by the government to project reassurance and certainty, and to make decisions on the basis of projections about which no one can be either sure or certain. Indeed, we are seeing a morphing of the discussion of the crisis from the financial realm to the realm of the real economy—to the realm of the economy of econometric projections and budget calculations, which underpin congressional expenditure programs such as the stimulus package.

The National Bureau of Economic Research (NBER) declared in late 2008 that we have been in recession since December 2007, maybe a little earlier. In the calculations that underpin a budgeting exercise, a certain length is attributed to recessions once they begin. The normal expectation, which will underpin a forecast such as released in January 2009 by the Congressional Budget Office, will lead the NBER to project a trough and an upturn, in this case at the end of 2009 and the start of 2010. And from that calculation, and a calculation of the depth of the fall, we will get a calculation about how much of an expenditure package is required to replace the fall of demand.

It's almost certainly wrong. It's as close to being certainly wrong as an economist who is versed in thinking about risk and uncertainty can say. Why? Because these are calculations that are entirely rooted in the postwar statistical record, and we are experiencing a phenomenon that we have not seen in that record, namely the complete and systematic disintegration of the normal relationship of credit and finance in the economy.

It's a phenomenon that we've not actually seen since 1929. It's in a different institutional context than in 1929, but it's still a phenomenon not seen since then, and, therefore, one can say almost for sure that the statistical relationships of the postwar period, when recessions were largely caused by external shocks or great increases in interest rates and efforts to control inflation, will not be strictly applicable to the current situation, particularly with the question of depth and longevity.

The package Congress enacted, while a good start, well-intentioned and in the right direction, was hampered by four problems:

1. Scaling to forecast, which gives you an answer that's too small.
2. A desire to be responsible and do useful things, which gives you an emphasis on projects that start too slowly and that are relatively difficult to administer—good and useful things, mind you, but far from being the major things that you need to do.
3. The need to work within existing laws so as to reduce the time needed to legislate. It takes longer to rewrite statutes than to put money into existing programs.
4. The instinct of all good politicians to return to normal as quickly as possible. They will want to accept the projection that the economy will recover in a year, and that they can get back to the business of balancing the budget and otherwise normal activity without undue delay.

The pessimistic view is that we will get too small a program and that when the administration realizes this and comes back to Congress for a second tranche, it will find an increasing skepticism about the proposed remedy. At that point, we may see snake oil salesmen proposing alternatives, making the whole process extremely difficult.

The optimistic view is that Congress does the right thing in spite of itself. Perhaps as a result of a bidding war among competing interests, they would form a sufficiently scaled program. As a model, Congress could draw from the successful experience of the Reagan administration, which in 1981 gave away one-third of the national tax revenues—much too much—and then spent five years taking part of it back. Everybody forgives or has forgotten the tax increases of 1982, 1984, and 1986, because they remember the economic recovery that occurred.

WHAT SHOULD BE IN THE NEXT PACKAGE?

The following items are suggested for inclusion in the next package of legislation.

1. Open-ended state and local revenue sharing to stop the persistent process of cuts in public services, such as teachers, fire and police, and parks and libraries. Infrastructure and "green" jobs should be included, particularly to the extent that they can be started quickly. Here, the recovery package already enacted, HR1, makes a very good beginning. But it's only a beginning.
2. Comprehensive relief in the housing sector from foreclosures and refinancing. This major task will have to be carried out on the retail level with a fair amount of due diligence that should have been exercised in the first place. Risk managers are needed in that sector.
3. Expansion of Social Security benefits to replace the purchasing power that the elderly population has lost in the collapse of the stock market.
4. Reduction in the age of eligibility for Medicare so as to allow workers to retire at 55 or so rather than hold on to their jobs 10 more years for the medical coverage.
5. A reconstruction finance corporation, again, with a good emphasis on risk management, to deal with the industrial problems that we're facing.
6. And finally, payroll tax relief to put cash in the pockets of working families to help them pay their mortgages, stabilize their credit card debts, and generally to get the banking system back on its feet. The banking system will not recover until the economy does. The idea that the economy could recover just through the banking system is illusory.

IN THE FUTURE

When the economy is righted again, the financial sector will be different from the one we've had for the past 30 years. It'll be a smaller one that works under considerably greater regulatory supervision that is considerably more sensitive to risk, and considerably more attentive to dealing with it. It'll also be considerably closer to home. The age of tax havens and regulatory arbitrage will have passed. But most of all, we are at the end, for the time being, of an economy that is driven by one unstable and unsustainable bubble after another. We will have to think very hard and very fresh about how to build a successful economy that can do the things we need to do and keep them going for a longer time.

NOTE

1. For a more complete discussion, see the paper "Time for a New New Deal," by Marshall Auerback, excerpted at: http://tpmcafe.talkingpointsmemo.com/2009/01/21/unemployment_statistics_of_the_new_deal_era/.

ABOUT THE AUTHOR

James K. Galbraith holds the Lloyd M. Bentsen, Jr. Chair of Government/Business Relations at the Lyndon B. Johnson School of Public Affairs at the University of Texas at Austin. His most recent book is *The Predator State: How Conservatives Abandoned the Free Market and Why Liberals Should Too* (Free Press). He is a senior scholar with the Levy Economics Institute, and chair of the Board of Economists for Peace and Security. Galbraith holds degrees from Harvard and Yale (Ph.D. in economics, 1981). He served on the staff of the U.S. Congress, including as executive director of the Joint Economic Committee, before joining the Texas faculty in 1985. His recent research has focused on the measurement of inequality in the world economy, while his policy writing ranges from monetary policy and the economic crisis to the economics of warfare, with forays into politics and history, especially that of the Vietnam war.

CHAPTER 7

Enron Rerun: The Credit Crisis in Three Easy Pieces

JONATHAN C. LIPSON
Peter J. Liacouras Professor of Law, Temple University Beasley School of Law*

SHOULD WE HAVE SEEN IT COMING?

Many claim that today's credit crisis was an unforeseen and unforeseeable catastrophe, no more predictable than the Asian flu or the Argentine debt crises of the 1990s and early 2000s.[1] In fact, however, it was entirely foreseeable, and was foreshadowed by the most infamous financial failure of recent years—Enron.

The Enron scandal has much in common with today's credit crisis. Enron offered many lessons that could have helped us to avert this crisis—if we had chosen to learn from those lessons. We did not, however, learn from Enron.

And, while the U.S. government agreed in the Emergency Economic Stabilization Act (EESA)[2] to finance a $700 billion bailout of banks holding troubled mortgage assets, very little in that legislation—or any government action since—has addressed the toxic trilogy of conditions that created both sets of failures: complexity, complacency among regulators and investors, and conflicts of interest. Although there are scores of proposals to reregulate the financial system, few recognize that this lethal mix was at the root of the crisis.[3] Thus, nothing will prevent this crisis from recurring.

Enron Rerun—The Credit Crisis in Three Easy Pieces

Enron's deals and today's crisis share three sets of features that created illusions of wealth that confounded even seemingly sophisticated investors.

Complexity
The first thing that Enron and today's crisis share is complexity. *Complexity* is obviously not a self-defining term. So as to avoid the thickets of epistemology and cognitive science, I limit the definition to entity and transaction structures with so many components that it would not have been realistic for investors or regulators to fully understand the risks being created (*transactional complexity*). I recognize

---

*An earlier version of this paper was presented at a conference on corporate governance at Tsinghua University, Beijing, China, in October 2008.

that many other forms of complexity matter here: the regulatory environment and interconnections among large financial institutions were also extremely—perhaps needlessly—complex. For this essay, however, transactional complexity will suffice. The credit crisis would not have been possible without it.

Convoluted Structures

The first type of transactional complexity we see is in the convoluted structures used by Enron and in the mortgage-driven deals at the heart of the current crisis.

For its part, Enron created thousands of subsidiaries that it used to "purchase" cash flows from Enron's operating businesses (for example, its gas pipelines) in asset securitizations. These subsidiaries then issued securities that investors ultimately purchased. But these structures and securities were so complex that it was difficult, if not impossible, for investors to understand that in some cases, Enron was really selling the same cash flows over and over to different subsidiaries. Complexity thus helped to conceal Enron's fraud, at least for a while.[4]

Today's transactions do not, to our knowledge, involve the outright fraud seen in Enron.[5] But, they nevertheless involved the creation of many entities by financial institutions for the sole purpose of purchasing cash flows (in particular, home mortgage payments), and issuing securities backed by the value of these cash flows. The securities themselves often had complex payment and other rights.

Both Enron's and today's transactions involved hundreds—perhaps thousands—of pages of dense legal documentation. These contracts, or sets of contracts, created many complex rights and responsibilities. While some people doubtless understood the details of these transactions, it is not clear that they were understood by the people who really mattered—investors and regulators.

Stealth Guarantees

But if the deals were too complicated to understand, why would anyone invest in them?

One answer involves what I call *stealth guarantees*. These were side agreements that were not actually called *guarantees*, but instead were called *swaps*, which are themselves needlessly complex transactions.

In Enron's case, in addition to purchasing securities allegedly backed by cash flows, the investors also obtained something called a Total Return Swap (TRS) from Enron. In essence, these swaps provided that if Enron's securitizations did not pay, then Enron itself would make the investors whole. Thus, they functioned like guarantees. But they were *stealth* guarantees because, being labeled *swaps*, Enron did not have to account for them like guarantees and, as investors later learned, Enron was not able to make good on its obligations under them.

Stealth guarantees appear to have played a critical role in today's transactions, too. Investors in mortgage-backed securities—among many others—apparently often purchased credit default swaps (CDS). Like Enron's total return swaps, these functioned economically like guarantees, but were structured and documented to be far more complex than a guarantee.

Nomenclature and documentation are not the only complicated features of credit default swaps. Compounding the complexity is the situation that no one really knows who is liable on these credit default swaps, or—most important—for how much. There are claims that as much as $60 trillion in face amount of CDS have been issued for many types of transactions.[6] But because no one knows how much will be owed, by whom or to whom, the credit markets panicked and ground to a halt in late 2008. There is legitimate concern that American International Group (AIG)—which is said to have issued more than $300 billion in CDS—may just be the tip of the iceberg.[7]

Mark-to-Market Accounting

A third complexity shared by Enron and today's deals involves the use of mark-to-market accounting. Under this accounting method, those who hold an asset can account for it at its market value, as determined by the holder.[8]

Enron used this to inflate the value of the subsidiaries that had supposedly purchased its cash flows. This enabled Enron to create securities that were allegedly backed by payment streams, and declare that they had a higher value than was realistic.

Today's investors (banks, in particular) apparently used mark-to-market accounting to book mortgage-backed securities at a value largely of their choosing. When there was a vigorous market for these transactions, they could claim these assets were valuable. But once the market froze, they had to recognize that they had little or no value—because there was no market.

The complexity here derives from acknowledging that market values are necessarily moving targets. It becomes much more difficult to judge a company's financial health if you know only that its value is determined by market forces outside the balance sheet.

While Enron and today's crisis may share needless transactional complexity, complexity alone is an incomplete explanation. It does not, for example, explain why sophisticated investors made the terrible investments that created today's crisis. Why would someone invest in something that was too complex to understand?

The answer turns on two other elements common to Enron and today's crisis—complacency and conflicts of interest. Complexity made both possible.

Complacency

Enron and the current crisis are marked by both regulatory and investor complacency.

Regulatory Complacency

The many state and federal regulators that should have checked Enron's misconduct did not because they were complacent. Enron manipulated these regulators through its political connections, taking advantage of a general trend toward deregulation in the U.S. commodities and securities markets. Among other things, regulators famously failed to stop Enron's manipulation of the California electricity market, and affirmatively chose not to regulate Enron's total return swaps.[9]

Today's credit crisis is marked by even greater regulatory complacency. Consider a few examples:

- *Mortgage Brokers.* Historically, homeowners in the United States purchased their homes with money borrowed from commercial banks, which are heavily regulated. Many of the mortgage loans in trouble today, however, were not made by banks, but by (or through) mortgage brokers, who were largely unregulated. Some activists had tried to get U.S. banking authorities to

regulate mortgage brokers, to subject them to the same underwriting standards as banks. But regulators apparently refused.[10]

- *Rating Agencies.* The securities backed by (that is, paid from) these loans
  were often rated by rating agencies such as Standard & Poor's and Moody's.
  Although not regulators in a traditional sense, their job was to place ratings
  on securities that would help investors understand the credit risk they were
  taking. The rating agencies repeatedly gave their highest rating (AAA, for
  example) to securities that they knew, or should have known, were too
  risky to deserve that rating.[11] Nor was this the first time they failed: rating
  agencies famously gave Enron's securities good ratings until it collapsed,
  too.[12] Despite this, the Credit Rating Agency Reform Act of 2006 significantly
  constrains regulators from addressing flawed ratings.[13]
- *Credit Default Swaps.* The credit default swaps that made the underlying
  deals more complex were also a product of regulatory complacency. In the
  year 2000, Congress decided in the Commodity Futures Modernization Act
  that swaps should not be regulated at all.[14] This means that even though
  they function like insurance, issuers do not have to hold reserves against
  these potential liabilities. And even though they heavily influence the public
  securities markets, they were rendered largely exempt from federal securities
  laws.
- *Artificially Low Interest Rates.* A central cause of the credit crisis was the
  persistent, artificially low prevailing rate of interest, caused by repeated cuts
  by the U.S. Federal Reserve in response to various financial and geopolitical
  crises. While some reductions may have been appropriate, in hindsight, it
  would appear that others were not. They created too much liquidity, which
  in turn artificially inflated asset (for example, home) prices.
- *The Net Capital Rule.* In 2004, the SEC loosened the net capital rule, which
  required that securities broker-dealers limit their debt-to-net capital ratio to 12-to-1.[15] The five investment banks that qualified for an alternative rule—Bear Stearns, Lehman Brothers, Merrill Lynch, Goldman Sachs,
  and Morgan Stanley—were allowed to increase their leverage ratios, sometimes, as in the case of Merrill Lynch, to as high as 40-to-1. Today, only two
  of these—Goldman and Morgan—appear to have survived, and there are
  doubts about Morgan's future.

In short, as with Enron, today's credit crisis resulted from many regulatory
lapses.

But regulatory complacency cannot explain why investors made such bad
decisions. In other words, if we believe that rational market actors will protect
themselves, then these regulatory failures should not have mattered much. But
they did. Why?

Investor Complacency
The answer, in part, is that, as in the Enron case, investors today were also complacent.

In the case of Enron, its investors and analysts often refused to press Enron
to explain its convoluted transaction structures. Indeed, in April 2001, Enron's
CEO, Jeff Skilling, verbally attacked Wall Street analyst Richard Grubman, who

had requested a balance sheet with the company's earnings statement in an effort to understand the company's cash flow.[16] While that investor saw this as a sign of trouble to come, many did not.

As described earlier, many of Enron's investors may not have cared about the quality of the securities they purchased in Enron's transactions because they believed they were going to be paid by Enron under its total return swaps. These swaps lulled them into a false sense of security.

Today's investor complacency appears to stem from a number of similar factors:

- *Ratings.* As noted, the securities in these deals frequently bore AAA ratings—the highest ratings available. This meant, in theory, that the securities were roughly as safe as government securities. While the ratings obviously proved to be flawed, investors nevertheless relied on them rather than doing their own analyses. As one banker I know told me: "You get ratings so you don't have to do your homework."
- *Liquidity.* A second form of complacency was the assumption that liquidity would always assure a vigorous market for these securities. Investors may have believed that because banks and financial institutions were so liquid they did not have to worry about the real quality of the securities they purchased because they expected that they could always sell them to someone else. This liquidity was, in turn, the product of both low interest rates and credit derivatives, such as credit default swaps.
- *Reputation.* Investors also likely relied on the reputations of the banks and other financial institutions that created these structures and issued these securities. Surely, they may have thought, if the securities are issued by institutions like Bear Stearns, Merrill Lynch, or Lehman Brothers, they must be safe.
- *Complexity.* Finally, complexity itself may have lulled investors into complacency. Because these deals were so convoluted, investors may have decided that it was not economical to dig deeply through the deals to understand them and gain a better handle on their risk. Moreover, complexity may have been considered an indirect sign of integrity. Deals this complex, investors may have thought, must surely be sound.

Conflicts

Complexity and complacency by themselves would not have been a problem if everyone had done what they were supposed to do. But, being greedy and fallible, people did not do what they were supposed to do. Rather, as in Enron, today's crisis reflects massive failures of integrity—that is, conflicts of interest—which were made possible by complexity and complacency.

For Enron, its deal structures were essentially built on a conflict of interest. By ostensibly selling cash flows to its own subsidiaries, it was simply moving money from one pocket to another, but calling that (and treating it for accounting purposes as) a sale, thus inflating the company's value.[17] More particularly, Enron's board apparently waived its conflicts policy to allow notorious insiders like Andrew Fastow to act as counterparties to cash in on these inappropriate transactions.

Today's crisis reflects a much broader and deeper array of conflicts of interest. Among others whose greed was unchecked by meaningful market or regulatory forces were the following:

- *Fraudulent Borrowers.* Many borrowers clearly should not have obtained mortgages. Yet, they easily obtained credit fraudulently, or without adequate documentation of creditworthiness.
- *Mortgage Brokers, and Others.* Mortgage brokers, originators, and appraisers all had conflicts of interest because their only real incentive was to book as many loans as possible: each loan produced a commission. They were indifferent to loan quality, however, because they had no liability if the borrower defaulted or the property was overvalued. Theirs was the conflict of moral hazard—reward without risk.
- *Investment Banks.* Like the mortgage brokers and others, investment banks and other financial institutions that created the securitization structures also had conflicts. They received large fees for constructing these deals, even if they were not going to be liable in the event the securities defaulted.
- *Rating Agencies.* Rating agencies may have had the most serious conflicts of interest, since they were apparently hired and paid by the investment banks that issued the securities—not the investors who purchased them.[18] They therefore had strong incentives to give the securities very high ratings (AAA), even if they were unrealistic. These rating agencies earned astronomical amounts of money from rating these deals, even though the ratings were seriously flawed. As previously noted, although the federal government moved in 2006 to give the SEC authority to stem some of the worst abuses, that legislation still makes it virtually impossible for the government to address flawed ratings.
- *Hedge Funds.* Hedge funds and other purchasing intermediaries also likely had serious conflicts. In many cases, it appears fund managers were paid large fees for purchasing these securities with the money of their investor clients, including banks and other financial institutions. If the securities defaulted, they might have to liquidate the funds, but we have no evidence that the managers returned fees to investors.

UNLEARNING FROM HISTORY

According to a *New York Times* op-ed by Ron Suskind, President Bush was warned as early as February 2002 by former Treasury Secretary Paul O'Neill and former Federal Reserve Chairman Alan Greenspan that needless transactional complexity was at the heart of debacles like Enron, Global Crossing, and Worldcom. According to Suskind, O'Neill and Greenspan "railed that day like a pair of blue-suited Jeremiahs" denouncing the financial shenanigans that complex accounting made possible. "'There's been too much gaming of the system,'" Mr. Greenspan is alleged to have said. "'Capitalism is not working! There's been a corrupting of the system. . . .'"[19]

The result? No action, except further relaxation of the very regulations that might have prevented the current crisis.

Reregulating financial markets will not be easy. Forbidding conflicts and motivating active regulation are fairly easy steps. But complexity is another matter. Yet, if complexity makes deals too difficult to understand, thus permitting complacency and conflicts to thrive, we may need to address that as well.

Whether—or to what extent—we can regulate complexity is beyond the scope of this essay. Suffice it to say, it is a daunting proposition. Reasonable minds can—and probably should—differ as to what constitutes a complex transaction. Nor is it clear what regulators are supposed to do about complexity. Disclosure—the presumptive remedy for financial system ailments—may not help. More information about a complex transaction does not necessarily make it easier to understand.

Some may want to ban some sufficiently complex transactions entirely. I think that is too harsh. New transactions often appear complex at first, but can have many benefits. Indeed, some types of complexity may actually have virtues. They can push us to work our brains harder, perhaps making us stronger in the long run.

At this point, it would be enough simply to understand the credit crisis—why it happened, and why we failed to learn from history. There obviously are no easy pieces here. But failing to see those pieces—complexity, complacency, and conflicted behavior—assures that they will continue to hobble our system.

NOTES

1. See, for example, Khor Hoe Ee and Kee Rui Xiong, "Asia: A Perspective on the Subprime Crisis," *Finance and Development*, June 2008, www.imf.org/external/pubs/ft/fandd/2008/06/khor.htm; Davide Furceri and Annabelle Mourougane, "Financial Crises: Past Lessons and Policy Implications," *Organisation for Economic Co-operation and Development Economics Department* Working Paper No. 668, February 17, 2009; Carmen M. Reinhart and Kenneth S. Rogoff, "What Other Financial Crises Tell Us," *Wall Street Journal*, February 3, 2009, http://online.wsj.com/article/SB123362438683541945.html.

2. H.R. 1424, 110th Cong. (Oct. 3, 2008) (as signed by the President).

3. Professor Steven Schwarcz is one of the few to do so. See Steven L. Schwarcz, "Protecting Financial Markets: Lessons from the Subprime Mortgage Meltdown," 93 Minn. L. Rev. 373 (2008). Professor Schwarcz very generously acknowledged the source of this triad. See the same at 404, n. 152 ("I am grateful to Professor Jonathan Lipson for suggesting these categories.").

4. First Interim Rpt. of Neal Batson, Court-Appointed Examiner 22 (September 21, 2002).

5. Query whether certain types of deals—especially the notorious CDO^n—involved the same sort of Enron resale tactic. The CDO^n is a securitization in which the underlying assets are securities issued in one or more prior securitizations. They thus contemplate the possibility that the same underlying stream of mortgage (or other) payments could be repackaged and resold many times. If nothing else, it is not clear that anyone stopped to consider whether the leakage of fees (investment bank commissions, legal fees, and so on) from the repackaging of this cash flow would exceed its likely value.

6. Intl. Swaps and Derivatives Assn., Inc., ISDA Market Survey, www.isda.org/statistics/pdf/ISDA-Market-Survey-historical-data.pdf (accessed July 10, 2009).

7. "Lessons from the Credit Crisis for the Future of Regulation," Testimony before the House Comm. on Oversight and Govt. Reform, 110th Cong., October 23, 2008 (testimony of Christopher Cox, Chairman of the Sec. and Exch. Comm.). See www.sec.gov/news/testimony/2008/ts102308cc.htm.

8. Financial Accounting Standards Board Statement of Financial Accounting No. 157, "Fair Value Measurements" 6 (September 2006).

9. Richard W. Stevenson and Jeff Gerth, "Web of Safeguards Failed as Enron Fell," January 20, 2002, www.nytimes.com/2002/01/20/us/enron-s-collapse-the-system-web-of-safeguards-failed-as-enron-fell.html.

10. The President's Working Group on Financial Markets, "Policy Statement on Financial Market Developments" 3–4 (March 2008).

11. Id. at 9.

12. Edward Wyatt, "Credit Agencies Waited Months to Voice Doubt About Enron," *New York Times,* February 8, 2002, www.nytimes.com/2002/02/08/business/enron-s-many-strands-warning-signs-credit-agencies-waited-months-voice-doubt.html?scp=3&sq=credit agencies and enron&st=cse& pagewanted=2.

13. Sen. 3850, 109th Cong. (September 29, 2006) (as signed by the President). Section (c)(2) of this Act provides that "Notwithstanding any other provision of law, neither the Commission nor any State (or political subdivision thereof) may regulate the substance of credit ratings or the procedures and methodologies by which any nationally recognized statistical rating organization determines credit ratings."

14. 7 U.S.C. § 2(g) (2006).

15. Securities and Exchange Commission, Release No. 34-49830, "Final Rule: Alternative Net Capital Requirements for Broker-Dealers That Are Part of Consolidated Supervised Entities," § 3.B.1 (effective August 20, 2004). See www.sec.gov/rules/final/34-49830.htm.

16. Kurt Eichenwald and Diana B. Henriques, "Enron Buffed Image to a Shine Even as It Rotted From Within," February 10, 2002, www.nytimes.com/2002/02/10/business/enron-s-many-strands-company-unravels-enron-buffed-image-shine-even-it-rotted.html?pagewanted=all.

17. Supra n. 5, at 3–4.

18. Securities and Exchange Commission, "Summary Report of Issues Identified in the Commission Staff's Examinations of Select Credit Rating Agencies" 23 (July 2008).

19. Ron Suskind, "The Crisis Last Time," *New York Times,* September 25, 2008, www.nytimes.com/2008/09/25/opinion/25suskind.html?_r=1&scp=1&sq=oneill%20green span%20enron&st=cse&oref=slogin.

ABOUT THE AUTHOR

Jonathan C. Lipson is the Peter J. Liacouras Professor of Law at Temple University James E. Beasley School of Law. He teaches contracts, corporations, and commercial law courses, as well as a deal-based simulation. In 2007, he was a visiting professor of law at the University of Pennsylvania. Before that, he was an assistant (1999–2002) and associate (2002–2004) professor of law at the University of Baltimore. He is a graduate of the University of Wisconsin, B.A., with honors (1986) & J.D. (1990), where he was a note editor of the Law Review. Lipson writes, speaks, and blogs frequently on business law subjects, including corporate reorganization and the credit crisis. His work has appeared in, among others, the *UCLA Law Review,* the *Notre Dame Law Review,* the *Business Lawyer,* the *University of Southern California Law Review,* the *Washington University Law Review,* the *Minnesota Law Review,* and the *Wisconsin Law Review.*

CHAPTER 8

The Global Crisis
and Its Origins

PETER L. SWAN
Australian School of Business, University of New South Wales, Sydney, Australia*

M arkets in the United States are almost as much instruments of governmental social policy as were the cadres dictated to by the Soviet Union before the collapse of the Berlin Wall. These forces dictating the development of markets in quite unnatural ways are exemplified by the 1938 decision by President Roosevelt to found Fannie Mae (Federal National Mortgage Association) to add to housing liquidity by purchasing and insuring home mortgages.

While the original aim was the apparently benign one of encouraging increased home ownership and more affordable housing, in more recent times under Presidents Clinton and George W. Bush it evolved into a more targeted policy of promoting increased home ownership by African-Americans and Latinos and, in general, people for whom rental would be a smarter option. Fannie was privatized in 1968 and in 1970 Freddie Mac (Federal Home Mortgage Corporation) was set up to extend the work of Fannie Mae and to offer mortgage-backed securities as a way of collateralizing home mortgages and spreading the risks.

This was a great innovation as it meant that banks could profit by making loans that they knew would never be repaid so long as they could either sell them to "bigger fools" or implicitly hid them from public view by selling them to themselves (special purpose vehicles (SPV)). Freddie pioneered the innovation of hiding debt and losses off-balance sheet, later to be copied in spectacular fashion by Kenneth Lay and Enron with the creation of thousands of SPVs before its collapse.

The principals, bank depositors, and shareholders, would like their agent, bank management, to make responsible loans by carrying the can if the borrower defaults. Self-interest by management then provides protection for depositors and shareholders alike. Securitization, with hidden clauses that brought toxic assets back on the balance sheet if default was threatened, and off-balance-sheet devices such as SPVs were greatly heralded financial innovations that undermined the very foundation of the global banking system.

*This contribution draws extensively on Peter L. Swan, "The political economy of the subprime crisis: Why subprime was so attractive to its creators," *European Journal of Political Economy 25*, March 2009, 124–132. This article provides a much fuller account.

The 1977 Community Reinvestment Act requires banks to subsidize low-income communities, and Fannie Mae and Freddie Mac were required to increase mortgages to low- and median-income borrowers. Under the Clinton administration, the growth in African-American home ownership was three times as fast as that for whites, and for Latinos, five times as fast. In a command-and-control economy such as the failed Soviet Union such hidden subsidies may survive for a long time because they are implicitly funded by the all-powerful state. In a supposedly capitalist economy such as the United States, unbudgeted subsidies to special interests contain the seeds of their own demise, as was evident in the subprime crisis. In the absence of direct and transparent budget subventions, implicit guarantee mechanisms such as Fannie and Freddie can only work to encourage home ownership to the extent that investors are fooled into thinking that the risk premium is far lower than it really is.

Elected officials like hidden subsidy mechanisms for several reasons. First, they offer their electorate something for nothing, that is, more "affordable" housing at no cost to them as taxpayers, and second, it provides a channel for campaign funds, as entities closely associated with government, Freddie, Fannie and, for that matter, Enron before its failure, have a lot to gain by favorable legislation, regulation, and oversight. Third, elected officials appear to be doing something for their constituents even if they are really not.

As if these measures to promote catastrophe were not enough, overinvestment in housing was encouraged by interest deductibility for owner-occupied home loans, despite the situation that the implicit rental income from home ownership was (and is) not taxed. Banks were essentially required to borrow short and lend long at fixed rates, ensuring the earlier S&L crisis. Loans were structured as *non-recourse*, encouraging borrowers to borrow to the hilt and refinance as much as possible. As soon as borrower's interest in a property became negative, they could walk away with no penalty.

Since the decks were as tilted against longer-term bank survival as was the deck of the Titanic, the Federal Deposit Insurance Corporation (FDIC) deposit insurance was (and is) required, ensuring that little or no scrutiny was given to lemming-like bank-lending practices that must inevitably lead to failure. The edifice was further propped up by the American International Group (AIG), which could provide insurance against default but only so long as they remained solvent. The state regulatory structure for insurance companies gave at least the appearance, if not the reality, of government backing. The reality came later when the taxpayer poured in hundreds of billions in bailout funds.

No bubble would be complete without immense state-sponsored credit creation. Alan Greenspan, as chair of the Federal Reserve, had practiced his craft to underwrite the high tech Internet asset bubble, which peaked in 1999–2000. He not only gave birth to this child but also adopted parental naming rights—"irrational exuberance." The subsequent meltdown and the September 11 assault on the World Trade Center provided the excuse he needed to have a second go at creating an even bigger bubble this time. He reduced short-term interest rates (the federal funds rate (FFR)) to record lows of around 1.1 percent by July 2003 but could not delude markets sufficiently to reduce long-term rates to such record low levels. This was despite inflating the money supply in an apparently successful effort to eradicate the business cycle.

In their Nobel Prize–winning article, Kydland and Prescott (1977) pointed out the inconsistency of "optimal plans" such as those employed by Greenspan. Discretionary interventions by Greenspan, rather than the adoption of rules such as a constant growth rate for credit creation, have fanned the flames of the global crisis.

Hayne Leland, UC Berkeley, in a recent keynote address (Leland 2009) gave Greenspan's apparent success in reducing market volatility before the crisis as one reason why credit models severely underpredicted both credit spreads and default probabilities. In his Princeton lectures (Leland 2007), he also pointed to fundamental flaws in existing credit risk models that had consistently underpredicted spreads even before the crisis. Artificially low short-term rates induced by Greenspan's attempt to eliminate the business cycle by discretionary intervention also gave investment banks further impetus to rely on short-term funding for subprime loans.

Greenspan not only gave a name to an era but presided over two of the biggest asset pricing inflations of all time. While the first one was for stock prices, the second was for housing and real estate. When the FFR started to decline in January 2001, the Miami House Price Index was at 110.3 and it peaked in December 2006 at 280.9, a gain of 155 percent. In March 2009, it had declined to 148.9, a fall of 47 percent from the peak. Commentators as early as 2008 noted that about $5 trillion had already been stripped from the value of the U.S. housing stock (Bardhan 2008).

During the period 2001 to 2005, the number of subprime loans issued increased by 451 percent, from 624,000 to 3,440,000, falling to 2,646,000 in 2006, while the average value increased by 72 percent from $151,000 in 2001 to $259,000 in 2006. Subprime loans issued in 2001 totaled $94 billion, but by 2006 this had risen by more than sevenfold to $685 billion (Demyanyk and Van Hemert 2008). Mr. Greenspan had almost single-handedly created one of the biggest money machines of all time. Banks like Washington Mutual and Lehman Brothers could effectively borrow funds at close to the (almost negligible) yield on Treasury bills and lend it out for subprime loans at close to 12 percent per annum. The margins were huge. The CEO of Washington Mutual not only paid himself huge bonuses while the bank was apparently solvent but received additional large payouts as it went into receivership.

The lender risk premium for subprime loans was negligible, as the possibility of default was never acknowledged. In part, this was due to the severe flaws in the models themselves, as already noted. Strong biases toward short-term incentives in CEO contracts encouraged management to ignore the risk. Other factors giving rise to bankruptcy or bailout are very rapid growth, very large size and, naturally, very high leverage in the form of debt. Since debts would be securitized and apparently passed on to others as quickly as possible, very little showed up on balance sheets. In 2006, new securitized loans amounted to 15 percent of GDP in the United States, 7 percent in Australia, and 4.4 percent in Europe (Taiwan Ratings 2006). The amount of reported debt for Lehman increased from $23.7 for each dollar of equity in 2001 to $34.9 in February 2008, just before declaring bankruptcy (Lehman Brothers 2007).

Subprime lenders such as Lehman Brothers specialized in locating borrowers to whom they could issue *liar loans*, with no money to put down, bad credit histories, unreported or insignificant incomes with a virtual incapacity to repay to whom excessively large loans would be made with initially deferred and discounted interest payments (teaser rates).

Other countries such as Australia also experienced sizable rises in real estate values, but borrowers paid the highest mortgage rates in the world as regulatory authorities did not emulate Greenspan in artificially reducing rates. Nor have there been any collapse in house prices or significant mortgage defaults. The regulatory differences are significant. Interest is not tax deductible for owner-occupiers. Mortgage rates are variable, rather than fixed. Loans are full-recourse. Low-doc and subprime loans are severely discouraged. Mortgages are largely held by banks until maturity rather than securitized. As noted earlier, securitization is second only to the United States but is still far less significant. Banks are required to have adequate reserves. Prudential regulation applies to all financial organizations, including investment banks and insurance companies. Australian banks remain the most profitable in the world. When state governments set up schemes along the lines of Freddie Mac to promote low-cost housing, they very quickly went bankrupt at a huge cost to the taxpayer.

The very efficiency of the U.S. system also told against it. In many U.S. states, there was a massive increase in the supply of housing in response to increased prices but the very slow approval process and limited resources for new house construction mean that housing rental rates have continued to rise in Australia.

Credit rating agencies such as Standard & Poor's and Moody's cannot entirely escape blame for the debacle. Computer programs were created to amalgamate heterogeneous mortgages with on-average (say) BBB ratings into exceedingly opaque packages. Mortgages are sliced and diced into tranches with about 60 percent rated AAA. Ratings were not stress-tested in a meaningful way as, until the onset of the housing price collapse, there were no systematic price falls across the nation. It was assumed, incorrectly as it turned out, that price fluctuations and defaults (if any) would be localized with asset values protected by state-, regional-, or nationwide diversification. Nationwide downward housing price movements were not contemplated.

Consistent with both formal economic modeling of credit risks and far less volatile stock markets reflecting the success of Alan Greenspan and the Fed in removing fears of business cycles, the spread between exceedingly risky subprime loans and prime loans had fallen to a negligible 0.6 percent (60 basis points) by 2004. Official U.S. governmental and regulatory policy that had gradually become more and more effectively administered over decades had finally achieved its objective of driving risk out of the system. If the most risky borrowers in the economy were to become homeowners, then this was clearly a necessary condition. It was not the failure of regulatory policy, but the very success of regulatory policy conducted by successive administrations and Congress that had created the subprime crisis. Nonetheless, the only bank management of substance that paid the price of deliberate government policy, Lehman Brothers, was blamed by Congress for being a victim of policies successfully implemented by the Congress. Richard Fuld, the CEO of Lehman Brothers, was dragged before Congress as the scapegoat. One Congressman told him publicly: "You're the villain today" (Fishman 2008).

There is a widespread perception in the population that well-intentioned and prestigious international bodies such as the International Monetary Fund (IMF) and Basel II accords, representing the international banking community, have the expertise to make predictions with reasonable accuracy. This has proved not to be the case. Ironically, the first collapse occurred in the United Kingdom, where the fifth-largest mortgage lender, Northern Rock, suffered a bank run in September 2007. This was the first bank run since 1866 for a British bank. The precipitating factor in the run was a much higher dividend payout due to relaxed capital adequacy requirements (Blundell-Wignall and Atkinson 2008).

Under the newly negotiated Basel II accords, home mortgage lending was deemed such a riskless activity that it was safe to reduce equity reserves. Even after Northern Rock was bailed out by the U.K. Treasury (taxpayer), taxpayer funds continued to be used to make loans at 125 percent of (optimistic) valuations (*The Guardian* March 20, 2009). Hence, it is not clear that the U.K. government has managed bailed out institutions any better than the old failed management. In 2007, the IMF announced that even if there were major house price falls, there would be negligible subprime losses (Blundell-Wignall and Atkinson 2008).

Exhibit 8.1 summaries policy responses to the economic crisis, according to the OECD. These responses are the sum of fiscal stimulus plus tax cuts over the period 2008–2010. Surprisingly, Australia, which is one of the countries least affected, is proposing to spend the highest proportion of its GDP on fiscal stimulus measures and one of the lowest on budget cuts. Billions have also been spent on a $900 handout to all qualified Australians, both living and dead. Australia will also devote 2.6 percent of its GDP to stimulus investment compared to 0.3 percent for the United States. Such packages attempt to bring forward expenditures and postpone the necessary tax increases to pay for it by huge borrowing programs. Once the effects on expenditure of increased borrowings are taken into account, I am not aware of evidence that such stimulus programs have anything other than a very short-term transitory effect.

In conclusion, the global economic crisis is an outgrowth of the U.S. subprime crisis. This crisis is really no accident but is rather the culmination of policies adopted by successive U.S. government administrations with the innocuous and, indeed, laudable aim of promoting greater home ownership and more affordable housing. Congress provides the appearance of giving its constituents something for nothing while setting in place systems and dependencies that assist campaign fundraising and promote a more corrupt environment.

Exhibit 8.1 The Absolute Size of Fiscal Packages (Revenue and Spending Measures) for the Top Six Countries, 2008–2010, in Absolute USD Millions

Country	Amount	% GDP
United States	804,070	5.4
Germany	107,789	3.0
Japan	99,992	2.5
Canada	61,551	4.2
Spain	56,754	4.2
Australia	45,673	4.8

Source: OECD, "Policy Responses to the Economic Crisis: Investing in Innovation for Long-Term Growth," June 2009, www.oecd.org/dataoecd/59/45/42983414.pdf.

The culmination of these laudable aims coincided with the interventionary policies of Alan Greenspan and the Fed that aimed to ameliorate the bursting of the Internet bubble and the September 11 terrorist attacks. With the active participation of the Fed, the SEC and other regulators, and the informal arms of government, Fannie Mae and Freddie Mac, a savage fire was lit under the subprime-financed housing bubble. The result was the housing bubble and its inevitable collapse.

Securitization of subprime loans hid debts notionally off-balance-sheet in special purpose vehicles while spreading the toxic waste to devastated lenders around the world. Even lenders as far away as local councils in Australia purchased hundreds of millions of dollars of AAA-rated subprime loans that are now worthless. Not content with the massive indebtedness that was a necessary part of the subprime-created global spending spree, governments have now embarked on trillion-dollar borrowing programs to fund stimulus programs that will almost certainly prove as ineffectual as they are wasteful.

REFERENCES

Bardhan, A. D. 2008. Of subprimes and subsidies: The political economy of the financial crisis. Working Paper, UC Berkeley.

Blundell-Wignall, A., and P. Atkinson. 2008. The subprime crisis: Causal distortions and regulatory reform. Reserve Bank of Australia Conference: Lessons from the Financial Turmoil of 2007.

Demyanyk, Y., and O. Van Hemert. 2008. Understanding the subprime mortgage crisis. Working Paper, Federal Reserve Bank of St. Louis.

Fishman, S., 2008. Burning down his house. *New York Times Magazine*, November 30, 2008. http://nymag.com/news/business/52603/.

Kydland, F., and E. Prescott. 1977. Rules rather than discretion: The inconsistency of optimal plans. *Journal of Political Economy*, 85: 473–490.

Lehman Brothers, 2007. 2007 Annual report.

Lehman Brothers, 2008. 10Q Filing. U.S. Securities and Exchange Commission. February quarter.

Leland, H. 2006. Structural models in corporate finance. Bendheim lectures in finance, Princeton lectures, September.

Leland, H. 2007. www.haas.berkeley.edu/groups/finance/WP/LECTURE1.pdf.

Leland, H. 2009. Keynote address to the 2009 China International Conference in Finance, July.

Northern Rock bailout: www.guardian.co.uk/business/2009/mar/20/northern-rock-loans-bailout.

Securitization globally: www.taiwanratings.com/en/analysis/structured%20finance/2006/securitization002.JPG.

ABOUT THE AUTHOR

Professor Peter L. Swan, AM, FASSA, is currently in the School of Banking and Finance, Australian School of Business, University of New South Wales. Swan completed his honors economics degree at ANU, his Ph.D. at Monash, and after visiting positions at the University of Chicago and Rochester, joined the economics faculty at ANU, then to a chair at AGSM, and was foundation professor in the finance department at the University of Sydney before returning to UNSW. Swan has published in the *Journal of Finance, American Economic Review, Journal of Political Economy* (three articles), *Econometrica* (two), *Journal of Business* (two), and 40-plus international journal articles. He has also gained recognition in the Queen's Birthday Honours list in 2003, *Who's Who in Economics*, second and third editions, as Scientia Professor, UNSW, 2003–2008, and in the popular press. Swan was elected as a fellow of the Academy of Social Sciences in Australia in 1997.

CHAPTER 9

Four Paradoxes of the 2008–2009 Economic and Financial Crisis

JOHN E. MARTHINSEN
Professor of Economics and International Business, The Distinguished Chair in Swiss Economics, Babson College

The financial and economic crisis of 2008–2009 had its origins in the subprime meltdown that began during late summer 2007. Since then, a wave of economic misfortune has spread worldwide through a thickly intertwined network of global trade and investment relations. If we have learned anything from this financial tempest, it is that economic recession and foreign contagion are virtually impossible to avoid when a severe financial crisis in the United States is at hand.

The road to economic turmoil was paved with cheap credit, underpriced risks, and other demand-based incentives that increased real estate prices to unprecedented, unrealistic, and unsustainable levels. Cheap credit was the result of high world saving rates, massive international capital flows, expansionary U.S. monetary policies (which should have been reversed far earlier), and cheap foreign imports that kept inflationary expectations low. Underpriced risks were the result of combined illusions that price movements in the future would be as they were in the recent past and global macroeconomic conditions were becoming more stable with time. Adding fuel to the fires of demand were other important factors, such as excessive financial leverage, opaquely valued financial instruments (e.g., credit default swaps, mortgage-backed obligations, and collateralized debt obligations), fragmented and ineffective bank regulation, arcane derivative strategies, poor corporate governance, fraud, incompetence, deception, speculation, and government housing and tax policies that aimed to increase both the number of families that could purchase homes and profits that could be earned on real estate investments. In the end, all these forces combined to create the perfect economic and financial storm.

When expansionary U.S. monetary policy was reversed in 2004, interest rates rose (see Exhibit 9.1), real estate values tumbled, economic activity declined, and mortgage default rates increased. To cover losses and restore desired levels of liquidity, financial institutions were forced to sell assets at fire-sale prices; risk premiums surged, consumer wealth plummeted, and business expectations diminished. The collapse in asset prices and subsequent recession caused the massive destruction of wealth and income as market disruptions spread from financial institutions

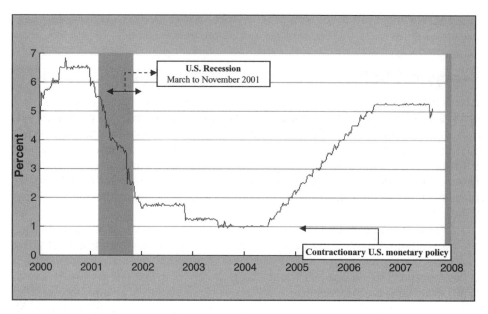

Exhibit 9.1   U.S. Federal Funds Rate: 2000 to Second Quarter 2007
Shaded areas indicate U.S. recessions.
Source: Board of Governors of the Federal Reserve System. 2009: http://research.stlouisfed.org/fred2/series/FF.

to industries, to countries, and to governments around the world. Public fears of cataclysmic failures and attempts by financial institutions to regain liquidity led to an unfortunate economic domino effect.

Governments and central banks responded to the *financial crisis* by recapitalizing domestic financial institutions and providing them with easy access to discount (window) loans. They addressed the *economic crisis* by reducing taxes, increasing government spending, and pursuing expansionary monetary policies that reduced interest rates (in some countries) nearly to zero percent.

FOUR MACROECONOMIC PARADOXES

When a statement seems self-contradictory or counter to common sense, it is called paradoxical. Macroeconomic paradoxes are often caused by the fallacy of composition, which occurs when false inferences about the sum of the parts are drawn from true observations about part (or parts) of the whole. These paradoxes remind us that countries are neither companies nor individuals.[1] Therefore, the tools and reasoning used to analyze the behavior of companies and individuals may not be (and often are not) appropriate for analyzing the economy as a whole. Of course, there are common factors that contribute to the success and economic well-being of countries, companies, *and* individuals, such as transparency, fairness, stability, and predictability; but beyond these basics, the differences can be large and significant.

Our current economic crisis has exposed four of these macroeconomic paradoxes, namely, the paradox of thrift, the paradox of leverage, the paradox of diversification, and the paradox of financial innovation. Understanding the conceptual and practical implications of them is an important first step toward finding appropriate remedies for nations under economic and financial stress.

Paradox of Thrift

At a personal level, thrift is considered by most of us to be a virtue because *a penny saved is a penny earned,* but at the macroeconomic level, saving is a double-edged sword. On one side, it provides the resources needed by nations to invest and grow. Saving can also help to keep real interest rates low, thereby encouraging business investment and household consumption. But on the other side, more saving means less consumption because a *penny saved is a penny not spent.* As spending falls, so do incomes, and, falling incomes reduce saving. As a result, frugal households may wind up saving a larger portion of a shrinking (income) pie.

An example may help demonstrate the aforementioned point. Gross domestic product can be defined as the sum of personal consumption expenditures, saving, and taxes. Suppose a nation's GDP was $1,000 billion, with $650 billion spent on consumption, $100 billion saved, and $250 billion paid in taxes. If saving increased from 10 percent to 20 percent of GDP, but GDP fell from $1,000 billion to $500 billion because of reduced demand, then net saving would remain constant at $100 billion (i.e., 20 percent × $500 billion = $100 billion). In short, a nation's attempt to save more would lead to the paradoxical result of no more or less saved.

Exhibit 9.2 shows the paradox of thrift at work in the context of the current economic crisis. As U.S. housing and stock market prices plummeted, households lost trillions of dollars in wealth and feared the worst was yet to come. They

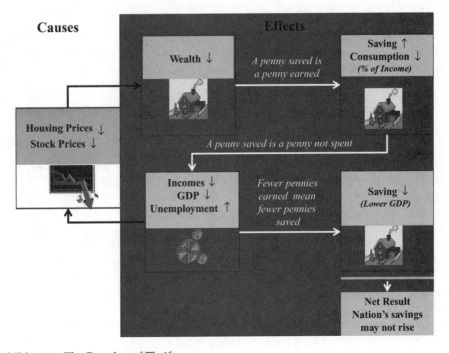

Exhibit 9.2 The Paradox of Thrift

reacted by saving larger portions of their incomes, but saving more meant con-
suming less, which had the secondary effect of lowering household incomes. Even
though increased saving may have helped reduce U.S. real interest rates, short-
term rates were already near zero because of aggressive Federal Reserve policies
and recession-led cuts in credit demand. Therefore, the additional liquidity had
only a marginal (if any) net effect on interest rates and spending, and, as a result,
economy-wide saving created macroeconomic conditions that, in the short run
(at least), partially or fully offset the increased saving rate.

Exhibit 9.3 shows the secular decline in the U.S. personal saving rate between
1970 and 2009. From an average of 9.6 percent during the 1970s, U.S. saving as a
percent of after-tax (disposable) income fell during the 1980s, 1990s, and 2000s to
9.0 percent, 5.2 percent, and, finally, 1.6 percent, respectively.[2]

The 2008–2009 recession in the United States abruptly reversed this downward
saving trend. From a diminutive 0.4 percent level in December 2007, the U.S. saving rate jumped to 6.9 percent in May 2009 (See Exhibit 9.4), which is a significant
change. To understand just how significant, consider that personal consumption
expenditures in the United States are about $10 trillion, which is approximately
70 percent of the nation's $14 trillion GDP. Assuming no secondary effects (e.g.,
multiplier, accelerator, or credit market), for every 1 percent increase in the annual
U.S. saving rate, household incomes fall by about $100 billion. Therefore, an in-
crease in the U.S. personal saving rate from 0.4 percent to 6.9 percent implies annual
income reductions of about $650 billion (i.e., 6.9 percent − 0.4 percent = 6.5 percent).

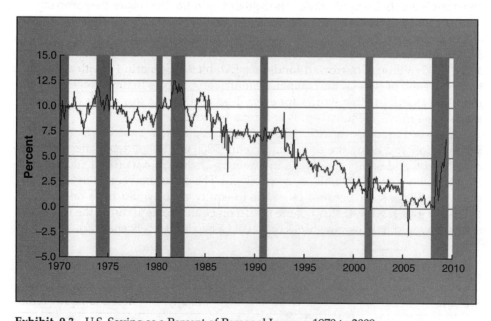

Exhibit 9.3 U.S. Saving as a Percent of Personal Income: 1970 to 2009
Shaded areas indicate U.S. recessions.
Source: U.S. Department of Commerce: Bureau of Economic Analysis. 2009, http://research.stlouisfed.
org/fred2/series/PSAVERT.

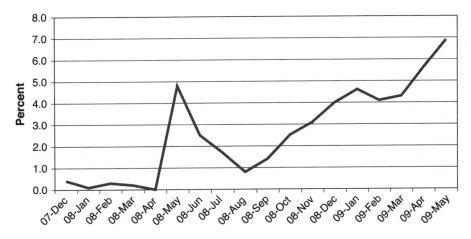

Exhibit 9.4   U.S. Saving Rate: December 2007 to May 2009

Paradox of Leverage

Leverage is using borrowed funds to magnify the potential gains and losses on invested equity. If the assets purchased with borrowed funds earn returns that are sufficient to cover their interest costs, then investors gain on both their invested equity *and* the borrowed funds. A commonly used measure of leverage is a company's assets-to-equity ratio. The higher this ratio, the riskier the company.

One way a company can reduce risk is to de-lever its balance sheet by selling assets and using the proceeds to retire debt. Take, for example, a company with $2,000 million of investment assets, which are financed by $200 million of equity and $1,800 million of borrowed funds (see Exhibit 9.5, Scenario 1). With an assets-to-equity ratio of 10-to-1, the company's return on equity is 10 times larger than its return on assets. In other words, for every 1 percent gain or loss on the company's assets, the return on equity is plus or minus 10 percent.

Suppose the company in Scenario 1 tried to reduce risk by selling assets worth $200 million and using the proceeds to retire $200 million of debt. Afterward, its assets, debt, and equity (as shown in Scenario 2) would be worth $1,800 million, $1,600 million, and $200 million, respectively. The de-levered company's balance sheet would be safer because its assets-to-equity ratio would have fallen from 10-to-1 to 9-to-1. Now, instead of the return on equity being 10 times the return on assets, it would only be nine times the level (see Exhibit 9.5, Scenario 2).

Exhibit 9.5   Successful Deleveraging Depends on Stable Market Prices

Scenario	Assets	=	Debt	+	Equity	Assets-to-Equity Ratio
1	2,000	=	1,800	+	200	2,000/200 = 10-to-1
2	1,800	=	1,600	+	200	1,800/200 = 9-to-1
3	1,800	=	1,700	+	100	1,800/100 = 18-to-1

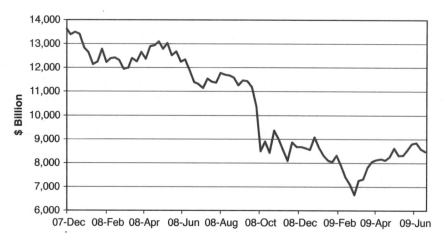

Exhibit 9.6   Dow Jones Industrial Average: December 2007 to June 2009

But what is true for an individual firm might not be true for an economy as a whole.[3] If all companies tried at once to reduce their balance sheet exposures, the prices of these investment assets would fall, which would hinder any individual firm's attempts to reduce risks. For example, suppose that industry-wide security sales caused our hypothetical company's assets to fall in value from $200 million to $100 million. By selling these assets, both liabilities *and* equity would fall by $100 million. As a result, the company's assets, debt, and equity would now be $1,800 million, $1,700 million, and $100 million, respectively. Instead of falling, the company's assets-to-equity ratio would rise from 10-to-1 to 18-to-1, which is a large increase that can be explained by the 50 percent reduction in equity (the denominator of the ratio) in contrast to Scenario 2, where the value of equity remained the same (see Exhibit 9.5, Scenario 3). In brief, for every 1 percent gain or loss on its assets, the company's return on equity would be 18 times that amount.

The paradox of leverage was at work in the United States during the 2008–2009 crisis. From early December 2007 to early March 2009, the Dow Jones Industrial Average fell by more than 51 percent (see Exhibit 9.6). This declining index was a reflection of broad-based reductions in stock market activity that wiped out trillions of dollars in household and business wealth. Reductions in asset values frustrated and mired attempts by many companies to decrease their leverage and, therefore, to reduce their balance sheet risks.

Paradox of Diversification

Portfolio diversification is supposed to provide investors with a degree of protection from changes in market prices. By owning assets with imperfectly correlated returns, investments suffering unexpected negative shocks should be offset (fully or partially) by investments experiencing unexpected positive shocks. But the protection afforded by diversification diminishes when systemic changes in market prices occur. During 2008 and 2009, dramatic reductions in market prices encouraged investors with well-diversified industry portfolios to dump their assets for the safety of U.S. Treasury securities and encouraged them to liquidate well-diversified foreign currency positions for the safety of the U.S. dollar.

The crisis revealed a simple, but powerful, truth, which is: *no portfolio can be completely diversified if it is duplicated by enough people.* When investors with similarly diversified portfolios unbundle and massively sell their assets, historical correlations among investment returns become meaningless and simultaneously approach one (i.e., perfect positive correlation). This diminishes the protective powers of diversification and weakens the value of frequently used risk management tools and measures.[4]

Paradox of Financial Innovation

The history of financial markets is a history of innovation and discovery that has resulted in new and better ways to manage the risk-and-return trade-off. Financial derivatives are a perfect case in point. Alan Greenspan, former chairman of the U.S. Federal Reserve, has heralded them as a way to distribute risks to the people who are best able to bear them, while Warren Buffett has demonized financial derivatives as "financial weapons of mass destruction, carrying dangers that . . . are potentially lethal."[5] Clearly, if these instruments provided no net benefits to their users, derivative markets would have shriveled and died, but they did not. Rather, derivative usage has thrived and grown exponentially. When they are used in moderation and fully understood, derivatives can provide significant benefits to users, but they can also be abused and misused, and, when they are, the consequences can be painful. In recent years, financial fiascos involving banks and hedge funds, such as Barings Bank, Long-Term Capital Management, Amaranth, and Société Générale, have demonstrated the swift and sometimes lethal blows that derivative instruments can deliver to overleveraged companies facing extreme movements in market prices.[6]

One might ask: *Why should regulators worry about losses incurred by overleveraged financial institutions if these losses are restricted to the companies' own shareholders, investors, and employees?* More pointedly: *Why should the actions of a few reckless investors trigger changes in rules and regulations that also affect disciplined and prudent users?* In general, financial regulators are not concerned with financial implosions that wind up destroying companies or financial institutions, but that attitude changes when implosions threaten to become explosions, causing unexpected, unwelcomed, and significant collateral damage.

The paradox of financial innovation is that financial products such as forwards, futures, swaps, and options, which are designed to optimize the risk-and-return trade-off for individual companies, can spill over and threaten the stability of the financial system as a whole. Novel products often layer a matrix of highly leveraged and puzzling financial uncertainties onto already complex risk management systems of individual companies, and add a network of hidden or obscure back alleyways between existing and new risks.[7] As a result, the pattern of historical price changes becomes a flawed guide to future risks.[8] For the financial system as a whole, new financial products (e.g., credit default swaps and collateralized debt obligations) can create systemic risks that may seem obvious after they occur but can have devastating effects on nations in which policy makers are still in the learning process.

In financial circles, the negative side effects of unmanaged risks are exacerbated by a culture of secrecy and opacity that prevents companies (and regulators) from understanding fully the net exposures of market participants. All that companies see and understand are their own exposures to business customers; so when the financial health and stability of these customers are questioned, a natural reaction is to demand more collateral and aggressively mark positions to market in the hopes of capturing as much of what is owed as quickly as possible. This *dash for cash* can lead to the death of even the most solvent companies and cause seizures in the credit markets, as lending dries up.

CONCLUSION

Financial crises have been a part of our global financial landscape for hundreds of years[9] and are likely to be recurring, irregular, and unsystematic parts of our future. Nevertheless, there is hope that this economic roller coaster can be tamed for the benefit of an increasingly integrated global economy. The key is not just to reduce the risk of recurrence but also to curtail the severity and duration of the economic fallout. Ways must be found to ensure that countries, like the United States, recover from the current financial crisis, prevent (or diminish the impact of) future recurrences, and create market-oriented solutions for systemic declines in asset prices. One of the prerequisites for making considered policy changes is to understand that a country is neither a company nor an individual. Therefore, the economic tools and reasoning used to analyze microeconomic and macroeconomic issues are bound to differ. Policy makers must understand the paradox of thrift if they wish to succeed in their attempts to influence domestic demand by implementing properly directed and adequately geared monetary and fiscal policies. Financial institutions, such as commercial banks, hedge funds, and investment banks, must understand how the paradoxes of leverage and diversification can severely compromise their risk management systems, and, finally, regulators must understand the paradox of financial innovation so they can better control and successfully promote the development of their financial markets.

NOTES

1. See Paul Krugman, "A Country Is Not a Company," *Harvard Business Review,* January–February 1996, product number 96108. Also see John E. Marthinsen, *Managing in a Global Economy: Demystifying International Macroeconomics* (Thomson South-Western, 2008), 724–730.

2. 1.6 percent includes the period from January 2000 to December 2007, when the current recession began.

3. See Hyman Minsky, "The Financial Instability Hypothesis: Capitalist Processes and the Behavior of the Economy," in Charles Kindleberger and J. Laffargue (eds.), *Financial Crisis: Theory, History, and Policy* (New York: Cambridge University Press, 1982), 13–38.

4. For example, *Value at Risk (VaR)* analysis quantifies the market risk of a portfolio based on historical returns and standard deviations. See René M. Stulz, "Ways Companies Mismanage Risk," *Harvard Business Review,* March 2009, 86–94.

5. Warren Buffett, Annual Letter to Shareholders, Berkshire Hathaway Inc., www. berkshirehathaway.com/letters/2002pdf.pdf (accessed July 8, 2009).

6. John E. Marthinsen, *Risk Takers: Uses and Abuses of Financial Derivatives* (Pearson Prentice-Hall, 2009).

7. It is for this reason that complicated risk-management systems usually need a set of simple rules to ensure that major blunders are avoided. This is also true in everyday life. As complicated as life has become, parents still lecture their children with time-proved rules such as: "Look both ways before crossing!" "Don't run with scissors in your hands!" "Fasten your seatbelt!" "Don't play with fire!" "Wear sunscreen!" "When in doubt, duck!" See Richard Bookstaber, "Risk Management in Complex Organizations," *Financial Analysts Journal* 55 (2) (March–April 1999), 18–20.

8. See Richard Bookstaber, *A Demon of Our Own Design: Markets, Hedge Funds, and the Perils of Financial Innovation* (Hoboken, NJ: John Wiley & Sons, 2007).

9. See Charles P. Kindleberger and Robert Z. Aliber, *Manias, Panics and Crashes: A History of Financial Crises* 4th ed., Wiley Investment Classics (Hoboken, NJ: John Wiley & Sons, 2005). See also Charles Mackay, *Extraordinary Popular Delusions and the Madness of Crowds* (New York: Three Rivers Press, 1980).

ABOUT THE AUTHOR

John E. Marthinsen is professor of economics and international business at Babson College in Babson Park, Massachusetts, where he holds the Distinguished Chair in Swiss Economics of the William F. Glavin Global Programs for Entrepreneurial Leadership. Dr. Marthinsen holds a Ph.D. from the University of Connecticut in Storrs (1974). He is an award-winning teacher and the author of many articles and books. Among his most recent books are *Risk Takers: Uses and Abuses of Financial Derivatives* 2nd ed. (Pearson Prentice-Hall, 2009) and *Managing in a Global Economy: Demystifying International Macroeconomics* (Thomson South-Western, 2008). Dr. Marthinsen has extensive consulting experience, working for both domestic and international companies, as well as the U.S. government. He has served on the United Nations Association's Economic Policy Council, lectured at the Universities of Bern and Basel in Switzerland and the University of Nuremberg, Germany, and he was a member of the board of directors of Givaudan SA, a Swiss-based flavors and fragrances company, from 2000 to 2009.

CHAPTER 10

Understanding the Subprime Financial Crisis

STEVEN L. SCHWARCZ
Stanley A. Star Professor of Law & Business at Duke University School of Law and Founding Director of Duke's Global Capital Markets Center*

HOW AND WHY DID THE FINANCIAL CRISIS HAPPEN?

Although we are now in a global credit and financial crisis, we refer to its earlier stages as a subprime mortgage crisis. The making and monetization of subprime mortgages, however, was not evil, per se. Mortgage loans were made available to even risky borrowers, but there were several reasons why, besides greed.

To some extent, lending to risky borrowers followed a time-tested credit card model in which credit is made easily available and high interest rates are charged, statistically, to offset losses. Furthermore, mortgage lenders, unlike credit card lenders, have not only one way out—cash flow—but also a second way out—collateral. This model worked brilliantly so long as home prices appreciated, as they had been doing for decades.

The model also was consistent with the government's strong encouragement of lenders to make mortgage loans to low-income (and often disproportionately minority) borrowers. In enabling the making of mortgage loans in many cases without documentation of borrower income, the model also recognized, at least implicitly, that many seemingly low-income borrowers are actually paid on a cash basis, without officially declaring their income. Therefore, not completely unlike the argument by economist Hernando de Soto that de facto property rights should be recognized so as to enable the poor to borrow and acquire capital, the model

---

*This article is based on the author's keynote speech, *Understanding the Subprime Financial Crisis*, published 60 S. C. L. Rev. 549 (2009). It is also available at http://ssrn.com/abstract_id=1288687.

Steven L. Schwarcz is the author of numerous articles and papers on the subprime financial crisis and systemic risk and has also testified before the Committee on Financial Services of the U.S. House of Representatives on "Systemic Risk: Examining Regulators' Ability to Respond to Threats to the Financial System," available at www.house.gov/apps/list/hearing/financialsvcs_dem/ht1002072.shtml.

enabled de facto income to be recognized, on a statistical basis, to enable the poor to borrow and acquire homes.

But the model failed for those borrowers who were relying on refinancing for loan repayment. For example, loans to risky borrowers were often made with the expectation that, because of home appreciation, the mortgagor would be able to refinance to a lower rate mortgage. And when the borrower had little de facto income, refinancing would be a significant means by which these mortgages would be paid. Due to the historically unanticipated depth of the fall in housing prices, however, these borrowers could not refinance.[1] In many cases, they defaulted.

These defaults in turn caused substantial amounts of low investment grade– rated mortgage-backed securities to default and the highest-rated securities (AAA) to be downgraded. That, in turn, spooked investors who believed that AAA meant ironclad safety and that *investment grade* meant relative freedom from default. Investors started losing confidence in ratings and avoiding debt securities.

Fewer investors meant that the price of debt securities started falling. Falling prices meant that firms using debt securities as collateral had to mark them to market and put up cash, requiring the sale of more securities, which caused market prices to plummet further downward in a death spiral. The refusal in mid-September 2008 of the government to save Lehman Brothers, and its resulting bankruptcy, added to this cascade. Debt markets became so spooked that even the commercial paper market virtually shut down. And the market prices of mortgage-backed securities collapsed substantially below the intrinsic value of the mortgage assets underlying those securities.

This collapse in market prices meant that banks and other financial institutions holding mortgage-backed securities had to write down their value. That caused these institutions to appear more financially risky, in turn triggering concern over counterparty risk: afraid these institutions might default on their contractual obligations, many parties stopped dealing with them.

In early October 2008, the U.S. government stepped in to the rescue with the Emergency Economic Stabilization Act of 2008. But its actions until September 2008 were spearheaded by the Federal Reserve Bank, which focused almost exclusively on protecting banks and other financial institutions against collapse. This narrow focus reflected the Fed's historical and legal mission, to act as a lender of last resort to banks and other financial institutions. Such a narrow focus worked well when banks and institutions were the primary source of corporate financing.

But as the financial crisis revealed, this focus has become insufficient now that companies obtain much of their financing directly through capital markets—a concept known as *disintermediation*.

WHAT SHOULD BE DONE TO AVOID FUTURE FINANCIAL CRISES?

It is impossible to know how future financial crises will arise. Ultimately, the key to protecting against future crises is to remain open, flexible, and aware of changing circumstances.

To this end, government should take a broad and flexible approach. I have mentioned how the Federal Reserve, initially tasked to address the building financial crisis, focused almost entirely on its narrow legal mandate. It may well be helpful to have a central governmental agency with a mandate to protect against financial crises of any type, including financial instability. In the United Kingdom, for example, the Financial Services Administration (FSA) is the single organization responsible for all financial institutions and markets. Several other countries, too, have their own governmental equivalents of the FSA.

Fully centralizing government responsibility in a single agency might, however, itself create an unintended degree of tunnel vision. It also would reduce competition among agencies, which might help to spur better regulation. It may well be better to have separate agencies with something like a centralized coordinating committee.

To protect against future crises, we also should try to learn from the nature of the fundamental failures causing the subprime crisis. In my article, "Protecting Financial Markets: Lessons from the Subprime Mortgage Meltdown,"[2] I have argued that most of the causes of the subprime financial crisis can be divided conceptually into three categories: conflicts, complacency, and complexity. These categories are broad, but they do not capture everything.

One might propose, for example, a fourth category: cupidity. Greed, however, is so ingrained in human nature and so intertwined with the other categories that it adds little insight to view it as a separate category. Government cannot meaningfully legislate against greed. Moreover, as the Gordon Gekko character famously said in the movie *Wall Street*, greed is (at least in moderation) good. Jewish law recognizes, for example, that human impulses are only problematic when yielded to in excess. In moderation, greed is positive, in the commercial sector stimulating trade and commerce through the profit motive.

These categories also do not capture the full problem of systemic risk, whose uniqueness arises from a type of tragedy of the commons. Because the benefits of exploiting finite capital resources accrue to individual market participants, whereas the costs of exploitation, which affect the real economy, are distributed among an even wider class of persons, market participants have insufficient incentive to internalize their externalities. I'm not claiming that lack of incentive to take care necessarily creates systemic problems, merely that lacking that incentive means the system isn't necessarily protected and is thus more exposed to problems that undermine it.

I address this more theoretical nature of the problem of systemic risk after addressing the fundamental categories of conflicts, complacency, and complexity, which themselves can lead, as in the current financial crisis, to systemic collapse. These categories embody market failures that firms should have protected against in their own self-interest. The interesting question is why firms failed to do so.

The first category, conflicts, is the most tractable because, once identified, conflicts can often be managed. For example, concerns about moral hazard resulting from the so-called originate-to-distribute model[3] can be managed by better aligning the interests of mortgage lenders and investors, such as by requiring the former to retain a risk of loss. And conflicts in the way that managers are paid, receiving high compensation and bonuses for arranging deals or investments that later fail, can be managed by firms taking a more long-term view of compensation. This should be done not only for top managers but also for secondary managers, who make many important decisions regarding investments.[4]

Complacency is a more difficult category because government cannot change human nature (although it can try to affect behavior). During a financial crisis, everyone becomes focused. But once the crisis recedes in memory and investors are again making money, the experience is that investors will always go for the gold.

Complexity is the most difficult category. It is increasingly a metaphor for the modern financial system and its potential for failure.[5]

Complexity comes in at least two forms. There is cognitive complexity: things are just too complex to understand. This manifests itself, for example, in the difficulty of achieving transparent disclosure for complicated securities and also in the difficulty of market participants to learn the financial condition of their counterparties (due, for example, to their entering into credit default swaps).

There is also temporal complexity: in a complex system, signals are sometimes inadvertently transmitted too quickly to control. This manifests itself, for example, in the tight coupling that causes markets to move rapidly into a crisis mode.

Consider first how to address cognizant complexity, initially addressing the failure of disclosure and then addressing the difficulty of market participants to learn the financial condition of their counterparties. Regarding the former, investors can try to demand more and better disclosure, including of contingent liabilities. As I've shown elsewhere, however, investors are sometimes lax, and there may well also be limits to the human ability to understand complex systems, no matter how well they are disclosed.[6]

There are at least two reasons why market participants have difficulty learning the financial condition of their counterparties: One reason is that it can be difficult to value a counterparty's assets. In the subprime financial crisis, this was illustrated by the difficulty of valuing the mortgage-backed securities owned by counterparties. The other reason for this difficulty is that a counterparty may have taken on undisclosed contingent liabilities such as over-the-counter credit derivatives under which firms bought or sold risk. Although a potential future solution to this problem is to centrally register credit-derivative transactions, I am skeptical of the solution's efficacy because the chameleon-like nature of derivatives makes it difficult to determine what constitutes a credit derivative, and thus what should be required to be registered.[7]

Turning next to the problem of temporal complexity (where signals are inadvertently transmitted too quickly to control), we need to loosen the tight coupling that causes markets to move rapidly into a crisis mode. I have argued that this can be done by a governmental or other entity acting as the equivalent of a market liquidity provider of last resort, to help stabilize irrationally panicked markets by purchasing securities.[8] This type of targeted market investment should generate relatively minimal costs, and certainly lower costs than those of a lender of last resort to financial institutions—the Fed's traditional role.

By providing a lifeline to financial institutions, a lender of last resort fosters moral hazard by encouraging these entities—especially those that believe they are too big to be allowed to fail—to be fiscally reckless. Loans made to these institutions also will not be repaid if they eventually fail. In contrast, a market liquidity provider, *especially if it acts at the outset of a market panic,*[9] can profitably invest in securities at a deep discount from the market price and still provide a floor to how low the market will drop. Buying at a deep discount will mitigate moral hazard and also make it likely that the market liquidity provider will be repaid. Such a market liquidity provider is needed because, among other reasons, in a panicked market, private investors may not act rationally.

Consider next the more theoretical nature of the problem of systemic risk. Recall that because the benefits of exploiting finite capital resources accrue to individual market participants, whereas the costs of exploitation are distributed among an even wider class of persons, market participants have insufficient incentive to internalize their externalities. *These are externalities that firms, out of self-interest, should not necessarily protect against.* Therefore, even if market participants fully understand that incurring certain risks may contribute to systemic risk, they will not be motivated, absent regulation, to internalize those risks. Conceptually, therefore, the solution to systemic risk is to impose regulation that internalizes those externalities.

It is unclear, however, what regulation can do to require market participants to internalize all their externalities because of the myriad ways in which externalities can arise. In the subprime financial crisis, for example, imposing suitability requirements on mortgage loans and otherwise restricting predatory lending may have helped to internalize externalities. These restrictions, however, almost certainly will not address the next crisis.

Market participants may also have created externalities by incurring too much debt. The liquidity glut that preceded the subprime financial crisis gave firms incentives to borrow at low cost. High leverage fosters systemic risk, and hence externalities, by making it more likely that a firm will fail, thereby triggering failures of other highly leveraged counterparty firms. Regulating leverage could create significant costs, however. Some leverage is good, though there is no optimal across-the-board amount of leverage that is right for every company. Regulation that attempts to track optimal leverage would thus be nuanced and highly complex, impairing a firm's ability to operate efficiently and impeding economic growth.

Absent effective means to avoid systemic risk by requiring market participants to internalize externalities, there still may be a pragmatic way to mitigate the likelihood of systemic collapse. Systemic collapses result from a chain of defaults; but if the chain can be broken, the defaults won't be transmitted.

A liquidity provider of last resort can break the chain of defaults. In the United States, the Federal Reserve traditionally has acted as such a liquidity provider to banks and other financial institutions to break the chain of institutional defaults. In contrast, a *market* liquidity provider of last resort, much along the lines previously discussed, can break the chain of financial market defaults by stabilizing irrationally panicked markets.[10]

Long term, to help address and solve capital market problems, we need fresh, unbiased ideas from an advisory group, like a brain trust, of scholars who have been studying these markets, as well as from experts with real-life market experience. Past knowledge is insufficient. For example, much of the present market crisis is tied to increasing market complexity, which causes unexpected consequences from otherwise routine and desirable actions. And these unexpected consequences are amplified by the very nature of modern financial markets, which causes events to move rapidly into crisis mode with little time or opportunity to intervene.[11]

Such a brain trust could function, formally or otherwise, by having access to government regulators at all levels and branches. Members of the group would suggest ideas and critique proposed government actions.

President Roosevelt took a similar approach in response to the Great Depression. One difference, though, is that because financial markets cross national borders, any brain trust should include at least some foreign experts in addition to Americans.

If government attempts to solve financial crises without this type of critical input, I fear that the solutions will continue to be makeshift, illusory, and costly—such as overregulation that causes our markets to lose their competitive edge.

NOTES

1. In one sense, the precipitous drop in home prices was unexpected, as in the Monty Python skit, "Nobody Expects the Spanish Inquisition." In another sense, though, the fall arguably should have been anticipated based on the earlier liquidity glut and its artificially low interest rates, driving up housing prices artificially.

2. 93 Minnesota L. Rev. 373 (2008), also available at http://ssrn.com/abstract_id=1107444.

3. Under the originate-to-distribute model, mortgage lenders sell off loans as they are made.

4. Consider, however, the extent to which super-large compensation, even if a portion can be clawed back (i.e., retroactively recovered) or contingently paid over time, creates inherent conflicts. For example, if an individual's compensation, even if it were to be fully adjusted downward, still enables that individual to be financially independent of the firm, that individual's incentives will not necessarily be aligned with the firm's incentives.

5. For a more detailed and complete analysis of the problem of complexity, see Steven L. Schwarcz, "Regulating Complexity in Financial Markets," 87 Wash. U. L. Rev., 2010; also available at http://ssrn.com/abstract_id=1240863.

6. See "Disclosure's Failure in the Subprime Mortgage Crisis," 2008 Utah L. Rev. 1109 (symposium issue on the subprime mortgage meltdown); also available at http://ssrn.com/abstract_id=1113034.

7. It also should be noted that risk transfer is not inherently bad. It can maximize efficiency if risk is transferred to parties better able to bear the risk. I am nonetheless concerned whether, in the subprime financial crisis, the degree of risk dispersion created a type of collective action problem, in that the ultimate risk-bearing parties did not always have sufficient amounts at risk regarding any given underlying credit risk to motivate them to engage in due diligence.

8. Testimony before the Committee on Financial Services of the U.S. House of Representatives on "Systemic Risk: Examining Regulators' Ability to Respond to Threats to the Financial System," available at http://www.house.gov/apps/list/hearing/financialsvcs_dem/ht1002072.shtml. See also "Regulating Complexity in Financial Markets," 87 Wash. U. L. Rev., 2010; also available at http://ssrn.com/abstract_id=1240863.

9. It is important to act before market prices collapse so far that banks and other financial institutions, forced to write down the value of their debt securities portfolios to market prices, appear inadequately capitalized, creating counterparty risk that shuts down the credit markets—which, in turn, harms the real economy because firms need credit to operate and grow. This occurred in the subprime financial crisis.

10. Consider how such a market liquidity provider of last resort could have helped to avoid the subprime mortgage meltdown. Once it recognized that panic was causing the market prices of mortgage-backed securities to fall materially below the level of their intrinsic value, the market liquidity provider could have stepped in to purchase sufficient quantities of those securities to stabilize the mortgage-backed securities markets. Even though the stabilized price would be deeply discounted from the intrinsic value of those securities, it still would be much higher than prices in a collapsed market.

11. "Regulating Complexity in Financial Markets," *supra* note v.

ABOUT THE AUTHOR

Steven L. Schwarcz is the Stanley A. Star Professor of Law & Business at Duke University and founding director of Duke's Global Capital Markets Center. Before joining Duke, he was a partner at two leading international law firms and also taught at the Yale and Columbia Law Schools. Schwarcz has advised the United States Congress and other government bodies on systemic risk and the recent financial crisis. His scholarly works include "Systemic Risk," 97 Geo. L. J. 193 (2008); "Protecting Financial Markets: Lessons from the Subprime Mortgage Meltdown," 93 Minn. L. Rev. 373 (2008); "Disclosure's Failure in the Subprime Mortgage Crisis," 2008 Utah L. Rev. 1109; "Understanding the Subprime Financial Crisis," 60 S. C. L. Rev. 549 (2009); "Conflicts and Financial Collapse: The Problem of Secondary-Management Agency Costs," 26 Yale J. on Reg. 457 (Summer 2009); "Too Big to Fail? Recasting the Financial Safety Net," in "The Panic of 2008," (Geo. Wash. Univ. symposium book); "Regulating Complexity in Financial Markets," 87 Wash. U. L. Rev. (2010); and *Regulating Financial Systems,* forthcoming from Oxford University Press (co-authored with Kenneth Anderson).

PART II

Causes and Consequences of the Financial Crisis

CHAPTER 11

The Origins of the Financial Crisis

MARTIN N. BAILY
Senior Adviser to McKinsey's Global Institute, an adviser to the Congressional Budget Office, and a Director of The Phoenix Companies

ROBERT E. LITAN
Vice President for Research and Policy at the Kauffman Foundation, and a Senior Fellow in Economic Studies at the Brookings Institution

MATTHEW S. JOHNSON
Research Associate, Harvard Business School*

The financial crisis that has been wreaking havoc in markets in the United States and across the world since August 2007 had its origins in an asset price bubble that interacted with new kinds of financial innovations that masked risk, with companies that failed to follow their own risk management procedures, and with regulators and supervisors who failed to restrain excessive taking.

A bubble formed in the housing markets as home prices across the country increased each year from the mid-1990s to 2006, moving out of line with fundamentals like household income and rents. While national in scale, the bubble varied in size by region, inflating enormously in states like California, Nevada, and Florida where housing demand far exceeded land supply, and stayed relatively mild in midland states where abundant land could accommodate increased housing demand.[1]

Like traditional asset price bubbles, expectations of future price increases developed and were a significant factor in inflating house prices. As individuals witnessed rising prices in their neighborhood and across the country, they began to expect them to continue to rise, even in the late years of the bubble when it had nearly peaked. Indeed, the boom in the subprime mortgage market was characterized by several features common to traditional asset price bubbles, such as rapidly rising asset prices, a surge in credit growth, declining risk perceptions, rising risk tolerance, and very high liquidity.

---

*This piece is based on Baily, Litan, and Johnson (2008).

Other than the surge in the ratio of real home prices to income, an expansion of credit was evident with the huge rise in mortgage originations (especially to subprime borrowers) and with the incredible boom in leverage in financial markets. Rising risk tolerance can be seen in the declining spread between subprime and conventional mortgage rates; as the boom went on, lenders were increasingly willing to accept lower rates of return for increasingly riskier assets. Finally, the ease with which homeowners could sell their homes during the time from 2000 to 2006, and the incredible ease with which homeowners, banks and nonbanks could borrow in credit markets, reflected the high liquidity during the housing bubble. Thus in many ways, the years preceding the crisis of 2007–2008 were characterized by features common to prior asset bubbles.

FINANCIAL INNOVATION AND THE RISE OF SUBPRIME LENDING

The rapid rise of lending to subprime borrowers since 2000 helped inflate the housing price bubble. Subprime borrowers—those with little or no history of income and with a FICO credit score below a certain threshold (typically below 620)—were historically considered much riskier borrowers than prime borrowers. Before 2000, subprime lending was virtually nonexistent, but thereafter it took off exponentially. The sustained rise in house prices, along with new financial innovations, suddenly made subprime borrowers—previously shut out of the mortgage markets—attractive customers for mortgage lenders. Lenders devised innovative Adjustable Rate Mortgages (ARMs)—with low teaser rates, with no down payments, and with some even allowing the borrower to postpone the interest due each month and add it to the principal of the loan—which were predicated on the expectation that home prices would continue to rise.

But innovation in mortgage design alone would not have enabled so many subprime borrowers to access credit without other innovations in the so-called process of securitizing mortgages: the packaging of mortgages and then selling securities backed by those packages, and with investors receiving pro rata payments of principal and interest by the borrowers. The two principal government-sponsored enterprises devoted to mortgage lending, Fannie Mae and Freddie Mac, developed this financing technique in the 1970s, adding their guarantees to these mortgage-backed securities (MBS) to ensure their marketability. Along the way, the private sector developed MBS backed by nonconforming loans that had other means of credit enhancement. In this fashion, Wall Street investors were providing the credit to finance homebuyers on Main Street. Banks, thrifts, and a new industry of mortgage brokers originated the loans but no longer kept them; rather, they sold the loans off their books to third parties who then pooled the loans to issue MBS, pocketing a fee along the way. Thus much more so than in the past, mortgage lenders had a big incentive to extend credit to subprime borrowers to maximize the volume of fees they received, as they no longer had a financial stake in the ultimate outcome of the loan.

Over the past decade, and especially since 2000, private sector commercial and investment banks developed new ways of securitizing subprime mortgages: by packaging them into collateralized debt obligations (sometimes with other asset-backed securities such as corporate bonds or auto loans), and then dividing the cash flows into different tranches to appeal to different classes of investors with different tolerances for risk. These tranches ordered the rights to the cash flows, meaning that a senior tranche was paid in full before a junior tranche was paid anything. By tranching the securities, along with using other forms of credit enhancement, CDO issuers were able to persuade the rating agencies to give AAA ratings to their senior tranches. Thus a CDO could turn lead into gold, or at least so it was thought, by pooling together low-grade MBS backed by subprime mortgages and convert some of them into new AAA-rated securities.

One such other form of credit enhancement was insurance that protected holders of CDOs (or other securities) in case the underlying loans went into default. In some cases, so-called monoline bond insurers (which had previously concentrated on insuring municipal bonds) sold this form of protection, but more recently insurance companies, investment banks, and other parties did the near equivalent by selling credit default swaps (CDS), which acted like insurance except that they did not require the seller to put up a large amount of capital to back up their claims. The market for CDS expanded very rapidly after 2000, as they increasingly became a way for traders to make bets on the outcome of a security rather than their original intention of pure insurance.

This new process enabled Wall Street to do for subprime mortgages what it had already done for conforming mortgages: channel funds of institutional investors to support the origination of mortgages to many more households than previously would have qualified for mortgage credit. These new innovations thrived as home prices continued to grow and credit was cheap. As the housing bubble continued to inflate, financial institutions borrowed more and more money (i.e., increased their leverage) to finance their purchases of mortgage-related securities. They especially turned to short-term collateralized borrowing like asset-backed commercial paper (ABCP) and repurchase agreements, so much so that by 2006 investment banks were, on average, using overnight loans to roll over a quarter of their balance sheet every night (Brunnermeier 2008). Also, banks increasingly used opaque off-balance-sheet instruments such as structured investment vehicles (SIVs) with which they could dodge capital requirements, increase their holdings of risky assets even more, and could operate under the radar of regulators.

This tenuous situation shut down and went into reverse once panic hit in 2007, however, as sudden uncertainty over asset prices caused lenders to abruptly refuse to roll over their debts, and overleveraged banks found themselves exposed to falling asset prices with very little capital. This sudden need to repay liabilities forced banks to de-leverage, or sell off their assets to raise capital. Since many banks had to do this at the same time, it depressed the price of those assets, which caused more demands and margin calls by lenders, creating a vicious cycle. Thus the unloading of leverage by individual institutions had systemic effects, meaning that the actions of one had implications for the system as a whole, A salient observation here is that while the deflation of the real estate bubble and the subsequent drop in asset prices catalyzed the panic that began in 2007, equally if not more central to the ensuring financial instability was the incredible systemwide reliance on short-term leverage that had been built up in the previous years.

HOW WERE SUCH DANGEROUS EXCESSES ALLOWED TO BUILD UP?

Regulatory failures undoubtedly were a factor. The Federal Reserve has received considerable criticism for having kept interest rates too low for too long after the 2001 recession, which encouraged the financial sector to take on especially risky assets and helped fuel the bubble. When measured by a standard Taylor Rule, monetary policy was only slightly over expansionary (Elmendorf 2007, 2008), but the situation of such dangerous financial excesses building up under the Fed's nose suggests the benchmark solely of output and inflation used to implement and judge monetary policy should be revisited.

Furthermore, the mélange of federal and state regulators who oversaw the mortgage and financial markets failed to rein them in as lending standards deteriorated and as dangerous amounts of leverage piled up in the financial sector. The Fed could and should have stepped in as loan-to-value (LTV) ratios shot up and other lending standards eroded in subprime lending in years preceding 2007. At the same time, though, a substantial amount of subprime lending took place outside of federal regulatory purview; half of subprime loans originated in 2004 and 2005 were originated by independent mortgage companies overseen only by state regulators, not federal ones. The patchwork of federal and state regulators resulted in a disjointed system of financial supervision whereby no regulator had clear authority. Furthermore, financial regulators unconcerned with systemic, or macro-prudential, risk looked on as increasing interconnectedness made the financial system incredibly unstable.

Third, the international Basel Capital Accord, while laudable in its attempt to standardize capital requirements across countries, had unintended consequences that further helped contribute to the housing bubble. For one, Basel legitimized SIVs by allowing them to be considered separate from the balance sheet of the bank that operated them, thus sanctioning the financial underworld that expanded enormously during the bubble. Furthermore, Basel actually encouraged the financial sector to hold securities backed by residential mortgages, even those that were subprime. The amount of capital that the accord required a bank to hold depended on the risk weight of its assets and, citing the "very low record of loss in most countries" of residential mortgages, gave a lower risk weight to securities backed by mortgages relative to other types of assets.

While it is clear various regulatory failures either encouraged or neglected to rein in on the bubble, they can explain only so much of the story. Even given these failures, what is especially shocking is how market participants along each link of the securitization chain failed so grossly to perform adequate risk assessment on the mortgage-related assets they held and traded. From the mortgage borrower and originator, to the loan servicer, to the mortgage-backed security issuer, to the CDO issuer, to the CDS protection seller, to the credit rating agencies, and to the holders of all those securities, at no point did any institution stop the party or question the little-understood computer risk models, or the blatantly unsustainable deterioration of the loan terms of the underlying mortgages.

Why would market participants fail so grossly to manage risk and perform due diligence? Partly to blame are the incentives in the securitization model itself. Each link of the securitization chain is plagued by asymmetric information—that is, one party has better information than the other. In such cases, one side is usually careful in doing business with the other and makes every effort to accurately assess the risk of the other side with the information it is given. With the ability to immediately pass off the risk of an asset to someone else (and collect a fee for doing so), however, institutions had little financial incentive to worry about the actual risk of the assets in question. Such a misalignment in incentives can help explain the collapse of due diligence across the financial system that characterized the bubble years.

But what about those who ultimately did hold the MBS, CDO, CDS, and other securities? The buyers of these instruments had every incentive to understand and manage the risk of the assets they held. Indeed, rather than spread out risk across the financial system, securitization actually *concentrated* risk, as it turned out that many of big banks that issued the subprime-backed securities actually kept them on (or off) their balance sheet. The skewed incentives of securitization can thus only explain so much of the story. What else explains such a widespread failure in risk management?

One factor that certainly contributed is the poor corporate governance embodied by the structure of compensation in the financial industry. Wall Street firms have rightly been blasted for compensation schemes that paid traders based on the short-term profits they made relative to their peers at other firms with no consideration of their longer-term performance. While his concerns were dismissed at the time, Rajan (2005) illustrates very clearly how such a compensation structure creates two perverse incentives that can feed off each other to fuel a bubble: First, it encourages traders to bet on tail risk, or buy assets that might blow up a few years from now, but in the meantime will reap high profits and boost compensation for the trader. Second, because performance is judged *relative* to peers, such compensation schemes encourage herding behavior, as no single trader wants to underperform her peers. Even if she thinks the price of subprime MBS are overvalued, she will feel compelled to swim along with the tide and buy them in case she is wrong. These two incentives reinforced each other to create an environment conducive to a bubble.

The overarching reason for such market failure, though, was that everyone was simply caught up in a bubble that enveloped the entire system. Homebuyers and highly paid financial execs alike believed that house prices could go nowhere but up. Investors saw the large profits from subprime mortgage-related assets and wanted to get in on the action. Consistent with what literature says about common features to asset bubbles, both the *perception* of risk went down, as investors came to view securities backed by subprime mortgages as safe, and the *tolerance* of risk went up, as investors increasingly were willing to accept lower returns for riskier assets. Adding to the mess was the sheer complexity and opacity of the securitized financial system, which meant that many people simply did not have the information or capacity to make their own judgment on the securities they held, relying instead on rating agencies and complex but flawed computer models.

In searching to understand the origins of this financial crisis, we must ask where to focus our efforts to ensure such a destabilizing crisis does not repeat itself. While reminiscent of previous asset bubbles in many ways, what made this crisis so uniquely destabilizing were the financial innovations that allowed the financial sector to accumulate such a massive amount of leverage under the nose of regulators. It would be misguided to label this financial crisis as either a crisis of regulation or a crisis of capitalism, for it surely had elements of both. Better regulation is needed across the financial spectrum, ranging from consumer protection laws that ensure mortgage borrowers are not misled into loans they cannot afford, to better monitoring of credit rating agencies, and all the way to capital requirements that do a better job to limit leverage and to rein in the shadow banking system. The patchwork of federal and state regulators of financial institutions must be reorganized to more clearly define responsibility. Likewise, a serious reassessment of corporate governance in the financial sector is just as important to align market incentives with the long-run health of the financial system. But when the next bubble comes, it will surely be of a completely different beast and be centered around something entirely different from subprime mortgages. Thus, perhaps the most important step of all is a general, widespread acknowledgment of the limitations of financial markets to correct themselves, and a greater commitment to understand what policy makers and market participants can do to prevent such destabilizing excesses from building up in the future.

REFERENCES

Baily, M. N., R. E. Litan, and M. S. Johnson. 2008. The origins of the financial crisis. The Brookings Institution, Fixing Finance Series: Paper 3 (November).

Brunnermeier, M. (2008). Thoughts on a new financial architecture. Remarks at Princeton University (September 28).

Elmendorf, D. W. 2007. Was the Fed too easy for too long? The Brookings Institution, unpublished paper. (November 9). Available at www.brookings.edu/opinions/2007/11_fed_elmendorf.aspx.

Elmendorf, D. W. 2008. Financial innovation and housing: Implications for monetary policy. The Brookings Institution, unpublished paper (April 21). Available at www.brookings.edu/papers/2008/0421_monetary_policy_elmendorf.aspx.

Rajan, R. 2005. Has financial development made the world riskier? National Bureau of Economic Research, working paper W11728 (November).

NOTE

1. Glaeser et al. (2008) illustrate that home price run-ups in supply-elastic areas like the Midwest were much milder than those in supply-inelastic regions, as price booms lasted on average for four years in the inelastic parts of the country, and only 1.7 years in the elastic parts.

ABOUT THE AUTHORS

Martin Neil Baily rejoined the Brookings Institution as a senior fellow in 2007 to develop a program of research on business and the economy. He is studying the financial crisis as well as productivity and technology. Baily is also a senior adviser to McKinsey's Global Institute, an adviser to the Congressional Budget Office, and a director of The Phoenix Companies. He serves as the co-chair of the Pew Task Force on Financial Sector Reform and is a member of the Squam Lake Group. Baily was chairman of the Council of Economic Advisers and as such enjoyed cabinet-level status in the Clinton administration from 1999 to 2001. He was a senior fellow at the Peterson Institute from 2001 to 2007. Baily earned his Ph.D. in economics at the Massachusetts Institute of Technology. He has taught at MIT, Yale, and the University of Maryland, and is the author of many articles and books.

Robert E. Litan is the vice president for research and policy at the Kauffman Foundation and a senior fellow in economic studies at the Brookings Institution. During his career, Dr. Litan has authored or co-authored 22 books, edited another 15, and authored or co-authored more than 200 articles in journals, magazines, and newspapers. Since the onset of the financial crisis, he has authored or co-authored a number of essays on financial reforms for the Brookings web site (www.brookings.edu). Dr. Litan has served in several capacities in the federal government: As associate director of the Office of Management and Budget, deputy assistant attorney general, antitrust division, Department of Justice; and staff economist, Council of Economic Advisers. He received his B.S. in economics (summa cum laude) from the Wharton School of Finance at the University of Pennsylvania; his J.D. from Yale Law School; and both his M. Phil. and Ph.D. in economics from Yale University.

Matthew S. Johnson is currently a research associate at Harvard Business School, and at the time this chapter was written he was a senior research assistant at the Brookings Institution. He received his B.A. from the University of California, Berkeley with honors and with a dual degree in economics and history.

CHAPTER 12

Ten Myths About Subprime Mortgages

YULIYA DEMYANYK
Senior research economist in the Research Department of the Federal Reserve
Bank of Cleveland

O n close inspection, many of the most popular explanations for the subprime crisis turn out to be myths. Empirical research shows that the causes of the subprime mortgage crisis and its magnitude were more complicated than mortgage interest rate resets, declining underwriting standards, or declining home values. Nor were its causes unlike other crises of the past. The subprime crisis was building for years before showing any signs and was fed by lending, securitization, leveraging, and housing booms.

Subprime mortgages have been getting a lot of attention in the United States since 2000, when the number of subprime loans being originated and refinanced shot up rapidly. The attention intensified in 2007, when defaults on subprime loans began to skyrocket. Researchers, policy makers, and the public have tried to identify the factors that explained these defaults.

Unfortunately, many of the most popular explanations that have emerged for the subprime crisis are, to a large extent, myths. On close inspection, these explanations are not supported by empirical research.

MYTHS

Myth 1: Subprime Mortgages Went Only to Borrowers with Impaired Credit

Subprime mortgages went to all kinds of borrowers, not only to those with impaired credit. A loan can be labeled subprime not only because of the characteristics of the borrower it was originated for, but also because of the type of lender that originated it, features of the mortgage product itself, or how it was securitized.

Specifically, if a loan was given to a borrower with a low credit score or a history of delinquency or bankruptcy, lenders would most likely label it subprime. But mortgages could also be labeled subprime if they were originated by a lender specializing in high-cost loans—although not all high-cost loans are subprime. Also, unusual types of mortgages generally not available in the prime market, such as "2/28 hybrids," which switch to an adjustable interest rate after only two years of a fixed rate, would be labeled subprime even if they were given to borrowers with credit scores that were sufficiently high to qualify for prime mortgage loans.

The process of securitizing a loan could also affect its subprime designation. Many subprime mortgages were securitized and sold on the secondary market. Securitizers rank-ordered pools of mortgages from the most to the least risky at the time of securitization, basing the ranking on a combination of several risk factors, such as credit score, loan-to-value, and debt-to-income ratios, and so forth. The riskiest pools would become a part of a subprime security. All the loans in that security would be labeled subprime, regardless of the borrower's credit scores.

The myth that subprime loans went only to those with bad credit arises from overlooking the complexity of the subprime mortgage market and the fact that subprime mortgages are defined in a number of ways—not just by the credit quality of borrowers. One of the myth's byproducts is that examples of borrowers with good credit and subprime loans have been seen as evidence of foul play, generating accusations that such borrowers must have been steered unfairly and sometimes fraudulently into the subprime market.

Myth 2: Subprime Mortgages Promoted Homeownership

The availability of subprime mortgages in the United States did not facilitate increased home ownership. Between 2000 and 2006, approximately one million borrowers took subprime mortgages to finance the purchase of their first home. These subprime loans did contribute to an increased level of home ownership in the country—at the time of mortgage origination. Unfortunately, many homebuyers with subprime loans defaulted within a couple of years of origination. The number of such defaults outweighs the number of first-time homebuyers with subprime mortgages.

Given that there were more defaults among all (not just first-time) home-buyers with subprime loans than there were first-time homebuyers with sub-prime loans, it is impossible to conclude that subprime mortgages promoted home ownership.

Myth 3: Declines in Home Values Caused the Subprime Crisis in the United States

Researchers, policy makers, and the general public have noticed that a large number of mortgage defaults and foreclosures followed the decline in house prices. This observation resulted in a general belief that the crisis occurred because of declining home values.

The decline in home values only revealed the problems with subprime mort-gages; it did not cause the defaults. Research shows that the quality of newly originated mortgages was worsening every year between 2001 and 2007; the cri-sis was brewing for many years before house prices even started slowing down. But because the housing boom allowed homeowners to refinance even the worst mortgages, we did not see this negative trend in loan quality for years preceding the crisis.

Myth 4: Declines in Mortgage Underwriting Standards Triggered the Subprime Crisis

An analysis of subprime mortgages shows that within the first year of origination, approximately 10 percent of the mortgages originated between 2001 and 2005 were delinquent or in default, and approximately 20 percent of the mortgages originated in 2006 and 2007 were delinquent or in default. This rapid jump in default rates was among the first signs of the beginning crisis.

If deteriorating underwriting standards explain this phenomenon, we would be able to observe a substantial loosening of the underwriting criteria between 2001 to 2005 and 2006 to 2007, periods between which the default rates doubled. The data, however, show no such change in standards.

Actually, the criteria that are associated with larger default rates, such as debt-to-income or loan-to-value ratios, were, on average, worsening a bit every year from 2001 to 2007, but the changes between the 2001 to 2005 and 2006 to 2007 periods were not sufficiently high to explain the near 100 percent increase in default rates for loans originated in these years.

Myth 5: Subprime Mortgages Failed Because People Used Homes as ATMs

Rising house prices and falling mortgage interest rates before 2006 gave many homeowners an opportunity to refinance their mortgages and extract cash. The cash extracted from home equity could be spent for home improvements, bill payments, or general goods and services. Among subprime mortgages that were securitized, more than half were originated to refinance existing mortgages into larger ones and to take cash out of home equity.

While this option was popular throughout the subprime years (2001 to 2007), it was not a primary factor in causing the massive defaults and foreclosures that occurred after both home prices and interest rates reversed their paths. Mortgages that were originated for refinancing actually performed better than mortgages originated solely to buy a home (comparing mortgages of the same age and origination year). The rates of default for cash-out refinance mortgages within one year of origination were 17 percent for mortgages originated in 2006 and 20 percent for those originated in 2007. In contrast, the rates of default within one year of origination for mortgages originated to buy a home were 23 percent and 27 percent for the origination years 2006 and 2007, respectively.

Myth 6: Subprime Mortgages Failed Because of Mortgage Rate Resets

Among subprime loans, the most popular type of adjustable rate mortgage (ARM) is a hybrid, a loan whose interest rate is reset after an initial two- or three-year period of fixed rates. A fixed-rate mortgage (FRM), on the other hand, never has its rate reset. The belief that rate resets caused many subprime defaults has its origin in the statistical analyses of loan performance that were done on these two types of loans soon after the problems with subprime mortgages were coming to light.

Those analyses compared loan performance in a way that was conventional at the time, but which turned out to be inappropriate for these loans.

To ascertain whether ARMs or FRMs were experiencing different levels of default, analysts compared the proportion of outstanding FRMs that were delinquent to the proportion of outstanding ARMs that were delinquent. Based on that comparison, the proportion of delinquent hybrid loans had begun to skyrocket after 2006, while that of fixed-rate loans looked as if it were fairly stable.

The problem with this type of analysis is that it hid problems with FRMs because it considered all outstanding loans; that is, it combined loans that had been originated in different years. Combining old with more recent loans influences the results, first, because older loans tend to perform better. Second, FRM loans were losing their popularity from 2001 to 2007, so fewer loans of this type were being originated every year. When newer loans were defaulting more than the older loans, any newer FRM defaults were hidden inside the large stock of older FRMs. By contrast, the ARM defaults were more visible inside the younger ARM stock.

To illustrate the problem, consider the following example. Suppose there are 1,000 FRMs and 100 ARMs outstanding in the market. In the current year, 100 new FRMs and 100 new ARMs are originated. Suppose the default rate for both types of new loans is 100 percent within a year and that old loans do not default. The observed default rate for FRMs is 100 out of 1,100 outstanding loans (9.1 percent), and the default rate for ARMs is 100 out of 200 outstanding loans (50 percent). Even though the level of default is the same for all new originations, the FRM pool looks much healthier.

If we compare the performance of adjustable- and fixed-rate loans by year of origination (which keeps new and old loans separate), we find that FRMs originated in 2006 and 2007 had 2.6 and 3.5 times more delinquent loans within one year of origination, respectively, than those originated in 2003. Likewise, ARMs originated in 2006 and 2007 had 2.3 times and 2.7 times more delinquent loans one year after origination, respectively, than those originated in 2003. In short, FRMs showed as many signs of distress as did ARMs. These signs for both types of mortgage were there at the same time; it is not correct to conclude that FRMs started facing larger foreclosure rates after the crisis was initiated by the ARMs.

Myth 7: Subprime Borrowers with Hybrid Mortgages Were Offered Teaser Rates

By design, a hybrid mortgage contract offers a fixed mortgage rate for a couple of years; after that, the rate is scheduled to reset once or twice a year to the current market rate plus a margin that is prespecified in the contract. A market rate combined with the margin may be lower or higher than the initial fixed mortgage rate, as it largely depends on the market rate that prevails at the reset time.

Hybrid mortgages were available in both prime and subprime mortgage markets, but at significantly different terms. Those in the prime market offered significantly lower introductory fixed rates, known as teaser rates, compared to rates following the resets. People assumed that the initial rates for subprime loans were also just as low and they applied the same label to them—teaser rates. We need to understand, though, that the initial rates offered to subprime hybrid borrowers may have been lower than they most likely would have been for the same borrowers had they taken a fixed-rate subprime mortgage, but they were definitely not low in absolute terms.

The average subprime hybrid mortgage rates at origination were in the 7.3–9.7 percent range for the years 2001 to 2007, compared to average prime hybrid mortgage rates at origination of around 2 to 3 percent. The subprime figures are hardly teaser rates.

Myth 8: The Subprime Mortgage Crisis in the United States Was Totally Unexpected

Observing the extent of the subprime mortgage crisis in the United States and the global financial crisis that followed, it is hard to tell that this turmoil and its magnitude were anticipated by anyone. The data suggest, though, that some market participants were likely aware of an impending market correction.

In a market with rapidly rising prices, mortgage contracts that cannot be sustained can be terminated through prepayment or refinancing. Borrowers can change houses and mortgage contracts easily in a booming environment, and defaults do not occur as frequently as they would without the boom. Because of this ability to dispose of unsustainable mortgages, signs of the crisis brewing between 2001 and 2005 were hidden behind a mask of rising house prices. Using a statistical model to control for rising housing prices, Otto Van Hemert and I determined that default rates were increasing every year for six consecutive years before the crisis had shown any signs. This deterioration is observable now, with the help of hindsight and research findings, but it was also known to some extent to those who were securitizing subprime mortgages in those years. Securitizers seemed to have been adjusting mortgage interest rates to reflect this deterioration in loan quality. In short, lenders' expectations of the increasing risk of massive defaults among subprime borrowers were forming for years before the crisis; most likely, it was not the crisis that was unexpected, it was its timing and magnitude.

Myth 9: The Subprime Mortgage Crisis in the United States Is Unique in Its Origins

The mortgage crisis in the United States is large and devastating, and it has led to global financial turmoil. In this sense, it is certainly unique. However, neither the origin of this crisis nor the way it has played out was unique at all. In fact, it seems to have followed the classic lending boom-and-bust scenario that has been observed historically in many countries. In this scenario, a lending boom of a sizable magnitude leads to a lending-market collapse if it is associated with a deterioration in lending standards, an increase in the riskiness of loans, and a decrease in the price markup of said risk. Argentina in 1980, Chile in 1982, Sweden, Norway, and Finland in 1992, Mexico in 1994, and Thailand, Indonesia, and Korea in 1997 all experienced a pattern similar to the U.S. subprime boom-and-bust cycle. The United Stated has had similar episodes, though on a smaller scale, as well: a crisis with farm loans in the 1980s and one with commercial real estate loans in the 1990s.

Myth 10: The Subprime Mortgage Market was Too Small to Cause Big Problems

Before the crisis, there was a conventional belief that a market as relatively small as the U.S. subprime mortgage market (about 16 percent of all U.S. mortgage debt in 2008) could not cause significant problems in wider arenas even if it were to crash completely. However, we now see a severe ongoing crisis—a crisis that has affected the real economies of many countries in the world, causing recessions, banking and financial turmoil, and a credit crunch—radiating out from failures in the subprime market. Why is it so?

The answer lies in the complexity of the market for the securities that were derived from subprime mortgages. Not only were the securities traded directly, they were also repackaged to create more complicated financial instruments (derivatives), such as collateralized debt obligations. The derivatives were again split into various tranches, repackaged, resplit and repackaged again many times over. This, most likely, was one of the mechanisms that amplified problems in the subprime securitized market, and the subsequent subprime-related losses. Each stage of the securitization process increased the leverage financial institutions were taking on (as they were purchasing the securities and derivatives with borrowed money) and made it more difficult to value their holdings of those financial instruments. With the growing leverage and inability to value the securities, uncertainty about the solvency of a number of large financial firms grew.

CONCLUSION

Many of the myths presented here single out some characteristic of subprime loans, subprime borrowers, or the economic circumstances in which those loans were made as the cause of the crisis. All these factors are certainly important for borrowers with subprime mortgages in regard to their ability to keep their homes and make regular mortgage payments. A borrower with better credit characteristics, a steady job, a loan with a low interest rate, and a home whose value keeps increasing is much less likely to default on a mortgage than a borrower with everything in reverse.

But the causes of the subprime mortgage crisis and its magnitude were more complicated than mortgage interest rate resets, declining underwriting standards, or declining home values. The crisis had been building for years before showing any signs. It was feeding off the lending, securitization, leveraging, and housing booms.

RECOMMENDED READING

Demyanyk, Y. 2009. Quick exits of subprime mortgages. *St. Louis Review* 91 (2): 79–93.

Demyanyk, Y., and O. Van Hemert. 2008. Understanding the subprime mortgage crisis. Forthcoming in the *Review of Financial Studies*. Working paper version available at http://ssrn.com/abstract=1020396.

ABOUT THE AUTHOR

Yuliya Demyanyk has a Ph.D. in economics from the University of Houston, an M.A. in economics from the Kyiv-Mohyla Academy, Economic Education and Research Consortium (EERC), Ukraine, and an M.A. in physics from the National University of Odessa, Ukraine. She is currently a senior research economist in the Research Department of the Federal Reserve Bank of Cleveland. Her research focuses on analysis of the subprime mortgage market, on the roles that financial intermediation and banking regulation play in the U.S. economy, and on analysis of financial integration in the United States as well as in the European Union. She recently co-authored articles published in the *Review of Financial Studies, Journal of Finance, Journal of International Money and Finance,* and several other journals and Federal Reserve outlets.

CHAPTER 13

The Financial Crisis: How Did We Get Here and Where Do We Go Next?

New Evidence on How the Crisis Spread Among Financial Institutions

JAMES R. BARTH
Lowder Eminent Scholar in Finance at Auburn University and Senior Finance Fellow at the Milken Institute

TONG LI
Senior Research Analyst at the Milken Institute

LU WENLING
Research Analyst at the Milken Institute

GLENN H. YAGO
Director of Capital Studies at the Milken Institute

For generations, the mortgage market has successfully extended credit to millions of families, enabling them to achieve the American dream of owning their own homes. Indeed, the home ownership rate reached a record high in 2004. The growth of subprime mortgages that contributed to this record, moreover, meant that many individuals deemed to be less creditworthy were provided with greater opportunities to purchase homes.

Unfortunately, a system born of good intentions veered horribly off track, derailed by poor risk-management and corporate governance practices, too many longer-term risky assets funded with too little owner-contributed equity capital and too much short-term wholesale debt financing, and lax regulatory oversight.

In the past, the vast majority of mortgages were more carefully vetted and extended on more stringent terms by neighborhood savings and loans, institutions that originated, held, and serviced these loans throughout their lifetimes. But in recent years, the mortgage industry increasingly moved toward securitization (that is, packaging mortgages into securities and selling them into the secondary market, thereby shifting credit risk).

This sweeping change provided the mortgage industry with greater liquidity. But by 2004, it was becoming ever more apparent that credit was expanding too rapidly, on terms that were too loose. What began as healthy growth in mortgage originations and housing starts swiftly became a home price bubble in most parts of the country.

As home values kept escalating, many borrowers were unable to obtain loans on the basis of traditional standards. Mortgage brokers and lenders were able to keep churning out seemingly profitable mortgages in such an environment by casting their nets even wider. Soon many loans were being written on such loose terms that they made homes more affordable, at least initially, but were clearly unsustainable unless home prices continued rising. Real estate agents and many of those originating mortgages earned fees and then passed the associated credit risk on to others without themselves retaining any skin in the game. In the reach for yield, many financial institutions made questionable loans, and many investors bought securities backed by questionable home mortgages, while the regulatory authorities failed to take steps to slow things down to a more normal pace.

When home prices did come plunging back to earth, too many homeowners found themselves in way over their heads, and too many home builders found themselves with an excess inventory of unsold homes. But this is not solely a tale of home buyers who overreached and home builders who overbuilt. The damage quickly spread far beyond the scope of the actual mortgage defaults and foreclosures.

Not only did financial institutions suffer losses on mortgages they held; so too did investors who bought mortgage-backed securities in the secondary market. The mortgage-backed securities in essence became *another* giant bubble, resting on the wobbly foundation of risky home loans. Investors from around the world were clamoring for a piece of the action—after all, ratings agencies, essentially blessed by the regulatory authorities, handed out AAA ratings on many of the investment vehicles ultimately backed in whole or in part by subprime mortgages. These agencies, moreover, are paid by the very parties that issued the securities. Also, a large but unknown amount was soon at stake in the form of newer derivatives known as credit default swaps that were issued to cover losses on these types of securities.

From Main Street to Wall Street, one common thread runs through all facets of this story: risky and excessive leverage. Homeowners and major financial firms alike had taken on too much debt while at the same time taking on too much risk.

The U.S. economy, as a result, is engaged in a massive wave of de-leveraging, a scramble to reduce debt and obtain new capital. Even solid companies with no direct connection to the real estate and finance sectors have been affected as credit markets seized up, liquidity became scarce, and a flight to safety ensued.

In many cases, the U.S. Treasury and the Federal Reserve intervened in the market in ways not seen since the New Deal. The sheer size of the government bailout, moreover, with $9.8 trillion or more committed in capital injections and various guarantees as of late April 2009, provoked a storm of controversy. Many critics cried foul about the government's lack of transparency in its strategy; others fumed that by rescuing firms and individuals that took on too much leverage, the government has created thorny new problems of moral hazard. Still others worried that insufficient effort and funds were devoted to halting the rising tide of home foreclosures.

BUILDUP AND MELTDOWN OF THE MORTGAGE AND CREDIT MARKETS

The demand for residential real estate was seemingly insatiable. After rising at an average annual rate of slightly less than 3 percent during the 1990s, home prices jumped nationally by an average of nearly 9 percent per year from 2000 to 2006—and much higher in some overheated regions.

Fueled by low interest rates, subprime home mortgage originations increased dramatically, rising from 8 percent in 2001 to 21 percent in 2005 of total originations. Mortgage brokers found subprime loans attractive because they could earn fees while passing along the credit risk to those who ultimately funded the loans. In hindsight, many participants in the housing market who should have known better clearly underestimated the risks associated with subprime loans—and there were undoubtedly some players who chose to purposefully exploit the situation for short-term gain. Increased mortgage originations, in turn, pushed housing prices to even higher levels.

As for the risks being incurred by lenders, some seem to have operated under the optimistic expectation that home prices would continue rising—or that mortgage loans could simply be securitized, shifting the credit risk to another party.

The run-up in prices quickly outstripped historical norms. Indeed, in roughly 40 percent of the years over more than a century, housing prices actually fell, which means that any business that relies for its success on an assumption that home prices rise year in and year out dooms that business to failure.

There were other warning signals. Median home prices rose sharply relative to median household income and rent-to-price ratios also experienced precipitous declines. Given these signs, it is appropriate to hold regulators and government officials accountable for having failed to take action to curtail the boom by, for example, tightening lending standards and increasing capital requirements.

By mid-2007, it was clear that the housing market had fallen into real distress. The most obvious sign was a long, steep plunge in home prices. Falling prices unleashed a cascade of consequences, as many homeowners, especially those who bought near the end of the boom, found themselves underwater.

There were 5.5 million foreclosures from 2006 to the first quarter of 2009, half of which were subprime mortgages. Behind these numbers are countless stories of families in crisis. In many neighborhoods, empty properties sit neglected, driving nearby home values down even further.

Given the increasing dollar amount and terms of subprime loans being made, regulatory authorities should have initiated corrective action well before August 2007. Indeed, why do we have numerous and well-staffed regulatory agencies at all if they are asleep at the wheel?

THE PAIN SPREADS THROUGHOUT THE FINANCIAL SECTOR AND BEYOND

The financial crisis began spreading more widely in August 2007, and suddenly, the crisis on Main Street had arrived on Wall Street's doorstep.

The liquidity freeze and credit crunch were on: the meltdown of the mortgage market had produced a widespread shortage of liquidity and credit in the financial system. Firms with cash were holding on to it, and other firms were rebuilding their capital, making them reluctant to lend. These multifaceted problems soon spilled over to the real economy. Credit spreads widened, and stock prices declined. The unemployment rate rose as recessionary effects set in.

The disruptions in the mortgage and credit markets have been accompanied by huge losses. Worldwide through June 22, 2009, financial institutions have taken cumulative losses and writedowns of $1.47 trillion. They have raised $1.25 trillion in capital and cut 324,246 jobs.

The pain has indeed spread far and wide. Even the yield spread between municipal bonds and 10-year Treasury bonds increased to its highest level since 1970, at almost 10 percentage points. Tightening market conditions also reduced the supply of credit available to state and local governments, which increasingly faced shortfalls.

Even the safety of money market funds was called into question when the Reserve Primary Fund suffered massive withdrawals—$24.8 billion from September 12 to 16, 2008, or nearly half of its assets—and on September 16 broke the buck, which means the value of its shares dropped below a dollar.

All of these factors shook confidence, but there was another looming cloud: the unregulated market for credit default swaps (CDS), which had grown enormously in recent years. A CDS is a private contract between two parties, traded over the counter, so no one could say with certainty just how big each firm's exposure might be. Not surprisingly, CDS spreads widened considerably for banks.

WHAT WENT WRONG . . . ? AND NEEDED REGULATORY FIXES!

The crisis in the housing and credit markets demands that one understand what went wrong. Only then can one take the appropriate steps to fix the regulatory apparatus to prevent a similar disruption in the future (or at least contain its severity).

... with Origination Practices and New Financial Products?

Part of what went wrong in the mortgage origination process is that originators receive fees without bearing any of the credit risk. Originators could be required to have skin in the game to provide them with incentive to be more selective in the loans they originate.

It is clear that origination practices did not always provide adequate information to potential borrowers that would enable them to make informed decisions, especially regarding new products. Some borrowers simply did not understand the terms of their loans.

Instead of trying to limit the products financial institutions can offer, however, it may make more sense to concentrate efforts on better informing potential customers about the available options and the specific terms of their loans.

As regards credit default swaps, which have received a substantial amount of attention in recent months, greater transparency can be achieved by requiring the clearing and setting of these derivatives through clearing houses or on exchanges. This also provides for greater monitoring of exposures and posting of necessary collateral.

... with Securitization and Rating Agencies?

The broad industry shift to an originate-to-distribute model relies on the ability to sell mortgage-backed securities (MBS) to investors. Rating agencies play a crucial role in providing information about the quality of such securities—but in the wake of the mortgage market meltdown, their performance has been called into question.

The rating process for securities backed by subprime loans was marked by a fundamental conflict: agencies received fees from the very issuers who requested the ratings—and almost everything wound up with AAA ratings through the issuance of complex new investment vehicles that were created from the slicing and dicing of earlier securities. In response to this situation, fee structures could be changed. Furthermore, the designation of credit rating agencies as National Recognized Statistical Rating Organization (NRSRO) could be eliminated and use of ratings in regulatory system decreased.

... with Leverage?

How could the $1.2 trillion in subprime mortgages outstanding at its peak trigger such a large global financial disaster? Leverage is certainly a part of the problem. If banks maintain a leverage ratio of 10:1, $120 billion of capital can support $1.2 trillion. With such a small amount of capital supporting such risky loans, a 10 percent decline in the $1.2 trillion of assets could wipe out all of the banks' capital. Of course, some of the institutions were more highly leveraged than 10:1, and in some areas, home prices have fallen much more than 10 percent; so too has the value of the subprime mortgages. This situation created widespread uncertainty over how big the losses were and where they were located. And the biggest enemy of well-functioning financial systems is uncertainty.

One fundamental truth governs all financial institutions: The greater the leverage, the smaller the decline in asset values that can be absorbed before insolvency sets in. This is why regulatory authorities overseeing financial institutions set minimum capital requirements. Letting regulated institutions grow too big with too little of a capital cushion is a policy for disaster.

There has been a dramatic decline in the capital-asset ratio or the correspondingly long-term increase in the leverage of commercial banks. Indeed, each dollar of capital supported $3.56 of assets in 1896, whereas the same dollar supported $9.89 of assets in 2007. The leverage issue for financial firms is compounded by the firms also having to rely on short-term borrowings to fund longer-term assets. In

1994, borrowed funds were 14 percent of total assets, but they had increased to 20 percent by the second quarter of 2008. Heavier reliance on borrowed funds means that banks must be able to roll over those funds to maintain the same total amount of assets, apart from any increases in equity. This puts banks in a more difficult position when asset values decline and the investors from whom they borrow become increasingly reluctant to lend. In such a situation, banks are required to raise additional capital or sell assets or a combination of the two, even just to be sure there is sufficient cash to meet payrolls and other ongoing operating expenses. Of course, the worst time to sell assets is during a crisis.

... with Fannie Mae and Freddie Mac?

These two government-sponsored enterprises (or GSEs) became the dominant players in the home mortgage market. But both Fannie Mae and Freddie Mac were enormously highly leveraged. With thin capital ratios, any significant decline in the value of their assets would wipe out their capital—and both institutions did indeed suffer substantial losses when housing prices began to decline.

This dire situation can largely be explained by understanding that both institutions have had a mandate not simply to focus on profits, but to provide funding for affordable housing. Also, both institutions were recently holding relatively large amounts of securities backed by subprime and Alt-A mortgages (Alt-A loans are a notch above subprime, but considered riskier than prime loans).

Going forward, one might consider merging Freddie Mac and Fannie Mae and limiting their activities to simply guaranteeing mortgages.

... with Regulation and Supervision?

The crisis cannot be chalked up to a *lack* of regulators. It is not even clear that the existing regulators need more powers. It is worth considering whether there are simply too many regulators with overlapping responsibilities—who did not adequately use the powers already granted to them to contain the emerging problems in the subprime mortgage market before they spread. There are also at least 10 U.S. congressional committees that have some jurisdiction over the financial services sector.

There were undeniable signs that a housing price bubble was growing, fueled by the excessive credit being provided to consumers to purchase homes, in many cases with little or no down payment. Going forward, much more effort should be devoted to preemptive actions that can prevent asset bubbles rather than to reactive actions designed to clean up the mess once the bubbles have burst. There must also be a much greater emphasis placed on systemic risk than the risk posed by individual institutions. At the same time, regulation must be more countercyclical and less procyclical through dynamic capital and provisioning requirements.

In recent years, FDIC-insured institutions, particularly commercial banks, were not only funding the subprime mortgage loans on their own balance sheets, but were also providing both on- and off-balance-sheet funding to other financial firms involved in subprime loans. They were also directly involved in securitizing such loans through special purpose entities.

Lastly, the crisis made clear that the "too big, too interconnected, or too important to fail" issue must be addressed by, for example, a regulation that internalizes (taxes) a financial institution's contribution to systemic risk.

CONCLUSION

We have attempted to provide an overview based on our book, *The Rise and Fall of the U.S. Mortgage and Credit Markets* (John Wiley & Sons, 2009), to explain how the growth of dangerous bubbles in the U.S. housing and credit markets occurred. On multiple levels, there was too much reliance on credit, which is essential for economic growth and development, but it was allowed to grow at unsustainable rates through risky and excessive leverage. When the housing bubble burst, the government took on enormous amounts of actual and potential debt in an attempt to shore up the financial system and real economy, which only worsened the already staggering deficit. Future administrations will be grappling with the ramifications of those decisions for years to come.

ABOUT THE AUTHORS

James R. Barth holds a Ph.D. in economics from Ohio State University and was chief economist of the U.S. Office of Thrift Supervision and Federal Home Loan Bank Board, a professor of economics at George Washington University, an associate director of the economics program at the National Science Foundation and a visiting scholar at the U.S. Congressional Budget Office, Federal Reserve Bank of Atlanta, Office of the Comptroller of the Currency, and the World Bank. Barth is currently the Lowder Eminent Scholar in finance at Auburn University and a senior fellow at the Milken Institute. Barth's writings include *The Rise and Fall of the U.S. Mortgage and Credit Markets* (John Wiley & Sons), *The Great Savings and Loan Debacle* (American Enterprise Institute), *The Reform of Federal Deposit Insurance* (HarperCollins), *Rethinking Bank Regulation: Till Angels Govern* (Cambridge University Press), and *Financial Restructuring and Reform in Post-WTO China* (Kluwer Law International). Barth also is overseas associate editor of *The Chinese Banker*.

Tong Li is a senior research analyst in the Capital Studies group at the Milken Institute. She specializes in hedge fund performance, the U.S. mortgage market, banking regulations, and Chinese capital markets. Her papers have been published and presented at major academic and regulatory conferences, including the 2006 American Economic Association annual meeting and the 2006 Federal Reserve Bank of Chicago Conference on "International Financial Instability: Cross-Border Banking and National Regulation." She is the author of *Financial Institutions in Rural China: A Study on Formal and Informal Credit* and a co-author of *The Rise and Fall of the U.S. Mortgage and Credit Markets: A Comprehensive Analysis of the Meltdown* (John Wiley & Sons, April 2009). She received her Ph.D. in economics from the University of California, Riverside, with research focused on microfinance and economic development, and special emphasis on China. She received a bachelor's degree in international finance from Peking University.

Lu Wenling holds a M.B.A. with a concentration in finance from Auburn University and a bachelor's degree in business from National Taiwan University of Science and Technology. She previously held positions with ACE Group and Dresdner Asset Management Corporation in Taipei, Taiwan, and is currently a research analyst at the Milken Institute. Her research interest focuses on financial institutions and mergers and acquisitions. Most recently, she co-authored *The Rise and Fall of the U.S. Mortgage and Credit Markets: A Comprehensive Analysis of the Meltdown* (John Wiley & Sons, April 2009).

Glenn H. Yago earned his Ph.D. at the University of Wisconsin, Madison in 1980. He is the director of capital studies at the Milken Institute and a visiting professor at Hebrew University of Jerusalem where he directs the Koret-Milken Institute Fellows program. Yago's work focuses on the innovative use of financial instruments to solve long-standing economic development, social and environmental challenges. His research and projects have contributed to policy innovations fostering the democratization of capital to traditionally underserved markets and entrepreneurs in the United States and around the world.

Yago is the co-author of several books, including *The Rise and Fall of the U.S. Mortgage and Credit Markets* (John Wiley & Sons, 2009), *Global Edge* (Harvard Business School Press, 2007), *Restructuring Regulation and Financial Institutions* (Kluwer, 2004) and *Beyond Junk Bonds* (Oxford University Press, 2005), and co-editor of the *Milken Institute Series on Financial Innovation and Economic Growth* (Springer).

CHAPTER 14

A Decade of Living Dangerously

The Causes and Consequences of the Mortgage, Financial, and Economic Crises

JON A. GARFINKEL
Associate Professor of Finance and Waugh Business Faculty Fellow in the Henry B. Tippie College of Business at the University of Iowa

JARJISU SA-AADU
Professor of Finance and Real Estate in the Henry B. Tippie College of Business at the University of Iowa

U.S. housing markets have experienced in recent decades two distinct boom-and-bust episodes, that is, periods of large and persistent increases (booms) followed by significant decreases (busts) in house prices. The earlier boom, which began in the 1980s, ended with a bust when real (that is, inflation-adjusted) house prices declined by 13 percent over a 12-month period ending January 1991 (see Shiller 2007).[1] The current housing episode appears significantly worse and is arguably unparalleled in U.S. history. It began with the subprime mortgage lending boom, followed by a significant rise in home ownership rates and a sharp appreciation in house prices.[2] The ensuing subprime mortgage crisis coincided with a real weakening of U.S housing markets beginning in the third quarter of 2006. From their peak in July 2006, U.S. housing markets declined through December 2008 by 33 percent in real terms. This was accompanied by widespread mortgage defaults, especially on homes financed with subprime mortgages, though prime mortgage foreclosures are also at historically high levels.[3]

The severe disruption in credit markets that started in August 2007 centered on the deterioration of U.S. housing markets, subprime mortgages, and mortgage-backed securities (MBS) linked to them. It then degenerated into financial and general economic crises, as evidenced by the subsequent credit crunch, asset price declines accompanied by illiquidity and a general weakening of balance sheets of banks, households, and businesses, which significantly slowed real economic activity. The depth of the crises, particularly the collapse or near collapse of major financial institutions (including nonbank financial institutions) compelled central banks around the globe, led by the U.S Federal Reserve and the Treasury, to intervene using an assortment of tools at their disposal. Their goal has been to recapitalize financial institutions and inject more liquidity into the financial systems to prevent even more severe disruptions in global financial markets and economies. These actions have significantly affected both the composition and size of the Federal Reserve balance sheet, which at roughly $2 trillion, is more than double what it was at the onset of the crisis.

There remains considerable uncertainty regarding resolution of the crises and the extent of their global repercussions. Perhaps this is because the current crises have proven harder to understand. For example, the following quote by Ben S. Bernanke, chairman of the Federal Reserve, at the Federal Reserve Bank of Chicago's 43rd Annual Conference on Bank Structure and Competition, on May 17, 2007, is illustrative. "... all that said, given the fundamental factors in place that should support demand for housing, we believe the effect of the troubles in the subprime sector on the broader housing market will likely be limited, and we do not expect significant spillovers from the subprime market to the rest of the economy or to the financial system." In other words, even scholars with long and storied histories of studying economic crises, failed to anticipate the impending storm.

We study the current crises with an eye toward understanding the surprising nature of their suddenness and strength. As part of our strategy, we compare the current housing crisis (arguably the precipitant) with the 1980s housing market boom that ended in a bust in the early 1990s. We believe this study of differences between the two housing episodes permits a more insightful analysis, in particular, helping to identify potential triggers that precipitated the current crises.

We proceed as follows. We first study some stylized facts from the two housing price bubbles, looking for incipient signs of the collapse of housing markets. We find that house prices have become more variable over time, particularly in the years leading to the 2006 peak in house prices. Prior academic work on asset prices (noted in the following paragraphs) suggests that underpricing of credit risk leads to inflated asset prices, which in turn exacerbates asset market crashes.[4] Thus, the higher volatility of house prices during the recent episode could have been an indicator that a housing market crash was imminent.

We then study whether borrower defaults were differentially sensitive to triggers such as heightened house price volatility and interest rates, across the two episodes. The intuition is as follows. Much of the increase in mortgage lending during the recent housing boom occurred at much higher loan-to-value (LTV) ratios; indeed, a significant number of mortgage loans were extended at 100 percent LTV.[5] This means that borrowers put little of their own money (and in some cases, none of their own money) into the purchase of the house. With so little (or none) of their own wealth at risk, borrowers would naturally be more inclined to walk away from the mortgage and the house (i.e., experience default) if the monthly mortgage payments became less affordable. In other words, default was made less painful because households would be giving up little to none of their own money that would have been in a down payment. Such borrowers essentially had no skin in the game, a position akin to that of a renter.

This is exactly what happened on many mortgage loans that were offered with low teaser rates for, say, the first few years. These so called hybrid adjustable rate mortgages (ARMs), which adjust to full market interest rates once the teaser period is over, carry excessive risk of rising interest rates, causing such mortgages to become less affordable. Indeed, we find that declines in house prices and increases in interest rates both led to more defaults by borrowers in the current episode than in the prior housing bubble and bust (of the late 1980s). This finding, coupled with the behavior of house prices documented earlier, further strengthens the notion that there were potential indications of the impending crisis at least from the behavior of house prices.

But how did the housing crisis metamorphose into full-blown financial and economic crises? U.S. banks are exposed to negative consequences of volatility in the housing markets because they make many of the mortgage loans that buyers use to purchase homes. Consequently, in the event of borrower defaults, particularly during periods of heightened illiquidity, banks lose money. Banks must respond to this loss because it reduces their equity capital. Given regulatory requirements on minimum amount of equity capital banks must always hold, banks typically respond to capital reductions by altering their lending behavior, which usually takes the form of a tightening of credit conditions.

We find that banks indeed reduced their lending, both consumer and real estate lending, in response to the current housing market debacle. More important, the reduction was much greater in the current crisis than in the previous housing downturn. How might this explain the economic collapse? Consumer spending constitutes roughly 70 percent of the U.S. economy. Reduced consumer spending directly feeds into less economic activity.

Also, many consumers relied on appreciating home values to draw equity from them and finance additional consumption, which is made possible through refinancing. When house prices collapsed, this removed an additional support of consumer spending. Finally, the U.S. national savings rate has ticked up during the recent economic malaise, perhaps due to households' concerns about the deteriorating employment situation. All in all, several factors contributed to the slide in consumer spending, which has certainly reduced economic activity.

The concomitant financial crisis can be partially explained by recognizing that financial markets are indicators of the health of the overall economy. However, there is more going on in the current crises. We study how housing markets, banks, and financial markets are all linked, both during the previous housing episode and during the current one. We find dramatically different linkages in the two episodes. Specifically, the influence of housing asset values on banks, and banks' influence on the stock market are much stronger in the current episode.

In sum, the severity of current crises can be understood as follows. The collapse of housing markets triggered by rising interest rates (making mortgage payments less affordable) also caused severe deterioration in households' balance sheets; in some cases, homeowners had negative equity positions. We find that the associated negative balance sheet effects were certainly more pronounced in the current episode than the housing crisis of the late 1980s and early 1990s. This higher sensitivity was arguably driven by the "already smaller than usual" equity position in homes that most buyers started with. Second, the collapse of housing markets fed into banks' balance sheets, which then reduced their consumer lending. As consumer spending shrank (for lack of financing by banks and other reasons), the economy contracted. This contraction led to further declines in financial markets.

Finally, stocks appear to be more sensitive to housing malaise (through the bank channel) than they used to be.

While the preceding findings are interesting in their own right, they also beg the question of whether there was something in the behavior of macroeconomic and financial aggregates to warn of epic crises of the sort that have unfolded. Consequently, we study the average behavior of a host of macroeconomic and financial variables before and after the previous and current house price busts. The analysis of the real and financial effects of the bursting of house price bubbles reveals that fluctuations and declines in economic activity are features of both the current and previous housing episodes. However, a different pattern emerges in the behavior of private consumption in the recent housing crisis that was absent in the previous housing episode. During the current housing episode, the relative contribution of personal consumption to GDP was significantly higher than in the previous housing episode. Even more surprising is the lack of evidence of material deterioration in the relative contribution of personal or private consumption to GDP, more than a year into the current house price bust. On the contrary, the relative contribution was positive and higher than in the two years up to the peak in house prices.

We also document important contrasts in the behavior of residential housing investments and private business investments in equipment and machinery, between the current and previous housing episodes. The relative contribution of residential housing investment to GDP in the two years preceding the peak in house prices (boom period) was negative in the previous housing episode. By contrast, in the current housing episode, the relative contribution of residential housing investment was positive up to the peak in house prices, before turning sharply negative only after the bursting of the bubble. Likewise, the relative contribution of private business investment to GDP displayed a different pattern, in that it was positive both before and after the bust in the current housing episode. In contrast, the behavior of this cyclical component of GDP was significantly negative during the previous house price bust.

Taken together, the unusually positive configuration of economic indicators during the current housing bust (private consumption, business investment, and residential investment) may have had dampening effects on the fluctuations of economic fundamentals, and this obfuscated the risk and potential fallout from the bursting of the housing bubble. Perhaps this dampening effect made it difficult to anticipate the timing and relative magnitude of the collapse of housing markets, as well as the subsequent weakening of the economy. This may explain the received wisdom at the outset of the current crisis, even from astute market observers, that the behavior of financial markets at the onset of the crisis was irrational, sentimental, and thus not supported by the condition of market fundamentals.

These findings on the unusual behavior of fluctuations in economic activity and financial markets development are important for another reason. To make rational decisions and choices about savings, investments, and asset allocation, market participants must understand the conditions that precipitated the crisis, how the crisis propagated, and what prospective market conditions may look like. The question that remains unanswered is whether recent innovations in financial markets may have reduced the reliability of business cycles as a barometer for current and future states of economic activity.

NOTES

1. Robert J. Shiller, "Historic Turning Points," *Cowles Foundation for Research in Economics Discussion Paper* No. 1610, Yale University (2007).

2. From 2001 to 2006, subprime mortgages grew from $160 billion (or 7.2 percent of all residential mortgage originations) to $600 billion (or 20.6 percent) of all mortgage originations). Home ownership rates rose from 65 percent to almost 70 percent by 2006. In nominal terms, house prices appreciated by about 160 percent from the late 1990s to June 2006.

3. For example, in the second quarter of 2008, the foreclosure rate on subprime mortgages was about 5 percent, compared to about 0.67 percent for prime mortgages. This .67 percent default rate on prime mortgages, however, is more than three times the national average over this decade.

4. See F. Allen, and D. Gale, "Optimal Financial Crises," *Journal of Finance*, 53: 1245–1283 (1998); R. Herring, and S. Wachter, "Bubbles in Real Estate Markets, *Asset Price Bubbles: The Implications for Monetary, Regulatory and International Policies*, Chapter 14: 217 (MIT Press, 2003); A. Pavlov, and S. Wachter, "Subprime Lending and House Price Volatility," *Wharton School Working Paper* (2008).

5. Subprime Heat (CSFB), September 5, 2007, 21. See also Y. Demyanyk, and O. Van Hemert, "Understanding the Subprime Mortgage Crisis," forthcoming in the *Review of Financial Studies* (2009).

ABOUT THE AUTHORS

Jon A. Garfinkel is currently associate professor of finance and Waugh business faculty fellow at the University of Iowa. Prior positions include assistant professor of finance at Loyola University Chicago and visiting academic fellow at the U.S. Securities and Exchange Commission. He earned his Ph.D. in finance from the University of Florida. His research has appeared in several academic journals, including the *Journal of Finance*, the *Journal of Financial Economics*, the *Journal of Accounting Research*, the *Journal of Financial and Quantitative Analysis*, and the *Journal of Money, Credit and Banking*. He is currently researching the housing and financial crises, as well as corporate investment and financing behavior.

Jarjisu Sa-Aadu is professor of finance and real estate in the Henry B. Tippie College of Business at the University of Iowa, where he holds the Chester A. Phillips Professorship of finance and real estate. He is currently associate dean of the Henry B. Tippie School of Management, where he oversees four programs, including the full-time MBA program, the executive MBA program, the MBA for professionals and managers (MBA-PM) and the international MBA program in Hong Kong. Professor Sa-Aadu serves on the editorial board of the *Journal of Real Estate Finance and Economics*. He has written and published extensively on several aspects of real estate finance and investments and his publications have appeared in several journals, including the *Land Economics, Journal of Money, Credit and Banking, Journal of Financial Research, Journal of Real Estate Finance and Economics, Journal of Urban Economics, Public Finance Quarterly*, and *Real Estate Economics*.

CHAPTER 15

Making Sense of the Subprime Crisis

KRISTOPHER S. GERARDI
Research Economist and Assistant Policy Adviser at the Federal Reserve Bank of Atlanta

ANDREAS LEHNERT
Assistant Director in the Division of Research and Statistics at the Federal Reserve Board, Washington, DC

SHANE M. SHERLUND
Senior Economist in the Household and Real Estate Finance section of the Division of Research and Statistics at the Board of Governors of the Federal Reserve System

PAUL WILLEN
Senior Economist and Policy Adviser in the Research Department of the Federal Reserve Bank of Boston*

M arket participants appear to have put low odds on the possibility that subprime mortgage defaults could rise as rapidly as they did in 2007 and 2008. Investors required low risk premiums on securities backed by such mortgages, and rating agencies required capital cushions that, in retrospect, proved to be inadequate. Had investors and others anticipated the possibility of a sharp jump in losses on subprime loans, they would have demanded greater compensation for holding such loans, and ratings agencies would have insisted on greater subordination; as a result, borrowers would not have found credit as cheap or easy to come by, potentially limiting the appeal of subprime mortgages. Thus, to make sense of the subprime crisis, one has to understand how market participants formed expectations about subprime defaults around the beginning of 2005, as they were originating and purchasing what proved to be extremely risky mortgages.

---

*Originally published in the Brookings Papers on Economic Activity Fall 2008 (69–145). Summary written by Andreas Lehnert (andreas.lehnert@frb.gov). The views expressed in the original paper and in this summary are the authors' and do not necessarily represent those of the Federal Reserve System or its staff.

Our bottom line is that the problem had largely to do with house price expectations. Had investors known the trajectory of house prices, they would have predicted large increases in delinquency and default, and losses on subprime mortgage-backed securities (MBS) roughly consistent with what we have seen. We show this by using two different methods to travel back to 2005, when subprime was still thriving. The first method is to forecast performance with only data available in 2005 and the second is to look at what market participants wrote at the time.

We proceed by first addressing the question of whether the loans themselves were *ex ante* unreasonable. Loans made in 2005 and 2006 were riskier than loans made earlier, but this difference is far from sufficient to explain the subsequent rise in defaults.

We then focus on the collapse in house price appreciation (HPA) that started in the spring of 2006. Lenders must either have expected that HPA would remain high, or have expected subprime defaults to be insensitive to HPA. We show that, using data available in 2005, it would have been possible, albeit difficult, to correctly estimate the sensitivity of default to house prices.

In the last section of the paper, we discuss what analysts of the mortgage market said in 2004, 2005, and 2006 about the loans that eventually got into trouble. Our conclusion is that investment analysts understood, with remarkable accuracy, how falling HPA would affect the performance of subprime mortgages and the securities backed by them.

UNDERWRITING STANDARDS IN THE SUBPRIME MARKET

In this section, we describe changes in the apparent credit risk of subprime mortgages originated from 1999 to 2007, and we link these to default rates. We argue that the increased number of subprime loans originated with high combined loan-to-value ratios (CLTVs) was the most important observable risk factor that increased over the period. Furthermore, we argue that the increases in leverage were to some extent masked from investors in mortgage-backed securities. A decomposition exercise indicates that the rise in defaults can be only partly explained by observed changes in underwriting standards.

To track changes in the kinds of loans made over the period from 1999 to 2007, we use loan-level data on mortgages sold into private-label mortgage-backed securities marketed as subprime. These data are provided by First American LoanPerformance and were widely used in the financial services industry; we refer to this database as *the ABS data* for simplicity. The outcome variable of interest is whether a mortgage defaults within 12 months of its first payment due date.

The observable risk characteristics we focus on are borrower credit scores (as measured by FICO score), loan documentation (i.e., full or incomplete verification of income and assets), leverage (as measured by the CLTV at origination), the loan's purpose (purchase versus refinancing), nonowner occupancy, and amortization schedules. We divide our sample into an early group of loans originated from 1999 to 2004, which performed reasonably well, and a late group of loans originated in 2005 and 2006, which defaulted at high rates. As shown in Exhibit 15.1, we find that

Exhibit 15.1 Summary Statistics for Variables from the ABS Data

	All Mortgages		Early Group[a]		Late Group[b]	
Variable	Mean	Standard Deviation	Mean	Standard Deviation	Mean	Standard Deviation
Outcome 12 Months After Origination						
Defaulted	6.57	24.78	4.60	20.95	9.28	29.01
Refinanced	16.22	36.86	15.96	36.63	16.57	37.18
Mortgage Characteristics						
Contract Interest Rate (percent a year)	8.21	1.59	8.38	1.76	7.97	1.27
Margin over LIBOR (percentage points)	4.45	2.94	4.28	3.11	4.69	2.67
FICO Score	610	60	607	61	615	58
CLTV (percent)	83	14	81	14	85	15
Mortgage Type						
Fixed Rate	28.14	44.97	32.30	46.76	22.43	41.71
2/28[c]	58.54	49.27	53.40	49.88	65.58	47.51
3/27	13.33	33.99	14.30	35.01	11.99	32.48
Documentation Status						
Complete	68.28	46.54	70.62	45.55	65.07	47.68
No Documentation	0.31	5.58	0.38	6.12	0.23	4.75
Low Documentation	30.71	46.13	27.82	44.81	34.68	47.60
Other						
Nontraditional Amortization[d]	16.04	36.69	6.93	25.40	28.53	45.15
Non-owner-occupied	6.57	24.78	6.51	24.68	6.66	24.93
Refinancing	67.00	47.02	70.95	45.40	61.58	48.64
Second Lien Present	14.59	35.30	7.50	26.34	24.32	42.90
Prepayment Penalty	73.55	44.11	74.00	43.87	72.93	44.43
No. of Observations	3,532,525		2,043,354		1,489,171	

[a]Mortgages originated from 1999 to 2004.
[b]Mortgages originated in 2005 and 2006.
[c]A 30-year mortgage with a low initial (teaser) rate in the first two years; a 3/27 is defined analogously.
[d]Any mortgage that does not completely amortize or that does not amortize at a constant rate.
Sources: First American LoanPerformance; authors' calculations.

borrower leverage, loans with incomplete documentation, loans used to purchase homes (as opposed to refinance an existing loan), and loans with nontraditional amortization schedules grew from the early to the late period. Borrower credit scores increased while loans to nonoccupant owners remained essentially flat.

Leverage was not perfectly observable by investors because of the use of junior liens. When making high CLTV loans, originators often preferred to originate two loans: one for 80 percent of the property's value, and the other for the remaining desired loan balance. Loans with reported CLTVs at origination of *exactly* 80 percent were riskier than loans with higher reported leverage, suggesting that not all junior liens were disclosed to investors.

We decompose the effect of underwriting changes between the two periods by estimating a probit model of default, using observed underwriting characteristics. Exhibit 15.2 shows the effect of incremental underwriting changes from the typical early period loan to the typical late period loan. If loans originated in 2006 were truly novel, there would be no unique decomposition between house prices and underwriting standards. We have shown that at least some of the riskiest loan types were already being originated (albeit in low numbers) by 2004. As shown in Exhibit 15.2, leverage (including hidden leverage), especially when combined with other risk factors, was the most important factor that changed between the early and late periods. However, even taken together, the increases in risk factors are able to explain only a small part of the rise in defaults between the early and late periods.

Exhibit 15.2   Effects of Selected Mortgage Characteristics on Default Probability for a Generic 2/28 Percent

Loan Characteristics	Estimated 12-Month Default Probability[a]
Base case[b]	1.96
Base case *except:*	
CLTV ratio = 80 percent	2.28
High CLTV ratio (= 99.23 percent, with second lien)	3.76
Low FICO score (FICO = 573)	2.47
Low documentation	2.88
Nontraditional amortization	1.96
Home purchase	2.41
High CLTV ratio *and* low documentation	6.17
High CLTV ratio *and* low FICO score	3.76
High CLTV ratio *and* home purchase	5.22

[a]Calculated using the model estimated from early period (1999 to 2004) data.
[b]The base case is a 2/28 mortgage originated in California for the purpose of refinancing and carrying an initial annual interest rate of 8.22 percent (and a margin over LIBOR of 6.22 percent), with a CLTV ratio of 81.3, a FICO score of 600, complete documentation, no second lien, and traditional amortization. Mortgages with these characteristics experienced an actual default probability of 11.36 percent. Each of the remaining cases differs from the base case only with respect to the characteristic(s) indicated. Values chosen for these characteristics are late-period (2005 to 2006) sample means or otherwise suggested by the experience in that period.
Source: Authors' calculations.

What Could Be Learned from the Data in 2005?

In our original paper we describe in some detail the estimation of two separate sets of competing hazards model. One set estimated against the commonly used ABS data described earlier, and another set estimated against a novel dataset of ownerships; that is, the tenure of a single owner in a given property across several loans. These latter data are drawn from records made available by the Warren Group, which collects mortgage and housing transaction data from Massachusetts registry of deeds offices. A complete description of the technical details on the estimation of, and related inference on the coefficients from, these models is beyond the scope of this summary. We describe here instead the exercise and results.

Our goal is to determine whether market participants could reasonably have estimated the sensitivity of foreclosures to house prices using only data on the performance of loans originated through the end of 2004; this is presumably the information set available to lenders, investors, and rating agencies as they were making decisions about loans originated in 2005 and 2006. We produce out-of-sample forecasts of foreclosures using coefficients estimated on data through the end of 2004, assuming the house price outcomes that the economy has actually experienced.

Estimating the relationship between prices and foreclosures requires, in principle, data that include a house price bust as well as a boom. Furthermore, analysts using loan level data must account for falling prepayments as well as rising foreclosures during a house price bust. Given that the ABS data did not contain a house price bust through the end of 2004, and that they could not track the experience of an individual borrower across loans, we expect (and find) that models estimated using the ABS data only through 2004 have a harder time predicting foreclosures in 2007 and 2008 than models that include a house price bust and can track ownerships.

In both sets of models, house prices play an extremely important role. In the models estimated against the ABS data, house prices work through an estimate of the mark-to-market CLTV. In the model estimated against the registry of deeds data, we include an estimate of the borrower's equity in the property.

Exhibit 15.3 shows the actual and forecast default rates on the 2004 and 2005 vintages of subprime originations, where the forecasts are from models estimated against the ABS data through the end of 2004. Comparing predictions for the 2004 and 2005 vintages of subprime mortgages is a particularly tough test of the model's ability to predict defaults. Any results we find here would be larger when comparing vintages further apart. The model overpredicts (underpredicts) defaults (prepayments) among the 2004 vintage and underpredicts (overpredicts) defaults (prepayments) among the 2005 vintage. In total, the simulations based on the ABS data predict an 18 percent increase in cumulative defaults and a 16 percent drop in cumulative prepayments for the 2005 vintage of loans relative to the 2004 vintage. These swings would have had a large impact on the cash flows from the pool of loans. The actual increase in defaults (decrease in prepayments), however, was much larger. In sum, models estimated against the ABS data as of 2005 would have predicted substantial losses on subprime MBS had analysts run the actual experience of house prices through them, although they would have underpredicted actual losses.

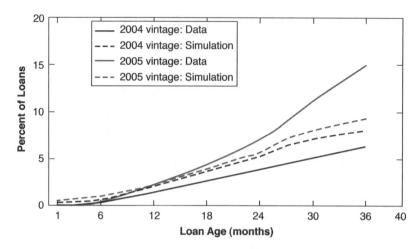

Exhibit 15.3 Default Simulations for the 2004 and 2005 Mortgage Vintages Using ABS Data

Simulations assume perfect foresight about home prices, interest rates, oil prices, and unemployment rates.

Sources: First American LoanPerformance; Authors' calculations.

We estimated similar models and conducted a similar exercise using data from the Massachusetts registries of deeds, collected by the Warren Group. Such data track when an owner purchased a home, some information on the type of loan used, and when and how the owner exited the property. If a foreclosure deed had been filed, we assumed a default; otherwise, we assumed a voluntary sale. These data are available back to January 1990 and track performance through a relatively severe local house price decline in the early 1990s. Although these data are typically not used by mortgage analysts, they are readily available, and, indeed, vendors sell national versions of the data (albeit at significant cost).

The major difference between the ABS specification and the registry of deeds specification comes in the treatment of refinances. In the loan-level analysis, when a borrower refinances, he drops out of the dataset, because the mortgage is terminated. However, in the ownership experience analysis, he remains in the data. Thus, perforce, for the same number of eventual foreclosures, the ABS data will show a lower apparent foreclosure rate.

Exhibit 15.4 shows the out-of-sample predicted foreclosure rates on the 2005 vintage of borrowers using coefficients estimated on the data from 2000 to 2004. We repeat the comparison of the model predictions for the 2004 and 2005 vintages. The model correctly predicted approximately 85 percent of cumulative foreclosures as of 2007:Q4 for the 2004 vintage. The model does not perform quite as well for the 2005 vintage, as it accounts for only 63 percent of cumulative foreclosures in 2007:Q4.

What Did the Participants Say in 2005 and 2006?

In this section, we attempt to understand why the investment community did not anticipate the subprime mortgage crisis. We do this by looking at analyst reports

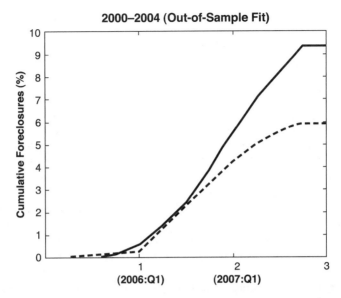

2000–2004 (Out-of-Sample Fit)

Exhibit 15.4 Foreclosure Simulations for the 2005 Subprime Purchase Vintage
Notes: This figure displays the results of an out-of-sample forecasting exercise conducted on Massachusetts registry of deeds data collected by the Warren Group. The solid line represents the cumulative percentage of foreclosure sales for home ownerships initiated in 2005. The dashed line represents the estimated cumulative incidence function for foreclosures from a competing risks model of home ownership termination. This is an out-of-sample forecast because the data used to estimate the parameters of the model came from the 2000-to-2004 period.
Source: Authors' calculations.

from investment banks, publications by rating agencies, and discussions in the media published between 2004 and 2006. We have chosen identify the five major banks we quote directly by alias (Bank A, Bank B, and so on). See the original paper for further citation information; many quotations in this summary are necessarily elided for brevity.

Five basic themes emerge. First, the subprime market was viewed by market insiders as a success story in 2005. Second, subprime mortgages were viewed, in some sense correctly, as lower risk than prime mortgages because of their more stable prepayment behavior. Third, analysts used fairly sophisticated tools, but were hampered by the absence of episodes of falling prices in their data. Fourth, many analysts anticipated the crisis in a qualitative way, but they never fleshed out the quantitative implications. Finally, analysts were remarkably optimistic about HPA.

In 2005, market participants viewed the subprime market as a success story. Bank A analysts referred to the subprime borrower as "Classic Middle America," writing that "[p]ast credit problems are the main reason why the subprime borrower is ineligible for a prime loan" and "[t]he deeply subprime borrowers of the late 1990s have been replaced by the average American homeowner." Analysts also noted the increasing sophistication of subprime market participants and their use of quantitative models estimated on loan-level data. Finally, market participants' experience with rating agencies through mid-2006 had been exceptionally good. Through 2004, subprime RMBS were seldom downgraded and more often upgraded.

Subprime borrowers were less likely to refinance their mortgages in response to a decline in interest rates than prime borrowers. As a result, subprime loans carried lower prepayment risk.

Of course, the absolute level of prepayment (rather than its sensitivity to interest rate changes) of subprime loans is quite high, reflecting that borrowers with such loans either resolve their personal financial difficulties and graduate into a prime loan or encounter further problems and refinance again into a new subprime loan, terminating the previous loan. However, this prepayment was also thought to be effectively uncorrelated across borrowers and not tightly related to changes in the interest rate environment. Mortgage pricing revolved around the sensitivity of refinancing to interest rates; subprime loans appeared to be a useful class of assets whose cash flow was not particularly correlated with interest rate shocks. Thus, Bank A analysts wrote, in 2005 "[subprime] prepayments are more stable than prepayments on prime mortgages, adding appeal to [subprime] securities."

Correctly modeling (and thus pricing) prepayment and default risk requires good data on the performance of loans in a variety of economic environments. While every major market participant routinely used loan-level data, these datasets typically started in the late 1990s and thus did not include any examples of sustained price declines. Most (but not all) analysts recognized this lacuna. Bank A analysts wrote in June 2005 "[w]e do not project losses with home appreciation below 2.5 percent because the dataset on which the model was fitted contains no meaningful home price declines."

Market participants clearly understood that HPA played a central role in the dynamics of foreclosures. They identified that HPA provided an exit strategy for troubled borrowers and that high HPA meant that loss severities would be small. Finally, they understood that the exceptionally small losses on recent vintage subprime loans were due to exceptionally high HPA and that a decline in HPA would lead to higher losses.

Virtually everyone agreed in 2005 that the record HPA pace was unlikely to last. However, many believed that price growth would simply revert to its long-run average without a big drop in national prices. At worst, some predicted a prolonged period of subpar nominal price growth. A December 2005 report by Bank A expressed the prevailing view that "[a] slowdown of HPA seems assured." In that report, the Bank A analysts stated ". . . the risk of a national decline in home prices appears remote. The annual HPA has never been negative in the United States going back at least to 1992."

ABOUT THE AUTHORS

Kristopher S. Gerardi holds a B.A. in economics and physics from Hamilton College (2002) and a Ph.D. in economics from Boston University (2008). He is currently a research economist and assistant policy adviser at the Federal Reserve Bank of Atlanta.

Andreas Lehnert is an assistant director in the Division of Research and Statistics at the Federal Reserve Board in Washington, DC. Lehnert earned an M.Sc.

degree in economics from the London School of Economics, and a Ph.D. in economics from the University of Chicago, where he was also a research affiliate at the Joint Center for Poverty Research. In 2006, he was a visiting scholar at the Urban Institute in Washington DC. His research focuses on household credit choices, consumption, and financial distress, including default, foreclosure, and bankruptcy. He has also written papers on optimal fiscal and monetary policy.

Shane M. Sherlund holds a Ph.D. from the University of Wisconsin-Madison (economics 2003) and is a senior economist in the household and real estate finance section of the division of research and statistics at the Board of Governors of the Federal Reserve System. Sherlund's recent work includes "The Rise in Mortgage Defaults," co-authored with Christopher Mayer and Karen Pence, "Making Sense of the Subprime Crisis," co-authored with Kristopher Gerardi, Andreas Lehnert, and Paul Willen, and "GSEs, Mortgage Rates, and Secondary Market Activities," coauthored with Andreas Lehnert and Wayne Passmore. His research focuses on mortgage markets, the housing government-sponsored enterprises, homeownership, and household choice.

Paul Willen is a senior economist and policy adviser in the research department of the Federal Reserve Bank of Boston. Willen's research focuses on household financial management; he has recently spent much of his time studying mortgage markets. His research appears in the *Review of Economics and Statistics, Economic Theory,* the *Journal of Finance,* the *Journal of Public Economics,* the *Journal of Urban Economics,* the *NBER Macro Annual,* the *Brookings Papers on Economic Activity,* and elsewhere. His research on the origins of the subprime crisis has appeared in scholarly journals and has been cited in virtually every major newspaper in the United States. Before joining the Boston Fed in 2004, Willen was on the faculty at Princeton and the University of Chicago. He did his undergraduate work at Williams College and earned his Ph.D. from Yale University.

CHAPTER 16

Miraculous Financial Engineering or Legacy Assets?

IVO PEZZUTO
Professor of Marketing, Strategy, and Business Development at the Swiss Management Center University of Zurich

This paper aims to demonstrate that the dramatic global financial crisis, generated by the U.S. subprime defaults in 2008, could have been addressed and managed earlier and better by many of the participants involved in the lending, securitization, and supervisory control processes had they implemented rigorous, systemic, and accountable controls. The article also shows how they succumbed to moral hazard, since it is quite likely that they understood what was happening in the market, but preferred not to intervene to change the course of events.

Most economists and financial analysts identify the following among the main causes of the current global financial crisis: the U.S. Federal Reserve's low interest rates policy since 2000, with the resulting credit euphoria of both lenders and borrowers; the more relaxed credit initiation and control policies and procedures of lenders; the overwhelmingly optimistic view of future house prices that prevailed in the market; and the widespread use of badly controlled innovative financial engineering tools (i.e., derivatives, securitizations, CDS, CDO, MBS, RMBS, CLO).

Although these causes reflect a portion of the big picture and help to identify and explain some of the key determinants of the global financial turmoil, the degree of complexity of the financial system coupled with its global reach imply a more interrelated and articulated set of responsibilities than those enumerated here.

There is no doubt that in today's globalized world and its highly integrated financial markets, the wave of profits and losses from financial markets moves very quickly across five continents. The speed of communication, online and real-time decision support systems, advanced computer architectures, and computer-based solutions have certainly simplified, but also amplified, the costs and benefits associated with global financial trading. In large part, this amplification is due to the much higher level of complexity in financial instruments and markets.

To fully understand what really happened in the financial crisis, it is important to identify the origins of the crisis. In the fall of 2008, the U.S. subprime mortgage loan defaults turned into Wall Street's biggest crisis since the Great Depression. As hundreds of billions in mortgage-related investments went bad, banks became suspicious of one another's undisclosed potential credit losses and preferred to reduce their exposure in the interbank markets. This withdrawal caused interbank interest rates and spread, along with credit default swap spreads, to increase. A liquidity shortage and tightened credit conditions for consumers and businesses quickly ensued. Central banks injected massive quantities of cash into money markets and reduced interest rates in an attempt to shore up banks and to restore confidence within the financial system. Governments implemented bailout agreements, issued protections from bankruptcies, and organized recapitalizations and bank nationalizations to rescue banks from disastrous bankruptcies to avoid an even worse economic recession, and to an anticipated systemic financial crisis. In the United States, the financial meltdown became so dramatic during the summer and fall of 2008 that it provided an effective additional spur to the election of Barack Obama as president of the United States.

The U.S. Federal Reserve laid the foundations of the credit crisis when it sharply lowered interest rates to a fed funds rate of 1 percent through a policy of monetary easing to spur the economy and to limit the damage of the stock market decline due to the 2000 dot-com crisis, the September 11 terrorist attacks, and the subsequent costs of the Iraq war. Furthermore, aggressive monetary policies were probably also introduced to reduce the GDP growth rate gap and to control monetary imbalances between the U.S. market and more dynamic emerging market economies.

In the years leading up to the crisis, high consumption and low savings rates in the United States contributed to significant amounts of foreign money flowing into the United States from faster-growing economies in Asia, as well as from oil-producing countries. This inflow of funds, combined with low U.S. interest rates, resulted in relaxed credit conditions, which fueled both housing and credit bubbles. It is well known that the consumer spending is the main driver of economic growth in the United States and that it represents more than two-thirds of the U.S. Gross Domestic Product (GDP). Just as in most other markets, the housing industry in the United States represents an important component of GDP and a major investment for households. The easiest and fastest way to increase housing sales, of course, is through very aggressive, convenient, and low-cost mortgage financing. Lower interest rates made mortgage payments cheaper, and the demand for homes began to rise, which helped to push up housing prices. In addition, millions of homeowners took advantage of low mortgage rates to refinance their existing mortgages.

The U.S. housing bubble rapidly escalated in those years in many local markets within the national housing market. At the national level, housing prices peaked in early 2005, according to the Case-Shiller Home Price Index. However, the rapid increase in housing prices caused many borrowers to be priced out of the market, and this led mortgage lenders to offer a wide variety of mortgage instruments, such as loans with low or no documentation of income, adjustable mortgages with low teaser rates, adjustable rate loans with low fixed rates for the first two to five years, loans requiring no down payment, loans with zero percent interest for the first year, and interest-only loans with negative amortization.

The resulting escalation in real estate values exacerbated unrealistic expectations about the future growth in prices for homes in the United States. There was overconfidence on the part of investment bankers, mathematicians, and finance specialists regarding their ability to offset any potential default risks through the use of state-of-the-art risk management techniques and the creation of innovative financial engineering instruments. These techniques and instruments included risk modeling, value-at-risk technology, securitization, portfolio diversification, and credit default swaps. This overconfidence further led to excessive borrowing based on wildly optimistic home price valuations as part of the residential home price bubble. Also, Americans allowed their savings rate to turn negative as they came to depend on their home's price appreciation to fund their retirements.

As the industry ramped up, however, mortgage quality fell because of poor credit origination standards, ineffective credit risk assessment, and an increasing number of low income and poor credit ratings on mortgage applications (i.e., Alt-A and subprime borrowers). Approximately 80 percent of U.S. mortgages issued in recent years to subprime borrowers were adjustable-rate mortgages. In June 2004, the Federal Reserve had begun to increase short-term interest rates, and the index for many adjustable rate mortgages, delinquency, and default mortgage rates soared as interest rates rose up to 5.25 percent in 2006. When U.S. house prices began to decline in 2006 and into 2007, adjustable-rate mortgages began to reset at higher rates, and refinancing became more difficult. The U.S. housing bubble started to deflate, causing poor households across the United States to struggle to keep up with their mortgage payments. The decreases in home prices resulted in many owners finding themselves in a position of negative equity—with mortgage debt exceeding the value of the underlying property. The dramatic rise in mortgage delinquencies and foreclosures in the United States triggered borrowers' defaults, bankruptcies, and repossessions, yet the pace of lending did not slow.

The subprime mortgage crisis would have remained a severe, but contained, crisis for the banking industry alone if the mortgages had not been securitized and systematically sold to other financial institutions, such as hedge funds, pensions funds, and investment banks, with all of this activity occurring in highly unregulated shadow banking markets.

Securitization is a process in which mortgage loans are pooled and act as collateral to back the issuance of other securities. The securitization process allows securitizers to transform a future stream of revenue into an asset base that can be used for further lending. With the sale of these structured asset-backed securities in the unregulated over-the-counter markets, banks have transferred the rights to the mortgage payments, along with the related credit risk, to the investors of the new securities. Through securitization, banks transformed much of the high-risk mortgage debt into structured asset-backed securities, mortgage-backed securities, and collateralized debt obligations, and they sold these assets in the financial markets around the world. Policy makers failed to recognize the increasingly important role played by the shadow banking system in the securitization process and the potentially devastating impact of their risky operations in adverse market conditions. As the evolution of the crisis proved, these institutions lacked a financial cushion sufficient to absorb large loan defaults or losses in the newly created mortgage-backed securities.

With the collapse of the first banks and hedge funds in 2007, the rising number of foreclosures helped to speed the decline in housing prices as the number of subprime mortgage defaults began to increase. As many CDO products were held on a mark-to-market basis (a fair value accounting rule that put a market price on any financial instruments held and traded), the paralysis in the credit markets and the collapse of liquidity in these products led to dramatic writedowns in 2007. When stock markets in the United States, Europe, and Asia continued to plunge, leading central banks took the drastic step of implementing a coordinated cut in interest rates. Governments also took equity stakes in major banks.

Despite uniquely adverse market conditions, which certainly contributed a great deal to these dramatic events, it appears quite evident that other factors also helped to cause the breakdown of the world banking and financial system. Furthermore, it appears that the financial crisis stemmed largely from the underestimated complexity of innovative financial engineering products and their trading in unregulated markets. The systematic use of SPVs (special purpose vehicles) and SIVs and the too ambitious short-term-oriented objectives and incentives schemes of the investment banks' management also contributed to the collapse. And last, but not least, even the roles of investment banks, credit rating agencies, and banking and financial markets' supervisory authorities have not been very transparent and proactive in providing and communicating timely assessments that might have mitigated the burgeoning crisis.

It seems quite unlikely that all the risk management specialists of banks and financial institutions involved in the subprime mortgage loans crisis simultaneously lost control of their portfolio risk and failed to understand what was really happening in their organizations. It is even more incredible that the subprime mortgage loan portfolios deteriorated so suddenly and unexpectedly that risk managers, internal auditing teams, external independent auditors, credit rating agencies, bank managers, industry and investment analysts and banking and financial markets supervisory authorities failed to perceive the increasing risk and potential danger.

The banks' subprime mortgage loan securitizations received investment grade ratings from the leading rating agencies (i.e., Standard & Poor's, Moody's, and Fitch). The generous ratings from the agencies has led to a widespread perception and a serious concern about conflicts of interests within the rating agencies. Ironically, securitization had been expected to make the markets safer through diversification and a more widespread distribution of risk.

Contrary to the familiar principle that low risk is accompanied by low expected returns, the presumed financial engineering miracle of securitization seemed to promise low risk accompanied by high expected returns. Most stakeholders in this innovative banking approach must have been very happy about the apparent miracle, at least in the beginning. Rating agencies' risk models certainly underestimated the impact that widespread defaults in an environment of declining home prices and rising interest rates could have on the value of complex financial engineering products.

Portfolio deterioration does not occur overnight if the risk management process is managed properly. At least risk managers should not receive significant, unexpected surprises simultaneously, given that their banks have different credit policies and corporate strategies. Even if the scoring, rating, and credit bureau models are not fully able to respond to rapid changes in market conditions, expert risk managers should be able to spot early warning indicators from unusual portfolio risk developments. Furthermore, risk managers might have also identified early warning risk factors through a variety of channels they monitor.

To summarize, the main factors that caused this crisis were:

- The low interest rates introduced in the U.S. market starting in 2000
- The high level of consumer leverage and the uncontrolled expansion of innovative financial engineering tools
- The activities of mortgage lenders, credit rating agencies, supervisory authorities, and policy makers in the U.S. market
- The high profitability objectives of banks

Today, governments and other institutions need to continue their efforts to save the global financial markets from collapse, strive to avoid a global recession, and seek to reestablish credibility and confidence in the banking sector and financial markets.

The following recommendations may help to avoid similar crises in the future: All financial instruments should be traded only in regulated markets. Contracts should be standardized and settled through clearinghouses, rather than being cleared directly between the contracting parties as they are in the over-the-counter market. The presently unregulated and uncontrolled shadow banking system should be dismantled. Banks and other financial institutions should implement more effective internal controls. The Basel II regulatory framework should be reworked to avoid procyclical effects and to reduce the risk of off-balance-sheet activities and securitizations. Regulators should review the requirement of mark-to-market accounting rules in times of crisis. All banks and financial institutions should be held responsible for the securitizations they create. Regulators should develop an integrated and international early warning system. Regulators should develop more transparent corporate governance rules for financial institutions and compensation schemes for the management of these organizations. Banks and financial institutions should focus more attention on business ethics and the development of a corporate culture of social responsibility.

The dramatic events of the subprime crisis have demonstrated that the global banking industry and financial markets have lost trust through their socially irresponsible behaviors. The lesson learned from this crisis is that regulations, ethics, transparency laws, corporate governance rules, systemic risk controls, and social responsibility principles are not just the job of bankers and supervisory authorities. They are critical elements of social justice in the interest of everyone in our society. If the global legislators and our regulatory authorities really aim to solve this crisis and avoid similar crises in the future, they must think seriously about creating a new generation of socially responsible leaders in all organizations and industries.

ABOUT THE AUTHOR

Ivo Pezzuto holds a D.B.A. from the Swiss Management Center University of Zurich (Switzerland), an M.B.A. from the Bocconi School of Management of Milan (Italy), a BS from the Stern School of Business, New York University, and several executive development programs. Born in Italy and raised in the United States, Pezzuto holds the position of professor of marketing, strategy, and business development at SMCU as well as other top European institutions. He is also an active partner in a management consulting firm. Pezzuto has a successful track record across a 15-year corporate career in Europe with leading global banks, financial services institutions, and multinational consulting firms such as ING Advisory, Citigroup, Diners Club, American Express, Accenture, and the Fiat Group. Pezzuto's most recent paper is "Miraculous Financial Engineering or Toxic Finance? The Genesis of the U.S. Subprime Mortgage Loans Crisis and its Consequences on the Global Financial Markets and Real Economy."

CHAPTER 17

The Making and Ending of the Financial Crisis of 2007–2009

AUSTIN MURPHY
Professor of Finance, Oakland University

T he credit crisis of 2008 has led to widespread financial distress throughout the world that may adversely affect aggregate international economic
activity for some time. While many blame lax regulation and borrower irre-
sponsibility, the true cause can be traced to inadequate credit analysis conducted
by the major insurance companies and banks before the crisis. Loans were insured
against default that never should have been guaranteed, and money was lent to
borrowers who never should have been granted so much credit. Also, in cases
in which loans and insurance on loans were offered to creditworthy debtors, the
interest rate charged was insufficient for the risk involved.

THE NEW VIRUS THAT INFLICTS CATASTROPHIC FINANCIAL DISEASES

It seems that many key financial managers involved in making and insuring loans
in recent years have been applying purely mathematical and statistical models to
the credit-granting decision. They have largely or completely ignored the practical
aspects of credit analysis that require educated or experienced human judgment
with respect to the future cash flow risks associated with debt repayments. Financial analysis without any evaluation by human beings is just one form of a larger
process of transforming financial decision making into just a numbers game that
can only result in catastrophe.

To the extent that the financial experts at the top of the world's financial institutions fail to learn from their past mistakes and correct their mechanical processes by
exercising some subjective human analysis, the financial crisis will persist longer
and deeper, cost more to resolve, and recur without end. Many of these experts
scapegoat various participants in the mortgage crisis, including lax regulators,
bought politicians, irresponsible and deceptive salespeople in the mortgage and
real estate industries, and reckless and deceitful homeowners for the financial
catastrophe. The elite of the financial services industry are rarely blamed, even
though it was they who provided the motivation for the questionable behavior

that led to the mortgage crisis. In particular, they lobbied against regulation of financial services, made legal campaign donations to influence important government votes on the regulation of their industry, created incentive systems that focused on short-term revenue and accounting profit targets, and at least tacitly condoned the widespread fraud that was public knowledge long before 2008. Most important, though, it was these elite experts who reduced financial analysis to a naive exercise in pure mathematics and statistics that ignored financial reality. They thereby created the foundation for a bubble in the debt markets that seemed almost designed to crash into a global disaster.

THE MORTGAGE CRISIS

The core mispriced instrument that led to the bubble and subsequent crash was the credit default swap (CDS). A CDS is essentially just a guarantee of specified debts against defaults that was given its special name largely to avoid the regulation and capital requirements associated with bond insurance. After lobbying by financial institutions to have their desired legislation passed by the U.S. government to enable such debt insurance with virtually no regulation whatsoever, CDSs exploded from a tiny market in the late 1990s to $60 trillion in guarantees by 2008 even though the aggregate value of actual debt being so insured was only a fraction of that amount. Many investors such as hedge funds bought and sold the insurance strictly for speculative trading purposes in highly levered gambles conducted with borrowed money.

Many financial institutions, including banks and insurance companies, sold the insurance contracts so they could record the periodic income from them without any capital investment, with little or no reporting requirements, and with virtually no regulatory oversight for the resulting excessive risk that was taken. The reported earnings of the financial institutions that participated in the massive scam were thereby enhanced in the short term with little or no disclosure of the risks involved. Without regulatory oversight, and with the financial institutions relying on experts using debt valuation models that ignored important risks, the competition for such easy profits put downward pressure on the price of the CDS insurance.

Within this environment, arbitrageurs such as hedge funds rushed to buy the cheap insurance called CDSs at the same time that they purchased the underlying risky debts in the actual bond markets to lock in guaranteed net returns that were significantly above U.S. Treasury yields. The extra demand for risky bonds raised their prices to levels that provided investors with yields only slightly above those on default-free Treasury bonds.

Such pricing also enabled debtors to issue new bonds and loans at yields that provided lenders with insufficient compensation for the risk. Having little or no knowledge of lending fundamentals but a blind faith in market pricing and mathematical models, the elite expert leaders of the world's lending institutions were willing to accept the yields offered in this market with little more than pure statistical credit-scoring systems without any subjective human judgment whatsoever. The effect of such inadequate credit analysis resulted in loans at artificially low interest rates as well as loans that should never have been made at all.

Compounding the problem was the development of a market for various new types of home mortgages for which past data on default rates were limited or nonexistent. The evaluation of loans by mechanical credit-scoring models based on inadequate numeric inputs resulted in lending decisions that varied even more from those that would have been made with human credit analysis. Most of the new types of residential mortgages, such as adjustable-rate mortgages (ARMs), which had fixed coupons and payments for as many as 5 to 7 years, had artificially low payments in the early years of the mortgages before they were scheduled to reset at higher payments and interest rates. Many no-doc loans were made without any checking verification of the loan application information that was put into the credit-scoring models, besides lacking any subjective human evaluation of the debtor's character, and so forth.

While many real credit analysts were able to forecast extremely high default rates on these loans long before the 2008 credit crisis, many of the leading financial institutions relied instead on their mathematical models that contributed to the market mispricing. These market prices were accepted by yet other ignorant lenders who blindly accepted them as gospel.

Also contributing to the problems in the mortgage market was the pricing of the guarantees on the various collateralized mortgage obligations (CMOs) that were widely sold by financial institutions in the form of CDSs. These CDSs on CMOs provided investors with the opportunity to buy into pools of risky mortgages that were widely perceived as virtually riskless because of the guarantees from insurance companies that had the highest credit ratings (like American International Group [AIG] with its sterling pre-crisis AAA that is equal to that of the U.S. government). Further protection against risk for the CMO investors was also available through the purchase of CDSs on the financial institution insuring the CMOs, thereby providing a private guarantee that another financial institution would pay off if the insurer of the CMO defaulted on its obligation to make good any losses resulting from homeowners defaulting on the mortgages in the CMO.

The insurance company AIG, which was in fact one of the institutions that relied too heavily on mathematical models and too little on human credit analysis, was an especially large player in the sale of the guarantees on the CMOs. It therefore no doubt greatly contributed to the mortgage catastrophe through its underpricing of the guarantees that it issued on those CMOs and that earned it a nice stream of profits for the first few years.

When payments and interest rates on the underlying risky mortgages began to rise by 2007, mortgage defaults started to skyrocket. Rapidly rising foreclosure rates on mortgaged homes followed shortly thereafter. A flood of foreclosed homes then popped the bubble in real estate prices that had been blown up by the extra demand resulting from the earlier conditions of the easy credit, which in turn had been inspired by the allegiance of financial institutions to pure mathematical models. Falling real estate prices caused more mortgage defaults, as the value of the home collateral fell below the amount owed on many mortgages, and the defaults and falling home prices began to feed upon and magnify each other.

THE LIQUIDITY CRISIS

As default rates on the mortgages underlying the CMOs rose, so did the price of guarantees on the CMOs. Financial institutions like AIG that had sold the guarantees were then faced not only with higher payoffs due to the defaults but also with higher collateral payments that were required according to the terms of the CDSs. In particular, many CDS contracts required the companies selling the insurance to post more security deposits when the market prices of such insurance rose, as the higher mortgage default rates were causing them to.

A liquidity crisis therefore ensued that first appeared in the summer of 2007 but was alleviated by massive interventionary help from the U.S. central bank (the Federal Reserve), which was widely thought to have averted a financial meltdown at the time because of its massive injection of liquidity. Because the $60 trillion in CDSs were widely contracted between many different financial institutions, the failure of one financial institution would inevitably lead to defaults on many of their CDS contracts and thereby lead to losses among other financial institutions that would be magnified by CDS guarantees issued by other financial institutions on the insolvent one, as well as by other liability relationships of the original failed institution. The failure of just one large financial institution might lead to the failure of one or more other institutions that would then spread to yet more financial institutions in a contagion that was feared might end in the collapse of the entire financial system.

Despite the Fed's successful intervention in 2007 to avert a major default at that time (and thereby prevent a systemic cascade of defaults), home mortgage foreclosures continued to escalate. The resulting continuing increases in the price of CDS guarantees on CMOs began to spread to the prices of CDSs on other debts as investors began to realize the original prices for insuring debt were too low, especially given that the risk of a recession increased the probability of default on all debts. Further CDS margin calls occurred, mandating posting of additional collateral by participating financial institutions.

In early 2008, a major investment bank, Bear Stearns, suffered a severe liquidity crisis resulting from mandatory collateral payments on CDSs that it couldn't make and that forced it to accept a merger arranged with the assistance of the Federal Reserve. After a short reprieve, a continued rise in mortgage defaults increased the prices of CDS insurance further, and the giant federal mortgage agencies FHLMC and FNMA, both of which were leveraged to the hilt, had to be seized by the U.S. government in the summer of 2008 because of insolvency.

Finally, another large investment bank, Lehman Brothers, was unable to raise capital to meet its own liquidity squeeze and went into bankruptcy in September 2008. The possibility of contagion and financial collapse suddenly became too real for many investors. This event catapulted the price of CDSs on all debts to extremes, while risky bond prices fell dramatically. The adverse effect was felt on CDS and bond prices on nonfinancial companies as well as on financial institutions, because the real possibility of a financial collapse increased the chances of a complete economic collapse that would result in defaults among companies throughout the economy.

THE WORLDWIDE ECONOMIC CRISIS

Yield premiums on loans rose dramatically as a result, leading to a drying up of lending activity. The mortgage defaults, along with the reduction in lending, created the conditions for a recession that caused yet greater increases in the price of risk and that thereby contributed to both a fall in stock market values and a further tightening of credit.

The collapse of the credit market bubble was felt worldwide, as the value of the assets of major financial institutions also fell with bond prices. A deep recession going into 2009 followed, but the various rescue programs launched by the governments worldwide that began in late 2008 probably spared the world a financial collapse at that time.

Nevertheless, despite government spending, lending, and loan guarantee programs that cumulate to approximately $10 trillion in the United States alone, it is not even completely sure if the situation has fully stabilized. While much of the money involved in these programs is composed of lending and loan guarantees that may eventually be paid back if the world economy does indeed stabilize by the end of 2009 as many predict, the size of the problem remains sizable. Some have estimated that there are about $3 trillion in credit losses at major financial institutions that may have to be funded to continue on the current rescue path, not to mention the cost of some of the other government programs that were initiated as a result of the crisis. While a complete financial and economic collapse may have been averted, it is quite possible that there will be several decades of stagnant economic growth in the future as a result, just as there have been in Japan following the collapse of its own real estate bubble in 1990.

SOLUTIONS

Better solutions exist that were proposed early in the crisis in 2008 and that still could be used to minimize the depth of both the resulting financial and economic disaster. These proposals include requiring lenders to accept shared appreciation mortgages with standardized terms on all mortgages that are in default (to remove the real estate overhang caused by the flood of foreclosures that is depressing home prices and further increasing mortgage defaults). Insolvent financial institutions need to be closed or nationalized instead of rescued (to save the government trillions of dollars as well as to enable just allocation of the costs of the crisis to those responsible). A massive stimulus package that focuses on federal and local government spending to make necessary improvements in both infrastructure and the environment, as well as on education and national health care, must be initiated (to maintain useful economic activity). Incentives could also be provided to insulate existing houses as well as to replace older cars contributing more to pollution with newer ones that are more environmentally friendly (to both avert the imminent catastrophes of global warming catastrophe and support economic activity in those depressed industries).

While such policies would likely minimize the costs of the current crisis, they will not prevent a new one that will almost surely reappear unless the core cause of the financial disaster is addressed. The only possible way to avoid recurrences of the 2008 crisis is for financial institutions to replace today's mechanical application of mathematical and statistical models for decision making with systems that incorporate at least some expert human judgment. No amount of government regulation or self-regulation within the financial services industry will succeed unless there is a return toward subjective human analysis that is grounded in financial common sense.

Having financial institutions run by human beings using financial common sense requires the education of managers with such sense. College business schools might seem to be the optimal source of such education, but a culture of elitism in academics that enshrines the mathematical rigor at the most prestigious universities as gospel has created a mold for business school teachers and students that emphasizes mathematics and statistics and strongly discourages human judgment, subjective forecasting, and business common sense. Without widespread change in at least the finance departments of business schools, there seems little hope for business school finance majors to contribute to solving the problem in a positive way.

While it may be virtually impossible to institute the necessary changes among the finance faculty at the most prestigious academic institutions, many professors at normal business schools may be quite open to teaching students something more practical than what is excreted from the most prestigious universities. If the financial crisis wakes them up, and if the horribly mismanaged financial institutions that dominate the world economy begin hiring their students (in lieu of the standard practice of recruiting strictly from the most prestigious institutions), the important pieces will be in place to resolve the current crisis as quickly and cheaply as possible and to avoid future recurrences. The government, which has been spending trillions of dollars bailing out the insolvent financial institutions run by robotic computer programs, should be in a position to use moral suasion and regulation to motivate such practices that would reinstitute human management of the financial services industry.

TEACHING FINANCIAL MANAGERS CREDIT ANALYSIS SKILLS

The crucial area in which financial managers of the future need to be educated to avoid another credit crisis is, of course, credit analysis. This key business function may be among the most important for financial managers in general to learn. However, with the exception of my own textbook (*Scientific Investment Analysis* that has been taught to my students since the publication of the first edition in 1994), I know of no other textbook that addresses the subject of credit analysis of individual debts on more than a purely statistical or superficial basis.

The widespread philosophy of credit analysis appears to be centered on the idea of finding statistical relationships between past default rates and various parameters such as accounting ratios, using the most advanced statistical methods and the most sophisticated mathematical analysis. The output of this philosophy is the magic credit-scoring system that provides a single number output for credit risk. While there are many different variables incorporated into the various credit-scoring models, relevant factors based on subjective forecasting, business common sense, and human judgment are generally not among them.

It has generally been shown that the human mind is more capable of incorporating many factors into decision making in a manner that is far more effective than even the most advanced computer models (e.g., see *Gut Feelings* by G. Gigerenzer). For example, to keep spurious correlations and noise from making statistical analysis totally meaningless and to avoid the nonsense of kitchen sink models, credit-scoring models generally contain only a limited number of variables. In contrast, the human brain evolved to be able to evaluate an almost unlimited number of variables using simple but highly effective algorithms.

A failure to use informed human minds at least as a check on the output of credit-scoring models is not only suboptimal but also a recipe for disaster. Any mechanical system is easily subject to human manipulation, and credit-scoring models are indeed manipulated by borrowers who can always use both conscious and subconscious human judgment to take advantage of the failure of such models to incorporate some relevant omitted variables and to misestimate the relative importance of other variables. Loans are thereby made when they shouldn't be, and others are made at interest rates below what should be required.

There are, of course, other problems associated with using pure statistical and mathematical analysis to evaluate credit, such as the failure to properly measure systemic risks and incorporate proper premiums for such risks. The important point being made, however, is that it is necessary to employ skilled human credit analysts in credit decisions. Such analysts may very well use computer models that incorporate complex mathematics and statistics, but they need to also have a core understanding of the cash flow and other requirements necessary to enable borrowers to make their contractual payments.

CONCLUSION

The current financial crisis was made by mechanical application of credit-scoring models without oversight by human beings skilled in credit analysis. That crisis and its recurrence will end when skilled humans are again put in charge of credit-granting and other financial decisions.

ABOUT THE AUTHOR

Austin Murphy has a Ph.D. from the University of Georgia (1984) and has been a professor of finance at Oakland University for the last 25 years. He was a visiting scholar at the Federal Home Loan Bank Board in 1988 and 1989 and a Fulbright professor in Berlin, Germany, in 1989 and 1990. His primary field of expertise is asset pricing and investments, and he provides continuing education classes on credit analysis. His writings include 75 published articles in academic journals and several books, including *Scientific Investment Analysis*. He was the editor of *Practical Financial Economics* in 2003. Current research includes working papers on the financial crisis, the psychology of financial cycles, shared appreciation mortgages, and mortgage refinancing.

CHAPTER 18

The Subprime Mortgage Problem

Causes and Likely Cure

RONALD D. UTT
Herbert and Joyce Morgan Senior Research Fellow at The Heritage Foundation

O ne of the fundamental issues often missing from most general discussions of the subprime mortgage collapse and the financial and economic troubles that soon followed was any clear acknowledgment of what exactly a subprime mortgage is. For the record, the term *subprime mortgage* defines any mortgage provided to a credit-impaired borrower with a FICO score below 660, and, of course, a prime mortgage is one provided to a borrower with a FICO score above that amount. Bank supervisors generally look for one or more of the following credit-risk characteristics when deciding to label a loan subprime:

- Recent payment delinquencies (30-day or 60-day, depending on recency)
- Judgment, foreclosure, repossession, or charge-off within the previous two years
- Bankruptcy within the previous five years
- Relatively high default probability (FICO below 660 or similar measure)
- Limited ability to cover living expenses after debts (debt-service-to-income ratio of 50 percent or more).

In sum, a subprime mortgage is a pretty risk proposition under any circumstances, and it is not surprising that they caused as many problems as they did.

For reasons most likely related to the pursuit of more profit in the otherwise dull, slow-growing, highly competitive, residential mortgage market, somewhere around the mid-1990s a number of financial institutions concluded that the higher risks of subprime mortgages could be offset by higher yields and fees, and began to offer mortgages to subprime borrowers who heretofore had been excluded from the market. And as home price inflation began to accelerate beginning in the mid-1990s through 2006, the perceived risk of a subprime loan declined in inverse proportion to the increase in the value of the asset that collateralized the loan.

And as perceived risks diminished with the rapid increase in the value of the collateral, many lenders began to tailor the loan and repayment terms to increase the pool of potential subprime borrowers with such devices as no down payment, interest-only, below-market teaser rates, second loans, and pay-whatever-you-want schemes. At the same time, many of these risky instruments were extended to prime borrowers, hence the Alt-A market and jumbo loans. It should also be noted that the expanded appetite for risk in the mortgage market also carried over into credit cards, car loans and leases, commercial loans, and cell phone subscriptions, to name just several industries where lax credit standards became more common.

With the benefit of hindsight, many looking back on this 10-year period of rapid credit growth now wonder how this collapse of credit standards could have happened, and why the many government financial market regulators and policy makers in Congress and the White House did nothing to stop it. While a definitive answer may be many years away, and require a detailed forensic analysis of the many institutions—both public and private—involved in the process, the simple fact is that many involved in the oversight process—including both liberals and conservatives—viewed this shift in risk appetite as a desirable trend that opened up the opportunity for ownership and asset accumulation to those of modest and financially troubled circumstances who heretofore had been excluded from this process because of impaired credit or minimal or nonexistent net worth.

Among some of the factors contributing to the institutionalization of diminished risk averseness was the "ownership society" policy of President George W. Bush, through which the privatization of Social Security and proposals to boost home ownership through no down payment FHA loans were designed to boost asset accumulation for African-Americans, whose home ownership rate today is not materially different from that of the nation as a whole in 1890.[1] As for the two government-sponsored enterprises (GSE)—Fannie Mae and Freddie Mac—legislation enacted in the early 1990s led the administrations of presidents Clinton and Bush to push both institutions to match the private market's share of originations of risky loans to lower-income borrowers or to borrowers buying homes in lower-income communities. Thus, as the private market pursued greater risks through offering more subprime loans, Fannie Mae and Freddie Mac were required to match the private sector's trends, thereby leading both to acquire riskier portfolios of mortgage loans than they might otherwise have wanted at the time.[2]

As a consequence of the more liberal lending policies by mortgage lenders and investors, by 2006, about 48 percent of the residential mortgages originated were subprime, Alt-A, or seconds (compared to 15 percent in 2001), and the impact of this trend on the housing market (and economy) was nothing short of spectacular.[3] Single-family housing starts increased to a record of 1.7 million units in 2005 compared to an annual average of 1.1 million during the decade of the 1990s, and the earlier peak of 1.3 million single-family starts in 1972 when generous federal subsidies were driving the market.[4] More significantly, the home ownership rate increased from 65 percent in 1995 to 69.1 percent by the first quarter of 2005—the highest in American history.[5] With the number of households in 2005 estimated at 110 million, the diminished mortgage credit standards can be said to have created an additional four to five million new homeowners that might otherwise not have existed. In this sense, the ownership society policy was an amazing success.

As attractive as this outcome was to policy makers and to those involved in many of the businesses serving the housing and housing finance market, these benefits spilled into the rest of the economy. Over the same period, mortgage refinancings and second loans were subject to the same liberal standards, and much of the cash pulled out of the house was used for other consumer spending purposes. And at the same time, and in a little understood process that suggested that consumers themselves had become less risk adverse in their own financial positions, the personal savings rate declined from 9 percent in 1989 to less than 1 percent in 2005,[6] while at the same time they were adding more debt. This, too, contributed to the economic expansion by allowing consumer spending to grow faster than incomes as consumers drew down their financial assets in favor of more consumption. How much of the economic growth over the period from 1995 to 2006 is attributable to these changes in credit markets and household dissaving is unknown at this time, but it seems likely that it was an important component of the growth that did occur during those years.

As the record reveals, subprime mortgages experienced high default and fore-closure rates in 2002 (15 percent and 9 percent, respectively) in the economic slowdown that followed the September 11 terrorist attacks.[7] As the economy improved, the subprime default rate soon fell below that on FHA mortgages, but the advantage was deceptive and largely reflects the rapid expansion in the number of outstanding subprime mortgages (the denominator) in comparison to those sufficiently seasoned to run into problems (the numerator). Moreover, inasmuch as subprimes were still a small part of the market, problems in that sector were thought unlikely to adversely affect the housing finance system as a whole, let alone the overall economy.

But this all soon changed. The financial underpinnings of this seeming buoyant prosperity began to unravel sometime in the beginning of 2006 when the default rates on subprime loans soared to 13 percent and then to 17 percent by the end of 2007,[8] while at the same time the value of the collateral securing these loans flattened and then began to decline as well, especially in the overheated markets of California, Florida, Arizona, and Nevada. According to the National Association of Realtors, the median home price in Los Angeles fell from $593,600 in 2007 to $303,500 in early 2009 and from $317,400 in Las Vegas in 2006 to $155,300 in early 2009. Miami peaked at $371,200 in 2006 and fell to $206,000 in 2009.[9] What is important to note here, and perhaps says volumes about just how poorly underwritten many of these mortgages were, is that the serious default and foreclosure problems first emerged when the economy was still growing, when the unemployment rate was below 5 percent, and when most of the defaulting borrowers were gainfully employed.

Highly leveraged mortgage lenders concentrating on subprime mortgages were to first to go under as defaults soared, but the contagion soon spread up the financial food chain because many of the nation's leading investment firms had incurred extensive obligations in support of the billions of dollars of mortgage-backed securities they had issued to global investors and that were largely collateralized by high-yield, subprime mortgages that were now defaulting at a frightening pace. Although many economists and financial market participants at the time believed that the subprime collapse could be contained, that the overall economy would continue to grow, albeit slowly, and that the housing market would soon recover, the financial market collapse during the second half of 2008 proved how wrong these optimistic forecasts had been.

By mid-2009, the housing and housing finance market was still declining, and the overall economy was in the midst of a serious recession. In turn, the housing finance collapse that occurred when the economy was relatively healthy has since been exacerbated by an economy that is anything but that. As unemployment hovered around 10 percent, attributes of the contagion have now spread to the prime mortgage market, and, for the first time since the advent of the subprime market, fixed-rate prime mortgages represented the largest share of new foreclosures during the first quarter of 2009. The overall mortgage delinquency rate in early 2009 stood at 9.12 percent, the highest rate since the Mortgage Bankers Association began calculating the measure in 1972. Including mortgages in foreclosure, the rate was 12.07 percent, more than 1 in 10 of outstanding residential mortgages. Subprime loan delinquency rates reached almost 25 percent, while FHA loans were at nearly 14 percent. The foreclosure rate on subprime loans was 14 percent, compared to 2.76 percent on prime loans. In sum, the housing market is the worst it has been since the Great Depression of the 1930s.[10]

Although there is a substantial amount of anecdotal evidence to indicate that home prices and land values were still falling in mid-2009, many economic forecasters and housing market analysts remain upbeat on the prospect of a near-term recovery in the residential housing market. Unfortunately, long-term patterns and relationships in the housing market suggest that such a turnaround is unlikely anytime soon.

As noted earlier, the advent of subprime and Alt-A mortgages helped propel the nation's home ownership rate from 65 percent in 1995 to 69.1 percent in early 2005, adding an additional four to five million new homeowners who achieved that status thanks to diminished credit standards. With many of these newly minted homeowners demonstrating by their actions that they were not in fact capable of fulfilling the financial responsibilities of home ownership, many of them are losing their homes and becoming renters through foreclosure, deed in lieu of foreclosure, or short sales. According to the U.S. Census Bureau, the home ownership rate in the first quarter of 2009 stood at 67.3 percent, nearly two percentage points below the 69.1 percent peak in 2005. As a consequence of this decline in home ownership and escalation in foreclosures, in 2008 there were 18.7 million vacant residential housing units in the United States.[11]

Based upon long-run housing market patterns and the restoration of less risky lending practices to the residential housing finance market, it seems likely that the homeownership rate will continue to drift downward to the 65 percent rate of 1995, and maybe even lower if the economy remains weak and the financial sector troubled. The home ownership rate in the United States before World War II hovered in the 40 percent range, but in the immediate postwar era, it soared to 63 percent by the early 1960s, thanks to rising prosperity and an improved housing finance system. Despite numerous periods of financial turmoil, rising incomes and several booms and busts, the home ownership rate remained within the 63-to-65 percent range during the 35 years between 1960 and 1995.[12]

For the most part, the market's long-term maintenance of this 63-to-65 percent range reflects several factors: the share of households wanting to be homeowners, the share of households that can afford to be homeowners, and the underwriting standards of the period that limited mortgage credit to prime borrowers who could afford a meaningful down payment (equity investment), and excluded those prospective borrowers now defined as subprime, that is, those with FICO scores below 660.

As the market and the market's many regulators react to these lessons by requiring a reversion to the stiffer underwriting standards common to the 1960-to-1995 period, credit will be hard to come by for many prospective buyers, and the growing volume of foreclosed and abandoned homes will meet a diminished number of eligible buyers thanks to these tougher standards. If in fact the market does trend to a 65 percent home ownership rate, then the number of current homeowners will have to decline by about another two million from the number of homeowners in early 2009, and this means that many more housing units will join the national inventory of vacant homes and apartments.

To the extent that such an outcome is likely to transpire, federal policy makers confront a troubling dilemma. Given the shattered state of U.S. and global financial markets, efforts by financial regulators (as well as by shareholders and other investors) to impose tougher underwriting standards on all financial institutions will hasten the recovery of the financial markets, and contribute to growing confidence and future economic growth and recovery. These tougher underwriting standards, however, will also sustain the current level of stagnation in the housing and construction market, thereby dulling the economic recovery as the housing market continues to deteriorate as it seeks a sustainable equilibrium at a lower rate of home ownership.

Unfortunately, a solution to this dilemma that the federal government is most likely to adopt is the socialization of housing finance risk by massively expanding the role of the federal government into the operation of the housing finance system. With Fannie Mae and Freddie Mac now largely owned and controlled by the federal government, and with a number of the mortgage relief programs dependent upon a revival of the once moribund Federal Housing Administration to refinance risky borrowers to deter foreclosures, it seems increasingly likely that subprime borrowers, borrowers with insufficient incomes, and borrowers without the wherewithal for a down payment will be welcomed by a federal government eager to stimulate the economy through the housing market at whatever the cost.

NOTES

1. See Ronald D. Utt, "Congress's Risky Zero Down Payment Plan Will Undermine FHA's Soundness and Discourage Self-Reliance," *Heritage Web Memo* 529, July 9, 2004, www.heritage.org/Research/Budget/wm529.cfm.

2. Harold L. Bunce, "The GSE's Funding of Affordable Loans: A 2004–2005 Update," *Housing Finance Working Paper Series*, Office of Policy Development and Research, United States Department of Housing and Urban Development, Working Paper No. HF-018, June 2007.

3. Darryl E. Getter, Mark Jickling, Marc Labonte, and Edward Vincent Murphy, "Financial Crisis? The Liquidity Crunch of August 2007," Congressional Research Service, *Report for Congress*, September 21, 2007, 3, http://assets.opencrs.com/rpts/RL34182_20070921.pdf.

4. Economic Report of the President: 2008, United States Government Printing Office, Washington, DC, 2008, Table B-56 (New Private Housing Units Started, Authorized and Completed and Houses Sold, 1959–2007), 291.

5. "Housing Vacancies and Home Ownership," Annual Statistics 2007, Table 12, U.S. Census Bureau, www.census.gov/hhes/www/housing/hvs/annual07/ann07t12.html.

6. Economic Report of the President: 2008, United States Government Printing Office, Washington, DC, 2008, Table B-30 (Disposition of Personal Income, 1959–2007), 262.

7. Mortgage Bankers Association, National Delinquency Survey, 4th quarter, 2007, December 31, 2007.

8. Mortgage Bankers Association, National Delinquency Survey, 4th quarter, 2007, December 31, 2007.

9. "Median Sales Prices of Existing Single-Family Homes for Metropolitan Areas: 2009:I," National Association of Realtors, www.realtor.org/wps/wcm/connect/882586804e108 aadb922ffec21680fb0/REL09Q1T.pdf?MOD=AJPERES&CACHEID=882586804e108aa db922ffec21680fb0.

10. "Delinquencies and Foreclosures Continue to Climb in Latest MBA National Delinquency Survey," Mortgage Bankers Association, Washington DC, May 28, 2009, www.mbaa.org/NewsandMedia/PressCenter/69031.htm.

11. "Housing Vacancy Survey—Historical Table 7, Housing Vacancies and Home Ownership, Table 7: Estimates of the Total Housing Inventory for the United States: 1965 to Present," U.S. Census Bureau, www.census.gov/hhes/www/housing/hvs/historic/ index.html.

12. "Housing Vacancies and Home Ownership," Annual Statistics 2007, Table 12, U.S. Census Bureau, www.census.gov/hhes/www/housing/hvs/annual07/ann07t12.html.

ABOUT THE AUTHOR

Ronald D. Utt is the Herbert and Joyce Morgan senior research fellow at the Heritage Foundation, and holds a doctorate in economics from Indiana University and a B.A. degree in business administration from Penn State University At Heritage, Utt conducts research on housing, transportation, and the federal budget, and also the application of privatization, restructuring, decentralization, and devolution of government programs. He also writes on the success and failure of policies for urban revitalization, land use, and growth management. Earlier, Dr. Utt served as director of the Housing Finance Division at the Department of Housing and Urban Development, and was senior economist at the Office of Management and Budget. In 1987, President Reagan appointed Utt to be the director of privatization to lead his administration's efforts to promote the transfer of some federal government functions to the private sector. Dr. Utt produced and edited two Heritage Foundation books: *A Guide to Smart Growth* and *21st Century Highways*. He lives on the Rappahannock River with his wife Michele in Fredericksburg, Virginia.

CHAPTER 19

Sequence of Asset Bubbles and the Global Financial Crisis

ABOL JALILVAND
Dean of the School of Business Administration and Professor of Finance,
School of Business Administration, Loyola University Chicago

A. G. (TASSOS) MALLIARIS
Professor of Economics and Finance, School of Business Administration,
Loyola University Chicago

The financial crisis that began in August 2007 evolved to become one of the worst since the Great Depression. Its severity within the financial sector and its significant impact on the real economy are extensive and well documented. Considerable research has also identified several contributing causes.

The likely causes can be categorized in subgroups including factors rooted in macroeconomics (the decline in real estate prices), monetary policy (low interest rates during 2002 to 2004), microeconomics (subprime lending, opaque derivative securities, excessive risk taking, failed risk management strategies), and government deregulation (the abolishment of the Glass-Steagall Act, absence of regulation for credit derivatives). There are also institutional issues (problems with rating agencies, originate-to-distribute), global considerations (savings glut, fixed exchange rates for certain countries such as China), ethical violations (greed and corruption), and even psychological attributes (animal spirits). The collection of papers in this volume explores these issues and several more.

The intensity, complexity, and length of the crisis justify the multiplicity and interrelatedness of causal factors. These factors are now weaved into analytical frameworks and empirical scenarios to facilitate our understanding of why and how it happened and to help us both discover ways to get out of it and avoid its reoccurrence. In this essay, we refocus the spotlight on a sequence of bubbles that were an integral part of the financial and economic landscape during the last decade and argue that their investigation can give us valuable clues, both about the occurrence of the crisis and its ultimate resolution. Another way to describe the contribution of this paper is to say that the global financial crisis of 2007–2009 has multiple subsets of causes, all contributing to an overall complex system, and we wish to propose that the formation of asset bubbles is a critical component that requires analytical attention.

ASSET BUBBLES

An *asset bubble* is the phenomenon of an upward price movement over an extended period of time that then crashes swiftly. Typical examples include the NASDAQ 100 Index that climbed rapidly from 1994 to 2000 from about 500 to 5,000 and then crashed from 2000 to 2002 to about 1,000. Several other stock market indexes in the United States and around the world have exhibited similar behavior with gradual increases and rapid declines. U.S. and global housing prices similarly increased from 2002 to mid-2007 and then began to decrease with declines continuing to date.

Historically, asset bubbles have occurred in many countries and numerous asset markets. Yet, economists and policy makers view bubbles with much skepticism because the definition and description of an asset bubble are not precise. What if an asset price increases rapidly because of economic fundamentals. Such an increase cannot be termed a bubble. More technically, a *bubble* is the difference between an asset's observed price and the price determined by economic fundamentals. The theory of market efficiency allows no room for a bubble since it claims that market prices correctly reflect all the information embedded in fundamentals. Yet, history has repeatedly demonstrated that market prices deviate from fundamentals and the bubble component of these prices often grows to become quite large. Thus, bubbles may populate the economic scene, and we often talk about them, but in the end we always disregard them. Unimpeded by its conceptual imprecision, economic historian Charles Kindleberger (1978) documents the existence and evolution of bubbles and the remarkably high costs associated with their crashes.

A wide range of favorable economic conditions is needed to influence the development and size of the bubble. During the post-World War II period, asset booms appear to have been driven by increases in the growth of real output, low unemployment, and increased productivity. If during such periods, inflation was also low, then nominal interest rates most likely were also relatively low. A strong economy growing rapidly with no concern for inflation and therefore with an easy monetary policy most often induces asset booms. Such stable economic conditions of employment and productivity growth with low inflation also influence the fundamentals of firms, which include higher earnings, lower costs of borrowing, larger earnings and dividends, and further positive stock price expectations. In 2004, Alan Greenspan, former chairman of the Federal Reserve, wrote "Perhaps the greatest irony of the past decade is that the gradually unfolding success against inflation may well have contributed to the stock market bubble of the latter part of the 1990s. Looking back on those years, it is evident that technology-driven increases in productivity growth imparted significant upward momentum to expectations of earnings growth and, accordingly, to stock prices." At the same time, an environment of increasing macroeconomic stability reduced perceptions of risk. In this article, we center the discussion on bubbles as substantial increases in asset prices that eventually crash, but we also include in our vision the notion of economic booms and busts, or as Kindleberger (1978) describes them, as manias and crashes. Asset booms and busts do not exclusively explain the financial crisis of 2007–2009. They are, however, an important component of the composite dynamics that led to the economic severity and duration of the economic recession.

ASSET BUBBLES AND THE FED

After asset prices decline significantly, central bankers are often taken to task for not having raised interest rates high enough during the formation of the bubble to moderate the growth of the bubble or even to deflate it. Usually in setting monetary policy, central bankers act asymmetrically; that is, they do not target asset prices in addition to their usual targets of inflation and the output gap. When an asset bubble bursts, there is wide agreement among economists that a central bank typically should ease monetary policy to dampen the negative impact of the bust on economic activity. However, before the bursting of the bubble, there is no consensus about the appropriate policy response to an emerging bubble. The Greenspan-Bernanke Fed argued that a bubble cannot be identified for certain and if recognized conclusively could not be effectively deflated without significant cost to the real economy. Recall the popular description "one could not do brain surgery with an ax." Numerous economists disagreed with the asymmetric approach and argued for Fed intervention to deflate the emergence of asset bubbles. They prophetically warned that uncontrolled bubbles cause significant damage to the financial stability of the system and substantial costs to the real economy.

SEQUENCE OF BUBBLES

The typical scenario of the current financial crisis viewed from the standpoint of asset bubbles unfolds as follows. Housing prices have been slowly increasing for a long time with essentially no correction. These increases were not uniform across the country. Certain states, such as California and Florida, experienced above-average appreciations in specific areas, but the general fact was that there were no areas with systematic declines. Around 2003 or 2004, these real estate appreciations accelerated, fueling expectations of further appreciation. With low inflation, constructions costs remained stable, while low interest rates stimulated further demand. A relatively easy monetary policy during 2002 to 2004 along with the savings glut of China and Japan induced financial institutions to increase the securitization of mortgages with an emphasis on subprime mortgages.

The easy monetary policy was driven by the bursting of the Internet bubble that caused a crash in both the NASDAQ and the S&P 500 Indexes. After the stock market crash in 2000, the economy slowed down significantly, and we even had a recession in 2001 beginning in March and ending in November. During 2002 and 2003 the economy was growing slowly, so the Fed kept interest rates very low. In retrospect, one may argue that for the Fed to minimize the impact on the real economy of the bursting of the stock market bubble of 2000–2001, it kept fed funds rates very low for too long. Putting it in the language of this essay, the Fed's motivation to minimize the risks from the bursting of one bubble contributed to the generation of another bubble. So the U.S. economy replaced the stock market bubble with a housing bubble. The financial press during this period described the Fed's policy toward asset markets as the "Greenspan put." This description captured the chairman's determination to use an easy monetary policy to place a floor on stock market declines. The unintended consequence of the Greenspan put was the fueling of the real estate bubble. This idea of a sequence of the two bubbles may be viewed with reservation by efficient market advocates.

The collapse of the Internet bubble and the significant decline of about 80 percent in the NASDAQ cannot easily be dismissed as a bubble having burst. After all, what dramatic changes in economic fundamentals could have caused such an incredible decline? The idea, however, that housing price increases during 2003–2005 could be interpreted while occurring as a bubble was viewed then as controversial. The fact that housing prices have dropped on average by 30 percent since their peak, with larger declines in certain states such as California, Nevada, and Florida, gives support to the notion that a housing bubble developed in sequence to the stock market bubble. Hayford and Malliaris (Chapter 58, this volume) elaborate this analysis in detail.

By mid-2006, monetary policy had become tighter, and Fed funds stood at 5.25 percent. Economic signs appeared then that the housing appreciation was not sustainable, at which point mortgage delinquencies and defaults were expected. These expectations did materialize in early 2007, and by summer 2007, the early signs of a subprime mortgage crisis became apparent.

Economists agree that the Fed correctly moderated the decrease in Fed funds to cushion against the NASDAQ crash. However, John Taylor (2007) argues that the Fed kept fed funds very low for too long and this relatively easy monetary policy fueled the housing boom and the growth of subprime mortgages. Controlled experiments are not possible in economics, and no one knows the degree of validity of this hypothesis, but what is certainly new and challenging in the form of analysis of financial instability is the novelty of linking one bubble to the next. If such a link exists between bubbles, then the static optimality of the Fed's asymmetric response is seriously questioned, posing a new challenge to the risk management approach to monetary policy and the evaluation of its action in a dynamic context. Chairman Bernanke has stated that this issue needs to be reconsidered.

TRAVELING BUBBLES

The stock market bubble of 1996 to 2000 and the housing bubble of 2003 to 2007 are not the only bubbles in the United States. The prices of several energy, metal-lurgical, and agricultural commodities have also exhibited bubble-type behavior. Currencies such as the euro and the Canadian dollar also increased dramatically. Also, these various bubbles were not unique to the United States. Globalization with rapid financial transfers, free capital mobility, coordinated monetary policies, and integrated financial markets contributes to the emergence and growth of bubbles across several nations and also to their simultaneous crashes. We have seen by now ample evidence that equity prices, home prices, and commodity prices have collapsed around the world. Although interpreting the dramatic rise and subsequent collapse in stock markets, housing markets, commodity markets, energy markets, and currency markets during the last several years in both the United States and numerous other countries as bubbles may be still viewed as controversial, it is conceptually impossible to imagine the financial crisis occurring if these bubbles did not exist. Could the global economy have generated the financial crisis if stability had prevailed in stock markets, housing markets, commodity markets, and energy markets?

FUTURE BUBBLES

During the past few months, the Fed as the lender of last resort has supplied reserves valued at over $1 trillion to financial institutions to stabilize the financial system. The U.S. government, through the Treasury Department, has supplemented this monetary policy with $350 billion of TARP (Toxic Asset Relief Program) financing. The administration that took office in 2009 has further secured a stimulus package of approximately $800 billion to counter the jobs lost because of the crisis. Opening the floodgates to put out the fire, do we have a strategy for draining the flood? Our thesis is that unlike the October 19, 1987, stock market crash, which was an isolated bubble bursting with no impact on the real economy, the March 2001 NASDAQ and S&P 500 Index crashes set the stage for a sequence of events leading to the financial crisis. The bursting of the U.S. stock market bubble in 2001 led to a U.S. recession in the same year that began a prolonged easy monetary policy that along with the global saving glut inflated house prices already accelerated because of a housing lending boom. Unlike the calculation of future positions of stars, economic predictions are subject to huge errors, because economic actors continuously revise their decisions and modify their actions. To reduce prediction errors, we assume that the Fed will continue to provide liquidity to financial institutions that need it. We assume that these loans to banks and primary dealers are overcollateralized and the Fed will not suffer any losses. It is estimated that real estate loans at all commercial banks are about $4 trillion and commercial and industrial loans are about $20 trillion. Lending by the Fed allows banks to avoid fire sales of assets and insolvencies, and gives them time to sell assets, merge, or raise capital.

There are several competing scenarios. One scenario is the smooth return of financial stability and economic recovery. Another scenario considers deflation as consumers, businesses, and foreigners reduce their spending that is not adequately offset by government stimulus programs. In such a scenario, investors accumulate safe government bonds, and a new bubble in Treasury bond prices could emerge. Third, the super-easy fiscal and monetary policies overcompensate for weakness in the real economy, thus putting pressure on prices. The rising inflation and the public debt bubble induce home and foreign investors to sell their holdings of bonds as they search for hedges against inflation. The U.S. government bond market then crashes, and prices of physical assets enter a bubble phase. Such assets include gold, oil, and real estate, among others. Put differently, there is a high probability that the sequence of bubbles continues to generate financial instability and volatility, which in turn will dampen economic activities.

STOPPING THE BUBBLES

The safety net of a circus is designed for the trapeze artist, not the elephants. The Fed and the Treasury have assumed enormous burdens. The Fed has not burdened the taxpayers and may continue providing liquidity for as long as it is needed. It can also reduce this liquidity swiftly as it reverses its steps. The situation at the Treasury is more challenging because large budget deficits may cause higher interest rates, potential inflation, and perhaps a weaker dollar. One strategy that has not been discussed is for the Treasury to sell a portion of its gold reserves, sell other government assets, and also propose a comprehensive plan of both short-term fiscal initiatives and long-term credible strategies to eventually contain future budget deficits. Silence about the long-term fiscal health of the U.S. economy will only fuel more speculative bubbles and volatility leading to an explosive growth of the public debt. It is unrealistic to assume that the bursting of several bubbles coupled with very easy monetary and fiscal policies will have no economic side effects on the road to an eventual return to stable growth. The economic subsystem that fueled the past sequence of bubbles needs to be studied, and ways must be found to restore global economic stability. In other words, the uncertainty the past sequence of bubbles has generated must be addressed for global stability to be restored.

REFERENCES

Kindleberger, C. 1978. *Manias, panics and crashes: A history of financial crises*. Hoboken, NJ: John Wiley & Sons.

Taylor, J. B. 2007. Housing and monetary policy. National Bureau of Economic Research Working Paper 13682.

ABOUT THE AUTHORS

Abol Jalilvand received his Ph.D. in finance from the University of North Carolina at Chapel Hill, a master of business administration from Oklahoma State University, and a B.A. in banking and finance from the Iranian Institute of Banking. His scholarly work in corporate debt structure, risk management, measurement of the cost of capital, and international capital flows has appeared in top refereed journals and major academic conferences. Professionally, he has been editor-in-chief of the *Canadian Journal of Administrative Sciences*, president of Mid-Continent East AACSB Conference, a consultant for major corporations, and has testified before a number of regulatory bodies. He is dean of the School of Business Administration and Graduate School of Business at Loyola University Chicago. He came to Loyola from Halifax, Nova Scotia, Canada, where he most recently was appointed to his second term as the dean of the faculty of management and the Herbert S. Lamb Chair in Business Education at Dalhousie University.

A. G. (Tassos) Malliaris is currently professor of economics and finance at Loyola University Chicago, and holds the Walter F. Mullady Sr. Chair in Business Administration. He has earned two Ph.D.s: one in economics from the University of Oklahoma and another in mathematics from the University of Chicago. He has authored and co-authored numerous articles in professional journals such as the *Society of Industrial and Applied Mathematics Review, Mathematics of Operations Research, Review of Economic Studies, Journal of Financial and Quantitative Analysis, Review of Quantitative Finance and Accounting, Journal of Futures Markets, Journal of*

Banking and Finance, Journal of Macroeconomics, Economic Modeling, Journal of Multinational Financial Management, International Review of Financial Analysis, European Journal of Political Economy, European Journal of Operations Research, International Journal of Finance, Multinational Finance Journal, Economic Inquiry, Neural Computing and Applications, and others. He has also edited and co-edited several books. He is currently interested in financial economics, monetary policy, and the formation of asset bubbles.

PART III

Borrowers

CHAPTER 20

The Past, Present, and Future of Subprime Mortgages

SHANE M. SHERLUND
Senior Economist, Board of Governors of the Federal Reserve System*

The performance of mortgages has come under intense scrutiny over the past couple of years. The proportion of subprime fixed-rate mortgages that were at least one payment behind schedule increased from a low of 13.6 percent in 2006 to over 28 percent by April 2009. Even more striking, the same rate for variable-rate subprime mortgages increased from a low of 14.7 percent in 2005 to over 55 percent by April 2009. These facts have caused policy makers to ask what factors led to the increased mortgage delinquency rates, what can be done to lessen the effects, and what can be done to ensure that future mortgage lending does not repeat the same mistakes.

Several major factors have been cited as having led to increased mortgage defaults. First, house price appreciation and its intricate link to homeowner equity has a large effect on the delinquency status of households (Gerardi, Shapiro, and Willen 2007; Sherlund 2008; Gerardi, Lehnert, Sherlund, and Willen 2008). As house prices stagnate or decline, some homeowners are left with little or no equity. This leaves borrowers with little or no incentive to remain current on their mortgage payments, especially for those who may have bet on continued house price gains. Borrowers may also be faced with more difficulty in refinancing or selling their homes. Nadauld and Sherlund (2009) show that house prices may have also influenced decisions in the market for securities backed by subprime mortgages.

Next, underwriting standards slackened considerably since at least 2000 (Demyanyk and Van Hemert 2008; Keys et al. 2008; Mian and Sufi 2008; Mayer and Pence 2008; Mayer, Pence, and Sherlund 2009). Median loan-to-value ratios on subprime mortgages rose from 90 percent in 2003 to 100 percent in 2005–2007, partly as a result of the more widespread use of second liens. Furthermore, the share of fully documented subprime variable rate mortgages declined from 75 percent in 2000 to 60 percent in 2005–2006. By 2005–2006, nearly one in six subprime variable rate mortgages was originated with low quality underwriting,

*The opinions, analysis, and conclusions of this paper are those of the author and do not necessarily reflect those of the Board of Governors of the Federal Reserve System, its members, or its staff.

meaning they had little or no loan documentation and loan-to-value ratios exceeding 95 percent.

Next, mortgage rate resets on subprime variable rate mortgages, and the associated change in monthly payments, have been widely viewed as leading to increased mortgage defaults (Mayer, Pence, and Sherlund 2009). If delinquency and default are driven by household cash flow problems, mortgage rate resets that result in higher mortgage payments could strain households to the point of delinquency or default.

Finally, the generally favorable economic environment of 2004–2006, including above-average house price appreciation, relatively low interest rates, and low unemployment, may have masked potential performance problems associated with subprime mortgages. Homeowners could easily refinance or sell their homes. But once house price appreciation slowed, some homeowners lost their ability to refinance or sell their homes, leading to a higher incidence of mortgage delinquency and default. Households faced with unemployment or other household shocks were less able to afford their monthly mortgage payments.

When faced with a shock, mortgage borrowers can exercise various options with respect to how they terminate, or finish, their mortgage contracts. First, borrowers can make timely mortgage payments until they pay off their mortgage balances, thereby satisfying their mortgage contracts. Second, borrowers can pay off their mortgage balances early, either through early payments, refinancing, or home sale. These borrowers are said to have prepaid their mortgages. Third, borrowers can fall behind on their mortgage payments and enter the process of foreclosure. These borrowers are said to have defaulted on their mortgages. The prepayment and default options, and how they are affected by house prices, mortgage underwriting, mortgage rate resets, and macroeconomic factors, are the focus of this paper.

I estimate a competing hazards model, using data on securitized subprime mortgages from 2000 to 2007 from First American LoanPerformance. The model includes various measures of house price appreciation, underwriting standards, mortgage rate resets, and macroeconomic factors. Ultimately, I find that borrower leverage is perhaps the most important factor explaining both mortgage prepayment and default for borrowers with subprime mortgages. Then, using several different assumptions about the future path of house prices, I simulate potential trajectories for subprime mortgage defaults from 2008 to 2010. I also examine the short-term sensitivities of prepayments and defaults to several policy proposals.

MODEL

The competing hazards model used here is fairly standard. Having arrived at any particular loan age, mortgage borrowers are assumed to prepay, default, or continue making timely mortgage payments according to the Public Securities Association (PSA) standard. Any proportional deviation from the PSA standard is assumed to be a function of house price appreciation, mortgage underwriting, mortgage rate resets, and macroeconomic factors. For example, borrowers facing higher-than-average house price appreciation might default at lower rates than those facing lower rates of appreciation. The prepayment and default hazard functions are estimated jointly, using maximum likelihood.

DATA

The primary data source is the First American LoanPerformance ABS database. These loan-level data track securitized mortgages in mortgage pools marketed as Alt-A and subprime. I restrict the analysis to first-lien, 30-year mortgages originated between 2000 and 2007 contained in subprime ABS pools. The data contain information on loan-to-value ratios, mortgage rates, credit scores, loan documentation, and occupancy status (all at origination), as well as prepayment penalties, interest-only features, piggyback mortgages, loan purpose, property type, and information on mortgage rate reset periods and terms.

The data also track the performance of these mortgages over time. Delinquency status (current, 30 days past due, 60 days past due, 90 days past due, or in foreclosure) is recorded monthly for all loans. The data are used to determine the type of mortgage termination: prepayment or default. Throughout this paper, default will describe any mortgage terminating after a notice of default was served, whereas prepayment will describe any mortgage terminating without such a notice (presumably through refinancing or home sale).

I augment the LoanPerformance data with ZIP code and state-level house prices, also from First American LoanPerformance. These data are used to construct estimates of current or mark-to-market loan-to-value ratios—in other words, the ratio of the loan balance to the property's current estimated value. I also include time-series data on oil prices, various interest rates, and state-level unemployment rates, and ZIP code–level demographic data from the 2000 Census.

Several mortgage products dominate our data: subprime 2/28s being the most popular. These mortgages have fixed interest rates for two years before resetting toward prevailing market rates (generally six-month LIBOR plus a margin averaging 6 percentage points) every six months thereafter. As shown in Pennington-Cross and Ho (2006), subprime 2/28s have a tendency to prepay rapidly immediately before and after the first mortgage rate reset (loan age 24 months). Similarly, subprime 3/27s tend to prepay most rapidly around their first mortgage rate reset (36 months). Subprime fixed-rate mortgages, however, face no mortgage rate resets and hence do not display the same sporadic prepayment behavior. Because of the differing prepayment and default behavior of these mortgage types, estimation is carried out on three subsamples: subprime 2/28, subprime 3/27, and subprime fixed-rate mortgages. I allow additional flexibility by further separating by refinance versus purchase originations.

RESULTS

House Price Appreciation

House price appreciation is primarily captured through the mark-to-market loan-to-value variable. Borrowers who experience a lot of house price appreciation have lower mark-to-market loan-to-value ratios than borrowers who experience less house price appreciation. As a result, those borrowers have more of an incentive to make timely payments and find refinancing easier, reducing the probability of default. Borrowers with negative equity (those who owe more than the property's value) have a higher probability of default. I find only weak evidence, at best, that investors are more likely to default when house price appreciation is low, so-called ruthless default.

Underwriting

Underwriting is captured through several variables, including credit scores, loan documentation, occupancy status, second liens, payment-to-income ratios, initial loan-to-value ratios, prepayment penalties, interest-only features, and initial mortgage rates. Of these, credit scores predict default and prepayment well, with higher credit scores defaulting less and prepaying more often. Somewhat surprisingly, the initial loan-to-value ratio has little effect on default and prepayment behavior. Low quality mortgages (those with high loan-to-value ratios and little or no loan documentation) tend to default more frequently. Loans made for non-owner-occupied properties, those made with simultaneous second liens, and those made to borrowers with higher payment-to-income ratios have higher default rates.

Mortgage Rate Resets

The effect of mortgage rate resets is captured in a highly complex manner through the current mortgage rate, the fully indexed rate (six-month LIBOR plus the margin), a payment shock variable, and indicator variables for the reset and post-reset periods. In short, prepayments jump during mortgage rate resets, while defaults remain largely unaffected.

Macroeconomic Factors

Higher unemployment rates tend to be associated with higher prepayments, but not necessarily higher defaults. Because I use only state-level unemployment rates, I could be missing much of the local variation in unemployment and thus the underlying effect on defaults. Furthermore, house prices could be capturing some of these more local effects. Higher oil prices, however, tend to be associated with higher rates of default. As the cost of necessities, such as oil, rises, the ability of some households to make their mortgage payments could be reduced, especially for higher payment-to-income households who may have stretched to afford their homes in the first place.

SIMULATIONS

Subprime Default Projections

I use house price, interest rate, and unemployment rate forecasts from public sources as of June 2008. Under the baseline simulation, aggregate house prices fall a total of 8.5 percent during 2008–2010. Mortgage rates increase from 6 percent in mid-2008 to 6.5 percent by the end of 2010. The unemployment rate declines from 5.6 percent to 5.4 percent from 2008 to 2010. Finally, oil prices exceed $100 per barrel over the simulation period. Under a "worst house price" scenario, house prices fall a total of 17 percent from 2008 to 2010.

Under the baseline simulation, nearly half of the subprime mortgages originated during 2006 and 2007 default by the end of 2010—twice the proportion for mortgages originated during 2005. Similarly, prepayments fall by about half for 2006 and 2007 originations relative to 2005 originations. Under the "worst house price" scenario, over half of the 2006–2007 originations default by the end of 2010. These simulations emphasize the importance of house prices in the current episode.

One important caveat is that house price declines and unemployment rates have exceeded June 2008 expectations. Thus, defaults can be expected to be higher. But oil prices and interest rates have been lower than expected.

Policy Implications

To single out some of the effects pertinent to policy makers, I conduct several simulations to examine the short-run sensitivity of predicted prepayments and defaults to several policy proposals. First, if prepayment penalties were removed in 2008, default and prepayment rates would initially increase, but would decline by 2010. Next, a principal write-down would decrease the chance of default and increase the chance of prepayment. Lower mortgage interest rates would also decrease the chance of default and increase the chance of prepayment. The introduction of interest-only periods during 2008 lowers the probability of default initially, but increases after the expiration of the interest-only period in 2010. Finally, the removal of mortgage rate resets really only affects prepayments.

CONCLUSIONS

In this chapter, I model the historical default and prepayment behavior for subprime mortgages from 2000 to 2007. The rise in mortgage defaults stems largely from unprecedented declines in house prices, along with slack underwriting and tight credit market conditions. I estimate a competing hazards model to identify the effects of house price appreciation, underwriting standards, mortgage rate resets, and macroeconomic factors on the likelihood of borrowers with subprime mortgages to default or prepay. I find that borrower leverage is perhaps the most important factor in describing subprime mortgage prepayment and default.

Using several different assumptions about the future path of house prices, I simulate potential trajectories for subprime defaults from 2008 to 2010. I also explore the short-term sensitivities of default and prepayment to several policy proposals. The results suggest that default and prepayment rates are most sensitive to house prices from 2008 to 2010. This is not to say that the other factors are unimportant and will not matter going forward. Rather, the largest effects are likely to come from the realized path for house prices.

Of course, these simulations rely heavily upon the assumed paths for house prices, interest rates, unemployment, and oil prices. To the extent that house prices are lower and unemployment higher, subprime mortgage defaults would likely be even higher, depending on the nature of the assumed paths and their interactions. Furthermore, policies designed to stem foreclosures by eliminating mortgage rate resets or lowering monthly payments could be more or less effective than suggested here, again depending on the realized paths for house prices, interest rates, unemployment, and oil prices.

REFERENCES

Demyanyk, Y., and O. Van Hemert. 2008. Understanding the subprime mortgage crisis. *Review of Financial Studies*, forthcoming.

Gerardi, K., A. Lehnert, S. M. Sherlund, and P. S. Willen. 2008. Making sense of the subprime crisis. In *Brookings Papers on Economic Activity*, eds. D. W. Elmendorf, N. G. Mankiw, and L. H. Summers. Washington, DC: Brookings Institution.

Gerardi, K., A. H. Shapiro, and P. S. Willen. 2007. Subprime outcomes: Risky mortgages, home ownership experiences, and foreclosures. Federal Reserve Bank of Boston, Working Paper 07-15.

Keys, B. J., T. K. Mukherjee, A. Seru, and V. Vig. 2008. Did securitization lead to lax screening? Evidence from subprime loans. *Quarterly Journal of Economics*, forthcoming.

Mayer, C., and K. Pence. 2008. Subprime mortgages: What, where, and to whom? In *Housing markets and the economy: Risk, regulation, and policy*, eds. E. L. Glaeser and J. M. Quigley. Cambridge, MA: Lincoln Institute of Land Policy, forthcoming.

Mayer, C., K. Pence, and S. M. Sherlund. 2009. The rise in mortgage defaults. *Journal of Economic Perspectives* 23: 27–50.

Mian, A., and A. Sufi. 2008. The consequences of mortgage credit expansion: Evidence from the U.S. mortgage default crisis. *Quarterly Journal of Economics*, forthcoming.

Nadauld, T. D., and S. M. Sherlund. 2009. The role of the securitization process in the expansion of subprime credit. Federal Reserve Board, Finance and Economics Discussion Series 2009-28.

Pennington-Cross, A., and G. Ho. 2006. The termination of subprime hybrid and fixed rate mortgages. Federal Reserve Bank of St. Louis, Working Paper 2006-42A.

Sherlund, S. M. 2008. The past, present, and future of subprime mortgages. Federal Reserve Board, Finance and Economics Discussion Series 2008-63.

ABOUT THE AUTHOR

Shane M. Sherlund holds a Ph.D. from the University of Wisconsin-Madison (economics 2003) and is a senior economist in the Household and Real Estate Finance section of the Division of Research and Statistics at the Board of Governors of the Federal Reserve System. Sherlund's recent work includes "The Rise in Mortgage Defaults," co-authored with Christopher Mayer and Karen Pence; "Making Sense of the Subprime Crisis," co-authored with Kristopher Gerardi, Andreas Lehnert, and Paul Willen; and "GSEs, Mortgage Rates, and Secondary Market Activities," co-authored with Andreas Lehnert and Wayne Passmore. His research focuses on mortgage markets, the housing government-sponsored enterprises, home ownership, and household choice.

CHAPTER 21

FHA Loans and Policy Responses to Credit Availability

DR. MARSHA COURCHANE
Vice President, Charles River Associates

RAJEEV DAROLIA
Senior Associate, Charles River Associates

DR. PETER ZORN
Vice President, Housing Analysis and Research, Freddie Mac*

The past decade has witnessed dramatic shifts in mortgage market structure along with substantial changes in underwriting standards for residential mortgages, volatile house prices, and increasing delinquencies and foreclosures. A major aspect of the evolving mortgage market was the general decline in market share for government-insured Federal Housing Administration (FHA) loans through 2006, and increased market share for conventional prime and subprime loans. A closer understanding of this decline in FHA share, and its determinants, may help policy makers better understand the FHA's current resurgence and more successfully navigate the current crisis.

The FHA insures mortgages made by approved lenders, providing an explicit government guarantee against borrower default risk. Borrowers incur the costs of the mortgage insurance, and in return face lower down-payment requirements and relaxed underwriting standards relative to the prime market. Congress limits the size of mortgages the FHA can insure to loan limits at or below those in the conforming, conventional market. While the FHA has traditionally served first-time homebuyers, minority borrowers, those in central cities, and those with less financial liquidity, the subprime market also grew to serve borrowers in those groups. Therefore, the FHA's decline may reflect the movement of its most qualified

---

*All views and opinions are those of the authors and do not reflect the view or opinions of Charles River Associates or its board of directors, of Freddie Mac or its board of directors, or of the Federal Housing Finance Agency. The authors thank participants and discussant Kathleen Engel at the Federal Reserve Board Conference on Innovative Financial Services for the Underserved, April 2009, for helpful comments. We also thank Brent Smith for his contributions to earlier work on FHA.

borrowers to the conventional, conforming prime market, and the movement of its least qualified borrowers to subprime lenders.

Understanding the historical fall and recent rise in FHA lending may be important to construct policy options aimed at rescuing delinquent borrowers and preventing future mortgage market crises. For example, success may have eluded the FHASecure and Hope for Homeowners (H4H) programs, designed to provide refinancing opportunities to homeowners as an alternative to foreclosure, because the policy objectives presupposed that borrowers with payment problems were FHA-eligible and would have had FHA loans, but for subprime. Many borrowers from the subprime sector in need of loan modifications or refinances, however, may not have credit profiles that make them eligible for FHA loans, or may not want to purchase properties for which FHA insurance is not available. Also, while the economywide tightening of credit availability and more stringent underwriting standards in the prime market may encourage some borrowers to shift to the FHA, such a move may appeal most to underwater borrowers—those for whom the mortgage exceeds the appraised value of their home.

In another example, while delinquency rates are currently lower in the FHA than in the subprime market, they are much higher than in the prime market. As of the first quarter of 2009, the prime rate delinquency was 6.06 percent, as compared to delinquency rates of 24.95 percent in subprime and 13.84 percent in the FHA (MBA 2009). Therefore, the ratio of borrowers moving into the FHA from prime and subprime markets may affect the overall level of mortgage delinquencies in the United States. To the extent that workout programs are better in the FHA than in the conventional market, the shift of borrowers from the subprime sector back to the FHA may help alleviate the U.S. housing crisis. On the other hand, if borrowers are moving to the FHA from the prime market, where Freddie Mac and Fannie Mae are already providing extensive loss mitigation efforts, this movement of borrowers may simply transfer the costs from the borrowers, lenders, and investors of the prime market directly to the taxpayers.

Before too much hope is placed on FHA lending as the solution to today's mortgage crisis, it is important to understand why the FHA failed to meet the needs of borrowers in either expanding home ownership opportunities in the early 2000s or in mitigating losses in 2008 and 2009. If private solutions are more adaptive, albeit at potentially higher risk, there is every reason to expect again a movement away from the FHA in the future.

RECENT FHA, SUBPRIME, AND PRIME MORTGAGE MARKET TRENDS

The FHA sector has experienced a substantial decline over the decade though 2007, most significantly among minority borrowers, who accounted for a growing share of subprime loans during that period. The FHA's market share of total mortgage market origination volume fell from 14 percent in 1997 to 5 percent in 2007, with almost the entire decline occurring since 2000.[1] After that time, in part due to the collapse of the subprime market and in part due to tightened prime market underwriting standards, FHA mortgage loan originations have surged. By the fourth quarter of 2008, FHA originations comprised 33.6 percent of the market, and reached an annual share for 2008 of almost 19.5 percent (Inside Mortgage Finance, *Statistical Annual*, 2009b).

The FHA's market share could have declined for two primary reasons. Possibly, locations with high FHA shares lost a share of the total mortgage market. Reductions in national FHA share may therefore reflect changes in the geographic concentration of where mortgages were originated (e.g., a shift of originations away from historically FHA share-rich tracts). Tracking FHA census tract changes over time indicates that the geographical concentration of originations did not drive the FHA share decline, but rather the loss of FHA share within each tract (Courchane, Darolia, and Zorn 2009). In fact, trends suggest that if FHA shares within tracts had not changed, the FHA's overall share would have remained steady or even increased slightly.

Thus, it appears that the decline of national FHA share was the result of a shift away from FHA originations to prime and subprime products within tracts. It is possible that FHA-insured products with stringent underwriting were less attractive when compared to product offerings in the subprime sector, as the FHA continued to have product restrictions dictating lower loan amounts and larger down-payment requirements. Unlike many subprime mortgage programs, the FHA required at least a 3 percent equity contribution to the deal. Alternatively, subprime lenders routinely offered 100 percent or more financing for properties. Moreover, low interest rates and rising house prices further increased demand for loan products offered by the conventional market, appealing to borrowers seeking flexible payment options, rapid approval rates, and low down payments that allowed them to qualify for mortgages despite higher housing costs. Finally, while many subprime and prime lenders relied heavily on broker-identified wholesale channel originations, the FHA has had, historically, more particular financial requirements for brokers writing FHA loans (FHA 2009b). Further research is needed to definitively determine whether the FHA share moved to the prime or subprime markets. The decline in FHA share is remarkably coincident, however, with the increase in subprime over the time period, with the results even more dramatic for those tracts with the highest 20 percent (top quintile) of FHA shares. In a result that mirrors the decline in FHA share, research demonstrates that the increase of national subprime share was also not geographically driven, but the result of a shift toward subprime products within tracts (Courchane, Darolia, and Zorn 2009).

Of particular interest is the growth of both prime and subprime loans for borrowers to whom the FHA has traditionally played a major role. By providing mortgages to borrowers with limited down payments, the FHA has served a high percentage of minorities, as well as younger, credit- and liquidity-constrained borrowers. The FHA has seen its share of loans among these populations decline substantially, however. For example, both African-Americans and Hispanics increased shares of prime and subprime loans from 1997 to 2007, while the FHA's market share of minority originations fell 18 percentage points (from 21 to 3 percent). The decline in the FHA's market share was particularly large among Hispanic borrowers, dropping from 37 percent to 3 percent of Hispanic-originated loans, while the subprime share of Hispanic-originated loans increased from 9 to 22 percent.

The FHA continues to originate around 30 percent of its loans to African-American borrowers, but over this period both the share of African-American and Hispanic borrowers in the prime and subprime sectors grew substantially.

From 1997 to the relative peak in 2006, Hispanic borrowers grew from 5 percent of subprime loans to 21 percent and African-Americans increased their share of subprime loans from 14 percent to 19 percent. Prime shares similarly rose for Hispanics (5 percent to 11 percent) and African-Americans (4 percent to 8 percent) from 1997 to 2006. As the minority shares of both the FHA and subprime markets were much higher than prime shares of minority loans, these market segments are likely part of the reason for the recent increase in the home ownership rate.

POLICY IMPLICATIONS AND COMMENTS

The FHA has historically met the needs of borrowers who may not have been able to qualify for loans in the prime, conventional market. These loans have helped first-time homebuyers, minorities, and low-income homebuyers access credit even when faced with down payment constraints or nontraditional credit histories. Many borrowers who would traditionally be served by the FHA sector appear to have shifted to subprime loans over the past decade. In response to subprime market share growth, the FHA expanded product offerings, streamlined the application process, and reduced initial outlay requirements from borrowers. Therefore, the issues that led to subprime's demise may also affect the FHA's future lending patterns, possibly leading to higher increases in delinquencies in the FHA market than in prime markets.

Whether or not the FHA continues to gain and hold market share will be a function of its cost and its ability to appeal to consumers. The FHA will also benefit from the decrease of viable conventional products. Since 2007, nearly all independent mortgage company subprime lenders have ceased operations, voluntarily or involuntarily, or sharply reduced their products offered. By mid-2008, the asset-backed securities market that provides liquidity to the mortgage market was substantially reduced, and subprime lenders found it nearly impossible to finance originations without going to FHA loans that could be pooled into Ginnie Mae securities. At the same time, the FHA has seen an increase in customers refinancing out of conventional loans into its insured mortgage programs. For the last two weeks of November 2008, total applications increased over 70 percent as compared to the same period in 2007 (U.S. Department of Housing and Urban Development 2008a). Some of that increase is due to the higher loan amounts allowable under the new FHA guidelines, but some of the gain represents borrowers hoping to move from subprime adjustable rate mortgage loans to fixed FHA loans.

The FHA likely also currently appeals to borrowers who do not qualify for prime mortgages. For example, some aspects of the FHA's underwriting process may allow borrowers with nontraditional credit to obtain financing. The FHA uses a type of automated underwriting system that incorporates an applicant's full credit history, employment, and nontraditional credit patterns such as rent and utilities payments (U.S. Department of Housing and Urban Development 2009). FHA guidelines allow for compensating factors to justify exceeding ratio guidelines or offset other negative factors, much like similar systems used in the conventional sector. For example, FHA guidelines allow factors such as large down payments, potential for increased borrower earnings due to job training, or substantial nontaxable income to justify mortgage approval. While a nontraditional credit report can be used to supplement a traditional credit report that lacks a sufficient number of reported trade items, however, it cannot enhance credit history for borrowers with a poor payment record or offset derogatory traditional credit references. Ongoing changes in its underwriting and pricing practices throughout 2009 continued to influence the share of the residential mortgage market held by the FHA.

Moreover, FHA loans may not be readily available for all types of properties. For example, while the FHA will insure some loans in cooperative housing projects through the Section 203(n) program, only a limited number of lenders appear to participate in the program. Additionally, the FHA needs to specifically approve condominiums for a borrower to receive financing, which may add time to the purchase process or disqualify some units. The FHA recognized in 2008 that condominiums may be more affordable and attractive to first-time homebuyers by simplifying the loan underwriting process for condominium purchases and no longer subjecting properties of this type to the same complex requirements of multifamily housing loans (U.S. Department of Housing and Urban Development 2008b).

However, public policy initiatives that encourage the substitution of FHA for subprime and prime loans may prove costly. The U.S. Department of Housing and Urban Development, HUD's, projected budget for the FHA in 2008 included a $143 million shortfall. This was the first time in three decades HUD has made a request to Congress for a taxpayer subsidy (U.S. Department of Housing and Urban Development 2007). Even though the FHA is statutorily required to be budget neutral, the GAO projected that taxpayer-funded subsidies of half a billion dollars over three years would be necessary if no changes are made to the FHA program.

Programs such as FHASecure and H4H potentially raise additional financial concerns that may have compromised their effectiveness. For example, at the end of 2008, HUD terminated FHASecure, a temporary program designed to allow families who had been making timely payments to qualify for refinancing if they were at risk for default upon reset of the adjustable rate of their mortgage. Typical underwriting standards were imposed, but the FHASecure initiative permitted new subordinate financing that exceeded customary maximum loan limits and relaxed loan-to-value ratios to cover any shortfall from the existing first lien, closing costs, and arrearages (FHA 2007, FHA 2008b). While HUD estimated the program would assist approximately 500,000 families by the end of 2008, fears of its damaging financial impact on the Mortgage Mutual Insurance fund spelled its demise (FHA 2008c).

FHA recommends the H4H program to borrowers who were delinquent on their mortgages. The H4H program allows refinancing loans into an FHA product for borrowers who cannot afford the terms of their previous mortgage. However, few borrowers have actually realized relief from the program because of onerous lender and borrower requirements, and as of January 2009, the program had generated only a handful of applications and loan approvals (Inside FHA Lending 2009). Guidelines were revised in January 2009 and revisited again in May 2009 as part of the Helping Families Save Their Homes Act, with the hope that the program will be more successful and provide greater incentives for mortgage servicers to participate in the program (FHA 2009a, FHA 2009b).

Most of the FHA's recent huge growth has been in traditional FHA loans (Inside Mortgage Finance 2008). These gains in the FHA reflect the tightened underwriting standards in the prime markets, with borrowers facing increased difficulty in obtaining higher LTV loans requiring mortgage insurance in any markets but the FHA. The magnitude of the continued movement of prime and subprime borrowers to the FHA partly depends on the efforts of conventional mortgage providers, including Freddie Mac and Fannie Mae, to offer viable alternatives to subprime borrowers. Notwithstanding the actions of conventional providers, the FHA could be a vehicle to provide lower-priced and more sustainable mortgage options for some at-risk borrowers holding higher-priced subprime loans. However, careful assessment and management of the risks associated with serving these borrowers would be necessary to avoid exacerbating problems in the financial performance of the FHA's insurance program.

NOTE

1. Shares calculated from Home Mortgage Disclosure Act (HMDA) data, various years. We define the market to include FHA and conventional, single family, home purchase, and refinance loans below the conforming loan limit, excluding manufactured housing loans or lenders. We restrict our analysis to the conforming market so that we can also look at the market with loan amounts within the reach of FHA-eligible borrowers. This also allows us to compare secondary mortgage market effects where Fannie Mae and Freddie Mac, the government-sponsored entities (GSEs), hold significant market shares. For our analysis, we use a panel of data obtained from Robert Avery of the Federal Reserve Board that defines subprime and prime lenders, relying on the HUD Subprime and Manufactured Home Lender List. From this, we exclude all manufactured housing lenders.

REFERENCES

Courchane, S., and P. Zorn. 2005. Subprime borrowers: Mortgage transitions and outcomes' *Journal of Real Estate Research* 29 (4): 365–392.

Courchane, S., R. Darolia, and P. Zorn. 2009. From FHA to subprime and back? Working paper.

Federal Housing Administration. 2007. The FHASecure initiative and guidance on appraisal practices in declining markets. Mortgagee Letter 2007-11, September 5.

Federal Housing Administration. 2008a. Temporary loan limit increase for FHA. Mortgagee Letter 2008-06, March 6.

Federal Housing Administration. 2008b. Expansion of FHASecure. Mortgagee Letter 2008-13, May 7.

Federal Housing Administration. 2008c. Termination of FHASecure. Mortgagee Letter 2008-41, December 19.

Federal Housing Administration. 2009a. Hope for homeowners origination and servicing guidance supplement. Mortgagee Letter 2009-03, January 6.

Federal Housing Administration. 2009b. The FHA Title II mortgagee approval handbook 4060.1, Rev-2. www.hud.gov/offices/adm/hudclips/handbooks/hsgh/4060.1/40601handbookHSGH.doc. (accessed March 3, 2009).

Inside FHA Lending. January 16, 2009.

Inside Mortgage Finance. October 24, 2008, 6.

Inside Mortgage Finance. February 20, 2009, 3.

Inside Mortgage Finance. 2009. *Mortgage market statistical annual, volume I: The primary market*, 4.

Mortgage Bankers Association. 2009. National delinquency survey results, first quarter 2009.

U.S. Department of Housing and Urban Development. 2007. www.hud.gov/offices/hsg/fhahistory.cfm.

U.S. Department of Housing and Urban Development. 2008a. Single family operations, November 16–30, *FHA Outlook*, 2.

U.S. Department of Housing and Urban Development. 2008b. *FHA annual management report, fiscal year 2008*, 6.

U.S. Department of Housing and Urban Development. 2009. Mortgage credit analysis for mortgage insurance handbook 4155.1. www.hud.gov/offices/adm/hudclips/handbooks/hsgh/4155.1/41551HSGH.pdf (accessed June 30, 2009).

ABOUT THE AUTHORS

Dr. Marsha Courchane, VP, leads the Financial Economics Practice at Charles River Associates (CRA). She is executive vice president of the American Real Estate and Urban Economics Association and a director of the American Real Estate Society. Her Ph.D. in economics is from Northwestern University. Dr. Courchane has published widely in the areas of consumer and mortgage credit with articles in *Journal of Real Estate Research, Journal of Economics and Business, Real Estate Economics, Housing Policy Debate, Real Estate Economics,* and *Journal of Real Estate Finance and Economics.*

Rajeev Darolia is a senior associate at CRA, currently completing a Ph.D. in public policy at George Washington University. He holds a master's degree in economics.

Dr. Peter Zorn, VP, heads housing analysis and research at Freddie Mac. He was formerly an associate professor at Cornell. He received his Ph.D. in economics from the University of California at Davis and a B.A. in history from Marlboro College. Dr. Zorn has published widely in the areas of consumer and mortgage credit with articles in the *Journal of Real Estate Research,* the *Journal of Economics and Business, Real Estate Economics, Housing Policy Debate, Real Estate Economics,* and the *Journal of Real Estate Finance and Economics.*

CHAPTER 22

The Single-Family Mortgage Industry in the Internet Era: Technology Developments and Market Structure

FORREST PAFENBERG
Senior Policy Analyst in FHFA's Office of Policy Analysis and Research*

T echnological innovation has had an important influence on the recent evolution of the single-family mortgage industry. Changes in technology have
made possible improvements throughout the lending process that allowed
prospective borrowers to apply for loans, and enabled lenders and investors to service, price, sell, and trade mortgages more quickly. The development of automated
underwriting systems (AUS) that use scoring models to measure the credit risk of
mortgages has completely changed how lenders underwrite loan applications and
handle delinquent loans, while other innovations have begun to change the way
the ownership of mortgages is recorded.

Since the mid-1990s, computer networks and the Internet have changed how
firms in many industries operate, both internally and in the markets in which they
do business. The costs of storing, transmitting, and processing information have
been dropping continuously by 25 to 35 percent per year for the last 30 years. Improvements in computing power, data storage, and data transmission bandwidth
have increased business profitability in several ways. They have lowered the cost of
information and, thereby, transaction costs. They have also contributed to changes
in workflow processing within firms. Such changes have led firms to change how
they are organized, which in turn has led to further reductions in transaction costs.
Lower information and transaction costs and greater organizational flexibility

---

*This article summarizes and then updates a paper published in January 2004 that explored
the impact of financial innovation and technological change on the economics and structure
of mortgage lending since the 1980s. The impact was profound and significantly changed
the way the participants in the mortgage industry did business. This article, however, does
not attempt to explain the causes of the current financial crisis that manifested in 2007. Other
articles in this volume address this in detail.

allow firms to reinvent the ways in which they do business, refocusing their activity on what they do best.

The goal of many mortgage lenders is to structure their business operations to be process-driven rather than business department–driven, consumer-oriented rather than firm-oriented, automated and collaborative rather than paper-based and competitive, and adaptable rather than hidebound. For many in the industry, full achievement of those goals will require moving from paper-based to electronic mortgages. Electronic mortgages will require an extensive, long-term effort to reengineer business processes as well as changes in consumer preferences.

TECHNOLOGY AND MORTGAGE LENDING

In the last 30 years, improvements in computer and communications technologies have reduced the cost of and time needed to conclude financial transactions. Lower transaction costs and greater transparency have transformed financial markets in many ways.[1] The four major changes to the single-family mortgage lending process made possible by improvements in technology are: the growth of mortgage securitization and the unbundling of the lending process, the automation of lender operations, consolidation in the origination market, and consolidation in servicing.[2]

THE GROWTH OF SECURITIZATION AND THE UNBUNDLING OF THE LENDING PROCESS

Improvements in information technologies first affected single-family mortgage lending by making securitization the preferred method of funding loans. Securitization was stimulated in the 1970s by the advent of computers and cheap data transmission. Rapid increases in computer processor speeds facilitated the development of multiclass mortgage securities in more active markets for mortgage securities in the 1980s and 1990s.

The growth of securitization greatly increased the liquidity of most single-family mortgages and made it easier for firms to unbundle the lending process. Instead of most firms making loans, keeping them in portfolio, and servicing them, the unbundled process allows separate firms to originate loans (functioning as mortgage brokers), service loans (servicers), securitize pools of loans for sale in the capital market (secondary market entities), and own claims to their cash flows (mortgage-backed security [MBS] investors). Since the late 1980s, most single-family mortgage lending has occurred through this unbundled model.

AUTOMATION OF MORTGAGE LENDER OPERATIONS

Single-family mortgage lenders began to automate their operations during the 1980s. At that time, the computer systems of most lenders were based on mainframe architecture with application software designed to meet the needs of individual departments within the firm but not integrated across the firm. For example, proprietary loan origination systems (LOS) were separate from servicing application software. Data definitions and standards were not consistent across departments of the firm because the segments of the lending process were operationally segregated, and each department defined its technology needs separately. Automation continued to occur largely at the department level until the second half of the 1990s.

Automation has allowed originators of single-family mortgages to transmit information quickly and easily, allocate staff more flexibly, and transform fixed costs into variable costs. One important effect of automation is that refinancing of single-family loans is cheaper and less time-consuming, which has made borrowers more likely to refinance when mortgage rates decline and to shop among originators for the best rates and terms. The development of electronic commerce—the process of evaluating, negotiating, executing, and managing business transactions electronically—has been an essential to the automation of mortgage originations. The largest single-family mortgage lenders have used Electronic Data Interchange (EDI) to exchange information and execute transactions with mortgage insurers, credit bureaus, and other business partners since the 1970s. Other lenders and firms in the industry began using EDI in the mid-1990s. Fannie Mae and Freddie Mac accelerated the automation of the mortgage origination process and the use of e-commerce by introducing their own proprietary automated underwriting systems (AUS) and electronic mortgage information networks in 1995.

The largest efficiency gains from automation have occurred in servicing departments. Since 1980, four different technologies—personal computers (PCs), local area networks (LANs) that link PCs, automated voice response technologies, and the Internet—have each reduced the cost of responding to customer inquiries. Another technology—document imaging—has allowed large servicers to retain much less paper for each individual loan and to access records quickly and cheaply. The adoption of those technologies has enabled servicers to achieve increasing economies of scale. Those economies were the principal factor in improving the operational efficiency of the mortgage industry in the last two decades, while at the same time, increasing their operational risk. Although some servicing functions remain labor intensive, the modern servicing department is highly automated in discharging its traditional responsibilities for overseeing tax and insurance payments, monitoring delinquent loans, managing foreclosures and real estate owned (REO), reporting to investors, and communicating changes in loan terms to consumers. The elimination of skilled labor from servicing departments has become a major problem in resolving the foreclosure and REO problems since 2008.

CONSOLIDATION IN THE ORIGINATION MARKET

The automation of the single-family mortgage origination process, including the emergence of AUS and e-commerce through the Internet, has facilitated significant consolidation among mortgage originators in recent years. The market share of the top 10 firms rose from over 17 percent in 1990 to nearly 72 percent in 2008, while the market share of the top 25 firms rose from 28 percent to 91 percent during the same period. Economies of scale achieved through the exploitation of new technologies were one of the primary reasons for that consolidation.

Another explanation for the consolidation trend is the growth in purchased production, which has been facilitated by technology.[3] Retail production of mortgage loans declined steadily during the 1990s, falling from 62 percent in 1990 to 40 percent in 2002, while purchased production rose during that period. Statistics compiled by the Mortgage Bankers Association of America (MBA) document that, as the share of purchased production by the firm increases, the cost per loan produced decreases. More important, firm size, as measured by the number of loans produced, is directly related to the share of purchased production.[4]

Why is it less expensive to buy externally produced mortgages than to originate those loans in-house? One reason is the large expense of establishing and maintaining a retail operation. Since the mortgage origination business is cyclical, mortgage lenders have found that it is costly to ramp up and down retail operations in response to changes in mortgage demand. Second, and related to this, the emergence of the Internet as a medium for transacting business has significantly reduced the cost of establishing meaningful business relationships between the mortgage brokerage community and mortgage companies and financial institutions. Third, the deployment of automated underwriting technology in multiple channels, including the Internet, has provided the lending community with widespread access to those systems and allowed mortgage bankers and brokers to contemporaneously share loan decisions. That has streamlined the process, reduced paperwork and errors, and has allowed for quicker execution of pending transactions.

Mortgage lending is a local transaction. The use of local mortgage brokers lowers the cost and risk of loan aggregation for regional and national lenders. Beginning in 1995, distant lenders began to rely heavily on AUS to perform the due diligence functions of credit risk, fraud risk, and collateral risk underwriting. Mortgage lenders now can run mortgage broker names through online fraud prevention services to determine if enforcement or de-licensing actions have been taken, further reducing their counterparty risk. Those technological innovations have significantly reduced the costs of transacting business with geographically distant parties and increased the willingness of mortgage lenders to use delivery channels other than retail production.

CONSOLIDATION IN THE SERVICING MARKET

The market for servicing single-family mortgages has consolidated far more quickly than the origination market. The market share of the top 10 firms rose from over 11 percent in 1990 to over 79 percent in 2008, while the market share of the top 25 firms rose from 17 percent to nearly 90 percent during the same period. The scale economies achieved through automation of servicing operations in the 1980s have allowed the most efficient lenders to increase the size of their servicing portfolios.

Sheer size has, in turn, required the largest servicers to make continual technology expenditures to process the growing number of loans in their portfolios. That investment further lowered unit costs and increased the rate of consolidation. Firms that were too small to achieve economies on their own left the servicing industry or outsourced the servicing function to very large servicers.

THE DEVELOPMENT OF NEW CREDIT RISK MANAGEMENT TECHNOLOGIES IN SINGLE-FAMILY MORTGAGE LENDING

The adoption of AUS was the single most important technology development in the mortgage lending industry in the 1990s. Those systems, which use scoring technology to evaluate the credit risk of individual mortgages and loan portfolios, revolutionized the underwriting of prime, conventional, and later all single-family mortgages. They have also led to sweeping changes in how servicers handle delinquent loans, including the elimination of skilled property disposal personnel—a change that lenders currently rue.

The combination of AUS and the Internet significantly reduces the costs of communicating and doing business among mortgage brokers, mortgage companies, Fannie Mae and Freddie Mac, and firms that provide settlement services for the mortgage or real estate transactions. Together, those two technologies have fostered new visions of how single-family mortgage lenders and secondary market entities can manage credit risk, communicate, and do business.

Automated underwriting revolutionized how residential mortgages were underwritten. There are three basic components of single-family mortgage underwriting:

1. Determining the ability of the consumer to make the monthly mortgage payment
2. Determining the willingness of the consumer to pay the debt in a timely manner
3. Determining the value of the collateral underlying the mortgage

Automated underwriting replaced rules-of-thumb human underwriters and detailed underwriting guidelines with computer-assisted decision tools that assess the ability and willingness of consumers to repay their loans.[5] The widespread adoption of automated underwriting was made possible by the dominance of Fannie Mae and Freddie Mac in the secondary market for conventional fixed-rate mortgages (FRMs).

In 1995, Fannie Mae and Freddie Mac each began using a proprietary AUS to assess the credit risk of single-family mortgages prior to purchase. Soon thereafter, each enterprise included its use in the conforming guidelines for its sellers and servicers. In doing so, the enterprises sought to increase business volumes and improve risk management.[6]

The ability of Fannie Mae and Freddie Mac to establish underwriting terms and conditions for conventional single-family mortgages allowed them to become the most significant providers of AUS and related credit risk management technology in the primary mortgage market. Lenders are using automated underwriting to help streamline work processes and risk management decisions. A consequence of the use of scoring and automated underwriting was the extension of mortgage credit to some households traditionally viewed as higher risk and to markets previously underserved by the mortgage lending industry.[7]

MORTGAGE LENDING AND THE INTERNET

The evolution of the Internet as a low-cost business medium and the use of automated underwriting systems and other automated credit risk management tools by lenders have had a major impact on the single-family mortgage lending industry. Many single-family mortgage lenders and other firms that provide services used in mortgage lending are pursuing e-business models. For some of those entities, the e-business model is their only business channel. For others, the Internet is viewed as one of many approaches to interacting with consumers or business partners.

The many e-business models being pursued by single-family mortgage lenders can be characterized generally as business-to-consumer (B2C) or business-to-business (B2B). B2C models focus exclusively on mortgage originations and the settlement services that are necessary to close the real estate or mortgage transaction. They bring automated underwriting to the point of sale. The most common B2B e-commerce models attempt to support back-office functions—servicing and secondary marketing. There are also B2B e-business models that focus on supporting the mortgage origination process.

THE OPPORTUNITIES AND CHALLENGES FOR MORTGAGE LENDERS CREATED BY THE INTERNET

A useful way to think about the impact of the Internet on single-family mortgage lending is in terms of the value chain formed by lenders and their business partners.[8] Outsourcing of functions previously performed by a lender is increasingly possible and offers a low-cost off-the-shelf option for both large and small firms. Disintermediation of firms—residential appraisers and settlement service providers, for example—by new business models is beginning and is likely to radically change the residential mortgage finance delivery system. The competitive advantage of proprietary software applications such as loan origination systems or servicing applications is disappearing, and the influence of e-commerce is changing competitors into suppliers of service.

Intercompany coordination is the heart of all B2B e-business models. The Internet provides a communications channel for information, decisions, transactions, and processes. B2B e-business models involve sharing operational and planning information with strategic business partners to coordinate the successful completion of activities. The Internet has changed the way consumers shop for financial services and the business models mortgage lenders are pursuing.

DATA AND COMMUNICATION STANDARDS

An important impediment to the development of e-commerce in single-family mortgage lending is a continued lack of industrywide data and communication standards. For most of the time that mortgage records have been computerized, there were no common definitions (or computer formats) for demographic data or information about the property, mortgage products, payment status, or settlement services across firms. Moreover, there often were no common formats between the origination and servicing departments of the firm.

The evolution in the attitude toward data and communication standards by the single-family mortgage industry has been gradual. As businesses began to adopt computer networks in the late 1980s, the first task that network administrators faced was establishing firm-specific data and communication standards. At that time, the objective was to increase internal firm productivity by, for example, creating a common standard across the firm so it could pass data among software applications. Little thought was given to establishing standards in common with other firms in the industry or with business partners.

EDI, first developed in the 1980s, has become the primary computer data interchange by which large data sets are transferred within a firm. The largest mortgage lenders, Fannie Mae and Freddie Mac, and mortgage insurers were quick to adopt EDI for internal operations, but there was no attempt to develop an industry standard for data definitions. The task of maintaining multiple EDI standards generally stretches the limited information technology resources of a mortgage lender. Not only are the technical requirements difficult to manage, they are expensive to maintain. That challenge is being addressed by the increasing use of the Internet to transfer data and eXtensible Markup Language (XML) to improve compatibility between disparate EDI standards.

In 1999, the Mortgage Bankers Association announced the formation of the Mortgage Industry Standards Maintenance Organization (MISMO) to develop universal standards for single-family mortgage lending. The mission of MISMO, which is a coalition of mortgage lenders, mortgage settlement service providers, and Fannie Mae and Freddie Mac, is to develop, promote, and maintain voluntary electronic commerce standards for the mortgage industry. MISMO publishes a Logical Data Dictionary and a version of XML data definitions (DTDs) for four different business areas: origination, mortgage settlement services, secondary marketing, and servicing.

E-MORTGAGE LENDING

Beginning in the late 1990s, a number of lenders, Fannie Mae and Freddie Mac, and technology providers began to advocate the concept of an entirely electronic mortgage that would all but eliminate the need for paper in the mortgage lending process. Interest in creating an electronic mortgage has increased significantly since the National Conference of Commissioners on Uniform State Laws (NCCUSL) approved the Uniform Electronic Transaction Act (UETA) for adoption by the states in July 1999, and the Electronic Signatures in Global and National Commerce Act (E-Sign) was enacted in June 2000.

An electronic mortgage envisions the use of a combination of new and existing technologies to provide an entirely paperless closing transaction, resulting in a loan evidenced solely by electronic records and signatures, often referred to as an e-mortgage. An e-mortgage is a mortgage by which the critical loan documents are created, executed, transferred, and ultimately stored electronically. The technologies required to facilitate that would include digital signatures; sophisticated encryption, authentication, and security strategies and standards; and data exchange with trusted systems through the Internet or private network connections among lenders, data repositories, closing agents, county recording offices, and investors.

Electronic mortgages promise to yield both a competitive advantage and savings for lenders that adopt them. Doing so is daunting to many lenders, however, given the amount of inefficiency still present in the current lending process. There are many areas in which competing standards paralyze decisions and choices, such as the choice between XML and EDI for transmitting data. Consumer acceptance is also an issue. Consumers, already feeling anxiety about obtaining a mortgage, may be uncomfortable with a process without paper, so the capability to print records must be provided.

CHANGED MORTGAGE MARKET: 2004 TO 2009

A lot has occurred since this paper was published in 2004, including a significant increase in origination volume of both alternative financing arrangements and nontraditional mortgages that differed in terms and conditions from the traditional fixed-rate loans and one-year Treasury ARMs purchased by Fannie Mae and Freddie Mac. Without the financial innovation made possible by automation, scoring technologies, and the Internet, the proliferation of nontraditional mortgage products and their securitization could not have occurred. For example, the Internet (used as an intranet) provided the connectivity within the mortgage firm that allowed the ability to add a hybrid mortgage product to the origination system and be able to support it in the servicing systems. This allowed mortgage lenders the ability to robustly scale up mortgage production in products that had never been previously offered to consumers.

Accompanying the rise in nontraditional loans and the growth of the nonconforming mortgage market was the vertical integration of firms in the primary and secondary mortgage markets, which allowed new entrants into the origination segment of single-family mortgage lending, changing the role of Wall Street investment banking firms and their mortgage conduits. At the same time, traditional lenders, like IndyMac and Countrywide, became major players in the secondary market.

Beginning in August of 2007, however, one year into a hard housing market correction, financial markets seized up, and nonconforming conventional mortgage lending became nonexistent. The recession that began in December 2007 continued throughout 2008. Not until the summer of 2009 did it begin to show signs of ending. Serious delinquencies and foreclosures that began in the subprime and nontraditional mortgage markets have spilled over into the real economy, and this has caused serious financial losses for all mortgage lenders and insurers.

Declines in the value and liquidity of asset-backed securities, including those backed by mortgages and credit losses, increased concerns about the solvency and liquidity of important financial institutions. Because of growing safety and soundness issues at both Fannie Mae and Freddie Mac, on September 6, 2008, the Federal Housing and Finance Agency (FHFA), placed each enterprise in conservatorship. This action was taken to enable the enterprises to continue to fulfill their mission of providing liquidity and stability to mortgage markets.

Why did the primary market change so quickly? One simple answer is that, with housing becoming less affordable since 2001, the alternative mortgages with teaser rates, interest-only payments or negative amortization options appeared to provide consumers with more affordable means of financing than the traditional 30-year fixed-rate mortgages and enterprise hybrid and one-year Treasury ARMs. Some consumers were willing to accept the increased interest rate risk associated with ARMs and the house price risk associated with negative amortizing loans.

Traditionally, single-family mortgages have been segmented into government-insured or -guaranteed, conforming conventional, and nonconforming conventional loans. Conforming conventional mortgages are defined as loans with unpaid principal balances below the conforming loan limit (which is $417,000 in 2009) that are underwritten to the guidelines of Freddie Mac and Fannie Mae. Nonconform-ing conventional loans are either jumbo mortgages or are not underwritten to the guidelines of the enterprises. Historically, the nonconforming conventional sector was relatively small compared to the origination volume of the conforming sector; however, beginning in the mid-1990s, the volume of nonconforming mortgages began to rise, first at the expense of the government-insured or -guaranteed sector, and later at the expense of the conforming conventional sector. Today, the major mortgage market sectors for single-family mortgages are government, prime con-ventional, jumbo, subprime, Alternative-A,[9] and home equity loan or home equity line of credit (HELOC).[10]

Beginning in 2000, both the government (FHA and VA) and prime conventional market shares declined significantly. In 2001, the government sector represented 7.9 percent and the prime conventional sector represented 57.8 percent of total single-family mortgage originations. In 2005, the market shares for those segments had declined to 2.9 and 35 percent, respectively. In 2009, after the collapse of the nonconforming market, government represents 22 percent and conforming conventional represents 70 percent of mortgage originations.

Both Freddie Mac and Fannie Mae participated in the nonjumbo segments of the nonconforming market by acquiring for portfolio senior, private label, AAA-rated Real Estate Mortgage Investment Conduit (REMIC) securities collateralized by pools of subprime, Alt-A, or home equity loans. The adjustable-rate share of single-family originations began to increase in 2001 in response to declines in the affordability of single-family housing. The ARM share of total single-family originations rose from 16 percent in 2001 to 48 percent in 2005, after peaking at 50 percent in 2004. The ARM share in 2009 is 4 percent.

A significant failure in mortgage lending after 2004 was an overreliance on automated underwriting systems and the underestimation of credit risk in non-traditional mortgage products. A major difficulty in evaluating the credit risk of the nontraditional mortgages originated from 2001 through 2006 was the lack of data regarding their performance during times of stress. Available information was skewed by the favorable interest rate and housing market conditions of the period. For many of those products, defaults and losses were quite low. The bulk of nontraditional loans originated between 2003 and 2005 exhibited extremely high prepayment speeds. As a consequence, the credit performance of those loans was extremely good. It was not until the spring of 2007 that market analysts and the general public realized the extent of the decline in underwriting standards.

Much of the public discussion of the performance of specific types of nontra-ditional mortgages failed to factor in the layering of risks. For example, option ARMs had performed well from 2003 through 2005. However, if a piggyback financial arrangement, a low borrower FICO score, limited or no documentation of income and assets, and a high LTV ratio are also present in the mortgage, the risk of default increases substantially. Most of the nonconforming mortgages were carefully introduced initially to low-risk borrowers, and the underwriting was very conservative. Over time, however, those loans were offered to less creditwor-thy borrowers, and underwriting became far less conservative. One lesson from the subprime meltdown is that there is significantly more model risk than was previously believed, since virtually none of the major credit risk scoring models captured in their scores the increasing risk layering that prevailed in the market.

Subprime and Alt-A mortgage lending were so profitable during the early part of this decade that new entrants were attracted to the origination, conduit,[11] and servicing segments of such lending. Several Wall Street investment banks vertically integrated into the production of subprime and Alt-A loans.[12] Those new entrants often entered all three segments. Bear Stearns and Lehman Brothers, for example, had generated such significant returns in issuing ABS and MBS in 2000 and 2001 that they changed their business models. Those firms shifted from just securitizing mortgages for large lenders to establishing wholly owned affiliates (Lehman Brothers owned Aurora Loan Services and Bear Stearns owned EMC Mortgage Company) that originated subprime loans, purchased those mortgages in bulk (i.e., function as conduits), and issued securities in their own name.

Such backward vertical integration enabled Wall Street firms to expand their business volumes. By 2005, Lehman Brothers was the second-largest private mortgage conduit, with 8.9 percent of that market, and Bear Stearns was the fourth-largest, with 6.4 percent of the market. In late 2005, both Bear Stearns and Lehman Brothers announced intentions to purchase national banks to feed their conduit and securitization activities. The bulk of activities at both firms was subprime, Alt-A, and HELs, with more limited activity in the jumbo segment. Both firms severely regretted their entry into these markets when they became insolvent in the financial collapse brought about by the subprime meltdown. Bear Stearns was rescued and sold to JPMorgan Chase in March 2008, while Lehman Brothers was forced into bankruptcy six months later, in September 2008.

NOTES

1. For a discussion of the effects of changes in technology on financial markets, see Frederick S. Mishkin and Philip E. Strahan, "What Will Technology Do to Financial Structure?" in Robert E. Litan and Anthony M. Santomero, eds., *Brookings-Wharton Papers on Financial Services 1999* (Washington, DC: The Brookings Institution, 1999), 249–277.

2. For an in-depth discussion of those changes, see Michael LaCour-Little, "The Evolving Role of Technology in Mortgage Lending," *Journal of Housing Research* 11 (2000): 173–205.

3. In the 1980s and early 1990s, mortgage originators adopted three business channels, characterized by their source of funding—retail, wholesale, and correspondent originations. Retail lending consists of loans made directly to a borrower whether through a branch office, a call center, the Internet, or some other direct means. Wholesale lending occurs when a mortgage broker uses table funding to close a loan. The broker finds the consumer, facilitates the closing, but uses a wholesale lender's money to fund the closing of the loan. In correspondent lending, a lender buys a loan after it is funded at the closing table. That purchase could occur immediately or after several weeks. See Thomson Financial Publications, *Mortgage Industry Directory, Lenders, Brokers & Servicers* 2002 ed., New York, 2–3.

4. See Mortgage Bankers Association of America annual reports, *2008 Cost Study: Income and Cost for Origination and Servicing of 1- to 4-Unit Residential Loans* (Washington, DC, December 2008).

5. See John W. Straka, "A Shift in the Mortgage Landscape: The 1990s Move to Automated Credit Evaluations," *Journal of Housing Research* 11 (2000): 207–232, for a history of the development of the automated underwriting system in mortgage lending.

6. See Robert Van Order, "The Structure and Evolution of American Secondary Mortgage Markets, with Some Implications for Developing Markets," *Housing Finance International* (2001): 16–31, for an extensive discussion of why the secondary market requires lenders to adopt secondary market standards and technology.

7. See John W. Straka, "A Shift in the Mortgage Landscape: The 1990s Move to Automated Credit Evaluations," *Journal of Housing Research* 11 (2000): 207–232.

8. Michael Porter, *Competitive Advantage* (New York: The Free Press, 1985) is widely credited for coining the phrase *value chain* while explaining the concepts of competitive advantage. In manufacturing, the equivalent term is *supply chain*.

9. There is no uniform definition of Alt-A loans across the single-family mortgage industry. According to bank regulators, however, Alt-A mortgages can be made to borrowers who have marginal to very good credit where traditional underwriting guidelines for standard complying loans have been expanded. Alt-A mortgages may include those with:
   - No credit score or credit scores higher than subprime
   - Nonowner-occupied homes
   - A loan-to-value ratio greater than 80 percent and no mortgage insurance
   - High debt-to-income ratios that are not considered subprime
   - Little or no documentation

10. Home equity lending comprises home equity loans (HELs) and home equity lines of credit (HELOCs). HELs are fixed- or variable-rate second mortgages with terms to maturity of 5 to 15 years.

11. Conduits are firms that purchase or package their own mortgages into mortgage- or asset-backed securities (ABS). Those firms often specialize in specific primary market segments. For example, there are conduits that purchase FHA or VA mortgages from small lenders and issue Ginnie Mae securities. Similarly, there are firms that purchase or package nonconforming mortgages in nonagency MBS and ABS.

12. Most of the reasons that firms choose to vertically integrate have to do with reducing costs or eliminating a market externality. A firm may vertically integrate to assure itself a steady supply of a key input, for example, vertically integrating backward to buy or build the capacity to produce that input. Additionally, a firm may vertically integrate to increase or create market power, for example, vertically integrate forward to monopolize the final product market and thereby increase its monopoly profits (by being able to price discriminate, eliminate competition, or foreclose entry into markets).

ABOUT THE AUTHOR

Forrest Pafenberg has more than 30 years of experience as a housing and mortgage finance economist. He has been a senior policy analyst in the FHFA's Office of Policy Analysis and Research since October 2000. Before joining the OFHEO, he was the director of real estate finance research for 17 years at the National Association of Realtors. Before joining the Realtors, he was a housing economist at Freddie Mac. Pafenberg began his career as a housing economist at the Bureau of Labor Statistics. He has a B.S. in economics from George Mason University and an M.A. in economics from the University of Massachusetts.

CHAPTER 23

Speed Kills?

Mortgage Credit Boom and the Crisis

GIOVANNI DELL'ARICCIA
Advisor in the Research Department of the International Monetary Fund

DENIZ IGAN
Economist in the Research Department at the International Monetary Fund

LUC LAEVEN
Deputy Division Chief in the Research Department of the International Monetary Fund*

T he global economy is still in the grip of the financial turmoil that started with problems in the U.S. subprime mortgage market. Over the last decade, this market has expanded dramatically, evolving from a small niche segment into a major portion of the overall U.S. mortgage market. Can the recent market turmoil—triggered by the sharp increase in delinquency rates—be related to this fast expansion? In other words, is the recent experience, in part, the result of a credit boom gone bad? Caught in the wind of the boom, did lenders expand credit

---

*The authors are all at the International Monetary Fund Research Department (Macro-Financial Linkages Unit). Dell'Ariccia and Laeven are also at the CEPR. We would like to thank Richard Baldwin, Tam Bayoumi, Stijn Claessens, Enrica Detragiache, Gianni De Nicolo, David Gussmann, Robert Hauswald, Patrick Honohan, Simon Johnson, Pete Kyle, Robert Marquez, Rebecca McCaughrin, Marcelo Pinheiro, Calvin Schnure, Rene Stulz, and seminar participants at the International Monetary Fund, Fannie Mae, Freddie Mac, George Washington University, American University, University of South Carolina, University of Houston, University of Virginia, University of Kansas, Homer Hoyt Institute Weimer School, Federal Reserve Bank of New York, Philadelphia, and Chicago, Bank of England, and BSI Gamma Foundation for helpful discussions and comments. We would also like to thank Chris Crowe for sharing his data. Mattia Landoni provided outstanding research assistance. The views expressed here are those of the authors and do not necessarily represent those of the IMF, its executive board, or its management.

This article is based on the empirical evidence presented in "Credit Booms and Lending Standards: Evidence from the Subprime Mortgage Market," available as IMF Working Paper 08/106 and CEPR Discussion Paper Series No. 6683, and "Lender Behavior over the Credit Cycle," IMF Working Paper, forthcoming.

recklessly? Did competitive pressures contribute to the alleged decline in lending standards because no lender wanted to be the first to quit in a game of musical chairs? While many would say yes to these questions, rigorous empirical evidence on the matter has thus far been lacking. This article summarizes research analyzing millions of loan applications to investigate the roots of the crisis. A credit boom and the resulting race to the bottom in credit quality may be to blame.

CREDIT BOOMS

There appears to be widespread agreement that periods of rapid credit growth tend to be accompanied by loosening lending standards. For instance, in a speech delivered before the Independent Community Bankers of America on March 7, 2001, former Federal Reserve chairman Alan Greenspan pointed to "an unfortunate tendency" among bankers to lend aggressively at the peak of a cycle and argued that most bad loans were made through this aggressive type of lending.

Indeed, most major banking crises in the past three decades have occurred in the wake of periods of extremely fast credit growth (Exhibit 23.1).

For some policy makers, this is enough reason to view credit booms as a recipe for disaster. Yet, not all credit booms are followed by banking crises. Actually, most studies find that, while the probability of a banking crisis increases significantly (by between 50 and 75 percent) during booms, historically, only about one in five boom episodes have ended in a crisis. For example, out of 135 credit booms identified in Barajas et al. (2007) only 23 preceded systemic banking crises (about 17 percent), with that proportion rising to 31 (about 23 percent) if nonsystemic episodes of financial distress are included. In contrast, about half of the banking crises in their

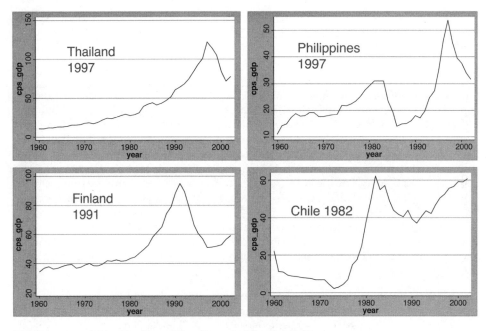

Exhibit 23.1   Major Banking Crises Preceded by Credit Booms

sample were preceded by lending booms. Not surprisingly, larger and longer-lasting booms, and those coinciding with higher inflation and, to a lesser extent, lower growth, are more likely to end in a crisis. Booms associated with fast rising equity and property prices are also more likely to turn bad.

Evidence on the linkage of credit booms to financial instability mostly depends on aggregate data from emerging market economies. This limits study of lender incentives and determination of causal relationships. The subprime market, in that sense, provides a good opportunity to look closely at a credit boom and use variation across regions and lenders based on loan-by-loan data.

THE MORTGAGE MARKET: REGIONAL ANALYSIS

Reminiscent of this pattern linking credit booms with banking crises, current mortgage delinquencies in the U.S. subprime mortgage market appear indeed to be related to past credit growth (see Exhibit 23.2).

In our working paper titled "Credit Booms and Lending Standards: Evidence from the Subprime Mortgage Market," we analyze data between 2000 and 2006 from over 50 million individual loan applications and find that delinquency rates rose more sharply in areas that experienced larger increases in the number and volume of originated loans (Dell'Ariccia, Igan, and Laeven 2008a). This relationship is linked to a decrease in lending standards, as measured by a significant increase in loan-to-income ratios and a decline in denial rates, not explained by improvement in the underlying economic fundamentals.

The deterioration in lending standards can be linked to five main factors. First, standards tended to decline more where the credit boom was larger. This is

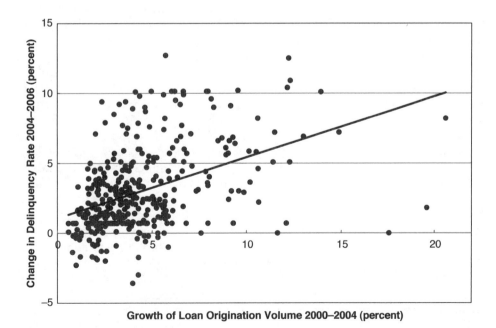

Exhibit 23.2   Another Credit Boom Gone Bad?

consistent with cross-country evidence on aggregate credit booms. Second, lower standards were associated with a fast rate of house price appreciation, consistent with the notion that lenders were to some extent gambling on a continuing housing boom, relying on the belief that borrowers in default could always liquidate the collateral and repay the loan. Third, there is evidence that changes in market structure mattered. Lending standards declined more in regions where large (and aggressive) previously absent institutions entered the market. Fourth, the increasing recourse by banks to loan sales and asset securitization appears to have affected lender behavior, with lending standards experiencing greater declines in areas where lenders sold a larger proportion of originated loans. Finally, easy monetary conditions seem to have played a role, with the cycle in lending standards mimicking that of the federal funds rate. In the subprime mortgage market, most of these effects appear to be stronger and more significant than in the prime mortgage market, where loan denial decisions seem to be more closely related to economic fundamentals.

THE MORTGAGE MARKET: LENDER ANALYSIS

In our second paper, "Lender Behavior during the Credit Cycle," we expand the data set to the period between 1996 and 2006, covering a full credit cycle in the mortgage market. Moreover, we combine these data with information on lenders' balance sheets and income statements. This allows us to study whether particular lenders behave differently over the cycle. We find that denial rates tend to decline with the number of loan applications. More precisely, denial rates tend to drop in regions where applications increased, as measured by the log number of applications to other lenders in a given area, but increased with the number of applications at each individual lender. The overall effect of an increase of loan applications on denial rates is strongly negative, as the first effect outweighs the second. These results are consistent with theoretical predictions suggesting that adverse selection problems decrease as a large number of previously unbanked borrowers enter the market, while at the same time banks become choosier as the number of potential clients rises. Also consistent with adverse selection stories, we find that lenders with larger market shares tend to be less choosy, as reflected in lower denial rates. Looking at the impact of lender characteristics on lending behavior, there is evidence that more capitalized banks are choosier than their less capitalized counterparts in their decisions to grant loans, suggesting that capital requirements may play a disciplining role for banks. Moreover, the regulator appears to make a difference, with lenders supervised under the Federal Reserve System being the ones with the least tendency to loosen lending standards. Lenders supervised by the Department of Housing and Urban Development tend to make loans at less strict standards. This group of lenders is mostly brokers operating under minimal licensing requirements and arguably less oversight.

These findings are consistent with the notion that rapid credit growth episodes, because of the cyclicality of lending standards, may create vulnerabilities in the financial system. The subprime experience demonstrates that even highly developed financial markets are not immune to problems associated with credit booms. There is some hope, though, in the sense that capital exhibits the expected disciplinary role and controlling for competitive pressures may help curb individual lenders' response to rapid credit expansion by others.

POSSIBLE SOLUTIONS

What can be done to curb bad credit booms? Historically, the effectiveness of macroeconomic policies in reducing credit growth has varied (see, for example, Enoch and Ötker-Robe 2007). While monetary tightening can reduce both the demand and supply of bank loans, its effectiveness is often limited by capital account openness. This is especially the case in small open economies and in countries with more advanced financial sectors, where banks have easy access to foreign credit, including from parent institutions. Monetary tightening may also lead to significant substitution between domestic and foreign-denominated credit, especially in countries with (perceived) rigid exchange rate regimes. Fiscal tightening may also help reduce the expansionary pressures associated with credit booms, though this is often not politically feasible.

While prudential and supervision policies alone may prove not very effective in curbing credit growth, they may be very effective in reducing the risks associated with a boom. Such policies include prudential measures to ensure that banks and supervisors are equipped to deal with enhanced credit risk (such as higher capital and provisioning requirements, more intensive surveillance of potential problem banks, and appropriate disclosure requirements of banks' risk management policies). Prudential measures may also target specific sources of risks (such as limits on sectoral loan concentration, tighter eligibility and collateral requirements for certain categories of loans, limits on foreign exchange exposure, and maturity mismatch regulations). Other measures may aim at reducing existing distortions and limiting the incentives for excessive borrowing and lending (such as the elimination of implicit guarantees or fiscal incentives for particular types of loans, and public risk awareness campaigns).

In response to aggressive lending practices by mortgage lenders, several states in the United States have enacted antipredatory lending laws. By the end of 2004, at least 23 states had enacted predatory lending laws that regulated the provision of high-risk mortgages. Research shows, however, that these laws have not been uniformly effective in limiting the growth of such mortgages, at least in those states (see, for example, Ho and Pennington-Cross 2007). At the end of 2006, U.S. federal banking agencies issued two guidelines out of concern that financial institutions had become overexposed to the real estate sector while lending standards and risk management practices had been deteriorating, but these guidelines were too little, too late. Of course, one could always put the blame on the regulators and policy makers for failing to see the buildup of risk. Yet, another explanation of why tighter regulations never got implemented could be related to the relationship between the financial industry and the policy makers. For example, Igan, Mishra, and Tressel (2009) show that lobbying is associated with more lax lending. To be able to do business as usual, the financial industry might be lobbying against any such regulations or laws. In other words, the influence of the finance industry in the political process might be one of the factors at the root of the crisis while the continued existence of such influence might sidetrack ongoing financial regulation efforts.

REFERENCES

Barajas, A., G. Dell'Ariccia, and A. Levchenko. 2007. Credit booms: The good, the bad, and the ugly. Washington, DC: International Monetary Fund, unpublished manuscript.

Dell'Ariccia, G., D. Igan, and L. Laeven. 2008a. Credit booms and lending standards: Evidence from the subprime mortgage market. Washington, DC and London, UK: International Monetary Fund, Working Paper 08/106, CEPR Discussion Paper 6683.

Dell'Ariccia, G., D. Igan, and L. Laeven. 2008b. Lender behavior during the credit cycle. Washington, DC: International Monetary Fund, unpublished manuscript.

Enoch, C., and I. Ötker-Robe (eds). 2007. *Rapid credit growth in central and Eastern Europe: Endless boom or early warning?* New York: International Monetary Fund and Palgrave Macmillan.

Ho, G., and A. Pennington-Cross. 2007. The varying effects of predatory lending laws on high-cost mortgage applications. *Federal Reserve Bank of St. Louis Review* 89 (1): 39–59.

Igan, D., P. Mishra, and T. Tressel. 2009. A fistful of dollars: Lobbying and the financial crisis. Washington, DC: International Monetary Fund, unpublished manuscript.

ABOUT THE AUTHORS

Giovanni Dell'Ariccia holds a Ph.D. in economics from the Massachusetts Institute of Technology and is currently advisor in the research department of the International Monetary Fund. He also is a research fellow of the Financial Economics Programme of the Centre for Economic Policy Research (CEPR) in London and a member of the editorial committee of the *IMF Staff Papers*. Dell'Ariccia's research has been published in top academic journals, including the *Journal of Finance*, the *Journal of Financial Economics*, and the *Review of Economic Studies*. His research interests include banking, the macroeconomics of credit, and issues in international finance.

Deniz Igan holds a Ph.D. in economics from Princeton University and is currently an economist in the research department at the International Monetary Fund. Igan's research has been published in several edited volumes and in academic journals such as the *Journal of Real Estate Research and Comparative Economic Studies*. Her research interests include international finance, banking, corporate finance, and real estate economics.

Luc Laeven holds a Ph.D. in economics from the University of Amsterdam and is currently deputy division chief in the research department of the International Monetary Fund and full professor of finance at CentER, Tilburg University. Before this, he was a senior economist at the World Bank. Laeven's research has been published in top academic journals, including the *Journal of Finance*, the *Journal of Financial Economics*, and the *Review of Financial Studies*. He has also co-edited a book titled *Systemic Financial Crises: Containment and Resolution* (Cambridge University Press) and a book titled *Deposit Insurance around the World* (MIT Press). He is a research fellow of the Financial Economics Programme of the Centre for Economic Policy Research (CEPR) in London and a research associate at the European Corporate Governance Institute (ECGI). His research focuses on international banking and corporate finance issues.

CHAPTER 24

Subprime Mortgages

What We Have Learned From a New Class of Homeowners

TODD J. ZYWICKI
George Mason University Foundation Professor of Law

SATYA THALLAM
Director of the Financial Markets Working Group at the Mercatus Center at George
Mason University*

A loss of confidence in rising home prices, exacerbated by precipitous losses from the portion of the mortgage market referred to as subprime loans, is widely considered to be one of the central culprits in perpetrating the financial catastrophe of 2007 and 2008. The huge growth and then collapse of the subprime market has led many to see opportunistic lenders as being culpable for the fraud, having tricked an increasing number of unwitting homebuyers into participating in their scheme.[1] But a full understanding of the subprime market, and indeed the crisis to which it is tied, requires balancing the benefits that accrued to millions of new American homeowners, increasing their economic well-being.[2] Thus, in applying lessons learned from the crisis, it will be necessary for new regulation of mortgage lending to preserve these benefits.

Indeed, there is little argument that a great deal of questionable behavior was present. But this cuts both ways. Some lenders preyed on borrowers with excessively costly loans in hopes of collecting high fees and interest payments. On the other side, many borrowers defrauded lenders by inflating the reported value of a house or misrepresenting income figures.[3] Its large impact notwithstanding, the subprime problem should be considered in the context of the overall housing finance picture. As of 2005, 34 percent of Americans owned homes outright. Of mortgage holders, about three-quarters had traditional fixed rates, about one-quarter adjustable rate mortgages (ARMs), and a smaller subset with subprime loans.[4] Moreover, an estimate from 2006 predicted U.S. homeowners would lose about $110 billion in home equity over the next several years because of

*Based on Todd J. Zywicki and Joseph Adamson, "The Law and Economics of Subprime Lending," *University of Colorado Law Review* 80 (Winter 2009): 1–86.

foreclosures, which amounts to about 1 percent of total accumulated home equity nationwide.[5]

But examination of the scope of the foreclosure problem itself begs another question: What is the appropriate number of foreclosures in the subprime market? Though the increased dislocation effects of foreclosures have caused hardship for some, the subprime market has, on net, increased home ownership overall.[6] As Lawrence Summers put it in 2007, "How much [foreclosure] are we prepared to accept?"[7] The answer is clearly more than zero, because a housing market in which there is no chance of foreclosure would require buyers to pay the entire price of the house up front in cash.

SUPERCHARGING THE SUBPRIME MARKET

Before the expansion of the subprime market, many subprime borrowers had been excluded from the mortgage market. Credit rationing occurred when lenders could not charge higher rates on mortgages to riskier customers because of interest rate caps. The expansion of the subprime market is a direct result of lenders' increased use of risk-based pricing in response to deregulated lending markets, technological changes in underwriting, and financial innovations in securities markets.[8]

Two federal laws allowed lenders to adopt risk-based pricing standards in their mortgages, which were requisite to subprime mortgage structures. First, the Depository Institutions Deregulation and Monetary Control Act of 1980 preempted state interest rate caps and allowed lenders to charge higher interest rates. Second, in 1982, the Alternative Mortgage Transactions Parity Act allowed lenders to offer adjustable-rate mortgages and balloon payments. Later came the Tax Reform Act of 1986, which allowed for the deductibility of mortgage interest payments (but not on consumer loans),[9] which made mortgage debt more attractive than other consumer debt, and thereby increased the demand for home ownership, mortgage refinancing, and borrowing against the equity in their homes. The 1997 change to capital gains taxation, allowing homeowners to take up to $500,000 from the sale of the price of a house tax free, further encouraged investment in residential real estate and pushed up prices.[10]

Before the introduction of risk-based pricing, mortgages were primarily originated by traditional savings and loans taking deposits that paid 3 percent and lent at 6 percent.[11] Risk-based pricing meant the possibility of a more efficient market through price discrimination. But because of information asymmetries, lenders rationed credit to reduce their risk of lending money to risky borrowers.[12] Some of the safest borrowers would be too risk-averse to borrow at the market interest rate, while some borrowers would appear less risky than they really were and be approved for loans with interest rates that were too low. As interest rates climb, those who are still willing to pay the higher interest rates will increasingly tend to be the riskiest borrowers, resulting in lower returns to the lender (despite the higher rates).

In addition to interest rate deregulation, two growing trends served to fuel growth in subprime lending: use of credit scoring and securitization. The use of credit scores allowed for an objective as well as a more granular test of borrower risk, leading to the schedule of interest rates and risk classes that currently make up the mortgage borrowers (e.g., prime A, A–, Alt-A, B, C, and D).

Securitization of mortgages began in the 1970s, with subprime securities available beginning in the 1990s.[13] Securitization is the "aggregation and pooling of assets with similar characteristics in such a way that investors may purchase interests or securities backed by those assets."[14] From 2000 to 2005, Wall Street had increased the pooling of subprime mortgages from $56 billion to $508 billion.[15] Pools of mortgages are split into different tranches whose characteristics are compared with historical data to predict its particular credit risk.[16] The tranches each have a different grade: from senior to mezzanine to junior. The senior tranche is paid off first and thus has the highest investment grade, with the junior tranche being last in line and thus the riskiest.

WHO'S AFRAID OF SUBPRIME LENDING?

Subprime loans fail more often than prime loans and are much more common in areas with large minority and low-income populations.[17] As a result, some consider subprime loans to be an example of predatory lending. Although this is certainly the case for some subprime loans, most are not. For every neighborhood facing a foreclosure crisis, there are others that have been resuscitated or families empowered by increased home ownership. Thus, regulations intended to prevent subprime lending must be carefully tailored so as to not unduly disrupt the market for legitimate subprime loans.[18]

In general, a *predatory* loan is one in which there is no reasonable anticipated financial benefit to the borrower. The Federal Reserve employs a slightly more specific, yet still invariably vague, definition of predatory lending.[19] Lacking a clear definition of predatory lending makes a measure of its extent impossible. Distinguishing a predatory loan from a legitimate subprime loan will therefore often be difficult. Empirical research indicates that although some loan terms may increase foreclosures in some contexts, those same terms may reduce foreclosures, and in still other contexts, their individual impact is contingent on their interaction with other loan terms.[20]

Similarly, although repeated refinancing may indicate predatory practices, consumers may refinance a given loan several times to their own advantage. As real estate prices were increasing during the first part of this decade, many consumers used home equity loans or mortgage refinancing to gain a lower interest rate, fund home improvements, consolidate debt (e.g., student loans, auto loans, credit card debt), diversify their wealth portfolio by reinvesting home equity into financial assets, and fund additional consumption.[21] So a consumer who refinances multiple times is not sufficient evidence of predatory practices.

The presence of prepayment penalties in a subprime loan is widely criticized by consumer advocates as predatory and unjustified.[22] But like multiple refinancings, a blanket condemnation inaccurately characterizes the use of this aspect of some mortgages. Prepayment risk is difficult to anticipate—there is no reliable model for predicting prepayment risk.[23] Because a lender must reinvest its capital at the prevailing market rates when prepayment occurs, the lender bears the risk that the new investment will provide a lower return than the existing investment.

Of course prepayment risk applies to both prime and subprime mortgage segments. When market interest rates fall, prime borrowers can be predicted to refinance their mortgages. Although changes in market interest rates are relevant for subprime borrowers as well, prepayment risk in the subprime market is more idiosyncratic than the prime market. Because credit score is a major component of the determination that lenders make of a borrower's interest rate—and the primary component for subprime loans—an increase in credit score can qualify a borrower for a much lower interest rate and monthly payments or even qualify a borrower for a prime-rated loan. Making on-time payments for even a short time can lead to a credit score upgrade and therefore an opportunity to reduce payments by refinancing.

Additional risk is just one reason why subprime loans are more costly. Sub-prime loans may be more expensive to underwrite in light of the heterogeneity of borrowers and the increased time required of lenders to service. One study estimated that servicing costs may in fact be two to three times higher for sub-prime loans than for prime loans, requiring an additional 50 basis points to the interest rate.[24] The rejection rate is also higher, which also increases the cost of each successfully endorsed loan.[25] The higher underwriting cost and the tendency to finance closing costs into the loan suggests that a prepayment penalty may be appropriate in subprime loans to ensure that the lender recoups up-front costs.[26] The bottom line is a significantly higher proportion of subprime borrowers prepay their mortgages when compared to prime borrowers.[27]

HAS THE BLOOM COME OFF THE ROSE?

Starting in late 2006, mortgage delinquencies and foreclosures in the subprime mar-ket began to rise dramatically. By February 2008, one source counted 226 lenders having imploded since 2006.[28]

But delinquency in the subprime market may not necessarily be a sign of financial distress. Because of the riskier credit history of subprime borrowers, some may actually choose to substitute the higher interest rates and late penalties of the loan for other more traditional, but more expensive, short-term liquidity options, such as payday lending or check bouncing. Indeed, in contrast to the prime market in which delinquency rate for mortgage payments decreases between 30-day delinquency to 60-day and 90-day delinquency, for the subprime market, the rates are highest for 30-day (7.35 percent), decline for 60-day (2.02 percent), and increase again for 90-day (4.04 percent). Ninety-day delinquency rates can exceed 60-day delinquency rates if borrowers fall three months behind in their loans, then begin to repay without catching up to the current month's payment. This is evidence that some subprime borrowers rationally choose to, in effect, take out short-term loans equal to one or two months of rent.[29]

Foreclosure itself, which may indicate financial distress, can be explained by two different, but conceptually related models. The first is the *distress model*, wherein a borrower desires to repay the loan, but is unable to do so because of an income or expense shock such as job loss or ARM rate increase.[30] Empirical support for this model is mixed.[31] The second is the *option model*, in which foreclo-sure is driven by a change in the underlying asset. A mortgage essentially gives the borrower an option—she can pay the mortgage as contracted and retain the property or default and surrender the property. If the house falls in value, this creates incentives for borrowers to exercise their option to default and surrender the collateral. So, under this theory, foreclosure is essentially a rational response to the incentives created by the change in value of the asset.

Determining which model has more explanatory power can be difficult because housing prices are inversely correlated with interest rates—as interest rates rise, housing prices fall. Nonetheless, empirical evidence seems to be on the side of the option theory.[32] To wit, even though interest rates rise uniformly nationwide, the foreclosure rate is lower where residential real estate prices have appreciated more.[33] One study found that in Massachusetts over an 18-year period, housing prices played the dominant role in generating foreclosures. They go on to point out that "subprime lending played a role but that role was creating a class of homeowners who were particularly sensitive to declining house price appreciation, rather than, as is commonly believed, by placing people in inherently problematic mortgages."[34]

Another major factor driving foreclosure is the presence or absence of equity in the property. Loans with little or no down payment—such as those with high loan-to-value ratios (LTV)—offer unusually strong incentives to default if property values fall, and thus lower down payments predict higher rates of default.[35] One study finds that "the increases in the adjusted delinquency and foreclosure rates are *almost exclusively* caused by the worsening of performance of loans with a combined LTV of 80 percent or more."[36]

Most outstanding mortgages remain traditional 30-year fixed-rate mortgages. Interest rate fluctuations for these mortgages present a risk for new purchasers, but not for those with established mortgages. Similarly, unless a given homeowner intends to sell, short-term changes in property values are fundamentally irrelevant. Traditional mortgage holders are more likely to have purchased a home as owner-occupied housing and to gain the amenities of home ownership. Homeowners also gain insurance against rent price volatility.[37] These conditions are reversed in the subprime market, however. Because many subprime loans are ARMs, an increase in market interest rates will lead to an increase in rates not only for new borrowers but existing borrowers, creating the condition for a payment shock, which can lead to foreclosure. Also, in areas where there are a higher percentage of subprime loans, this increase in interest rates will have a more dramatic effect on pushing down house prices—the reverse of the effect of low interest rates in pushing up market prices. Higher rates and declining values feed off one another to exacerbate default rates. Keep in mind though, that although ARMs appears unreasonably risky when interest rates rise, they are also equally beneficial when they fall, and thus cannot be generalized as unreasonably risky.

Those who feel that subprime lending is nearly synonymous with predatory lending would like to see much stricter controls over the types of loans that can be offered and the methods that brokers and lenders use to advertise them.[38] But this position ignores the benefits of legitimate subprime lending. The broad presence of ARMs contributed to the crisis because of broad market conditions: stagnant and declining home values,[39] rising interest rates,[40] and slowing economic growth that was especially acute in some specific regions.[41]

CONCLUSION

Attempts to solve the problems of the subprime market must be tempered with the reality that it has likely boosted home ownership levels, and that strict antipredatory regulations can raise the costs of mortgage credit, thereby reducing legitimate lending. Current lending disclosure requirements are not ideal, and some disclosure reform may go a long way toward helping borrowers make more informed decisions.

The subprime bust was not caused exclusively by unscrupulous lenders pushing borrowers to sign unsuitable loans. Exuberant borrowers, lenders, and investors combined with macroeconomic conditions to inflate housing prices and lure individuals to make what turned out to be bad bets. Without detailed knowledge of why certain loans went bad, a drastic reshaping of the mortgage market could hurt millions of homeowners afforded opportunities through expanded credit availability, foregoing a great deal of welfare gains to those individuals and their communities.

NOTES

1. See, for example, Center for Responsible Lending, CRL Issue Paper No. 14, "Subprime Lending: A Net Drain on Home Ownership" (2007), www.responsiblelending.org/pdfs/Net-Drain-in-Home-Ownership.pdf.

2. Thomas P. Boehm and Alan Schlottmann, U.S. Department of Housing and Urban Development, "Wealth Accumulation and Home Ownership: Evidence for Low-Income Households" (2004), www.huduser.org/Publications/pdf/WealthAccumulationAnd Homeownership.pdf.

3. Income or asset misrepresentation makes up 38 percent of fraud cases, and false property valuation accounts for 17 percent of fraud. Fannie Mae, Fannie Mae Mortgage Fraud Update 1 (2007), www.efanniemae.com/utility/legal/pdf/fraudupdate0507.pdf [hereinafter Fraud Update].

4. Preserving the American Dream: Predatory Lending and Home Foreclosures: Hearing before the Sen. Comm. on Banking, Housing and Urban Affairs, 110th Cong. 13 (2007). (Statement of Douglas G. Duncan, chief economist, Mortgage Bankers Association.)

5. Christopher L. Cagan, "Mortgage Payment Reset: The Rumor and The Reality," 6, Fig. 1 (First American Real Estate Solutions, February 8, 2006).

6. See James R. Barth et al., "Despite Foreclosures, Subprime Lending Increases Homeownership," Subprime Market Series, Milken Institute (2007).

7. As former Treasury Secretary Lawrence Summers recently stated the question, "We need to ask ourselves the question, and I don't think the question has been put in a direct way and people have developed an answer; what is the optimal rate of foreclosures? How much are we prepared to accept?" Lawrence Summers, Remarks at the Panel Discussion on Recent Financial Market Disruptions: Implications for the Economy and American Families, Washington, DC: The Brookings Institution, September 26, 2007.

8. Souphala Chomsisengphet and Anthony Pennington-Cross, "The Evolution of the Subprime Mortgage Market," Federal Reserve Bank of St. Louis Review 32 (2006): 88.

9. Jeff Nielsen, "Looking at Subprime Clouds from Both Sides Now," Navigant Consulting Presentation (February 28, 2008): 38 (citing Inside Mortgage Finance).

10. See Vernon L. Smith, "The Clinton Housing Bubble," Wall Street Journal, December 18, 2007, A20.

11. Kristopher Gerardi, Harvey S. Rosen, and Paul Willen, "Do Households Benefit from Financial Deregulation and Innovation? The Case of the Mortgage Market" (Federal Reserve Bank of Boston, Public Policy Discussion Papers 06-6, June 2006, 1).

12. Joseph E. Stiglitz and Andrew Weiss, "Credit Rationing in Markets with Imperfect Information," American Economic Review 71 (1981): 393.

13. Kathleen C. Engel and Patricia A. McCoy, "Turning a Blind Eye: Wall Street Finance of Predatory Lending" *Fordham Law Review* 75 (2007): 107.

14. David Reiss, "Subprime Standardization: How Rating Agencies Allow Predatory Lending to Flourish in the Secondary Mortgage Market," 33 *Florida State University Law Review* 985, n. 95 (2006), quoting "Securitization: Asset-Backed and Mortgage-Backed Securities" §9.04, 9-21 (Ronald S. Borod, ed., 2003).

15. Michael Hudson, "Debt Bomb—Lending a Hand: How Wall Street Stoked the Mortgage Meltdown," *Wall Street Journal,* June 27, 2007, A1.

16. Michael Hudson, "Debt Bomb—Lending a Hand: How Wall Street Stoked the Mortgage Meltdown," *Wall Street Journal,* June 27, 2007, A1.

17. Souphala Chomsisengphet and Anthony Pennington-Cross, "The Evolution of the Subprime Mortgage Market," *Federal Reserve Bank of St. Louis Review* 32 (2006): 88.

18. Kathleen C. Engel and Patricia D. McCoy, "A Tale of Three Markets: The Law and Economics of Remedies for Predatory Lending," *Texas Law Review* 80 (2002): 1255, 1260 (separating mortgage markets into prime, legitimate subprime, and predatory segments).

19. Office of the Comptroller of the Currency, Board of Governors of the Federal Reserve System, Federal Deposit Insurance Corp. and Office of Thrift Supervision, SR 01-4, Expanded Interagency Guidance for Subprime Lending Programs (2001), www.federal reserve.gov/boarddocs/srletters/2001/sr0104a1.pdf [hereinafter Guidance].

20. Morgan J. Rose, "Predatory Lending Practices and Subprime Foreclosures: Distinguishing Impacts by Loan Category," *Journal of Economics and Business* 13 (2008): 60. For example, while a three-year prepayment prohibition is associated with a higher probability of foreclosure for purchase money fixed-rate mortgages and refinance adjustable-rate mortgages, that same provision has no impact on increased foreclosures for refinance fixed-rate mortgages.

21. See Alan Greenspan and James Kennedy, "Sources and Uses of Equity Extracted from Homes" (Division of Research and Statistics and Monetary Affairs, Federal Reserve Board, Finance and Economics Discussion Series, Working Paper 2007-20); Margaret M. McConnell, Richard W. Peach, and Alex Al-Haschimi, "After the Refinancing Boom: Will Consumers Scale Back Their Spending?" *Current Issues in Economics and Finance* 1 (2003): 9.

22. Keith S. Ernst, Center for Responsible Lending, "Borrowers Gain No Interest Rate Benefits from Prepayment Penalties on Subprime Mortgages" (2005): 5.

23. Joseph R. Mason and Joshua Rosner, "Where Did the Risk Go? How Misapplied Bond Ratings Cause Mortgage-Backed Securities and Collateralized Debt Obligations Market Disruptions" (May 2007): 54.

24. See "Economic Issues in Predatory Lending" (July 30, 2003): 12 (Office of the Comptroller of the Currency Working Paper).

25. Testimony of Anthony M. Yezer, U.S. House of Representatives, Committee on Financial Services, Subcommittee on Housing and Community Opportunity, Subcommittee on Financial Institutions and Consumer Credit (March 30, 2004).

26. Amy Crews Cutts and Robert A. Van Order, "On the Economics of Subprime Lending," *Journal of Real Estate Finance and Economics* Special Issue (2005): 175, Table 1.

27. Fred Phillips-Patrick, Eric Hirschorn, Jonathan Jones, and John LaRocca, "What About Subprime Mortgages?" *Mortgage Market Trends* (2000): 4.

28. The Mortgage Lender Implode-O-Meter home page, http://ml-implode.com/. Imploded, meaning gone bankrupt, halted major lending operations, or been sold at a fire sale price.

29. Amy Crews Cutts and Robert A. Van Order, "On the Economics of Subprime Lending," *Journal of Real Estate Finance and Economics* Special Issue 30 (2005): 173.

30. This can also be referred to as the "ability to pay" model, which "views home ownership as a consumption good, and borrowers default when they can no longer make the payments." William P. Alexander, Scott D. Grimshaw, Grant R. McQueen, and Barrett A. Slade, "Some Loans Are More Equal than Others: Third-Party Originations and Defaults in the Subprime Mortgage Industry," *Real Estate Economics* 30 (2002): 667.

31. Compare Michelle A. Danis and Anthony Pennington-Cross, "The Delinquency of Subprime Mortgages," Federal Reserve Bank of St. Louis (March 2005) (finding an *inverse* relationship between local unemployment and delinquencies) with Kristopher Gerardi, Adam Hale Shapiro, and Paul S. Willen, "Subprime Outcomes: Risky Mortgages, Home Ownership Experiences, and Foreclosures," Federal Reserve Bank of Boston (December 3, 2007) (finding a positive relationship between unemployment and delinquencies but a negative relationship between unemployment and foreclosure).

32. See Kerry D. Vandell, "How Ruthless Is Mortgage Default? A Review and Synthesis of the Evidence," *Journal of Housing Research* 6 (1995): 245; James B. Kau and Donald C. Keenan, "An Overview of the Option-Theoretic Pricing of Mortgages," *Journal of Housing Research* 6 (1995): 217; Patrick H. Hendershott and Robert Van Order, "Pricing Mortgages: An Interpretation of the Models and Results," *Journal of Financial Services Research* 1 (1987): 19.

33. Mark Dorns, Frederick Furlong, and John Krainer, "House Prices and Subprime Mortgaged Delinquencies," FRBSF Economic Letter, November 2007-14 (June 8, 2007); Ellen Schloemer, Wei Li, Keith Ernst, and Kathleen Keest, "Losing Ground: Foreclosures in the Subprime Market and Their Cost to Homeowners," *Center for Responsible Lending* (December 2006): 13.

34. Kristopher Gerardi, Adam Hale Shapiro, and Paul S. Willen, "Subprime Outcomes: Risky Mortgages, Home Ownership Experiences, and Foreclosures," Federal Reserve Bank of Boston (December 3, 2007): 1. More particularly, those who suffer a drop in value of greater than 20 percent have a 0.70 percent probability of defaulting, between negative 20 percent and zero have a 0.30 percent probability of defaulting, those who have an increase in value of zero to 20 percent have a 0.10 percent probability of defaulting, and those whose homes appreciate in value by more than 20 percent have only a 0.05 percent probability of defaulting.

35. Joseph R. Mason and Joshua Rosner, "How Resilient Are Mortgage-Backed Securities to Collateralized Debt Obligation Market Disruptions?" Hudson Institute, Washington, DC (February 15, 2007).

36. See Yuliya Demyanyk and Otto Van Hemert, supra note 94, at 4.

37. Todd Sinai and Nicholas S. Souleles, "Owner-Occupied Housing as a Hedge Against Rent Risk," *Quarterly Journal of Economics* 120 (2005): 763.

38. Catherine Rampell, "Elizabeth Warren on Consumer Financial Protection," Economix blog, June 17, 2009, http://economix.blogs.nytimes.com/2009/06/17/elizabeth -warren-on-consumer-financial-protection/.

39. Nationwide, annualized house price appreciation dropped from 11.88 percent in the fourth quarter of 2005 to 1.81 percent in the first quarter of 2007. See Press Release, Office of Federal Housing Enterprise Oversight, "U.S. House Price Appreciation Rate Remains Slow, but Positive," May 31, 2007, on file with author.

40. The federal funds rate has risen from 1 percent in June 2004 to a plateau of 5.25 percent beginning in June 2006. The Federal Reserve Board, Open Market Operations (2008), www.federalreserve.gov/FOMC/fundsrate.htm.

41. In the four quarters between the third quarter of 2006 and the second quarter of 2007, GDP grew at rates of 1.1 percent, 2.1 percent, 0.6 percent, and 3.4 percent. Data from the Bureau of Economic Analysis.

ABOUT THE AUTHORS

Todd J. Zywicki is George Mason University Foundation professor of law, a senior scholar at the Mercatus Center, and co-editor of the *Supreme Court Economic Review*. From 2003 to 2004, Professor Zywicki served as the director of the Office of Policy Planning at the Federal Trade Commission. He is a member of the board of directors and governing board of the Financial Services Research Program. Professor Zywicki clerked for Judge Jerry E. Smith of the U.S. Court of Appeals for the Fifth Circuit, and practiced law in Atlanta. He received his law degree from the University of Virginia, where he was a John M. Olin Scholar in law and economics, a master's degree in economics from Clemson University, and his undergraduate degree cum laude with high honors in his major from Dartmouth College. He has lectured and consulted with government officials around the world, including Iceland, Italy, Japan, and Guatemala. Professor Zywicki has testifed before Congress several times on issues of bankruptcy law and consumer credit and is a frequent commentator on legal and business issues in the print and broadcast media. In 2006, Professor Zywicki served as a member of the United States Department of Justice Study Group on "Identifying Fraud, Abuse and Errors in the United States Bankruptcy System."

Satya Thallam is director of the Financial Markets Working Group at the Mercatus Center at George Mason University, an interdisciplinary group of 16 scholars working collaboratively to understand financial crises, conduct original research, and advise policy makers. He was previously the Hernando de Soto Fellow and author of the 2008 International Property Rights Index. He completed his graduate studies in economics at Emory University and received his B.A. (cum laude) in economics from Arizona State University. He has authored numerous op-ed pieces that have appeared in publications such as the *Arizona Republic* and the *Orange County Register*. He is a senior editor of the financial regulation journal *Lombard Street*.

CHAPTER 25

Rating Agencies

Facilitators of Predatory Lending in the Subprime Market

DAVID J. REISS
Professor of Law at Brooklyn Law School*

As the credit crisis unfolds, credit rating agencies have been properly identified as playing a central role in causing the crisis and misleading investors. What has been forgotten in this acrimonious environment is that in their quest to increase the market for their services, rating agencies also took positions that were particularly bad for many homeowners.

Standard & Poor's, Moody's Investors Service, and Fitch Ratings (collectively, the "Big Three") utterly dominate the credit rating market, particularly that for mortgage-backed securities. The Big Three provide ratings for pools of mortgages that are converted to securities and sold to investors around the world, a process known as *securitization*. The Big Three claim that they are merely editorializing about the credit quality of the securities that they rate and do not take an active role in the structuring of the securities. For their labors, the Big Three are compensated by fees from the issuers of securities that solicit ratings from them.

Certain rating agencies, including the Big Three, are what are known as National Recognized Statistical Rating Organizations (NRSROs). The Securities and Exchange Commission (SEC) first granted NRSRO status in 1975. NRSRO status initially referred to those rating agencies whose ratings could be used in implementing the net capital requirements (the minimum ratio of indebtedness to liquid assets) for broker-dealers, a very modest incorporation of ratings into financial regulation.

As NRSROs, the Big Three have since been granted a privileged status by numerous financial services regulators. This privileged status results from the incorporation of the Big Three's ratings throughout a vast web of government

*Rating Agencies and Reputational Risk, "Rating Agencies and Reputational Risk," 4 Maryland J. Bus. & Tech. L. 295 (2009), http://ssrn.com/abstract=1358316 [hereinafter Reiss, *Reputational Risk*]; *Regulation of Subprime and Predatory Lending*, International Encyclopedia of Housing and Home (forthcoming 2010), http://ssrn.com/abstract=1371728. Thanks to Philip Tucker and Jason Gang for excellent research assistance.

regulation of private companies—requiring or encouraging market players such as broker-dealers, banks, money market funds, insurance companies, and pension funds to purchase financial instruments endorsed by an NRSRO.

As a result of their regulatory privilege, the Big Three operate as an oligopoly. The lack of a rating from at least one of the Big Three, which effectively grant regulatory licenses to institutions that wish to issue securities, is the financial equivalent of a death sentence for a residential mortgage-backed securities (RMBS) offering. Thus, the Big Three's NRSRO status makes them gatekeepers to other private financial entities attempting to access the financial markets. While the Big Three thereby bestow significant regulatory benefits upon issuers of securities, they themselves have not been subject to significant regulation of their own activities.

The most vehement criticism of the Big Three is that they do not provide accurate and valuable information to the markets. The Big Three also faced popular criticism for failing to warn of dramatic failures such as that of Enron. Lost within the ongoing debate over the flaws of the Big Three is that they have also taken anticonsumer positions that were aligned with the interests of their own industry and the securitization industry as a whole. In particular, the Big Three took positions against a variety of consumer protection statutes that were intended to assist subprime borrowers and curb predatory lending because such statutes might slow the growth of the subprime RMBS market, thereby slowing the growth of the Big Three themselves.

THE EXPLOSIVE GROWTH OF THE SUBPRIME MORTGAGE MARKET

The way that U.S. homebuyers borrow money to buy homes has changed radically since the 1980s. Before that time, Americans who wanted to buy a home would typically walk into their local savings and loan and speak to a loan officer who would evaluate their application. Usually, only those with a healthy, or prime, profile were approved. That is, they had a steady work history, a large down payment, and no problems with their credit.

Thrifts (a catchall phrase that includes savings and loans, savings banks, and mutual savings banks) were not only the dominant type of residential lender, but they also vertically dominated the residential mortgage market. They originated and serviced the mortgage, typically holding it until it was paid off by the borrower. Now, technological, financial, and legal innovations allow global finance companies to offer a range of mortgage services to a broad array of potential residential borrowers.

A mortgage now can be:

- Originated by a mortgage broker who makes money only from origination
- Serviced by a mortgage banker who did not originate the loan and may have bought the right to service the loan from another mortgage banker
- Originated with the credit risk taken by one of the secondary market institutions, perhaps along with a mortgage insurance company

- Funded by a mortgage-backed security (MBS) sold into the capital markets, and the MBS can be packaged as a bundle of derivative securities that separate interest rate and prepayment risk among different investors[1]

Subprime lending had been a significant and growing portion of this activity, reaching a peak of 20 percent of all originations in 2006 before the subprime market crashed. Subprime lending is the extension of credit to those with lower incomes, less wealth, and riskier credit profiles than traditional, prime borrowers. The secondary market provides much of the liquidity and capacity for growth for the subprime market, with 75 percent of the subprime market being securitized in 2006. As the mortgage industry moved away from the dominance of heavily regulated thrifts and toward that of relatively unregulated mortgage firms, severe consumer abuses arose in the subprime sector.

Although mortgage default and delinquency rates began to rise in 2006, subprime lenders kept lending. Lenders made loans on very easy terms during initial teaser periods to borrowers with poor credit, low income, and low assets. By 2007, the subprime market began to look disastrous as a wave of foreclosures quickly built and swept across the nation. The subprime bubble had gone bust, taking the rest of the credit markets with it.

The subprime market has been far less regulated and standardized than the prime market. As such, it presented an opportunity for those seeking to separate financially unsophisticated borrowers from the equity that they have in their homes. That is, it presents an opportunity to engage in predatory lending. The U.S. General Accounting Office (GAO) has cobbled together a good working description of predatory lending: it is "an umbrella term that is generally used to describe cases in which a broker or originating lender takes unfair advantage of a borrower, often through deception, fraud, or manipulation, to make a loan that contains terms that are disadvantageous to the borrower."[2] Accordingly, the GAO has defined predatory lending to include the following abusive practices and loan terms:

- Excessive fees
- Excessive interest rates
- Single-premium credit insurance
- Lending without regard to ability to repay
- Loan flipping
- Fraud and deception
- Prepayment penalties
- Balloon payments

Predatory practices were present in much of the subprime market, where low- and moderate-income borrowers are concentrated. They are used to prey on unsophisticated homeowners, often those who are not integrated into the sphere of mainstream financial institutions such as banks and credit unions. Most predatory behavior takes place between a mortgage broker or mortgage banker and the borrower. But such thinly funded entities could not exist without funding from secondary market investors. As gatekeepers to the financial markets, the Big Three provided predatory lenders with ready access to investors the world over.

THE ROLE OF RATING AGENCIES
IN RMBS SECURITIZATIONS

Real estate has always been considered good collateral because it needs little monitoring compared to other types of collateral, such as inventory, equipment, and other personal property. Yet, Wall Street investors had historically viewed mortgages as riskier investments than those assets because they were regulated by a patchwork of local and state laws. It is in large part because of this aversion that, before the 1970s, all real estate lending was local. This state of affairs was to change with the birth of securitization and the growth of the secondary market.

For mortgage originators, the securitization of residential mortgages, in particular, is attractive because these mortgages themselves are not easily traded in a secondary market. To be attractive to investors, each mortgage would require its own extensive and expensive evaluation and monitoring, as each typically has its own unique terms and risks. These characteristics would make residential mortgages, which are typically much smaller than commercial mortgages, of limited interest on secondary markets that rely on standardization to reduce the transaction costs associated with conveying assets from one party to another. Since the 1970s, investors have become quite comfortable investing in RMBS because the standardization of mortgage terms overcame many of these problems. Nonstandardized state law relating to lending practices and foreclosures, however, remained a problem from the perspective of the financial services industry, including the rating agencies.

Nonstandardized state law makes it more difficult for the Big Three to rate RMBS; it can also make RMBS less attractive to the Big Three's clients, RMBS issuers. Nearly every securitization of mortgage-backed securities is rated by one, and often two, of the Big Three. The rating that the agency provides "is an assessment of the likelihood of timely payment on securities."[3] The rating process is typically initiated by or on behalf of a securities issuer. The issuer provides the rating agency with information regarding the issuer's background, strategy, operations systems, historical performance data, and any other information that may be relevant. The issuer then typically meets with the rating agency to explain the proposed structure of the deal, the nature of the underlying assets, and the operations of the originator of the assets.

Standard & Poor's, Moody's, and Fitch each had its own approach to rating RMBS pools, but they all pay particular attention to the impact of consumer protection statutes on such pools. One key concern is whether a particular mortgage might be the subject of a lawsuit by the borrower and whether the ultimate holder of that mortgage, a securitized pool, might face liability as a result.

The Big Three rate RMBS transactions by categorizing each state statute on the basis of the nature and degree of the assignee liability and damages provisions of its consumer protection law. In states where there is both assignee liability and unquantifiable damages, various members of the Big Three have refused to rate various transactions containing mortgage loans from such jurisdictions. Thus the Big Three can effectively shut down the entire mortgage market of a state that passes strong predatory lending legislation.

In 2004, New Jersey felt compelled to amend one of its premier consumer protection laws, the Home Ownership Security Act, even though it was enacted with broad bipartisan support just one year before. The New Jersey law was designed to control a small number of unscrupulous brokers and lenders that originate extremely predatory loans. That same year, Georgia found itself doing the same thing—amending its own antipredatory lending law, the Fair Lending Act, that it had enacted mere months before. Twenty other states would watch and learn from the pressure the Big Three exerted against New Jersey and Georgia, modifying their own pending predatory legislation to meet the Big Three's standards.

Historically, the Big Three had promoted themselves as no more than information-analyzing handmaidens to the invisible hand of the market. Whether driven by bias or merely by their own mandate to protect investors first and foremost, however, it is now clear that the Big Three hold a veto over state legislators who have attempted to stop predatory practices in their jurisdictions. This veto by unelected, unaccountable private corporations is highly disturbing, to say the least.

THE FAILURE OF RATING AGENCY REGULATION

While regulators have incorporated the ratings of the Big Three into their regulations, the Big Three largely escaped effective regulation. Thus, to the extent that they made systemic mistakes or demonstrated systemic biases, they were not held accountable to anyone. The business model of the Big Three has been found to be rife with problems: conflicts of interest, lack of transparency, and lack of leadership being some of the most serious.

Their business model was based on serious conflicts of interest, conflicts that should and did undermine the trust that others had in them. The Big Three were paid by the issuers who needed their ratings. As a result, the profit motive drove the agencies to recklessly expand the market for their services.

The Big Three were also deficient when it came to transparency. They helped investment banks structure the transactions to be rated to an extent not known to the rest of the world. They were integrally involved, for instance, in legitimizing subprime debt instruments like the collateralized debt obligation (CDO) securities that make up many of the toxic assets that have dragged down the balance sheets of so many financial firms. The rating agencies also claimed that their very sophisticated rating models were reliable enough to predict with great accuracy the risk of default and delayed payment. It turns out however, that "sophisticated" was just a way of saying complex and confusing. Like many other financial players, it appears that their complex risk management models had some very simplistic assumptions undergirding them—national housing prices will never go down on a year-to-year basis, for one.

Finally, the leadership at the rating agencies set an ethos that clearly distorted the mission of these firms. The rating agencies did not properly monitor their employees to ensure that they avoided even the most obvious conflicts of interest. Clearly, the Big Three's worst excesses went unchecked by regulators, and the public paid the price.

CONCLUSION

The bust of the subprime market in the mid-2000s led to the global financial crisis of the late 2000s. This crisis has virtually ended subprime lending for the current credit cycle. Most subprime lenders have gone out of business or merged with other financial institutions. The remaining financial institutions have tightened their underwriting so that they no longer lend to those with subprime credit profiles. It is likely, however, that subprime lending will return in some form once the credit cycle turns.

Rating agencies were historically considered to be mere commentators on the comings and goings of the players in our free market economy while ensuring that objective information is widely disseminated to all. This view, however, fails to take into account the privileged regulatory status that the SEC and other government regulators have granted to the Big Three. It also fails to take into account the role that the Big Three have in structuring RMBS transactions. Moving forward, effective regulation of the NRSROs must take into account their gatekeeper function, and ensure that their systemic biases are not permitted to trump state consumer protection initiatives.

NOTES

1. See Robert Van Order, "The U.S. Mortgage Market: A Model of Dueling Charters," *Journal of Housing Research* 233 (2000): 233–34.
2. U.S. General Accounting Office, Consumer Protection, "Federal and State Agencies Face Challenges in Combating Predatory Lending" 18 (2004).
3. Steven L. Schwarcz, *Private Ordering of Public Markets: The Rating Agency Paradox*, 2002 U. Ill. L. Rev. 1, 15.

ABOUT THE AUTHOR

David J. Reiss is a professor of law at Brooklyn Law School and has also taught at Seton Hall Law School. His research focuses on the secondary mortgage market. He was previously an associate at Paul, Weiss, Rifkind, Wharton & Garrison in its real estate department and an associate at Morrison & Foerster in its land use and environmental law group. He was also a law clerk to Judge Timothy Lewis of the United States Court of Appeals for the Third Circuit. He received his B.A. from Williams College and his J.D. from the New York University School of Law. His article, "Subprime Standardization: How Rating Agencies Allow Predatory Lending to Flourish in the Secondary Mortgage Market," in the *Florida State University Law Review,* was granted an award as the best article of 2006 by the American College of Consumer Financial Services Lawyers.

PART IV

The Process of Securitization

CHAPTER 26

A Primer on the Role of Securitization in the Credit Market Crisis of 2007

JOHN D. MARTIN

Carr P. Collins Chair in Finance in the Hankamer School of Business at Baylor University*

Once upon a time credit markets were dominated by lenders who both originated loans and held them to maturity. Today, the majority of credit is created using an originate-to-distribute model in which the originator of the loan sells it to someone who combines it in a portfolio of similar loans and then issues new securities that hold a claim against the income provided by the loan portfolio. This process is called *securitization*. The growing importance of securitization gave rise to three issues that form the basis for this paper:

1. First, whereas loans were once held by the lender until repaid, with securitization, these loans are pooled, and claims on their cash flows are sold to investors around the world. As a consequence, the impact of credit origination problems is no longer limited to the originating institution but is diffused throughout the credit markets.
2. Second, since the loan originator does not actually hold the credit it originates, but distributes the loans to others through securitization, the originator has a reduced incentive to monitor the credit-granting process. This is a classic principal-agent problem that arises whereby the incentives of the originator of credit are not aligned with those of the entity that ultimately holds the loan.
3. Third, the credits are securitized in pools with new securities that have claims on the pooled cash flows. This means that these new securities do not have a direct claim on any specific loan or credit. This complexity makes it difficult to sort out the claims in the event of a specific credit default.

*I want to thank Mark McNabb for his comments on earlier drafts of this paper; responsibility for any remaining errors is mine, however.

WHAT IS SECURITIZATION?

Securitization is a form of asset-backed finance that involves the pooling of a set of credits or debt securities whose acquisition is financed by the issuance of new debt securities. The new securities go by various names, depending on the type of assets in the pool. For example, if the pooled assets consist of residential home mortgages, then the new securities are residential mortgage-backed securities (RMBS); if the pooled assets consist of business loans, then the new securities are known as collateralized loan obligations (CLO); and so forth. The payments of principal and interest on the securities issued in the securitization are derived from the cash flows generated by pools of assets.

Both consumer debt and corporate debt have been securitized. Consumer credit is divided into mortgage loans and all other types of consumer debt. For example, when residential mortgages are securitized, the entity that performs the securitization issues residential mortgage-backed securities (RMBS). When credit card debt or other forms of consumer debt are securitized, the securities issued against these pools are referred to simply as asset-backed securities (ABS).

The term *collateralized debt obligation* (CDO) is sometimes used as the broad umbrella term to refer to all types of securities issued in securitizations involving corporate debt. For example, a collateralized loan obligation (CLO) is issued in conjunction with the securitization of corporate loans, whereas collateralized bond obligations (CBO) are issued when the securitization involves a portfolio of corporate bonds.

The Mechanics of Securitization

To illustrate how securitization works, consider the mortgage-backed securitization process. The mortgage banker originates mortgage loans in the ordinary course of business. Once a sufficient block of mortgages has been originated, the mortgage banker initiates the securitization process by selling or assigning the mortgages to a special purpose vehicle (or SPV). The SPV can be a trust, corporation, or partnership that is set up by the mortgage broker or an investment bank specifically to purchase the originator's mortgages and act as a conduit for the mortgage payment flows. An investment banker then sells mortgage-backed securities to investors and uses the proceeds to purchase the mortgages from the mortgage originator.

Credit Enhancement

Virtually all MBS are rated by one of the major credit rating agencies (Moody's, Standard and Poor's, or Fitch). Achieving a high rating for the securities is critical to the marketability of the issues, and the MBS issue will often receive some type of credit enhancement that helps raise the credit quality of the securities in an attempt to attract investors.

The credit enhancement can come from the assets themselves or from an external source. Examples of the former include the subordination of different tranches to higher rated tranches and overcollateralizing the asset pool, (i.e., issuing a smaller dollar value of securities against the pool of mortgages).

Alternatively, the SPV can seek out external credit enhancements such as purchasing a surety bond or a letter of credit from a financial institution. Both of these alternatives provide guarantees to investors that they will receive the promised payments associated with the MBS. An important source of credit enhancement involves the purchase of credit insurance from monoline insurance companies (so named since they offer insurance in only one industry). These firms (Ambac Financial Group Inc and MBIA Inc. are the dominant firms, and both were formed in the 1970s to insure municipal bonds) sold credit default insurance to bond issuers. If the issuer failed to make a principal or interest payment, the insurance company would step in and make it.

Secondary Market for Securitization Issues

The secondary market for the securities issued in securitizations is a dealer market. That is, just like bond markets, dealers make a market so that the securities are traded over the counter rather than on one of the exchanges. Therefore, it is the willingness of dealers to maintain an inventory, or make a market, as well as their financial position that provides liquidity to this market. Moreover, the continued existence of this market, like any financial market, is contingent on maintaining some symbolism of informational symmetry between buyers and sellers. If either party feels they are less well-informed than the other, there is the very real possibility that the less well-informed party will not transact in fear of being taken advantage of by the better-informed party. This is precisely the market for lemons problem described by George Ackerlof.[1]

Why Do Firms Securitize Assets?

Note that the originating firm that creates the mortgage loan, credit card receivable, or commercial bank loan that makes up the securitization pool, assigns or sells the loan to an entity that then securitizes it along with a portfolio of similar credits. This, in turn, monetizes the asset and frees up the cash the originator had tied up in the loan. Once the asset has been monetized, it is no longer on the books of the originating firm, and the originator now has liquidity that can be used to originate new loans and investments.

Alternatively, the firm could issue debt or equity to raise additional capital to fund new investments while holding the investments it has already made. Thus, a very important question to ask ourselves is the following: When would we expect securitization to be a more cost-effective form of financing than firm or corporate financing? To gain some perspective on this issue, let us consider the possible advantages and disadvantages of asset-based finance or securitization as opposed to firm financing.

There are two potential benefits to the originating firm that can be derived from securitization as opposed to firm financing:

1. *Lower-cost financing*—It is possible that firms with relatively poor credit histories can acquire assets (receivables, loans, leases, etc.) that are of high quality. If the financial markets are unable to discern the quality of these assets when combined with the firm's other investments, then it may be possible to obtain better financing terms through a securitization than as part of a corporate financing. Specifically, by securitizing the firm's assets, they are separated from the originating firm, thereby making the quality of the asset-backed security issued in the securitization independent of the

creditworthiness of the originator. This argument would suggest that firms that securitize would tend to have weaker credit quality than comparable firms that do not securitize their assets.[2]

2. *Comparative advantage*—Some firms may be very good at originating investments but because of their small size or lack of expertise in obtaining financing, may not be good at arranging financing. Moreover, compared to the originators of the underlying loans, financial institutions that manage securitizations may possess a comparative advantage in structuring and managing securitization pools.

On the negative side, securitization may lead to a severe principal-agent problem whereby the firm that originates the credits that will ultimately be sold and securitized retains little or no interest in the pool of securitized assets. If bad loans can be passed on through the securitization process, the loan originator does not have the same incentive to pay attention to the creditworthiness of its customers as would be the case when the loan is not passed on for securitization. In fact, many now attribute much (if not most) of the blame for the collapse of the securitized mortgage market to the low quality of subprime mortgages originated in the waning years before the market's collapse. The notion that securitization reduces the incentive to monitor the screening process has gained a lot of support as an important contributor to the collapse of the subprime mortgage market.[3]

Who Purchased MBS and Why?

Following the dot-com crash in 2000 and the attacks on the World Trade Center in 2001, the Federal Reserve Bank followed a policy of maintaining low rates of interest in an attempt to provide a growth stimulus to the economy. As a result of this policy, interest rates offered to savers in the economy remained very low. With the banking system offering very low rates, the nonbanking component sought ways to enhance returns to attract savers through the use of financial leverage.[4]

How was it that MBS could offer higher, safe rates of interest through securitization? There are two possible responses to this question. First, the mortgages that were combined in a securitization were not free of default risk and carried correspondingly higher rates of interest. By issuing MBS in tranches and using credit enhancement, the securitization was able to offer very low default risk AAA/Aaa tranches that offered attractive yields. Moreover, so long as the credit enhancements built into the securitization were in place, the risk of owning the highest-rated tranches seemed very low to yield-starved investors.

The second method for enhancing yields on securitized portfolios relates to the use of financial leverage. For example, collateralized debt obligations were issued to purchase portfolios of RMS in which the majority of the funds came from fixed-return CDOs.

DID SECURITIZATION CONTRIBUTE TO THE CREDIT MARKET CRISIS?

Although the root causes of the credit market crisis of 2007 and 2008 are only now being ferreted out, there is growing support for the theory that changes in the debt markets over the last 25 years led to deterioration in the quality of the credit-granting process.

Potential Agency Problem in the Originate-to-Distribute Model

Under the originate-to-distribute model, lenders originate loans that are then distributed through securitization such that the lender retains little or no exposure to the loan. This change, many now argue, gave rise to the problems that are at the very heart of the credit crisis. Specifically, Mishkin (2008) summarizes the problem as follows:

> *The originate-to-distribute model, unfortunately, created some severe incentive problems, which are referred to as principal-agent problems, or more simply as agency problems, in which the agent (the originator of the loans) did not have the incentives to act fully in the interest of the principal (the ultimate holder of the loan). Originators had every incentive to maintain origination volume, because that would allow them to earn substantial fees, but they had weak incentives to maintain loan quality. . . .*

Support for this idea is not universal, however. Gorton (2008) rejects this theory based on the following observations:

- First, the originate-to-distribute theory proposes nothing to explain why problems arose with the securitization of subprime mortgages. It would seem that the agency problem created by the originate-to-distribute model would apply to all forms of securitization, not just subprime mortgages.
- Second, significant losses have been incurred throughout the subprime mortgage chain. In fact, many originators, securitization structurers, and underwriters have gone bankrupt. Those that did not go bankrupt have had to do massive writedowns.

Why were the originators, securitization structurers, and underwriters subjected to the risk of bankruptcy? The originate-to-distribute model argues that any bad risks they created through lax lending policies were simply passed on to investors in the securitization process. Obviously, this was not the case. Specifically, there were two sources of risk to the originators and facilitators of the securitization process:

- *Warehousing risk*—The originator must warehouse the mortgages it originates until a sufficient volume of mortgages is accumulated so that they can be transferred to an underwriter for securitization.
- *Residual interest risk*—Originators of mortgages end up retaining a residual interest in the mortgages they originate in the form of valuable servicing rights as well as retained interest. The latter refer to the lower tranches of the securitization that are most difficult to sell.[5]

The Evidence: Declining Credit Standards for Mortgages

If the originate-to-distribute model is the real culprit in the credit crisis, then there should be evidence of deteriorating credit standards for mortgages originated in

2006 that ultimately performed so poorly in 2007 and 2008. There is anecdotal evidence to support this thesis. For example, the percentage of low or no documentation (both Alt-A and subprime mortgages) rose dramatically over the period from 2001 to 2006. These loans constituted 28.5 percent of new subprime mortgages in 2001 and 50.8 percent in 2006. At the same time, adjustable rate mortgages (ARMs) rose from 73 percent to 91.3 percent of all subprime mortgages. Interest-only loans were zero percent of subprime mortgages in 2001 but rose to 37.8 percent in 2005 before dropping to 22.8 percent in 2006.

Keys et al. (2008) provides direct empirical evidence that securitization did reduce the quality of loan screening for subprime loans. They found that a portfolio of subprime mortgages that is more likely to be securitized defaults around 20 percent more than a similar risk profile group with a lower probability of being securitized. The implication being that securitization does have an adverse effect on the screening incentives of lenders.[6]

Complexity and Loss of Information

We described earlier the creation of mortgage-backed securities and the securitization process. This is not the complete story, however, since there is yet another layer of securitization for these mortgage-backed securities in the form of collateralized debt obligations (CDOs) that were formed to purchase mortgage-backed securities by issuing tranches of long-term securities that were themselves reliant on the cash flows from prior securitizations. The increasing complexity of the structures and opaqueness of the connection of the financial claim on a specific mortgage makes it extremely difficult to trace a third-tier securitization CDO back to a particular mortgage on which it has a partial claim.

Gorton (2008) argues that a root cause of the current crisis was in fact the loss of information due to the complexity that arises with multiple levels of securitizations. CDO investors and investors in other instruments that have CDO tranches in their portfolios (so-called CDO squares or CDO^2) cannot penetrate the chain backward and value the chain on the basis of the underlying mortgages. They relied on modeled values and the certification of a credit rating agency.

TRIGGERING THE PANIC OF 2007–2008

The forces underlying the collapse of the market for securitization were in place for a number of years. However, the resulting financial crisis was triggered by changing economic conditions in the residential real estate market and the subsequent forced revaluations of mortgage-backed security portfolios by the financial institutions that held them.

Falling Real Estate Prices

So long as the value of residential real estate continued to rise, home mortgages and the securities issued against them in the securitization market remained solvent. However, when real estate prices began to fall in mid-2006, the lower quality mortgages (those with little or no down payment) became insolvent. Thus, falling residential real estate prices put in motion a sequence of events that eventually led to panic in the RMBS market that spread throughout the credit markets. Falling housing prices in and of themselves should not lead to panic and a collapse of mortgage-backed security markets. However, as we noted earlier, the complexity of the residential mortgage-backed security market and the resulting loss of information may have been such that a market for lemons type of problem may have arisen in which buyers of mortgage-backed securities would not trade at any price once flaws in the system became obvious.

Mark-to-Market Accounting and the Absence of Market Prices

Most firms' balance sheets report assets based on the price the firm paid for them less any depreciation in value since their acquisition. This is the historical cost method of accounting. However, for those assets that are held for resale such as mortgage- or asset-backed securities, firms must account for the values of those assets on their books using mark-to-market accounting under FAS 157. This method of accounting assigns a value to an asset (usually a financial instrument or security) based on its current market price or an estimated price based on similar assets.

Proponents of mark-to-market accounting argue that it promotes transparency in that firms that hold investments whose value has declined must reflect this drop in value of these assets in their financial statements. The problem that arose with the recent credit crisis is that the market for mortgage-backed securities ceased to function such that there were no market prices with the exception of fire sale prices. Consequently, when firms marked their investments in mortgage-backed securities to market, they were forced to use fire sale or liquidation prices, as these were the only ones available.[7]

In response to this problem on September 30, 2008, the Securities and Exchange Commission (SEC) issued a clarification of fair value accounting.[8] Among other things, the clarification stated that in the absence of an active market for a security, the firm could substitute management estimates that incorporate current market participant expectations of future cash flows, and appropriate risk premiums. The important point was that fire sale or liquidation prices did not have to be used to value the affected assets. Under Financial Accounting Standard (FAS) 157 many companies had been forced to mark down the value of their mortgage-backed security portfolios drastically. The clarification recognized that such writedowns were not orderly and that the mark-to-market rules should be more liberally applied so as to reflect the expected cash value of the underlying assets.

CONCLUSION

So what are we to conclude about the role of asset-backed finance or securitization in the financial crisis of 2007–2008? First of all, the securitization of mortgages, in particular subprime mortgages, was at the very heart of the crisis. The downturn in real estate prices made it impossible for subprime borrowers (who put down little or no down payment) to refinance their homes. Second, although many attribute the problems in the securitization market to the separation of credit origination from investing that occurs with securitization, it is not clear that this was the only problem since the subprime mortgage originators were also driven out of business with the collapse of the market. Another possible contributor to the problems of subprime mortgage securitizations is the sheer complexity of the structures that were being built and the resulting loss of information that accompanied it. With multiple levels of securitization, it was no longer possible to trace the securities back to specific assets. Although this certainly appears to be the case, one has to wonder why it took so long to cause a problem. The trigger for the collapse of the securitization market came when real estate prices started to decline. So long as real estate prices were rising there was no reason to be concerned about the ambiguity of claims of the securities on specific assets.

Finally, mark-to-market accounting may well have failed where the market for securities issued by the loan securitizers collapsed. Nonetheless, firms continued to mark down the value of their asset-backed securities to distress prices since no orderly market existed. The SEC recognized the problem belatedly and offered holders of asset-backed financing securities the opportunity to estimate market values in the absence of normal prices.

NOTES

1. Akerlof (1970).

2. Anecdotally, this appears to be the case for Chrysler back in 1992 when it securitized its auto loan portfolio. The firm had been downgraded to B+ earlier in the year.

3. The principal-agent problem becomes an issue when a principal hires an agent and cannot monitor the activities of the principal perfectly.

4. Finance 101 tells us that if we can earn a rate of return on our investments that exceeds the cost of borrowing money, then borrowing (i.e., using financial leverage) can lead to a higher return on our equity invested in a project. Of course, financial leverage is a double-edged sword that reduces the equity rate of return when the investment no longer earns a rate higher than the cost of borrowing.

5. In its 2007 annual report, Merrill Lynch (357) reported a $137 million exposure related to warehouse lending and losses for the year of $31 million. The exposure to residuals at year-end was $855 million. Losses for the year, however, were $1.582 billion.

6. There have been other studies that have documented the effects of securitization on other aspects of banking behavior. For example, Loutskina (2005) found that securitization serves as a substitute for traditional liquid funds on banks' balance sheets.

7. Merrill Lynch's sale of its portfolio of risky mortgage debt for $0.22 on the dollar in July 2008 is an often-cited incident that could well have contributed to wholesale write-downs among other financial institutions. http://money.cnn.com/2008/07/29/news/newsmakers/thain.denial.fortune/index.htm?ref=patrick.net.

8. http://sec.gov/news/press/2008/2008-234.htm.

REFERENCES

Akerlof, G. 1970. The market for "lemons": Quality uncertainty and the market mechanism. *Quarterly Journal of Economics* 84 (3): 488–500.

Gorton, G. 2008. The panic of 2007. Unpublished paper, Yale School of Management and NBER. Prepared for the Federal Reserve Bank of Kansas City, Jackson Hole Conference, August.

Keys, B. J., T. Mukherjee, A. Seru, and V. Vig. 2008. Did securitization lead to lax screening? Evidence from subprime loans. Unpublished working paper, University of Michigan, April.

Loutskina, E. 2005. Does securitization affect bank lending? Evidence from bank responses to funding shocks. Unpublished working paper, Boston College, September.

Mishkin, F. 2008. On leveraged losses: Lessons from the mortgage meltdown. Speech at the U.S. Policy Forum, New York City, February 29.

ABOUT THE AUTHOR

John D. Martin holds the Carr P. Collins Chair in Finance in the Hankamer School of Business at Baylor University, where he teaches in the Baylor EMBA programs. He has published over his career more than 50 articles in the leading finance journals and served in a number of editorial positions, including the co-editorship of the FMA *Survey and Synthesis Series* published by the Oxford University Press. His current research spans issues related to the economics of wind and other alternative energy sources, the role of securitization in the financial panic of 2007, and the role of corporate social responsibility in managing for shareholder value. He is also a co-author of several books, including *Basic Financial Management* (11th ed.), *Foundations of Finance* (7th ed.), *Theory of Finance, Financial Analysis* (3rd ed.), *Valuation: The Art and Science of Corporate Investment Decisions, and Value-Based Management with Social Responsibility* (2nd ed.).

CHAPTER 27

Incentives in the Originate-to-Distribute Model of Mortgage Production

ROBERT W. KOLB
Professor of Finance and Considine Chair of Applied Ethics, Loyola University Chicago

One of the most fundamental beliefs among economists is that humans respond to incentives. This simple intuition has been given increasing prominence in economic thought in recent years, and it would not be too much of an exaggeration to say that this model has been pressed into service to explain an increasing share of economic behavior.

In the residential mortgage market in the United States, the transformation of mortgage technology from an originate-to-hold model (OTH) to an originate-to-distribute model (OTD) profoundly altered the incentives of all of the actors in the process. Furthermore, the rise of the OTD introduced a host of new participants with their own incentives, which turned out to be quite perverse and proved to be a significant contributor to the subprime crisis, which in turn led to the worldwide systemic financial crisis that has transformed our lives. This article sketches the incentives in the OTH and then the incentives in the OTD with a view to showing how these incentives contributed to a disaster of enormous proportions. This brief article draws on two more substantial efforts, an article that is forthcoming in *Business Ethics Quarterly*, "Incentives in the Financial Crisis of Our Time," and a book on the financial crisis that is forthcoming from Oxford University Press, *Understanding Our Financial Crisis*.

In the OTH, there were few actors, and their incentives were simple, as the diagram of Exhibit 27.1 indicates.

In the United States from the aftermath of the Great Depression until about the 1980s, mortgage lending was dominated by savings and loan institutions (S&Ls) that operated within the confines of a strict regulatory regime, but were granted a privileged market position in many respects.[1] For a prospective homeowner seeking a loan, the mortgage origination process typically began with an application to a local S&L. Reasons for seeking such a loan were few, but they were compelling. In the most ordinary case, of course, the prospective borrower wanted to secure funds to purchase a home in which to live. Other reasons for requesting a loan

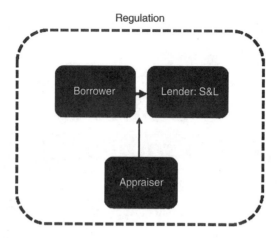

Exhibit 27.1 The Originate-to-Hold Model of Mortgage Production

were to secure more favorable financing terms and replace an existing loan or to finance a home renovation, but these motivations were relatively infrequent.

The S&L, for its part, wanted to lend at as high an interest rate as the market would bear, but for most of the period dominated by the OTH interest rates were relatively stable. The financial soundness of the borrower was also critical to the S&L, so they took care to inquire carefully into the assets and employment of the prospective borrower. The S&L also wanted to ensure that the property was worth more than the loan amount, because the lender would look to the property to recoup its funds if the borrower failed to perform as promise. To that end, the S&L typically demanded at least a 20 percent down payment, which was thought to ensure that the property's value would exceed the loan balance even in harsh economic times.

The last significant actor in the OTH was the appraiser. The prospective lender would hire an appraiser to investigate the condition of the property and to report to the S&L on its value. For the S&L, it was important to be sure that the property was worth at least the loan amount, so the S&L would instruct appraisers to give unbiased estimates of the property's value, or perhaps, even to provide a conservative estimate. The appraiser serves at the pleasure of the S&L, and thus has a strong incentive to provide the kind of appraisal that the client demands. After all, there are many appraisers, and if the S&L demands an unbiased or conservative estimate, then the appraiser's chance for repeat business depends on providing the specified appraisal.

All of these precautions in the lending process made a great deal of sense, because the S&L would typically hold the mortgages it granted among its own assets for the life of the mortgage loan, which was typically 30 years. These practices explain the name of the OTH—the lender would originate the mortgage by making a loan, and would hold that mortgage for the life of the loan.

In the fully developed OTD, as shown in Exhibit 27.2, there are many actors in the mortgage origination process. Perverse incentives infected virtually every linkage in the entire chain—from the prospective borrower through the ultimate investor, as I argue more fully in *The Financial Crisis of Our Time.*

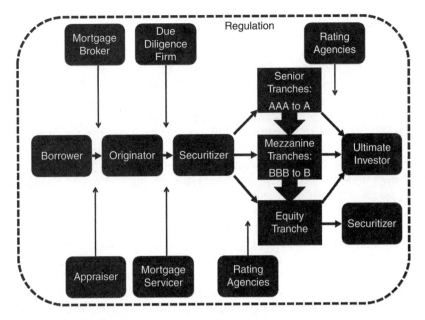

Exhibit 27.2   The Originate-to-Distribute Model of Mortgage Production

For the prospective borrower in the new world of the OTD, the old motivations continued to prevail—to secure a home to live in, to secure better financing, and to finance a home renovation. But under the new model of mortgage origination, the prospective borrower has new motivations that were not previously available. Most important among these was the prospect of cash-out refinancing—a type of mortgage on an existing home in which the homeowner replaces an old mortgage with a new mortgage at a higher balance and receives cash from the new loan to use for any purpose. In other words, in an era of steadily rising home prices, a homeowner could take a series of new loans on the same home with higher balances and receive cash with each refinancing. This process of repeated cash-out financing has been likened to using one's home as a piggy bank.

Beyond the cash-out motivation, a perception that home prices will continue to rise significantly provides an incentive to buy a house as an investment property rather than as a home. And if prices are always rising, then one can make even more money by successively (or concurrently) buying and selling any number of houses—a process known as flipping properties. From long experience, financial institutions know that borrowers who buy homes they will actually occupy tend to honor their mortgage commitments more readily. Consequently, lenders have long required borrowers to live in the homes they finance, or they at least offer more favorable financial terms for owner-occupied homes.

But if a borrower wants to buy a number of homes simultaneously to exploit rising prices, he or she will not be able to occupy them all. This desire to purchase several houses on the most favorable financial terms gives borrowers an incentive to lie about their occupancy intentions, a form of mortgage fraud or predatory borrowing—borrowing that exploits a financial institution. Occupancy fraud is one of the most common types of mortgage fraud. The other most prevalent kind of mortgage fraud occurs when a prospective borrower misrepresents income or financial assets.

Another kind of fraud in the mortgage process has received more attention. In predatory lending, the financial institution exploits a borrower by making a loan that damages the borrower in some way. For instance, the loan may have unfairly high costs, or the lender may make a loan believing that the borrower will be unable to make the payments the loan demands.

In the OTD, the financial institution[2] that originates the mortgage never intends to retain the mortgage on its own balance sheet. Instead, the goal is to originate a mortgage, to capture some fee income in the origination process, and to sell the mortgage into the securitization process at a profit. While the OTD gives the borrower additional incentives that were not present under the OTH, many of the lender's incentives are radically altered in the movement from the OTH to OTD.

The lender still wants to grant a loan on the most favorable financial terms— with a high interest rate and lucrative fee potential. But some considerations that were extremely important under the OTH become unimportant or even undesirable under the OTD. Because the lender plans to sell the mortgage, the borrower's ability to repay, a high value of the house relative to the mortgage principal, and the collection of a large down payment all become less important. Furthermore, the price for the mortgage will be larger the larger the principal balance on the mortgage, so the lender actually has a positive incentive to make loans with small down payments and high loan-to-value ratios. Both practices increase the principal balance of the loan and the lender's payday when it sells the loan into the securitization process. Thus, under the OTD, the initial lender has an incentive to disregard the borrower's capacity to pay on the loan, to ignore the value of the home relative to the loan amount, and to grant loans with little or no down payment.

Under the OTD, the business of lending institutions is initiating and selling mortgages, so a growing supply of borrowers is necessary to fuel this process. Lending institutions found it quite efficient and lucrative to allow mortgage brokers to bring prospective borrowers to them. A mortgage broker is essentially an information intermediary that connects prospective borrowers and lenders. As such, the mortgage broker can potentially provide three services that benefit the borrower: help borrowers find a lender; help the borrower complete the mortgage application; and, possibly, help the borrower negotiate more favorable terms than the borrower could secure alone. These services, of course, are more valuable for the financially naïve, because people of even modest financial sophistication would have little trouble negotiating the mortgage process on their own.

Thus, the mortgage broker occupies a sensitive middle ground between borrower and lender and faces two completely different sets of perverse incentives. First, the mortgage broker can cooperate with the financial institution to engage in predatory lending and to exploit the borrower. One of the most common abuses occurs when the mortgage broker engages in "steering"—the guiding of the prospective borrower to a less suitable and more expensive borrowing option. This steering benefits the lender and the mortgage broker at the expense of the borrower. The mortgage broker receives a higher fee, and the lending institution receives a better profit on the sale of the mortgage.[3]

Because the mortgage broker occupies a middle position between the borrower and lender, the mortgage broker can also cooperate with the prospective borrower to defraud the lender. For example, the mortgage broker can coach the borrower in completing a fraudulent application and can use his knowledge to help present the borrower in dishonestly more favorable light in the mortgage application. In short, the mortgage broker has two sets of perverse incentives, to cooperate with the financial institution to defraud the borrower and to cooperate with the borrower to defraud the financial institution.

Appraisers almost universally work for financial institutions and receive a fixed fee for rendering an appraisal. If a lender wants to make a loan, it is necessary that the property have a sufficient appraised value. Thus, the lending officer may encourage (or even demand) that the appraiser deliver an appraised value that is higher than a property actually deserves. In such an environment, an appraiser has limited choices. She can either deliver the desired type of appraisal or leave the industry and find other employment. Accordingly, in the OTD the appraiser often faced strong incentives to submit false appraisals, whereas in the OTH, the appraiser received incentives that encouraged professionalism and honest appraisals.

Similar conflicting and perverse incentives infect the remainder of the securitization chain. A lender sells the mortgage to a financial institution, or *securitizer*, that gathers many home mortgages and uses the cash flows from those mortgages as the basis for offering other securities. As Exhibit 27.2 shows, these new securities, or *collateralized debt obligations* (CDOs), can have many different forms and may have cash flows that differ from the underlying cash flow patterns being received from the pool of home mortgages. It is typical for the securitizer to issue a variety of securities, or *tranches*, and for a variety of tranches to be based on the cash flows from one pool of mortgages. Most commonly, the various tranches of securities are ordered in terms of priority of payments, with the claims of the most senior tranche of securities being paid in full before the next tranche receives any payment. This gives rises to a waterfall of cash spilling down into the empty bucket held out by the senior tranche. When the bucket of the most senior tranche is filled (that is, when the claims of the most senior tranche are completely honored) the excess cash spills to the next most senior tranche, and so on, until either the cash flows are exhausted or until even the bucket of the most junior tranche is filled.[4]

Key to the entire process is the purchase of mortgages from initial lenders as individual mortgages constitute the mortgage pool, and the pool provides the cash flows that will ultimately flow to the several tranches of new securities. Employees of the securitizing financial institution are instructed to investigate and purchase mortgages. In this process, the securitizer performs due diligence on the loans to ensure that they are as described and worth the price being demanded. If we think of the securitizing firm as monolithic, the firm certainly has an interest in buying good mortgages at favorable prices. But the firm is not monolithic, of course. At a minimum, we can distinguish the firm itself as an entity, the senior managers of the firm, and the employees who actually investigate and purchase the mortgages.

In the normal event, the employees who purchase these loans get a substantial portion of their compensation in the form of bonuses to reward them for meeting their targeted level of purchases. This puts these employees in an awkward position. The securitizing firm (presumably) wants the mortgages to be of high quality, but it pays this cadre of its employees based on its volume of purchases. This compensation arrangement gives those involved in the purchase of these mortgages a very bad set of incentives. They can maintain high quality, purchase fewer loans, and receive less compensation, or they can surreptitiously purchase many low quality loans and receive more compensation. Thus, these rank and file workers who actually inspect and purchase mortgages face strong and perverse incentives that conflict with the interests of their firm.

The managers of the securitizing firm are not immune to their own special incentives, for they too often get rewarded on the basis of short-term performance of the firm. If the stock market rewards favorable quarterly earnings and if a high volume of securitization contributes to high earnings, many top executives will be tempted to sacrifice the true interest of the firm for it to achieve the best possible short-term performance. One of the easiest ways to pump up immediate performance is to buy many mortgages and issue many securities allowing the booking of immediate profits. Such a process can lead easily to a too casual investigation of the quality of the mortgages that the firm is purchasing.

Continuing to move through the process shown in Exhibit 27.2, we next come to the securitization process in which rating agencies play a critical role. The entire securities market relies on ratings provided by organizations such as Standard & Poor's, Moody's, and Fitch, which grade securities from the best quality with the least chance of default (Triple-A), down through lesser grades (e.g., Triple-B), to below investment grade (e.g., C).[5]

Given a particular mortgage pool, the securitizer has many alternatives for the kinds of different securities it can issue on the basis of cash flows from the pool. For the securitizer, the goal is to create a package of securities that will secure the best total price, and securing this best price turns on the ratings that the securities will receive. Not surprisingly, many securitizers hire rating agencies as consultants to advise them on the creation of the tranched securities. Because the value of the securities it will issue depends on the rating those securities receive, the securitizer really needs the agencies to tell them how to create securities that will get the best possible rating. For example, making a security just barely good enough to get a Triple-A is highly desirable, because no rating is better than Triple-A and putting more value into the security than the minimum necessary to secure the desired rating is just wasting resources. Of course, the securitizer pays the rating agency a significant consulting fee for the valuable guidance it provides.

When the tranched securities are issued, they must be rated. Without a rating, many prospective purchases are prohibited from buying those securities. So the securitizer pays the same rating agency to rate the securities. As a consequence, the rating agency gets a payday for helping to design the security and a second payday for rating the security.

Even though there were only five significant rating agencies during the heyday of the subprime market and even though S&P, Moody's, and Fitch together accounted for more than 90 percent of the rating business, there was still competition among these firms. The securitizer had an incentive to shop for the best rating available. This competition encouraged the rating agencies to cooperate with the securitizer and to work with the securitizer to give the new securities the best possible rating. This incentive for the securitizer and the chosen rating agency to work together toward high ratings stands in stark contrast to the rating agency's responsibility to be objective in its work and to provide honest ratings. In many instances, the rating agencies succumbed to lucrative incentives to provide higher ratings.

This is evidenced in part by the very large number of downgrades issued by the rating agencies as the financial crisis has developed and by the consequence that many tranched securities would pay a much higher yield than their awarded rating would suggest.[6] For example, a tranched security that is rated Triple-B may pay a rate of interest that was unusually high for a security of that grade, suggesting that the market was aware that the security perhaps did not deserve its Triple-B rating.

Once the tranched securities are created and rated, they are sold to the ultimate investors. For an investment manager who buys securities, the goal is to achieve a high performance for a given investment policy. Consider for a moment an investment firm that can invest only in Triple-A instruments. The investment manager for the firm will generally be rewarded by the profitability of its portfolio. This gives the manager an incentive to purchase the highest-yielding Triple-A securities he can find in order to achieve the greatest investment return and to capture the personal rewards that accompany high profits. Thus, in many instances, investment managers succumbed to the temptation to stretch for yield and buy securities that seemed to be too good to be true in that they were yielding returns that were exorbitantly high for their assigned ratings. We now know that the market realized, at least to a partial extent, that many of these tranched securities were not fully worthy of their assigned ratings and expressed this view by demanding a higher yield from the tranched securities than from a regular corporate bond with the same rating.

As this article has briefly discussed, a host of conflicting incentives pervaded the entire chain of the securitization process. Borrowers, mortgage brokers, initial lenders, appraisers, securitizers (including their managers and employees), rating agencies, and ultimate investors all faced incentives that led them to behave in a perverse and uneconomic manner that ultimately played a significant role in the subprime disaster. And it is this subprime debacle that fed immediately into the severe financial distress that has affected so many around the world.

NOTES

1. For most of the period, commercial banks were restricted from home lending by regulation, and savings and loans were allowed to pay higher interest rates on deposits than were commercial banks. Savings and loans were restricted from commercial lending and were required to focus on home lending within a geographical area near their office. In simple terms, commercial banks were thought to be more sophisticated, but savings and loan associations were more of an institution that served its own community.

2. From 1982 onward, financial regulation of depository institutions was liberalized to make the various kinds of institutions (e.g., commercial banks and S&Ls) more similar in their powers. As a result, the financial institution that originated a home mortgage in the OTD model was very often a commercial bank or a nonbank financial institution as well as an S&L.

3. For example, a mortgage broker usually receives payment from the lender when the loan closes that is expressed in some number of points—a point being one percent of the principal balance of the loan. A normal loan might garner 1 to 2 percent for the broker, but an especially profitable loan for the lender might give a payoff of 4 to 7 points for the broker. Of course, such high payoffs for the broker mean high payoffs for the lender and abusive terms for the borrower.

4. The process of securitization and the creation of various tranches is explained elsewhere in this text.

5. Each rating agency uses its own scheme of ratings, but they are quite similar. The privileged role of these rating agencies is enshrined in government regulation, the explicit investment policies of many financial institutions, and market custom.

6. In fairness to the rating agencies, it now becomes increasingly clear that a part of the downgrades resulted from honest errors in the rating process. Most participants in the market did not fully understand the risks, as unfolding events have demonstrated.

ABOUT THE AUTHOR

Robert W. Kolb holds two Ph.D.s from the University of North Carolina at Chapel Hill (philosophy 1974, finance 1978) and has been a finance professor at the University of Florida, Emory University, the University of Miami, the University of Colorado, and currently at Loyola University Chicago, where he holds the Considine Chair of Applied Ethics. He is the author of more than 50 refereed finance articles. Kolb's recent writings include *Understanding Futures Markets* (6th ed.), and *Futures, Options, and Swaps* (5th ed.), co-authored with James A. Overdahl. Edited volumes include *The Ethics of Executive Compensation, The Ethics of Genetic Commerce, Corporate Retirement Security: Social and Ethical Issues, Corporate Boards: Managers of Risk, Sources of Risk,* and the *Encyclopedia of Business Ethics and Society,* a five-volume 1.5-million-word work. Current projects include: *Employee Stock Options: Financial, Social, and Ethical Issues* and *The Financial Crisis of Our Time,* forthcoming from John Wiley & Sons, Inc. and Oxford University Press, respectively.

CHAPTER 28

Did Securitization Lead to Lax Screening?

Evidence from Subprime Loans

BENJAMIN J. KEYS
Economist, Research and Statistics, Board of Governors of the Federal Reserve System

TANMOY MUKHERJEE
Managing Director at Sorin Capital Management, LLC

AMIT SERU
Professor of Finance at the University of Chicago, Booth School of Business

VIKRANT VIG
Assistant Professor of Finance at London Business School

I n the wake of the subprime mortgage crisis, a central question confronting market participants and policy makers is whether securitization had an adverse effect on the ex ante screening effort of loan originators. Securitization, converting illiquid assets into liquid securities, grew tremendously during the subprime boom, with the securitized universe of mortgage loans reaching $3.6 trillion in 2006. The option to sell loans to investors transformed the traditional role of financial intermediaries in the mortgage market from "buying and holding" to "buying and selling."

The perceived benefits of this financial innovation, such as improving risk sharing and reducing banks' cost of capital, are widely recognized. However, delinquencies in the heavily securitized subprime housing market increased by 50 percent from 2005 to 2007, forcing many mortgage lenders out of business and setting off a wave of financial crises that spread worldwide. In light of the central role of the subprime mortgage market in the current crisis, critiques of the securitization process have gained increased prominence.

For lenders to screen and monitor borrowers, they must be given appropriate incentives to do so. By creating distance between a loan's originator and the bearer of the loan's default risk, however, securitization may have potentially reduced lenders' incentives to carefully screen and monitor borrowers. On the other hand, proponents of securitization argue that reputation concerns, regulatory oversight, or sufficient balance sheet risk may have prevented moral hazard on the part of lenders. What the effects of existing securitization practices on screening were, thus, remains an empirical question.

Our paper (Keys et al. 2010) investigates the relationship between securitization and screening standards in the context of subprime mortgage loans. There are two reasons why making a causal link between securitization and screening is particularly challenging. First, the analysis must isolate differences in loan outcomes that are not simply due to differences in contract terms or borrower characteristics. Those loans that are securitized may differ on observable and unobservable risk characteristics from loans that are kept on the balance sheet (not securitized). Second, simply documenting a correlation between securitization rates and defaults relies on establishing the optimal level of defaults at any given point in time. Moreover, this approach ignores macroeconomic factors and policy initiatives that may be unrelated to lax screening and yet may alter the composition of mortgage borrowers over time. For instance, house price appreciation and the changing role of government-sponsored enterprises (GSEs) in the subprime market may also have accelerated the trend toward originating mortgages to riskier borrowers in exchange for higher payments.

We attempt to overcome these challenges by taking advantage of a specific rule of thumb in the lending market, which created variation in the ease of securitization of loans with similar characteristics. This rule of thumb is based on the summary measure of borrower credit quality known as the FICO score. Since the mid-1990s, the FICO score has become the credit indicator most widely used by lenders, rating agencies, and investors. Underwriting guidelines established by the GSEs, Fannie Mae and Freddie Mac, standardized purchases of lenders' mortgage loans. These guidelines cautioned against lending to risky borrowers, the most prominent rule of thumb being not to lend to borrowers with FICO scores below 620. While the GSEs actively securitized loans when the subprime market was relatively small, this role since 2000 has shifted entirely to investment banks and hedge funds (the nonagency sector).

We argue that persistent adherence to this ad hoc cutoff by investors who purchase securitized pools from nonagencies generates a differential increase in the ease of securitization for loans. That is, loans made to borrowers that fall just above the 620 credit cutoff have a higher unconditional likelihood of being securitized and are therefore more liquid relative to loans below this cutoff. To evaluate the effect of securitization on screening decisions, we examine the performance of loans originated by lenders around this threshold.

As an example of our methodology, consider two borrowers, one with a FICO score of 621 (620+) while the other has a FICO score of 619 (620−), who approach the lender for a loan. To evaluate the quality of the loan applicant, screening involves collecting both hard information, such as the credit score, and soft information, such as a measure of future income stability of the borrower. Hard information by definition is something that is easy to contract upon (and transmit), while the lender has to exert an unobservable effort to collect soft information.

We argue that the lender has a weaker incentive to base origination decisions on both hard and soft information, screening the borrower less carefully, at 620+ when there is a higher likelihood that this loan will be eventually securitized. In other words, because investors purchase securitized loans based on hard information, the cost of collecting soft information is internalized by lenders to a lesser extent when screening borrowers at 620+ than at 620−. Therefore, by comparing the portfolio of loans on either side of the credit score threshold, we can assess whether differential access to securitization led to changes in the behavior of lenders who offered these loans to consumers with nearly identical risk profiles.

FINDINGS

Using a sample of more than one million home purchase loans during the period from 2001 to 2006, we empirically confirm that the number of loans securitized varies systematically around the 620 FICO cutoff. For loans with a potential for significant soft information—*low documentation* loans—we find that there are more than twice as many loans securitized above the credit threshold at 620+ versus below the threshold at 620−. Exhibit 28.1 illustrates this pattern for loans originated in 2003, with a similar relationship appearing in the other years in our sample.

Since the FICO score distribution in the population is smooth, the underlying creditworthiness and demand for mortgage loans (at a given price) is the same for prospective buyers with a credit score of either 620− or 620+. Therefore, these differences in the number of loans confirm that the unconditional probability of securitization is higher above the FICO threshold, that is, it is easier to securitize 620+ loans.

Strikingly, we find that while 620+ loans should be of slightly better credit quality than those at 620−, low documentation loans that are originated above the credit threshold tend to default within two years of origination at a rate 10 to 25 percent higher than the mean default rate of 5 percent, which amounts to roughly

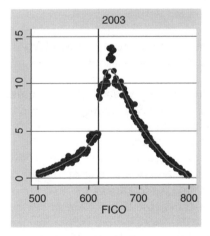

Exhibit 28.1 Thousands of Low Documentation Loans Originated in 2003 by FICO Score
Presents the data for number of low documentation loans (in thousands) originated in 2003. We plot the average number of loans at each FICO score between 500 and 800. As can be seen from the graphs, there is a large increase in the number of loans around the 620 credit threshold (i.e., more loans at 620+ as compared to 620−). More details on sample selection can be found in this chapter.

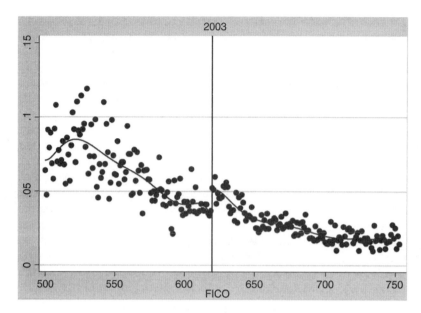

Exhibit 28.2 Percentage of Low Documentation Loans Originated in 2003 With Rapid Deliquency

Exhibit 28.2 presents the dollar-weighted fraction of low documentation loans originated in 2003 that became delinquent between 10–15 months after origination for one point FICO bins between scores of 500 and 750. The vertical line denotes the 620 cutoff, and a seventh order polynomial is fit to the data on either side of the threshold. More details on sample selection can be found in this chapter.

a 0.5 to 1 percent increase in delinquencies. Exhibit 28.2 illustrates this result for loans originated in 2003, which is representative of the other sample years.

As we find that the loans have very similar terms (which we empirically account for), the only remaining difference between the loans around the threshold is the increased ease of securitization. Therefore, the greater default probability of loans above the credit threshold must be due to a reduction in screening by lenders.

We rule out various alternative explanations that might explain our results. First, we find that loan terms and borrower characteristics are smooth around the 620 threshold. This suggests that the differences in default rates around the threshold cannot be attributed to similar screening applied to borrowers of differential risk levels around the threshold.

Second, strategic adverse selection on the part of lenders may also be a concern. However, lenders offer the entire pool of loans to investors, and, conditional on observables, securitizers largely follow a randomized selection rule to create bundles of loans out of these pools, suggesting that securitized loans would look similar to those that remain on the balance sheet. Furthermore, if at all present, this selection will tend to be more severe below the threshold, thereby biasing the results against us finding any screening effect. We also constrain our analysis to a subset of lenders that are not susceptible to strategic securitization of loans. The results for these lenders are qualitatively similar to the findings using the full sample, highlighting that screening is the driving force behind our results.

Could the 620 threshold be set by lenders as an optimal cutoff for screening that is unrelated to differential securitization? We investigate further using a natural experiment in the passage and subsequent repeal of antipredatory laws in New Jersey (in 2002) and Georgia (in 2003) that varied the ease of securitization around the threshold. If lenders use 620 as an optimal cutoff for screening unrelated to securitization, we expect the passage of these laws to have no effect on the differential screening standards around the threshold. However, if these laws affected the differential ease of securitization around the threshold, our hypothesis would predict an impact on the screening standards followed by lenders.

Our results confirm that the discontinuity in the number of loans around the threshold diminished during a period of strict enforcement of antipredatory lending laws. There was also a rapid return of a discontinuity after the law was revoked. Importantly, our performance results follow the same pattern, that is, screening differentials attenuated only during the period of enforcement. Taken together, this evidence suggests that our results are indeed related to differential securitization at the credit threshold and that lenders did not follow the rule of thumb in all instances. Importantly, we find no such pattern in the prime segment of the housing market around the 620 threshold, suggesting that strategic selection from the prime part of the market is not at play.

Once we have confirmed that lenders are screening more rigorously at 620− than 620+, we assess whether borrowers were aware of the differential screening around the threshold. Although there is no difference in contract terms around the cutoff, borrowers may have an incentive to manipulate their credit scores so they can take advantage of differential screening around the threshold (consistent with our central claim). Aside from outright fraud, it is difficult to strategically manipulate one's FICO score in a targeted manner, and any actions to improve one's score take relatively long periods of time, on the order of three to six months (according to Fair Isaac). Nonetheless, we investigate further using the same natural experiment evaluating the performance effects over a relatively short time horizon. The results reveal a rapid return of the discontinuity in loan performance around the 620 threshold, which suggests that rather than manipulation, our results are largely driven by differential screening on the part of lenders.

As a test of the role of soft information on screening incentives of lenders, we investigate the *full documentation* loan lending market. These loans have potentially significant hard information because complete background information about the borrower's ability to repay is provided. In this market, we identify another credit cutoff, a FICO score of 600, based on the advice of the three credit repositories. We find that twice as many full documentation loans are securitized above the credit threshold at 600+ versus below the threshold at 600−. Interestingly, however, we find no significant difference in default rates of full documentation loans originated around this credit threshold. This result suggests that despite a difference in ease of securitization around the threshold, differences in the returns to screening are attenuated because of the presence of more hard information. Our findings for full documentation loans suggest that the role of soft information is crucial to understanding what worked and what did not in the existing securitized subprime loan market.

CONCLUSION

While we cannot infer what the optimal level of screening at each credit score ought to be, we conclude from our empirical analysis that there was a causal link between ease of securitization and screening. That we find any effect on default behavior in one portfolio compared to another with virtually identical risk profiles, demographic characteristics, and loan terms suggests that the ease of securitization may have a direct impact on incentives elsewhere in the subprime housing market, as well as in other securitized markets.

The results of the paper, in particular from the antipredatory lending laws' natural experiment, confirm that lender behavior in the subprime market did in fact change on the basis of ease of securitization. This suggests that existing securitization practices did not ensure that a decline in screening standards would be counteracted by requiring originators to hold more of the loans' default risk. If lenders were in fact holding on to optimal risk when it was easier to securitize, there should have been no differences in defaults around the threshold. This finding resonates well with concerns surrounding the subprime crisis that, in an environment with limited disclosure on who holds what in the originate-to-distribute chain, there may have been insufficient skin in the game for some lenders (Blinder 2007; Stiglitz 2007). At the same time, the results further suggest that the breakdown in the process occurred only for loans for which soft information was particularly important. With enough hard information, as in the full documentation market, there may be less value in requiring market participants to hold additional risk to counteract the potential moral hazard of reduced screening standards.

In a market as competitive as the market for mortgage-backed securities, our results on interest rates are puzzling. Lenders' compensation on either side of the threshold should reflect differences in default rates, and yet we find that the interest rates to borrowers are similar on either side of 620. The difference in defaults, despite similar compensation around the threshold, suggests that there may have been some efficiency losses. Of course, it is possible that from the lenders' perspective, a higher propensity to default above the threshold could have exactly offset the benefits of additional liquidity—resulting in identical interest rates around the threshold.

Our analysis remains agnostic about whether investors accurately priced the moral hazard aspects of securitization. It may have been the case that moral hazard existed in this market even though investors appropriately priced persistent differences in performance around the threshold (see Rajan et al. 2008). On the other hand, developing an arbitrage strategy to exploit this opportunity may have been prohibitively difficult given that loans are pooled across the FICO spectrum before they are traded. Also, these fine differences in performance around the FICO threshold could have been obscured by the performance of other complex loan products in the pool. Understanding these aspects of investor behavior warrants additional investigation.

It is important to note that we refrain from making any welfare claims. Our conclusions should be directed at securitization practices as they were during the subprime boom rather than at the optimally designed originate-to-distribute model. We believe securitization is an important innovation and has several merits. It is often asserted that securitization improves the efficiency of credit markets. The underlying assumption behind this assertion is that there is no information loss in transmission, even though securitization increases the distance between borrowers and investors. The benefits of securitization are limited by information loss, and in particular the costs we document in the paper. More generally, what types of credit products should be securitized? We conjecture that the answer depends crucially on the information structure: loans with more hard information are likely to benefit from securitization as compared to loans that involve soft information. A careful investigation of this question is a promising area for future research.

More broadly, our findings caution against any policy that emphasizes excessive reliance on default models. Our research suggests that by relying entirely on hard information variables like FICO scores, these models ignore essential elements of strategic behavior on the part of lenders, which are likely to be important. The formation of a rule of thumb, even if optimal (Baumol and Quandt 1964), has an undesirable effect on the incentives of lenders to collect and process soft information. As in Lucas (1976), this strategic behavior can alter the relationship between observable borrower characteristics and default likelihood. Incorporating these strategic elements into default models, although challenging, is another important direction for future research.

REFERENCES

Baumol, W. J., and R. E. Quandt. 1964. Rules of thumb and optimally imperfect decisions. *American Economic Review* 54: 23–46.

Blinder, A. 2007. Six fingers of blame in the mortgage mess. *New York Times*, September 30.

Keys, B. J., T. Mukherjee, A. Seru, and V. Vig. 2010. Did securitization lead to lax screening? Evidence from subprime loans. *Quarterly Journal of Economics*, forthcoming.

Lucas, R. E., Jr. 1976. Econometric policy evaluation: A critique. In K. Brunner and A. H. Meltzer, eds. *The Phillips curve and labor markets*. Carnegie-Rochester Conferences on Public Policy. Amsterdam: North Holland Press.

Rajan, U., A. Seru, and V. Vig. 2008. The failure of models that predict failure: Distance, incentives and defaults. Chicago Graduate School of Business research paper 08-19.

Stiglitz, J. 2007. Houses of cards. *The Guardian*, October 9, 2007.

ABOUT THE AUTHORS

Benjamin J. Keys joined the Board of Governors of the Federal Reserve System as an economist in the Division of Research and Statistics in August 2009. His research interests include consumer finance, behavioral economics, labor economics, and the housing and financial opportunities of the poor. Keys received his bachelor's degree in economics and political science from Swarthmore College and his Ph.D. in economics from the University of Michigan.

Tanmoy Mukherjee is a managing director at Sorin Capital Management, LLC, a fixed-income hedge fund based in Stamford, Connecticut. He is a senior member of the investment team for Sorin Capital Management and heads the quantitative research group at Sorin. Mr. Mukherjee joined Sorin in September 2005 from Capital One Finance Inc., where he spent three years as a senior quantitative analyst developing strategies to predict default risk and prepayments in consumer receivables. Also, Mr. Mukherjee developed hedging strategies using interest rate derivatives for Capital One's consumer loan portfolios. Before joining Capital One, Mr. Mukherjee was a senior consultant for Bearing Point, an analyst with Standard Chartered Bank, and an operations engineer with Hindustan Petroleum Corp. Mr. Mukherjee graduated from the Indian Institute of Technology with a bachelor's of technology degree in chemical engineering. He also has a master's degree in financial engineering from Cornell University and an M.B.A. from the University of Delhi. Mr. Mukherjee has written two academic papers that have been published in the *Journal of Monetary Economics* and approved for publication in the *Quarterly Journal of Economics*. The two academic papers have received widespread citations from established publications including, the *Economist* and *Financial Times* and from the ECB president Jean Claude Trichet.

Amit Seru holds a Ph.D. in finance from the University of Michigan. He has been a professor of finance at the University of Chicago, Booth School of Business since 2007. Before his Ph.D., Seru earned a bachelor's degree in electronics and communication and an M.B.A. in finance from the University of Delhi. Amit Seru's primary research interest is in corporate finance. He is interested in issues related to financial intermediation, entrepreneurial finance, emerging market financial systems, incentives, and performance evaluation. His papers have been published in the *Journal of Finance, Journal of Financial Economics, Review of Financial Studies, Quarterly Journal of Economics,* and *Journal of Monetary Economics.*

Vikrant Vig has been an assistant professor of finance at London Business School since July 2007. He received his Ph.D. from Columbia Business School and holds a master's degree in engineering and finance from the University of Illinois at Urbana-Champaign. His research interests lie in the area of financial contracting and include financial intermediation, firm's choice of optimal debt structure, corporate governance, and law and finance. He was most recently a visiting scholar at the Reserve Bank of India and was awarded a CIBER (Center for International Business Education and Research) grant for his research on the role of legal institutions in emerging markets. His current research focuses on the subprime mortgage market in the United States, where he investigates how securitization affects the incentives of different market participants.

CHAPTER 29

Tumbling Tower of Babel

Subprime Securitization and the Credit Crisis

BRUCE I. JACOBS
Co-founder and principal of Jacobs Levy Equity Management*

T he credit crisis was characterized by a lack of due diligence on the part of mortgage brokers, lenders, and investors; a lack of oversight by banks and credit rating agencies; and a lack of regulation and enforcement by government agencies. The low interest rates set by the Fed following the tech stock bubble of the late 1990s and the events of September 11, 2001, prepared the foundation for hundreds of billions of dollars in untenable loans. The overblown edifice itself, however, was built on a tower of structured finance products based on subprime mortgage loans. These instruments—RMBS, CDOs, SIVs, and CDS—shifted the risk of mortgage lending, especially the default risk, from one party to another, until many lost sight of the real risks of the underlying loans.

RISK-SHIFTING BUILDING BLOCKS

Essential differences exist between risk sharing and risk shifting (see Jacobs 2004). Risk sharing works by combining risk exposures in such a way that they offset one another to some degree. Risk shifting works by moving risk from one party to another. Mortgages are essentially risk shifting with regard to underlying housing prices.

A mortgage loan provides the homebuyer with a put option that allows the risk of a decline in the value of the house to be shifted to the mortgage lender. If the value of the house declines below the value of the mortgage, the homebuyer can default on the loan. The down payment relative to the value of the mortgaged house is generally smaller for a subprime than for a prime borrower (Gorton 2008). Furthermore, a substantial portion of subprime borrowers took out piggyback loans of home equity or second mortgages to cover down payments. These borrowers were highly leveraged and, barring price appreciation, had little or no equity in their homes.

---

*Full article originally appeared in *Financial Analysts Journal*, March/April 2009. Copyright © 2009 by CFA Institute.

Having made a smaller down payment than the prime borrower, the subprime borrower has less to lose by defaulting. Furthermore, with a decline in housing prices, the subprime borrower, with a higher loan-to-value (LTV) ratio, is more likely than a prime borrower to owe more on the mortgage than the home is worth. Subprime loan default rates are thus more sensitive than prime loan default rates to declines in underlying housing prices.

Borrower defaults pass the risk of price declines on to lenders. Diversification of mortgage loans can reduce a lender's exposure to default by a given homeowner when that default is the result of a specific, diversifiable event—say, the borrower's loss of a job. Risk of default resulting from housing price declines, however, is unlikely to be that specific a risk. The risk-reducing benefits of diversification are more limited when the underlying risk is more systematic.

Mortgage lenders do not have to retain this systematic risk. Mortgages can be pooled, repackaged, and sold. Mortgages are generally securitized and sold through special purpose vehicles (SPVs) established by mortgage originators or by banks that buy mortgages from the originators. SPVs pool hundreds or thousands of residential mortgages to create residential mortgage-backed securities (RMBS). Moving mortgages to an SPV removes them—and their risk exposures—from the lender's balance sheet. With less risk on its balance sheet, the lender is subject to lower capital requirements. Capital is thus freed up for making more loans.

RMBS rely on *structured* securitization, which takes the payments on the underlying mortgages and redirects them, along with any associated losses, to three basic levels, or tranches. The senior tranche at the top offers the lowest interest rates and is the least risky because it is protected from loss by the tranches below it. Any losses are absorbed first by the bottom, or equity, tranche; if losses totally erode that tranche, further losses are directed to the next-lowest tranche, and so on. The equity tranche is the riskiest, but if the underlying assets perform well, it can offer very high returns. The mezzanine tranche falls between the equity and senior tranches in terms of both risk and return.

Subordination shifts risk within the RMBS structure and allows the transformation of subprime mortgages into AAA-rated senior tranches and BBB-rated mezzanine tranches, with a generally small, unrated equity tranche bearing the brunt of the risk. The sale of RMBS tranches then shifts the risks and the returns of the underlying mortgages from lender to RMBS investors. In particular, it shifts the largely nondiversifiable, systematic risk of default due to a decline in housing prices. The sale also provides the lender with funds for the purchase of more mortgages for more RMBS issuances.

Potential buyers of RMBS include packagers of collateralized debt obligations (CDOs). These CDOs represent a pool of underlying assets, such as RMBS, which are carved into tranches of differing risk-and-return profiles. As with RMBS, CDOs shift risk from the upper to the lower tranches. And the sale of CDOs provides CDO issuers with funds to buy more RMBS, or to underwrite more mortgages.

RMBSs and CDOs can be protected by their sellers or buyers through the purchase of credit default swaps (CDS) sold by monoline insurers, banks, and hedge funds. In exchange for a negotiated premium, the CDS seller agrees to make whole the buyer of the contract if the latter suffers because a default or other specified credit event causes a loss on a specified underlying asset. The underlying asset may be a particular debt issue, a tranche, or an index of RMBS tranches.

CDS are largely unregulated derivatives, and multiple CDS can be sold on a given underlying asset. Thus, a market for CDS exists, with prices that reflect the perceived financial health of the underlying asset. As surrogates for the underlying assets, CDS can be used to create synthetic CDOs, which serve in place of actual RMBS tranches.

One point that seems to have been forgotten in this long chain of structured products and structuring mechanisms is that shifting risk does not eliminate or even reduce it. For the most part, the underlying systematic risk is merely shifted from borrower to lender, from tranche to tranche, from lender to investor, from investor to guarantor. Although hidden, the risk remains.

THE RISE OF SUBPRIME

In mid-2003, subprime mortgages started to gain ground quickly, with the level of subprime originations rising from about $200 billion to more than $500 billion by mid-2004 (Federal Reserve Bank of San Francisco 2008). At their height (2005 and 2006), subprime originations totaled roughly $600 billion a year. In 2001, subprime mortgages accounted for less than 9 percent of mortgages issued and about 6.5 percent of mortgage-backed securities; by 2005, subprime made up more than 22 percent of mortgages and almost 23 percent of mortgage-backed securities (Ashcraft and Schuermann 2008).

Between 2004 and 2006, the issuance of CDOs more than tripled globally, to nearly $552 billion; more than half of these CDOs incorporated structured finance securities, such as subprime RMBS (Gorton 2008). The mezzanine tranches of RMBS were particular favorites of CDO packagers because they offered relatively high returns and could be transformed through subordination into AAA-rated products. The popularity of these instruments was so great that the demand outstripped the supply of raw material. CDO exposure to mezzanine RMBS issuance grew from 65 percent in 2004 to 160 percent in 2005 and 193 percent in 2006 (Bank for International Settlements 2008). The excess exposure was created synthetically using CDS.

Initial fixed rates on subprime mortgages were roughly 200 basis points higher than rates on fixed prime mortgages (Federal Reserve Bank of San Francisco 2008). The rate differential, especially meaningful in a low interest-rate environment, gave RMBS and CDO packagers healthy profit margins while offering product purchasers competitive returns. Subprime loans were thus extremely attractive both as candidates for securitization and as investments.

The relatively high yields on underlying subprime mortgages—and on structured finance products that included subprime mortgages—were accompanied by irresistibly low perceived risk. (In fact, the spread between subprime and prime mortgage rates declined by almost 250 basis points between 2001 and mid-2004 (Demyanyk and Van Hemert 2008).) For lenders and many financial intermediaries, this perception was fostered by their ability to shift some or all of the credit risk of the mortgages to RMBS and CDO buyers. For those buyers, risk perception was distorted by several factors.

Diversification offered buyers some protection. The structured instruments seemed to offer smoother payouts because the effects of refinancings and defaults were more diversified (Gerardi et al. 2008). The pooling of the mortgages also provided buyers some protection against adverse selection, whereby sellers with superior information cherry-pick for their own accounts those mortgages that appear least likely to default. Credit rating agencies played a crucial role, too, as an investment-grade rating from one of the rating agencies came to be viewed as a virtual guarantee of investment quality by insurance companies, mutual funds, pension funds, third-party banks, and other potential buyers. Finally, CDS seemed to offer the ultimate protection from defaults resulting from housing price declines.

The perceived lowering of risk encouraged an increase in leverage throughout the system. In 2007, about 40 percent of subprime mortgage exposure—50 percent if government-sponsored Fannie Mae (Federal National Mortgage Association) and Freddie Mac (Federal Home Loan Mortgage Association) are included—was held by U.S.-leveraged financial institutions, mostly commercial and investment banks and hedge funds (Greenlaw et al. 2008). These institutions tend to increase their leverage levels as their measured risk levels fall (Adrian and Shin 2008). Not surprisingly, Greenlaw and colleagues (2008) document a sharply positive relationship between total asset growth and leverage growth for both commercial and investment banks over the 1998-to-2007 period.

Securitization also allowed the funding for subprime mortgages to move beyond the leveraged financial sector to such traditionally unleveraged investors as insurance companies, pension funds, and mutual funds. These incremental sources of credit increased the supply of funding for subprime loans. At the same time, an expansion in the loan supply was perceived as an increase in funding liquidity, which reduced the perception of risk and the probability of default.

The structured finance instruments and mechanisms manipulating the cash flows to and from mortgage loans formed a positive feedback system that magnified underlying trends and their effects. The disconnect between the relatively high returns offered by subprime-mortgage-based products and their perceived low risk fueled demand for the products, thereby increasing funding for mortgages, facilitating home purchases, and raising housing prices. The complexity and opacity of the instruments and mechanisms, and the web of interrelationships they constructed between firms and between markets, magnified the effects.

Of course, the entire leveraged system rested on a shaky foundation: loans to high-risk borrowers. Furthermore, subprime loans had themselves become increasingly leveraged, with LTV ratios rising more than 6 percentage points between 2001 and 2006 (Demyanyk and Van Hemert 2008).

THE FALL

The S&P/Case-Shiller U.S. National Home Price Index (seasonally adjusted) shows that the average price of U.S. homes rose by 10.6 percent, 10.7 percent, 14.6 percent, and 14.7 percent annually from 2002 through 2005. In 2006, prices were essentially flat (–0.2 percent) for the year but actually began declining from the second quarter on. The LTV ratio of the average subprime mortgage issued that year was nearly 86 percent (Demyanyk and Van Hemert 2008).

Delinquency rates on subprime loans, which had picked up in mid-2005, continued to build in 2006 (Federal Reserve Bank of San Francisco 2008). In mid-2006, foreclosure rates on subprime mortgages started to increase significantly (OFHEO 2008). Subprime mortgage originations subsequently dropped off by more than half through mid-2007 (Federal Reserve Bank of San Francisco 2008).

The feedback between risk and leverage, which had helped inflate the subprime bubble when risk was perceived as low, now acted to deflate it. As default rates on subprime mortgages increased, risk increased. The credit ratings of subprime-based RMBS and CDOs were downgraded. Companies holding these products were required by regulation or internal risk control systems to increase their levels of capital in response to the increased risk. And entities that had leveraged mortgage-based products or sold CDS based on these products had to put up more collateral. These firms had to come up with additional capital by raising it from investors, borrowing it, or selling assets; alternatively, they had to reduce their leverage levels by closing positions.

In a market characterized by heightened risk and pressure from forced sales, the appetite for securitized products declined. The flow of funds to securitized product providers, lenders, and mortgage borrowers slowed. The decline in housing prices accelerated, further dampening demand for the products. Further losses led to further increases in required capital and even more pressure to delever.

Subprime mortgage originations fell from $93 billion in the first quarter of 2007 to $14 billion in the fourth quarter and all but disappeared by 2008 (Greenlaw et al. 2008). The S&P/Case-Shiller U.S. National Home Price Index shows that home prices dropped steeply from their peak in the second quarter of 2006, falling 32.2 percent by the end of March 2009. In the fourth quarter of 2008, the U.S. economy contracted at a sharp annual rate of 6.3 percent, and the recession continued into 2009. The Standard & Poor's 500 fell to a 12-year low in March 2009, 57 percent below its October 2007 peak.

CONCLUSION

Structured finance products helped inflate the housing-price bubble by providing ready funding for subprime loans. That market was enlarged through securitization, leverage, and extension to unleveraged economic sectors. As prices rose, however, the pool of possible homebuyers began to be exhausted, and prices eventually started to decline. With declines, many subprime borrowers found themselves underwater. Some exercised the put options in their mortgages. At that point, the real underlying risk of subprime mortgages, hidden for so long by the instruments used to shift that risk, became apparent.

The downside risk of housing-market prices was shifted to lenders and, magnified by vast amounts of leverage, spread up through the tower of structured instruments to investors in CDOs and sellers of CDS. Demand for the products was sharply curtailed. This led to further declines in housing prices, more defaults and foreclosures, and more losses for mortgage holders and investors in mortgage-related products. The solvency of some critical institutions began to be questioned, counterparty risk came to the forefront of decision making, and liquidity dried up as banks hoarded their capital and declined to lend.

Sophisticated, highly complex financial instruments and mechanisms were devised to shift risk from one part of the financial system to another (similar to portfolio insurance, a protective put option strategy, in the 1980s; see Jacobs 1998 and 1999). As in a shell game, the risk itself seemed to disappear in the shifting. But the underlying systematic risk remained, and, magnified by leverage, blew up the very foundations of the financial system and, in turn, threatened the entire economy.

REFERENCES

Adrian, T., and H. S. Shin. 2008. Liquidity and financial contagion. *Financial Stability Review*, 11: 1–7.

Ashcraft, A. B., and T. Schuermann. 2008. Understanding the securitization of subprime mortgage credit. Federal Reserve Bank of New York Staff Report 318.

Bank for International Settlements. 2008. Credit risk transfer: Developments from 2005 to 2007. Consultative document.

Demyanyk, Y., and O. Van Hemert. 2008. *Understanding the subprime mortgage crisis*. Federal Reserve Bank of St. Louis.

Federal Reserve Bank of San Francisco. 2008. *The subprime mortgage market: National and twelfth district developments*. 2007 Annual Report.

Gerardi, K., A. Lehnert, S. Sherlund, and P. Willen. 2008. *Making sense of the subprime crisis*. Washington, DC: Brookings Papers on Economic Activity.

Gorton, G. 2008. *The panic of 2007*. Yale School of Management and NBER.

Greenlaw, D., J. Hatzius, A. K. Kashyap, and H. S. Shin. 2008. *Leveraged losses: Lessons from the mortgage market meltdown*. U.S. Monetary Policy Forum, 8–59.

Jacobs, B. I. 1998. Option pricing theory and its unintended consequences. *Journal of Investing*, 7 (1): 12–14.

———. 1999. *Capital ideas and market realities: Option replication, investor behavior, and stock market crashes*. Oxford, U.K.: Blackwell.

———. 2004. Risk avoidance and market fragility. *Financial Analysts Journal*, 60 (1): 26–30.

OFHEO. 2008. *Mortgage markets and the enterprises in 2007*. Office of Federal Housing Enterprise Oversight. www.ofheo.gov/media/research/MME2007.pdf.

ABOUT THE AUTHOR

Bruce I. Jacobs is co-founder and principal of Jacobs Levy Equity Management, a leading provider of quantitative equity strategies. Jacobs has a B.A. from Columbia College, an M.S. in Operations Research and Computer Science from Columbia University, an M.S.I.A. from Carnegie Mellon Graduate School of Industrial Administration, and an M.A. in applied economics and a Ph.D. in finance from the Wharton School. Jacobs is author of *Capital Ideas and Market Realities: Option Replication, Investor Behavior, and Stock Market Crashes* (Blackwell), co-author with Ken Levy of *Equity Management: Quantitative Analysis for Stock Selection* (McGraw-Hill), and co-editor with Ken Levy of *Market Neutral Strategies* (Wiley). He was a featured contributor to *How I Became a Quant: Insights from 25 of Wall Street's Elite* (Wiley). He is an associate editor of the *Journal of Trading* and serves on the *Journal of Portfolio Management* advisory board and the *Financial Analysts Journal* advisory council.

CHAPTER 30

The Incentives of Mortgage Servicers and Designing Loan Modifications to Address the Mortgage Crisis

LARRY CORDELL
Federal Reserve Bank of Philadelphia

KAREN DYNAN
Brookings Institution

ANDREAS LEHNERT
Federal Reserve Board of Governors

NELLIE LIANG
Federal Reserve Board of Governors

EILEEN MAUSKOPF
Federal Reserve Board of Governors*

I n the current mortgage crisis, much attention has focused on the origination and securitization of residential mortgages, with little attention paid to mortgage servicing. Yet, mortgage servicers are the front line in resolving delinquencies and avoiding unnecessary foreclosures in the interests of lenders and investors. We examine in this paper the incentives of servicers to work out troubled mortgages, particularly those that are packaged in private-label mortgage-backed securities (MBS) and sold to investors.[1] We argue that while servicers substantially increased loss mitigation efforts in 2008, the costs of loss mitigation are high, and servicers had

---

*For a more complete discussion, see Larry Cordell, Karen Dynan, Andreas Lehnert, Nellie Liang, and Eileen Mauskopf, "The Incentives of Mortgage Servicers: Myths and Realities," *Uniform Commercial Code Law Journal* 41 (Spring 2009): 347–374. The opinions expressed here are those of the authors and do not necessarily represent those of the Federal Reserve System.

little financial incentive to invest heavily in the staff and technology to provide these services. Moreover, lack of clear guidance from investors about acceptable loan modifications, uncertainty about the success of modifications, conflicting interests of holders of different tranches of MBS, and obstacles related to junior liens have led to foreclosures even when both borrower and investor would benefit if such an outcome were avoided.

Many of these obstacles were recognized by and, indeed, helped shape the Obama administration's Making Home Affordable (MHA) program, which was designed to reduce preventable foreclosures by encouraging loan modifications and refinancings. That said, job losses have led to a sharp deterioration in the financial situations of many households, leaving them unable to sustain even the reduced mortgage obligations associated with a prudently modified loan. Close monitoring of the progress of MHA and making adjustments as necessary will help to ensure that resources are being directed most effectively to address the ongoing distress among borrowers, and to support a broad and sustained economic recovery.

FORECLOSURES, MORTGAGE WORKOUTS, AND LOSSES FROM FORECLOSURE

The number of foreclosures initiated by lenders soared from an annual average of less than 1 million from 2004 through 2006 to 1.6 million in 2007 and 2.4 million in 2008. Through the third quarter of 2009, foreclosure starts reached an annual rate of about 3 million, boosted by a steep rise in starts among prime mortgages. Foreclosure starts are likely to remain extremely elevated by historical standards into 2010, amid high levels of unemployment and large numbers of homes with negative home equity.

Mortgage workouts, defined as repayment plans or loan modifications, also increased but did not keep pace with the rise in distress among homeowners. Data from the OCC show that the annualized pace of workouts at the largest banks increased by 540,000 to 1.3 million in the first quarter of 2009 from a year earlier, but seriously delinquent loans at these banks increased over the same period by almost 800,000.[2] Hope Now—a joint government-industry program designed to help distressed homeowners—reports that the annualized pace of workouts for the industry as a whole increased about 800,000 over the four quarters ending in the first quarter of 2009 to 2.5 million, while delinquent loans rose over the same period by 1.2 million, to 2.9 million. Repayment plans are typically offered to borrowers to resolve temporary financial difficulties, while modifications involve a permanent change to the mortgage contract, such as a reduction in interest rate or an extension of the term. While modifications have risen more sharply than repayment plans since 2007, they have still accounted for less than half of total workouts since 2008.

Loss severities on foreclosed subprime mortgages are high and involve substantial deadweight losses. Loss severity rates on subprime mortgages averaged about 50 percent in 2008, with much higher rates in areas with significant job losses. More recent data suggest that severity rates on subprime mortgages are now close to 70 percent.[3] These extremely high loss rates suggest that the potential savings from more efficient loss mitigation could be significant.

Little information is currently available on the rate at which borrowers redefault on modified loans. But anecdotal evidence suggests that redefault rates may be as high as 50 percent within six months to a year of modification. High redefault rates boost the expected costs to servicers of a modification and are cited by investors as a reason why loan modifications may not be in their best interests.

Mortgage Servicer Costs and Revenues

The mortgage servicing industry has consolidated substantially over the past 20 years. The largest five firms accounted for nearly 60 percent of mortgage servicing assets in 2008, up from 7 percent in 1989. Consolidation has created substantial economies of scale in processing payments and managing collections for loans. However, such economies of scale are not present in loss mitigation, which generally requires more labor-intensive processes.

The revenue and cost structures of the mortgage servicing business shed some light on why mortgage servicers might foreclose upon a distressed borrower rather than pursue an alternative, such as a loan modification. Servicers collect a monthly fee for every dollar of loan serviced, ranging from 25 basis points for prime fixed-rate loans to 50 basis points for subprime loans. For borrowers who fall behind on their payments, offering an alternative to foreclosure such as a repayment plan, a modification, or a short sale is costly and yields little economies of scale, as these services are tailored to the individual borrower and are therefore labor intensive. The foreclosure process, in contrast, is efficient because it is well understood and may not even require direct contact with borrowers. Moreover, many foreclosure expenses incurred by servicers, such as property disposition and legal expenses are out of pocket, and thus chargeable to investors, whereas the labor expenses associated with modifying loans are expected to be covered by the standard fees paid to servicers.

Also, mortgage servicers are typically required to initiate foreclosures on defaulted mortgages held in private-label MBS by the governing pooling and servicing agreement (PSA), even if they are also pursuing workouts. In this important respect, offering an alternative to foreclosure is an *added* cost to servicers.

Servicers' investment in capacity has lagged behind the need for workouts. Servicers were generally ill-equipped at the onset of the crisis because past losses were not large enough to justify a sustained high level of investment in loss mitigation resources. As the crisis expanded, obstacles presented impediments to ramping up such resources. For one, the parents of some servicers became financially constrained. Also, with the collapse of private-label MBS issuance in the second half of 2007, prospects for servicing significant volumes of subprime loans in the future disappeared.

Loss Mitigation for Mortgages in Private-Label MBS

PSAs generally obligate servicers of mortgages in private-label MBS to follow customary and usual standards of prudent mortgage servicing. Few PSAs prescribe explicit actions on loss mitigation beyond the requirement that workouts and loan modifications pass a net present value (NPV) test. Indeed, the language typically only covers limitations on amount and types of modifications that are permitted.

Private-label securities are typically carved up into tranches, with ratings from AAA down through B with residual (or equity) classes. Conflicting interests among the different tranche holders has led to "tranche warfare." While PSAs obligate a servicer to maximize the returns to investors as a whole, not just returns to the more senior securities holders, they are silent on how to act when modifications benefit one tranche at the expense of another. For example, junior tranches benefit from a loan modification that prevents default, while higher-rated tranches might be better off with a foreclosure if losses are absorbed by junior bondholders.

In the past, investors have not generally questioned servicers about their actions. This behavior may owe to a lack of coordination among the investors, as they can number in the hundreds, tend to be dispersed, and may be uninformed about how servicing works. As a result, servicers of MBS have some discretion when calculating the best way to proceed with a troubled loan.

One way servicers have exercised discretion is through the choice of parameters in the NPV test, as PSAs leave most such choices to servicers. These parameters include the house price likely to be obtained in a foreclosure, the rate used to discount payment streams under workout options, and the probability of redefault. A sizable amount of subjectivity figures into the choice, especially in the current environment of high delinquencies and falling house prices.

Investors have not conveyed widespread concern that servicers have been executing too many foreclosures. Indeed, in conversations with investors, they have not expressed a high degree of enthusiasm for offering additional payments to servicers to undertake modifications or other workouts. The concern appears to be that such payments might lead to workouts not in the best interest of senior bondholders.

Junior Lien Holders

Servicers' efforts to work out delinquent loans are complicated by the preponderance of junior liens on mortgages originated during the mortgage boom. In 2006, more than one-third of subprime adjustable-rate loans were originated simultaneously with a junior lien (most commonly an 80 percent first lien and a 20 percent second lien). We estimate that subprime borrowers with second liens are significantly more likely to be seriously delinquent on their first-lien mortgage.

Holders of first liens may worry that a significantly modified lien might be considered a new lien and become subordinate to the existing junior lien. The probability of this occurring is highly uncertain, as it is related to state legal traditions and local case law. Even so, senior lien holders are reportedly reluctant to agree to a significant loan modification without resubordination by the junior lien holder. With substantial negative equity positions, much of the current economic value of the junior lien comes from the ability to extract payments from first lien holders. Many servicers do not have the operational controls or experience to get junior lien holders to agree to resubordinate or release their claims.

SELECTED RECENT LOAN MODIFICATION PROGRAMS

Congress, the Bush and Obama administrations, and industry participants have offered numerous plans aimed at stemming the surge in foreclosures. We now discuss some of the programs that specifically address the obstacles to modifications discussed earlier.

Late in 2007, Hope Now, working closely with the American Securitization Forum and the U.S. Treasury, introduced a fast-track plan to help borrowers avoid interest rate resets. The Teaser Freezer plan allowed servicers to use a set of agreed-upon criteria to offer certain borrowers with subprime adjustable-rate loans a modification that extended their initial low interest rates for an additional five years. These streamlined modifications helped address the capacity constraints discussed before, as they could easily be implemented by servicers that did not have the staff or technology to modify the mounting number of distressed loans on a case-by-case basis. Also, because the plan was designed with broad-based support from investors, servicers should have been less worried about being sued by investors.

In November 2008, Fannie Mae and Freddie Mac, working with Hope Now, offered the Streamlined Modification Program (SMP) for loans that they guaranteed. The program defined uniform borrower eligibility requirements and a specific protocol for modifying loans.[4] Payments were to be reduced to 38 percent of income through a waterfall that included interest rate reductions, extending the term, and (as a last resort) allowing principal forbearance. Like the Teaser Freezer plan, the program lowered the costs and the risks to servicers making such modifications. As an additional inducement, the program agreed to pay servicers $800 for each mortgage modified to offset some of the costs of doing so.

In early 2009, the Obama administration launched the Making Home Affordable (MHA) plan as part of its broader Homeowner Affordability and Stability plan. The MHA plan is the most comprehensive to date in addressing servicer impediments to modifying loans.[5] First, it provides clear standardized guidelines for conducting loan modifications to mitigate legal risks and make it easier for servicers with limited capacity to modify loans. As with the SMP, servicers follow a protocol to achieve a certain reduction in payments. Second, it subsidizes the modifications to allow for more generous reductions in payments and thus limits costly redefaults. In particular, investors absorb the cost of lowering the mortgage payment to 38 percent of income, and the Treasury absorbs half the costs of additionally reducing payments down to a 31 percent debt-to-income ratio. Third, the program provides even larger payments to servicers to offset the costs of conducting the modification—$1,000 for each modified mortgage, and up to $1,000 more per year (for up to three years) for each modified mortgage that stays current. Fourth, incentives are paid for modifications made before a mortgage enters delinquency. Fifth, to further reduce the likelihood of redefault, the principal balances of modified mortgages will be reduced by $1,000 per year for up to five years as long as the borrower remains current. Finally, the program recently announced steps to address the impediments that servicers face with respect to junior liens.

The MHA program also has features that encourage servicers to pursue other alternatives to foreclosure with troubled mortgage holders. For example, the program includes a streamlined procedure and payments to servicers for completing short sales. The program also has features that should encourage use of the Hope for Homeowners (H4H) program, which Congress created in mid-2008 to provide a new way for borrowers to refinance into an FHA-insured fixed-rate mortgage. Under the original H4H, a mortgage could be refinanced into an H4H loan if the lender agreed to write down the mortgage balance to no more than 90 percent of the home's value and extinguished any subordinate liens. In exchange for being put above water on the mortgage, the borrower was required to share some of the subsequent appreciation of the value of the home with the government. H4H refinancing has been extraordinarily low to date (despite some changes in late 2008), however, reportedly because of the complexity of the program and the unwillingness of lenders to write down principal. To increase servicers' use of the program, the MHA requires that servicers evaluate borrowers for an H4H loan.

It is too early to judge the success of MHA. As of November 2009, 78 servicers, including the five largest, had signed up for the program and more than one million trial modifications had been offered to borrowers. However, whether the program is sufficient to curtail the surge in foreclosures remains to be seen. Of the more than 700,000 active modifications as of November 2009, servicers had only converted 38,000 to the permanent phase. Moreover, borrowers who have substantial negative equity may not be interested, and borrowers who have experienced a significant reduction in income may not qualify. Despite the better design of the program, the likelihood that many borrowers cannot be helped under MHA remains a risk to the recovery of the housing market.

NOTES

1. *Private label* in this case means securities not issued by Fannie Mae, Freddie Mac, or Ginnie Mae. Most private-label MBS include loans that are subprime, near-prime (or Alt-A), or jumbo prime securities.
2. See www.occ.treas.gov/ftp/release/2009-77a.pdf.
3. See Credit Suisse, "ABX May 2009 Remits Update" (May 27, 2009).
4. The protocol built off a similar protocol developed earlier in the year by the FDIC for IndyMac Bank.
5. Details are provided at www.financialstability.gov.

ABOUT THE AUTHORS

Larry Cordell is currently at the Federal Reserve Bank of Philadelphia working on initiatives related to the mortgage crisis, including participation on the Treasury Department's stress test exercises; the examination team that evaluated Fannie Mae and Freddie Mac; a task force to manage parts of the Bear Stearns portfolio; and several research projects. Larry is also an adjunct professor in Penn State University's master's of finance program. He previously served as vice president of risk analytics and chief economist at Radian Group. He also spent 11 years at Freddie Mac, where he was among the team of economists that developed the first commercially available automated underwriting scoring model for the U.S. mortgage market and headed up the team that developed behavioral scoring software to assist mortgage servicers in managing delinquent accounts. He received his Ph.D. in economics from the University of North Carolina at Chapel Hill.

Karen Dynan is vice president, co-director of the Economic Studies program, and the Robert S. Kerr Senior Fellow at the Brookings Institution where she focuses on macroeconomic and household finance issues. Karen joined the Brookings Institution in September 2009. She came from the Federal Reserve Board, where she worked for 17 years, including most recently as a senior advisor. She also served as a senior economist at the White House Council of Economic Advisers, from 2003 to 2004, and a visiting assistant professor at Johns Hopkins University. She received her Ph.D. in Economics from Harvard University. Karen has published papers in numerous leading journals on a range of issues including household consumption and saving decisions, household financial security, and the effects of financial innovation on economic volatility.

Andreas Lehnert is an assistant director in the Division of Research and Statistics at the Federal Reserve Board in Washington, D.C. Lehnert earned an M.Sc. degree in economics from the London School of Economics, and a Ph.D. in economics from the University of Chicago, where he was also a research affiliate at the Joint Center for Poverty Research. In 2006, he was a visiting scholar at the Urban Institute in Washington, DC. His research focuses on household credit choices, consumption, and financial distress, including default, foreclosure, and bankruptcy. He has also written papers on optimal fiscal and monetary policy.

Nellie Liang is a Senior Associate Director in the Division of Research and Statistics at the Federal Reserve Board where she conducts research and policy analysis related to financial markets and institutions, and monetary policy. She has been part of the leadership team for a number of the Federal Reserve Board's responses to the current financial crisis, including the Supervisory Capital Assessment Program, known as the "stress tests" of the largest banking institutions, facilities to provide liquidity to the commercial paper market, and efforts to address the mortgage foreclosure crisis. In recent years, Nellie's research has focused on investor runs in short-term funding markets, incentives of mortgage servicers, debt covenants on employment risk, the effects of tax changes on corporate payout policies, corporate funding of defined benefit pension plans, and defined contribution pension plans and company stock, and has published papers in a range of leading journals. She received her Ph.D. in Economics from the University of Maryland.

Eileen Mauskopf is an economist at the Federal Reserve Board, with specialties in macroeconomic modeling and corporate taxation. In recent years, her interests have focused on real estate and mortgage delinquencies. She has served as an advisor to the Australian Department of the Treasury, the Central Bank of Israel, and the Czech National Bank. She also served as a senior economist at the White House Council of Economic Advisors under President Clinton and was a visiting professor at the University of New South Wales in Sydney, Australia. She received her Ph.D. in Economics from Johns Hopkins University. Eileen has published papers on a range of issues, including macroeconomic modeling, the monetary transmission mechanism, corporate taxation, and mortgage servicing. She has recently co-authored a proposal for government aid to financially distressed homeowners who have lost their jobs.

CHAPTER 31

The Contribution of Structured Finance to the Financial Crisis

An Introductory Overview

ADRIAN A.R.J.M. VAN RIXTEL
Head of the International Financial Analysis Unit, International Financial Markets Division, Associate Directorate General International Affairs, Bank of Spain

SARAI CRIADO
Staff Economist in the Financial Institutions Department, General Directorate of Regulation, Bank of Spain*

G lobal financial market conditions deteriorated sharply in the summer of 2007, triggered by concerns about exposures of financial institutions to U.S. subprime mortgage markets and related financial instruments. As risk assessments were adjusted, the financial turmoil spilled over to other financial market segments, and risky assets—particularly those linked to structured finance—were abandoned in favor of safe instruments such as government bonds. Uncertainty was particularly pronounced in the short-term money markets, as evidenced by a marked increase in risk aversion in the asset-backed commercial paper (ABCP) market and rather unprecedented rises in interbank money market interest rates. This financial turmoil developed in the third quarter of 2008 into a full-blown financial crisis of unprecedented proportions.

There is broad consensus that structured finance played an important role in the development and propagation of the financial turmoil and subsequent financial crisis (see, for example, IMF 2008). Hence, our paper published in the Occasional Paper Series of the Bank of Spain, and which is the basis of this contribution, aims to provide an introductory overview of structured finance, so that the reader may better understand its role and importance in the financial crisis of 2007–2008 (Criado and van Rixtel 2008). Structured finance has developed very fast in recent years and often involves highly complex financial instruments and techniques, which may not be understood completely beyond a small circle of financial market

---

*The views expressed in this contribution are personal and do not necessarily reflect those of the Bank of Spain.

experts. Therefore, we present in Section 2 our overview of structured finance and its main instruments and techniques. Section 3 provides a concise analysis of the most important channels linking specific structured finance instruments to the financial crisis.

A CLASSIFICATION OF STRUCTURED FINANCE

Structured finance relates to a group of complex financial instruments and mechanisms that defies a simple universal definition, but broadly defined, it could be described as referring to the repackaging of cash flows that can transform the risk, return, and liquidity characteristics of financial portfolios (Issing 2005; Fabozzi et al. 2006). A more straightforward interpretation is provided by the Bank of International Settlements (2005), through which structured finance is defined as a form of financial intermediation that is based on securitization technology: Structured finance "... involves the pooling of assets and the subsequent sale to investors of claims on the cash flows backed by these pools. Typically, several classes (or *tranches*) of securities are issued, each with distinct risk-return profiles." This definition clearly involves the elements of forming a pool of assets (either cash-based or synthetically created) and the tranching of liabilities that are backed by the asset pool. Also, the credit risk of the collateral asset pool is separated from the credit risk of the originator, through the involvement of a special purpose vehicle (SPV) or special purpose entity (SPE).

It is evident from this interpretation of structured finance that it is strongly interrelated with securitization. According to Fabozzi and Kothari (2007), structured finance, in a narrow sense, is used almost interchangeably with securitization. Traditionally, *securitization* can be defined as the formation of a pool of financial assets, such as, for example, mortgages, and their subsequent true sale (or only the transfer of their credit risk by using credit default swaps in so-called synthetic securitizations) by the bank that originated them to a SPV, which then issues debt securities—known as asset-backed securities (ABS)—for sale to investors (for an overview, see Exhibit 31.1). The principal and the interest of the ABS issued by the SPV depend on the cash flows produced by the pool of underlying financial assets (such as mortgages) (ECB 2008). In our Occasional Paper, we present an extensive example of the creation of residential mortgage-backed securities (RMBS) (see Exhibit 31.1) and the related process of dividing these securities in specific parts (or tranches) with different ratings. We also present statistical information on the development of the global securitization market by currency and underlying assets.

Exhibit 31.2 provides our overview of the main structured finance instruments. In essence, these instruments can be divided in securitizations and credit derivatives. Securitizations consist of short-term asset-backed securities (short-term ABS, which predominantly are asset-backed commercial paper or ABCP) and longer-term asset-backed securities (ABS), defined from a broad perspective. Broadly defined, asset-backed securities include three main categories: mortgage-backed securities (MBS), asset-backed securities in a narrow sense (ABS, which are essentially collateralized by all kinds of assets except mortgages, such as car loans, student loans, and so forth) and cash flow collateralized debt obligations (CDOs) (Jobst 2003, 2006; Vink and Thibeault 2007). In market practice, when the term

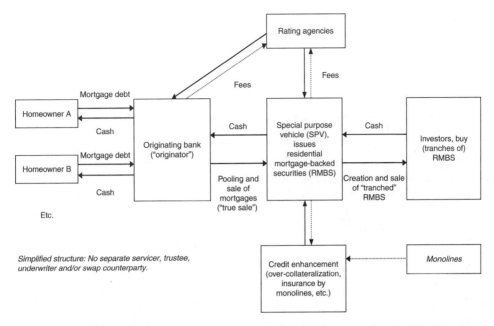

Exhibit 31.1 Example "True Sale" Securitization—The Creation of Residential Mortgage-Backed Securities (RMBS)

asset-backed securities or the abbreviation ABS is used, the narrow interpretation is often followed, thus implying asset-backed securities (ABS) with the important exception of mortgage-backed securities (MBS) and cash flow CDOs. In addition to securitizations or asset-backed securities, our Occasional Paper provides detailed explanations of the mechanisms involved in various structured finance products such as ABCP and CDOs.

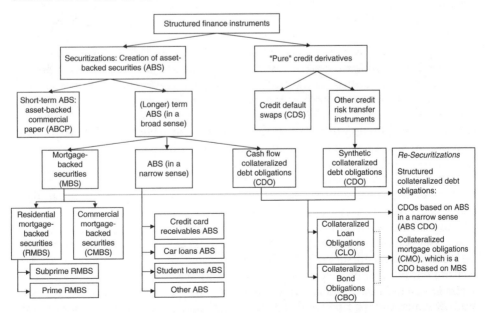

Exhibit 31.2 Structured Finance Instruments and Securitization

The mortgages underlying residential mortgage-backed securities (RMBS) may be of either prime or subprime quality, depending on the creditworthiness of the respective borrowers, or combinations of both. The financial turmoil that started in the summer of 2007 originated in the subprime mortgage markets and affected in particular those structured finance instruments that were collateralized by these assets (Ashcraft and Schuermann 2007).

Asset-backed commercial papers (ABCP) are collateralized short-term debt instruments (commercial paper, or CP), which are constantly rolled over and issued by so-called conduits (which include structured investment vehicles, or SIVs) to finance investments in often longer-term securities. These securities can be regarded as the collateral underlying the ABCP issued, or in other words, are the asset-backed component of ABCP. The ABCP market has been at the heart of the financial crisis. More specific, in August 2007, when pressures stemming from the U.S. subprime mortgage markets spilled over to structured finance products directly or indirectly linked to these markets, issuers of ABCP started to increasingly experience problems in finding investors willing to purchase these securities even for a short period. The problem was that the exposure of ABCP programs to mortgage-related financial instruments (which were included in the assets sold to conduits by collateral providers) had grown very fast to an estimated $300 billion (Bank for International Settlements 2007), so that investors lost confidence in ABCP when the subprime mortgage market tensions mounted.

Collateralized debt obligations (CDOs) are securities that are based on the packaging of, in particular, higher risk assets such as risky loans, mortgages, bonds and asset-backed securities, into a new security. Thus, a pool or number of debt contracts is grouped within a SPE/SPV. The CDO's liabilities are divided into tranches of different credit quality, and therefore of different subordination, as is the case with the asset-backed securities discussed before. The investors in the tranches of a CDO have the ultimate credit risk exposure to the underlying reference entities.

Different classifications of CDOs exist, and we chose to classify cash flow CDOs predominantly as securitizations, with only an indirect link to credit derivatives (see Exhibit 31.2). The reasons for this choice are twofold: First, their main characteristic is the explicit use of securitization techniques in transforming a pool of assets into new securities, and second, various statistical sources include cash flow CDOs in asset-backed securities (and not in credit derivatives). At the same time, we include synthetic CDOs in pure credit derivatives (see Exhibit 31.2), which are based on securitization techniques, but are much more very specific instruments to transfer credit risk from one party to another without transferring the underlying asset. The classification of synthetic CDOs as pure credit derivatives is also done mainly to follow statistical market practices. For example, the credit derivatives statistics published by the British Banking Association include only synthetic CDOs and not cash flow CDOs.

So-called structured CDOs are essentially securitizations of other securitizations, for example, of mortgage-backed securities (i.e., CDOs of MBS, or collateralized mortgage obligations, or CMOs) or of other CDOs, which are called CDO^2s (see Exhibit 31.2). Thus, structured CDOs constitute an element of resecuritization. Structured CDOs played a key role in the 2007–2008 financial crisis, as they were heavily collateralized by U.S. (subprime) residential mortgage-backed securities.

Thus, when problems in U.S. subprime mortgage markets mounted in the course of 2007, investors in CDOs based on tranches of subprime mortgage-backed securities incurred substantial losses. In the end, in parallel due to growing uncertainty of exposures and transparency concerns, the issuance of CDOs collapsed and by the end of 2008, the CDO market had virtually ceased to exist.

HOW STRUCTURED FINANCE CONTRIBUTED TO THE FINANCIAL CRISIS

As a summary overview, Exhibit 31.3 presents in a stylized format the main channels through which structured finance instruments played a role in the financial crisis. Although not all possible channels are shown, the figure depicts the essential interaction between the use of structured finance, the banking sector and the development of the financial crisis.

Channel 1 involves the creation of subprime mortgage-backed securities by a U.S. commercial bank, which are bought by ABCP conduits, for example, a SIV belonging to a German bank. The example of a German bank has been chosen because a number of German banks, such as IKB and Sachsen Landesbank, were particularly affected by the turmoil in this way. When because of the subprime crisis the value of these assets declined substantially, the collateral values of the SIV eroded, resulting in major refinancing difficulties.

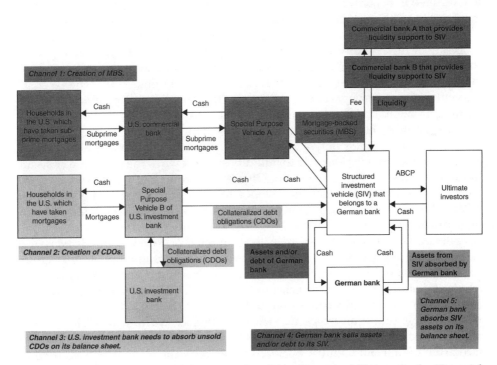

Exhibit 31.3 The Channels of Contagion Involving Structured Finance in the Financial Crisis

In a similar fashion, Channel 2 shows the creation of cash flow CDOs by a U.S. investment bank, which are collateralized by residential mortgage loans that also are bought by the SIV of the German bank. Here, too, the collapse of the price of these instruments created major problems and losses for the SIV.

Channel 3 involves the creation of the same CDOs as in Channel 2, but now the U.S. investment bank needs to absorb these instruments on its balance sheet. Namely, the financial turmoil completely eroded investor confidence in CDOs, and banks were no longer able to sell these instruments to investors. As a result, some SPVs of banks became saddled with CDOs because they could not get rid of them, forcing their sponsoring banks to absorb these instruments. Merrill Lynch has been one of the banks hit in particular through this channel (Cassidy 2008).

Channel 4 is a channel more directly linked to the banks and their ABCP conduits. Numerous banks used these conduits—here, the SIV belonging to a German bank—to put specific assets off their balance sheet or to absorb debt securities that they issued. Some of these assets proved to be relatively risky when the financial turmoil evolved, generating losses for the SIV. Moreover, when the crisis of confidence in financial markets hit the banking sector, the debt securities issued by the sponsoring bank that the SIV purchased dropped in value as well.

Channel 5 is related to the previous channels and essentially involves the absorption of the impaired assets from the ABCP conduits by the sponsoring banks, again here by the German bank that owns the SIV. Ultimately, the problems spilled over to the banks arising from the obligation to bail out their SIVs, for example, by taking over the impaired assets that had declined significantly in value, a process that resulted in major write-downs and losses for the banks involved. Some banks that have been hit through this channel are HSBC, Citigroup, and WestLB.

Finally, Channel 6 is also related to the first four channels and consists of the process that the liquidity facilitating banks actually needed to provide liquidity support to the ABCP conduits. As the ABCP issued by conduits is of very short maturity, they almost constantly are in need of new funding. Thus, when a crisis hits and no investor wants to buy ABCP, almost immediately conduits face major funding problems and need to sell their assets or need to obtain liquidity support from the liquidity facilitating banks. Of course, in a collapsing market, it is very difficult to sell assets or only at a substantial loss, so in fact many SIVs had no choice than to recourse primarily to liquidity support when the subprime crisis hit the market. This resulted in major liquidity strains for the banks involved, because they had not anticipated that they would have to provide such large amounts of liquidity, and the process consequently resulted in considerable disarray in interbank markets.

All in all, the financial crisis revealed a number of weaknesses related to the use of structured finance, which can be summarized as follows. In numerous cases, banks underestimated their exposures to structured finance products and to specific off-balance-sheet vehicles that play an important role in this type of finance. Moreover, certain banks invested heavily in structured finance products, retaining large exposures to specific structured finance instruments such as collateralized debt obligations, but without sufficiently understanding their impact on the banks' capital and liquidity positions. Also, banks, in general, had resorted to more volatile funding sources, including structured finance products. When the financial turmoil hit and structured credit markets came to a virtual standstill, the funding capability of specific banks—such as Northern Rock in the United Kingdom—was impaired significantly. Furthermore, many of the globally operating banks had offered liquidity standby facilities to off-balance-sheet vehicles engaged in structured finance, but generally underestimated the liquidity risk arising from off-balance-sheet exposures. Finally, the financial turmoil has raised concerns that the process of securitization may have generated unwelcome incentive problems, in the sense that banks may not assess the credit risk of specific borrowers accurately because they put these loans off the balance sheet anyway through their securitization techniques.

REFERENCES

Ashcraft, A. B., and T. Schuermann. 2007. Understanding the securitization of subprime mortgage credit. Wharton Financial Institutions Center Working Paper 07-43.
Bank for International Settlements. 2005. *The role of ratings in structured finance: Issues and implications.* Basel, Switzerland: BIS, Committee on the Global Financial System.
———. 2007. *BIS Quarterly Review.*
Cassidy, J. 2008. Subprime suspect: The rise and fall of Wall Street's first black CEO. *The New Yorker,* March 31, 78–91.
Criado, S., and A. van Rixtel. 2008. *Structured finance and the financial turmoil of 2007–2008: An introductory overview.* Banco de España Documentos Ocasionales 0808.
European Central Bank. 2008. Securitization in the euro area. *Monthly Bulletin,* 81–94.
Fabozzi, F. J., H. A. Davis, and M. Choudhry. 2006. *Introduction to Structured Finance.* Hoboken, NJ: John Wiley & Sons, Inc.
Fabozzi, F. J., and V. Kothari. 2007. Securitization: The tool of financial transformation. Yale International Center for Finance Working Paper 07-07.
International Monetary Fund. 2008. *Global Financial Stability Report: Containing Systemic Risk and Restoring Financial Soundness.* Washington, DC: IMF.
Issing, O. 2005. Opening remarks at the 4th Joint Central Bank Research Conference on Risk Measurement and Systemic Risk. Frankfurt am Main, November 8–9.
Jobst, A. 2003. Collateralized Loan Obligations (CLOs): A primer. *The Securitization Conduit* 6 (1-4): 7–14.
———. 2006. What is structured finance? *The Securitization Conduit* 8: 1–9.
Vink, D., and A. E. Thibeault. 2007. *ABS, MBS and CDO compared: An empirical analysis.* mimeograph, August 28.

ABOUT THE AUTHORS

Adrian A.R.J.M. van Rixtel is head of the International Financial Analysis Section at the Bank of Spain. He previously held positions at the Netherlands Central Bank and the European Central Bank and in private financial institutions in Amsterdam and London. He also has been a visiting scholar at the Japanese Ministry of Finance and a visiting researcher at the Bank of Japan. Van Rixtel took his Ph.D. at the Tinbergen Institute, Free University Amsterdam. He has published in a wide range of journals and books. His publications include *Informality and Monetary Policy in Japan: The Political Economy of Bank Performance,* published by

Cambridge University Press. His research has been discussed in *The Economist* and *Wall Street Journal*.

Sarai Criado is a senior economist at the Financial Institutions Department in the Regulation Directorate of the Bank of Spain. She previously held positions in the European Central Bank, PriceWaterhouseCoopers, and AFI. She holds an M.Sc. in economics from the London School of Economics and Political Science. Criado's recent writings include "Some critics to the contagion correlation test" (Working Papers on International Economics and Finance 05-01 at FEDEA) and "Banking Fees as a strategic variable: Trends and structure." Edited volumes include *World Exchange Regimes* and *Financial Systems of the East European Countries*.

CHAPTER 32

Problematic Practices of Credit Rating Agencies

The Neglected Risks of Mortgage-Backed Securities

PHIL HOSP
Associate, Los Angeles Office of Stroock & Stroock & Lavan, LLP*

The credit rating agencies occupy a special place in our financial markets. Millions of investors rely on them for independent, objective assessments. The rating agencies broke this bond of trust and federal regulators ignored the warnings signs and did nothing to protect the public.[1]

The adverse effects of the financial crisis began in 2007 with the fallout of the U.S. housing market. Effects of decreasing home prices spilled over to the broader economy because large financial institutions were heavily invested in credit instruments called mortgage-backed securities. These complex investments proved riskier and less profitable than investors initially thought, and their decline in value has caused financial institutions to write down trillions of dollars in assets, incur massive amounts of losses, and halt lending to other banks and businesses.[2]

Mortgage-backed securities are created through a process called *securitization*. The process of securitizing mortgages is complex and involves many players within the financial markets. The financial system currently counts on these players to independently assess the risks of the mortgages that back each security sold. However, instead of conducting their own due diligence, market participants

*This contribution is an abridged version of *Problems and Reforms in Mortgage-Backed Securities*, 79 Miss. L.J. (forthcoming 2010).

Associate, Stroock & Stroock & Lavan L.L.P–Los Angeles. B.S., 2002, Boston University School of Management; J.D., 2009, Loyola Law School, Los Angeles. I thank my family for their support—my wife Vivian; my parents, Phil and Maureen; and my sister, Megan. I also thank the faculty at Loyola, especially Professors Lauren Willis and Gia Honnen-Weisdorn, for their encouragement and dedication to students.

overly relied on credit rating agencies (CRA).[3] This proved problematic because CRAs used outdated models that failed to account for changing conditions in the U.S. housing market.[4]

This paper provides a general background of the evolution and importance of CRAs in the financial industry, and argues that a lack of regulatory sanctions, along with the absence of incentives for accuracy helped create the problem. This paper then argues that the imposition of a handicapping system similar to those used to handicap professional sports would provide a solution.

CREDIT RATING AGENCIES AS GATEKEEPERS

CRAs play an important role in U.S. financial market. They serve as important gatekeepers that investors and regulators rely on to provide objective, timely, and accurate financial information.[5] CRAs are among a number of different professions that act as gatekeepers in the financial markets. The most common gatekeeper professions include auditors, CRAs, securities analysts, and attorneys.[6]

Generally, market participants use gatekeepers in two primary capacities.[7] First, market participants use gatekeepers in a reputational capacity. A reputational gatekeeper is a professional (individual or company) who is well known among market participants for providing neutral and accurate assessments of financial information.[8] This status allows a reputational gatekeeper to lend its credibility to information that is communicated by a company to other market participants.[9] With the reputational gatekeeper's seal of approval, market participants are more willing to rely on that information in making investment or business decisions.

Second, market participants use gatekeepers in a regulatory capacity because the government requires their consent, approval, or certification in certain transactions.[10] For example, securities regulations require that CRAs rate debt securities being issued in the financial markets. The government requires this because ratings theoretically provide an objective assessment of the risks inherent in the securities being offered.[11] Unlike an issuer who has a financial incentive to exaggerate the profitability of securities being sold, CRAs are neutral because they have no financial ties to a security's profitability. Thus, the government uses CRAs to guard against inaccurate information from misleading decisions by market participants.[12]

Currently, CRAs act in both a reputational and gatekeeper role. However, in the late nineteenth century, CRAs initially began as pure reputational gatekeepers in selling business publications to investors. These publications contained assessments of commercial paper and other financial instruments.[13]

Nonetheless, following the stock market crash of 1929, CRAs rapidly transitioned into a more regulatory capacity. This transition began in 1931 when the Comptroller of the Currency required banks to hold extra capital for bonds rated non-investment grade.[14] Because the Comptroller defined the term *non-investment grade* as a security rated BBB and lower, credit ratings became essential to investors in the bond market.[15]

Since that initial regulation, CRAs' regulatory influence has spread while their reputation for accuracy has decreased.[16] Currently, CRAs have been incorporated into hundreds of regulations, some of which directly concern the buying and selling of mortgage-backed securities.[17]

CREDIT RATINGS IN MORTGAGE SECURITIZATION

Mortgage-backed securities are composed of thousands of individual home loans, pooled into one security, and sold in shares to investors.[18] They are created in a process called securitization.

Securitization starts when an originator (i.e., a lender) agrees to lend money to homebuyers in return for principal and interest payments.[19] The originator then sells its rights to these payments to an arranger, typically a major bank.[20] After purchasing thousands of loans from different originators, the arranger divides the loans into individual loan pools.[21]

After consolidating the loans into pools, the arranger sells each pool to a special purpose vehicle (SPV), which is a separate legal entity that cuts off the arranger's vulnerability to losses incurred from the loan pool.[22] Ultimately, the SPV sells shares of the loan pool to investors. However, before it sells any shares, the SPV structures the loan pool into a series of tranches.[23]

Tranches are pieces of the loan pool that the SPV separates according risk.[24] Tranches with the least amount of risk are referred to as senior tranches.[25] Tranches with more risk are called junior tranches.[26] Senior tranches are less risky than junior tranches because SPVs structure the security so that junior tranches incur losses before senior tranches. In this, SPVs allocate senior tranches with different forms of credit enhancement.[27]

Credit enhancements can be internal contractual rights with respect to other tranches in the loan pool, or external arrangements with third parties that protect investors against financial losses. The most common forms of internal credit enhancements are subordination—in which junior tranches incur losses before the senior tranches, overcollateralization—in which the SPV creates an equity tranche that absorbs losses before the investor tranches, and excess spread—in which the SPV creates loss reserves or pays off delinquent payments with interest payments that exceed the payments owed to investors.[28]

The most common form of external credit enhancement is the credit default swap. Effectively, a credit default swap is an insurance policy formed through an agreement between the SPV and a third party.[29] Under this agreement, the SPV pays the third party to cover potential losses to investors of a particular tranche.[30] Coverage under the credit default swap agreement is usually triggered by specified credit events.[31] These events are usually defined as a percentage of homeowners defaulting on their mortgage payments owed to that tranche.[32]

In 2008, credit default swaps became increasingly controversial. Because of bankruptcies or large financial losses in the financial sector, companies heavily involved in selling credit default swaps, like Lehman Brothers—one of the 10 largest sellers of credit default swaps—were unable to fulfill their contractual obligations to investors.[33] Consequently, investors covered by swaps sold by those companies were exposed to unexpected financial risks.

After structuring the loan pool into tranches, the SPV hires CRAs to assign each tranche a credit rating. Mortgage-backed securities generate revenue from the principal and interest payments made by homeowners on the underlying mortgages.[34] The CRAs' purpose in rating these securities is to consider whether the security as a whole will meet payment and performance obligations—that is, whether the homeowners will collectively make good on their payments.[35]

The ratings process can be divided into four steps.[36] First, the SPV sends information of the issuer's background and the loan pool to a CRA analyst.[37] Second, the CRA analyst uses that information to forecast the performance of the loan pool. In forecasting the security's performance, the analyst inputs the information into a mathematical formula that replicates the loan pool's revenue stream during a series of economic scenarios.[38]

Third, the analyst evaluates the qualitative, quantitative, servicing, and legal aspects of the security.[39] This includes information concerning security's capital structure, its revenue stream, the loan pool's underwriting criteria, the quality of the servicer, and the loan pool's legal risks (e.g., the effects of bankruptcy, regulatory issues concerning the issuer and the industry, the legal structure of the sale, the requirements necessary for a perfection of security interests, and taxes).[40]

Fourth, the analyst recommends a rating for each tranche and presents it to a rating committee.[41] The committee votes on the merits of each rating and notifies the issuer of its decision.[42] After the initial rating is issued and the securities are sold, CRAs monitor each security and general market conditions. If the CRA discovers that new information could have a "material impact on a security's creditworthiness," it reconvenes the rating committee and reconsiders the rating.[43]

Through this process, CRAs have become essential parties in managing risks of mortgage-backed securities. A recent SEC investigation, however, has shown that CRAs have ineffectively performed in that role.

PROBLEMS IN THE CREDIT RATING INDUSTRY

In 2007, after a sudden increase in foreclosures, the SEC decided to investigate the rating practices of the three largest CRAs—Moody's, S&P, and Fitch. From its investigation, the SEC concluded that CRAs issued inaccurate ratings because they used antiquated formulas that did not account for evolving market conditions.[44] The SEC also concluded that CRAs knew their formulas' were inaccurate and continued to issue ratings despite knowing that market participants relied on them.[45]

Among the evidence supporting the SEC's conclusions were internal e-mails that were discovered during the investigation. One e-mail summed up the problems with CRAs in a nutshell. In that e-mail, a CRA analyst stated to a colleague that her agency's model did not "capture half of [the deal's] risk," but that "it could be structured by cows and we would rate it."[46]

So why did CRAs fail in assessing the risks of mortgage-backed securities? As an initial assessment, commentators suggested that the current fee structure, in which the issuer pays for the rating, creates a conflict of interest between the CRAs' desire to obtain issuer business and the CRAs' ability to render objective ratings.[47] This idea is supported by other internal documents uncovered by the SEC. In an e-mail titled "Competition with Moody's," two S&P officers expressed their frustration in losing a deal to Moody's. To prevent any future problems, these S&P officers discussed the possibility of diluting S&P's rating requirements.[48]

Commentators also suggest that security information and CRA rating methodologies are too opaque.[49] In fact, even the raters have trouble gaining access to the necessary loan data to calculate a rating. For example, in another e-mail, an S&P analyst requests loan documentation to review risks of a security being rated. A senior manager abruptly replied to his request by stating that, "Any request for loan level tapes is TOTALLY UNREASONABLE!!! Most investors don't have it and can't provide it. Nevertheless, we MUST produce a credit estimate."[50]

In all, these issues are a result of the government's inadequate oversight of the credit rating industry. In this, regulators fail to deter CRA misconduct because they impose inconsequential penalties on CRAs that issue inaccurate ratings. Moreover, the current regulatory environment does not encourage the market to economically value accurate ratings over inaccurate ratings.

With respect to penalties, the SEC has demonstrated little backbone in deterring CRAs from issuing inaccurate ratings. For example, after its 2007 investigation, the SEC failed to recommend any punitive action against the CRAs involved. Instead, the SEC recommended only remedial measures, which the CRAs agreed to before the investigation's findings were published.[51]

Nevertheless, even if the SEC wanted to penalize inept CRAs, it would be difficult to do so because Moody's, S&P, and Fitch dominate the ratings business. In fact, in 2007, the so-called Big Three agencies rated 98 percent of the asset-backed securities issued in the United States.[52] This market dominance has stifled competitive pressures in the industry, causing CRAs to become complacent in not updating and improving rating methodologies.

The dominance of the Big Three is a direct result of the Nationally Recognized Statistical Rating Organization (NRSRO) designation. This designation is required by the government for CRAs to be used for regulatory purposes.[53] From the time of its creation in 1975 until 2002, the SEC only granted NRSRO status to seven CRAs.[54] Because the Big Three subsequently acquired four of those agencies, the industry transformed itself into a virtual oligopoly.[55] Since 2002, the SEC has taken steps to increase competition and reduce regulatory reliance on NRSROs.[56] However, those actions have had little effect on the dominance of the Big Three.

In addition to insufficient penalties, current regulations fail to provide economic value in accurate ratings. On the sell side, issuers want the best rating possible (accurate or not) because a good credit rating permits the issuer to sell its security to large institutional investors.[57] And because issuers retain no interest in the profits or losses of that security, they are more concerned about the marketability of the security rather than the likelihood of its profitability.

On the buy side, one would think that investors would pay more money for accurate ratings. However, in a market bubble environment like that of the housing market, investors are less averse to risk.[58] Accordingly, many institutional investors disregard proper due diligence and instead demand securities with the highest credit rating, regardless of its accuracy. High credit ratings are attractive to investors because, when the bubble bursts, good credit ratings provide corporate officers with an excuse for bad investment decisions and poorly executed risk management procedures.[59]

For their part, CRAs claim that ratings accurately capture risk over time when compared to other relevant public information.[60] However, this argument falls

short in today's market because mortgage-backed securities are complex investment vehicles whose structure and risk many market participants do not understand. Furthermore, as discussed before, buy-side entities have little access to
information about the security's underlying assets.

PROPOSAL: HANDICAPPING THE CREDIT RATING AGENCIES

Indeed, the SEC has taken steps to encourage competition in the credit rating
industry by increasing the number of NRSROS and reducing reliance on those
designated CRAs. However, more must be done to inject economic value into
a rating accuracy. To accomplish that goal, this paper proposes to handicap
CRAs by imposing a regulatory disadvantage to CRAs with less accurate rating
histories.[61]

Handicapping the CRAs could be similar to the system used by the United
States Golf Association in regulating the game of golf.[62] Generally, the purpose of a
golf handicap is to level the playing field between players of different skill levels.[63]
It accomplishes this by giving less skilled golfers a numerical advantage over a
competitor. This numerical advantage is determined by the difference between
each golfer's playing ability and it is deducted from the less skilled golfer's final
score at the end of the round.

For example, if Golfer A averages 75 strokes on a par 72 course, he has a
handicap of 3. If Golfer B averages 80 on a par 72, he has a handicap of 8. When
Golfer A plays against Golfer B, Golfer B receives a five-stroke advantage. After
completing the round, both golfers add up their individual scores. Golfer B then
subtracts five strokes from his score and compares that score with Golfer A's score.
The lowest score wins.

Regulators could apply a similar concept to CRAs. To calculate a CRA's handicap, the SEC would take that CRA's average accuracy in rating a particular type of
security (e.g., asset-backed securities). Based upon the accuracy of its past ratings,
and other relevant historical data, the CRA's handicap will be the best predictor
of the likelihood that the rating will be accurate. After calculating the handicap,
the SEC would apply the CRA's handicap to the ratings that it issues. Depending
on the CRA's past accuracy its handicap could lower or increase the overall rating
that is used for regulatory purposes.

To illustrate, if a CRA initially rates a particular security AAA, the SEC will take
the AAA rating and apply the CRA's handicap. If the CRA has a poor track record
in rating similar securities the handicap could potentially reduce the gross rating
from AA to A, depending on the severity of the CRA's past inaccurate ratings. As
such, if the CRA's track record demonstrates total unreliability, the handicap could
even reduce the rating below BBB. In that case institutional investors would be
barred from buying shares in that security.

Ultimately, this proposal will improve the credit rating industry. As an initial
matter, handicapping CRAs will allow investors to easily compare the accuracy
of each CRA. This will negate the blame game and increase the economic value
of CRAs that accurately assess risk. Handicapping CRAs will also create regulatory penalties for CRAs that consistently issue bad ratings. Such penalties will

encourage CRAs to improve both their ratings methodologies and due diligence standards. Ultimately, these penalties will offset any adverse monetary incentives presented by the issuer-pays model.

CONCLUSION

In conclusion, CRAs are essential to maintaining market transparency and managing the market risk. However, CRAs have taken advantage of this influential position by using inaccurate rating methods that failed to capture foreseeable market risks. Regulations and regulators overseeing the credit rating industry allowed this to happen by failing to penalize incompetent CRAs and failing to create an environment that economically values rating accuracy. Policymakers can remedy these problems by implementing a handicapping system that integrates the accuracy of a CRA's past ratings into the regulatory and economic value of its future ratings.

NOTES

1. Credit Rating Agencies and the Financial Crisis: Hearing Before the House Committee on Oversight and Government Reform, 110th Congress 1–4 (2008) [hereinafter Credit Rating Agencies and the Financial Crisis] (opening statement of Rep. Henry Waxman, Chairman, House Committee on Oversight and Government Reform).

2. Ben Bernanke, Chairman, Federal Reserve, "The Crisis and the Policy Response" (January 13, 2009). In a statement before the House Committee on Financial Services, Dean Baker reiterated that estimates have placed losses of the banks at more than $2 trillion. See TARP Oversight: Is TARP Working for Main Street? Hearing Before the House Committee on Financial Services, 111th Congress 1 (2009) (statement of Mr. Dean Baker, Ph.D., Co-Director, Center for Economic and Policy).

3. On February 8, 2009, Lloyd Blankfein, CEO of Goldman Sachs, wrote an article in the *Financial Times* in which he commented on seven lessons that he learned from the current economic crisis. Specifically, he noted that "too many financial institutions and investors simply outsourced their risk management. Rather than undertake their own analysis, they relied on the rating agencies to do the essential work of risk analysis for them." Lloyd Blankfein, "Do not destroy the essential catalyst of risk," *Financial Times*, February 8, 2009, 7.

4. See Richard Cantor and Frank Packer, *The Credit Rating Industry*, 19 FRBNY Q. Rev. 2–4 (1994) (discussing regulatory role of CRAs).

5. See Cantor and Packer, supra note 4, at 4 (discussing reliance on CRAs).

6. John C. Coffee, Jr., "Gatekeeper Failure and Reform: The Challenge of Fashioning Relevant Reforms," 84 B.U. L. Rev. 301, 309 (2004).

7. The term *market participant* generally refers to persons buying, selling, and marketing financial products.

8. See Coffee, supra note 6 at 308.

9. Id.

10. See id. at 308–309; Partnoy, "The Siskel and Ebert of Financial Markets? Two Thumbs Down for the Credit Rating Agencies," 77 Wash. U.L.Q. 619, 623 (1999) [hereinafter Partnoy, *Siskel and Ebert*] (describing the effects of regulatory reliance on the CRAs).

11. See Frank A. Bottini, Jr., "An Examination of the Current Status of Rating Agencies and Proposals for Limited Oversight of Such Agencies," 30 San Diego L. Rev. 579, 603–08 (1993) (describing the use of ratings in issuing new securities).

12. The SEC recognizes the dangers of "publicity efforts" that will "condition the public mind or arouse public interest" in a particular security before verified information is provided to investors. See *In the Matter of Carl M. Loeb, Rhoades & Co. and Dominick & Dominick*, Securities Act Release No. 34-5870 (February 9, 1959).

13. See Cantor and Packer, supra note 4, at 4.

14. Id. at 5–7.

15. Id.

16. A 2004 survey by the Association for Financial Professionals found that only 53 percent of professionals believed that the ratings of their organization were accurate. Although this is up from 2002, when only 29 percent of professionals indicated that their ratings are accurate, the numbers have most likely declined since events after the housing market crash have revealed rating inaccuracy. See 2004 Credit Rating Agency Survey 6-7 (2004), www.afponline.org/pub/pdf/2004_10_research_cra_report.pdf. However, with more regulations requiring their use, CRAs could afford to sacrifice their reputations in realizing increasing profits. See Partnoy, *Siskel and Ebert*, supra note 10, at 684.

17. See Partnoy, *Siskel and Ebert*, supra note 10, at 690.

18. SEC web site: Mortgage-Backed Securities, www.sec.gov/answers/mortgagesecurities .htm (last visited July 9, 2009).

19. See Securities and Exchange Commission, "Summary Report of Issues Identified in the Commission Staff's Examinations of Select Credit Rating Agencies" 6 (2008) [hereinafter SEC Summary Report], www.sec.gov/news/studies/2008/ craexamination070808.pdf; Int'l Org. of Sec. Comm'n, "The Role of Credit Rating Agencies in Structured Finance Markets" 7 (2008) [hereinafter IOSC], www.cmvm.pt/NR/ rdonlyres/85312A11-A927-4F63-810A-082C1A2CF5F8/9759/RelIOSCOsobrePapelCRAMercProdEstrut.pdf.

20. See, for example, In re Worldcom, Inc. Sec. Litig., 346 F. Supp. 2d 628, 652 (S.D.N.Y. 2003) (discussing the role of the Bank of America as a lead arranger and its due diligence requirements). See also John Patrick Hunt, "Credit Rating Agencies and the 'Worldwide Credit Crisis': The Limits of Reputation, the Insufficiency of Reform, and a Proposal for Improvement," 2009 Colum. Bus. L. Rev. 109, 136 (noting the dominance of a few major banks that act as arrangers); SEC Summary Report, supra note 19, at 6.

21. Id.

22. Kathleen C. Engel and Patricia A. McCoy, "Turning a Blind Eye: Wall Street Finance of Predatory Lending," 75 Fordham L. Rev. 2039, 2045–46 (2007) (discussing how SPVs protect assets from creditors)

23. IOSC, supra note 19, at 9.

24. Id.

25. Calvin R. Wong, *Emerging and Nonstandard Products: A Rating Agency's Perspective*, 759 PLI/COMM 347, 350 (1997).

26. President's Working Group on Financial Markets, "Policy Statement on Financial Market Developments" 8 (March 2008) ("The subprime RMBS and the ABS CDOs were structured in tranches and a very large share of the total value of the securities issued was rated AA or AAA by the credit rating agencies.").

27. SEC Summary Report, supra note 19, at 6.

28. Id.

29. Aaron Unterman, "Exporting Risk: Global Implication of the Securitization of U.S. Housing Debt," 4 Hastings Bus. L. J. 90–91 (2008) (discussing general concepts of credit default swaps).

30. Id.

31. Id.

32. Id.

33. Julie Satow, "Derivatives Pose New Wrinkle in Lehman Case," *New York Sun*, September 25, 2008, B1.

34. Stephen J. Choi and A. C. Pritchard, "Securities Regulation: Cases and Analysis" 146–148 (2008).

35. See Claire A. Hill, "Regulating the Rating Agencies," 82 Wash. U. L. Q. 43, 71–73 (2004) (discussing the nature of information provided by credit ratings).

36. SEC Summary Report, supra note 19, at 7; IOSC, supra note 19, at 9; see also Claire A. Hill, "Securitization: A Low-Cost Sweetener for Lemons," 74 Wash. U. L.Q. 1061, 1070–74 (1996) (discussing the CRAs' role in securitization).

37. SEC Summary Report, supra note 19, at 7; IOSC, supra note 19, at 9.

38. See IOSC, supra note 19, at 9 ("This analysis also includes assumptions as to how much principal would be recovered after a defaulted loan is foreclosed."); Wong, supra note 25, at 351.

39. See David Reiss, "Subprime Standardization: How Rating Agencies Allow Predatory Lending to Flourish in the Secondary Mortgage Market," 33 Fla. St. U. L. Rev. 985, 1014 (2006) (describing four steps in the analyses); compare with SEC Summary Report, supra note 19, at 7–8 (describing only three categories of information).

40. In Professor Reiss's article, he discusses the effect that antipredatory lending laws in Georgia, New Jersey, and North Carolina have on the legal risks associated with mortgage-backed securities. He argues that because these states passed laws making investors liable for lending law violations, mortgages from those states were not sold on the secondary market because CRAs would not assign them a favorable rating. Id.

41. SEC Summary Report, supra note 19, at 9; IOSC, supra note 19, at 7–10.

42. SEC Summary Report, supra note 19, at 9; IOSC, supra note 19, at 7–10.

43. Gretchen Morgenson, "Debt Watchdogs: Tamed or Caught Napping?" *New York Times*, December 17, 2008, A1.

44. One of the changing conditions in the U.S. home mortgage market has been the sudden influx of subprime and near-prime loans. In 2007, the Federal Reserve Bank of Dallas noted that subprime and near-prime loans increased from 9 percent of newly originated securitized loans in 2001 to 40 percent of newly originated securitized loans in 2006. See Danielle DiMartino and John V. Duca, "The Rise and Fall of Subprime Mortgages" 2 (2007), www.dallasfed.org/research/eclett/2007/el0711.pdf.

45. In hearings before the Congressional Committee on Government Oversight and Reform, Congressman Henry Waxman suggested that the CRAs focused on profits rather than actual risks of the securities they rated. In this, Congressman Waxman noted that "The total revenues for the three firms doubled from $3 billion in 2002 to over $6 billion in 2007. At Moody's, profits quadrupled between 2000 and 2007. In fact, Moody's had the highest profit margin of any company in the S&P 500 for five years in a row." *Credit Rating Agencies and the Financial Crisis*, supra note 1, at 5.

46. Credit Rating Agencies and the Financial Crisis, supra note 1 (Instant message conversation between Shannon Mooney and Ralul Dilip Shah, April 5, 2007); SEC Summary Report, supra note 19, at 12 & n.8.

47. Id. at 23.

48. Credit Rating Agencies and the Financial Crisis, supra note 1 (E-mail from Yo-Tsung Chang to Joanne Rose et al., May 25, 2004).

49. See Hunt, supra note 20, at 126–27 (defining transparency as "investors' ability to understand how agencies arrive at ratings and their ability to monitor how ratings perform").

50. Credit Rating Agencies and the Financial Crisis, supra note 1 (E-mail from Frank Raiter to Richard Gugliada et al., March 20, 2001).

51. SEC Summary Report, supra note 19, at 6.

52. In a 2008 proposal, the SEC noted that "According to their most recent Annual Certifications on Form NRSRO, S&P rates 197,700 issuers of asset-backed securities, the category that includes RMBS, Moody's rates 110,000 such issuers, and Fitch rates 75,278 such issuers. No other registered NRSRO reports rating more than 1,000 issuers of asset-backed securities." SEC, Proposed Rules for Nationally Recognized Statistical Rating Organizations, Release No. 34-57967, File No. S7-13-08, at 5 (June 16, 2008), www.sec.gov/rules/proposed/2008/34-57967.pdf.

53. The Treasury Department recently enacted the Term Asset-Backed Securities Loan Facility, which provides government loans to investors of asset-backed securities. To be eligible to receive these loans, securities must "have a long-term credit rating in the highest investment-grade rating category (for example, AAA) from two or more major [NRSROs]." See press release, SEC, "Talk Task Force Expanded to Address Public-Private Investment Plan" (April 28, 2009), www.sigtarp.gov/... /TALF_Task_Force _Expanded_to_Include_PPIP.pdf; See also SEC, TALF FAQs 1, www.federalreserve .gov/newsevents/... /monetary20090303a2.pdf.

54. Hill, supra note 35, at 54.

55. See *Rating the Rating Agencies: The State of Transparency and Competition: Hearing Before the Capital Markets Subcommittee of the House Financial Services Commitee*, 108th Congress 34–35 (2003) (Statement of Lawrence J. White, Professor of Economics, Stern School of Business, New York University), http://financialservices.house.gov/media/pdf/108-18.pdf (last visited July 11, 2009); Hill, supra note 35, at 54–55.

56. As of July 9, 2009, the SEC designated a total of 10 rating agencies as NRSROs—A.M. Best Company, Inc., DBRS Ltd., Egan-Jones Rating Company, Fitch, Inc., Japan Credit Rating Agency, Ltd., LACE Financial Corp., Moody's Investors Service, Inc., Rating and Investment Information, Inc., Realpoint LLC, and S&P Ratings Services. See SEC web site, "Credit Rating Agencies—NRSROs," www.sec.gov/answers/nrsro.htm (last visited July 9, 2009) (on file with author). On July 1, 2009, the SEC proposed to reduce reliance on NRSROs by eliminating references to them in the Investment Company Act (Rules 2a-7, 3a-7, 5b-3, and 10f-3), and the Investment Advisers Act (Rule 206(3)-3T). See SEC Release No. IC-28327 (July 1, 2008).

57. Professor Reiss states that "The lack of a rating from at least one of the privileged raters... is the financial equivalent of a death sentence for a residential mortgage-backed securities offering." See Reiss, supra note 39, at 988. See also Unterman, supra note 29, at 90–91 (discussing the role of institutional investors in buying mortgage-backed securities).

58. Professor Robert Shiller suggests that investor confidence is not always rationally based in a market bubble environment. Rather, he suggests that investor confidence is

sometimes based on blind emotional trust that dismisses instinctive doubts about other players in the market. See Robert Shiller, "Animal Spirits Depend on Trust," *Wall Street Journal,* January 27, 2009, A15.

59. See, for example, "The Charlie Rose Show: A Conversation with Vikram Pandit, CEO of Citigroup," (KCET television broadcast Nov. 25, 2008), www.charlierose.com/view/interview/9653.

60. See Gregory Husisian, "What Standard of Care Should Govern the World's Shortest Editorials? An Analysis of Bond Rating Agency Liability?" 75 Cornell L. Rev. 411, 440–42 (1990) (discussing the accuracy of bond ratings); Eamonn K. Moran, "Wall Street Meets Main Street: Understanding the Financial Crisis," 13 N.C. Banking Institute 5, 40 (2009) (discussing the difficulty in judging the risks of collateralized debt obligations).

61. The handicapping concept is further explained in "Problems and Reforms in Mortgage-Backed Securities: Handicapping the Credit Rating Agencies," 79 Miss. L. J. (forthcoming 2010).

62. See, generally, United States Golf Association web site, "Handicaps," www.usga.org/playing/handicaps/handicaps.html.

63. See John Paul Newport, "The Genius of Handicapping—The Beauty of Golf's Scoring System Is That It Levels the Field for All Players," *Wall Street Journal,* November 1, 2008, W6.

ABOUT THE AUTHOR

Phil Hosp is an associate in the Los Angeles office of Stroock & Stroock & Lavan, LLP. He has a law degree from Loyola Law School–Los Angeles and a bachelor's degree in business administration from Boston University School of Management. Hosp recently wrote "Problems and Reforms in Mortgage-Backed Securities: Handicapping the Credit Rating Agencies," which was published in the *Mississippi Law Journal.* Before attending law school, Hosp served four years as an armor officer in the U.S. Army and was awarded the Bronze Star for his service in Iraq.

CHAPTER 33

Did Asset Complexity Trigger Ratings Bias?

VASILIKI SKRETA
Assistant Professor of Economics, NYU Stern School of Business

LAURA VELDKAMP
Associate Professor of Economics, NYU Stern School of Business

Most market observers attribute the recent credit crunch to a confluence of factors: excess leverage, opacity, improperly estimated correlation between bundled assets, lax screening by mortgage originators, and market-distorting regulations. It was the job of the credit rating agencies to create transparency, to provide the basis for risk management regulation, and to discipline mortgage lenders and the creators of structured financial products by rating their assets. Understanding the origins of the crisis requires, at least in part, understanding the failures of the market for ratings.

POTENTIAL SOURCES OF RATINGS BIAS

Proposed explanations for ratings bias have broadly fallen into three categories.

It Was an Honest Mistake

New financial instruments were being traded, and rating agencies had no historical return data for these instruments on which to base their risk assessments.

These new instruments had a degree of complexity that even financial professionals acknowledged was "far above that of traditional bonds,"[1] or "dizzying."[2] But complexity alone would generate independent errors in ratings, not ratings that were systematically upward biased and subsequently downgraded in 2008. For this story to make sense, it must be that many raters made the same mistake. For example, they underestimated the correlation of defaults, particularly in residential mortgage-backed securities. This led them to underestimate the risk of a geographically diverse pool of mortgages and to assign such assets inflated ratings.

Agencies Were Beholden to Asset Issuers

A host of recent papers explore the conflict of interest that arises when rating agencies' fees are paid by asset issuers. Damiano, Li, and Suen (2008), Bolton, Freixas, and Shapiro (2008) Becker and Milbourn (2008), and Mathis, McAndrews, and Rochet (2008) investigate the extent to which reputation effects can discipline rating agencies who may feel compelled to deliberately inflate their ratings, either to maximize their consulting fees or because the issuer could be shopping for the highest rating.

Asset Issuers Shopped for Ratings

Since, with few exceptions, an asset issuer decides which ratings will get published, he can publish only the most favorable one(s). An article in the *New York Times* explains: "The banks pay only if [the ratings agency] delivers the desired rating.... If Moody's and a client bank don't see eye to eye, the bank can either tweak the numbers or try its luck with a competitor like S&P, a process known as ratings shopping."[3]

   While all three of these explanations likely played some role in creating ratings bias, only the first explains why upward bias appeared recently. Asset issuers have been paying for credit ratings since the 1970s,[4] and until recently ratings upgrades were more common than downgrades. Does this mean that the conflict of interest and ratings shopping were not possible sources of the ratings inflation of the last few years and should therefore not be the subject of new regulation?

OUR EXPLANATION

Our work (Skreta and Veldkamp 2009) looks for a trigger that could explain why the incentive to shop for and bias ratings might have remained dormant until recently. The trigger we identify is an increase in asset complexity. As Mark Adelson testified before Congress,

> *The complexity of a typical securitization is far above that of traditional bonds. It is above the level at which the creation of the methodology can rely solely on mathematical manipulations. Despite the outward simplicity of credit ratings, the inherent complexity of credit risk in many securitizations means that reasonable professionals starting with the same facts can reasonably reach different conclusions.*[5]

However, the credit market crisis was not generated by independent ratings errors. Only systematic upward ratings would produce a widespread rise in the prices of credit products. This raises the question: Is it possible that more dispersion in ratings can translate into higher ratings on average?

   We show that the combination of an increase in asset complexity and the ability of asset issuers to shop for ratings can produce ratings inflation, even if each rating agency produces an unbiased rating. The intuition behind our results is as follows: Each rating agency issues an unbiased forecast of an asset's value. However, if the announced rating is the maximum of all realized ratings, it will be a biased signal of the asset's true quality. The more ratings differ, the stronger are issuers' incentives to selectively disclose (shop for) ratings. For simple assets, agencies issue nearly identical forecasts. Asset issuers then disclose all ratings because more information reduces investors' uncertainty and increases the price they are willing to pay for the asset. For complex assets, ratings may differ, creating an incentive to shop for the best rating. There is a threshold level of asset complexity such that once this threshold is crossed, shopping becomes optimal and ratings inflation emerges. Furthermore, the link between asset complexity and ratings shopping can work in both directions. An issuer who shops for ratings might want to issue an even more complex asset, to get a broader menu of ratings to choose from. This, in turn, makes shopping even more valuable.

Biased ratings affect securities prices if investors are unaware of the bias. If past data led investors to believe that the complexity of assets was low, then they would rationally expect ratings to be unbiased. Once complexity increased, this belief would persist until the investors observe a sufficient amount of data to detect the bias.

A similar effect might have prompted a recent resurgence in asset issuers pressuring rating agencies to generate favorable ratings. If the guidelines for rating an asset are straightforward and all rating agencies must rate an asset the same way, then there is little pressure an issuer can exert. But if assets become more complex and there are now judgment calls to be made, the agency can legally come to many possible conclusions about what the rating should be. This creates the possibility for rating agency conflicts of interest that were not present, or not as severe, before. Thus, an increase in asset complexity could have prompted rating shopping by asset issuers and manipulation by ratings agencies.

Two types of evidence support this explanation. First, asset complexity increased. We do not argue that the complexity of any given asset increased. Rather, the composition of assets being sold changed so that the more complex type of asset, the structured financial products—particularly those that were mortgage-backed—became more prevalent. For example, while under $10 billion in structured finance collateralized debt obligations (CDOs) were distributed in 2000, nearly $200 billion were issued in 2006 (Hu 2007).

Second, the pattern of downgrades and defaults in the last few years confirms this relationship between asset complexity and overoptimistic ratings: Complex CDOs had significantly higher default rates than simple corporate bonds with identical ratings. Similarly, mortgage-backed securities whose underlying credit risk, correlation risk, and prepayment risk are notoriously difficult to assess, experienced more widespread downgrades than did assets based on other collateral types.[6]

EVALUATING POLICY RECOMMENDATIONS

Issuer-Initiated Ratings

One possible solution to the problem of ratings bias is to replace issuer-initiated ratings with investor-initiated ratings. We show that even though some investors—those who, by law, can hold only highly rated securities—would prefer biased ratings, they cannot shop for ratings. To make this argument, we use the well-known model of information acquisition formulated by Grossman and

Stiglitz (1980). We then add to that framework a requirement that some investors buy investment-grade assets with sufficiently high ratings, as well as a market price, rather than a fixed cost, for information. We see that investor-initiated ratings bias has limited price impact. This is because if the investors shop for ratings, it is to find a rating agency that gives the asset an investment-grade rating. But once the investor finds that the asset is in a feasible investment set, she does not ignore the other ratings she has observed. Rather, she uses all available information to value the asset. Thus, all observed ratings, not just the publicly disclosed ones, affect the asset's price. The only price effect of ratings shopping is to increase demand for some borderline assets that would not be investment grade, were it not for their inflated ratings.

The drawback of investor-initiated ratings is the potential for underprovision of information. Since information requires a fixed cost to discover and is free (or, at least, quite cheap) to replicate, efficiency dictates that a discovered piece of information should be distributed to every asset investor so that all investors benefit from lower asset payoff risk. Yet, when investors have to pay for ratings themselves, either no investors or too few investors may end up being informed.

Increasing Competition among Rating Agencies

Because market failures are often associated with a lack of free competition, policy makers have taken measures to increase competition. While this might cure some problems with ratings provision, it does not remedy ratings shopping. In fact, it worsens the problem. When the issuer shops for ratings, the more draws the issuer can observe before choosing a rating—that is, the larger the number of rating agencies—the higher this bias will be. This result follows from the simple observation that the more rating agencies available, the greater the possibilities of ratings shopping. Of course, having more rating agencies does not ensure that an asset issuer will observe more ratings. If not, then the bias will stay constant. However, if some issuers prefer to obtain more ratings than what were previously available to them, increasing the number of agencies will increase the number of observed ratings and the bias from shopping for the best one. It is also possible that the price of ratings falls because of higher competition, encouraging asset issuers to sample more ratings, which would increase ratings bias even more.

The Design of Risk-Management Legislation

Another target for criticism in the ratings scandal has been the design of risk management rules and the emphasis they put on ratings. Many banks and pension funds can hold only assets that earn sufficiently high ratings from one of the nationally recognized statistical ratings organizations. This rule puts an enormous amount of pressure on asset issuers to ensure that their assets achieve this rating. Without a high rating, the pool of potential investors is considerably smaller, and the asset's prices will be considerably lower. By itself, revising this regulation will not solve the problem of ratings shopping. As we argued before, bias in issuer-initiated ratings can arise, even in the absence of such regulation. It is likely, however, that risk management regulation further encouraged ratings shopping by increasing the payoff from acquiring a high rating.

Mandatory Disclosure Laws

Perhaps an obvious suggestion is to mandate disclosure of all ratings. While, in theory, that is a cure, in practice, it is difficult to directly regulate the transmission of information. For example, the line between informal advice and a rating can be easily blurred. Prohibiting a discussion of how various assets might be rated if they were issued could easily be ruled an infringement on free speech. An additional problem is that when undesirable ratings are proposed, the asset in question is frequently restructured. A tiny change in asset structure would make the previous rating no longer applicable and could effectively hide that rating.

GOING FORWARD

What does the relationship between asset complexity and the incentives to bias ratings mean for future regulatory efforts? First, the incentive for rating agencies to inflate ratings and the ability of asset issuers to shop for the best rating can each independently produce ratings bias. Dealing with one of these problems without addressing the other is unlikely to solve the problem. Second, just because these effects did not produce upward bias in ratings in the 1980s and 1990s does not mean that the problems in the rating market structure are harmless. There is good reason to think that such incentives were latent and only emerged when assets were sufficiently complex that regulation was no longer detailed enough to keep them in check. Finally, the ability of ratings manipulation and shopping to affect asset prices only exists when the buyers of assets are unaware of the games being played by the issuer and rating agency. While that was likely the case for some buyers two years ago, today major market participants must have some awareness of the perils of relying on selectively disclosed ratings. If investors mentally discount ratings, then this problem has corrected itself. However, if we forgo this opportunity to re-think how ratings are provided, the next bout of financial innovation could trigger another round of ratings inflation and the financial market turmoil that ensues.

More broadly, our findings highlight the role that institutions, rules, and market structure play in an industry that produces information. A central question in the mechanism design literature is: Which institutions are most desirable when information is asymmetric or dispersed? The reverse question is equally important: What information do agents choose to observe or disclose in a given institution and market structure? As the recent crisis highlights, understanding the information provision is as important as understanding the institutions. When information production runs amok, large economic fluctuations can result.

NOTES

1. Adelson: Director of structured finance research at Nomura Securities. Testimony before the Committee on Financial Services, U.S. House of Representatives, September 27, 2007. On January 26, 2008, the *New York Times* quoted Moody's CEO, saying, "In hindsight, it is pretty clear that there was a failure in some key assumptions that were supporting our analytics and our models." He said that one reason for the failure was that the information quality given to Moody's, both the completeness and veracity, was deteriorating. See also page 10 of the "Summary Report of Issues Identified in the Commission Staff's

Examinations of Select Credit Rating Agencies," United States Securities and Exchange Commission, July 8, 2008.

2. Mark Zandi, "Financial Shock," FT Press, July 2008.

3. Quote from the *New York Times Magazine*, "Triple-A-Failure," April 27, 2008. Other articles making similar arguments include "Why Credit-rating Agencies Blew It: Mystery Solved," available from http://robertreich.blogspot.com/2007/10/they-mystery-of-why-credit-rating.html; "Stopping the Subprime Crisis," *New York Times*, July 25, 2007; "When It Goes Wrong," *The Economist*, September 20, 2007; and "Credit and Blame," *The Economist*, September 6, 2007.

4. The credit rating industry switched from the investor-pays to the issuer-pays model in the early 1970s. This is believed to have happened because of the widespread availability of photocopier technology. See, for instance, White (2007).

5. Supra, Note 1.

6. The first nonmortgage securitization was equipment leases, followed by credit cards and auto loans, and, more recently, home equity, lease finance, manufactured housing, student loans, and synthetic structures. All of those types of collateral used tranching structures that were measurably simpler than those for RMBS. They had correspondingly lower default rates for similarly rated assets (Mason and Rosner 2007).

REFERENCES

Becker, B., and T. Milbourn. 2008. Reputation and competition: Evidence from the credit rating industry, HBS Finance Working Paper 09-051.

Bolton, P., X. Freixas, and J. Shapiro. 2008. The credit ratings game. Working Paper.

Damiano, E., H. Li, and W. Suen. 2008. Credible ratings. *Theoretical Economics* 3: 325–365.

Grossman, S., and J. Stiglitz. 1980. On the impossibility of informationally efficient markets. *American Economic Review* 70 (3): 393–408.

Hu, J. 2007. Assessing the credit risk of CDOs backed by structured finance securities: Rating analysts' challenges and solutions. Moody's Investors' Service working paper.

Mason, J. R., and J. Rosner. 2007. Where did the risk go? How misapplied bond ratings cause mortgage-backed securities and collateralized debt obligation market disruptions. SSRN Working paper 1027475.

Mathis, J., J. McAndrews, and J. C. Rochet. 2008. Rating the raters. Toulouse working paper.

Skreta, V., and L. Veldkamp. 2009. Ratings shopping and asset complexity: A theory of ratings inflation. *Journal of Monetary Economics* 56: 5.

White, L. 2007. A new law for the bond rating industry. *Regulation* 30 (1): 48–52.

ABOUT THE AUTHORS

Vasiliki Skreta is an assistant professor of economics at New York University's Stern School of Business. Before going to teach there, Professor Skreta was an assistant professor at the University of Minnesota and at the University of California, in Los Angeles. Professor Skreta's main research contributions are on mechanism design with limited commitment: This area presents special difficulties because the celebrated revelation principle is inapplicable. She has also published in other aspects of mechanism design. More recently, she has been working on the optimal design of industries that produce information, such as the credit rating agencies and other certification intermediaries. Her research has been supported by the National Science Foundation and by other grants. Professor Skreta holds a B.A.

in economics from Athens University of Economics and Business, and a Ph.D. in economics from the University of Pittsburgh.

Laura Veldkamp earned her Ph.D. in economics from the Stanford Graduate School of Business in 2001 and has taught economics at INSEAD in France, at Princeton University, and is currently at New York University's Stern School of Business, where she is a tenured associate professor. Professor Veldkamp's recent work focuses on how information is acquired by producers and financial market participants and how that information affects production and investment decisions. This work has been published in leading economics and finance journals such as *American Economic Review, Journal of Finance, Review of Financial Studies,* and the *Journal of Monetary Economics.* She is currently working on a book for Princeton University Press titled *Information Choice in Macroeconomics and Finance.*

CHAPTER 34

The Pitfalls of Originate-to-Distribute in Bank Lending

ANTJE BERNDT, Ph.D.
Assistant Professor of Finance at the Tepper School of Business,
Carnegie Mellon University

ANURAG GUPTA, Ph.D.
Associate Professor of Finance at the Weatherhead School of Management,
Case Western Reserve University

The historic credit crisis of 2007 and 2008 brought an important question sharply into focus—to what extent should bank credit be allowed to change from the traditional relationship banking model to an originate-to-distribute model?[1] Over the last 15 years, an active over-the-counter market has emerged for the sales and trading of syndicated corporate loans. Fueled by securitization and the tremendous growth in collateralized loan obligation funds, the secondary syndicated loan market has grown in annual trading volume almost sixfold from $60b in 1997 to $342b in 2007. This transaction-oriented model has transformed bank credit to an originate-to-distribute model, by which banks can originate loans, earn their fees, and then distribute them to third-party investors.[2] This distribution of syndicated loans is largely opaque since there is no centralized exchange or clearinghouse in which such transactions are recorded.

The shift to the originate-to-distribute model of bank credit has important implications for all market participants, including the originating banks, the loan investors, the borrowing firms, and the regulators. The banks' superior information about their borrowers gives rise to concerns about adverse selection—are the banks selling off loans about which they have negative private (unobservable) information? In a perfect market, this should lead to a breakdown of the secondary loan market because of the classic lemons problem. The issue of adverse selection is important from the perspective of the loan investors as well—can they trust that the bank selling the loan is doing so because of legitimate motives (like capital relief and risk management) rather than because of negative private information? Alternatively, does it lead to a moral hazard in the form of an impairment in the monitoring function of banks, thereby having a negative effect on the borrowers?

After all, once a bank has sold off its portion of the syndicated loan, it would have little incentive to monitor the borrower.

There are several policy questions that arise from this debate. Should the regulatory authorities restrict the originate-to-distribute activities of banks? Should they enforce enhanced disclosure of the banks' activities in the loan sales market? How are the borrowing firms being affected, in the long run, by banks moving from relationship lending to the originate-to-distribute model of credit? Does this shift lead to value creation or value reduction in the corporate sector? These questions are, ultimately, empirical ones. Using extensive data from the syndicated loan market, we conduct the first empirical investigation of these important but as yet unanswered questions.

Banks could sell loans in the secondary market because of negative private information about the borrower, or for legitimate reasons such as capital relief, risk diversification, improving balance sheet liquidity, and reducing financing frictions and their cost of capital. These latter, potentially positive effects of loan sales on banks have led to a point of view that the originate-to-distribute model of bank credit is socially desirable. There is also a vast academic literature on banks being special, since they generate proprietary information about the borrowers in the course of lending to them. The secondary market loan buyers who do not have a lending relationship with the borrowers are then likely to be at an information disadvantage when buying a loan originated by a relationship bank. This could lead to moral hazard and adverse selection problems that have been discussed by Gorton and Pennacchi (1988), Pennacchi (1988), and others. Banks that sell loans would have little incentive to engage in costly screening and monitoring of the borrowers. In addition, they would have an incentive to sell the loans of the borrowers about whom they have negative private information.

From a borrower's perspective, there are potentially positive as well as negative consequences of their loans being sold in the secondary market. As shown by Gupta, Singh, and Zebedee (2008), banks charge a lower interest rate on loans that they can readily sell, thereby lowering the cost of capital of such borrowers. Other studies have shown that the liquidity of their loans increases the access to debt capital for such obligors, and has positive information effects. Loan sales lead to a breakdown of the lending relationship between the bank and the borrower, however, which could be detrimental for the borrower. It has been shown that stable lending relationships could enhance the availability of credit for some borrowers, reduce the requirement of collateral, and reduce the costs of financial distress for borrowers. Studies have also shown that loan liquidity comes at the price of harsher covenants for the borrower. It also makes it more difficult for the borrower to renegotiate with the lender if the loan has been distributed to a large number of loan investors.

Theoretical models in this area (for example, Parlour and Plantin 2008) incorporate some of these opposing effects. However, from an empirical standpoint, it is not clear which of these effects dominate. If the originate-to-distribute model of credit creates perverse incentives for banks to originate bad loans and then sell them off in the secondary market, such borrowers should underperform their peers in the long run. Since theoretical arguments on this issue can go either way, it needs to be resolved empirically. Our study is the first one to empirically examine this issue by analyzing the long-run performance of borrowers with and without an active secondary market for their loans.

We analyze a set of 1,054 borrowers, the largest sample in this strand of literature thus far. These are all U.S. publicly listed firms that borrowed in the syndicated term loan market from January 1, 2000, until December 31, 2004. We do not consider more recent originations since we need three years of stock-return data after loan origination to analyze the long-run equity performance of all borrowers. The loan origination data are obtained from the DealScan database from the Loan Pricing Corporation. We also use the secondary loan market database from the Loan Syndication and Trading Association (LSTA) to classify borrowers into two groups, those with and without an active secondary market for their loans.

LSTA receives bid-and-ask quotes on several thousand loans on a daily basis from over 35 dealers that represent the loan trading desks of virtually every major commercial and investment bank. These dealers account for more than 80 percent of the secondary market trading in syndicated loans. Therefore, the LSTA quotes provide an adequate representation of the trading activity in the secondary syndicated loan market. Using these quotes, LSTA offers a daily mark-to-market pricing service on several thousand syndicated loans to numerous institutions that manage bank loan portfolios. Following Gupta, Singh, and Zebedee (2008), if a borrower's term loans are quoted in our secondary market database by at least two dealers, and the first quoted bid price is greater than 98 (i.e., it is a *par* loan at the initiation of trading), we assign the borrower to the *LIQ* group, which identifies borrowers who have loans with an active secondary market. If there were at least two dealers that quoted bid prices for a loan, it is reasonable to infer that it was possible to trade the loan on that day. Furthermore, if the loan is first quoted at par, it was not a distress sale, since the loan did not have to be discounted to be sold. All other borrowers are assigned to the *NoLIQ* group. *NoLIQ* borrowers do not have an active secondary market for their loans.

Based on this classification, we find that 309 out of the 1,054 borrowers belong to the *LIQ* group. The remaining 745 have syndicated term loans originated from 2000 to 2004, but they are never liquid as per our definition. Our total sample of 1,054 borrowers represents a large proportion of firms in the corporate universe—they have, in the aggregate, about $3.3 trillion in market capitalization, $5.1 trillion in total assets, and over $800 billion in net sales. The median firm in the *LIQ* group is about three times larger than the median firm in the *NoLIQ* group. In addition, most *LIQ* firms are speculative grade (89 percent, versus 66 percent for *NoLIQ* firms), highlighting that loan investors are primarily interested in buying speculative grade loans because of their higher yields.

We then estimate the risk-adjusted long-run abnormal stock returns for these two portfolios, *LIQ* and *NoLIQ*, using a battery of tests that have been used in prior studies on measuring long-run abnormal performance (quite often in the IPO and SEO literature). We use calendar-time methods that allow simulation of investment strategies that could be implemented by a portfolio manager as well as event-time methods that focus on the aftermarket performance of event firms. Studies have found that the event-time methods may overstate the long-run performance of a firm, and, since they have time-period overlap, can introduce cross-sectional dependence that could lead to poorly specified test statistics. Therefore, we base

Exhibit 34.1   Long-Run Abnormal Returns of Different Borrower Groups

12 months		24 months		36 months	
EW	VW	EW	VW	EW	VW
Active Loan Market (*LIQ*)					
−0.73	−1.09	−0.93	−1.06	−0.75	−0.74
(−1.57)	(−2.29)	(−2.62)	(−2.27)	(−2.79)	(−1.93)
No Active Loan Market (*NoLIQ*)					
0.30	−0.21	0.39	−0.18	0.40	−0.19
(1.87)	(−1.10)	(2.37)	(−0.89)	(2.32)	(−0.92)
NoLIQ-LIQ					
1.19	0.99	1.36	0.97	1.18	0.67
(2.34)	(2.06)	(3.47)	(2.05)	(3.81)	(1.79)

our inferences primarily on calendar-time methods, using the event-time methods as a robustness check.

Our primary abnormal return measure is the alpha coefficient from the monthly time-series regression of excess returns on the three Fama-French factors MKT, SMB, and HML, and on the momentum factor UMD. The table in Exhibit 34.1 shows the monthly alphas from regressing the *LIQ* and *NoLIQ* portfolio returns on these four factors along with their t-statistics in parentheses, for equally as well as value-weighted portfolios. We also report the alpha for a portfolio that is long in borrowers with no active loan market and short in borrowers that have an active loan market, which is indicative of the abnormal return of an admissible trading strategy based on the liquidity of the borrowers' loans in the secondary market.

The results in Exhibit 34.1 show that the borrowers whose loans are sold in the secondary market underperform their peers by an economically large and statistically significant magnitude of about 9 percent annually, on a risk-adjusted basis, over the three-year period following the initial sale of their loans. The result is similar using value-weighted or equally weighted portfolios. On the other hand, borrowers who do not have an active loan market do not underperform in the long run. The long-short portfolio performance indicates that the strategy would yield an abnormal annual return of between 8 and 14 percent, depending on the method of construction of the portfolios.

To examine the robustness of our risk-factor adjustment, we expand the four-factor model to up to eight factors by including liquidity, term, default, and volatility factors. The results for all of these models are similar to the ones reported for the four-factor model described earlier—borrowers with an active secondary market for their loans underperform their peers, while borrowers without an active loan secondary market do not underperform. The magnitude and statistical significance of this underperformance also remains remarkably stable across the different factor models tested in this study. Censoring the data to remove the smallest quintile (or decile) of firms does not change the results, which shows that our results are not driven by the smallest firms in our sample.

Stratification at the median shows that the underperformance in the *LIQ* firms is concentrated within speculative grade, small firms with high leverage. These firms are likely to be more opaque, with less public information about them. Therefore, the private information advantage of the bank is likely to be greater, resulting in a greater ability of the banks to sell the loans of firms that they internally believe will perform poorly in the future (adverse selection). Alternatively, these firms are more likely to benefit from the discipline of bank monitoring, since they may not have effective corporate governance mechanisms in place, or as much public scrutiny as the other firms. In this case, the weakening of their relationship with their lenders could affect them negatively because of weaker monitoring by the banks (moral hazard). We stratify by industry as well, and find that our results are not being driven by borrowers in any particular industry.

For additional robustness, we estimate the mean calendar-time abnormal returns (MCTARs) for the *LIQ* and the *NoLIQ* groups. We construct 125 reference portfolios based on size, book-to-market ratio and momentum, subtract the reference portfolio's return from each firm's return, average these abnormal returns each calendar month for the cross-section of firms in the sample in that month, and then estimate a grand mean monthly abnormal return by averaging through time. These MCTARs serve as an alternative to the alphas obtained from factor regressions. We find very similar results—firms with an active secondary market for their loans underperform their peers by a statistically significant margin of between 8.8 percent and 10.2 percent per year over a three-year period subsequent to the sale of their loans. Firms without an active secondary market for their loans do not underperform their peers over a similar horizon. Further robustness checks using event-time methods such as cumulative abnormal returns as well as buy-and-hold abnormal returns yield similar results.

In addition to abnormal stock returns, we also examine the relative changes in the valuation of the borrowers in these two groups using the Tobin's q (ratio of the sum of the market value of equity plus the book value of debt to total assets), which is a widely used proxy for firm valuation. The changes in Tobin's q are match adjusted relative to nonborrowers with the same two-digit SIC code and Tobin's q (within 90 percent and 110 percent), as recommended by prior studies. The 36-month-ahead difference in Tobin's q relative to the reference group firms is calculated using levels as well as changes in levels of Tobin's q. The results are striking—we find that, on average, borrowers with an active secondary loan market lose between 11.5 and 14 percent of their value (as a percentage of total assets) when compared to the reference group firms over the three-year period subsequent to the initial sale of their loans. This result is significant for both average and median long-run changes in Tobin's q. Borrowers without an active loan market do not show any abnormal changes in Tobin's q.

The significant long-run underperformance and value reduction of borrowers with an active secondary loan market is a striking result, for which we offer two possible explanations. First, banks may be cherry picking by preferentially selling loans of the borrowers about whom they have negative private information that is unobservable to outsiders. Alternatively, banks may be knowingly originating some lemons, primarily to expand their origination-fee-based income, since they are able to sell these loans in the secondary market to outside investors (mostly nonbank financial institutions and hedge funds). In a perfect market, reputation concerns should prevent a bank from cherry picking or selling lemons on a systematic basis. If it is still happening, it is perhaps an indication of a market failure, in which investors have not (yet) recognized the adverse selection that they are facing in the secondary syndicated loan market. This bears a remarkable resemblance to the events that have unfolded in the monumental subprime mortgage crisis that began in 2007.

Our second explanation is based on the moral hazard argument. Perhaps the weakening of the bank-borrower relationship due to the sale of the loan leads to diminished monitoring of the borrowers. This may hurt the borrowers, since banks play an important corporate governance role, help borrowers make optimal investment and operating decisions, restrict excessive risk taking and opportunistic managerial behavior on the part of the borrowers, and thus have a positive wealth effect on them, as documented in prior studies.

Based on our tests and results, it is not possible to clearly distinguish which one of the two explanations dominates. It is likely that both of these mechanisms play some role in explaining our results. Also, despite our extensive robustness tests, there is always a possibility that some of the abnormal returns that we observe may be partly due to inadequate risk adjustments.

Our results have important policy implications for regulators. Whether the underperformance and value reduction of borrowers with an active secondary loan market is due to banks originating and selling lemons, or due to diminished monitoring, it raises serious questions about the extent to which the originate-to-distribute model of bank credit is socially desirable. While there are clear benefits of enhancing the liquidity of the secondary syndicated loan market, we demonstrate some of its long-term undesirable consequences. It is likely that one of the major reasons for the latter is the highly deregulated nature of the secondary syndicated loan market. Should the regulators impose restrictions on the sales of bank loans by originating banks? Perhaps. At the minimum, they could require the originating banks to retain a certain proportion of the loans on their balance sheet to limit the moral hazard and adverse selection problems. A similar proposal has been put forward in the recently announced new regulations for financial institutions in the area of mortgage loans. In addition, there must be additional disclosure requirements about the loans being traded in the secondary market, along with disclosure about the market participants that are trading them. A loan trading exchange with a clearinghouse could be a possible solution, somewhat similar to the platform recently created for the trading of credit default swaps. It is certainly clear that the originate-to-distribute model of bank credit needs to be modified, and the transactions made more transparent.

NOTES

1. This article is based on Berndt and Gupta (2009).
2. The risk of these borrowers can also be distributed, in an opaque manner, through the credit default swap (CDS) market. We do not include this channel in our study because of the unavailability of a sufficiently large overlapping sample of obligors that have traded syndicated loans as well as CDS contracts written on their corporate debt. During our sample period, the loan sales market was concentrated among speculative-grade obligors, whereas the CDS market was largely an investment-grade market.

REFERENCES

Berndt, A., and A. Gupta. 2009. Moral hazard and adverse selection in the originate-to-distribute model of bank credit. *Journal of Monetary Economics* 56: 725–743.

Gorton, G., and G. Pennacchi. 1988. Banks and loan sales: Marketing non-marketable assets. *Journal of Monetary Economics* 35: 389–411.

Gupta, A., A. K. Singh, and A. Zebedee. 2008. Liquidity in the pricing of syndicated loans. *Journal of Financial Markets* 11: 339–376.

Parlour, C. A., and G. Plantin. 2008. Loan sales and relationship banking. *Journal of Finance* 63: 1291–1314.

Pennacchi, G., 1988. Loan sales and the cost of bank capital. *Journal of Finance* 43: 375–395.

ABOUT THE AUTHORS

Dr. Antje Berndt is an assistant professor of finance at the Tepper School of Business, Carnegie Mellon University. She holds a master's degree in mathematical finance from Columbia University and a Ph.D. in statistics from Stanford University. Berndt's research focuses on the econometric analysis of financial markets, with concentrations in four areas: banking, the valuation of corporate debt and credit derivatives, the interaction of market and credit risk, and the effect of fiscal policy on financial markets. She has published articles in top finance journals such as the *Review of Financial Studies*, the *Review of Finance*, and the *Journal of Monetary Economics*. Her work has been featured in a number of media outlets, including the *Wall Street Journal*, CNBC, NPR Marketplace, Reuters, and Bloomberg News. Dr. Berndt was the recipient of the Fulbright Enterprise Scholarship, the Moody's research award and the GARP risk management research award. She was awarded the PNC professorship in computational finance for 2007 through 2010.

Dr. Anurag Gupta is an associate professor of finance at the Weatherhead School of Management, Case Western Reserve University. His research and teaching interests include corporate risk management, fixed-income option pricing models, capital adequacy of financial institutions, liquidity risk analysis, and credit risk management in the banking industry. Dr. Gupta's research work has been published in top finance journals like the *Journal of Financial Economics*, *Journal of Finance*, *Journal of Monetary Economics*, *Journal of Financial Markets*, *Journal of Banking and Finance* and the *Journal of Derivatives*. His work has been written about in mainstream global media (*Wall Street Journal*, Reuters, Bloomberg, Financial Post, and so on), and he has been interviewed live on CNBC's Squawk Box on the financial crisis. Much of his current ongoing research is focused on the problems in the banking industry in the aftermath of the financial crisis. He earned his Ph.D. in finance from the New York University Stern School of Business, his M.B.A. from the Indian Institute of Management in Calcutta, and his B.S. in chemical engineering at the Indian Institute of Technology in Delhi.

PART V

Risk Management
and Mismanagement

CHAPTER 35

Behavioral Basis of the Financial Crisis

J. V. RIZZI
Senior Investment Strategist, CapGen Financial*

M ajor strides were made in risk management during the 1990s. Yet despite these advances, financial institutions suffered large losses following the collapse of the subprime and structured products markets. Although we know how risk decisions should be made, less is known on how these decisions are actually made.

Risk management should encourage profitable risk taking while discouraging unprofitable and catastrophic risk. Our existing risk measures account for perhaps 95 percent of what occurs. The major catastrophic risks lurk in the fat tails of the remaining 5 percent. We tend to underestimate these improbable risks because of behavioral biases.

Institutions and regulators are changing their risk systems and personnel to address this issue. The problem, however, is not only with the systems or the quality of the personnel but within the individuals themselves. Most individuals have a model of how the world works. When challenged by events, we try to explain away the events. Behavioral economics provides insights into risk-assessment errors and possible remedies.

This article outlines a behavioral risk framework to address judgment bias and develop appropriate responses. The framework supplements current quantitative risk management by improving responses to risk changes over time. It also helps explain how the market crisis caught experts by surprise.

BEHAVIORAL FINANCE FRAMEWORK

Risk is exposure to the consequences of the unknown. Risk can be classified along two dimensions. The first concerns high frequency events with relatively clear cause-and-effect relationships like missing your connecting flight. Other risks such as health problems occur infrequently. Consequently, the cause-and-effect relationship is unclear. The second dimension is impact severity. No matter how remote,

---

*The views expressed here represent those of the author, and not CapGen Financial.

high impact events cannot be ignored because they can threaten an institution's existence as was demonstrated in the current market crisis.

Cyclical risks are low frequency–high impact events characterized by their fat-tailed loss distributions. Investors incurring such risk can expect mainly small, positive events but are subject to a few cases of extreme loss. These risks are difficult to understand. First, there are insufficient data to determine meaningful probability distributions. In this case, the statistics are descriptive, not predictive. Consequently, no amount of mathematics can tease out certainty from uncertainty. Second, and perhaps more important, infrequency clouds perception. Risk estimates become anchored on recent events. Overemphasis on recent events can also produce an underappreciation of risk during a bull market because instruments are priced without regard to the possibility of a crash. These facts lead to risk mispricing and the procyclical nature of risk appetite.

Behavioral finance examines how risk managers gather, interpret, and process information. Specifically, it concentrates on perception and cognitive bias. It recognizes models can influence behavior and shape decisions. These biases can corrupt the decision process, leading to suboptimal results as emotions override self-control.

Overconfidence

Overconfidence occurs when we exaggerate our predictive skills and ignore the impact of chance or outside circumstances. Risk managers who took credit for results during the boom failed to consider the impact of randomness and mean reversion, creating an illusion of control. Compounding this is their selective recall of confirming information to overestimate their ability to predict the correct outcome, which inhibits learning. Disappointments and surprise are characteristics of processes subject to overconfidence.

Industry and product experts are especially prone to overconfidence on the basis of knowledge and control illusions. Knowledge is frequently confused with familiarity. This is reflected in the number of industry experts, including, most famously, the former Federal Reserve chairman who missed the collapse of the housing and structured credit bottoms.

Control reflects the unfounded belief of our ability to influence or structure around risk. Risk is accepted because we believe we can escape its consequences because of our ability to control it. Examples include the perceived ability to distribute or hedge risk independent of the likelihood of being better or faster at identifying risk than the market.

This reflects an optimistic underestimate of costs while overestimating gains. Optimism is heightened by anchoring when disportionate weight is given to the first information received. This is usually based on the original plan, which tends to support the transaction. These time-delayed consequences magnify overconfidence as individuals weigh short-term performance at a higher level than longer-term consequences.

Statistical

Statistical bias involves confusing beliefs for probability and skill for chance by selecting evidence in accordance with our expectations. Economics is a social science based on human behavior. Prices are not determined by random number machines. Rather, they come from trades by real people.

Statistically based risk management practices are inherently limited. They are unable to reflect the hidden risk that the market conditions may change, such as formerly diversified positions that begin moving together, triggering unexpected losses. The changes are unexpected because such movements are unfamiliar. We tend to view the unfamiliar as improbable, and the improbable is frequently ignored.

Another statistical error prevalent during a boom is extrapolation bias. This occurs when current events or trends are assumed to continue into the foreseeable future independent of historical experience, sample size, or mean reversion. Undoubtedly, this resulted in many of the projections underlying structured credit models.

Since the subjective probability of an event depends on recent experience, expectations of low frequency events, like a market or firm collapse, are very small. These types of events are ignored or deemed impossible, particularly when recent occurrences are lacking. This causes a false sense of security as risk is underestimated, or assumed away, and capital is misallocated. Unlikely events are neither impossible nor remote. In fact, unlikely events are likely to occur because there are so many unlikely events that can occur. Thus, the longer the time period, the higher the likelihood of a *Black Swan* event, like a nationwide house price decline, occurring.

Herding

There are also social aspects to decision making, such as when individuals are influenced by the decisions of others as reflected in herding and groupthink. Herding occurs when a group of individuals mimic the decisions of others. Through herding, individuals avoid falling behind and looking bad if they pursue an alternative action. It is based on the social pressure to conform, and reflects safety by hiding in the crowd. In so doing, you can blame any failing on the collective action and maintain your reputation and job. Even though you recognize market risk, it pays to follow the crowd. This is referred to as a positive feedback loop or momentum investing, which can produce short-term self-fulfilling prophecies.

Herding amplifies credit cycle effects, as decisions become more uniform. The cycle begins with a credit expansion leading to an asset price increase. Investors rush in to avoid being left behind, using rising asset values to support even more credit. This explains why bankers continued questionable risk practices even though they feared this was unsustainable and leading to a crisis. Eventually, an event occurs, such as a move by the central bank, which triggers an asset price decline. This causes losses, a decline in credit, and an exit of investors, which strains market liquidity.

Groupthink

Groupthink, or organizational pressure, enhances cognitive biases. It occurs when individuals identify with the organization and uncritically accept its actions. Once the commitment is made, inconsistent information is suppressed. Consequently, mutually reinforcing individual biases and unrealistic views are validated.

Experts are prone to groupthink. They tend to limit information from all but other expert sources. Thus, they repeat statements until they become accepted dogma, regardless of their validity, because of a lack of critical thinking.

The subprime collapse illustrates this. The industry participants used the same consultants and models for their projections. The consultants based their reports and recommendations on the surveys of industry participants. Once the perception of a bull market took hold, it was reinforced and accepted uncritically. When the crash occurred, the experts were taken by surprise by a supposed perfect storm.

This is illustrated in a June 2006 *BusinessWeek* cover story that surveyed risk officers at numerous institutions, including Bear Stearns and Lehman Brothers. They believed that despite the risks taken, they were safer than ever. This belief was based on complex risk models and market diversification. The faith in risk management encouraged institutions to increase their risk exposures because they believed the risks were under control.

During a late-stage boom with high sentiment levels, behavioral risk factors will dominate and quantitative risk measures will be unreliable. This is reflected by Charles Prince, the former CEO of Citigroup, who famously said, "As long as the music is playing, you have to get up and dance." This is characterized as irrational exuberance, whereby prices are driven principally by momentum and herding is reflected in high liquidity levels.

CURRENT CRISIS

Setting

A declining economy and falling markets triggered aggressive Federal Reserve interest rate cutting and liquidity injections in 2001 to 2002. Liquidity-driven technicals improved, resulting in falling risk premiums, increasing credit asset prices. Institutions responded by adopting an asset-intensive carry trade strategy, which involves borrowing for the short term to invest in longer-term risk assets.

A credit bubble formed as liquidity-driven technicals surpassed fundamentals. This was reflected in historically low credit-risk spreads in the real estate, leveraged buyout, and structured credit markets. Spread narrowing and a flattening yield curve reduced the attractiveness of the carry trade, putting pressure on institutional accrual and trading budgets.

In the search for yield, institutions adopted a procyclical asset heavy strategy.

This strategy involved going long on higher-risk assets for the institution's own account instead of distribution. The strategy is reflected in principal finance, merchant banking, bridge loans, and warehousing activities. These activities represented up to 75 percent of revenues at some institutions.

This caused a major credit boom, during which prices exceeded underlying fundamental economic values. Such cycles, while predictable, are difficult to manage for several reasons. First, financial institution compensation is tied to peer group comparisons. Thus, firms and individuals not following their peers suffer. Next, organizations frequently discourage pessimism. Therefore, conservative risk managers and bankers are pressured to become optimistic or leave. Finally, institutions risk losing bankers if their risk activities are curtailed.

Positive short-term results frequently mask long-term risks. Seemingly high returns can reflect the subjective probability of an event that has not occurred in the time period studied. Investing in such instruments is profitable most of the time. Eventually, a beyond-the-data event occurs. Individuals and institutions succumbed to a bias of assuming that the absence of evidence implied evidence of risk absence.

Concerns

The appropriateness of the asset heavy portfolio strategy depends on several factors. Pricing and trading discipline is needed to ensure an adequate risk premium is earned. Maintaining discipline becomes increasingly difficult as the cycle continues.

Next, the strategy involves incurring increased systematic or beta risk exposure versus value-adding alpha returns. Structured products are less liquid than market-traded investments. The return on structured products consequently reflects compensation for liquidity risk. The liquidity premium was mischaracterized as alpha. Thus, liquidity risk was underreported. This was subsequently discovered during the crisis.

Unfortunately, apparent success breeds an inability to imagine the possibility of failure, and warnings were ignored. Firms continued to underestimate the likelihood and impact of unlikely events. Widespread credit risk underpricing existed because of an emphasis on nominal returns.

It is difficult to price rationally when risk seems remote and hard to measure, and when conditions seem favorable. The last market correction had occurred more than three years before and was largely forgotten by the first half of 2007. Thus, risk sensitivity had diminished. This recognition problem is rooted in the complex nature of cyclical risk.

Reinforcement

The complexity of low frequency–high impact cyclical risk is compounded by institutional factors such as budgets and compensation systems that reinforce the behavioral bias effect. These systems favor consistent earnings and misread low frequency–high impact risk profitability.

Risk models also contribute to the problem by presenting the illusion of safety and control leading to overoptimism. Consequently, models underestimated low frequency–high impact cyclical risk. The underlying exposure builds during a bull market as apparent risk declines, while the losses materialize in the bear market cycle. This anomaly is due to social and psychological biases resulting in bounded rationality. Ignoring these facts substitutes an inaccurate normative model for the real world.

The objective is to supplement existing quantitative risk management with developments taken from the evolving field of behavioral finance. In so doing, it can reduce future losses during the credit cycle as risk management evolves to a more balanced system incorporating human behavior. This requires taking low probability worst case scenarios seriously, and developing appropriate responses. The process is similar to earthquake engineering, which does not attempt to predict a shock. Rather, the focus is on constructing a structure to withstand a certain shock level.

CONCLUSION

The market appears to be thawing. While no two cycles are identical, we must resist the temptation to say, "This time is different." The deeper we are into illiquid credits, products, and structures, the more difficult it becomes to manage risk. The key is to identify potential adverse scenarios, apply a stress test to determine their impact, compare the test results to our risk appetite and take appropriate portfolio decisions. This entails adopting countercyclical portfolio strategies despite negative short-term revenue implications. This requires adopting difficult infrastructure changes.

Organizational obstacles inhibit appropriate responses to high impact–low probability risks. Chief among the obstacles are short-term compensation systems that reinforce behavioral biases. This leads to a potentially fatal neglect of the longer-term build of risk. As Robert Merton noted, "The amount of risk we take personally, individually, or collectively is not a physical given constant. We chose it. Behavioral finances offer a means to choose wisely as it affects both individual decision making and market efficiency. You ignore behavioral risk at your own peril."

ABOUT THE AUTHOR

Joseph V. Rizzi is a senior investment strategist for CapGen Financial, a private equity firm focusing on financial institutions. Before that, he worked at ABN AMRO for a number of years in both the United States and Holland in the areas of risk management, structured finance, acquisition finance, and asset liability management. The author of numerous articles on lending, risk management, and financial accounting, he is also a frequent lecturer to academic and professional groups. He holds a B.A. degree (summa cum laude) from DePaul University, an M.B.A. from the University of Chicago, and a J.D. degree from Notre Dame University Law School (magna cum laude).

CHAPTER 36

Risk Management Failures During the Financial Crisis

DR. MICHEL CROUHY
Head of Research & Development, NATIXIS Corporate and Investment Bank

INTRODUCTION

Many people saw this crisis coming and sounded warning bells ahead of the sub-prime crisis, but they were ignored. Policy makers as early as 2006 had warned of the emerging weaknesses in financial markets and the global economy. But nobody listened. Too many people were busy making money originating mortgages, warehousing assets to be securitized, structuring CDOs, and distributing these structured credit products to investors desperately seeking investments that offer yield enhancement in an environment of low interest rates and low volatility.

The current crisis was thus an accident waiting to happen. The trigger was a series of events that struck out of the blue in the summer of 2007. First, the attempt by Bear Stearns to bail out two hedge funds hurt by subprime mortgage losses. Then, the first bailout by German regulators of IKB, a German regional bank that specialized in lending to small companies and not involved in mortgage lending at all. Finally, the freeze by BNP Paribas of three investment funds with assets of 2 billion euros because the bank could not value the subprime assets in the funds.

It seems that all of a sudden the market realized that mortgage-backed securities (MBS), collateralized debt obligations (CDOs) of asset-backed securities (ABS), and other structured products were mispriced. This led to information problems and liquidity problems that helped cause markets for important securities to freeze up and models to fall apart.

Information Problems

- Information was inadequate about the quality of the underlying mortgage loans and the borrowers, especially for subprime mortgages and affordability products that required little or no down payment, as well as no documentation of the borrower's income. These loans were also known as *liar loans.*
- Market participants lost confidence in the accuracy of the credit ratings of CDO tranches given by the rating agencies as a huge fraction of tranches of CDOs of ABS saw their ratings downgraded sometimes from AAA to non-investment grade, including default, in one shot.

- Market prices became unavailable or unrealistic for many securities, including those rated Triple-A.
- There was a lack of knowledge about the positions and liabilities of the major banks and other players, such as hedge funds and insurance companies.

Liquidity Problems

- Home buyers could not refinance their loans as they had expected, and they could not make the required payments when their mortgages reset at much higher interest rates.
- Hedge funds could not roll over the financing of their leveraged positions. As their losses increased, they had to sell off securities to meet demands for cash from lenders and investors who were trying to withdraw capital. Compounding the problem was the demand from primary dealers for more collateral. Hedge funds were forced, as a result, to unwind positions in illiquid markets, feeding a downward spiral in asset prices.
- SIVs (special investment vehicles) could not roll over their asset-backed commercial paper (ABCP), as rating agencies started to downgrade these structures. Most sponsoring banks ended up bailing out their SIVs and took over their assets on their balance sheet.
- Some investors, like money market funds, may hold only Triple-A rated securities. As these securities, in particular, Triple-A-rated super-senior tranches of CDOs, were downgraded, these investors were forced to sell these securities in illiquid markets putting more downward pressure on the price of structured credit products.

As more and more complex securities, such as MBS, CDOs of ABS, and so on, and later on, monolines, were downgraded, banks experienced huge amounts of losses and writedowns. These losses are far in excess of what pricing models, rating models, and risk models would have predicted. Risk measurement models totally underestimated the risks, and many risk managers didn't see it coming.

In this chapter, we first analyze what went wrong in risk management and risk modeling, and we then draw some lessons from this fiasco.

WHAT WENT WRONG IN RISK MANAGEMENT AND RISK MODELING

Major weaknesses in risk assessment and risk modeling are at the origin of the credit losses in financial institutions, worldwide, which mostly originate from an overreliance on:

- Misleading ratings from rating agencies
- Unrealistically simple risk models, that is, models that were not designed to deal with the complexity of structured credit products
- Inaccurate data
- Short-term financing with too little consideration for liquidity risk

Overreliance on Misleading Ratings from Rating Agencies

Rating agencies are at the center of the current crisis because many investors relied on their ratings for many diverse products. Money market funds are restricted to investing only in Triple-A assets and pension funds. Municipalities are restricted to investing in investment grade assets and base their investment decisions on the ratings attributed by the rating agencies. Many of these investors invested in assets that were both complex and contained exposure to subprime assets mainly because these assets benefited from an investment grade rating and were promising a yield higher than traditional assets, such as corporate and Treasury bonds, with an equivalent rating.

Investors in complex credit products had considerably less information at their disposal to assess the underlying credit quality of the assets they held in their portfolios than the originators. As a result, these end-investors often came to rely heavily on the risk assessments of rating agencies. Implicit in the investment decision is the assumption that ratings are timely and relatively stable. No one was expecting, until recently, a Triple-A asset to be downgraded to junk status within a few weeks or even a few days. The argument could be made that as the yields on these instruments exceeded those on equivalently rated corporations, the market knew they were not of the same credit or liquidity risk. But investors still misjudged the risk.

Large numbers of rating downgrades on structured credit products, in particular tranches of subprime CDOs, have thus revived the questions about the nature of structured finance ratings, their sensitivity to changes in credit fundamentals, the degree to which rating transitions should be expected to differ from those of corporate bonds, and the extent to which ratings can serve as universal measures of credit risk.[1]

In particular, the nature of the risks involved in holding a Triple-A-rated super-senior tranche of a subprime CDO was completely missed by all the players: rating agencies, regulators, financial institutions, and investors. Subprime CDOs are in fact CDO-squareds, because the underlying pool of assets of the CDO is not constituted of individual mortgages, but instead is composed of subprime residential mortgage-backed securities (RMBS), or mortgage bonds, that are themselves tranches of individual subprime mortgages.

Cliff Effects, or Nonlinearities, in the Risk of Subprime CDO Tranches

Perhaps one of the biggest failings in the subprime crisis was the failure to understand the binary (zero-one) nature of the senior tranches of subprime CDOs. The problem is that the initial level of subordination for a Triple-B mortgage bond is relatively small, between 3 and 5 percent and the width of the tranche is very thin, 2.5 to 4 percent maximum.

As prepayments occur, the level of subordination of the lower tranches increases, in relative terms, and can reach 10 percent over time. Assuming a recovery of 50 percent on the foreclosed homes means that a default rate of 20 percent on subprime mortgages, which is realistic in the current environment, will most likely hit most of the Triple-B tranches. Moreover, it is also most likely that in the current downturn in the housing market and recessionary economic environment, the loss correlations across all the Triple-B tranches will be close to one. As a consequence, if one Triple-B tranche is hit, it is most likely that most of the Triple-B tranches will be hit as well during the same period. And, given the thin width of the tranches, it is most likely that if one MBS bond is wiped out, they will all be wiped out at the same time, wiping out the super-senior tranche of the subprime CDO.

In other words, we are in a binary situation in which either the cumulative default rate of the subprime mortgages remains below the threshold that keeps the underlying RMBS bonds untouched and the super-senior tranches of subprime CDOs won't incur any loss, or the cumulative default rate breaches this threshold and the super-senior tranches of subprime CDOs could all be wiped out.

Wrong Estimates of Default Rates and Default Correlations[2]

Rating agencies based their ratings on wrong estimates of the underlying securities' default risks, and how likely defaults were to be correlated in a stressed environment. Rating agencies based their estimates of default rates on a very short history, going back to 2001, characterized by a fairly benign environment for the real estate market. They did not take into account two major changes in their rating model: the rupture in the delinquency statistics starting in 2005 and the inflection in the real estate market and the economic environment that made defaults on mortgages no longer an isolated phenomenon, but rather a systemic event with borrowers defaulting in clusters in some geographic areas such as parts of California and Florida.

Delinquencies on subprime mortgages rose significantly after mid-2005 for at least four reasons:[3]

First, subprime borrowers are typically not very creditworthy, often highly leveraged with high debt-to-income ratios, and the mortgages extended to them have relatively large loan-to-value ratios.

Second, in 2005 and 2006 the most common subprime loans were 2/28 or 3/27 hybrid subprime ARMs. These loans had a relatively low fixed teaser rate for the first two or three years, and then reset semiannually to a much higher rate. Debt service burdens for loans eventually increased, which led to financial distress for some of this group of borrowers.

Third, many subprime borrowers had counted on being able to refinance or repay mortgages early through home sales and at the same time produce some equity cushion in a market in which home prices kept rising. As the rate of U.S. house price appreciation began to decline after April 2005, it became more difficult for subprime borrowers to refinance, and many ended up incurring higher mortgage costs than they had expected to bear at the time of taking their mortgage.

Fourth, a decline in credit standards by mortgage originators in underwriting over the previous three years was a major factor behind the sharp increase in delinquency rates for mortgages originated during 2005 and 2006.

According to rating agencies, ratings assumed a default correlation of 20 percent, which is probably a high estimate in a benign economic environment in which defaults are essentially due to idiosyncratic factors: job loss, unanticipated medical expenses, divorce, and so on, which are specific to an individual or family and won't affect the other borrowers in the same geography. When a recession hits the economy, as it started in late 2007, it is a different story. Whole industries are affected, with companies going bankrupt and having to lay off thousands of people, which makes the impact of the recession even more severe in the geographic areas affected by these corporate bankruptcies. Delinquencies occur in waves, and defaults are becoming a systemic phenomenon with defaults becoming highly correlated at least in some locations.

Rating agencies, as well as structurers and investors totally occulted that the securitization process substitutes idiosyncratic risks that are largely diversifiable in a benign economic environment for systemic risks that are not diversifiable during a severe economic downturn.

Sensitivities of the Rating of Senior Subprime CDO Tranches to Estimation Errors of Delinquency Rates, Recovery Rates, and Default Correlations

Ratings of tranches of CDOs and other credit instruments, such as corporate debt, are indicators of default risk based on expected loss (Moody's) or probabilities of default (Standard & Poor's and Fitch Ratings).[4] Rating agencies rely on Monte Carlo–type simulations to simulate cash flows and correlated defaults of the assets in the pool, and allocate the cash flows to the various tranches according to the waterfall. This simulation produces a loss distribution for the pool and an expected loss for each tranche of the capital structure of the securitization transaction. These expected losses are then mapped into the letter-based rating scale. The tranching is structured so that the senior tranches obtain a Triple-A rating.

Simple simulations show that small errors in the evaluation of the delinquency rate of the underlying mortgages, recovery rates, and default correlations can result in major changes in the expected loss of the senior tranches of a CDO, and its consequent rating.[5] Rating transitions for structured credit products, such as tranches of subprime CDOs, differ substantially from those of corporate bonds. It is therefore misleading to use the same rating scale for bonds and structured credit products. They may have the same expected loss at the time the rating is produced, but their future dynamics may differ substantially.

It is therefore important for rating agencies, investors, and regulators to understand the fundamental difference between the rating of a corporate bond and the rating of tranches of CDOs when it comes to exposure to systemic risk. Corporate bonds are mainly exposed to idiosyncratic risks, that is, risks specific to the firm, the quality of its management, and the positioning of the company within its industry. The risk of a company will be affected by the economic environment, but systemic risk is not the dominant factor in assessing the risk of an individual company. On the contrary, a senior tranche of a CDO has the features of a catastrophe bond, which is strongly affected in extreme scenarios. Investors in those securities wrote insurance against a major recession but were not properly compensated for the associated risk.

Overreliance on Unrealistically Simple Risk Models

Value-at-risk (VaR) has become the universal risk measure for financial institutions in understanding their sensitivity to changes in market risk drivers such as interest rates, asset prices, correlations, and volatilities.

Given the amount of calculations involved in running a VaR model, the pricing of securities within a VaR model requires some shortcuts. Since structured credit products are rated using the same rating scale as for corporate bonds, banks have naturally taken as proxy for these securities in their VaR models corporate bonds with similar ratings. We have demonstrated in the previous section that this approach is fundamentally flawed and may lead to major underestimation of the risks involved with holding these complex securities.

Overreliance on Inaccurate Data

For reasons indicated earlier, the delinquency rate for subprime mortgages increased significantly after 2004. The market experienced a major change of regime in 2005, which was totally occulted in the risk measures, not only by the rating agencies, but also by the banks and other investors holding subprime structured credit products.

Overreliance on Short-Term Financing with Too Little Consideration for Liquidity Risk

Since the beginning of the 1990s, banks have gradually shifted away from the traditional business model of *originate and hold* toward the new *originate-to-distribute* business model. Under this new business model, the bank services the loans, but the funding of the loans is sourced out to investors, and the risk of default is also transferred out to these investors, without recourse.[6] This new business model was supposed to disperse credit risk throughout the financial system and make financial institutions safer and less sensitive to credit crises, as well as provide banks with additional sources of funding for their lending activities.

This is the theory. In practice, the implementation of this business model was flawed, and this crisis demonstrated that the redistribution of credit risk among final investors that it was supposed to achieve was only an illusion.

Banks moved away from their balance sheets the assets to be securitized to locate them into structured investment vehicles (SIVs) that are limited-purpose, bankruptcy-remote companies. Their purpose is to fund the purchase of the assets, which are primarily long-term assets, with short-term asset-backed commercial paper (ABCP) and some medium-term notes and capital.

Liquidity risk arises because of the need to refinance because of the maturity mismatch between assets and liabilities. The SIV must demonstrate that apart from the vehicle's cash flows that provide liquidity, it has backstop lines of credit from different institutions, and highly liquid assets that can be sold, so that it is able to deal with market disruptions.

When banks were unable to roll the ABCP funding these SIVs, and market liquidity had totally evaporated for subprime related assets, banks had no other alternative to preserve their reputation but to take back the assets onto their balance sheet and face funding liquidity issues of the sort that led to the bankruptcy of Lehman Brothers and the rescues of Bear Stearns, Merrill Lynch, and American International Group (AIG) in the United States and Northern Rock in the United Kingdom.

LESSONS FROM THIS FIASCO

A number of important lessons can be drawn from this postmortem analysis of the failures of risk management during the crisis.[7]

Differentiate the Ratings of Corporate Bonds and Structured Credit Products

To have confidence in a model, it is necessary to have a clear definition of what a rating means for a particular type of instrument, the factors that an agency considers when assigning a rating and how well a rating model performs in different economic environments.

Subprime ABS ratings differ from corporate debt ratings in a number of different dimensions. Corporate bond ratings are largely based on firm-specific risk, while CDO tranches represent claims on cash flows from a portfolio of correlated assets. Thus, the rating of CDO tranches relies heavily on quantitative models while corporate debt ratings rely essentially on the analyst judgment. While the rating of a CDO tranche should have the same expected loss as a corporate bond for a given rating, the volatility of loss, that is, the unexpected loss, is quite different and strongly depends on the correlation structure of the underlying assets in the pool of the CDO.[8] This in itself warrants the use of different rating scales for corporate bonds from that of structured credit products.

It is also critical to assess the sensitivity of tranche ratings to a significant deterioration in credit conditions affecting creditworthiness and default clustering. As discussed earlier, the impact of the shocks affecting creditworthiness on CDO tranche ratings is very different from that for a corporate bond. It critically depends on the magnitude and the clustering of the shocks, and it tends to be nonlinear.[9]

For the last few years, the characteristics of subprime mortgage borrowers were undergoing major changes due to declining underwriting standards and fraud. The failure to explicitly recognize the changing nature of the underlying data used in model estimation implied that the probabilities of default, recovery rates, default dependence, and the dependence between default and recovery rates were poorly estimated. Models need to capture default contagion that exists in local housing markets.

Check the Quality of the Data about the Underlying Assets and Make Sure It Is Complete and Timely

It is essential to perform due diligence on the raw data—neither the rating agencies nor the banks that structured the CDOs have done it.

The rating agencies clearly state that they do not perform due diligence on the raw data. The current situation is analogous to accountants accepting at face value the figures given to them by firms. There is no auditing function. The current situation is problematic. In moving forward, if data auditing is required, then the issue of compensation both for rating and for auditing needs to be addressed. It is not clear that regulating the originators will solve the problem of faulty data unless there is adequate enforcement.

Clarity is required about the data sources used to reach a rating. Is the agency accepting data from a third party, and has the agency done anything to ascertain whether there have been structural changes in the data sources? Has it checked the data to justify the validity of its distributional assumptions?

For asset-backed securities, the government should sponsor an agency that collects information on a timely basis about the collateral pools and make it available to market participants. This will facilitate an independent party's ability to reproduce the credit ratings.

Complement the Traditional VaR Risk Measure with Worst-Case Scenario Analysis and Stress Testing

Value-at-risk (VaR) is a useful measure of risk in normal market conditions and over a very short-term horizon. But it is well documented that VaR does not perform well in exceptional market conditions characterized by unprecedented price moves and significant tail risk. VaR must be complemented by other risk metrics such as worst-case scenario analysis and stress testing to better assess the extent of losses consecutive to extreme market conditions that may have a very low probability of occurrence but are still realistic.

The subprime crisis introduced new risk features that are not captured in VaR models:

- Liquidity risk, that is, the phenomenon that trading liquidity dries up so suddenly that traders cannot adjust their hedging portfolios.
- Strong nonlinearities in risk for complex structured products such as subprime CDO tranches. We discussed earlier what we called the *cliff effect* for senior tranches of subprime CDOs. This risk is not captured by VaR models.
- Contagion risk also cannot be accounted for in a VaR model.

Shortcuts proposed to deal with these complexities within the framework of VaR have lead to major underestimations of risk. For example, some banks have taken as a proxy for a rated CDO tranche a corporate bond with the same rating. This is flawed for the reasons discussed earlier.

If it was not obvious before, this crisis has revealed the necessity to design stress tests and worst-case scenarios that include business cycle stresses as well as event-specific tail risks.

Risk management should also run worst-case scenarios to measure the risk of future collateral calls and writedowns, which can have a devastating effect on the finances of the firm.

NOTES

1. Moody's first took rating action on 2006-vintage subprime loans in November 2006. In 2007, Moody's downgraded 31 percent of all tranches for CDOs of ABS it had rated, and 14 percent of those initially rated AAA. This raises questions about the rating methodologies employed by the different agencies. See Ashcraft and Schuermann (2007) for a detailed description of the rating of subprime MBS.

2. A third factor, that is, the amount recovered in the event of default also named recovery rate, affects the expected loss. Very few data are available to calibrate this parameter for subprime loans, and it was estimated across the board at 40 percent.

3. See Crouhy et al. (2008).

4. Contrary to a corporate bond, an MBS or a tranche of a CDO does not default in the sense of a corporate default event. Instead, depending on the rate of delinquencies on

the underlying pool of assets, these securities will experience cash flow shortfalls and principal writedowns over the life of the transaction.

5. See Coval et al. (2008) and Fender et al. (2008).

6. See Crouhy et al. (2006, Chapter 12).

7. See also Crouhy et al. (2008) for a more exhaustive and detailed analysis of the steps to prevent a repeat of such a crisis.

8. See the discussion in Ashcraft and Schuermann (2007).

9. See Fender et al. (2008) and Coval et al. (2008).

REFERENCES

Ashcraft, A. B., and T. Schuermann. 2007. Understanding the securitization of subprime mortgage credit. Federal Reserve Bank of New York working paper.

Coval, J. D., J. Jurek, and E. Stafford. 2008. The economics of structured finance. Harvard Business School working paper 09-060.

Crouhy, M. G., D. Galai, and R. Mark. 2006. *The essentials of risk management.* New York: McGraw-Hill.

Crouhy, M. G., R. A. Jarrow, and S. M. Turnbull. 2008. The subprime crisis of 2007. *Journal of Derivatives* 16 (1): 81–110.

Fender, I., N. Tarashev, and H. Zhu. 2008. Credit fundamentals, ratings and value-at-risk: CDOs versus corporate exposures. *BIS Quarterly Review,* March: 87–101.

Honohan, P. 2008. Bank Failures: The limitations of risk modelling. Working paper.

Standard and Poor's. 2008. *Structured finance rating transitions and default updates as of June 20, 2008.*

ABOUT THE AUTHOR

Dr. Michel Crouhy is head of research and development at NATIXIS. He has bankwide oversight on all quantitative research and the development of new products and applications supporting the trading and structuring businesses. He is also responsible for implementing a bankwide risk-adjusted return on capital (RAROC) system. He is the founder and president of the NATIXIS Foundation for Quantitative Research, which promotes and supports academic research and world-class events in the area of mathematical finance. Crouhy was formerly senior vice president for business analytic solutions in the risk management division at the Canadian Imperial Bank of Commerce. Before his career in the industry, Crouhy was a professor of finance at the HEC School of Management in Paris and has been a visiting professor at the Wharton School of the University of Pennsylvania and at the University of California, Los Angeles. Crouhy is the author and co-author of several books, the most recent ones being *Risk Management* (McGraw-Hill, 2001) and *The Essentials of Risk Management* (McGraw-Hill, 2006). Crouhy holds a Ph.D. from the Wharton School of the University of Pennsylvania and has a Doctoris Honoris Causa from the University of Montreal.

CHAPTER 37

The Outsourcing of Financial Regulation to Risk Models

ERIK F. GERDING
Associate Professor, University of New Mexico School of Law*

T he widespread use of computer-based risk models in the financial industry during the last two decades enabled the marketing of increasingly complex financial products to consumers, the growth of novel financial instruments, such as asset-backed securities and derivatives, and the development of sophisticated risk management strategies by financial institutions. These models helped create a web of risk transfers in the economy that allowed investors in financial markets to invest in consumer loan markets and hedge the risks of these investments with derivatives. By linking consumer lending to capital markets, these models fueled explosive growth in mortgages and other consumer loans.

Awed by this growth and reassured by the ability of risk models to help financial institutions measure and manage risk, regulators outsourced vast responsibility for regulating risk in consumer finance and financial markets to privately owned industry models. Proprietary risk models of financial institutions came to serve as a new financial code that regulated transfers of risk among consumers, financial institutions, and investors. The global financial crisis proved that this faith in risk models was spectacularly misplaced. This chapter examines several explanations for the failures of models that contributed to the crisis and outlines regulatory reforms.

THE RISE OF RISK MODELS

In the 1980s, mathematicians revolutionized how Wall Street manages and prices risk and makes complex investment decisions. These individuals (called *quants* because their approach is known as quantitative finance) combined innovations in finance theory with advances in computing power to develop complex models that could churn through massive amounts of market data to forecast financial risks. By quantifying risk, these models enabled financial institutions to develop more complex financial instruments, including asset-backed securities and derivatives.

---

*This chapter is based on an article that appeared in Volume 84 of the *Washington Law Review* (2009).

Asset-backed securities are created by pooling large numbers of mortgages, loans, or other assets that produce a stream of future cash payments. An investment vehicle purchases these assets from lenders and then uses the cash streams to make payments on securities sold to investors. This transformation of payments on loans into securities, called *securitization*, allows investors in capital markets to invest in consumer lending markets. Investors in asset-backed securities bear considerable risks, particularly that defaults on the underlying mortgages or other assets will cause defaults on the securities. To measure these risks and price securities appropriately, investors rely on the risk models described earlier, including models used by credit rating agencies that often evaluate asset-backed securities. Risk models also enable the pricing and development of derivatives. One form of derivatives, credit default swaps, functions as a kind of insurance policy that protects against defaults on asset-backed securities, other bonds, and loans. For example, an investor worried about nonpayment on an asset-backed security (the credit protection buyer) can agree to make premium payments to another party (the credit protection seller) in return for the credit protection seller agreeing to make payments should the security default.

Credit default swaps thus represent another link in a chain of risk transfers running from the original borrowers to lenders (who bear the risk of borrower default until they sell the loans in a securitization) to investors in asset-backed securities to credit protection sellers in a credit default swap. But the chain metaphor does not capture the full complexity of asset-backed securities and derivatives. Just as mortgages are securitized, so too are asset-backed securities from various investment vehicles often pooled and used to back a new issuance of asset-backed securities (called *collateralized debt obligations*, or CDOs). CDO securities can themselves be pooled with other asset-backed securities and be securitized (a CDO squared). Similarly, the credit protection seller in a credit default swap can hedge the risk it assumes of default on the underlying debt by entering into a second credit default swap with another party. Thus asset-backed securities and derivatives are linked in not only chains, but tangled webs of risk transfers, all of which rely on financial models to evaluate and price risk.

The complex system of risk transfers created by asset-backed securities and derivatives offers several benefits. First, these transfers enable the risks of defaults on consumer loans to be spread widely and allocated to parties that theoretically can bear risk most efficiently. Second, transferring risk fueled spectacular growth in mortgage and other consumer lending and lowered interest rates for borrowers. By selling consumer loans, lenders offload concentrated risk of consumer defaults to the investors in asset-backed securities and can take on the risk of new loans. Furthermore, lenders exchange illiquid, long-term assets (loans) for liquid, short-term assets (cash), which could be used to make additional loans. Similarly, investors in asset-backed securities can offload risk by selling their securities. Sales give investors cash, which can be reinvested in new asset-backed securities, giving lenders additional resources. The hedging provided by credit default swaps lowers the risk for investors and allows them to purchase additional asset-backed securities.

THE OUTSOURCING OF REGULATION

The dazzling potential of these models to forecast and price risk prompted financial regulators to outsource to these models and the financial institutions that use them considerable responsibility for regulating risk in financial markets. This regulatory outsourcing ranges from refusal to regulate certain financial instruments or practices to the explicit delegation of regulatory functions. Outsourcing has occurred all along the risk chain from consumer lending to asset-backed securities to credit default swaps.

Consumer lending: In the last decade, federal bank regulators refused to regulate new consumer lending practices in the mortgage and credit card industries that shifted risk to consumers. These practices included mortgage lenders marketing exotic mortgages to high-credit-risk borrowers. Lenders and mortgage brokers employed sophisticated data mining and credit scoring software to target riskier borrowers. Many of these exotic mortgages included interest rates that reset from a low fixed rate to a higher floating rate after an initial teaser period. High-credit-risk borrowers would be unable to pay the higher rate, but could refinance or sell the mortgaged property *as long as housing prices continued to rise.* Federal bank regulators, including Federal Reserve chairman Alan Greenspan, expressed reluctance to regulate these practices, citing a belief that the models used by lenders both effectively policed risk and enabled many high-credit-risk borrowers to afford their first homes.

Pricing of securitizations and rating agencies: The outsourcing of financial regulations with respect to the pricing of asset-backed securities is even more explicit. This outsourcing takes the form of regulations that restrict the securities investments of many financial institutions to bonds rated investment grade by credit rating agencies. These credit rating agencies are licensed by the U.S. Securities and Exchange Commission (SEC), which gives them a quasi-oligopoly power. These investment grade regulations delegated to rating agencies—and their models—the responsibility to determine which investments are safe for financial institutions. These rating agencies gave investment grade ratings to asset-backed securities even as these securities increasingly became backed by risky exotic mortgages. Without these ratings, regulated financial institutions could not have invested in these securities, and the securitization market would have shrunk considerably.

Financial institution risk management: Financial institutions employ their own proprietary computer-based risk models to make investment decisions and manage firmwide financial risk. A 2004 international accord known as Basel II allows bank regulators in the United States and other nations to delegate regulatory responsibility to the internal risk models of banks. Basel II gives certain large banks the ability to set regulatory capital—a bank's cushion against major losses, insolvency, bank runs, and financial crises—according to internal risk models. Some European bank regulators implemented the accord quickly. U.S. bank regulators passed regulations implementing the accord in December 2007 (even as the financial crisis accelerated). But the SEC applied the accord to large investment bank conglomerates in 2004 as part of a new regulatory scheme called the Consolidated Supervised Entity (CSE) program. Critics note that the CSE program allowed investment bank conglomerates to increase leverage dramatically and take on large risk.

Credit default swaps and hedge funds: Their faith in financial risk models also animated the refusal of federal regulators to regulate credit default swaps and other over-the-counter (OTC) derivatives (derivatives not traded on an exchange). Again, regulators such as Alan Greenspan expressed a belief that sophisticated risk models priced the risk of these derivatives appropriately. Over the past decade, regulations were relaxed or reinterpreted to allow banks and other regulated financial institutions to enter into OTC derivatives, including credit default swaps. These institutions found counterparties in hedge funds, unregulated investment firms that could take on the risk of credit default swaps and other derivatives without restriction.

These multiple forms of regulatory outsourcing reflect a deep faith in risk models to quantify and mitigate financial risk. Risk models thus have assumed many of the functions of regulation to oversee transfers of risk in the marketplace and risk-taking by banks and other important institutions. These models serve as a new financial code, a metaphor that captures both their reliance on computing power and their law-shaping function.

THE FAILURE OF MODELS IN THE CRISIS

This new financial code crashed spectacularly in the global financial crisis. The risk models used by financial institutions failed to predict the cascade of financial risk that began in 2007, including the following:

- Waves of consumer defaults on exotic mortgages as teaser rates expired, market interest rates rose, housing prices stagnated, and borrowers could no longer refinance or resell mortgaged properties
- Massive mortgage defaults, creating massive losses on mortgage-backed securities
- Feedback loops that formed as decreased lending drove market interest rates higher, started a credit crunch, and worsened default rates on mortgages
- Fire sales of mortgages and asset-backed securities by financial institutions that suffered significant losses
- Problems valuing asset-backed securities as buyers disappeared and the layers of securitization on securitization prevented investors from calculating potential losses
- Modern-day bank runs on major financial institutions by panicked creditors and investors

Of particular note, some of the most prominent financial institutions that foundered in the crisis were the financial conglomerates that lowered their regulatory capital and increased their leverage under the SEC's CSE Program.

The "new financial code" failed to predict this cascade of risk because of cascading errors in risk models. These errors can be broadly classified into technological failures, or errors in the design of models, and human failures, or errors in the selection and use of models.

Technological Failures

The risk models used by financial institutions failed in part because they were based on flawed assumptions that did not capture the complexity and dynamism of modern financial markets. Many models used historical data to calculate probabilities of future risk. But many users of models failed to go back far enough in time in gathering data and missed important periods in which markets suffered large losses. For example, a 2006 model that used five years of data would have missed the 1998 Asian financial crisis. Fifteen years of data would have missed the 1987 U.S. stock market crash. Moreover, there is also the possibility that historical data cannot fully capture new forms of risk and random, unexpected events.

Economists have also noted that securitizing and resecuritizing assets in multiple layers exacerbates the risk of errors; small errors in measuring the risk of underlying assets, like mortgages, are magnified at each subsequent level of securitization or hedging. Moreover, risk models often fail to capture the problems caused by a high correlation of losses on underlying assets. When losses on assets become highly correlated, losses on one asset are no longer offset by profits on other assets; losses occur in waves. This frustrates measuring and mitigating risk. Losses on mortgages and securities can become increasingly correlated because of spillover effects (for example, the default on one mortgage lowering surrounding property values and increasing the probability of default on other mortgages) and feedback loops (for example, widespread defaults on mortgages constricting lending, which increases interest rates, which leads to a new round of defaults).

Models used to price asset-backed securities or derivatives can also fail because they require high quality information on the risks of the underlying assets at the beginning of the securitization chain (the mortgages or other loans), but this information progressively deteriorates the further up the chain one moves from those underlying assets. When pricing a credit default swap based on a CDO, the modeler needs information on the risks of the diverse asset-backed securities underlying the CDO, which ideally would require information on all the assets underlying those asset-backed securities, which ultimately requires understanding the risks associated with the mortgages backing those securities. The modeler of the CDO faces extreme difficulty compiling all of this information and often takes short cuts, such as relying mainly on rating agency ratings on the immediate assets being securitized. But rating agencies have often fared quite poorly in predicting risk.

Even if a modeler had access to data on the ultimate underlying assets such as mortgages, evaluating the risk of nonpayment on these assets requires modeling individual behavior. Unfortunately, individual behavior often veers from the rationality assumed by many economists, frustrating prediction. Finally, the risk models of individual institutions fail to capture the risk of homogeneity among the models of multiple firms. If many different institutions use similar models, they may have similar blind spots and make similar errors. Furthermore, these models would translate into similar risk management strategies. This could cause many institutions to buy (or sell) the same assets simultaneously and trigger market booms (or crashes).

Human Failures

Even good risk models can falter because individuals, with their failings and self-interest, select, run, and use risk models. The individuals at financial institutions may fail to realize the limitations of a particular risk model or select a model's parameters to justify a risky investment already decided upon. Traders at financial institutions have also learned to game established models. One strategy is to "stuff risk into the tails," which means to make investments that usually earn small returns, but in rarer instances can suffer colossal losses. These low probability–high magnitude losses escape detection by many risk models.

Even well-designed and well-selected models prove useless if the data being inputted are faulty. The chain of risk transfers, though, undermines the incentives of parties to gather and pass on accurate data on risk. For example, mortgage lenders increasingly made loans to high risk borrowers without requiring documentation of employment. These lenders had less incentive to ensure the creditworthiness of borrowers because the risk of default was transferred when the mortgages were securitized.

As noted earlier, many models relied heavily on rating agency determinations, but critics have questioned both the competency and impartiality of rating agencies. Rating agencies are paid not by investors, but by the firms that sponsor and profit from securitizations. Moreover, rating agencies face little consequence for making bad forecasts because of their oligopoly power and lack of legal liability.

PRECURSORS

The confluence of a financial crisis and a failure of risk models is not unprecedented in the United States even in the last 20 years. The 1987 stock market crash was exacerbated by a new quantitative finance-driven investment strategy called *program trading*. With program trading, many financial institutions placed their investment strategies on virtual auto-pilot, allowing computer-based risk models to determine when to buy or sell securities. Many institutions used similar models, and thus, when a market blip occurred, these same firms sold simultaneously, causing the stock market to plummet. In 1998, the federal government orchestrated an industry bailout of a prominent hedge fund, Long-Term Capital Management (LTCM), whose quantitative, finance-driven investments suffered large losses during market turbulence. LTCM's looming insolvency threatened major Wall Street firms.

SOLUTIONS

This history of spectacular failures of risk models from 1987 to the current crisis argues that regulators must reverse the trend of outsourcing risk regulation to these financial industry models. Financial regulations should rely less on rating agency ratings to determine how much risk financial institutions can bear. The provisions of the Basel II Accord that allow banks to set their capital requirements according to their internal models should be scuttled.

If industry models continue to substitute for regulation, regulators must enhance their ability to audit these sophisticated models. Regulators will struggle, however, to command the resources and expertise to audit each financial institution and its models thoroughly and to keep pace with continuing industry innovations. Regulators must also compare risk models of different institutions to evaluate whether they suffer from excessive homogeneity. Moreover, it is difficult for the marketplace and the public to know if regulators are auditing any individual financial institution adequately. This lack of transparency undermines international regulatory cooperation; regulators in other countries cannot be assured that a regulator is not allowing its home country financial institutions to use loose models to take on excessive risk and earn higher profits.

Therefore, if industry models continue to substitute for regulation, regulators must insist that financial institutions publicly disclose the inner workings of these models. Borrowing from computer science, open source risk models, that is, models whose assumptions and methodologies are publicly disclosed would allow the marketplace and the public to debug models for errors, detect excessive homogeneity, and police financial institutions and regulators.

ABOUT THE AUTHOR

Erik F. Gerding was graduated with a J.D. from Harvard Law School and afterward practiced securities and corporate law in the New York and Washington, D.C., offices of a large international law firm. In 2006, he joined the faculty of the University of New Mexico School of Law, where he is now an associate professor. Gerding has written several law review articles on financial regulation during asset price bubbles and financial crises. He is working on a book tentatively titled *Law, Bubbles, and Financial Regulation* for Routledge Press.

CHAPTER 38

The Future of Risk Modeling

ELIZABETH SHEEDY
Macquarie University

T his chapter examines two questions regarding market risk models. First, are they fixable, or are they fundamentally flawed as some claim? Second, if they are fixable, do they have a useful role to play in financial risk management? But first, I explain the role of risk models in financial risk management.

Risk models have assumed growing importance in risk management since the mid-1990s, when Value at Risk (or VaR) gained prominence. VaR models are used to measure the potential for losses over a given time from trading portfolios. VaR models typically use statistical methods to assess relatively unlikely outcomes that may occur on only a couple of business days per year, that is, on 1 percent of days. Such models are used by financial institutions and others as an input to decisions concerning capital structure and for setting limits on trading positions. Measures of risk (such as VaR) may also be taken into consideration when determining the appropriate pricing of financial products (to compensate for the risks taken) and also in risk-adjusted performance measures that can determine bonus payments.

VaR measures risk with, say, 95 percent or 99 percent confidence. Risk managers must also consider the possibility of even more extreme or improbable losses. Stress tests are designed to assess the impact on trading portfolios of these plausible but highly improbable events. Stress testing is arguably even more difficult than VaR modeling from a statistical perspective since we have only a small sample of these extreme events from history. Stress tests are considered complementary to VaR models; both risk measures are used to guide decisions regarding capital structure, trading limits, and so forth.

In light of the events of 2007 and 2008, both VaR models and stress testing practices have come under scrutiny. In the *Turner Review* (Turner 2009), Lord Turner, chairman of the U.K. banking regulator, sees misplaced reliance on sophisticated math as a causal factor in the global crisis. He goes on to question the empirical method that is the foundation of all risk modeling, that is, our ability to observe markets historically and draw robust inferences about the future.

Nassim Taleb, author of *The Black Swan* (Taleb 2007) is another commentator who has been highly critical of risk models. In late 2008, when interviewed on CNBC, he said, "Wall Street underestimates the role of extreme events, and risk management systems are completely defective. The problems we have now come from these risk management systems that cannot detect the risk of rare events."

(interview on CNBC, November 8, 2008). On Bloomberg, he is quoted as saying, "We would like society to lock up quantitative risk managers before they cause more damage" (October 14, 2008).

The global financial crisis exposed a number of interconnected market risk modeling challenges:

- The number of days on which extreme losses occurred was much higher than predicted by the risk models, and such high-loss days often occurred in quick succession (Campbell 2008). This caused capital to be rapidly exhausted, in some cases necessitating government intervention to prevent a systemic collapse.
- Risk measures in many cases did not sufficiently adapt to changing conditions as the crisis unfolded (Senior Supervisors Group 2008). They typically did not adequately reflect feedback effects, that is, the impact of changing behavior following the initial price shocks.
- Stress tests were unduly reliant on and made inappropriate use of historical data (Supervision 2009). They assumed, for example, that statistical relationships observed during tranquil periods would be maintained.

In responding to these criticisms of risk modeling, it should first be pointed out that the industry uses a variety of risk models. They can broadly be categorized as conditional models (that is, conditional on and sensitive to very recent history) or unconditional models (applying equal weighting to all data in the sample and therefore relatively insensitive to very recent history). This turns out to be a very important distinction because one of the most important and ubiquitous characteristics of financial markets is the tendency for one large market move (whether up or down) to be followed by more large market moves—so-called volatility clustering. The implication of this is that risk is forecastable to some degree; in particular, the pattern of prices today has implications for risk on subsequent days. The conditional risk models exploit these relationships that are observed in all financial markets.

Volatility clustering can be explained by the behavior of market participants in response to an initial price shock. Funding pressures (induced, for example, by margin calls and demands for additional collateral), increased uncertainty, and breaches of trading and credit limits lead to panic buying and selling by those seeking to hedge, unwillingness to open new positions, withdrawal of some participants from the market altogether, and a flight to quality (Borio 2000; Poole and D'Arcy, 2008). Market liquidity is thereby reduced so that the market impact of trading is exacerbated and we observe further large price moves (increased volatility) following the initial shock. Conditional risk models potentially reflect these market characteristics and adapt to changing market conditions following a market shock.

The merits of the conditional risk models (in comparison to unconditional risk models) can be assessed using the empirical method. That is, we can test the hypothesis that conditional risk models better explain historical price data by looking at what would have happened historically if such risk models had been applied. To do this, we recalculate VaR every day over a period of, say, 20 years using only data that was available at the time. This is important so that the VaR model is always tested using out-of-sample data. We then look to see how often the subsequent portfolio losses exceeded the VaR estimate. If VaR is calculated with 99 percent confidence, then we expect that portfolio losses should exceed VaR in 1 percent of cases. We can perform statistical tests to determine whether the actual number of exceptions was significantly higher than expected (or, less importantly, lower) and whether the exceptions are randomly scattered. The issue of randomness is crucial; if exceptions occur close together, then insolvency is far more likely to occur as capital cannot quickly be replaced.

Such empirical research has shown that conditional risk models are superior to their unconditional counterparts (Hull and White 1998; Berkowitz and O'Brien 2002; Alexander and Sheedy 2008). Research also shows that it is important to avoid assuming that the (conditional) return distribution is normal. This is because the normal distribution tends to underestimate the potential for extreme market movements. In contrast, Alexander and Sheedy (2008) have shown that unconditional models (even those that eschew the normality assumption) tend to perform poorly. In particular, they tend to produce clustered exceptions (that is, lots of days with unexpectedly high losses close together). My recent paper (Sheedy 2009) reexamines these issues using data to the end of 2008. Even during the turbulent period of 2007 and 2008, the conditional risk models performed adequately (that is, they cannot be rejected statistically), while the unconditional risk models clearly understated risk. The same paper also shows how stress testing practices can be improved to better reflect the characteristics of volatility clustering and to avoid the problems observed in 2007 and 2008.

What does all this mean for the industry? The pattern of losses experienced by financial institutions in 2007 and 2008 is consistent with the widespread use of unconditional risk models in the industry. We know from survey results that unconditional risk models are the most popular in the industry (Perignon and Smith 2006; Deloitte 2009), despite not having any solid empirical support.

My paper argues that it is not the empirical method that is at fault, but rather the failure to use it appropriately. The problems observed in risk modeling in 2007 and 2008 are fixable at least for markets with a reasonable price history through cycles of both high and low volatility. Existing models can be radically improved by adopting the conditional risk models that are supported by empirical research.

So why aren't conditional risk measures more widely used by financial institutions? My own hypothesis is that the incentives in financial institutions are wrong. Financial institutions have a fundamental disincentive to invest in risk management. Investing in the best risk management people and systems, supporting risk research, and providing quality risk training are all expensive. In the short run, they increase costs, but the offsetting benefits are experienced in the long term and are difficult to quantify. There will always be the temptation to cut costs in the risk management area to boost short-term profits. This is especially true if bankers believe that the taxpayer will come to the rescue in a disaster scenario. Another concern is the possibility that banks avoid risk models that might necessitate additional capital. Extra capital means lower return on equity in the short term (for a given level of earnings), which does not win any plaudits.

Having established that market risk models are fixable, I now turn to the second question: Do risk models play a useful role in risk management? Would we be better to abandon quantitative risk models as Taleb suggests? Should we find some other way of making decisions about capital, limits, pricing, and so forth. This is a more difficult question to answer empirically, and the answer will depend on what alternative is proposed. Some propose a move to more subjective measures of risk, based on the opinion of supposedly seasoned experts.

My concern is that relying on subjective measures of risk rather than quantitative risk models could be even worse than the status quo. Just because an expert comes up with a subjective measure of risk doesn't mean there is no risk model. It's just that the model exists in the mind of the expert and is therefore not transparent. We have no data on how the expert's model will perform in extreme conditions, so this approach requires a great deal of faith in the expert, which may or may not be justified.

In contrast, a risk model written out in mathematical notation is at least open to scrutiny, and its assumptions can be debated in the community of risk managers and scholars. We have the ability to test the model and understand how it works. Models provide an objective measure of risk, relatively free of biases, which can be a starting point for discussion. We can be confident that the risk models with empirical support have proven their ability to explain market movements even in rapidly changing market conditions. Having said that, some important lessons must be learned about our market risk models and the way we use them.

1. *Liquidity Risk.* More research is needed to better understand how to model market liquidity risk. The good news is that with the advent of automated exchanges and high-frequency datasets, we have far more information than ever before about the nature of liquidity. The potential is now there to analyze how liquidity varies, and to what extent it is linked to volatility. This is currently one of the hottest areas in market risk research.

Securities with poor liquidity probably ought not to be included in the trading book, at least in the short term. The conservative approach is to assume that they will remain on the bank's balance sheet until they either mature or are written off. That is, we need to treat these assets more like old-fashioned loans.

We also need to be more realistic about our ability to model the risk of new products and markets. We saw in the recent crisis that the use of proxy data—taking data from established securities and assuming that the same patterns apply for newly engineered securities—proved to be a flawed strategy. It may be that these products need to be handled differently, that is, excluded from the risk model and treated as illiquid assets. We need to be careful only to apply market risk models to markets and products that are truly traded, that is, to liquid, mature products.

2. *Education.* Model users need to be far better educated regarding their interpretation. First, any risk estimate is just that, an estimate, with a confidence interval around it. Second, models are not intended to fully describe reality; they capture certain features of reality only. We therefore need to ensure that users understand the assumptions of the model (and therefore what has not been modeled). The obvious corollary of this is that the models need to be kept as simple as possible. Third, remember the model ignores the unknown unknowns. Whenever model results are presented, the users ought to be specifically reminded of this point. The implication is that our risk measures will inevitably be understated. In sum, risk reports should come with health warnings in large print.

Are risk models fixable? Research shows that conditional risk models perform well, even during periods of high turbulence such as those experienced in 2007 and 2008. Unfortunately, these risk models are not yet widely adopted in the financial industry for reasons that remain unclear, but could be explained by incentive failures. It appears therefore, that risk modeling problems are fixable rather than fundamentally flawed, provided financial institutions are willing to commit adequate resources to risk modeling.

Are they worth fixing? Yes, they provide a useful structure and objectivity for analysis of risk. But they must be used sensibly. A risk model is the starting point for analysis, not the end point. We use technology as an aid but not as a substitute for thinking. People often use models inappropriately; they follow them slavishly without an understanding of their assumptions and limitations. It's primarily not the risk model that's at fault but the way that we as humans respond. We need more research into certain areas of market risk (especially market liquidity). More crucially, however, we need better educated risk managers, and we need senior managers and directors with a better understanding of risk. Investment in risk education will, I hope, encourage right thinking about risk models and better risk management decisions.

REFERENCES

Alexander, C., and E. Sheedy. 2008. Developing a stress testing framework based on market risk models. *Journal of Banking and Finance* 32 (10): 2220–2236.

Berkowitz, J., and J. O'Brien. 2002. How accurate are value-at-risk models at commercial banks? *Journal of Finance* 57 (3): 1093–1111.

Borio, C. 2000. Market liquidity and stress: Selected issues and policy implications. *BIS Quarterly Review*, 38–51.

Campbell, A. 2008. The year of living riskily. *Risk* 21: 28–32.

Deloitte. 2009. *Global risk management survey: Risk management in the spotlight*: New York: Deloitte.

Hull, J., and A. White. 1998. Incorporating volatility updating into the historical simulation method for value-at-risk. *Journal of Risk* 1 (Fall): 5–19.

Perignon, C., and D. Smith. 2006. *The level and quality of value-at-risk disclosure by commercial banks*. Vancouver, Canada: Simon Fraser University.

Poole, E., and P. D'Arcy. 2008. Liquidity in the interdealer foreign exchange market. *Reserve Bank of Australia Bulletin*, 1–6.

Senior Supervisors Group. 2008. Observations on risk management practices during the recent market turbulence.

Sheedy, E. 2009. Can risk modeling work? http://ssrn.com/abstract=1398486.

Supervision, B. C. o. B. 2009. Principles for sound stress testing practices and supervision. Basel, Switzerland: Basel Committee on Banking Supervision, consultative paper.

Taleb, N. 2007. *The black swan: The impact of the highly improbable*. London: Penguin.

Turner, L. 2009. *The Turner review: A regulatory response to the global banking crisis*. London: Financial Services Authority.

ABOUT THE AUTHOR

Elizabeth Sheedy has a Ph.D. in finance from Macquarie University, where she currently teaches courses in financial risk management. Her research focus is on market risk modeling. She is on the academic advisory committee for PRMIA (Professional Risk Managers International Association) and has co-edited *The Professional Risk Manager's Handbook.* Sheedy previously worked in the finance industry for a number of institutions, including Macquarie Bank and Westpac. Her industry experience was primarily in engineering structured derivative products for corporate and institutional clients. She had a special interest in the management of currency risks, developing the first Australian currency overlay product for asset portfolios.

CHAPTER 39

What Happened to Risk Management During the 2008–2009 Financial Crisis?

MICHAEL MCALEER
Econometric Institute, Erasmus University, Rotterdam, and Department of Applied Economics, National Chung Hsing University, Taiwan

JUAN-ANGEL JIMÉNEZ-MARTIN
Department of Quantitative Economics, Complutense University of Madrid

TEODOSIO PÉREZ-AMARAL
Department of Quantitative Economics, Complutense University of Madrid*

W hen dealing with market risk under the Basel II Accord, variation pays in the form of lower capital requirements and higher profits. Typically, generalized autoregressive conditional heteroskedasticity (GARCH)-type models are chosen to forecast value at risk (VaR) using a single risk model. We illustrate in this paper two useful variations to the standard mechanism for choosing forecasts, namely: combining different forecast models for each period, such as a daily model that forecasts the supremum or infinum value for the VaR; alternatively, select a single model to forecast VaR, and then modify the daily forecast, depending on the recent history of violations under the Basel II Accord. We illustrate these points using the Standard and Poor's 500 Composite Index. In many cases we find significant decreases in the capital requirements, while incurring a number of violations that stays within the Basel II Accord limits.

INTRODUCTION

A financial crisis occurs when there is a significant fall in stock prices and a marked increase in the uncertainty about the value of financial assets. A crisis may also be

*The first author is grateful to the Australian Research Council for financial support. The second author wishes to thank the Secretaría de Estado de Universidades of Spain through project SEJ206-14354 and Complutense University through project UCM-940063, and the third author wishes to thank the Secretaría de Estado de Universidades of Spain through project ECO2008-06091/ECON.

accompanied by panic, which can be contagious. During a financial crisis, the risks associated with investing increase substantially. The financial crisis of 2008 and 2009 has left an indelible mark on economic and financial structures worldwide, and left an entire generation of investors wondering how things could have become so bad. Many questions have been asked about whether appropriate regulations were in place, especially in the United States, to permit the appropriate monitoring and encouragement of (possibly excessive) risk taking.

The Basel II Accord (see Basel Committee on Banking Supervision 1996) was designed to monitor and encourage sensible risk taking by using appropriate models of risk to calculate value-at-risk (VaR) and subsequent daily capital charges. The Basel II Accord, however, does not apply to the United States.

VaR is defined as an estimate of the potential loss to be expected over a given period, and is a standard tool in financial risk management. It has become especially important following the 1995 amendment to the Basel Accord, whereby banks and other authorized deposit-taking institutions (ADIs) were permitted (and encouraged) to use internal models to forecast daily VaR (see Jorion (2000) for a detailed discussion). The last decade has witnessed a growing academic and professional literature comparing alternative modeling approaches to determine how to measure VaR, especially for large portfolios of financial assets.

The amendment to the initial Basel Accord was designed to encourage and reward institutions with superior risk management systems. A back-testing procedure, whereby actual returns are compared with the corresponding VaR forecasts, was introduced to assess the quality of the internal models used by ADIs. In cases in which internal models lead to a greater number of violations than could reasonably be expected, given the confidence level, the ADI is required to hold a higher level of capital (see Exhibit 39.5 for the penalties imposed under the Basel II Accord). Penalties imposed on ADIs affect profitability directly through higher capital charges, and indirectly through the imposition of a more stringent external model to forecast VaR. This is one reason why financial managers may prefer risk management strategies that are passive and conservative rather than active and aggressive.

Excessive conservatism can have a negative impact on the profitability of ADIs, as higher daily capital charges are subsequently required. Therefore, ADIs should perhaps consider a strategy that allows an endogenous decision as to how many times ADIs should violate in any financial year (for further details, see McAleer and da Veiga (2008a, 2008b), McAleer (2008), Caporin and McAleer (2009), and McAleer et al. (2009a)). This paper suggests alternative aggressive and conservative risk management strategies that can be compared with the use of one or more models of risk throughout the estimation and forecasting periods. We also discuss the strategy of choosing one risk model at the beginning of the period, and subsequently modifying the forecast depending on the recent history of violations of the model (see McAleer et al. 2009b).

In this paper we define *risk management* as choosing sensibly from a variety of risk models. We discuss the selection of optimal risk models by considering a combination of alternative risk models, and modifying the forecasts of a given risk model depending on the recent history of violations of the model. We evaluate the effects of the Basel II Accord on risk management, and how risk management strategies performed during the 2008–2009 financial crisis.

These issues are illustrated using Standard and Poor's 500 Composite Index, with an emphasis on how risk management practices were encouraged by the Basel II Accord regulations during the financial crisis.

THE FAST RECESSION OF 2008 AND 2009 IN PERSPECTIVE

The recession of 2008 and 2009 is undoubtedly severe, but not as much as the Great Depression. During the Great Depression of 1928 to 1934, Standard and Poor's 500 Composite Index (S&P 500)[1] and the Dow Jones Industrial Average (DJIA), using daily data for the period March 1, 1928, to January 7, 2009, fell by 86.18 percent and 89.19 percent, from a peak of June 9, 1929, to a trough of January 6, 1932, and a peak of March 9, 1929, to a trough of August 7, 1932, respectively, whereas the comparable figures for 2008 and 2009 for the S&P 500 and the DJIA were falls of 53.25 percent and 49.86 percent from a peak of March 1, 2008, to a trough of September 3, 2009, and from a peak of February 5, 2008, to a trough of September 3, 2009, respectively (see Exhibit 39.1).

The average daily falls in returns of the S&P 500 and the DJIA were 0.23 percent and 0.25 percent during the Great Depression, from a peak of June 9, 1929, to a trough of January 6, 1932, and from a peak of March 9, 1929, to a trough of August 7, 1932, respectively, while the average daily falls in returns of the S&P 500 and the DJIA were 0.25 percent and 0.32 percent in 2008 and 2009, from a peak of March 1, 2008 to a trough of September 3, 2009, and from a peak of February 5, 2008, to a trough of September 3, 2009, respectively, as illustrated in Exhibit 39.2.

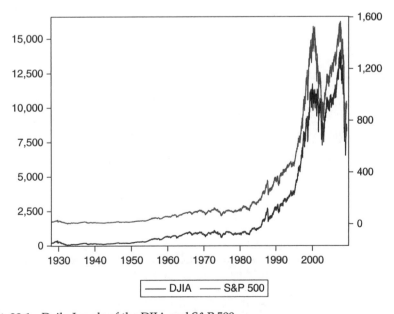

Exhibit 39.1   Daily Levels of the DJIA and S&P 500

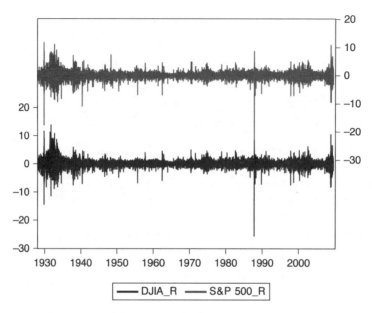

Exhibit 39.2   Daily Returns of the DJIA and S&P 500

The standard deviation of the S&P 500 and the DJIA returns reached 15 percent and 14 percent during the Great Depression, respectively, while in 2008 and 2009, both indexes reached only 11 percent, as illustrated in Exhibit 39.3.[2]

A caveat is that the Great Depression lasted for six years, while the most recent recession, which began in December 2007, may have ended by June 2009. This recession is less pronounced but somewhat faster than the Great Depression.

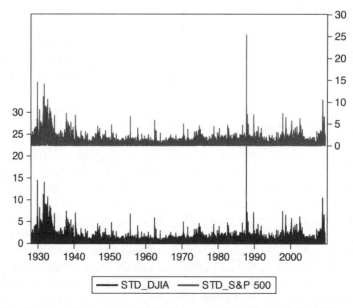

Exhibit 39.3   Standard Deviation of Daily Returns of the DJIA and S&P 500

Exhibit 39.4 Correlations between the DJIA
and the S&P 500

Correlations	Daily
Index (level)	0.996068
Return	0.940417
Standard deviation	0.999212

The DJIA and S&P 500 indexes are very highly correlated with each other, as seen in Exhibit 39.4, and tell a similar story in levels, returns, and volatility. The use of either is likely to be sufficient for analyzing the issues at hand.

As we have seen, the indexes fell by around 90 percent during the Great Depression, while they decreased by around 54 percent during the 2008–2009 crisis. Volatility reached 15 percent during the Great Depression while it reached 11 percent during the 2008–2009 crisis. The Great Depression was about five times deeper when measured by prices and 36 percent bigger when measured by volatility.

Once we have placed the 2008–2009 crisis into greater perspective, we will be able to discuss how market risk has been managed during it under the Basel II Accord.

RISK MANAGEMENT DURING THE 2008–2009 FINANCIAL CRISIS UNDER THE BASEL II ACCORD

When ADIs manage risk within the framework of the Basel II Accord, they can choose a model of risk for predicting their VaR. Then they have to communicate their forecasts on a daily basis to the relevant monetary authority.

The ADIs usually choose autoregressive conditional heteroskedasticity (ARCH)-type models (such as generalized autoregressive conditional heteroskedasticity (GARCH), the Glosten-Jagannathan-Runkle (GJR) model, the exponential general autoregressive conditional heteroskedasticity (EGARCH) model, and the exponentially weighted moving average (EWMA) model), all of which relate future risk to current and past risk (for a discussion of these and other models, see McAleer et al. (2009b)).

The Basel II Accord stipulates that daily capital charges (DCC) must be set at the higher of the previous day's VaR or the average VaR over the last 60 business days, multiplied by a factor $(3 + k)$ for a violation penalty (see Exhibit 39.5), wherein a violation involves the actual negative returns exceeding the VaR forecast negative returns for a given day. A description in detail of DCC can be seen in the appendix.

The multiplication factor (or penalty), k, depends on the central authority's assessment of the ADI's risk management practices and the results of a simple back test. It is determined by the number of times actual losses exceed a particular day's VaR forecast (Basel Committee on Banking Supervision 1996). The minimum multiplication factor of three is intended to compensate for various errors that can arise in model implementation, such as simplifying assumptions, analytical approximations, small sample biases and numerical errors that tend to reduce the true risk coverage of the model (see Stahl 1997). Increases in the multiplication factor are designed to increase the confidence level that is implied by the observed number

Exhibit 39.5   Basel II Accord Penalty Zones

Zone	Number of Violations	k
Green	0 to 4	0.00
Yellow	5	0.40
	6	0.50
	7	0.65
	8	0.75
	9	0.85
Red	10+	1.00

of exceptions to the 99 percent confidence level, as required by the regulators (for a detailed discussion of VaR, as well as exogenous and endogenous violations, see McAleer (2008), Jiménez-Martin et al. (2009), and McAleer et al. (2009b)).

This back-testing procedure intends to encourage appropriate risk management by ADIs, while ensuring their liquidity and solvency. In the next section, we discuss strategies that can be adopted by the ADIs to enhance risk management practices by minimizing their daily capital charges while restricting the number of violations to lie within the Basel II Accord limits.

PROPOSALS FOR SOPHISTICATING THE FORECASTS OF VAR TO MINIMIZE DCC WITHIN BASEL II

In this section, the forecast values of VaR for different forecast models and daily capital charges are analyzed before and during the 2008–2009 financial crisis.

In Exhibit 39.6, VaR forecasts are compared with S&P 500 returns for the period January 2, 2008, through July 2, 2009. The vertical axis represents returns, while the horizontal axis represents time. Returns of S&P 500 are given as the darker, variable line, which fluctuates around zero. The lighter, solid line represents the infinum of the VaR calculated for individual models of volatility (VAR upperbound), which reflects an aggressive risk management strategy, whereas the lower, light and broken line represents the supremum of the VaR calculated for the individual models of volatility (VAR lowerbound), which reflects a conservative risk management strategy. These two lines correspond to a combination of alternative risk models (see McAleer et al. (2009b) for further details).

As can be seen in Exhibit 39.7, VaR forecasts obtained from the different models of volatility have fluctuated, as expected, during the first few months of 2008. It has been relatively low, at below 5 percent, and relatively stable between April and August 2008. Around September 2008, VaR started increasing until it peaked in October 2008, between 10 and 15 percent, depending on the model of volatility considered. This is essentially a fivefold increase in VaR in a matter of two months. In the last two months of 2008, VaR decreased to between 5 and 8 percent, which is still twice as large as it was just a few months earlier. It continued to decrease in the first six months of 2009 toward values similar to those immediately before September 2008.

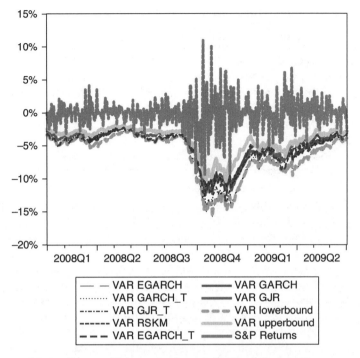

Exhibit 39.6 VaR for S&P 500 Returns, January 2, 2008 to July 2, 2009

In McAleer and colleagues (2009b), we developed a risk management strategy that used combinations of several models for forecasting VaR. It was found that an aggressive risk management strategy (namely, by choosing the infinum of VaR forecasts, or upperbound) yielded the lowest mean capital charges, and had the highest frequency of minimizing daily capital charges throughout the forecasting period, but which also tended to violate too often. On the other hand, a conservative

Exhibit 39.7 Percentage of Days Minimizing Daily Capital Charges, Mean Daily Capital Charges, and Number of Violations for Alternative Models of Volatility

Model	% of Days Minimizing Daily Capital Charges	Mean Daily Capital Charges	Number of Violations
Riskmetrics	14.0 %	0.163	10
GARCH	0.0 %	0.161	13
GJR	10.0 %	0.157	7
EGARCH	1.70%	0.146	13
GARCH_t	0.00%	0.171	3
GJR_t	0.00%	0.167	3
EGARCH_t	34.0 %	0.153	3
Lowerbound	0.00%	0.177	3
Upperbound	39.6 %	0.143	16

Note: The models of volatility chosen are the most frequently used in this literature. The figures are for the S&P 500 Index from January 2, 2008, to February 12, 2009.

risk management strategy (namely, by choosing the supremum, or lowerbound) had far fewer violations, and correspondingly higher mean daily capital charges. This can be seen in Exhibit 39.6, taken from McAleer et al. (2009b).

The area between the bounds provided by the aggressive and conservative risk management strategies would seem to be a fertile area for future research.

We could also compare the previous strategies with a dynamic learning strategy, DYLES, developed in McAleer et al. (2009a). For that strategy, we disclose a market risk (MRD) that is the one given by a risk model that was modified by a weight factor.

The DYLES strategy leads to capital requirements that are significantly lower than those of competing models that stay within the Basel II limits. In particular, for a period of one year, when DYLES is used, it can improve on EGARCH t, which, as seen in Exhibit 39.3, is one of the leading competitors, decreasing the average credit requirement by up to 96 basis points. See McAleer et al. (2009a).

The Basel II Accord is currently under scrutiny, with the purpose of enhancing its effectiveness for multinational financial regulation, as can be seen in the Consultative Document of the Basel Committee on Banking Supervision (2009). The document contains proposals for changes to Pillars 1 to 3, namely minimum capital requirements, supervisory review process, and market discipline.

The document discusses the application of more stringent risk weights, the management of liquidity risks and of solvency risks, and the use of stress tests (pages 2, 23, and 25), among other proposed regulatory measures.

CONCLUSION

We analyzed in this paper the construction of risk management strategies that used combinations of several models for forecasting VaR. It was found that an aggressive risk management strategy yielded the lowest mean capital charges, and had the highest frequency of minimizing daily capital charges throughout the forecasting period, but which also tended to violate too often. On the other hand, a conservative risk management strategy would yield far fewer violations, and correspondingly higher mean daily capital charges.

We also compared the previous two strategies with the DYLES strategy of McAleer and colleagues (2009a). In this case, we found slightly higher mean capital charges than in the aggressive strategy, while the number of violations remained within the Basel II Accord limits.

Note: The analysis presented here strongly suggests that, in seeking to manage market risk optimally, it can pay to vary risk management models on a daily basis.

APPENDIX

$$DCC_t = \sup \left\{ -(3+k)\,\overline{\text{VaR}}_{60}, \ -\text{VaR}_{t-1} \right\} \qquad (39.1)$$

where:

DCC = daily capital charges, which is the higher of $-(3+k)\,\overline{\text{VaR}}_{60}$ and $-\text{VaR}_{t-1}$,

VaR_t = Value-at-Risk for day t,

$$VaR_t = \hat{Y}_t - z_t \cdot \hat{\sigma}_t,$$

$\overline{VaR}_{60} =$ mean VaR over the previous 60 working days,

$\hat{Y}_t =$ estimated return at time t,

$z_t = 1\%$ critical value of the distribution of returns at time t,

$\hat{\sigma}_t =$ estimated risk (or square root of volatility) at time t,

$0 \leq k \leq 1$ is the Basel II violation penalty (see Exhibit 39.7).

NOTES

1. Some changes in the definition of the S&P 500 Index over time:

   1923—Standard & Poor's develops its first stock market indicators. The new stock indexes cover 26 industry groups and 233 companies. Also, S&P introduces base-weighted aggregate techniques to gauge stock market performance.

   1926—Standard & Poor's creates a 90 Stock Composite Price Index, comprising 50 industrials, 20 rails, and 20 utilities. The new composite has a base period of 1926 = 100 and is calculated and published weekly. Historical values are available going back to 1918. The 233 and the industry group indexes are rebased to 1926 = 100 and are calculated and published weekly.

   1928—Standard & Poor's 90 Stock Composite Price Index is calculated and published daily.

   1941—The 233 grows to 416, comprising 72 industry subgroups. The new 416 and the 90 Stock Composite are rebased to 1935–1939 = 100.

   1957—The 416 becomes the Standard & Poor's 500 Composite Stock Price Index. Thanks to technological advancements, computers are introduced and permit the 500 to be calculated and disseminated at one-minute intervals throughout the trading day. In order to create a lengthy historical time series, the new 500 is linked to the 90 Stock Composite Price Index daily. S&P 500 Index prices become available back to 1928. The original 233 and 90 stock indexes have evolved into the modern 500. The 500 now consists of 425 industrials, 60 utilities, and 15 rails, and has a base period of 1941–1943 = 10.

2. On October 19, 1987 (Black Monday) stock markets crashed and fell a huge value in a very short time. As shown in Exhibit 39.1, the S&P 500 and the DJIA fell by 23 percent and 26 percent just in one day, respectively. The standard deviation of both S&P 500 and DJIA returns reached 25.5 percent. The Black Monday decline was the largest one-day percentage decline in stock market history.

REFERENCES

Basel Committee on Banking Supervision. 1996. Supervisory framework for the use of back-testing in conjunction with the internal model-based approach to market risk capital requirements. Basel, Switzerland: BIS.

———. 2009. Proposed enhancements to the Basel II framework. Basel, Switzerland: BIS, consultative document. www.bis.org/publ/bcbs150.pdf?noframes=1.

Caporin, M., and M. McAleer. 2009. The ten commandments for managing investments. *Journal of Economic Surveys*, forthcoming. http://ssrn.com/abstract=1342265.

Jiménez-Martín, J.-A., M. McAleer, and T. Pérez-Amaral. 2009. The ten commandments for managing value-at-risk under the Basel II Accord. *Journal of Economic Surveys*, forthcoming. http://ssrn.com/abstract=1356803.

Jorion, P. 2000. *Value at risk: The new benchmark for managing financial risk*. New York: McGraw-Hill.

McAleer, M. 2008. The ten commandments for optimizing value-at-risk and daily capital charges. *Journal of Economic Surveys*, forthcoming. http://ssrn.com/abstract=1354686.

McAleer, M., J.-Á. Jiménez-Martin, and T. Pérez-Amaral. 2009a. *A decision rule to minimize daily capital charges in forecasting value-at-risk*. Madrid, Spain: Complutense University Department of Quantitative Economics. http://ssrn.com/abstract=1349844.

———. 2009b. Has the Basel II Accord encouraged risk management during the 2008–2009 financial crisis? Madrid, Spain: Complutense University Department of Quantitative Economics. http://papers.ssrn.com/sol3/papers.cfm?abstract_id=1397239.

McAleer, M., and B. da Veiga. 2008a. Forecasting value-at-risk with a parsimonious portfolio spillover GARCH (PS-GARCH) model. *Journal of Forecasting* 27: 1–19.

———. 2008b. Single index and portfolio models for forecasting value-at-risk thresholds. *Journal of Forecasting* 27: 217–235.

ABOUT THE AUTHORS

Michael McAleer holds a Ph.D. in economics from Queen's University, Canada. He is a professor of quantitative finance at the Econometric Institute, Erasmus School of Economics, Erasmus University Rotterdam, in the Netherlands; a fellow of the Tinbergen Institute in the Netherlands; distinguished chair professor in the department of Applied Economics at National Chung Hsing University, Taiwan; and distinguished professor, faculty of economics at Chiang Mai University in Thailand as well as adjunct professor at universities in Spain, Japan, and New Zealand. He has published more than 500 journal articles and scientific monographs in econometrics, economics, finance, and statistics, and is a member of the editorial boards of *Econometric Reviews, Journal of Economic Surveys, Mathematics and Computers in Simulation,* and *Environmental Modelling and Software.*

Juan-Angel Jiménez-Martin is an associate professor of econometrics at Complutense University. He previously held positions as an assistant professor at the European University of Madrid and visiting scholar at George Washington University. He holds a Ph.D. in economics from Complutense University. Professor Jimenez-Martin has published in academic journals, including *Journal of Economic Surveys, Open Economies Review, Applied Economics, International Business & Economics Research Journal, Journal of Commercial Biotechnology, Papeles de Economía Española,* and *Estudios de Economia Aplicada*. Professor Jimenez-Martin's research covers a variety of topics in econometrics, finance, and international finance, including exchange rate models, risk premium in exchange rate markets, and VaR.

Teodosio Pérez-Amaral is an associate professor of economics at Complutense University in Madrid. He previously held the position of staff economist at the Bank of Spain. He has been a visiting scholar at the University of California, San Diego. He has also been a consultant to DIW of Berlin, Deutsche Telekom, and Telefónica. Professor Pérez-Amaral holds a Ph.D. in economics from the University of California, San Diego. He has published in academic journals, including the *Oxford Bulletin of Economics, Econometric Theory, Applied Economics,* and *Information Economics and Policy*. His research covers topics in telecommunications economics and model construction and selection.

CHAPTER 40

Risk Management Lessons from the Global Financial Crisis for Derivative Exchanges

JAYANTH VARMA
Professor in the Finance and Accounting Area, Indian Institute
of Management, Ahmedabad*

D uring the global financial crisis, no major derivative clearinghouse in the world encountered distress, while many banks were pushed to the brink and beyond. This was despite the exchanges having to deal with more volatile assets—equities are about twice as volatile as real estate, and natural gas is about 10 times more volatile than real estate. Clearly, risk management at the world's leading exchanges proved to be superior to that of the banks. The global financial crisis has shown that the quality of risk management models does matter. Three important lessons have emerged from this experience:

1. The quality of risk management models can be measured along two independent dimensions: crudeness versus sophistication and fragility versus robustness. The crisis of 2007–2009 has shown that of these two dimensions, the second dimension (robustness) is far more important than the first dimension (sophistication).
2. An apparent structural change in the economy and the financial markets may only be a temporary change in the volatility regime. Risk models that ignore this can be disastrous.
3. Risk models of the 1990s, based on normal distributions, linear correlations, and value at risk, are obsolete not only in theory but also in practice.

Most of this paper deals with these lessons from the crisis of 2007–2009. In the final section, the paper argues that as derivative exchanges prepare to trade and clear ever more complex products, it is important that they refine and develop their risk models even further so that they can survive the next crisis.

---

*This chapter is based on Varma, J. R. 2009. *Risk management lessons from the global financial crisis for derivative exchanges.* IIMA Working Paper 2009-02-06. SSRN: http://ssrn.com/abstract=1376276.

LESSON 1: ROBUSTNESS

The contrast between the performance of banks and derivative exchanges during the crisis of 2007–2009 illustrates the difference between fragile models and robust models.

Fragile Models Failed: Bank Regulation

The evolution of banking regulation provides a good example of what happens when robustness is ignored. The Basel I system of bank regulation, based on a simple leverage ratio, was both crude and fragile. It was crude in that it did not distinguish between safe loans and risky loans, nor did it account for the degree of diversification of the bank's assets. It was fragile because these deficiencies could be easily gamed by the banks that it was trying to regulate. In other words, Basel I was highly vulnerable to Goodhart's law: when a measure becomes a regulatory target, it ceases to be a good measure. The simple leverage ratio is a useful metric only when no regulator is using it!

In response to the problems of the crude leverage ratio, Basel II introduced a complex model running into hundreds of pages to account for the quality of assets and of their correlations. Unfortunately, these sophisticated models were based on normal distributions, linear correlations, and value at risk, all of which failed during the crisis (see Lesson 3). Basel II was highly sophisticated, but it was still fragile.

Crude Models Succeeded: Derivative Exchanges

In contrast to the banks, most derivative exchanges today use crude but robust margining systems. For example, the Standard Portfolio Analysis of Risk (SPAN) is a portfolio margining method developed by the Chicago Mercantile Exchange in 1988. It calculates the portfolio loss under several price and volatility scenarios and determines the margin based on these loss levels. These models do not explicitly take correlations into account. Ad hoc offsets are used to provide margining benefits for spread positions (offsetting positions in closely related assets as well as offsetting positions in the same asset at different maturities). Though correlations are by no means constant, the spread margins or offsets are typically kept constant for long periods of time. Moreover, they are set at levels that lead to overmargining of spread positions relative to what might be indicated by estimated correlations.

The big advantage of this crude model is that the margining system is very robust in the face of correlation breakdowns and correlation instability. Moreover, by eliminating the use of correlations, these models are also able to avoid a dependence on the normal distribution. It is very easy to use a fat-tailed distribution while choosing the scenarios for a SPAN-based model.

The greater importance of robustness rather than sophistication is one of the ways in which risk management models are very different from valuation models. By their very nature, valuation models need to be heavily parameterized and calibrated to market prices. Increasing sophistication and complexity do lead to greater model risk, but this is unavoidable, because trading at even slightly wrong prices can be disastrous for a financial intermediary.

Risk management models on the other hand do not need to be so highly calibrated and parameterized. Crudeness (leaning toward conservatism) is less of a problem in risk management, because unlike in valuation, here it only locks up capital for some time; it does not affect the transaction price itself.

For example, nobody would dream of valuing stock index options using a fixed unchanging volatility. In risk management, however, Korea has been very successful in its index futures market with a flat 15 percent margin that was kept unchanged for a very long time despite fluctuations in market volatility. Average margin levels in Korea are excessive compared to many other markets in the world—even those markets (like India) where the average volatility is comparable. Yet, Korea has developed one of the largest index futures markets in the world. What this shows is that a crude model can provide very high risk protection while not impeding market development.

Compared to Korea, Indian derivatives regulation is at the other end of the spectrum—the volatility is estimated every day using the RiskMetrics (exponentially weighted moving average) methodology. Margins are adjusted every day based on the latest estimate of the volatility. It could be argued that the more sophisticated margining system in India is actually a source of systemic risk for the exchange. If margins are revised at a frequency that exceeds the ability of the payment system to mobilize funds from the ultimate client, then large price movements can result in panic unwinding of levered positions that exacerbates the original price movement. There is anecdotal evidence to suggest that this is what has happened.

Robust Sophistication: The Long Run Goal

To summarize: risk management models can be classified into four possible combinations of crudeness and sophistication and robustness and fragility, as shown in Exhibit 40.1.

I believe that risk models must evolve first toward robustness and then toward sophistication, as shown in Exhibit 40.2, because the movement to robust and sophisticated models is bound to be long and difficult. In this light, the evolution from Basel I (crude and fragile) to Basel II (sophisticated and fragile) was a move in the wrong direction. In the long run, risk management models must become both robust and sophisticated. This transition will be slow because of the mathematical

Exhibit 40.1   Classification of Risk Management Models on the Basis of Crudeness/Sophistication and Robustness/Fragility

	Fragile	Robust
Crude	Simple leverage ratios as in Basel-I treatment of the banking book	Simple scenario-based models like SPAN used by derivative exchanges
Sophisticated	Complex models based on normal distribution like Basel-II	Fat-tailed nonlinear dependence models—the long-term goal of risk management

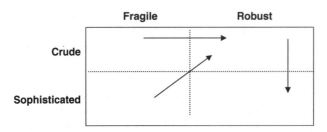

Exhibit 40.2 Risk Management Models Must Evolve Toward Greater Robustness and Then to Greater Sophistication

complexity of modeling risk in a robust way when distributions are fat-tailed (not normal) and exhibit nonlinear dependences.

LESSON 2: REGIME SWITCHING VERSUS STRUCTURAL BREAKS

Another important lesson from the ongoing global financial crisis is that models calibrated to short time periods from a benign economic environment can fail disastrously when the economic environment becomes more adverse. During the period of the "Great Moderation" (from the late 1990s to 2007), macroeconomic and systemic volatility was quite low. Haldane[1] provides Exhibit 40.3 for macroeconomic volatility in the United Kingdom.

We would all agree that margin levels should have been lower during the Great Moderation than earlier. The question is whether the margins during this period should have been based only on the observed volatility during this period or whether the margins should also have been influenced by the past experience.

The structural-break perspective would have argued that there was a structural transformation in the economy in the late 1990s, which made the earlier data irrelevant and meaningless. In this perspective, the margins would be based only on data from the Great Moderation.

The regime-switching perspective would argue that the economy operates under different regimes at different points of time and that there is a nontrivial probability of the regime switching to a more volatile one. In this perspective, the long-run data are extremely useful and important because it indicates the average volatility across several different regimes.

Exhibit 40.3 Volatility of U.K. Macroeconomic Variables During the Great Moderation Compared with 150-Year Average

Variable	Volatility (1998–2007)	Volatility (1857–2007)
GDP growth	0.6%	2.7%
Earnings growth	0.5%	6.4%
Inflation	0.9%	5.9%
Unemployment	0.6%	3.4%

Source: Haldane (2009) Annex Exhibit 40.1.

I believe that prudent risk management should be based on a regime switching framework and not on a structural break framework. In practice, one may not go so far as to estimate a formal statistical model (for example, a Markov switching model) for the regime switching. What is essential is that the risk management model must be robust under the assumption that regime switching could occur.

A simple and robust solution is to calibrate to very long times even if such a time period cuts across one or more structural breaks in the data. What can be regarded as a structural break in a valuation model is often best regarded as a regime switching in a risk management model—the implication being that regime switches could reverse as well. Risk management is designed to deal with rare events, and the probability of such events can be estimated only by examining long historical stretches of data.

LESSON 3: PITFALLS OF 1990S-ERA RISK MANAGEMENT SYSTEMS

The risk management systems of Basel II and of many banks were based on 1990s-era risk models. Since the early 1990s, there have been three major advances in the theoretical foundations of risk management:

1. Value at Risk (VaR) has been abandoned in favor of coherent risk measures like expected shortfall (ES)
2. The normal distribution has been discarded in favor of fatter-tailed distributions
3. Linear correlation measures have been replaced by copula-based models of tail dependence

The cumulative effect of these three advances is so great that we must today regard the risk measurement methodologies developed in the early 1990s as theoretically obsolete. The global financial crisis has shown that in practice, too, these models have failed.

The major problems with VaR, normal distributions, and linear correlations can be summarized as follows:

1. The inadequacy of VaR becomes obvious when one thinks of the 99 percent VaR as the best of the worst 1 percent of possible outcomes. For example, if one considers 1,000 days of data, the worst 1 percent corresponds to the worst 10 days. The 99 percent VaR is the loss on the best of those 10 bad days while expected shortfall is the average of the 10 bad days. VaR works reasonably well when the 10 worst days are all more or less alike, and the VaR is therefore not too different from the expected shortfall. Otherwise, VaR is a bad measure of risk.
2. Normal distributions are ubiquitous in the natural world and in social phenomena because of a simple statistical fact (the central limit theorem): any phenomenon that is the result of a large number of small causes obeys the normal distribution. Asset price changes are often affected by a multiplicity of small causes, and the normal distribution appears to be a good fit.

However, once in a while we do get a large cause that causes big moves in asset prices. This means that the normal distribution fails and we have fat tails instead. Moves that are supposed to happen only once in a century start to happen every day.

3. Correlation is a measure of the linear relationship between two assets, and is quite meaningful during normal times. During periods of turmoil, however, correlations are often unstable and the assumed diversification benefits may disappear. Extreme price movements are more correlated than usual (for example, the crash of 1987, the dot-com bubble of 1999, and the turmoil of 2007 and 2008). Instability of correlations often reflects the inadequacy of correlation as a measure of dependence. In reality, the dependence between two assets could be stable but nonlinear. Nonlinear dependence can account for the high correlation of extreme movements and the modest correlation of mild movements. It can also account for asymmetric dependence relationships when the dependence is different in rising and falling markets.

TOWARDS ROBUST SOPHISTICATION: THE FUTURE OF RISK MANAGEMENT

By using crude models, derivative exchanges have by and large avoided the three pitfalls of value at risk, normal distributions, and linear correlations that have sunk other risk management systems. There are, however, significant advantages in designing risk management systems that explicitly incorporate coherent risk measures (expected shortfall), fat-tailed distributions, and nonlinear dependence structure.

Advances in computing power over the last two decades make it feasible to use risk models that require a thousand times as many computations as the models of the early 1990s. It is relatively easy to convert SPAN into an explicit expected shortfall measure for a single asset. This will require several changes: we must use vastly more scenarios than SPAN; we need analytical approximations to interpolate and integrate between scenarios; even after adding scenarios with low weights in the fat tails, it would be necessary to use a power law approximation to extrapolate and integrate beyond the most extreme scenario.

The real difficulties are in going beyond one asset without relying on ad hoc margin offsets as exchanges do today. Copulas provide the mathematical machinery to model nonlinear dependence, and the t-copula is potentially tractable enough to make the task feasible.

Finally, exchanges need to be wary of adverse selection—positions that are undermargined would be heavily used while those that are overmargined would be less popular. Even if the margins were right on average for randomly chosen positions, they would be too low for the actual positions chosen by traders. Borrowing from the idea of reverse stress tests, the exchange could identify scenarios that would bankrupt the clearing corporation and then add them to the SPAN scenarios used for margining. Some mathematical techniques for doing this reverse stress test are available.

Derivative exchanges should not become complacent after surviving the crisis of 2007–2009. They have to keep improving their risk models as they start trading more and more complex products in ever greater volume. If they do not do so, the next crisis may not be as kind to them as this crisis has been.

NOTE

1. Haldane, A. G. 2009. *Why banks failed the stress test.* Bank of England, www.bankofengland .co.uk/publications/speeches/2009/speech374.pdf.

ABOUT THE AUTHOR

Jayanth Varma holds a doctorate in management from the Indian Institute of Management, Ahmedabad, and is a professor in the finance and accounting area at the same institute. He has served on the board of India's securities market regulator (SEBI) and has chaired several regulatory committees on risk management in the equity and commodity derivatives markets in India. He is also on the board of one of India's large private sector banks. The books that he has authored or co-authored include *Derivatives and Risk Management, Strategic Corporate Finance: Managing under Economic Crises, Portfolio Management,* and the *Great Indian Scam.* The last-mentioned book (on the Indian securities scam of 1992) was a national best seller. He has carried out extensive research in the field of Indian financial markets and finance theory and published extensively in academic journals.

PART VI

The Problem of Regulation

CHAPTER 41

Regulation and Financial Stability in the Age of Turbulence

DAVID S. BIERI

School of Public & International Affairs, Virginia Tech, Blacksburg, Virginia

P ossibly one of the most perplexing puzzles of the global financial crisis is that nobody saw it coming. Gale-force winds, yes. A storm, perhaps. But neither policy makers, market participants, nor experts anticipated the tsunami that ravaged financial markets. Given the abundance of safeguards, a collapse of the global financial system seemed unthinkable. Yet still, "How could this happen?" asks the Bank for International Settlements (BIS) disarmingly in its most recent annual report (BIS 2009). Not since its own foundation during the Great Depression had a crisis of similar proportions engulfed the global economy, leaving vast segments of the financial system dysfunctional.[1] This chapter illustrates how the crisis has pushed financial (in)stability to the very top of the agenda for policy reforms and discusses how it has come to constitute the litmus test for effective regulation.

ANATOMY OF A CRISIS

From a historic perspective, one can broadly distinguish between three types of financial instability. First, there is volatility-based instability, such as the ERM crises in 1980s and 1990s, the 1987 stock market crash, the 1994 emerging market bond market instability, the 1998 Russian default, the Argentinean default in 2001, and, in part, the U.S. subprime crisis that started in 2007. A second type of instability is stress-based instability, usually triggered by the default of an individual institution such as the insolvency of Credit-Anstalt in 1931, the collapse of Bankhaus Herstatt in 1974, the folding of BCCI in 1991, the Barings scandal in 1995, the failure of LTCM in 1998 and the most recent string of institutional failures, from Northern Rock to Bear Stearns, Lehman Brothers, and American International Group (AIG). Lastly, there are instances of crisis-based financial instability, the causes of which usually emanate from the real economy or the financial system. Costly bank insolvencies and major adjustments in the level of asset prices tend to follow. During this type of financial instability, there is often a very strong (reinforcing) interaction between the financial sector and the real economy, with strong contagion effects both domestically and internationally.

A Minskian Meltdown

Together with the Great Depression and the Asian financial crisis, the current global financial crisis displays all the hallmarks of this last category: A perfect storm in financial markets triggered a massive global credit crunch, which was soon followed by a global recession. This, in turn, deepened the credit crunch as demand and employment fell, and credit losses of financial institutions surged. An unlikely Minskian scenario had become unsettling reality: The intensifying process of financialization across the global economy had led to an increase in the amplitude of its cyclical fluctuations, culminating in the current episode of financial instability (Minsky 1991).

Diagnosing the Causes

The causes of the current crisis can be divided into two broad categories: macroeconomic and microeconomic. The macroeconomic causes are twofold: problems associated with the buildup of imbalances in international claims and difficulties created by the long period of low real interest rates. The microeconomic causes can be grouped into three areas: incentives, risk measurement, and—the focus of this chapter—regulation. In this context, financial institutions found it relatively easy to move activities outside the regulatory perimeter. Worse still, financial regulation was not equipped to see the risk concentrations and flawed incentives behind the financial innovation boom. The perimeter of regulation was poorly drawn in most countries, leaving large risk concentrations and leverage buildups out of regulators' sight. Financial supervisors were preoccupied with the formal banking sector, not with the risks building in the shadow financial system.

At the same time, other critical microprudential issues, such as overall leverage, and macroprudential aspects, such as the impact of the economic cycle on systemic risks, were ignored. Macroeconomic policies did not take into account the buildup of systemic risks in the financial system and in housing markets. Lastly, the global financial architecture still only encompasses a fragmented surveillance system that compounded the inability to see growing vulnerabilities and links. After all, despite an increasingly integrated global financial system, much of its institutional governance structure still hinges on national institutions.

IN SEARCH OF FINANCIAL STABILITY

Over the last decade or so, addressing financial instability has become a policy priority. The current crisis serves as a painful reminder of how far policy makers are still away from developing a satisfactory operational framework. To some extent, progress remains constrained by the fuzziness with which financial (in)stability can be measured (Borio and Drehmann 2009).

Consensus with regard to the definition of monetary stability is well established, with notions ranging from stability of the (anticipated) value of money to price level stability or low levels of inflation. Monetary stability is a vital ingredient for sustainable economic growth, and its unique institutional responsibility resides with the central bank.

Definitions Matter

The story for financial stability, however, is somewhat different; there is a much broader spectrum of definitions, and consensus seems to exist only insofar as financial stability is deemed a good thing, and that it is mostly noticed by its absence.[2]

Broadly speaking, one can distinguish between a systems approach—primarily linking financial stability to a well-functioning financial system[3]—and a more narrow definition relating to the (excess) volatility of an observable financial variable, such as asset price volatility or interest rate smoothness. The debate around finding a suitable definition is more than a semantic one, particularly since any given definition predetermines the role assigned to monetary policy in contributing to financial stability.

From the perspective of policy makers, however, it is clear that some of the elements that might potentially harbor a threat to financial stability are actually very desirable for achieving the goal of monetary stability. Financial innovation, for example, has been key to making the transmission mechanism for monetary policy more effective.

A Trade-Off between Monetary and Financial Stability?

In the sense of Tinbergen (1956), if monetary authorities have control over only one policy instrument, namely monetary policy, they can achieve only one independent goal, for example, price stability. By delegating the broader objective of financial stability to a regulatory or supervisory body, time inconsistency complications of a direct trade-off between the two goals can be avoided. In turn, this raises the challenge for policy makers to identify suitable trade-offs between monetary and financial stability.[4]

The mainstream policy consensus is highly skeptical concerning the existence of such a trade-off. Monetary instability is regarded as the main threat to financial stability, because inflation distorts perceptions about future return possibilities. Price stability is thus deemed a sufficient condition for financial stability. In this sense, central banks should not focus on gauging the effects of asset price inflation on core inflation, but they should instead place their focus on capital requirements that increase with the growth of credit and are collateralized by inflated assets.[5]

More recently, as inflation rates have reached historic lows in most industrialized economies, a new school of thought has emerged that suggests that low and stable inflation can make financial systems even more vulnerable because of the threat of asset price bubbles and the associated irrational exuberance of market participants. Indeed, the current crisis seems to be a very powerful case in point in favor of this so-called new environment hypothesis.[6]

In an attempt to reconcile these conflicting views, Issing (2003) concludes that the strict systems-based definition of financial stability excludes any trade-off between monetary and financial stability by definition. The key to solving this apparent contradiction lies in shifting the focus to the role of the policy horizon: A short-term conflict between monetary and financial stability may indeed be

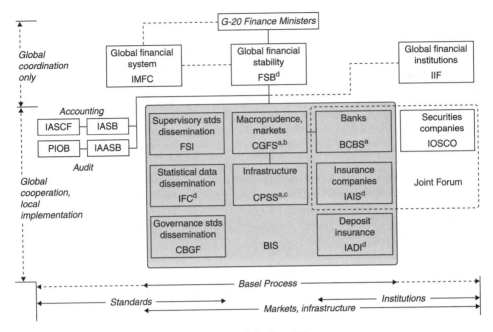

Exhibit 41.1 Global Regulatory System and the Basel Process
[a]Permanent committee hosted at the BIS, originally established by the G10 central banks. The BCBS, CGFS, and CPSS are relatively autonomous from the BIS with regard to setting their agendas and activities.
[b]Including the Markets Committee (formerly the Gold and Foreign Exchange Committee).
[c]Also handles the secretariat functions for the Central Bank Counterfeit Deterrence Group.
[d]Independent organizations with secretariat that is hosted by the BIS, but does not directly report to the BIS or its member central banks.
Source: Reproduced with permission from Bieri (2009).

possible, as long as it is optimal for the authorities to deviate from the desired rate of inflation to maintain price stability over a medium run. With a clear definition of an appropriate horizon to which policy objectives should apply, the conflict disappears.[7]

The institutional responsibilities for financial stability are traditionally shared across different institutions, namely finance ministries, central banks, and regulators. While clearly defined accountabilities for each of these institutions is a sine qua non, the actual goal of financial stability can be brought about only by an effective coordination of their efforts. This is the role of the so-called Basel Process, which is illustrated in Exhibit 41.1.

REGULATORY CHALLENGES IN THE AGE OF TURBULENCE

Implicitly or explicitly, the promotion of both monetary and financial stability has been a key goal for national authorities in developed economies for much of the post–Bretton Woods era. From the inflationary scares of the late 1970s well into the 1990s, the policies of the "Washington consensus" implied a nearly exclusive focus by central banks on monetary stability. Central banks' budgetary and institutional independence from political processes became the dominant governance paradigm. At the same time, several bouts of financial instability leading up to the Asian financial crisis demonstrated the importance of independence of regulatory and supervisory agencies for financial stability (Quintyn and Taylor 2002). In parallel, the move toward unified financial sector supervision became more pressing.

Governance and Regulatory Best Practice

Indeed, the systemic banking crises of the last 30 years can largely be attributed to weak, fragmented, and ineffective regulation that was shaped by the political interference of special interests. The current crisis should be no different. As in previous episodes of instability, it is the highly toxic cocktail of investor exuberance and regulatory complacency that brought the mighty global financial system crashing to its knees this time.

Today, a vast majority of the world's financial supervisory agencies are separate stand-alone agencies, while most bank supervisors are still part of a central bank. Most of these agencies now have operational independence, yet bank supervisors are still unique in viewing financial stability as part of their mandate (Seelig and Novoa 2009). After almost two years of global financial market upheaval, this much seems clear today: best practice with regard to the governance structure and the prudential mandate of national financial supervisors are at best a necessary, and by no means sufficient, condition for financial stability.[8]

In his aptly titled memoirs-cum-economic treatise, Alan Greenspan, the former chairman of the Federal Reserve, offers some rules of thumb as guidance for the (re)design of regulation in a globalized financial system (Greenspan 2007, 374–375). First, "Regulation approved in a crisis must be subsequently fine-tuned" and second, "Regulations outlive their usefulness and should be renewed periodically."

Financial Stability as a Public Good

The rationale for financial regulation rests ultimately on two objectives: the desire to maintain financial stability by mitigating systemic risk and the desire to protect consumers (investors). Consumer protection and mitigation of systemic risk are mostly complementary, but they can also conflict. The current crisis has shown that measures taken to protect particular market participants (e.g., homeowners in the United States or depositors in the United Kingdom) may sometimes have unintended consequences, increasing systemic risk.

Financial stability carries all the textbook hallmarks of a public good: first, it is nonrival, as its benefits to one consumer are not limited by the simultaneous consumption by other consumers. Second, financial stability is nonexcludable, as its benefits are available to all economic agents, even to those who do not pay for them (i.e., entities that are not regulated). Lastly, individual agents cannot actively withdraw themselves from the influence of financial stability.

Public finance theory has long established that the private sector production of public goods yields an undersupply with respect to its optimal quantity. For this very reason, financial stability has traditionally been produced by and provided by national governments. Globalization, however, has brought about a partial shift in the optimal locus of production, since financial stability is no longer a fully spatially delineated public good. This has considerably raised the stakes in the ordoliberal challenge for well-coordinated international policy cooperation in the age of turbulence.

Global Change, Local Challenge

As the financial landscape of the post–Bretton Woods era has changed, and banks, insurers, and securities firms have begun to offer similar or even identical products, central banks and regulatory authorities have recognized the growing need for a central vehicle for coordinating their efforts. With their various regulatory and supervisory initiatives and by providing the institutional building blocks, the Basel-based committees form the natural home for such a global coordination exercise. Collectively, the interaction of the committees and their working groups is referred to as the Basel Process. As such, it encompasses a global framework aimed at harmonizing regulatory and supervisory processes and standards.

Exhibit 41.1 gives a schematic overview of the specialized division of labor between the various committees and regulatory bodies that are involved in the Basel Process. This chart highlights that although the global financial system is increasingly interlinked, much of the international regulatory system still operates on a sectoral level. While this dichotomy is ever more problematic, the Basel Process provides a unique institutional framework for future regulatory and supervisory coordination.[9] See Exhibit 41.2 for a list of entities involved and the abbreviations.

REGULATORY LESSONS AND OUTLOOK

The economic theory of regulation pioneered by Stigler (1971) stipulates that regulation often induces changes in behavior that go against the very effects that regulation intended in the first place. During periods of investor exuberance and comparative regulatory complacency, these adverse effects of regulation are very likely to be muted if not invisible altogether. Any new regulation, such as Basel II, will bring with it the so-called boundary problem of regulation, that is, the problem that institutions in the regulated sector and those in the unregulated sector face different incentives.[10] Supervisors must thus attempt to learn how the regulated are seeking to avoid the constraints placed upon them. During the Great Moderation in the run-up to the crisis, the boundary problem profoundly misaligned incentives in the financial sector. This induced large-scale regulatory capital arbitrage, for example, in the form of securitization, which offset some or all of the intended regulatory effects. Regulation failed to take account of the risks that can emerge from the interaction between regulated and unregulated institutions, activities, and markets. In particular, bank regulation did not reflect risks from off-balance-sheet vehicles, monoline insurance companies, or loan originators with weak underwriting standards. Equipped with the analysis from ratings agencies, even sophisticated investors could not be relied on to assess risk accurately on more complex financial products.

In very broad terms—as the global economy no longer stares into the abyss of a financial market fallout and the first green shoots of a tentative recovery are

Exhibit 41.2 List of Entities Related to the Basel Process

Acronym	Full Name	Scope	Reporting Entity	Location[a]
BCBS	Basel Committee on Banking Supervision	Banks	G10 Governors	BIS, Basel
CBCDG	Central Bank Counterfeit Deterrent Group	Bank notes	G10 Governors	BIS, Basel
CBGF	Central Bank Governance Forum	Operation and governance	BIS	BIS, Basel
CGFS	Committee on the Global Financial System	Financial markets	G10 Governors	BIS, Basel
CPSS	Committee on Payment and Settlement Systems	Markets infrastructure	G10 Governors	BIS, Basel
FSB[b]	Financial Stability Board	Global financial stability	G20 Ministers and Governors	BIS, Basel
FSI	Financial Stability Institute	Supervisory standards	BIS	BIS, Basel
IAASB	International Auditing and Assurance Standards Board	Audit standards	PIOB, IFAC	New York
IADI	International Association of Deposit Insurers	Deposit insurance	Member agencies	BIS, Basel
IAIS	International Association of Insurance Supervisors	Insurance supervision	Member agencies	BIS, Basel
IASB	International Accounting Standards Board	Accounting standards	IASCF	London
IASCF	IASC Foundation	Accounting standards	Member institutions	London
IFC	Irving Fisher Committee on Central Bank Statistics	Statistical issues	Central bank members	BIS, Basel
IIF	International Institute of Finance	Financial institutions	Member institutions	Washington, DC
IOSCO	International Organisation of Securities Commissions	Securities regulation	Member agencies	Madrid
JF	Joint Forum	Financial conglomerates[c]	BCBS, IOSCO, IAIS	—
PIOB	Public Interest Oversight Board	Audit standards	IFAC	Madrid

[a]The location either indicates the seat of an organization's headquarters (i.e., where its most important functions are concentrated) or the location of a committee's permanent secretariat. The BIS Quarterly Review regularly provides an overview of the most recent activities of the Basel-based committees and the FSF. These activities are also reviewed in the BIS Annual Report, for example BIS 2009, 153–186.

[b]In April 2009, the membership of the Financial Stability Forum (FSF) was enlarged to include the current FSF members' jurisdictions plus the rest of the G-20, Spain, and the European Commission. In addition, the expanded FSF was re-established as the Financial Stability Board (FSB) with a broadened mandate to promote financial stability.

[c]This term is used by the Joint Forum to denote "any group of companies under common control whose exclusive or predominant activities consist of providing significant services in at least two different financial sectors (banking, securities, insurance)."

Source: Reproduced with permission from Bieri (2009).

visible—the principal regulatory lesson is twofold. First, at a microprudential level, the regulatory perimeter needs to be strengthened and extended. Indeed, it was excessive risk taking by global financial actors outside this very perimeter that lies at the origin of the current crisis. Going forward, this implies both expanding the scope of regulation of institutions (improved disclosure, limits on leverage, liquidity requirements, governance standards) and a tighter regulation for markets and individual financial products (Carvajal et al. 2009). At the same time, macroprudential regulation ought to incorporate the idea that systemic risk is an endogenous component of the global financial system; the seamless monitoring of the growing interconnectedness of its various institutional building blocks forms a central part of this new regulatory paradigm. The new financial supervisory framework for the European Union (EU) that was endorsed in June 2009, consisting of a macro- and a microprudential pillar, represents a first comprehensive supranational attempt in this direction (Masciandaro et al. 2009).

Yet better regulation will not be enough; complementary adjustments to macroeconomic policy frameworks are equally essential. These adjustments would call for a more symmetric response to the build-up and unwinding of financial imbalances. The BIS (2009) sees a need to explore how to incorporate credit and asset price booms and the associated risk taking more meaningfully in monetary policy frameworks. Likewise, additional consideration to the possible role of fiscal policy, including that of the tax system and fiscal balances, seem inevitable.

NOTES

1. Unprecedented global bank writedowns in excess of $1.2 trillion (or 12 percent of U.S. GDP) and the massive policy interventions are just some of the superlatives of the current crisis. Policy rates in the United States and Europe are at historic lows. With nominal rates at or close to zero, central banks are employing alternative policy tools on a large scale to combat the crisis. For example, in the six months between October 2008 and April 2009, the Federal Reserve expanded its balance sheet from around $850 billion to just over $2 trillion. In addition, the Fed committed a further $1.75 trillion to the purchase of large quantities of longer-term Treasury debt to help bring down corporate bond and other rates that are linked to Treasury yields by the end of 2009.

2. One of the earliest definitions of financial stability is given by Bagehot (1873): "[It is . . .] not a situation when the Bank of England is the only institution in which people have confidence." More recently, at the 1997 Jackson Hole conference dedicated to "Maintaining Financial Stability in a Global Economy," Crockett (1997) introduces the distinction between two types of financial instability: that of institutions and that of markets.

3. Mishkin (1992) offers a systems-based definition, describing a stable financial system as one that ensures " . . . without major disruptions an efficient allocation of savings to investment decisions."

4. If financial stability is indeed defined as interest rate smoothness, a trade-off with price stability immediately follows from the result of Poole (1970) whereby in the face of an aggregate demand shock, monetary authorities need to choose the degree to which they want to stabilize interest rates or output and inflation.

5. See Schwartz (1995, 2002) for one of the most prominent proponents of this school of thought.

6. Borio et al. (2003) provide an overview of how the new environment hypothesis relates to the continuity view.

7. In a more radical interpretation of the issue, Laidler (2004) argues that the authorities should stick to the basic task of targeting inflation, while holding the lender of last resort powers in reserve. Consequently, policy makers should not be tempted by any form of trade-off simply for the sake of achieving financial stability.

8. Nier (2009) discusses four types of regulation and the two main examples of regulatory structures, which comprise two agencies (in addition to the treasury and a deposit insurance fund): the single integrated regulator model and the twin peaks model.

9. As a complement to this section, I recommend to the interested reader a very comprehensive guide by Davies and Green (2008) that covers the inner workings of the international regulatory system in a level of detail that is well beyond the scope of what is possible here. With regard to the Basel Process, Bieri (2009) contains a detailed overview of its place in the global financial system and its role for financial stability.

10. Brunnermeier et al. (2009) offer a more detailed discussion on the boundary problem of financial regulation.

REFERENCES

Bagehot, W. 1873. *Lombard street: A description of the money markets*. London: Henry S. King and Company.

Bieri, D. S. 2009. Financial stability, the Basel process and the new geography of regulation. *Cambridge Journal of Regions, Economy and Society* 2 (2): 303–331.

BIS. 2009. *79th Annual report*. Basel, Switzerland: Bank for International Settlements.

Borio, C. E., and M. Drehmann. 2009. *Towards an operational framework for financial stability: Fuzzy measurement and its consequences*. Basel, Switzerland: Bank for International Settlements, working paper 265.

Borio, C. E., W. English, and A. Filardo. 2003. *A tale of two perspectives: Old and new challenges for monetary policy*. Basel, Switzerland: Bank for International Settlements, working paper 127.

Brunnermeier, M., A. D. Crockett, C. A. E. Goodhart, A. D. Persaud, and H. S. Shin. 2009. *The fundamental principles of financial regulation*. Geneva, Switzerland: International Center for Monetary and Banking Studies, Geneva reports on the world economy 11.

Carvajal, A., R. Dodd, M. Moore, E. Nier, I. Tower, and L. Zanforlin. 2009. *The perimeter of financial regulation*. Washington, DC: International Monetary Fund, staff position note SPN/09/03.

Crockett, A. D. 1997. Why is financial stability a goal of public policy. In *Maintaining financial stability in a global economy*, 7–36. Federal Reserve Bank of Kansas City: Proceedings from the Jackson Hole symposium.

Davies, H., and D. Green. 2008. *Global financial regulation: The essential guide*. Cambridge, England: Polity Press.

Greenspan, A. 2007. *The age of turbulence: Adventures in a new world*. New York: Penguin Press.

Issing, O. 2003. Monetary and financial stability: Is there a trade-off? In *Monetary stability, financial stability and the business cycle* 18, 16–24. Basel, Switzerland: Bank for International Settlements, BIS papers.

Laidler, D. 2004. Sticking to its knitting: Why the bank of Canada should focus on inflation control, not financial stability. *Commentary* 196, Toronto, Canada: C. D. Howe Institute.

Masciandaro, D., M. Nieto, and M. Quintyn. 2009. *Will they sing the same tune? Measuring convergence in the new European System of financial supervisors.* Washington, DC: International Monetary Fund, working paper WP/09/142.

Minsky, H. P. 1991. The risk of economic crisis. In *The financial instability hypothesis: A clarification*, 56–71. Chicago: University of Chicago Press.

Mishkin, F. S. 1992. Anatomy of a financial crisis, *Journal of Evolutionary Economics* 2: 115–130.

Nier, E. W. 2009. *Financial stability frameworks and the role of central banks: Lessons from the crisis.* Washington, DC: International Monetary Fund, working paper WP/09/70.

Poole, W. J. 1970. Optimal choice of monetary policy in a simple stochastic macro model. *Quarterly Journal of Economics* 84 (2): 197–216.

Quintyn, M., and M. W. Taylor. 2002. *Regulatory and supervisory independence and financial stability.* Washington, DC: International Monetary Fund, working paper WP/02/46.

Schwartz, A. J. 1995. Why financial stability depends on price stability. *Economic Affairs* 1: 21–25.

———. 2002. *Asset price inflation and monetary policy.* Cambridge, MA: National Bureau of Economic Research, working paper series 9321.

Seelig, S. A., and A. Novoa. 2009. *Governance practices at financial regulatory and supervisory agencies.* Washington, DC: International Monetary Fund, working paper WP/09/135.

Stigler, G. J. 1971. The theory of economic regulation. *Bell Journal of Economics and Management Science* 2 (1): 3–21.

Tinbergen, J. 1956. *Economic policy: Principles and design.* Amsterdam: North-Holland Publishing.

ABOUT THE AUTHOR

David S. Bieri is at the School of Public & International Affairs at Virginia Tech in Blacksburg. He holds degrees in economics from the London School of Economics (LSE) and international finance from Durham University (U.K.). Bieri's current research focuses on equilibrium models of locational sorting and nonmarket interactions. He also pursues research on regulatory aspects of international finance, monetary economics, and applied econometrics. From 1999 until 2006, Bieri held various senior positions at the Bank for International Settlements (BIS), most recently as the adviser to the general manager and CEO. As head of business development in the BIS banking department, he was responsible for financial services and reserve management advisory for central banks before joining the BIS Monetary and Economics department, where he worked as an economist. Prior to the BIS, Bieri worked as a high-yield analyst at Banker's Trust in London and in fixed-income syndication at UBS in Zurich.

CHAPTER 42

The Financial Crisis of 2007–2009

Missing Financial Regulation or Absentee Regulators?

GEORGE G. KAUFMAN
John Smith Professor of Banking, Loyola University, Chicago, and consultant to the Federal Reserve Bank of Chicago

A. G. MALLIARIS
Professor of Economics and Finance, and Walter F. Mullady Sr. Chair in Business Administration, School of Business Administration, Loyola University, Chicago

The financial crisis that began in August 2007 is now in its third calendar year and has evolved into the most severe recession since the Great Depression of the 1930s. This brief discussion examines some of the causes of the crisis and in particular the role of financial regulation, financial regulators, and the problem of both defining and containing systemic risk. The discussion concludes that many of the difficulties that arose during the financial meltdown may be attributed to the reluctance of bank regulators to enforce the regulations that were in place. Such enforcement could have reduced, if not prevented, systemic risk from occurring.

Most economists agree that the trigger of the current crisis may be found in the reversal of the rapid increase of housing prices in both the United States and in many other industrial countries. John Taylor (2007, 2009), Hayford and Malliaris (2009), and others have argued that the housing bubble was driven by an easy monetary policy that kept interest rates too low for too long, while Alan Greenspan and Ben Bernanke, the former and current chairmen of the Federal Reserve, claim that the global character of the housing bubble should be attributed largely to a global savings glut, primarily from Asia. Financial innovation in packaging together large numbers of individual mortgages, rating such financial instruments, and distributing them among a large class of investors helped to finance the boom in housing price increases. At the same time, the price of risk was underestimated because the historical data used in testing the banks' risk models was too short to contain national housing price crashes. Housing prices began to escalate rapidly during the period from 2000 to 2006. By 2005, the proportion of risky subprime mortgages had increased sharply relative to the total pool of mortgages and increased overall financial leverage. When defaults on these mortgages jumped sharply in 2007, the crisis began. In ending the crisis and repairing the financial system, it is important that we do not throw out the baby with the bathwater.

FINANCIAL REGULATION

Banking has a history of several centuries and serves a number of valuable functions that have raised wealth. The banking system plays a central role in pooling capital and funding economic activities in a way that allocates financial resources efficiently and promotes maximum economic growth and prosperity. As the banking system has evolved and become more complex and diverse, the central role of allocating scarce capital has not changed. Although highly leveraged banking institutions contribute to accelerated economic growth, they are also associated with costly financial instabilities and often contribute to significant economic recessions and depressions. To ensure that their positive contribution to a nation's economic growth outweighs the adverse impact of bank failures and economic crises, banks may need to be regulated by the government. Such regulation supplements self-regulation that comes from market discipline.

In the United States, the goals of government banking regulation include the safety and soundness of bank operations, the promotion of competition and efficiency in the banking sector, the stability of the broader financial system, the efficiency of the payments system, consumer protection, and more social goals such as nondiscrimination in lending.

CRITIQUE OF CURRENT REGULATION

Recent analyses identify three fundamental failures of the existing regulatory framework. First, current bank regulations put almost exclusive emphasis on how to limit each bank's risk in isolation from the risk of the banking and financial system as a whole. Second, the present regulations do not call for desirable cyclical adjustments. Indeed, the very success of prolonged periods of low goods and services inflation and low economic volatility during the 1990s and early 2000s reduced statistical measures of risk, underestimated risk premiums, and contributed to excessive risk taking and asset price inflation (bubbles), which reinforced rather than countered the boom. This is a phenomenon that Hyman Minsky called "financial stability causes instability"—the success of one policy unintentionally causes problems in another policy area. Third, regulators have not been very good at enforcing the regulations that were in place in a timely and effective manner. The regulators have not always been faithful agents for their healthy bank and taxpayer principals.

SYSTEMIC RISK

Systemic risk was perceived as a major source of concern in the period leading up to and during the crisis. Systemic risk refers to the risk or probability of breakdowns in an entire system, as opposed to breakdowns in individual parts or components, and is evidenced by high co-movements (correlation) among most or all the parts. In particular, systemic risk in banking is evidenced by high correlation and clustering of bank failures in a country, a number of countries, or globally. Systemic risk may also occur in other parts of the financial sector, for example, in securities markets, as evidenced by simultaneous declines in the prices of a large number of securities in one or more markets in a country or across countries. Systemic risk may be both domestic and transnational. Acharya (2009) and Kaufman and Scott (2003) provide a detailed discussion of systemic risk.

Defining *systemic risk* precisely is a challenging task. There appear to be three frequent definitions. The first refers to a big, or macro, shock that produces nearly simultaneous adverse effects for most or all of the domestic economy or system. That is, *systemic* refers to an event having effects on the entire banking, financial, or economic system, rather than just one or a few institutions. Such an event disrupts information in financial markets, making them unable to channel funds efficiently to those parties with the most productive investment opportunities. How the transmission of effects from a macro shock to individual units occurs is unspecified.

Two other definitions focus on potential spillover from one economic agent to others. For example, systemic risk may be defined as the probability that cumulative losses will accrue from an event that sets in motion a series of successive losses along a chain of institutions or markets comprising a system that results in multiple failures. That is, systemic risk is the risk of a chain reaction of falling interconnected dominos. This definition is consistent with that of the Bank for International Settlements (BIS) that describes systemic risk as "the risk that the failure of a participant to meet its contractual obligations may in turn cause other participants to default with a chain reaction leading to broader financial difficulties." This definition emphasizes causation as well as correlation and assumes strong direct interconnections or linkages among institutions or markets. When the first domino falls, it falls on others in the chain, causing them to fall and in turn knock down others in a chain or knock-on reaction. Losses and failures are passed on down the line.

A third definition of systemic risk also focuses on spillover from an initial shock, but does not involve direct causation and depends on weaker and more indirect interconnections. It emphasizes commonalities in third party risk exposures among the firms involved. When one unit experiences an adverse shock from, say, the failure of a large financial or nonfinancial firm that generates severe losses, uncertainty is created about the values of other units potentially subject to the same shock. To minimize additional losses, market participants will examine the other entities, such as banks, in which they have economic exposures to see whether and to what extent they are at risk. The more similar the risk exposure profile to that of the initial entity, the greater is the probability of loss and the more likely are the participants to withdraw funds from the exposed entity as soon as possible. Until the damaged institutions are sorted out and separated from the unaffected or mildly affected institutions, financial markets freeze up, and liquidity and solvency problems arise across the board.

MARKET FAILURE

Conventional wisdom claims that the current attack of systemic risk and the resulting financial meltdown may be attributed largely to market failure. That is, free market forces were not able to prevent excessive risk taking, poor lending practices, and other forms of misbehavior and abuses by market participants, particularly in the mortgage market. As a result, the remedy frequently proposed is more government regulation to minimize, if not prevent, such practices in the future. But more careful examination of the crisis suggests that a strong case can be made that regulatory failure was as much, if not more, to blame as market failure. It is also useful to distinguish between regulatory failure due to inadequate rules contrasted with an insufficient application of the existing rules by the regulators.

The direct underlying causes of the crisis generally highlight excessive leverage by both lending institutions (insufficient capital) and borrowers (insufficient down payment), excessively complex mortgage instruments, deficient stress testing of both the institutions and securities under suitably adverse economic and financial conditions, the failure by regulators to be adequately concerned with the banks' off-balance-sheet activities, the failure of regulators to be sufficiently concerned about the likely consequences of a bursting of the bubble in real estate prices, and possibly fraud. But there was little or nothing to prevent the bank and other financial regulators from acting to try to correct these problems before the meltdown.

There is neither a law nor a regulation that prevents bank regulators from requiring banks to maintain higher regulatory capital ratios. Ironically, before the meltdown, some regulators actively argued for lowering the minimum regulatory capital requirements for many large U.S. commercial banks through the adoption of Basel II regulatory capital requirements, despite many recognized bank analysts and scholars arguing that the banks were already at that time undercapitalized, not overcapitalized. The lack of regulatory agency attention to financial stability is reflected in the situation that the United States is the only major country that neither publishes a financial stability report that analyzes the fragility and vulnerability of banks and the financial system to shocks, such as the bursting of a real estate price bubble, nor participates in the IMF–World Bank Financial Sector Assessment Program, which evaluates bank fragility. Only recently have the regulators focused on stress tests for individual banks and the financial system as a whole. Ironically, financial stability was the major reason for the establishment of the Federal Reserve in 1913. Nor were regulators hampered by barriers to deal with troubled banks on a timely and effective basis. Indeed, the prompt corrective action provisions of the FDIC Improvement Act (FDICIA) of 1991 mandated that they do so and to declare troubled banks that failed to respond and regain their financial health insolvent and place them in receivership.

Moreover, the Federal Reserve had regulatory authority over bank holding companies on a consolidated basis for many years and could have collected data on and monitored the performance of the off-balance-sheet activities of these banking organizations. The insufficient testing of securities and models for tail shocks was readily evident from the questionable results large banks reported to the regulators from their testing of the models required for the Basel II regulatory capital requirements, which were based on their own internal models and credit ratings.

This is not to argue that market failure did not occur or to assert that had the regulators performed their duties well the meltdown would have been prevented. But we do maintain that it was not a lack of regulations or legal authority that prevented them from doing so and possibly preventing, or at least mitigating, the meltdown. It was primarily a lack of will. What was encountered was not a regulatory failure but a failure of regulators. This failure reflected poor corporate governance of the agencies and a serious principal agent problem. Improved agency behavior awaits improved corporate governance regimes that better align the incentives of taxpayer principals and their regulator agents.

In the rush to introduce legislated cures, it is important to first identify and pinpoint the problem correctly so that the recommended cure fits the disease. At this time, this likely requires additional research to identify the precise causes of the crisis as distinguished from first reactions and hasty judgment calls. Such reflection will help to ensure that the cure is not worse than the disease. Excessive or ill-conceived regulations can wipe out all or much of the upside in aggregate wealth that is created by a market-driven financial sector. Somewhat delayed correct actions trump hurried actions that later prove to be incorrect, even if political pressures try to push policy makers to "not just stand there, do something!"

CONCLUSION

The financial crisis of 2007–2009 had multiple causes. It represented a financial perfect storm. If any component had been missing, the depth of the crisis and its adverse feedback on the real economy would have been considerably milder. What triggered the crisis in both the United States and most other industrial countries was the bursting of the residential real estate price bubble. Had there been no real estate price bubble, there would have been no bursting of the bubble and no financial crisis. The financial regulators were amiss both in permitting the bubble to develop to the extent it did and in permitting excessively high leverage in the banking system and the remainder of the economy to amplify the damage caused by its bursting. Regulations were in place that could have reduced, if not, prevented, both conditions and thus diminished, if not totally eliminated, systemic risk. But they were not effectively enforced. Thus, unless a way is found to make the regulators more accountable, introducing additional regulations to attempt to prevent similar crises in the future may not be expected to be very effective. Public policies must be designed and adopted that will make the regulators more effective and more transparent agents.

In mid-2009, the Obama administration published a report presenting its recommendations for changes in financial regulation to improve the performance of the U.S. financial system (U.S. Treasury Department 2009). The current crisis is blamed primarily on a failure of regulation, and recommendations focus on reregulation. In brief, the recommendations propose extending prudential regulations to some currently more lightly regulated institutions and markets; rearranging some of the regulatory agencies; granting additional powers to the Federal Reserve, particularly with respect to monitoring and preventing systemic risk potential at large (systemic) banks, bank holding companies, and bank-like institutions; and accelerating the resolution process for insolvent systemic institutions to minimize disruptions. Unfortunately, the report does not discuss how these changes would have either prevented the current crisis or future crises. The report does not define systemic risk or discuss the implications of identifying some institutions as systemic for the purpose of allocating losses to their creditors and other counterparties in the case of insolvency. It is likely that to reduce contagion, the losses will be shifted to the government, and by making the counterparties whole provide these institutions with a competitive advantage in raising funds relative to their smaller, nonsystemic competitors and increase their moral hazard risk-taking behavior.

Lastly, the report considers only in passing the potential problem of regulators failing to effectively enforce any new regulations imposed. In this paper, we have identified such failure as a major cause of the current crisis. We found that the problem in achieving better public policy performance was more with the regulators than with the regulations. Until this problem is resolved, greater regulations are a weak foundational piece on which to base effective reform.

REFERENCES

Acharya, V. 2009. A theory of systemic risk: Risk and design of prudential bank regulation. *Journal of Financial Stability* 5 (3): 224–255.

Hayford, M., and A. G. Malliaris. 2009. Risk management by central banks: Lessons from the financial crisis of 2007–2009. In Robert Kolb (ed.). *Lessons from the financial crisis: Insights and analysis from today's leading minds*. Hoboken, NJ: John Wiley & Sons.

Kaufman, G. G., and K. E. Scott. 2003. What is systemic risk. *Independent Revie*, Winter: 371–391.

Taylor, J. B. 2007. *Housing and monetary policy*. Cambridge, MA: National Bureau of Economic Research, working paper 13682.

———. 2009. *The financial crisis and the policy responses: An empirical analysis of what went wrong*. Cambridge, MA: National Bureau of Economic Research, working paper 14631.

U.S. Treasury Department. 2009. *Financial regulatory reform: A new foundation*. Washington D.C.

ABOUT THE AUTHORS

George G. Kaufman is the John Smith Professor of finance and economics at Loyola University Chicago. He previously taught at the University of Oregon and was a visiting professor at Stanford University and the University of California at Berkeley. Kaufman has also been associated with the Federal Reserve Bank of Chicago as both a full-time employee in the research department and as a consultant. Kaufman has been president of the Western Finance Association, Midwest Finance Association, the North American Economic and Finance Association, and a director of the American Finance Association and the Western Economic Association. Kaufman is co-chairman of the Shadow Financial Regulatory Committee and was executive director of the Financial Economists Roundtable. Kaufman has published widely in professional journals and books, and his money and banking textbook went through six editions. He is co-editor of the *Journal of Financial Stability* and is on the editorial boards of a number of other professional journals.

A. G. (Tassos) Malliaris is currently a professor of economics and finance at Loyola University Chicago, and holds the Walter F. Mullady Sr. Chair in Business Administration. He has earned two Ph.D.s: one in economics from the University of Oklahoma and a second in mathematics from the University of Chicago. He has authored and co-authored numerous articles in professional journals such as the *Society of Industrial and Applied Mathematics Review, Mathematics of Operations Research, Review of Economic Studies, Journal of Financial and Quantitative Analysis, Review of Quantitative Finance and Accounting, Journal of Futures Markets, Journal of*

Banking and Finance, Journal of Macroeconomics, Economic Modeling, Journal of Multinational Financial Management, International Review of Financial Analysis, European Journal of Political Economy, European Journal of Operations Research, International Journal of Finance, Multinational Finance Journal, Economic Inquiry, Neural Computing and Applications, and others. He has also edited and co-edited several books. He is currently interested in financial economics, monetary policy, and the formation of asset bubbles.

CHAPTER 43

The Demise of the United Kingdom's Northern Rock and Large U.S. Financial Institutions

Public Policy Lessons

ROBERT A. EISENBEIS
Chief Monetary Economist, Cumberland Advisors, and former Executive
Vice President and Director of Research at the Federal Reserve Bank of Atlanta

GEORGE G. KAUFMAN
John Smith Professor of Banking, Loyola University Chicago, and consultant
to the Federal Reserve Bank of Chicago

In the late fall of 2007 and early spring of 2008 both the United Kingdom and the United States experienced the collapse of several major financial institutions, including Northern Rock in the United Kingdom and Countrywide, Independent National Mortgage Corporation (IndyMac), Bear Stearns, Lehman Brothers, Wachovia, and American International Group (AIG) in the United States. In the United Kingdom, a very visible retail depositor run occurred on Northern Rock, which led the government to extend 100 percent deposit guarantees for depositors. No similar visible runs occurred in the United States in the sense that depositors did not line up outside of banks demanding their funds, but the U.S. institutions did experience declines in access to money market funding, and banks saw outflows of large, uninsured wholesale deposits (Gorton 2008).

Besides excessive risk taking, three regulatory problems contributed to their collapse: the defective structure of U.K. deposit insurance guarantees, lax regulatory oversight in both the United States and the United Kingdom, and the lack of an adequate legal structure governing the windup of failures. When subject to a careful forensic investigation, these failures provide valuable insights as to how deposit guarantee systems and the monitoring and regulatory structures for large complex financial institutions failed and should be restructured.

In the aftermath of the crisis, finance ministers and regulators have called for more regulations, more coordination to deal with future crises and changes in the regulatory and legal structures. The debate has just begun. In the United States, the Obama administration has released a broad-based set of proposals for regulatory reform, largely rooted in the belief that the financial collapse was due to insufficient regulations, lax and inefficient regulation and supervision, incentive problems within institutions resulting from executive compensation schemes that encouraged excessive risk taking, deficiencies in the way large interconnected financial institution failures could be resolved, and the complexity of regulatory oversight. We begin by briefly comparing the circumstances surrounding the failures of large financial institutions in the United States and the United Kingdom and then turn to the lessons that should be drawn from them.

BACKGROUND

The large financial institutions that failed were of several different types. Northern Rock (NR) in the United Kingdom and Countrywide and IndyMac in the United States were thrifts. Wachovia was a large commercial bank. Lehman Brothers and Bear Stearns were investment banks, and AIG was the world's largest general insurance company. Despite these differences in institutional form, all were heavily concentrated in mortgage-related assets—direct loans, mortgage-backed securities, collateralized debt obligations, and credit default swaps. Northern Rock, Countrywide, IndyMac, and Wachovia largely pursued the recently popular originate-and-distribute business model. They originated whole mortgage loans—which were largely of relatively low credit quality—securitized them and sold most of them to other parties. For these services they collected fees. Until sale, they funded the warehousing of their longer-term mortgage assets with shorter-term liabilities obtained primarily on the wholesale market. AIG, Bear Stearns, and Lehman Brothers were heavily invested in the kinds of securities that the originate-and-distribute model generated and in some instances provided credit enhancements or served as conduits for placing the securities so generated with investors. But as interest rates began to rise and mortgage markets began to weaken, participants in that business were subject to significant market chatter about their deteriorating financial conditions and all began to experience significant problems in rolling over their outstanding funding.

Northern Rock started life as a mutual building society but converted into a stock bank in 1997. Thereafter, it grew rapidly, doubled from $16 billion in mid-2005 to $32 billion at year-end 2007, and it more than tripled its share of the U.K. mortgage market between 1999 and 2007 from 6 percent to 19 percent (Bank of England 2007). At the same time, the bank increased both its capital leverage and its dependence upon short-term wholesale funding as part of its mortgage warehousing process until the individual mortgages could be packaged and sold. Its regulator, the Financial Services Authority (FSA), saw it as being well-run and well-capitalized in 2007. However, by September 2007, severe difficulties were encountered in rolling over its short-term financing. Northern Rock's board sought and was given assurance by the FSA, the Chancellor of the Exchequer, and the Bank of England that the latter would provide the necessary liquidity support.[1] However, a depositor run ensued, and the government responded first, by extending deposit guarantees to all deposits at NR, and then in February 2008 with nationalization.

Until 2005, Countrywide was a designated "financial services holding company," which required relatively high capital ratios, and its bank was a chartered national bank. The bank was also a primary dealer with the Federal

Reserve Open Market Desk. However, in December 2006, Countrywide converted the bank to a federal savings bank, and it became a savings and loan holding company. The change switched its primary regulator from the Comptroller of the Currency for the bank and the Federal Reserve for the holding company to the Office of Thrift Supervision (OTS), which was widely perceived to be a less stringent supervisor. OTS permitted Countrywide to delay and understate its loan loss reserving and charge-offs, which effectively lowered its required regulatory capital.[2]

Like Northern Rock, Countrywide employed the originate-and-distribute model. But the freezing up of the short-term asset-backed commercial paper market in August of 2007, due to problems in the U.S. subprime mortgage market, made it extremely difficult for Countrywide to finance its mortgage warehousing business. As its funding dried up, Countrywide turned to the Federal Home Loan Bank of Atlanta for short-term funding and increased its collateralized advances from approximately $30 billion to over $50 billion at the end of September 2007. These advances accounted for nearly a quarter of its total liabilities and were over-collateralized. By the beginning of 2008, it became apparent to the federal regulators that the institution would not be viable, and a sale was encouraged by the Federal Reserve to the Bank of America.

IndyMac was initially organized as a subsidiary of Countrywide but was spun off as an independent entity in 1997. The institution specialized in the origination, servicing, and securitization of Alt-A (low documentation) mortgage loans. Similar to Countrywide, IndyMac grew rapidly and nearly doubled its size from $16.8 billion to $32.5 billion between March 2005 and December 2007. Like Countrywide, its funding depended heavily on Home Loan Bank advances, which accounted for from 32 to 45 percent of its total liabilities in any one recent quarter.[3]

IndyMac's critical problems began to surface in mid-2007, when it reported a significant decline in its capital. Uninsured deposits began to run off. The bank replaced these funds with insured brokered deposits. The bank's earnings turned negative in the fall of 2007. Its regulator, the OTS, was aware of its financial difficulties in early 2008, but steadfastly maintained that it was well capitalized. It was later learned that this classification was in part due to the OTS permitting IndyMac to backdate to March 2008 a capital contribution from the parent holding company made in May. This accounting manipulation enabled it to meet OTS criteria for being "well capitalized."[4] Had IndyMac's true capital position on March 31, 2008, been accurately reported, the OTS would have been required to impose sanctions limiting its ability to accept brokered deposits, which had become a critical component of its funding base.

In June, following the release of a letter from U.S. Senator Charles Schumer to the Office of Thrift Supervision questioning the viability of IndyMac, it experienced an outflow of funds. The OTS concluded that the bank was no longer viable, and it was closed on July 11, 2008, and turned over to the FDIC as conservator. The FDIC has estimated that it lost over $10 billion in the failure on an asset base of $40 billion. This is not the kind of loss performance envisioned in FDICIA 1991!

Wachovia was a regulated commercial bank that developed large major stakes in mortgage origination and securitization through a series of acquisitions. It too experienced funding problems as the mortgage market declined, and it was subsequently sold in 2009, under the threat of closure by U.S. regulators, to Wells Fargo Co., a bank holding company.

Although AIG was an insurance company whose insurance products were regulated by the individual states or countries in which it operated, it also owned thrift institutions and was therefore also regulated as thrift institution holding company. As such, it was under the consolidated supervision of the Office of Thrift Supervision, whose oversight was recognized as meeting the requirements of the international regulatory community, especially the European Union. Finally, Lehman Brothers and Bear Stearns were investment banks, and as such were not subject to federal prudential regulation or oversight to the same degree as U.S. commercial banks.

Although there are many similarities among these four types of institutions, there are also important differences in how they were resolved, the risks that have been assumed by the taxpayers, and how the systems will function prospectively. Furthermore, a number of weaknesses have been exposed in the legal and regulatory structure of the guarantees and how failing institutions are handled.

SIMILARITIES AND DIFFERENCES AMONG THE THREE CASES

The most striking difference between the United Kingdom's experience with Northern Rock and the United States's experience was that public run on Northern Rock in the United Kingdom was shown on national TV. There were also differences in the quality of the supervisory processes and in the misplaced reliance in the United Kingdom on the courts and general bankruptcy procedures to resolve problem institutions in a timely manner, whereas the United States had a system that enabled regulators to resolve bank failures (but not non-bank failures) promptly and efficiently. This is not to suggest, however, that the U.S. structure always fostered better outcomes. Indeed, the U.S. supervisory structure was designed around prompt corrective action (PCA) and least cost resolution (LCR) provisions of FDICIA, which conceptually should have minimized losses to the FDIC. However, the losses experienced by IndyMac, for example, were huge and represented a breakdown due in part because the process was implemented using flawed accounting principles and in part to flawed regulatory incentives that encourage forbearance.

The Deposit Insurance Contract

At the time of the NR retail run, the U.K. deposit insurance contract only covered 100 percent of the first £2,000 (about $4,100) and 90 percent of the next £33,000 (about $67,500). This structure was based on the principle of co-insurance by which depositors with funds in excess of $4,100 bore 10 percent of any loss. Because of the co-insurance, depositors should have had an incentive to monitor the performance of their bank and serve as a source of market discipline. This co-insurance contract contrasts sharply with that of the United States, where there was no co-insurance for small depositors and full coverage per account at the time for the first $100,000.

Importantly, unlike the case with U.S. bank depositors, U.K. depositors of NR also could not count on receiving even their insured funds quickly if NR had been legally closed and placed in receivership. They faced possible waits of many months to be fully compensated. Thus, like the uninsured creditors, insured depositors in the United Kingdom had a significant incentive to run both to avoid credit losses (possible 10 percent loss from par value) and liquidity losses (delays in gaining full access to their fully insured funds). However, compared to many uninsured creditors in both U.K. and U.S. institutions, the insured depositors were late to the table in seeking to obtain their funds. Many of the large, insured creditors were long gone. This suggests that it is impractical to rely upon small depositors to exert a significant amount of market discipline compared to large depositors.

Failure Resolution Process

The low full coverage and co-insurance features of the U.K. deposit insurance contract were only partly responsible for the run on Northern Rock. In the United Kingdom, the resolution of insolvent institutions falls under the general corporate bankruptcy procedures administered by bankruptcy courts. Unlike in the United States, where regulatory authorities can essentially resolve a bank failure in a day or over the weekend, the United Kingdom's reliance upon the general bankruptcy procedure can impose significant potential delays in when and how much of their deposit funds they will be able to access. U.K. law provides only that insured deposits are paid fully within three months, but additional stays are possible under both U.K. and EU protocols if the bankruptcy courts determine it is necessary.

Because of the potential long delays in depositors being able to access their funds, the run on Northern Rock was a natural response to those problems. This was not an issue in the United States because the bank chartering authority, the primary federal regulator, or the Federal Deposit Insurance Corporation may intervene to broker a merger or legally close a bank whenever its book value equity is still positive but declines below 2 percent of its assets or other threats to its safe and sound operations arise. Indeed, Countrywide was sold to the Bank of America, and IndyMac was legally closed and opened the next business day as a newly chartered FDIC-operated institution. In both instances, customers experienced minimal inconvenience. They suffered no major disruptions to banking services, although IndyMac's large depositors received immediate access to only 50 percent of their uninsured funds and could expect to suffer large losses. However, the large loss the FDIC experienced in the IndyMac case suggests that the OTS waited far too long to legally close the institution, contrary to the intent of FDICIA. Subsequent hearings and investigation by the Treasury's Inspector General indicated that there were significant breakdowns in OTS's supervision of the institution and irregularities in how the OTS permitted the institution to backdate capital injections downstreamed by the parent holding company.

These same bank-type resolution options, however, were not available to U.S. regulators in the case of Bear Stearns, Lehman Brothers, or AIG, because they were not commercial banks. The options available to U.S. authorities in resolution of these institutions were under the jurisdiction of the courts and general bankruptcy statutes of the United States, which was similar to the option for resolving Northern Rock faced by U.K. authorities. As a result, the Federal Reserve invoked the "exigent circumstances" clause of Section 13 of the Federal Reserve Act, which provided the Fed the authority to make the loan that facilitated the takeover of Bear Stearns by JPMorgan Chase in March 2008 and to provide loans to AIG.

The Breakdown in Supervision

In the wind-down of Northern Rock and U.S. institutions, serious weaknesses were exposed in the monitoring and supervision of these institutions by the regulators. In the case of Northern Rock, supervisory deficiencies led to U.K. taxpayer exposure to losses. In the United States, contrary to the intent of FDICIA, supervisory failures exposed the FDIC to large losses from the failure of IndyMac. The inability to quickly resolve Bear Stearns, Lehman Brothers, and AIG resulted in the liquidation of Lehman Brothers and large losses from Bear Stearns and AIG to the Federal Reserve. These problems included reliance upon seriously deficient accounting and capital adequacy standards, failure to monitor institutions in a timely, effective, and ongoing fashion; failure to intervene appropriately when problems were identified; and promoting the welfare of the regulated institutions and the regulatory agency rather than the insurance fund or the taxpayer.

For example, hearings by a committee of the U.K. House of Commons on the problems surrounding Northern Rock focused on the actions of the Bank of England (BOE), the FSA, and the Treasury, which collectively shared responsibility for financial stability in the United Kingdom. The hearings clearly revealed that the FSA did not perform as it should have, failed to monitor the institution and even allowed Northern Rock to increase its dividends despite its troubled financial position. The FSA's own internal audit of the experience exposed the lack of rigor in the analyses conducted and the agency's failure to devote sufficient resources to monitoring high-impact institutions.[5] The report points to internal organizational problems, to skill gaps in its supervisors, and to problems in how the supervision of large institutions was conducted. It also describes process problems and deficiencies in the flow of information from the NR to the FSA and within the FSA itself. The FSA supervisory reviews of Northern Rock paid too little attention to liquidity issues, were inconsistent in their application and coverage, were spaced too far apart, and too little time and effort was devoted to stress testing Northern Rock's financials. Finally, not only was it clear that the FSA ignored numerous early warning signs of troubles with Northern Rock, it apparently also ignored a breach of required minimum capital standards early in 2007.

In the United States, AIG, Countrywide, and IndyMac were supervised by the Office of Thrift Supervision. The OTS proved to be an ineffective regulator that permitted and even abetted in improper actions by the institutions. Bear Stearns and Lehman Brothers were under the jurisdiction of the SEC, which did not conduct safety and soundness examinations of investment banks. Its major focus was on investor protection. As a result, the permissible leverage ratios of investment banks were considerably higher than for commercial banks or thrifts.

WHAT THE UNITED STATES AND THE UNITED KINGDOM SHOULD HAVE LEARNED FROM FAILURES OF NORTHERN ROCK AND MAJOR FINANCIAL INSTITUTIONS IN BOTH COUNTRIES

The United States savings and loan and banking mess of the 1980s and early 1990s should have served as an important laboratory from which both U.K. and U.S. officials could have learned regulatory lessons in structuring a regime and methods both for reducing failures and their consequences and for resolving financial institution failures in crisis and noncrisis periods. In 1991, Congress enacted the FDIC Improvement Act (FDICIA). This law introduced provisions for regulatory actions to attempt to turn troubled banks around before insolvency and, if this failed, to legally close and recapitalize, sell, or liquidate a bank before its capital was fully depleted. The underlying theory was that, if successful, losses could be confined to shareholders; depositors and other creditors would remain whole. The structure of FDICIA reflected the experience that as they approach insolvency troubled banks tend to overstate their revenues, income, and capital; understate their expenditures and loss reserves; and to blame their problems on lack of market liquidity. Thus, FDICIA assumed that both low levels of capital and so-called liquidity problems frequently masked underlying insolvency problems that required prompt regulatory actions, including, ultimately, resolution.

The United States also realized that insolvent banks needed to be legally closed more quickly than other firms to reduce both depositor runs and losses and to maintain uninterrupted operation of the payments systems, and that the closure decision should be made by regulators and not by the courts. Thus, Congress enacted a special bank bankruptcy code separate and different from the general corporate bankruptcy code (Bliss and Kaufman 2007). Legal closure powers to cancel a bank's charter and place it in receivership were given to the bank regulators, not the courts. With rare exceptions, losses would be assigned to the insured claimants and the FDIC, standing in the shoes of insured depositors in absolute priority order. In addition, in the late 1980s, the FDIC also received authority to charter a temporary bridge bank to assume the activities of an insolvent large bank if a buyer could not be found sufficiently quickly. The United Kingdom had no such provisions in place in the first half of 2007. Nor were similar options available in the United States to deal with Bear Stearns, Lehman Brothers, or AIG.

Were these institutions solvent at the time the regulators acted to resolve them, or were they victims of short-term liquidity crises and only suffering temporarily depressed asset values? The answer depends on the capital measures and accounting procedures applied. Clues can be gained from several pieces of evidence which ex post at least suggest the answers. For example, the inability of U.K. regulators to find a buyer for Northern Rock, which did not demand significant government financial compensation, implies that, at least in market value terms, NR was not solvent.

Similarly, IndyMac reported leverage and risk-based capital ratios well above the minimum requirements. Yet, like FSA's problems with selling NR, the OTS had a difficult time finding a buyer for IndyMac when it tried shopping the institution before resolution. This supports the argument made earlier that as a bank approaches insolvency, it tends to overstate its revenues and understate its expenses, thereby overstating both its income and capital. The delay caused by the search enlarged the losses substantially. On the other hand, the successful sale of Countrywide to the Bank of America without financial assistance suggests that it was perceived to be market value solvent or close enough to it to make it attractive to at least one potential buyer.[6] Bear Stearns was a more difficult case, but given the losses the Federal Reserve was accruing on the assets it guaranteed in the rescue, it is likely that Bear was insolvent as well.

The problems of reliance upon book value accounting and regulatory accounting standards plague effective U.S. implementation of the PCA and FDICIA closure rules. Some proponents of the FDICIA PCA procedures argued that the capital tranche triggers for regulatory intervention and closure rules should be based upon fair market values rather than book values, which lag changes in market conditions.[7] The fact that the OTS could claim that IndyMac was not only adequately capitalized, but well capitalized just a few days before its closure and yet the FDIC could estimate at closure that it would lose between $4 billion to $8 billion is *res ipsa loquitur,* and points to the critical need for further evaluation of how FDICIA should be implemented.

Given the lines of U.K. depositors in the street and no feasible alternatives to promptly close or otherwise resolve Northern Rock's problems, the government was forced to guarantee all deposits and attempt to broker a merger or acquisition of the troubled institution. However, uncertainty about the value of the bank's assets reduced its market value and made brokering a deal acceptable to most current shareholders, who, unlike in the United States, have a strong voice in the resolution process, doomed to failure. These actions introduce potential serious moral hazard problems by encouraging institutions with government guarantees to take on more risk and time inconsistently problems in that prevention of failure in the short run only promises to increase the magnitude of problems in the future with higher costs of failure. Losses will surely also be visited upon taxpayers.

CONCLUSION

The combination of poorly designed deposit insurance, poor regulatory supervision, and a poor insolvency resolution regime led to a very visible and disruptive run on Northern Rock in the United Kingdom and larger-than-necessary losses in the failure of IndyMac, Bear Stearns, Countrywide, and AIG in the United States. The run on Northern Rock has resulted in broad changes in the existing U.K. deposit insurance contract, the supervisory structure, and the bank bankruptcy code. The recent failure and large losses at U.S. institutions have accelerated a reconsideration of its supervisory and regulatory systems. It has also resulted in a white paper on financial regulatory reform issued by the Treasury Department that contains a long list of suggested reforms.

This paper has described the more important faults in the bank regulatory structure in the United States and the United Kingdom that suggest areas in which reform would be most beneficial in reducing the number of bank failures and costs of those failures to taxpayers. Inefficient or unlucky banks should be permitted to fail, as in any other industry, but at low cost to the economy. But regardless of how well any regulatory legislation is drafted, without the support of the regulators in implementing the required actions effectively, the promised favorable outcomes are unlikely to by fully achieved. It should, however, be noted that these recommendations work best in noncrisis periods when large number of banks are not simultaneously endangered. In crisis periods, game books are generally thrown out in favor of quick, intuitively appealing ad hoc actions.

NOTES

1. HM Treasury, Bank of England, and Financial Services Authority (2007).
2. See *Financial Week* (2007).

3. Data from FDIC Quarterly Reports of Condition and Income.

4. Indeed, the Treasury's Inspector General's Material Loss Review on IndyMac, which is required by FDICIA 1991, is highly critical of the OTS and its supervisory performance in the IndyMac case. The IG indicates that the OTS identified problems in IndyMac early on but never followed up to ensure appropriate corrective actions were taken, despite a history on the part of the institution of not addressing problems raised in examinations. In some instances, identified problems weren't always reported in the Reports of Examination of IndyMac. See Office of Inspector General (2009).

5. See FSA Internal Audit Division (2008).

6. However, recent mortgage losses imply that BofA may have overestimated the true value of Countrywide's assets.

7. Shadow Financial Regulatory Committee (2000).

REFERENCES

Bank of England. 2007. Financial Stability Report. October.

Bliss, R. R., and G. G. Kaufman. 2007. U.S. corporate and bank insolvency regimes: a comparison and evaluation. *Virginia Law and Business Review* 2 (1): 143–177.

Financial Week. 2007. Bank-to-thrift shift helps countrywide sneak by. *Financial Week,* July 30.

FSA Internal Audit Division. 2008. " The Supervision of Northern Rock: A Lessons Learned Review," March.

Gorton, G. 2008. The Panic of 2007. in *Maintaining Stability in a changing Financial System.* A Symposium sponsored by the Federal Reserve Bank of Kansas City. Federal Reserve Bank of Kansas City.

HM Treasury, Bank of England, and Financial Services Authority. 2007. *Liquidity support facility for Northern Rock PLC,* 14.

Office of Inspector General, U.S. Department of the Treasury. 2009. *Safety and soundness: material loss review of IndyMac bank.* Federal Savings Bank, OIG-09-032, February 26.

U.S. Shadow Financial Regulatory Committee. 2000. *Reforming bank capital regulation.* Washington, D.C.: American Enterprise Institute, Policy Statement 160.

ABOUT THE AUTHORS

George G. Kaufman is the John Smith professor of finance and economics at Loyola University Chicago. He previously taught at the University of Oregon and was a visiting professor at Stanford University and University of California at Berkeley. Kaufman has also been associated with the Federal Reserve Bank of Chicago as both a full-time employee in the research department and as a consultant. Kaufman has been president of the Western Finance Association, Midwest Finance Association, and North American Economic and Finance Association and a director of the American Finance Association and the Western Economic Association. Kaufman is co-chairman of the Shadow Financial Regulatory Committee and was executive director of the Financial Economists Roundtable. Kaufman has published widely in professional journals and books and his money and banking textbook went through six editions. He is a co-editor of the *Journal of Financial Stability* and is on the editorial boards of a number of professional journals.

Robert A. Eisenbeis has Ph.D. and master's degrees in economics from the University of Wisconsin-Madison and a B.S. from Brown University. He is presently chief monetary economist at Cumberland Advisors. He has held positions at the Federal Reserve Board, the FDIC, and most recently at the Federal Reserve Bank of Atlanta, where he was executive vice president and director of research. He has held academic positions as the Wachovia professor of banking and associate dean for research in the Kenan-Flager Business School, UNC-Chapel Hill. His published research includes work on banking structure and regulation in the *Journal of Finance;* the *Journal of Financial Services Research;* the *Journal of Money, Credit, and Banking;* and the *Journal of Regulatory Economics.* Current research examines the financial crisis, regulatory reform, and the development of methods for evaluating the forecasting performance of economic forecasters. He was named a fellow by the National Association for Business Economics in 2004.

CHAPTER 44

Why Securities Regulation Failed to Prevent the CDO Meltdown

RICHARD E. MENDALES
Visiting Professor of Law, Penn State Dickinson School of Law,
Supreme Court Fellow, 1999–2000

T he spark that set off the 2007–2008 explosion in the world financial markets was the failure of the market for collateralized debt obligations (CDOs),[1] starting with one sector of that market, the one based on subprime mortgages. Proposals to deal with the financial crisis often focus on measures drawn from bank regulation, such as capital requirements and leverage ratios. In fact, however, the crisis began when highly rated CDOs that formed significant parts of the capital of financial institutions turned out to be toxic: there was not enough information to fairly value them, although it was clear they were worth significantly less than their face value. This failure in transparency is a classic securities law problem, but SEC regulations failed to prevent it. Nonetheless, the underlying problems that led to the meltdown can best be addressed by giving the SEC the right tools for the job.

Mortgage lenders have long relied on a secondary mortgage market, enabling them to sell mortgages to investors and relend the proceeds to new mortgagors. At least as early as the 1880s, investors bought mortgages from lenders, assembled them into pools, and sold participations in the pools as securities. The market for mortgage-backed securities collapsed with the Panic of 1893, but revived during the 1920s, and widespread defaults on these securities following the Crash of 1929 were noted in the Pecora Committee hearings that led to the Securities Act of 1933.

The New Deal recognized the need for a secondary mortgage market to promote lending to homeowners. The National Housing Act of 1934 authorized one or more national associations to buy and sell mortgages, and Congress created the Federal National Mortgage Association (Fannie Mae) in 1938. It was authorized to buy and sell mortgages insured by the Federal Housing Administration. After World War II, veterans' need for housing led Congress to authorize Fannie Mae to buy and sell mortgages insured by the Veterans Administration as well.

In 1966, the U.S. Treasury, facing costs such as that of the Vietnam War, found itself bumping against the upper limit fixed by Congress for the national debt. One of the ways in which it dealt with this was to reinvent mortgage-backed securities. Under this program, Fannie Mae pooled mortgages it had purchased and placed them in trusts, which sold participation certificates, giving buyers fractional interests in each pool. Payments of principal and interest on the underlying mortgages flowed through to participation holders. The obligations represented by the participations were considered those of the mortgagors and not counted toward the federal debt, so the Treasury had not only reinvented mortgage-backed securities, but introduced off-balance-sheet financing.

Two years later, Congress removed more exposure from the federal balance sheet by splitting Fannie Mae in two. Half retained the Fannie Mae name and charter, but became a quasi-independent corporation, and continued to buy qualifying mortgages to collateralize securities. The other half became the Government National Mortgage Association (Ginnie Mae), which remained a government agency, with the function of guarantying securities backed by pools of FHA and VA mortgages.

Congress chartered another corporation, the Federal Home Loan Mortgage Corporation (Freddie Mac), in 1970, to package conventional mortgages (those not backed by the FHA or VA, and thus ineligible for Fannie Mae purchase) into mortgage-backed securities for sale on the securities markets. Although Fannie Mae and Freddie Mac gradually moved to private ownership, their government charters, federal regulation, and lines of credit from the government led to their designation as "government sponsored entities" (GSEs), and their securities were initially exempt from registration with the SEC.

Over the next decade, the GSEs were unable supply the demands of the mortgage market. This was partly due to retrenchment in federal spending on housing, and partly to the failure of some mortgages to qualify for purchase by the GSEs, such as jumbo mortgages, whose size exceeded FHA guidelines. As a result, beginning in 1977, investment banks began to pool mortgages (and other sources of periodic payments such as car loans), and transfer them to entities designated as "special purpose vehicles." These issued "private label" securities, which passed payments from underlying mortgage pools through to security holders. Unlike GSE securities, these were registered with the SEC. The process is called *securitization*, or more generally, *structured finance*.

The Secondary Mortgage Market Enhancement Act of 1984 (SMMEA) aided securitization by removing securities law impediments to private label securities; for example, it removed them from regulation under state securities laws. With the act's definition of qualifying securities, however, a snake slithered under the rock: to be a mortgage-related security for purposes of SMMEA, a security had to be rated at one of the two highest levels provided by at least one major credit rating agency, which the SEC called Nationally Recognized Statistical Rating Organizations (NRSROs).

Rating agencies had rated the creditworthiness of corporations and their securities for close to a century, and were originally paid for their ratings by subscribing investors. In the 1970s, however, they changed their business model to payment by the issuers whose securities they were rating. This obvious conflict of interest was aggravated by an absence of competition: there were only three agencies accredited by the SEC, with Moody's and Standard & Poor's getting most of the work, and Fitch bringing up the rear. Ironically, the SEC was the first government body to give these unregulated ratings official cachet, by using them as criteria for securities that broker-dealers could use to satisfy their capital requirements, beginning in 1975. During the next 30 years, the SEC did nothing substantial to regulate the rating process, and blocked potentially corrective competition by failing to accredit new agencies.

In the issuance of asset-backed securities, the rating system became a substitute for careful examination of the mortgages in pools being securitized. Rating agencies did not examine individual mortgages in a pool, but instead rated securities based on applying proprietary statistical models to collective characteristics reported on the loan tape, an unverified summary of the assets in a pool. The agencies were largely unregulated until Congress passed the Credit Rating Agency Reform Act of 2006 (CRARA) in the wake of the agencies' failure to issue timely downgrades of failing corporations such as Enron. CRARA provided only minimal regulation. It was chiefly intended to force the SEC to accredit more agencies, although in fact it failed to produce a meaningful increase in competition. Though it barred some abusive practices such as threatening to give an adverse rating unless an issuer hired an agency, it was counterproductive in more important ways. It barred the SEC from substantively regulating the rating process, giving the agencies a privileged position not shared by other participants in the process of issuing securities, which are generally required by the Securities Act of 1933 to employ due diligence to ensure that information they provide concerning newly issued securities is accurate.

By the time CRARA was enacted, flaws based on defective ratings were embedded in billions of dollars' worth of CDOs and their derivatives, particularly those issued after the turn of the century. Mortgage-backed securities received top ratings even though none of the mortgages that backed them had strong repayment ability.

The alchemy by which securities based on pools of low-grade mortgages received top ratings took several forms. First, there were credit enhancements, guarantying payments of the securities, such as standby letters of credit issued by banks and insurance policies from monoline insurers such as Ambac Financial Group. These guarantees were no stronger than the institutions that issued them. Monoline insurers in particular had no alternate insurance business to support them if enough mortgage-backed securities defaulted. When the crisis broke, Ambac lost its own AAA rating.

Pools of low-grade collateral were also turned into AAA-rated securities by dividing the securities into tranches, through which holders of a first tranche held first priority on payments due from mortgagors, followed by holders of a second tranche, and so on. The rating agencies created models under which, because holders of higher-ranking tranches held first priority rights to payments from all successive tranches—what was called the *waterfall effect*—they would supposedly be assured of payment even if some mortgages in a pool defaulted, and first-priority tranches received top ratings, even though their cash flow came entirely from high-risk mortgages.

Matters became more complex when investment banks pooled hundreds of tranches of asset-backed securities into pools that provided cash flow for other securities, known as collateralized debt obligations, or CDOs. CDOs include not only interests in pools of mortgages and securities based on them, but also derivative obligations such as credit default swaps, or contracts to pay a holder of a debt instrument such as a mortgage-backed security in event of its default. CDOs were rated solely on the basis of ratings of the instruments on which they were based, since they were too complex for the agencies rating them to review the soundness of the base-level collateral providing the cash flow.

This problem was magnified when financial institutions operating outside regulated markets created derivative obligations based on CDOs. The result was to multiply the exposure of the financial system to a failure of CDOs, often by many layers of derivatives. Because these transactions were not made on recognized markets, the amount outstanding was unknown, and when the instruments providing the underlying cash flow began to default, the amount of institutional liability on derivatives such as credit default swaps became both enormous and incalculable.

The waterfall model failed in part because it was not based on real-world default data. Moreover, as the SEC found when it studied agency practices, the agencies failed to adjust their statistical models when the housing market shifted to a riskier pattern. Beginning in the 1990s, government agencies such as the FHA began to insure mortgages whose obligors had progressively less equity in their homes. Required down payments declined from the once sacrosanct 20 percent to 5 percent in the 1990s and then to a mere 3 percent after the turn of the century. Technically, these were not subprime loans, but default rates rose to the point at which the FHA had to draw on general government funds for the first time in its 74-year history.

Despite these problems, the SEC issued only superficial rulings to deal with the special characteristics of asset-backed securities, which were finally compiled in Regulation AB in 2005. Regulation AB failed to require basic safeguards such as due diligence concerning individual mortgages in a pool to verify mortgagors' ability to make payments on interest and principal. Unlike normal securities law disclosure concerning conventional debt, it did not require the disclosure of information that could have been used to check the accuracy of ratings on mortgage-backed securities.

The easing of FHA down payment requirements contributed to a larger housing bubble inflated by easy credit that the Federal Reserve made available after the crash in technology stocks. Unlicensed mortgage brokers appeared and competed with traditional mortgage lenders—and mortgage-backed securities pushed the market from an originate-to-hold model, characteristic of earlier institutional mortgage lending, to an originate-to-sell model, which minimized concern for the ability of borrowers to repay. This spurred the proliferation of subprime mortgages, particularly after 2004.

Subprime mortgages started as mortgages that did not meet FHA criteria, because their borrowers could not make minimum down payments, failed to meet certain income tests, or had deficient credit histories. Originally, they were merely loans to borrowers with weaker capacities to make consistent payments than those with prime mortgages, and repayment patterns studied by the rating agencies showed that predictable numbers would make timely payments. Mixing them with prime mortgages in a pool, therefore, could reasonably allow high ratings for the top tranches of securities backed by the pool based on the waterfall effect.

This changed with the turn of the century, however. Driven by easy credit from the Federal Reserve, which was trying to stave off a recession following the collapse of technology stocks, and pressure from the Department of Housing and Urban Development to make mortgages more available, subprime mortgages multiplied beyond traditional proportions—up to 50 percent of the U.S. market—and mutated into more malignant forms. These included liar loans, whose borrowers misstated or failed to document their income, or where the mortgaged homes were appraised at higher than actual value; and loans offering low teaser interest rates that after a short period would reset upward beyond the mortgagors' ability to pay. In contrast to earlier subprime loans, these were not just somewhat weaker than prime loans, but had a high probability of default. Loans of this kind could not support a waterfall effect.

Nonetheless, the rating agencies gave AAA ratings to securities based on pools that sometimes contained only subprime mortgages. Even before subprime loans became a major part of the market, the agencies' ratings understated the risk of mortgage-backed securities. In Moody's system, for example, 2.2 percent of the corporate bonds rated Baa (the lowest investment-grade rating) failed over the period 1983 to 2005. For CDOs with the same rating, however, the average five-year default rate from 1993 to 2005 was 24 percent. Despite this, Moody's did not change its models from the one it adopted, undisclosed, in 2002, until the crisis broke when subprime mortgages began to default in substantial numbers late in 2006. By then, financial institutions around the world found themselves holding CDOs whose nominal values rested on ratings that were demonstrably inaccurate; and without the ratings, it was impossible to value the CDOs and derivative obligations based on them. Since these instruments were now embedded in the capital of financial institutions around the world, their holders' solvency came into question, destroying the trust that enabled them to deal with each other. World credit markets seized up, detonating the worst financial crisis since the Great Depression.

At great cost, the world's governments appear to have stabilized credit markets, and we must now consider how best to prevent a recurrence of this debacle. Although the SEC contributed to the dependence on the rating system that led to the crisis, it is better equipped to prevent future crises of this kind than any other federal agency. Housing finance requires mortgage-backed securities, and the SEC, unlike bank regulators, has had long experience in prescribing carefully structured public disclosure concerning the features and risks of registered securities. It also has far more experience in enforcing the law and regulations that assure accurate disclosure.

A good solution would apply principles from the Securities Act of 1933—which were devised, *inter alia*, to deal with conflicts of interest by underwriters of securities—by requiring the use of due diligence in rating asset-backed securities. While the agencies themselves are too small to be required to examine all the underlying documentation in each pool of several thousand mortgages, the professionals retained by issuers and underwriters normally examine large numbers of documents to assure accurate disclosure concerning conventional securities. They can be required to do so here to verify the contents of each pool, and the agencies should be required to use due diligence in applying their models to the verified characteristics of each pool to formulate their ratings.

The conflict of interest inherent in the agencies' function also calls for external supervision of the models used in formulating ratings. An independent regulatory board comparable to the Public Company Accounting Oversight Board, established by the Sarbanes-Oxley Act, should be established to oversee the rating models established by the rating agencies, the application of the models, check them against evolving conditions, and review their performance over time.

Finally, it is also important to require derivative transactions to be made on recognized exchanges. This is important to inform regulators of the identity of participants in derivative transactions and their exposure to potential liabilities, and to limit the ability of institutions to engage in transactions beyond their financial ability. The SEC can play an important role in determining whether derivative instruments created in these transactions should be registered as securities, and to prevent fraud. In doing so, it will need to cooperate with other agencies—those engaged in regulating financial institutions—that will decide matters such as requirements for capital needed to back derivative obligations.

NOTE

1. CDOs represent a large set of securities giving their holders interests in pools of income-producing assets such as mortgages and commercial loans, as well as derivatives of asset-backed securities.

ABOUT THE AUTHOR

Richard E. Mendales received BA and MA degrees from the University of Chicago, and a JD from Yale Law School. Following law school, he practiced law at the firms of Cravath, Swaine & Moore and Skadden, Arps, Slate, Meagher & Flom in New York, and at Crowell & Moring in Washington. Between his New York and Washington practice, he was appointed to a Supreme Court Fellowship in Washington for 1999–2000. In addition to his practice, he has served as Associate Professor and Professor of Law at the University of Miami in Coral Gables, FL, as Visiting Professor of Law at Widener University in Harrisburg, PA, and currently teaches as Visiting Professor of Law at Penn State Dickinson School of Law in University Park, PA. He has published numerous articles on securities law and structured finance.

CHAPTER 45

Curbing Optimism in Managerial Estimates Through Transparent Accounting

The Case of Securitizations

STEPHEN BRYAN
Professor of Accountancy at Fordham University Schools of Business

STEVEN LILIEN
Weinstein Professor of Accountancy at the Zicklin School of Business,
Bernard M. Baruch College

BHARAT SARATH
Vice-Chair of the Accounting, Business Ethics, and Information Systems
Department of Rutgers University

O ur article considers the role of accounting in the subprime crisis. Although the major part of the crisis occurred in 2007 and 2008, we examined data over a longer time period. Commencing in 2002, we witnessed a growing trend in the value of retained interests in securitized mortgages on the balance sheets of major banking institutions. These retained interests later became substantially impaired and even worthless in many instances. We were reminded of the classic inventory problem, in which a company buys large quantities of inventory, for which the market dries up. The company is forced to warehouse the goods and eventually recognize write-offs.

Continuing from the perspective of inventory accounting, we noted another significant issue, namely the allocation of values between the amounts of securitized mortgages that the banks sold and amounts retained (the retained interests). As we illustrate in an upcoming example, the values that were split between the sold and retained portions were fair values, rather than costs. These fair values were determined with internal valuation models that were heavily dependent upon assumptions made by management, and these values also appeared to have affected compensation paid under bonus plans. Drilling further, we also observed the role played by *special purpose entities* (SPEs) to carry out the sales of securitized mortgages. SPEs (or QSPEs, qualified special purpose entities) are off-balance-sheet entities, created by banks, to which the banks transferred or sold the mortgages. These transactions were made in an environment of substantial liquidity contingencies. Well-established accounting theory generally requires sales with numerous uncertainties (contingencies) to be postponed.

Testimony before the United States Congress and several academic studies have already provided many different reasons for the financial crisis. As a result, regulatory changes will be implemented. Some of the new oversight will be a rational response, based upon empirical data and analysis. Some may be purely political manifestations to placate constituencies hurt by the meltdown. Whatever changes are made will likely be partly temporary as unintended consequences invariably appear from the mixture of best intentions, rational thinking, and political forces. We add our point of view to the mix and believe a relatively simple accounting change would mitigate some of the issues that contributed to the crisis.

Accounting standard setters have grappled for years with a slippery problem of maintaining internal consistency in accounting standards while simultaneously meeting investor demands for information about expected future cash flows. For example, the prevailing use of historical cost, as the predominant basis for measurement and recognition, had to make room for the use of fair value accounting, which is theoretically based upon estimates of future cash flows. Beginning with the conservatism principle, fair values were recognized in the case of unrealized losses (expected reductions in future cash flows). Unrealized gains (expected increases in future cash flows) were deferred until realized. Subsequently, however, accounting standards began to recognize appreciation of value as well, in violation of conservatism. It was deemed that fair values, both those that resulted in gains and losses, were more relevant than historical cost, because fair values are explicitly tied to estimates of future cash flows. This explanation seemed satisfactory because, coupled with the concept of relevance is the notion of reliability, and therefore only those assets whose market values could be measured reliably were to be maintained on balance sheets at fair value. The assets that received fair value accounting were, therefore, essentially plain vanilla, actively exchange-traded investments in debt and equities.

The growth of more exotic and non-exchange-traded securities accelerated during the 1990s, as new securities were created from repackaged claims on cash flows, including collateralized debt obligations. Notwithstanding the lack of quoted market prices for many of these securitized assets, the market for them had been relatively liquid, at least up until about 2005 (and served as a reasonable basis for determination of fair value). However, for a variety of causes, the market started slowing down considerably over the next few years.

In the absence of an active market, holders of these mortgages, or securities backed by them, were faced with an accounting measurement problem. The determination of fair values now required new methodologies, including modeling techniques that were often proprietary to the firm. For purposes of comparability and consistency, fair value measurements and disclosures were codified in Statement of Financial Accounting Standard No. 157, "Fair Value Measurements." Three levels of assets were delineated under this standard, each of which received different valuation guidance. Level 1 asset values are based upon the values of identical assets (and liabilities) that are quoted in active markets. Level 2 valuations are one step removed in that they are based upon observable values for similar (rather than identical) assets and liabilities. Level 3 valuations are the furthest removed from quoted prices or observable inputs. These assets are valued using the company's own assumptions. Firms also had to disclose the amounts of each asset level. The disclosure rules showed that firms in the financial sector were using proprietary models in valuing these assets, necessarily, because the markets for these assets had become illiquid.

This is where we identify an unintended consequence, particularly for banks and other financial institutions. Banks had initiated or purchased large amounts of mortgages, which they repackaged into tranches that were distinguished mostly by underlying credit quality. Many of these tranches were sold to investors or transferred to a conduit that in turn sold new securities to investors using the transferred tranches as collateral. The financial institutions typically retained a tranche (the retained interest), as well as servicing rights on the sold securities. The portfolio of retained interests, servicing rights, and the tranches to be sold were all recorded at fair value.

Initially, financial institutions retained relatively small amounts of the repackaged mortgages because the investor demand for these products was relatively high. These securities were also deemed to be relatively safe in that the credit rating agencies gave investment grade ratings to them and the securities were often insured. However, as the market for securitized assets slowed down, banks retained ever larger shares of their asset-backed securities. Eventually, when housing prices collapsed and an increasingly large number of mortgagees became delinquent, the fair values of the retained interests came crashing down (and they had a long way to fall).

Whether these fair values were inflated cannot be known for certain, but the moral hazard was severe. These valuations were based on Level 3 valuations, which means that the valuations were based on proprietary models. In addition, bankers' compensation is largely bonus-based. Bonuses were tied to earnings, which included the realized gains recognized on the sales of the tranches, the fees earned on the sales, and the unrealized gains recognized on mark-to-market accounting on the servicing right and on the retained tranches. Moreover, the financial institutions were allowed to be involved in the creation of the SPEs to which they sold the tranches.

Therefore, the unintended consequence from trying to create more relevant information through fair value accounting was the relinquishing of control of setting fair values to employees whose pay was directly affected. Part of having reliable information is that the information should be unbiased. By moving from external, liquid markets to internal models to determine fair values, because the external markets became illiquid, the potential for biased values is increased. The issue of in-sourcing valuations is problematic, as stated by the chairman of the FASB, Robert Herz:

> To be sure, there is no question that implementing fair value in illiquid markets can be challenging and difficult and there are important questions to be asked. Does it lead, reflect, or lag reality? Are there genuine concerns over procyclicality? These are important questions and issues; but I would ask, what are the alternatives? ("Lessons Learned, Relearned, and Relearned Again from the Global Financial Crisis," AICPA National Conference on Current SEC Issues, December 8, 2008).

The writedowns of the portfolios on the balance sheets of financial institutions amounted to several hundreds of billions by mid-2008. The magnitude of these writedowns means that the accounting procedures, or their applications (or both) badly mismeasured values. Therefore, the accounting profession came under intense scrutiny and criticism.

Research from psychology suggests that in times of euphoria, internally determined valuations will be overly optimistic. In addition, the decision to continue buying mortgages was done with little regard for the downside risk that the mortgages were of little quality. When everyone is partying, no one wants to say, "Last call" or turn out the lights. This human tendency reinforced and exacerbated problems with fair value accounting. Nevertheless, we believe that there is merit in maintaining the practice of using fair values, even for those assets that are hard to value. Research has shown that the market finds that fair values convey meaningful information to market participants. However, we believe that a practice that is used in the accrual system should be applied to the fair values system. In the accrual system, revenues can be booked in advance of cash collections, but reserves are established for uncollectible receivables. In the fair value system, similarly, gains are booked in advance of realization, but no corresponding reserves are established, leading to overvalued assets, especially in boom times. The following examples (Exhibits 45.1 to 45.4) illustrate the process of setting up reserves against fair values.

Assume a company has two mortgage classes, Class 1 and Class 2, with principal amounts and fair values shown in Exhibit 45.1. Assume that the book values of the two classes totals $40,000,000. The company repackages the mortgages and retains a newly formed Class 3, and the company retains the servicing rights. Class 3 and the servicing rights are assigned fair values based upon internal models. The $40,000,000 of book value is reallocated among the three classes, plus servicing rights, based upon their relative fair values.

The journal entry (in intuitive form) to record the gain on sale to the SPE is shown in Exhibit 45.2.

Also, Class 3 and the servicing right must be updated to their respective full fair values of $1,000,000 and $500,000, respectively, resulting in another gain, as shown in Exhibit 45.3.

Combining the gain on sale with the gain on revaluing the retained items yields a total gain of $4,440,000, which is the difference between the book value of $40,000,000 and the total fair value of $44,440,000. The gain on sale was

Exhibit 45.1 Mortgage Classes, Principal Amounts, and Fair Values

	Principal	Price	Fair Value	Relative % of Fair Value	Relative Fair Value Allocation of Book Value
Class 1	40,000,000	100	40,000,000	90.01%	36,003,600
Class 2	3,000,000	98	2,940,000	6.62%	2,646,265
Class 3	0		1,000,000	2.25%	900,090
Servicing	0		500,000	1.13%	450,045
Total	43,000,000		44,440,000	100.00%	40,000,000

Exhibit 45.2 Journal Entries for Sale of SPE

Assets		Liabilities		Owners' Equity	
+42,940,000	Cash			+4,290,135	Gain
−40,000,000	Class 1 and 2				
+900,090	Class 3				
+450,045	Servicing				

facilitated by the QSPE, and the fair values of the retained assets (Class 3 and servicing), resulting in the second (unrealized) gain, were determined using proprietary models.

Given the potential for biased estimates of the unrealized gain, we recommend that a reserve for unrealizability be recorded. Under existing accounting standards, when the fair values of assets are determined using internal models, firms are required to disclose how those fair value estimates would be changed adversely if the critical parameters were to be changed. The combined recognized fair value of Class 3 and the servicing right is $1,500,000. Assume that an adverse change in the parameters resulted in an adverse reduction in value of the estimates of fair value of 20 percent, or $300,000. We would then propose that the firm accrue a reserve against its fair value estimates (see Exhibit 45.4).

The Valuation Allowance shown in Exhibit 45.4 would be a separate account (a so-called contra account) on the balance sheet that would show the fair value estimate at $1,200,000, net. The reserve would require full transparency and external validation to mitigate any potential for abuse. For example, it has been documented in academic literature that firms have managed their reserves opportunistically, reversing them to boost earnings in future periods.

We acknowledge and commend the banks for attempting to institute procedures to mitigate unbiased estimates of fair values, as shown in the following, an excerpt from Citigroup:

> When available, the Company generally uses quoted market prices to determine fair value, and classifies such items within Level 1 of the fair value hierarchy. If quoted market prices are not available, fair value is based upon internally developed valuation models that use, where possible, current market-based or independently sourced market parameters, such as interest rates, currency rates, option volatilities, etc. More than 800 models are used across Citigroup. Where a model is internally developed and used to price a significant product, it is subject to validation and testing by independent personnel. Such models are often based on a discounted cash flow analysis (2007, 10-K).

Exhibit 45.3 Class 3 Mortgage with Servicing Rights at Fair Value

Assets		Liabilities		Owners' Equity	
+99,910	Class 3			+149,865	Gain
+49,955	Servicing				

Exhibit 45.4 Valuation Allowance and Reserve

Assets		Liabilities		Owners' Equity	
−300,000	Valuation Allowance			−300,000	Expense

Our proposal extends this practice and the accounting literature by requiring formal balance sheet recognition, as well as income statement recognition, of an estimate of an adverse change on the fair values. This will mitigate the procyclical swings in fair values, particularly those based upon internal models. Also, the moral hazard that arises from compensation arrangements that are based on unrealized gains that are determined internally would be mitigated if these reserves were incorporated into the bonus-based earnings measures.

In conclusion, we identified two major accounting issues that contributed to the crises. First, we observed possible premature recognition of revenues. Under contemporary accounting rules, sales accounting can be achieved, even with the retention of tranches that were created by breaking up mortgages in bundles with different attributes. The huge writedowns of retained tranches and warehoused mortgages suggests that they were significantly overvalued, which thereby suggests the tranches transferred to others were undervalued, because of the allocations between retained and sold amounts. The accounting standard setters have also observed the problems raised by this accounting treatment, and they have reacted by providing a temporary solution. They have changed the measurement and recognition of securitizations by instituting a new accounting concept, which they refer to as *participating interests*. When a firm retains a portion of the securitization, the retained interest must identically resemble the portions transferred to others. To achieve sales accounting (that is, recognition of profit through transfers), more senior or lower interest rate tranches cannot be retained. Participating interest is equivalent to everyone getting an identical slice of the pie (apples and crust but not necessarily the same size slice). We are concerned, however, because if there are valid economic reasons to break up pools of mortgages and other receivables with differing priorities and attributes, the new accounting may end a practice that has valid economic reasons. Admittedly, however, premature recognition of gross profit should be curtailed.

The second major issue was the creation of QSPEs to move mortgages off the transferor's books, again to facilitate gross profit recognition. Coupled with this transaction were "liquidity puts" that could force the transferor to put monies into the QSPE, or in some instances take back the securities. We believe that the valuations of such liquidity puts were optimistically determined (i.e., the potential obligation was understated). There were substantial uncertainties accompanying such puts. In the meantime, the accounting standard setters have recently eliminated the accounting vehicle involved in such transactions, that is the QSPEs, by essentially requiring consolidation of the QSPEs, when there are large possible losses, even if unlikely. This will curtail upfront recognition of profit. However, where similar transactions occur without the use of QSPEs, it may still be possible to obtain results equivalent to those reported in this paper.

Our proposed solution uses reserve accounting on fair value estimates. We would also suggest that a company's risk group be actively engaged with the establishment of the reserve and work directly with a firm's board of directors to provide ongoing oversight. Such reserves can be used to curtail up-front profit recognition and the payment of bonuses attributable to opportunistic estimates.

ABOUT THE AUTHORS

Stephen H. Bryan, Ph.D. is a professor of accountancy at Fordham University School of Business. He received his Ph.D. from New York University. His articles have appeared in the *Accounting Review; Journal of Business; Journal of Corporate Finance; Harvard Business Review; Journal of Accounting, Auditing, and Finance;* and *Financial Management*. His research areas encompass corporate governance, compensation policies, and firm disclosures.

Steven B. Lilien, Ph.D., CPA, is the Weinstein Professor of Accountancy at the Zicklin School of Business, Bernard M. Baruch College, City University of New York. He was previously chairman of the Stan Ross Department of Accountancy, and director of the Robert Zicklin Center for Corporate Integrity. He received his Ph.D. from New York University. His articles have appeared in the *Accounting Review; Financial Analysts Journal; Journal of Accounting and Economics; Journal of Business; Journal of Accounting, Auditing and Finance;* the *CPA Journal; Harvard Business Review;* and *Management Accounting*. He has edited *The Accountants' Handbook* and co-authored books on financial accounting and auditing practice and on the discovery of accounting information in litigation actions.

Bharat Sarath holds two Ph.D.s, from the University of Calgary (mathematics, 1976) and Stanford University (accounting, 1988). He is currently vice-chair of the Accounting, Business Ethics, and Information Systems department of Rutgers University (New Brunswick). Sarath has published articles in mathematics, physics, economics, finance, and accounting. His main interests are in applying game theory to explain observed market microstructure, particularly with regard to the function of auditors. Some of the current projects Sarath is working on include an analysis of the effects of short-selling on price reactions around earnings announcements and the dynamics of price movements in incomplete markets.

CHAPTER 46

Basel II Put on Trial

What Role in the Financial Crisis?

FRANCESCO CANNATA
Head of the Regulatory Impact Assessment Unit in the Regulation
and Supervisory Policies Department of Banca d'Italia

MARIO QUAGLIARIELLO
Senior economist in the Regulation and Supervisory Policies Department
of Banca d'Italia*

T he subprime financial crisis has stimulated an intense debate on the rationale
of financial regulation and the role it has played in one of the worst financial
meltdowns in economic history. The Basel II framework on bank capital
adequacy has been put on trial as a major cause for the crisis. As usually happens,
the scapegoat has not found many advocates. However, in spite of that, some
questions deserve some attention before the verdict is returned. Can we just ascribe
the financial crisis to Basel II? Is it correct to focus on elements of the new framework
that, to a deeper analysis, are not strictly linked to the financial turmoil? Should
regulators discard the whole Basel II framework or, rather, try to overcome its
limits while preserving the backbone of the new discipline?

We discuss in this chapter the main accusations to Basel II and provide some
evidence for the defense.

THE ROLE PLAYED BY BASEL II
IN THE FINANCIAL CRISIS

The Average Level of Capital Required by the New Discipline
Is Inadequate and This Is One of the Reasons for the Recent
Collapse of Many Banks

The first accusation is that Basel II would have contributed to the undercapitaliza-
tion of many banks. Among others, Onado (2008) claims that regulators did not

---

*The views expressed in the paper are those of the authors and do not necessarily reflect
those of Banca d'Italia.

properly exploit the Basel II reform for raising the capital base of the international banking system. This is correct, but a few points should be clarified.

First of all, it is fair to remind ourselves that the objective of keeping the level of capital unchanged was thought of as a pragmatic way to foster a gradual transition from the old to the new framework, thus avoiding remarkable variations in capital requirements and potentially in credit supply. Indeed, if the new rules had required a stronger capital base, the risk of credit rationing would have been apparent, with possible effects on the real economy (EU Economic and Financial Affairs Council 2004).

The strong willingness within the Basel Committee to find an agreement among G-10 countries has advised to strike a balance among different financial systems and business practices. As with every compromise, this may have led to suboptimal solutions.

Finally, it is important to highlight that the Basel II framework, while stressing the role of adequate capital requirements, has also underlined the role played by banks' organization and risk management processes in maintaining sound economic and financial conditions. For certain risks, robust internal controls are more effective than large capital cushions.

Other economists wonder whether the objective of capital invariance with respect to Basel I has been actually accomplished. For example, Benink and Kaufman (2008) remark that for many banks, capital requirements measured according to the new rules turned out to be lower than those computed under Basel I. This is indeed true, but—if real data will confirm the results of QIS simulation—this is another confirmation of the willingness of regulators to provide banks with incentives for the adoption of the more advanced risk measurement methods. In any case, this does not prevent the revision of the rules and formulae that are used for determining banks' minimum capital levels.

The New Capital Accord, Interacting with Fair Value Accounting, Has Caused Remarkable Losses in the Portfolios of Intermediaries

The second charge for the Basel II rules is that they would have badly interacted with the international accounting principles that introduced fair value accounting (Zingales 2008). Actually, fair value assessment has certainly played a major role during the financial crisis, pushing banks to raise new capital to cover losses and avoid possible defaults. However, in our opinion, the Basel II rules did not play a specific role in this process. Such arguments would apply also to the 1988 Capital Accord. As a matter of fact, this would definitely apply to any regulation requiring banks to meet minimum capital levels.

On the other hand, it is true that the simultaneous implementation of Basel II and the new accounting standards has made banks' balance sheets more vulnerable to assets' value fluctuations. With respect to minimum capital requirements, such an effect has been smoothed by the introduction of prudential filters, that is, adjustments made to balance-sheet capital items in order to protect the quality of supervisory capital. However, such a mechanism has been designed asymmetrically: while fair value re-evaluations are not considered for prudential purposes, fair value devaluations are generally required to contribute to the calculation of supervisory capital. The experience gathered in the financial crisis may call for some form of correction to this mechanism.

Capital Requirements Based on the Basel II Regulations Are Cyclical and Therefore Tend to Reinforce Business Cycle Fluctuations

Basel II is also frequently blamed for being procyclical (Goodhart and Persaud 2008). Notwithstanding the lack of robust empirical evidence, it is undeniable that the Basel II framework may entail procyclical effects.

The new Accord does take explicitly into account the interaction between the micro and macro perspectives. Already during the preparatory work, specific solutions under Pillar 1 have been adopted so as to reduce the possible procyclical impact of the prudential rules, particularly for small and medium enterprises. In addition, within Pillar 2, the new framework requires banks to carry out a forward-looking assessment of their capital adequacy, also under stress conditions, and to build up capital buffers to be used in bad times and restored in good ones. Unfortunately, the timing of the crisis has prevented banks from fully carrying out this self-assessment and increasing capital cushions as well as supervisory authorities to check their adequacy.

However, we do not dispute that—notwithstanding these improvements—the potential risk of procyclicality of the new Accord remains remarkable. We also believe that the tools provided for by Pillar 2 might play a major role in dampening procyclicality risk. The effectiveness of such tools will largely depend on the quality of intermediaries' self-assessment and on the effectiveness of enforcement and supervisory control.

In the Basel II Framework, the Assessment of Credit Risk Is Delegated To Institutions such as Rating Agencies, Subject to Possible Conflicts of Interest

The assessment of borrowers' creditworthiness provided by credit rating agencies (CRAs) plays a significant role in the Basel II regulations, particularly under the standardized approach for credit risk. Doubts on the quality and reliability of such assessment emerged, not only in the aftermath of the subprime crisis, but also when some major corporations defaulted in the United States and Europe.

Two main criticisms have been raised.

The first one concerns the degree of independence of the rating agencies' judgment, particularly in the case of securitizations and structured products (Financial Stability Forum 2008).

The second criticism is more focused on rating methodologies. Indeed, the assignment of ratings is subject to many challenges; for complex financial instruments, the limitations of statistical models have become even more evident since such products are often illiquid and, in certain market conditions, they do not have a market price.

Having said that, it is hard to imagine, at this stage, plausible alternatives to the involvement of rating agencies in the assessment of credit quality. We believe that, at least for plain vanilla corporate debt, the shift from a system of fixed risk-weights to a ratings-based assessment of borrowers' creditworthiness—although inaccurate and, admittedly, sometimes fraudulently mistaken—represents a step forward in risk management practices.

The story is different for structured products. In this case, there is little room for buoyancy. Indeed, the limitations of agencies' methodologies seem mainly related to poor data sets and excessive trust in purely mathematical tools (FSF 2008).

On the other hand, some proposals to deal with such shortcomings have been already put forward. In November 2008, the European Commission finalized a proposal aimed at introducing specific rules for rating agencies; the agencies themselves have started rethinking their methodologies. It is certainly too early to assess the impact that such initiatives may have, but we believe that this is a constructive way to address existing concerns.

The Key Assumption That Banks' Internal Models for Measuring Risk Exposures Are Superior to Any Other Has Proved Wrong

During the crisis, banks' internal models for measuring risk exposures revealed serious shortcomings. This has led to a fierce debate on their use for regulatory purposes.

Benink and Kaufman (2008) highlight that a supervisory approach based on internal models may imply perverse incentives, which would induce banks to underestimate their exposure to risk. By the same token, Onado (2008) disagrees that the market is more efficient than regulatory authorities in detecting the adequate capital level.

Some of these charges are undoubtedly true, but a few points deserve some clarifications.

The Basel II framework is inspired by the principle that risk measurement for regulatory purposes should be based to the extent possible on the best practices adopted by the intermediaries themselves. Such a principle has been considered as a significant innovation in the way regulators have defined the rules to be applied by financial firms.

On the other hand, Basel II does not state the absolute supremacy of internal methodologies with respect to those developed by supervisors. Rather, it considers that any sensible risk assessment for prudential purposes should go hand in hand with the evaluation carried out by intermediaries with the same tools that are also employed for risk management, pricing, and capital planning purposes. We believe that such an approach is still convincing.

Moreover, supervisors are not passive recipients of the outcome of banks' models. Both the methods used and the results of the risk assessment process are to be examined by supervisory authorities. Internal models may be used for regulatory purposes only after they pass a multifaceted validation process. This is clearly a new process for both banks and the supervisory authorities, which requires a gradual learning-by-doing. The poor performance of some internal models calls for an improvement of methodologies, not for blaming the entire philosophy of the new framework (Sironi 2008).

Conversely, we think that it is crucial that sufficient emphasis be placed on the quality of the supervisory action that leads to the validation of banks' internal models. In a few countries, validation standards may have not always been sufficiently rigorous; some banks may have underestimated the importance of developing strong risk management and audit functions. This calls for a better and more harmonized enforcement of the existing rules rather than for their radical revision.

As far as the underestimation of risk by intermediaries is concerned, we do not believe that this is something that can be ascribed to Basel II, which, conversely, requires banks to define internal processes so it can continuously evaluate the consistency between capital endowment and the exposure to risk. In principle, such an assessment should cover a very wide spectrum of risks, not only the traditional ones. One can certainly be skeptical of the actual possibility of measuring some types of risk, such as the risk underlying innovative financial products, where data shortages are considerable. While we agree that Basel II has probably been too ambitious in requiring banks to quantify all the risks they are exposed to, we also believe that the greater attention paid to nontraditional risks is a merit of the Accord. What can turn into the main limit of Basel II is, in our view, the unjustified sense of safety that a system that pretends to measure all risks may induce. Such risk can be, however, reduced through the pragmatic and mindful application of the regulation.

Another criticism of banks' methodologies is that they would privilege the use of standardized and quantitative information, neglecting the soft information that is a key driver in bank-customer relationships. This is definitely a problem that should not be underestimated. On the other hand, it is fair to mention that a more widespread use of quantitative techniques for measuring credit risk tends to make the relationship between banks and firms more transparent and the selection criteria more objective. The need to use an internal rating would have probably limited the supply of the so-called Alt-A or no-doc loans, which played a significant role in the subprime crisis.

The Basel II Framework Provides Incentives to Intermediaries to Deconsolidate from Their Balance Sheets Some Very Risky Exposures

A last charge to Basel II is that it would have left room for regulatory arbitrages, leading intermediaries to set up off-balance-sheet vehicles so they could reduce the capital charge against some types of risk. However, the Financial Stability Forum (2008) provides a possible explanation. "*Public authorities recognised some of the underlying vulnerabilities in the financial sector but failed to take effective countervailing action [. . .]. Limitations in regulatory arrangements, such as those related to the pre–Basel II framework, contributed to the growth of unregulated exposures, excessive risk-taking and weak liquidity risk management.*" The main responsibilities should be therefore ascribed to the prudential regime in force prior to the introduction of Basel II and, in some cases, to poor supervision. Also, not always rigorous implementations of the international accounting standards in a few countries may have played a role.

Obviously, the transition from Basel I to Basel II does not completely eliminate the opportunities for regulatory arbitrage, and some features of the new Accord require rapid interventions. The initiatives undertaken over the last months at the G-20 and EU levels, along with an effective enforcement of the new rules, aim at reducing the risk of regulatory arbitrage.

THE ULTIMATE PIECE OF EVIDENCE

We left the final piece of evidence to the end of our defense: Basel II, our suspect, was not on the crime scene or, rather, showed up later. In the United States, the epicenter of the financial crisis, the introduction of the new prudential discipline has been postponed (so far) to 2010. In Europe, the actual use of the new rules was very limited in 2007, when the crisis erupted.

Therefore, the financial turbulence occurred under the old Basel framework, making very palpable its shortcomings, particularly its low risk sensitivity and the scarce adaptability to financial innovation.

Certainly, many banks, while still meeting Basel I minimum requirements, had already reviewed their credit standards so they could make them consistent with the incoming Basel II discipline. It is therefore likely that some (or many) banks, in the attempt to transform well-established credit processes and risk management methodologies, may have misjudged the actual exposures to new risk types (or new manifestations of traditional risks). In our view, this does not imply that the new framework should be discarded, but rather it confirms the need that the testing phase of the new rules be quickly completed.

CONCLUSION

The Basel II prudential framework for banks has been often identified as one of the major, if not the major, driver of the turmoil. In this chapter, we have tried to show that not all arguments raised by Basel critics are well-founded. We have argued that some of the regulatory failures that have been highlighted are failures of Basel I, rather than of the new framework. In other cases, they are indeed related to Basel II, but international and domestic regulators are already in the process of making important adjustments. Finally, other issues, such as fair value assessment, have nothing to do with prudential regulation. Last, but not least, we have loudly emphasized something that should be plain enough, but that it is very often forgotten: the Basel II rules were not actually applied in major countries when the crisis erupted.

Clearly, we do not deny that the financial turmoil has highlighted some drawbacks of the new framework. As a matter of fact, in the last months, international regulators have been intensively working on some of these issues: among others, Pillar 1 rules for structured products; the treatment of credit lines to off-balance vehicles; the prudential framework for trading book assets; a stricter regulatory regime for rating agencies. Last but not least, the two consultative documents published by the Basel Committee in December 2009 aim at strengthening banks, liquidity risk management and capital levels.

Against this background, we think that it is not sensible to blame Basel II because it did not prevent unregulated intermediaries from excessive leveraging and risk taking. It is much more meaningful to propose the extension of the scope of application of the new prudential regime to those intermediaries. With regard to simplified supervisory tools, such as the leverage ratio, which are becoming increasingly popular, we do believe that these are likely to raise the same problems posed by Basel I. While we cannot exclude that such tools could be used as a complement to Basel II, we are skeptical that they can serve as a full substitute for a risk-sensitive regulation.

At this point, we stop and leave the reader free to surmise. If our arguments have been convincing, it should be clear that it is urgent to strengthen Basel II, but there are not sound reasons for abandoning the philosophy underlying the new framework. Conversely, if Basel II is judged guilty, the only remedy is not going forward to Basel III but going back to Basel I.

REFERENCES

Benink, H., and G. Kaufman. 2008. Turmoil reveals the inadequacy of Basel II. *Financial Times*, February 28.

Borio, C. 2008. *The financial turmoil of 2007–? A preliminary assessment and some policy considerations*. Bank for International Settlements, working papers 251.

Draghi, M. 2009. *The Governor's Concluding Remarks*.

EU Ecofin. 2004. *Press Release—2628th Council Meeting*.

FSF (2008), Report of the Financial Stability Forum on Enhancing Market and Institutional Resilience, Basel.

Goodhart, C., and A. Persaud. 2008. How to avoid the next crash. *Financial Times*, January 30.

Onado, M. 2008. *Il problema è il capitale (Capital is the problem)*. www.lavoce.info.

Sironi, A. 2008. *Addio a Basilea II (Farewell to Basel II)*. www.lavoce.info.

Tarullo, D. 2008. *Banking on Basel: The future of international financial regulation*. Washington, DC: Peterson Institute for International Economics.

Zingales, L. 2008. La sospensione del mark-to-market (The suspension of mark-to-market). *Il Sole24Ore*, October 15.

ABOUT THE AUTHORS

Francesco Cannata holds a M.Sc. in finance from the Cass Business School (United Kingdom) and a Ph.D. in banking and finance from III University of Rome (Italy). He is the head of the Regulatory Impact Assessment Unit in the Regulation and Supervisory Policies Department of Banca d'Italia, the Italian central bank. His interests concern mainly economics of financial regulation, Basel II, and risk management. He has published several articles in Italian and international journals. He is also the editor of a comprehensive book on internal ratings (*The IRB Method*, Bancaria Editrice). A new edition is forthcoming.

Mario Quagliariello holds a Ph.D. in economics from the University of York (United Kingdom) and is a senior economist in the Regulation and Supervisory Policies Department of Banca d'Italia, the Italian central bank. His interests concern macroprudential analysis and stress tests, Basel II, and procyclicality, the economics of financial regulation. He has published several articles in Italian and international journals, including the *Journal of Banking and Finance*, the *Journal of Financial Services Research*, the *Journal of International Financial Markets, Institutions and Money, Applied Economics, Applied Financial Economics* and *Risk*. He is the editor of the volume *Stress Testing the Banking System: Methodologies and Applications*, published by Cambridge University Press.

CHAPTER 47

Credit Rating Organizations, Their Role in the Current Calamity, and Future Prospects for Reform

THOMAS J. FITZPATRICK IV
Economist in the Office of Policy Analysis at the Federal Reserve Bank of Cleveland

CHRIS SAGERS
Associate Professor of Law at the Cleveland-Marshall College of Law, Cleveland State University*

In light of the present economic crisis and their role in it, the world has taken a sudden interest in a small group of private corporations, often referred to as bond rating agencies, credit rating agencies, or credit rating organizations (CROs). Two significant CROs dominate the CRO market worldwide: Moody's Investors Services and Standard and Poor's.[1] Their debt ratings are incorporated into numerous federal and state regulations, granting them regulatory control over certain financial institutions. CROs have frequently been criticized by observers for failing to warn of major bond defaults, while simultaneously earning substantial profits for rating and monitoring bond issuances on their probability of default. Most recently, CROs have drawn criticism for their active complicity in the meltdown in structured finance and related investment vehicles that are at the heart of the current economic crisis.

Historically, the CROs have operated free of regulation. This is now changing, as policy makers and academics struggle with how to effectively regulate CROs.

---

*This paper briefly summarizes our more extensive treatment of the credit rating organizations and their role in the present economic crisis, Thomas J. Fitzpatrick IV and Chris Sagers, *"Faith-Based Financial Regulation: A Primer on Oversight of the Credit Rating Organizations,"* 61 Admin. L. Rev. 557 (2009).

The views and opinions expressed are those of the authors and not necessarily those of the Federal Reserve Bank of Cleveland, the Board of Governors, or other banks in the Federal Reserve System.

This debate has been dominated by two policy concerns: whether private credit ratings improve capital asset pricing efficiency and whether they reduce systemic risk. Noticeably absent from the debate, however, is an assessment of the current and proposed law surrounding the CROs and their likely future regulability. In this paper we provide this assessment and posit two propositions. First, the industry in its current posture cannot be meaningfully regulated. Second, it is likely to remain this way under proposed policy changes that contemplate a major private role in the formal assessment of credit risk.

HOW THE CROs CAME TO BE

Providing credit ratings is an old business in the United States. Companies provided reports on the creditworthiness of merchants as early as the 1840s,[2] and both of the major CROs started rating debt in the early 1900s. The role of credit ratings in capital markets was expanded numerous times by U.S. government regulations, beginning in 1936 when the Office of the Comptroller of the Currency incorporated credit ratings into federal banking capital requirements and peaking in the 1970s when the Securities and Exchange Commission (SEC) began making regulatory use of credit ratings when setting capital requirements for securities firms.[3] It was in this latter period that the SEC created the familiar "Nationally Recognized Statistical Rating Organization" (NRSRO) designation.[4]

The regulatory use of credit ratings today, which essentially outsources regulatory risk assessment to CROs, abounds: NRSRO ratings can be found in eight federal statutes and more than 60 regulations.[5] States, courts, private parties, and even foreign governments have also outsourced risk assessment to CROs. This regulatory use of NRSRO ratings has dramatically increased demand for them, making them necessary even when no independent reason for their use exists.

In addition, CROs have benefited from three major trends in capital markets since the 1970s. The first is the significant amount of deregulation that has taken place over the past 30 years,[6] and the second is the creation of increasingly complex financial products that deregulation facilitated. The third critical trend is disintermediation, which is the erosion of the buffer that once existed between investors and investment products. Instead of savings and relatively low-risk institutional investments, retail investors increasingly invest directly in riskier channels in hopes of greater returns. As the complexity of financial products has increased, the sophistication of parties investing in them has decreased. Information asymmetries increase demand for third-party risk assessment, which has increased demand for and regulatory reliance on CRO debt ratings.

The problems caused by regulatory outsourcing, deregulation, disintermediation, and complex financial innovation came to a head with the recent failings in structured finance.[7] CROs found themselves at the center of the creation of asset-backed securities (ABS)—debt issues unlike traditional corporate debt—and derivatives thereof. ABS markets like those for mortgage-backed securities and collateralized debt obligations could thrive only with high credit ratings.

OVERARCHING PROBLEMS IN THE CRO SYSTEM

The dramatic delegation of regulatory judgment to the CROs begs the question of whether their work improves capital market efficiency or reduces systemic risk.

Most research has found that highly rated bonds have low default rates and yields consistent with low risk,[8] but also that CROs just barely meet the market's own success at predicting bond values. In fact, observers have questioned the value that credit ratings add to the market since 1938. It appears the CROs likewise failed to reduce systemic risk. During the past several decades they failed to predict a series of bond defaults of systemic significance, and in the present crisis they materially contributed to *creating* systemic risk.

The causes of this poor performance could be many. Critics often point to conflict of interest, because debt issuers ordinarily pay for ratings. A recent investigation by the SEC found that issuers would play the CROs off of each other in an effort to obtain more favorable ratings. The CROs responded to this behavior by competing for issuer business by loosening their own standards so they could ensure that issues obtained the highest possible rating. Conflicts reached new highs in the structured finance arena, in which CROs began to rate issues they knew were poorly conceived. Because each structured debt issue required a CRO rating to be sold, it was in the CROs' interests to see the market for those products succeed. Thus, CROs rated them highly despite serious doubts about both their riskiness and their legal soundness. Additionally, CROs sold consulting services instructing issuers on how to structure pools of assets for them to achieve the highest rating, and then rated the same issues. They were unlikely to tell issuers how to structure pools and then rate them poorly.

Many argue that the reputational capital of the CROs should be sufficient to regulate their behavior. If any one CRO consistently issued inaccurate credit ratings, markets would simply demand ratings from other CROs. There are a few problems with this theory of market regulation, however. For example, this presumes a competitive market for debt rating, a situation that does not exist and is impeded by substantial difficulties of entry. Moreover, there is some evidence that capital market participants, possibly including the CROs, display herding behavior. That is, the CROs seem to feel safe rating issues poorly as long as they are both doing it.

CHECKS ON CRO POWER

Despite the significant problems inherent in the current credit rating system, the CROs face surprisingly little oversight. Until recently they were completely unregulated. This changed, though not dramatically, with the passage of the Credit Rating Agency Reform Act of 2006 (CRARA). CRARA is a pointedly free-market piece of legislation that actually insulates the CROs from securities law liability and prohibits both the SEC and state governments from regulating the substance of ratings. While some of the rules proposed under CRARA have more bite, it is unclear whether they will become law. The European Union passed a series of rules governing CROs that are slightly more restrictive, but for the most part, the CROs are still not subject to any meaningful oversight.

Of the other laws and regulations under which private parties might sue, all have proven ineffective. As pointed out by Frank Partnoy, "[t]he common element" in lawsuits against the CROs "is that the rating agencies win."[9] Worse yet, U.S. courts have held that the CROs are protected by the free speech protections of the First Amendment, so regulation of or litigation against the CROs for their ratings might be unconstitutional.

PROPOSALS FOR REFORM

Proposals for reform each face their own challenges. Perhaps the longest-standing proposal has been to remove CROs from any regulatory role and replace them with some market measure of risk, such as yield spread. While removing CROs from their regulatory role is an important step, it is not clear if or how they should be replaced. Market measures may be overly susceptible to manipulation, and they may be difficult to accurately calculate on a regular basis. In any case, replacing credit ratings with market measures is not as simple as it sounds.

Another suggestion with increasing support is to develop an investor-pays model, whereby investors pay for CRO ratings on an ex post basis. However, such a solution must first overcome tremendous free-riding and collective action problems, whereby many will attempt to reap the benefits of CRO ratings without paying for them. Even elegant and detailed systems in which issuers would pool money to pay CRO fees and investors would select the CROs that receive payment ex post raise more questions than they answer, and may contribute to problems by adding unnecessary complexity to CRO markets.[10]

Similar suggestions attempt to counterbalance CRO incentives to favor issuers with incentives to favor investors. For instance, one could require CROs to take a pecuniary stake in their own accuracy by requiring them to invest in each debt issue they rate. But this is probably impossible given to the sheer volume of debt issued and rated each year. A more feasible approach might rely on default insurance, effectively calling on insurers to replace CROs. This proposition is also dubious, as numerous entities with significant skin in the game (including insurers) suffered tremendous losses in the current crisis. A third suggestion is to require issuers to pay for investor-controlled CROs that would have a bias to favor investors and would issue ratings along with the traditional CROs. While this could theoretically counterbalance issuer and investor biases, it is unlikely that the additional costs would yield benefits to scale. Alternatively, CROs could be made liable for inaccurate ratings, but this runs the risk of either creating potential damages that are too large to make rating debt a profitable business or too small to dissuade CROs from inaccurate ratings.

Finally, the government could directly intervene in the process by either regulating the substance of credit ratings or creating a utility-model government CRO that would rate debt in competition with or in place of private CROs. The former would require change in recent legislation, as CRARA explicitly prohibits SEC regulation of the substance of credit rating methodologies, and the SEC is the primary regulator of CROs. The latter suggestion is politically infeasible, and is not clearly desirable. A government credit rater would likely be expensive and would have to cope with a lack of price signals to guide efficient investment of resources in securities research.

CONCLUSION

The CRO industry as it stands today is profoundly unregulable. Although it now seems fairly clear that change will come, proposed reforms are poised to fail. Before new pieces are added to the CRO regulatory puzzle, numerous pieces need to be changed, such as regulatory reliance upon CRO ratings, and the substantial legal protections CROs currently enjoy.

NOTES

1. As of 2006, these two CROs had 80 percent of the market, as measured by revenue, and rated as much as 99 percent of publicly traded debt issues and preferred stock in the United States. Their largest competitor, Fitch Ratings, holds an additional 15 percent of the market, as measured by revenue. See S. Rep. No. 109-326, 109th Congress, 2d Sess., at 4 (2006). Historically, the number of major CROs has fluctuated between three and five throughout the industry's history. See Lawrence J. White, *Good Intentions Gone Awry: A Policy Analysis of the SEC's Regulation of the Bond Rating Industry* (New York Univ. Law and Economics Working Papers, 69, 2006).

2. See Frank Partnoy, "The Siskel and Ebert of Financial Markets? Two Thumbs Down for the Credit Rating Agencies," *Wash. U.L.Q.* 77 (1999): 619, 636–637.

3. See Partnoy, supra, note 3, at 690–691.

4. See, generally, Fitzpatrick and Sagers, supra note 1.

5. See Frank Partnoy, "The Paradox of Credit Ratings," in *Ratings, Rating Agencies and the Global Financial System,* eds. Richard M. Levich et al. (Norwell, MA: Kluwer Academic Publishers, 2002), 74–75.

6. See, for example, Congressional Oversight Panel, *Special Report on Regulatory Reform: Modernizing the American Financial Regulatory System: Recommendations for Improving Oversight, Protecting Consumers, and Ensuring Stability* (2009).

7. Structured finance refers to debt products that are issued by a passive trust holding assets, such as mortgages, and are paid off using the revenue streams from those assets (as people pay their mortgages, those payments are forwarded on to investors). These differ from traditional debt products, such as corporate bonds, which are issued by a company and paid off out of company profits.

8. See, for example, Louis H. Edrington and Jess B. Yawitz, "The Bond Rating Process," in *Handbook of Financial Markets and Institutions* 41 (New York: John Wiley & Sons, Edward I. Altman ed., 6th ed., 1987); Pu Liu and Anjan V. Thakor, "Interest Yields, Credit Ratings, and Economic Characteristics of State Bonds: An Empirical Analysis" *Journal of Money, Credit and Banking* 16 (1984): 344.

9. Partnoy, supra note 5, at 79.

10. See, for example, Stephen J. Choi and Jill Fisch, "How to Fix Wall Street: A Voucher Financing Proposal for Securities Intermediaries," *Yale Law Journal* 113 (2003): 269.

ABOUT THE AUTHORS

Chris Sagers is an associate professor of law at the Cleveland-Marshall College of Law, Cleveland State University; He earned J.D. and M.P.P. degrees in 1997 from the University of Michigan. He writes and teaches in administrative law, antitrust, business organizations, and economic regulation. He is a member of the American Law Institute and is an active member of the antitrust section of the American Bar Association.

Thomas J. Fitzpatrick IV, is an economist in the Office of Policy Analysis at the Federal Reserve Bank of Cleveland. His primary fields of interest are in the origination channels of housing market structured finance, consumer finance and protection, financial regulation, and community development. Before joining the bank, Tom received his B.A. from the College of Wooster and his J.D. from Cleveland-Marshall College of Law at Cleveland State University, both with honors and awards. Tom's recent writings have focused on credit rating organizations, land banking, loan modification, and the home mortgage loan origination channel. He is an advisory board member for the Kirwan Institute at Ohio State, a member of the American Bar Association, Ohio Bar Association, and is actively involved in the alumni and pre-law programs at the College of Wooster.

CHAPTER 48

Global Regulation for Global Markets?

MICHAEL W. TAYLOR
Adviser to the Governor, Central Bank of Bahrain; formerly Head of Banking Policy, Hong Kong Monetary Authority; Senior Economist, International Monetary Fund; and Reader in Financial Regulation, ICMA Centre, University of Reading

DOUGLAS W. ARNER
Director, Asian Institute of International Financial Law (www.AIIFL.com), Director, LLM (Corporate and Financial Law) Program and Associate Professor, Faculty of Law, University of Hong Kong; Co-Director, Duke University-HKU Asia-America Institute in Transnational Law; and Visiting Research Fellow, University of New South Wales

More than 40 years ago, the economist Richard Cooper commented on the disjunction between what he called *domain* (the geographical area over which financial institutions and markets operate) and *jurisdiction* (the machinery of legislation and regulation that ensures the orderly operation of markets).[1] Since then the gap between domain and jurisdiction has grown ever wider. In the past 40 years, the abolition of exchange controls and the growth of new financial markets and new mechanisms for managing, measuring, and pricing risk have created an integrated, global financial system characterized by large financial conglomerate groups with extensive cross-border operations. Although the public policy issues created by these financial groups have long been recognized, the global financial crisis has demonstrated the necessity of a more robust and prompt response than has previously been the case.[2] The crisis has, in particular, posed the fundamental question of whether global financial markets now require global regulation.

The global financial crisis was caused more by deficiencies in national regulatory systems than it was due to any shortcomings in the current international arrangements for regulation. National deficiencies were particularly pronounced in the United States, where they included inadequate (or nonexistent) regulation of the mortgage brokers that were responsible for the origination of many subprime assets (the Federal Reserve delayed implementation of its regulatory authority over this market until 2008); inadequate surveillance of the credit default swaps market due to the deficiencies of the Commodities Futures Modernization Act 2000;[3] and the inadequate regulation of systemically important firms, especially insurance companies, owing to the lack of a federal charter for such companies.

Within this catalogue of deficiencies, the problems of international coordination were of lesser significance. However, as these domestic origins increasingly affected cross-border financial institutions, problems originating from deficiencies in the United States (and also the United Kingdom) quickly affected other markets, both directly through failures of cross-border institutions from the United States and through the impact on institutions in other jurisdictions operating in global markets.[4]

As a result of contagion from weaknesses in one market into global markets and also because of difficulties in resolving problems affecting complex global financial institutions, policy makers have placed considerable emphasis on the need for greater post-crisis coordination of regulation and further steps to harmonize regulatory standards.[5] For example, in his report on behalf of the United Kingdom's Financial Services Authority, Lord Turner provides the following recommendations:

International coordination of bank supervision should be enhanced by:

- The establishment and effective operation of colleges of supervisors for the largest complex and cross-border financial institutions
- The pre-emptive development of crisis coordination mechanisms and contingency plans between supervisors, central banks, and finance ministries[6]

In other words, the current framework for the coordinated supervision of cross-border financial groups needs to be enhanced both in respect of their ongoing supervision—through colleges of supervisors—and, in the event that banks or other financial institutions fail, more detailed crisis management arrangements, together with, potentially, advance agreement on sharing the burden of rescuing or resolving a cross-border banking or financial group.

The latter has emerged as one of the leading problems of international regulation in the wake of the crisis. However, the problem is far from new. The difficulties associated with the orderly resolution of a cross-border banking group have long been understood, and there have been several, largely inconclusive, attempts to develop an international consensus on how best to deal with them. Nonetheless, the collapse of Lehman Brothers in September 2008 provided a vivid illustration of the ineffectiveness of current international arrangements and created a more urgent need to address this long-standing problem. Commenting on this episode, Turner remarks:

The failure of Lehman Brothers demonstrated . . . that decisions about fiscal and central bank support for the rescue of a major bank are ultimately made by home country national authorities focusing on national rather than global considerations. It also illustrated that separate legal entities and nationally specific bankruptcy procedures have major implications for creditors.[7]

In short, although banks and other financial institutions are international in life, they are national in death.[8] Developing agreements in advance on how to handle the failure of a major bank or other financial institution might go some way to alleviate this problem. Ground rules on whom to tell, and when, concerning an imminent closure would certainly help. At the same time, however, purely voluntary agreements on burden-sharing are unlikely to be effective. There are good reasons for expecting that a *sauve qui peut* strategy will dominate in handling the failure of a cross-border institution; as Charles Goodhart has remarked "whether on purpose, or not, in a globalized financial system losses occurring in a bank in one country could be effectively passed through to the depositors or to the fiscal authorities in another country."[9]

Moving from the present voluntary framework to one that is capable of imposing binding obligations on national authorities would represent a change from what lawyers term *soft law* to *hard law*. At present, the framework of international regulation is a soft law framework in that it primarily takes the form of a network of agreements, developed by bodies like the Basel Committee, that do not create legally binding obligations.[10] The Basel II capital adequacy standard is a leading example of this approach in that it was the result of an agreement among the 12 members (at that time) of the Basel Committee. However, the agreement has no binding force in law, and compliance with it is mainly a matter of pragmatism and peer pressure, including the assessments performed under the auspices of the joint IMF and World Bank Financial Sector Assessment Program (FSAP). In the absence of any binding international obligations attached to such agreements, lawyers refer to them as *soft law*.

Hardening the current international arrangements would involve the creation of more effective arrangements for ensuring national compliance with international standards through procedures set out in a new international treaty. This would mean, for example, that if a national regulatory authority failed to comply with international agreements to which it was a party, another regulatory authority would possess the means to take the first national regulator to an international tribunal that could rule on the issue of compliance, and in addition impose penalties for noncompliance. Such a treaty-based arrangement exists already at a regional level in the European Union (EU) and in the World Trade Organization (WTO). How suitable might such organizations be either as models for new arrangements or possibly to take on this role themselves?

The European Union offers perhaps the most extensive and well-established hard law framework of agreements in financial services. Since the adoption of its internal market program, the EU member states have reached agreement on an extensive framework of directives that provide minimum standards for financial intermediaries, securities regulation, accounting, company law, and regulation of institutional investors, based on intermediation being unfettered by national borders or restrictions on activity, and an open internal market. These directives are binding on member states, which are therefore under an obligation to implement them in their domestic laws and regulations. Failure to do so can attract penalties for noncompliance, both in the form of fines and other sanctions imposed by the European Commission and in providing grounds for legal proceedings by individuals whose interests are adversely affected by noncompliance. If there is a working example of a hard law framework for financial services, the EU would appear to be it.

Nonetheless, the financial crisis has illustrated that even within the EU's hard law framework there have been some serious shortcomings in cross-border regulation and crisis management. The relative lack of consensus among the EU leaders during the final quarter of 2008 on the EU's crisis management response was highlighted by the unilateral actions by several member states, such as the decision by the Irish government to offer a general guarantee of deposits with its banks. This forced other member states to follow suit, often quite reluctantly, owing to the competitive distortions this introduced into the single banking market. Although the EU can boast of one relatively successful example of cross-border cooperation in dealing with a failing banking group—the troubled Fortis group—this involved countries with a long history of mutual cooperation. With a different constellation of countries involved, even the EU's arrangements would not have been capable of providing effective crisis management. This point is explicitly recognized by the de Larosiere report, which has, accordingly, recommended enhancements to the institutional structures for regulatory coordination in the EU.[11]

The WTO has also sometimes been invoked as a possible mechanism for hardening the current soft law of international regulation. The WTO structure is based on three main aspects: provision of an institutional framework for negotiated trade liberalization, with hard law commitments from members subject to a formal dispute resolution mechanism (DRM). Overall, the WTO itself has very limited authority and direct monitoring power, with responsibility for monitoring placed on individual members' use of the DRM to police commitments. Although some form of dispute resolution mechanism would have a useful role to play in managing cross-border banking problems, on balance, however, it appears to make little sense to incorporate financial regulation into the WTO framework. This is both because the WTO system is already overburdened and also because of its focus on negotiated liberalization. The framework is an important starting point in supporting foreign competition in financial services, but because of its essential focus on liberalization, it is probably not an ideal framework to address financial stability and financial regulation issues.

There are, of course, other existing international organizations and treaties that might perform the function that is required. For example, the IMF is also sometimes suggested as a body that could police international financial regulatory standards and bring greater coordination to managing cross-border bank failures. This would require amendments to be made to the IMF articles of agreement, to provide the Fund with a specific mandate and related tools in relation to financial regulatory surveillance (its current role in the FSAP process has been justified on the grounds that this is an extension of the fund's macroeconomic surveillance role rather than stemming from a commitment to financial stability as an objective in itself). Unless such an amendment were to be made—comparable to the recent changes to the legislation governing national central banks to provide them with an explicit financial stability remit—it is difficult to see how the IMF would possess the mandate, objectives, and resources necessary to take on this role.

In the absence of a clear and effective model for hardening the soft law of international regulation, the Group of Twenty (G-20) has opted instead for an intermediate arrangement in which no new binding obligations have been created but the mechanisms for peer review and oversight have been enhanced and formalized. At the center of this arrangement is the international body formerly known as the Financial Stability Forum. Now renamed the Financial Stability Board (FSB), its membership has been expanded to encompass all G-20 nations, Spain, and the European Commission. The FSB has also been granted a significantly enhanced mandate that includes, inter alia, coordinating the work of the various international standard-setting bodies, supporting the establishment of supervisory colleges, conducting early warning exercises (jointly with the IMF), and contingency planning for cross-border crisis management.

Overall, the FSB might be reasonably effective in the coordination and prevention functions without it being a hard law institution, but the issue that remains is how to handle cross-border financial institution failures. Although the FSB will play a role in facilitating discussion among its members, what is lacking from the system is the ability to put its members under binding obligations that will lead to a greater willingness to burden-share the costs of cross-border bank failures. Some form of binding arbitration mechanism might be the best way to achieve this (and this in fact is the approach being pursued in the European Union), but without a more formal and binding arrangement for burden sharing and dispute resolution arrangement, probably through a formal treaty or international organization, the problems raised by the failure of global financial institutions will not be adequately addressed by the current approach to international financial regulation.[12]

Inevitably, however, we return to the fundamental problem in all discussions of this issue. As long as the only resources for bank rescues come from nation-states (ultimately the taxpayers of each country) politicians will not allow the responsibility for regulating banks to pass from domestic agencies that are responsible to them. National politicians and national agencies remain liable for the costs if regulation fails, and this reality determines the extent to which regulatory functions can be shifted to an international level. These considerations are also the decisive objections to the often-discussed notion of a global financial regulator.

This same imperative to keep regulations domestic, however, requires that processes for international coordination need to be developed and that they must be given some binding force. As we have seen, no voluntary agreement can ever be expected to remain effective given the very strong incentives for national authorities to seek to pass the costs of a cross-border bank failure to other jurisdictions. Only a binding international treaty would be sufficient to counteract these incentives, but despite the severity of the global financial crisis there has been no political will to develop such a treaty-based approach. At the same time, existing treaty-based institutions are unsuitable for the role. As a result, we will continue to be confronted by an inherently unstable situation in which cross-border banks will be international in life and national in death, a situation that is doubtful could survive another round of financial instability. If there is no will to create international mechanisms for handling such bank failures, national authorities may by default be forced to require banks to return to their national roots with all that this would entail for global economic prosperity.

NOTES

1. R. Cooper, *The Economics of Interdependence* (New York: Columbia University Press, 1968).
2. See D. Arner and J. Norton, "Building a Framework to Address Failure of Complex Global Financial Institutions," *Hong Kong Law Journal* 39 (2009): 95.

3. For an account of the lobbying effort that resulted in this Act, see G. Tett, *Fool's Gold: How Unrestrained Greed Corrupted a Dream, Shattered Global Markets and Unleashed a Catastrophe* (New York: Little, Brown, 2009), 75.

4. See D. Arner, "The Global Credit Crisis: Causes and Consequences," *The International Lawyer* 43 (2009): 91.

5. See D. Arner and M. Taylor, "The Global Credit Crisis and the Financial Stability Board: Hardening the Soft Law of International Financial Regulation?" *UNSW Law Journal* (2009).

6. Lord Turner, "The Turner Review: A Regulatory Response to the Global Banking Crisis" (London: Financial Services Authority, 2009), 7, Recommendation 25.

7. Id., 37.

8. Although at least one of the authors has included this explicitly in teaching since the early part of the century, the first quotation of the idea is difficult to find. While Mervyn King and Charles Goodhart are both frequently cited as the source, the earliest quotation appears from *The Economist:* "Banks may be global in life but are national in death." "Homeward Bound," February 5, 2009 (available at www.economist.com/displaystory .cfm?story_id=13057265).

9. C. Goodhart, "Some New Directions for Financial Stability?" in *Towards a New Framework for Financial Stability,* eds. David Mayes, Robert Pringle, and Michael Taylor (London: Central Banking Publications, 2009).

10. See D. Arner, *Financial Stability, Economic Growth and the Role of Law* (Cambridge: Cambridge University Press, 2007); J. Norton, *Devising International Bank Supervisory Standards* (London: Kluwer Law International, 1995).

11. J. de Larosière et al., *High Level Group on Financial Supervision in the EU: Report* (European Commission, 2009).

12. For discussion of possible domestic responses, see Turner Review, note 6; Arner & Norton, note 2 (arguing that, in the absence of effective international arrangements, individual jurisdictions should adopt an approach based on requirements for separately capitalized and regulated subsidiaries for foreign financial institutions).

ABOUT THE AUTHORS

Michael Taylor is currently adviser to the governor of the Central Bank of Bahrain. He has previously held a variety of senior positions at the Hong Kong Monetary Authority, the International Monetary Fund, and the Bank of England. He has published widely in the field of financial regulation, including the influential 1995 "Twin Peaks" paper, which proposed a radical reform of regulatory structures and has again been featured in the recent debate on regulatory reform in Britain and the United States. His most recent publications include *Global Banking Regulation* (with Heidi Schooner, Academic Press, 2009) and *Towards a New Framework of Financial Stability* (editor with David Mayes and Robert Pringle, Central Banking Publications, 2009).

Douglas W. Arner is the director of the Asian Institute of International Financial Law (www.AIIFL.com), director of the LLM (corporate and financial law) program and a professor with the faculty of law of the University of Hong Kong. Before joining HKU, Douglas studied literature, economics, political science, and law in the United States and United Kingdom and taught at the University of London. He has served as a consultant with, among others, the World Bank, Asian Development Bank, European Bank for Reconstruction and Development, and APEC, and has worked on financial sector reform projects in more than 20 economies in Africa, Asia, and Europe. He has published nine books (including *Financial Stability, Economic Growth and the Role of Law*) and more than 80 articles, chapters, and reports on financial law, regulation, and development.

CHAPTER 49

Financial Regulation, Behavioral Finance, and the Global Financial Crisis

In Search of a New Regulatory Model

EMILIOS AVGOULEAS
Senior Associate Professor (Reader) School of Law, University of Manchester

The global financial crisis brought into sharp focus the inadequacies of the contemporary model of financial regulation at both the national and the global level. However, many of the reforms currently suggested by national regulators and the G-20 may prove inadequate, since they largely ignore the behavioral elements of the crisis. This paper argues that there is an urgent need for a radical rethinking of the contemporary model of national and international financial regulation. In this context, the paper offers a set of proposals for far-reaching reforms.

The global financial crisis brought into sharp and painful focus the inadequacies of the current (virtually) global model of financial regulation, defined here as the set of rules used to license and supervise the continuous operation of banks, securities firms, and investment funds at the national and international level. In the case of banks, the current regulatory model is characterized by its reliance on a set of internationally accepted supervisory standards dealing with institutional safety and soundness, such as the Basel capital adequacy standards and solvency ratios, and limited regulatory interference. It emerged as a result of the liberalization of banking business models in the 1990s and the international consensus reached within the Basel Committee on Banking Supervision as regards the acceptable model of prudential supervision of banks.[1]

Enabling banking institutions to merge their investment and commercial banking activities, following the gradual eradication of its restrictions and final repeal of the Glass-Steagall Act[2] and the implementation of the European Second Banking Directive,[3] allowed banks to reap serious economies of scale in their operations. These efficiencies significantly raised their profitability. At the same time, liberalization allowed global banks to exploit their safe funding (deposits) base and the implicit guarantee they enjoyed from their national central banks in order to speculate at a vast scale. The global financial crisis is to a large extent the result of this attitude.

The vast expansion of international investment funds has been the result of the abolition of restrictions on capital flows in the 1990s and of the investment opportunities created by the rapid development of global capital markets. International investment funds (IIFs), especially highly leveraged ones, such as hedge funds, were frequently established in tax havens, escaping, to a significant extent, regulatory oversight. Thus, largely unregulated IIFs borrowed and invested hundreds of billions of dollars, piling up, in the process, systemic risk of colossal proportions *and* contributing to the massive growth of the *shadow banking* sector, which was a significant cause of the crisis.

THE CAUSES OF THE CRISIS

From 1998 to 2007, global credit markets experienced a period of rapid expansion and widespread euphoria. The main reason for this credit expansion, which led the global financial system to unsustainable levels of gearing, was a combination of:

- Benign macroeconomic conditions and monetary policies favoring low and relatively stable long-term interest rates.
- Significant trade imbalances, which meant vast financial surpluses were being accrued to countries such as China, which have underdeveloped domestic financial systems. These countries invested their surpluses to deficit countries with highly developed financial systems like the United States.
- Financial innovation: The use of novel techniques for the laying off of credit risk and the active involvement of investment funds in the relevant market meant that credit risk spread much more widely to the global investment community, but it did not disappear.
- The significant increase of institutional investors participating in global financial markets.

Unrestrained availability of credit due to excessive liquidity led to the creation of a bubble in almost every asset market in the world (including commodities) starting with the U.S. housing market. The burst of these asset bubbles was the main trigger of the global financial crisis. Other reasons that are specific to the financial sector, which had a very considerable role in building the conditions that led to the global financial crisis, were:

- A breakdown in underwriting standards for subprime mortgages
- Flaws in the originate-and-distribute model, especially misaligned incentives that led to a significant erosion of market discipline in the lending process[4]
- Flaws in credit rating agencies' assessments of structured credit products
- Risk management weaknesses at major U.S. and European financial institutions

The underlying causes of several of these dysfunctions of the financial system were owed to behavioral[5] as well as to rational factors, although the former tend to be forgotten by the formal analyses of the crisis.

Behavioral Finance and the Global Financial Crisis

The obvious reasons for the phenomenon of excessive liquidity and credit expansion of the past decade were gigantic international trade imbalances and low interest rates. However, credit expansion may also be attributed to behavioral factors. Market actors, having a short memory and being in a state of financial euphoria, became increasingly, and irrationally, *overconfident* that liquid markets would continue indefinitely. As a result, "underwriting standards for U.S. adjustable-rate subprime mortgages weakened dramatically between late 2004 and early 2007" and mortgages were extended to borrowers with dubious credit histories.[6]

The behavioral factors that seemed to be in operation here were again *overconfidence* and *bounded rationality*.[7] First, in the prevailing conditions of market euphoria and *overconfidence*, falling risk premia, a traditional measure of risk, were taken to mean actual reduction of credit risk. Second, *bounded rationality* meant that, as securitization markets grew and products became more complex, expert investors showed limited capacity for understanding structured credit products and developing tools to value them. Instead, influenced by the *availability* and *representativeness heuristics*, investors replaced rigorous credit controls and valuation mechanisms with an overreliance on credit ratings.

Another major cause of the global credit crisis was that the market lost confidence in credit ratings. In the decade preceding the crisis credit rating agencies (CRAs) were seen as the cornerstone of the effective operation of credit markets and of the capital market activities relating to them. Investors used credit ratings in the valuation of structured credit products and in pricing them when reliable price quotations were unavailable.[8] As a result, credit ratings came to play a key role in the "valuation of customized or illiquid structured credit products."[9] These highly sophisticated market participants knew all too well, however, that the ratings produced by the major CRAs suffered several shortcomings.

Arguably, there are two ways to explain why big institutions chose to substitute proper analysis and due diligence for "a subscription to a ratings publication."[10] The rational choice explanation is that, in order to economize in substantial research costs and thus facilitate transactions, investors choose to ignore the known flaws of credit ratings. Yet given how pronounced, serious, and well known those flaws were, this explanation does not sound convincing.

It is possible that investor irrational reliance on credit ratings was the result of the operation of the *availability* and *representativeness heuristics*.[11] Namely, market participants relying much more heavily on heuristics than on rational computations came to the conclusion that painstaking and accurate calculations of market value were not necessary for structured credit products. Thus, market actors' cognitive limitations and focus on short-term profit meant that sophisticated investors chose to ignore the warning signals. This explains both the incredible amount of trust placed on the ratings of CRAs and why these "had grown more powerful than anyone intended."[12]

Finally, institutional investors' money is managed today by expert individuals who allocate, as agents, the money of their principals. Their interests, as in most principal-agent relationships, are not perfectly aligned and sometimes diverge considerably. While shareholders or fund investors are concerned with an optimal

inst ≠ indiv

mixture of risk and return that ensures sustained profitability, bankers' and fund managers' concerns relate to a need to show that their performance is equal to or better than the rest of the market. As a result, they are very likely to follow the herd, playing the momentum game in the hope that they will be able to sell and materialize their gains, before markets fall (Chevalier and Ellison 1999; Gompers and Metrick 2001; Wermers 1999). In doing so, however, fund managers exacerbate asset bubbles and market inefficiency.

A NEW MODEL FOR THE REGULATION OF BANKS AND INTERNATIONAL INVESTMENT FUNDS

A number of international summits have endorsed proposals for the introduction of countercyclical capital adequacy standards and international supervision of systemically important institutions, including the upgrading of the functions of the Financial Stability Forum. Both of these measures, if implemented, could be a significant improvement in the international supervision of global financial institutions. However, such improvement will prove insufficient to prevent those institutions from building very risky positions that may lead to a systemic crisis, unless the current model of banking regulation is subjected to radical rethinking and an international regime is established that is designed to deal with the systemic risks posed by the market activities of IIFs.

A Proposal for Reform of Banking Business

The regulatory reforms endorsed in the London and Washington summits, while constituting substantial improvement, do not address the impact of the discussed above sociopsychological aspects of market behavior. Therefore, more radical proposals must be considered, which should also take into account the cognitive limitations of market actors. In the paragraphs that follow, I provide a model for the radical reform of banking regulation and the establishment of a global regime for the prudential regulation of IIFs.

Under Exhibit 49.1, current account deposits that are more susceptible to bank runs are received only by Tier I banks and savings institutions that operate under the strictest regulatory framework. Also, the securitization of bank loans (assets) that may weaken a bank's balance sheet and make creditors unwilling to lend to it is substantially restricted. Finally, cross-shareholdings between the institutions of each Tier should not exceed 20 percent. These restrictions ensure that systemic risk does not return to the savings and loans industry by virtue of substantial cross-shareholdings (ownership participations).

A Global Licensing Regime for Systemically Important Investment Funds

The systemic importance of big hedge funds and their widespread involvement in credit markets, as well as their role in exacerbating the present crisis, has highlighted the need to design a suitable regulatory regime dealing with these highly leveraged investors. A regulatory regime extending to hedge funds may only

Exhibit 49.1 A New Model for Bank Authorization and Supervision

Permitted Activities	Type of License	Deposit Insurance	Capital Adequacy	Liquidity Insurance	Prohibited Activities
• Deposit taking • Consumer lending • Mortgage Lending • Corporate Lending • Leasing • Treasury & FX Operations • Lending to Inter-bank markets up to *e.g.*, 30% of total deposits	Tier I Savings and Loans Institution	90%+ up to a limit that covers all small and medium size deposits Prefunded but coinsurance scheme	Basel II (as revised)	Lender of Last Resort (inevitably at subsidized rates) but prefunded scheme	Balance sheet securitization up to 30–40% of total assets Treasury and FX operations only in connection with balance sheet management

Permitted Activities	Type of License	Deposit Insurance	Capital Adequacy	Liquidity Insurance	Prohibited Activities
• Issuing of short-term certificates of deposit and bills, and long-term bonds to the public • Mortgages • Corporate Lending, Leasing • Treasury & FX Operations • Asset Management • Client Broking • Limited ability to underwrite securities issues/take proprietary positions	Tier II Bank	50% of total short-term debt issued to savers Prefunded Scheme	Basel II (as revised)	Lender of Last Resort (inevitably at subsidized rates) but prefunded scheme	No under writing of securities or proprietary trading exceeding a ratio over (*e.g.*, 300%) shareholders' equity No current account deposits

Permitted Activities	Type of License	Deposit Insurance	Capital Adequacy	Liquidity Insurance	Prohibited Activities
• Full range of capital market activities • Trading (proprietary) in derivatives • Trading (proprietary) in securities • Underwriting • Broking	Tier III Firm Investment Bank, or Investment (Securities) Firm	None	Basel II (as revised)	Liquidity insurance from Central Bank or private provider at market rates	No deposit taking No short-term debt issued to the public

prove successful, however, if it has a global reach. It is therefore suggested that a World Investment Funds Authority (WIFA) be established that would deal with the licensing and supervision of certain aspects of the operation of systemically important international investment funds.

The criteria for bringing within the WIFA scheme funds engaging in investment and trading activities with an international focus should relate to the size of funds' balance sheet and gearing ratios. Admittedly, such a scheme would prove totally ineffective if sovereign wealth funds, some operating with substantial borrowings (leverage), were not also brought within the regulatory reach of the WIFA, in spite of such a suggestion creating serious political opposition and controversy.

The scheme would work on the basis of a global common operating license (passport), and the funds that have opted to stay outside the scheme could be legally disbarred from undertaking significant (above a specified threshold) trading or investment activities in the markets of participating states.

IIFs should be allowed to register with the scheme under two conditions: (a) provide the WIFA with full access to information regarding the composition and structure of their balance sheets (but not to the composition of their membership, which is a sensitive issue, especially for SWFs) and (b) prove that they have (i) subscribed with a new (pre-funded) global liquidity or systemic risk insurance scheme for IIFs, administered by the IMF, or (ii) entered into pre-funded liquidity support or systemic risk insurance arrangements provided by central banks from a G-20 country or by a credible private organization. The more leveraged the positions that the funds wished to take, the higher the systemic risk premium that the suggested liquidity insurance scheme would charge.

A New Approach to Financial Regulation

Systemic instability can cripple a country's economic life and threaten the health of the global financial system, including a cessation of payments and other transnational flows of funds, if it has international dimensions. It may also adversely affect global growth. The model of national and international financial regulation presented here successfully addresses several of these concerns. The proposed scheme's advantages may be summarized as follows:

- *It battles homogenisation:*[13] Segregation seems to be the only effective policy tool that can lead the global financial services firms to diversify their activities, lowering the destructive potency of endogenous risk.[14]
- *Better management of risk:* It sends credit risk to savings and lending institutions, where it can be best measured and managed, preventing AIG-type collapses.
- *Improved consumer service:* Creating banks that specialize in certain areas of consumer and business lending might mean better services for bank customers.
- *Protection of public funds:* The suggested model of segregation drastically limits the ability of banking institutions to free ride on the public guarantee. Implementation of the Exhibit 49.1 model would lead to the ring-fencing of the loans and savings sector from excessive speculation.

- *Complexity reduction and effective supervision:* The limits placed by the present proposal on the ability of savings and lending institutions to securitize their assets and engage in derivatives trading would drastically reduce the complexity of their operations. As a result, the effectiveness of regulatory supervision would improve dramatically.
- *A transparent and workable global regime for IIF supervision:* The objective of the suggested regime for IIFs targets the social costs of IIF activities. An obligation to buy liquidity insurance, for instance, would curb their ability to free ride on the implicit public guarantee enjoyed by their lender banks.
- *Restraining the "animal spirits" of the market:* Segregation, position limits, and liquidity insurance would drastically restrain the otherwise uncontrollable behavioral tendency of bankers and fund managers to focus on short-term profit.

CONCLUSION

The global financial crisis has shown that the systemic threats posed by irresponsible practices within the financial services industry can cause the collapse of the international financial system. Because of the behavioral factors discussed earlier, many of the current reforms will prove insufficient to prevent excessive risk taking. This will especially be the case during the next period of market euphoria.

This paper has argued for a new global regulatory consensus with respect to the radical redrawing of the current model of national and international financial regulation. It has proposed mandatory institutional segregation for the banking industry along business lines. The paper has also suggested the establishment of a global licensing and supervisory scheme for international investment funds. The reforms suggested here are expensive, but, if adopted, they would also prove to be effective at averting another crisis of this magnitude.

NOTES

1. *Core Principles for Effective Banking Supervision* (Basel Committee on Banking Supervision, September 1997, revised in October 2006). *International Convergence of Capital Measurement and Capital Standards, A Revised Framework* (Basel Committee on Banking Supervision, updated November 2005).

2. Gramm-Leach-Bliley Financial Services Modernization Act, Pub. L. No. 106–102, 113 Stat. 1338 (1999).

3. Directive 89/646/EEC [1989] OJ L 386/1, replaced by Directive 2006/48/EC [2006] OJ L 177. The Second Banking Directive allowed deposit-taking European banks to also engage in the kind of investment market activities that were usually reserved, at least outside of Germany, for securities firms and non-deposit-taking investment banks.

4. Normally, the original lender (the *originator*) is also responsible for carrying out due diligence regarding borrowers' creditworthiness and ensuring that the terms of the mortgage appropriately reflect the risks of the transaction. However, at the point of origination, credit controls gradually became increasingly compromised. *Originators* were paid by reference to the amount of loans generated, regardless of the repayment rate of those loans. As a result, they had every incentive to maximize the volume of loans granted independently of controls on borrower creditworthiness.

5. The fundamental assumption of rational choice theory about financial markets is that markets move only on the basis of rational expectations, namely, asset prices are set by rational investors. Based on rational choice theory, the efficient market hypothesis (EMH) assumes that market prices reflect equal fundamental value and change because of new information. Thus, in an efficient market, no investment strategy can yield average returns higher than the risk assumed ("there is no free lunch") and no trader can consistently outperform the market or accurately predict future price levels, because new information is instantly absorbed by market prices. Another EMH assumption is that markets give professional traders the opportunity to quickly observe and exploit through arbitrage trading any price deviations from fundamental value. Behavioral finance challenges most of the assumptions of EMH. The main tenets of behavioral finance are that: certain market phenomena called *anomalies* or *puzzles* may not be explained by the EMH, whereas the use of psychology can provide convincing explanations and the corrective influence of arbitrage trading is limited because of a number of restrictions.

6. President's Working Group Report, 16, 8.

7. This concept describes individuals' limited ability to process information because they possess "limited computational skills and seriously flawed memories." *Bounded rationality* was first discussed as a potential determining factor in decision making by Herbert Simon.

8. IMF, 55.

9. Ibid.

10. Carney, 3–4.

11. The *representativeness heuristic* is used by individuals to evaluate probability. Much of the time, *representativeness* is a helpful *heuristic*, but it can generate some severe biases. The *availability heuristic* controls estimates of the frequency or probability of events, which are judged by the ease with which instances of such events come to mind. *Anchoring* refers to the process by which an individual decision maker gravitates to a reference point that she subsequently uses as an initial condition for arriving at a final decision.

12. IMF, 56.

13. This is the term used for the widespread tendency of market players to all move in the same direction at once. This tendency was significantly exacerbated by financial conglomeration, which resulted in the formation of megabanks.

14. '[E]ndogenous risk means that any financial assets fluctuations are ... explained only by the very behavior of the participant or the participants that prize that financial asset, and not by exogenous factors...' Fischer, 124–125.

REFERENCES

Avgouleas, E. 2009. The global financial crisis, behavioural finance and financial regulation: In search of a new orthodoxy. *Journal of Corporate Law Studies* 9:121.

Barberis, N., and R. Thaler. 2002. *A survey of behavioral finance*. National Bureau of Economic Research, working paper 9222.

Basel Committee on Banking Supervision. 1997, 2006. *Core principles for effective banking supervision*.

———. 2005. *International convergence of capital measurement and capital standards: A revised framework*.

Brunnermeier, M., A. Crockett, C. Goodhart, A. D. Persaud, and H. Shin. 2009. *The fundamental principles of financial regulation*. Geneva Reports on the World Economy.

Carney, M. *Addressing financial market turbulence*. Remarks of the Governor of the Bank of Canada to the Toronto Board of Trade, March 13, 2008.

Chevalier, J., and G. Ellison. 1999. Career concerns of mutual fund managers. *Quarterly Journal of Economics* 114 (2): 389–432.

Fischer, L. 2007. Major risks of international banking. In *Law and economics of risk in finance*, P. Nobel and M. Gets (eds.). Zürich: Schulthess.

Financial Services Authority. 2009. *The Turner review: A regulatory response to the global banking crisis*. London: FSA.

G-20 Washington Summit. 2008. *Declaration of the Summit on Financial Markets and the World Economy*.

G-20 London Summit. 2009. *Joint Communique*.

Gompers, P., and A. Metrick. 2001. Institutional investors and equity prices. *Quarterly Journal of Economics* 116: 229–259.

International Monetary Fund. 2008. *Global financial stability report: Containing systemic risks and restoring financial soundness*. Washington, DC: IMF.

———. 2008. *Financial stress and deleveraging: Macrofinancial implications and policy*. Washington, DC: IMF, Global Financial Stability Report, (IMF2).

The President's Working Group on Financial Markets (PWGFM). 2008. *Policy Statement on Financial Market Developments*.

Schwarcz, S. 2008. Disclosure's failure in the subprime mortgage crisis. *Utah L. Rev.* 1109–1122.

———. 2008. Protecting financial markets: Lessons from the subprime mortgage meltdown. *Minn. L. Rev.* 93 (2): 373–406.

Simon, H. A. 1955. A behavioral model of rational choice. *Quarterly Journal of Economics* 69 (1): 99–118.

United Nations Conference on Trade and Development (UNCTAD). 2009. *The global economic crisis, systemic failures and multilateral remedies*. Geneva: UN.

Wermers, R. 1999. Mutual fund herding and the impact on stock prices. *Journal of Finance* 54 (2): 581–622.

ABOUT THE AUTHOR

Emilios Avgouleas is a reader (senior associate professor) in international financial law at the School of Law, University of Manchester. Emilios holds an L.L.M. in banking and finance law (1995) and a Ph.D. in law and economics (1999) from the London School of Economics. He has very extensive academic and legal practice experience in the field of financial markets. He is the rapporteur of the International Securities Regulation Committee of the International Law Association. In the spring term of 2009 he was the global capital markets center fellow at Duke University Law School. His publications include: *The Mechanics and Regulation of Market Abuse: A Legal and Economic Analysis* (Oxford University Press, 2005); *The Governance of Global Financial Markets and International Financial Regulation* (Cambridge University Press, 2010); "The Global Financial Crisis, Behavioural Finance and Financial Regulation: In Search of a New Orthodoxy," *Journal of Corporate Law Studies* 9 (2009): 121–157; "A New Framework for the Global Regulation of Short Sales: Why Prohibition is Inefficient and Disclosure Insufficient," *Stanford Journal of Law Business and Finance* 15 (1) (2010).

PART VII

Institutional Failures

CHAPTER 50

Why Financial Conglomerates Are at the Center of the Financial Crisis

ARTHUR E. WILMARTH JR.
Professor of Law, George Washington University Law School*

T he global economy is currently experiencing the "most severe financial crisis since the Great Depression."[1] The ongoing crisis has battered global financial markets and has triggered a worldwide recession. Global stock market values declined by $35 trillion during 2008 and early 2009, and global economic output was expected to fall in 2009 for the first time since World War II.[2]

In the United States, where the crisis began, markets for stocks and homes suffered their steepest downturns since the 1930s and drove the domestic economy into a steep and prolonged recession. The total market value of publicly traded U.S. stocks slumped by more than $10 trillion between October 2007 and February 2009. In addition, the value of U.S. homes fell by an estimated $6 trillion between July 2006 and the end of 2008. U.S. gross domestic product declined sharply during 2008 and the first quarter of 2009, and five million jobs were lost during the same period. Many sectors of the credit markets essentially ceased to function.[3]

The turmoil in global and domestic financial markets reflected deep concerns among investors about the viability of major financial institutions. Commercial and investment banks and insurance companies around the world reported more than $1.1 trillion of losses between August 2007 and March 2009. To prevent the collapse of the global financial system, central banks and governments in the United States (U.S.), United Kingdom (U.K.) and Europe provided almost $9 trillion of financial support in the form of emergency liquidity assistance, capital infusions, asset purchase programs, and guarantees. U.S. federal agencies extended about half of that support. Nevertheless, the ability of global financial markets to recover from the crisis remained in serious doubt in May 2009.[4]

This chapter documents that 17 major financial conglomerates accounted for a majority of the losses reported by global banks and insurers from the beginning

---

*This essay is adapted from portions of the following article: Arthur E. Wilmarth Jr., "The Dark Side of Universal Banking: Financial Conglomerates and the Origins of the Subprime Financial Crisis," *Conn. L. Rev.* 41 (2009): 963, available at http://ssrn.com/abstract= 1403973.

of the crisis through April 2009. In view of the huge losses suffered by these giant institutions, and the extraordinary governmental assistance they received, they clearly were the epicenter of the crisis. They were also the primary private-sector catalysts for the credit boom that led to the crisis.

During the past two decades, governmental policies in the United States, the United Kingdom, and Europe encouraged massive consolidation and conglomeration within the financial services industry. The Gramm-Leach-Bliley Act of 1999 (GLBA), which authorized U.S. banks to affiliate with securities firms and insurance companies, was part of a strong international regulatory trend in favor of universal banks.[5] Domestic and international mergers among commercial and investment banks and insurers produced a dominant group of large complex financial institutions (LCFIs). By 2007, 17 LCFIs effectively controlled domestic and global markets for debt and equity underwriting, syndicated lending, asset-backed securities (ABS), over-the-counter (OTC) derivatives, and collateralized debt obligations (CDOs).[6]

Universal banks exploited their dominance of global financial markets by pursuing an originate-to-distribute (OTD) strategy. The OTD strategy included:

- Originating and servicing consumer and corporate loans
- Packaging those loans into ABS and CDOs
- Creating additional financial instruments, including credit default swaps (CDS) and synthetic CDOs, whose values were derived in complex ways from the underlying loans
- Distributing the resulting securities and financial instruments to investors

LCFIs used the OTD strategy to maximize their fee income, reduce their capital charges, and transfer to investors (at least ostensibly) the risks associated with securitized loans and other structured-finance products. However, because many financial conglomerates followed similar OTD strategies, their common exposures to a variety of financial risks—including credit risk, market risk, and liquidity risk—produced a significant rise in systemic risk in global financial markets.[7]

Even before the subprime lending boom began in 2003, some observers raised questions about the risks and conflicts of interest created by the new universal banks. For example, LCFIs played key roles in promoting the dot-com-telecom boom in the U.S. stock market between 1994 and 2000, which was followed by a devastating bust from 2000 to 2002. Many leading universal banks were also involved in a series of scandals involving Enron, WorldCom, investment analysts, initial public offerings, and mutual funds during the same period. However, Congress did not seriously consider whether financial conglomerates posed a serious threat to the stability of financial markets and the general economy. Instead, political leaders assumed that federal regulators and market participants would exercise sufficient control over universal banks.[8]

The United States experienced an enormous credit boom between 1991 and 2007. Household debt rose by $10 trillion (to $13.8 trillion), nonfinancial business debt grew by $6.4 trillion (to $10.1 trillion), and financial sector debt increased by $13 trillion (to $15.8 trillion). As a result of this credit boom, the financial services industry captured an unprecedented share of corporate profits and gross domestic profit. Governmental policies (including the Federal Reserve's overly expansive monetary policy, as well as currency exchange rate policies pursued by foreign governments) were important factors that encouraged credit growth within the United States. At the same time, universal banks were the leading private-sector catalysts for the credit boom.[9]

During the boom, LCFIs used nationwide mass marketing, automated loan processing, and securitization to provide huge volumes of high-risk home mortgage loans and credit card loans to nonprime borrowers. The federal government facilitated the creation of nationwide consumer lending programs by LCFIs, because federal laws preempted state usury laws and other state laws that had traditionally shielded consumers from predatory lending. Unfortunately, Congress and federal regulators failed to establish adequate safeguards to protect consumers against abusive lending practices by federally chartered depository institutions and their subsidiaries and agents.[10]

Originations of nonprime mortgages rose from $250 billion in 2001 to $1 trillion in 2006. Nearly 10 million nonprime mortgages were originated between 2003 and mid-2007. LCFIs used securitization to spur this dramatic growth in nonprime lending. By 2006, more than four-fifths of nonprime mortgages were packaged by LCFIs into residential mortgage-backed securities (RMBS). As the securitized share of nonprime lending increased, lending standards deteriorated. For example, lenders increasingly offered subprime mortgages with low teaser rate payments for two or three years, followed by a rapid escalation of interest rates and payments. As a practical matter, subprime borrowers were forced to refinance their loans before the teaser rate period expired. However, refinancing was possible only as long as home prices kept rising. LCFIs effectively created a system of Ponzi finance, in which nonprime borrowers had to keep taking out new loans to pay off their old ones. When home prices stopped rising in 2006 and collapsed in 2007, nonprime borrowers were no longer able to refinance their debts. Mortgage defaults skyrocketed, and the subprime financial crisis began.[11]

Financial conglomerates aggravated the risks of nonprime mortgages by creating additional financial bets based on those mortgages. LCFIs resecuritized lower-rated tranches of RMBS to create CDOs, and then resecuritized lower-rated tranches of CDOs to create CDOs-squared. LCFIs also wrote CDS and synthetic CDOs to create additional financial bets based on nonprime mortgages. By 2007, the total volume of financial instruments derived from nonprime mortgages was more than twice as large as the $2 trillion in outstanding nonprime mortgages. LCFIs persuaded regulators and credit rating agencies that the securitization process transferred the risks of nonprime lending to far-flung investors. In fact, however, LCFIs retained significant exposures to nonprime mortgages. LCFIs kept RMBS and CDOs in their warehouses, and LCFIs also transferred RMBS and CDOs to off-balance-sheet conduits that relied on the sponsoring LCFIs for explicit or implicit financial support. Thus, many LCFIs pursued an originate-to-*not-really*-distribute strategy, because they retained significant residual risks so they could complete more transactions and earn more fees.[12]

Universal banks created similar risks with their credit card operations. While the housing boom lasted, universal banks aggressively expanded credit card lending to nonprime borrowers and encouraged borrowers to use home equity loans to pay off their credit card balances. As in the case of nonprime home mortgages, LCFIs discounted the risks of nonprime credit card loans as long as they could securitize most of the loans. The securitization market for credit card loans shut down in 2008, just as it had done for subprime mortgages in 2007, leaving LCFIs with large exposures to nonprime loans.[13]

Universal banks also pursued reckless lending policies in the commercial real estate and corporate sectors. LCFIs used securitization techniques to promote a dramatic increase in commercial mortgage lending and leveraged corporate lending between 2003 and mid-2007. LCFIs used many of the same risky loan terms (including interest-only provisions and high loan-to-value ratios) for commercial mortgages and leveraged corporate loans that they used for nonprime home mortgages. In all three markets, securitization created perverse incentives for universal banks. LCFIs believed that they could originate risky loans without properly screening borrowers and could also avoid costly post-loan monitoring of the borrowers' behavior, as long as the loans were securitized and transferred to investors. However, LCFIs often retained exposures to residual risks. This was particularly true in the market for leveraged corporate buyouts (LBOs), because LCFIs frequently agreed to provide bridge financing if they could not locate enough investors to fund the deals. Once again, the ability of LCFIs to control their risks was undercut by their emphasis on maximizing transactions and fees. When the securitization markets for commercial mortgages and leveraged corporate loans collapsed in mid-2007, universal banks were exposed to significant losses in addition to their problems with nonprime consumer credit.[14]

The huge losses reported by financial conglomerates after the outbreak of the financial crisis confirmed that LCFIs were leading catalysts for the credit boom that led to the crisis. Between August 2007 and April 2009, commercial and investment banks incurred more than $910 billion of losses, and insurance companies suffered an additional $220 billion of losses.[15] More than half of those losses were reported by 17 of the world's leading financial conglomerates.[16]

Thirteen of those 17 conglomerates suffered severe damage. Of those 13 LCFIs, six institutions (American International Group [AIG], Bear Stearns, Lehman Brothers, Merrill Lynch, Royal Bank of Scotland [RBS], and Wachovia) either failed or disappeared in government-assisted mergers or were nationalized. Three other institutions (Bank of America, Citigroup, and UBS) continued to operate under private management but with government-funded life support and close supervision; and four other institutions (Barclays, Goldman Sachs, HSBC, and Morgan Stanley) reported serious losses and were forced to make major changes to their operations.

Governments and financial regulators took extraordinary steps to prop up their leading financial institutions. In April 2009, the International Monetary Fund (IMF) reported that U.S., U.K., and European central banks and governments had provided nearly $9 trillion of support to financial institutions, including $2 trillion of emergency central bank liquidity assistance, $2.5 trillion of government asset purchase commitments, and almost $4.5 trillion of financial guarantees. U.S. authorities extended about half of that support.[17]

The current crisis has revealed a stunning failure of financial regulation. During the past two decades, regulators in developed nations (particularly the

United States and the United Kingdom) generally implemented the following policies:

- To rely primarily on market mechanisms and soft supervisory guidance as methods for directing and restraining the conduct of LCFIs, while reducing the use of binding regulations (including consumer protection laws)
- To promote the use of quantitative risk models as substitutes for traditional methods of evaluating the risks of customers and financial institutions
- To encourage LCFIs to replace traditional methods of credit intermediation— in which banks screen and monitor borrowers and hold loans on their balance sheets—with an OTD strategy that transferred loans to widely dispersed investors who had little opportunity to evaluate the creditworthiness of borrowers
- To encourage LCFIs to pursue additional fee-based business lines tied to the capital markets
- To promote continued consolidation within the financial services industry, based on the belief that larger and more diversified financial conglomerates offered greater safety and profitability.

Critics have alleged that the foregoing regulatory policies actually impaired the safety of financial institutions and undermined the stability of financial markets, because such policies encouraged:

- An excessive reliance on quantitative, market-sensitive measures of risk and capital, which accentuated booms and aggravated busts in the business cycle
- An overuse of structured finance securitizations and OTC derivatives, which created complex and opaque risk exposures and a fragile web of interconnections among LCFIs and various sectors of the financial markets
- A greater dependence by LCFIs on funding from the capital markets, which increased the vulnerability of the financial system to liquidity shortages and panics
- A failure to restrain the growth of systemic risk within LCFIs
- A misplaced confidence in market discipline as an effective restraint on excessive risk taking and abusive practices by LCFIs[18]

With respect to the last criticism, observers have pointed out that market discipline is inherently procyclical and is too lax during euphoric bubbles and too extreme during panic-induced busts. The effectiveness of market discipline is also undermined by self-reinforcing herd and momentum effects, which cause market participants to follow the herd even when they have doubts about the wisdom of the course the herd is pursuing.[19]

Two striking examples of the power of herd mentality appeared in statements made by the chief executive officers of Bank of America and Citigroup shortly before the financing boom for LBOs collapsed in the late summer of 2007. In May 2007, Kenneth Lewis boasted during a speech that Bank of America had participated in 7 of the 15 largest LBOs during that year. However, during the question-and-answer period following his speech, Mr. Lewis acknowledged that "[w]e are close to a time when we'll look back and say we did some stupid things. . . .

We need a little more sanity in a period in which everyone feels invincible."[20] Two months later, Chuck Prince of Citigroup famously declared during an interview with the *Financial Times* that "[w]hen the music stops, in terms of liquidity, things will be complicated. But, as long as the music is playing, you have got to get up and dance. We are still dancing."[21] Thus, even the top executives of the largest banks in the world felt compelled to follow the herd.

The current financial crisis has led to an unprecedented expansion of governmental support for LCFIs. In an article published in 2002, I maintained that the too-big-to-fail (TBTF) policy was "the great unresolved problem of bank supervision."[22] I argued that the passage of GLBA made the TBTF problem much worse, because GLBA's authorization of financial holding companies increased the likelihood that "major segments of the securities and life insurance industries will be brought within the scope of the TBTF doctrine, thereby expanding the scope and cost of federal 'safety net' guarantees."[23] I also warned that the risk control measures relied upon by GLBA's supporters—including market discipline—were plainly inadequate.[24] I predicted that the new financial holding companies would successfully exploit TBTF subsidies because "the unmistakable lessons of the past quarter century are that regulators will protect major financial firms against failure whenever such action is deemed necessary to preserve the stability of financial markets; and financial institutions will therefore pursue riskier and opaque activities and will increase their leverage, through capital arbitrage, if necessary, as they grow in size and complexity."[25]

The current financial crisis has confirmed all of the foregoing predictions. During the past decade, regulators in developed nations encouraged the expansion of large financial conglomerates and failed to restrain their pursuit of short-term profits through increased leverage and high-risk activities. LCFIs were allowed to promote an enormous credit boom that led to a worldwide financial crisis. Governments adopted extraordinary measures to support major banks, securities firms, and insurance companies to prevent a complete collapse of global financial markets. Those support measures, which are far from over, establish beyond any doubt that the TBTF policy now covers the entire financial services industry.[26] Consequently, one of the most pressing policy imperatives is to reform the regulation of financial institutions and financial markets with the goal of eliminating TBTF subsidies and their moral hazard effects, and establishing effective restraints on risk taking by LCFIs.

NOTES

1. Markus K. Brunnermeier, "Deciphering the Liquidity and Credit Crunch, 2007–08," *Journal of Economic Perspectives* 23 (2009): 77–100.

2. Arthur E. Wilmarth Jr. "The Dark Side of Universal Banking: Financial Conglomerates and the Origins of the Subprime Financial Crisis," *Conn. L. Rev.* 41 (2009): 963–1050, available at http://ssrn.com/abstract=1403973.

3. Id. at 967–68; James C. Cooper, "The Great Adjustment Is Well Under Way," *Business-Week*, April 13, 2009, 6.

4. Wilmarth, supra note 2, at 968, 1043–1046.

5. Id. at 972–980. As used in this essay, the term *universal bank* refers to an organization that has authority to engage, either directly or through affiliates, in the banking, securities, and insurance businesses. See Arthur E. Wilmarth Jr., "The Transformation of the U.S. Financial Services Industry, 1975–2000: Competition, Consolidation, and Increased Risks," *U. Ill. L. Rev.* 215 (2002): 223 n. 23, available at http://ssrn.com/abstract=315345. Also, the terms *universal bank, financial conglomerate* and *large complex financial institution* are used interchangeably.

6. Wilmarth, supra note 2, at 980–995.

7. Id. at 994–997, 1020–1037.

8. Id. at 996–1002.

9. Id. at 1002–1012.

10. Id. at 1011–1015, 1035–1036.

11. Id. at 1015–1027.

12. Id. at 1027–1035.

13. Id. at 1035–1037.

14. Id. at 1037–1043.

15. Id. at 1043–1044.

16. See id. at 994–995 (explaining that, in 2007, the world's leading financial conglomerates included the four largest U.S. banks—Bank of America (BofA), JPMorgan Chase, Citigroup, and Wachovia; the five largest U.S. securities firms—Bear Stearns, Goldman Sachs, Lehman Brothers, Merrill Lynch, and Morgan Stanley; seven major foreign universal banks—Barclays, Credit Suisse, Deutsche Bank, HSBC, Royal Bank of Scotland (RBS), Societe Generale, and UBS; and American International Group (AIG)—the largest U.S. life insurer and second-largest U.S. property and casualty insurer. By April 2009, AIG had recorded $87.3 billion of losses resulting from the financial crisis, compared to $544 billion of losses for the remaining 16 institutions Id. at 1044 n. 423.

17. Id. at 1044–1046.

18. Id. at 1047–1048; see also Daniel K. Tarullo, "Banking on Basel: The Future of International Financial Regulation" (2008): 98–108, 120–121, 131–135, 139–141, 149–190 (criticizing the Basel II capital accord, particularly the accord's heavy reliance on quantitative risk-based models developed by LCFIs).

19. Arthur E. Wilmarth Jr. "How Should We Respond to the Growing Risks of Financial Conglomerates?" in *Financial Modernization After Gramm-Leach-Bliley* ed. Patricia A. McCoy 65 (2002) 110–13; see also Robert J. Shiller, "Irrational Exuberance" (2nd ed., 2005): 157–172.

20. Greg Ip, "Fed, Other Regulators Turn Attention to Risk in Banks' LBO Lending," *Wall Street Journal,* May 18, 2007, C1 (quoting Mr. Lewis's remarks as reported by Bloomberg News).

21. Investment Adviser, "Counting the reasons not to be cheerful," *FT Business,* July 23, 2007 (quoting from Mr. Prince's interview).

22. Wilmarth, supra note 5, at 475.

23. Id. at 446–447.

24. Id. at 454–475.

25. Id. at 476.

26. Wilmarth, supra note 2, at 1049–1050. The comprehensive reach of the TBTF policy is confirmed by the federal government's recently completed stress test for the 19 largest U.S. banking organizations (each with more than $100 billion of assets). In announcing the stress test, regulators emphasized that none of the banks would be allowed to fail the test, because the federal government would provide any capital that was needed to ensure the survival of all 19 banks. Id. at 1050 n. 449.

ABOUT THE AUTHOR

Arthur E. Wilmarth Jr. is a professor of law at the George Washington University Law School in Washington, D.C. He has published numerous law review articles and book chapters dealing with banking law and constitutional history, and he has co-authored a book on corporate law. In 2005, the American College of Consumer Financial Services Lawyers awarded him its prize for the best law review article published in the field of consumer financial services law during 2004. Professor Wilmarth received his B.A. degree from Yale University and his J.D. degree from Harvard University. He has testified on issues concerning banking regulation before committees of the United States Senate, the United States House of Representatives, the California state legislature, and the District of Columbia City Council. He is a member of the editorial board of the *Journal of Banking Regulation* (Palgrave Macmillan, United Kingdom).

CHAPTER 51

Corporate Governance and the Financial Crisis: A Case Study From the S&P 500

BRIAN R. CHEFFINS
S. J. Berwin Professor of Corporate Law at the Faculty of Law,
University of Cambridge

How did corporate governance function in U.S. public companies as the financial crisis that swept the world in 2008 moved into full swing? Many are convinced the stock market meltdown the United States experienced proved that current corporate governance arrangements are not fit for the purpose. The prescription that most obviously follows is that lawmakers should introduce changes to strengthen corporate boards, address concerns about executive pay, and enhance shareholder rights. Indeed, for advocates of corporate governance reform, the financial turmoil provides a golden opportunity to press the case for change. After all, as Rahm Emanuel, Barack Obama's new chief of staff, said shortly after the 2008 presidential election, "You never want a serious crisis to go to waste."[1]

Despite much speculation that corporate governance shortcomings contributed to the 2008 stock market meltdown, systematic analysis of how corporate governance functioned during this turbulent year has thus far been lacking. "Did Corporate Governance 'Fail' During the 2008 Stock Market Meltdown? The Case of the S&P 500",[2] the paper on which this chapter is based, constitutes a pioneering effort to address this gap in our understanding, with the approach adopted being to examine corporate governance in the 37 companies removed from the S&P 500 index during 2008. The study reveals corporate governance functioned tolerably well in the sample companies. This implies that the case is not yet made out for fundamental overhaul of corporate governance arrangements in U.S. public companies.

THE DEVELOPMENT OF CORPORATE GOVERNANCE IN U.S. PUBLIC COMPANIES

A striking aspect of the stock market meltdown of 2008 is that it occurred despite considerable strengthening of corporate governance over the past few decades. During the 1970s, ill-advised conglomerate building and revelations of widespread questionable payments by U.S. public companies prompted a corporate governance counterreaction revolving around the promotion of shareholder value. By the end of 1990s, boards had been strengthened, executive compensation had been restructured to align pay more closely with performance and institutional shareholders, heretofore almost entirely passive, appeared ready to begin stepping forward to protect their interests.

As the 2000s opened, a series of major corporate governance scandals combined with a sharp decline in share prices to rock investors. Federal lawmakers, aiming to restore confidence in the markets, enacted the Sarbanes-Oxley Act of 2002 (SOX),[3] which introduced controversial new regulations governing board structure, accounting, and auditing. Share prices rallied in the mid-2000s, and a surge in private equity buyouts and shareholder activism by hedge funds provided a fresh market-oriented impetus for the promotion of shareholder value. Correspondingly, Christopher Cox, chairman of the Securities and Exchange Commission, seemed on the mark when he told Congress in 2006 "We have come a long way since 2002. Investor confidence has recovered. There is greater corporate accountability. Financial reporting is more reliable and transparent. Auditor oversight is significantly improved."[4] Then the bottom fell out.

THE 2008 STOCK MARKET MELTDOWN

2008 was the worst year for the S&P 500 since 1937, with share prices plummeting 38.5 percent, and the worst for the Dow Jones Industrial Average since 1931, with a 33.8 percent decline. Among the S&P 500 the financials were particularly hard hit (share prices dropped 57 percent), but all sectors suffered major price declines. Using the stock market as the sole barometer, corporate governance clearly failed. There is more to the story, however. Corporate governance is not the primary determinant of share prices, as reflected by an academic testing of the hypothesis that good corporate governance improves corporate financial performance and getting inconclusive results. It is therefore possible that corporate governance in public companies generally operated satisfactorily amid general market trends that inexorably drove share prices downward.

SAMPLE SELECTION AND SEARCH STRATEGY

Over the next few years, there will likely be numerous studies of how corporate governance functioned during the financial crisis. However, the 37 companies removed from the S&P 500 in 2008 (see Appendix) provide an apt departure point for analysis. One reason is that big public companies are markedly more important from an economic and investment perspective than their smaller counterparts—the S&P 500 Index covers approximately 75 percent of the total value of the U.S. equities market. Another is that among any sample of publicly traded firms, troubled companies will likely be the center of the action with respect to corporate governance controversies (e.g., scandal-ridden Enron at the beginning of the 2000s), and companies dropped from the S&P 500 index are apt to fall into this category. Among the 37 companies removed in 2008, 20 can be categorized as "at risk" (see Appendix), with 13 of the companies having been dropped because of a dramatic fall in their market value, six due to rescue mergers (i.e., mergers in which the company would have likely otherwise ended up bankrupt) and one (Lehman Brothers) due to actual bankruptcy. Of the 10 industrial sectors represented in the S&P 500, firms from the financials sector dominated the overall sample (15 out of 37 firms) and particularly the at-risk cohort (12 out of 20).

To assess the operation of corporate governance in the 37 companies removed from the S&P 500 during 2008, a wide-ranging set of searches was conducted using Factiva, which offers extensive coverage of newspapers, business magazines, and trade journals. The searches were structured to find out what corporate governance mechanisms were activated in the six months before and six months after a company's removal from the S&P index, with the objective being to assess how responsive and effective corporate governance was during the stock market turmoil. Because of the prominence of companies that are part of the S&P 500, the Factiva searches should have brought to light most material corporate governance developments concerning the sample companies. Nevertheless, the Factiva searches were supplemented by an analysis of Georgeson's *2008 Annual Corporate Governance Review*,[5] the Stanford Law School Securities Class Action Clearinghouse database, and an AFL-CIO web site offering data on CEO pay for 2007.[6]

CORPORATE GOVERNANCE AND S&P 500 REMOVAL, 2008

The searches conducted were drawn upon to analyze corporate governance in the companies removed from the S&P 500 in 2008 along the following dimensions: fraud, board issues, managerial turnover, executive compensation, private equity, and shareholder activism. The key findings were as follows.

Fraud. Senior executives with incentive-laden compensation packages may well have been tempted to cook the books or spin the facts to ensure they hit targets as share prices fell during 2008. However, as of June 2009, securities class actions alleging false or misleading disclosure had been filed against only 13 of the 37 companies removed from the S&P 500, most of which were at-risk financials (see Appendix). Moreover, there was an absence of evidence in press reports of the sort blatant manipulation of financial statements that went on at Enron or WorldCom in the early 2000s.

Board of directors. One public indication of board failure is criticism reported in the media and trade publications. Another is boardroom turnover, at least when doubts about the capabilities of incumbents prompt a change. With the partial exception of at-risk companies (particularly financials), public criticism of corporate boards and out-of-the ordinary board turnover was very much the exception to the rule among companies removed from the S&P 500 in 2008 (see Appendix). It correspondingly appears that while directors were not a bulwark against the sharp decline in share prices that occurred in 2008, at least in the companies removed from the S&P 500 boards did not compound the problem.

Managerial Turnover. Among the 37 companies removed from the S&P 500 during 2008, there was publicized CEO turnover in nine firms, publicized non-CEO managerial turnover in eight, and turnover of both sorts in four companies (see Appendix). The managerial turnover that occurred was not randomly distributed. Instead, all but two of the companies involved were financials, and the action focused almost exclusively on at-risk companies, 40 percent of which experienced CEO turnover. The latter finding is what would have been anticipated with well-functioning corporate governance, since imposing discipline and providing fresh leadership are particularly important when corporations are afflicted by poor performance.

Executive Pay. In 2008, the economy's downward spiral put executive pay in the spotlight as never before, with feelings running high because of expectations that executives would feel the pain along with the shareholders experiencing dramatic declines in stock prices and employees losing their jobs. Nevertheless, there was no random backlash among the 37 companies removed from the S&P 500 for 2008. Instead, with a sizable majority of the firms (23), there were no public complaints about arrangements in place. Moreover, in those instances in which executive compensation was criticized publicly, the targeting was apt in the sense that the companies were typically at-risk firms that had paid their CEOs greater than the norm for the S&P 500.

Private Equity. With corporate governance facing its most robust challenge in modern times because of the 2008 stock market meltdown, private equity went AWOL. Due primarily to a credit crunch beginning in mid-2007, public-to-private transactions became difficult to orchestrate, and the only two removals from the S&P 500 attributable to private equity buyouts resulted from finalizing deals struck in 2006 (see Appendix). Private equity firms did take minority stakes in two banks, but these forays worked out badly—the Texas Pacific Group even lost its entire $1.35 billion investment in Washington Mutual.

Shareholder Activism. Given the massive erosion of shareholder value that occurred during the stock market meltdown of 2008, it might have been anticipated that shareholders would have protested vocally and sought to orchestrate fundamental changes to improve matters. However, of the 37 companies removed from the S&P 500, with only one—Washington Mutual—did complaints by mutual funds or pension funds generate significant publicity. Hedge fund activism also proved to be the exception to the rule. Only 6 of the 37 firms experienced publicized interventions of this nature, though the interventions produced results when they occurred (e.g., board turnover at Circuit City, Unisys, and Dillard's).

POLICY IMPLICATIONS

With respect to corporate governance in the companies removed from the S&P 500 during 2008, financial companies were a breed apart. The financials aside, securities fraud lawsuits, criticism of the board, publicized board turnover, and criticism of executive pay policies were rarities, with the partial exception of firms at risk. In contrast, among the financials, securities fraud lawsuits and criticism of the board were fairly routine, and bonus-driven executive pay may well have provided senior managers with incentives to take risks that were ill-advised because of the hit their firms would take if things went wrong. Moreover, there were instances in which substandard corporate governance may well have had serious adverse knock-on effects due to systemic risk. Most notably, investment banks Bear Stearns and Lehman Brothers reputedly were run by overbearing, unjustifiably bullish CEOs insufficiently constrained by the board of directors, and the travails of these firms generated a negative ripple effect due to strong connections to other major players in the financial system.

To the extent that size, complexity, and interconnectedness with the financial system imply that major financial companies might be too big to fail, policy makers may be justified in imposing rigorous corporate governance standards so as to protect the implicit stake taxpayers have because of the government being a *de facto* guarantor against bankruptcy. On the other hand, the governance challenges financial services firms pose are likely to be less potent going forward. Self-imposed upgrading of risk management practices, market pressure, and tougher regulation will likely foster managerial conservatism on the part of executives running large, complex financial services firms. Since the corporate governance lapses that occurred among the companies removed from the S&P 500 during 2008 typically involved freewheeling financials, a change of this sort would mean a dramatic increase in corporate governance regulation would be superfluous.

Once the financials are removed from the equation, the case in favor of a regulatory overhaul of corporate governance is weakened considerably. To the extent that the 22 nonfinancial companies removed from the S&P 500 during 2008 were representative, corporate governance functioned tolerably well despite the pressures imposed by the most dramatic fall in share prices in modern times. Moreover, while the United Kingdom already has in place a number of the features of corporate governance popular among those who advocate reform in the United States (e.g., an annual advisory vote on executive compensation policy and a regulatory endorsement for splitting the roles of chief executive and chairman of the board), the stock market meltdown was worse in Britain than in the United States. Future studies perhaps will uncover damning evidence of corporate governance breakdowns during the stock market meltdown of 2008. However, at this point the case for radical reform has not been made out.

Please see Exhibit 51.1 for supplemental information on companies by sector.

Exhibit 51.1 Corporate Governance Features of Companies Removed from S&P 500, 2008 (in order of removal)

Company/Date of Removal	Sector	At Risk?	Securities Class Action(s)	Public Criticism of Board	Publicized Director Turnover	Publicized Executive Turnover	CEO Executive Pay Controversy	Private Equity Involvement	Hedge Fund Activism
Harrah's Entertainment (Jan. 28)	Consumer Discretionary	No						Taken private (2006 deal finalized)	
Circuit City Stores Inc. (March 28)	Consumer Discretionary	Yes			Yes	Yes			Yes
Commerce Bancorp (March 28)	Financials	No				Yes	Yes		
The Bear Stearns Companies Inc. (June 2)	Financials	Yes	Yes	Yes		Yes	Yes		
Trane Inc. (June 6)	Industrials	No							
Ambac Financial Group Inc. (June 10)	Financials	Yes	Yes		Yes	Yes			
Brunswick Corp. (June 20)	Consumer Discretionary	Yes			Yes				
OfficeMax Inc. (June 20)	Consumer Discretionary	Yes			Yes				
Countrywide Financial Corp. (June 30)	Financials	Yes	Yes	Yes			Yes		
E.W. Scripps (June 30)	Consumer Discretionary	No							
ACE Ltd. (June 30)	Financials	No							
Clear Channel Comm. Ltd. (July 30)	Consumer Discretionary	No						Taken private (2006 deal finalized)	
IAC/InterActive (Aug. 20)	Consumer Discretionary	No					Yes		
Electronic Data Systems (Aug. 26)	IT	No					Yes		
Federal Home Loan Mortgage Corp. (Sept. 10)	Financials	Yes	Yes				Yes		

Company	Sector			Minority stake acquired			Minority stake acquired
Federal National Mortgage Association (Sept. 10)	Financials	Yes	Yes		Yes	Yes	
Lehman Brothers (Sept. 16)	Financials	Yes	Yes	Yes	Yes	Yes	
Safeco Corp. (Sept. 22)	Financials	No	Yes	Yes			
Washington Mutual (Sept. 29)	Financials	Yes		Yes	Yes	Yes	
Wendy's International Inc. (Sept. 29)	Consumer Discretionary	No					Yes
Wm. Wrigley Junior Co. (Oct. 3)	Consumer Staples	No					
Dillard's Inc. (Oct. 21)	Consumer Discretionary	Yes		Yes		Yes	Yes
MGIC Investment Corp. (Oct. 30)	Financials	Yes	Yes				
Terex Corp. (Nov. 5)	Industrials	Yes	Yes				
Unisys Corp. (Nov. 10)	IT	Yes	Yes		Yes		Yes
General Growth Properties Inc. (Nov. 12)	Financials	Yes	Yes		Yes	Yes	Yes
Ashland Inc. (Nov. 13)	Materials	Yes	Yes				
Hercules Inc. (Nov. 13)	Materials	No					
Anheuser-Busch (Nov. 18)	Consumer Staples	No		Yes			
Applied Biosystems Inc. (Nov. 21)	Health Care	No					
Liz Claiborne Inc. (Dec. 1)	Consumer Discretionary	Yes	Yes		Yes	Yes	Yes
Allied Waste Industries Inc. (Dec. 4)	Industrials	No					
Transocean Inc. (Dec. 18)	Energy	No					
Barr Pharmaceuticals Inc. (Dec. 22)	Health Care	No					
Wachovia Corp. (Dec. 31)	Financials	Yes	Yes		Yes	Yes	
National City Corp. (Dec. 31)	Financials	Yes	Yes	Yes	Yes	Yes	
Merrill Lynch (Dec. 31)	Financials	Yes	Yes	Yes	Yes	Yes	

NOTES

1. Gerald F. Seib, "In Crisis, Opportunity for Obama," *Wall Street Journal*, November 21, 2008, A2.

2. ECGI—Law Working Paper No. 124/2009, available at SSRN: http://ssrn.com/ abstract=1396126; (2009) 65 *Business Lawyer* 1. Interested readers can find in this paper the extensive citations that are customary in legal scholarship. Citations have been kept to the bare minimum for the purposes of this chapter.

3. Pub. L. 107–204, 116 Stat. 745.

4. Quoted in Zabihollah Rezaee, *Corporate Governance Post-Sarbanes-Oxley* (Hoboken, NJ: John Wiley & Sons, 2007), 36.

5. Georgeson, *2008 Annual Corporate Governance Review: Annual Meetings, Shareholder Initiatives, Proxy Contests* (2009).

6. See www.aflcio.org/corporatewatch/paywatch/ (accessed April 2, 2009).

ABOUT THE AUTHOR

Brian R. Cheffins is the S. J. Berwin professor of corporate law at the Faculty of Law, University of Cambridge. Before coming to Cambridge, he taught at the University of British Columbia's Faculty of Law. Cheffins has held visiting appointments at Duke, Harvard, Oxford, and Stanford and is a fellow of the European Corporate Governance Institute. Professor Cheffins is the author of *Company Law: Theory, Structure and Operation* (Oxford, 1997; co-winner, Society of Public Teachers of Law Prize for Outstanding Legal Scholarship), *Corporate Ownership and Control: British Business Transformed* (Oxford, 2008) and numerous articles on corporate law and corporate governance.

CHAPTER 52

Secondary-Management Conflicts

STEVEN L. SCHWARCZ
Stanley A. Star Professor of Law and Business at Duke University
and Founding Director of Duke's Global Capital Markets Center*

INTRODUCTION

I have recently argued that financial market failures can be attributed, in large part, to three causes: conflicts, complacency, and complexity.[1] This chapter engages the first cause, focusing on a subset of conflicts that in the past has been regarded as relatively harmless: conflicts between a firm and its middle- to lower-level management (hereinafter *secondary management* or *secondary managers*). The chapter's thesis is that, as financial markets and the securities traded therein become more complex and as firms become more highly leveraged, these conflicts are increasingly likely to trigger the collapse of firms that invest in those securities and possibly also of the markets themselves.

Corporate governance scholarship has long grappled with conflicts of interest between a firm (meaning its owners, typically shareholders) and the firm's top managers, such as chief executive officers. Costs associated with this conflict are referred to as agency costs because managers are agents of the firm. It is widely acknowledged that top managers sometimes act to benefit themselves, to the detriment of the firm. To mitigate these agency costs, corporate governance scholars traditionally focus on two topics: reducing top-management conflicts of interest, and improving board governance.

*Copyright © 2009 by Steven L. Schwarcz. This chapter is based on "Conflicts and Financial Collapse: The Problem of Secondary-Management Agency Costs," *Yale Journal on Regulation*, 26 (2) (Summer 2009 symposium issue on "The Future of Financial Regulation," co-sponsored by the Yale Law School Center for the Study of Corporate Law), also available at http://ssrn.com/abstract_id=1322536.

Steven L. Schwarcz is the author of numerous articles and papers on the subprime financial crisis and systemic risk and has also testified before the Committee on Financial Services of the U.S. House of Representatives on "Systemic Risk: Examining Regulators' Ability to Respond to Threats to the Financial System," available at www.house.gov/apps/list/hearing/financialsvcs_dem/ht1002072.shtml.

Scholars have largely ignored, however, conflicts of interest between a firm and its secondary managers. There appear to be several reasons for this oversight. Most obviously, secondary managers report to, and thus are already theoretically subject to control by top managers. Moreover, to the extent decisions of secondary managers are not deemed to be pivotal to the direction of a firm or its strategic goals, the consequences of secondary management conflicts would not be deemed to be—and in the past probably were not—significant.

This chapter contends that the increasing complexity of financial markets and of the securities traded therein makes secondary managers more likely to act in conflict with interests of their firms, and that the increasing financial leverage of firms in the modern credit economy exacerbates the consequences of these conflicted actions. The chapter therefore argues for the importance of reducing secondary management conflicts of interest.

The chapter's scope is limited to conflicts of interest between firms and secondary managers that could trigger the collapse of firms or financial markets. Secondary managers likely to have that power include those who structure, sell, or invest in market securities on behalf of the firm, such as analysts responsible for making decisions about the firm's investments. Similarly, the types of firms likely to be seriously adversely affected by these conflicts include banks or other financial institutions whose assets are significantly invested in, or whose business is significantly concerned with structuring or selling, financial market securities. This chapter's examples therefore concentrate on secondary managers who structure, sell, or invest in market securities on behalf of financial institutions. Nonetheless, portions of this chapter might well have application to secondary managers in other types of firms.[2]

More of a problem for LCFI

ANALYSIS

The Nature of the Conflict

The conflict centers on compensation. Secondary managers are typically compensated for performing their assigned tasks, without regard to the long-term consequences of the tasks to their firms. For example, secondary managers who structure, sell, or invest in market securities on behalf of a firm are customarily compensated for those tasks even if, ultimately, the structure proves inadequate or the securities turn out to be poor investments.

This conflict can create perverse incentives. For example, as the VaR, or value-at-risk, model for measuring investment portfolio risk became more accepted, financial firms began compensating secondary managers not only for generating profits but also for generating profits with low risks, as measured by VaR. Secondary managers therefore turned to investment products with low VaR risk profile, like credit default swaps that generate small gains but only rarely have losses. The managers knew, but did not always explain to their seniors, that any losses that might eventually occur would be huge.[3]

Why, then, are secondary managers typically compensated without regard to long-term consequences of their performance? One reason is that secondary managers are subject to supervision and management control by top managers, who in turn are subject to direction by the board of directors. Top managers therefore are supposedly responsible for ensuring, and thus monitoring, that the tasks performed by secondary managers take into account long-term consequences to the firm.

The recent financial crisis has graphically demonstrated, though, that the conflict causes secondary managers to sometimes act in ways that create adverse long-term consequences to their firms, despite top management monitoring and supervision. The next part of this chapter examines why.

Complexity Causes Overreliance on Signals, Making the Conflict Worse

Why does monitoring and supervision by top management fail to prevent secondary managers from acting in conflict with their firms? I believe the answer is rooted in the increasing complexity of financial markets and of market securities, which causes overreliance on signals. Such overreliance, in turn, worsens the conflict, making secondary managers more likely to act on the conflict and also making it difficult for top managers to properly monitor secondary management action.

Complexity causes overreliance on signals. Consider first why complexity causes overreliance on signals. In the face of complexity, human beings often resort to simplifying heuristics. For example, even though different people mature at different ages, the age for alcohol consumption in the United States is fixed at 21 for everyone. The heuristics here, or the rule of thumb, is that by the age of 21 a person is mature enough to responsibly consume alcohol. In the context of structuring, selling, or investing in complex market securities, these heuristics include the signals provided by rating-agency ratings and by mathematical models.[4]

As the following discussion shows, such reliance—or overreliance, because the signal is an imperfect indicator of the underlying complexity—can worsen the conflict between a firm and its secondary managers by making such managers more likely to act in conflict with the firm and also by making it difficult for top managers to adequately monitor secondary management action.

Overreliance makes secondary managers more likely to act in conflict with their firms. Being compensated for performing specific tasks without regard to long-term consequences to the firm, secondary managers are tempted to take a relatively short-term view when performing tasks. This temptation makes secondary managers especially susceptible to overrely on signals, particularly when the signals align their performance with their economic benefit. Overreliance then makes those managers more likely to act in conflict with their firms.

In the recent financial crisis, for example, secondary managers overrelied on signals, in the form of rating-agency ratings and mathematical models, which aligned secondary-manager performance and economic benefit. Thus, "[a] lot of institutional investors bought [mortgage-backed] securities substantially based on their ratings [without fully understanding what they bought], in part because the market has become so complex." Similarly, there "was an enormous faith in the market's ability to analyze and measure risk" through mathematical models.

That overreliance by secondary managers was clearly in conflict with the long-term interests of their firms. Although ratings provide a useful yardstick by which to compare the safety of a debt security, ratings are imperfect measures, not even taking into account the possibility of fraud. In the recent financial crisis, many mortgage-backed securities turned out to be incorrectly rated. Similarly, although mathematical models can bring insight and clarity if the model is realistic and the inputted data are reliable, they can be misleading if the model is unrealistic or the inputted data are unreliable. In the recent financial crisis, it was not only the VaR model that was misleading; the cash-flow models underlying many mortgage-backed securities were also misleading because they turned out to rely on incorrect assumptions and data.

Overreliance makes it difficult for top managers to adequately monitor secondary management action. Overreliance also makes it difficult for top managers to adequately monitor secondary management action. In the face of complexity, top managers, like secondary managers, will be tempted to overrely on simplifying heuristics, like the signals provided by ratings and mathematical models. Although top managers will not be as susceptible as secondary managers to overrely because of conflicts, top managers will be susceptible to overrely for another reason: when the task being performed is highly technical, they will know less, and thus find the task more complex, than secondary managers will.

Consider this chapter's example of a secondary manager who structures, sells, or invests in complex market securities on behalf of his firm. This manager will typically have considerable technical training or experience regarding the securities. Yet even with that training and experience, he will probably not completely understand everything about those securities. The top manager supervising him is likely to know even less, though. If, therefore, the secondary manager recommends that the firm invest in a given amount of those securities rated investment grade, the top manager will have little basis to veto that recommendation. Similarly, top managers will probably have little expertise to go beyond VaR or other mathematically modeled risk profiles.

The complexity of modern financial markets, and resulting overreliance on signals such as ratings and models, thus makes it difficult for top managers to adequately monitor secondary management action.

Financial Leverage Exacerbates Problems Caused by Overreliance

This chapter so far has demonstrated that the increasing complexity of financial markets and the securities traded therein makes secondary managers more likely to act in conflict with the interests of their firms. I now show that the increasing financial leverage of firms in the modern credit economy exacerbates the consequences of these conflicts.

Increased financial leverage means that a firm will be less financially robust. Absent leverage, a firm "can absorb losses linearly, dollar for dollar."[5] The less leverage, the less likely it is, other factors being equal, that a firm would fail to pay its debts as they mature. When a firm is highly leveraged, though, losses beyond a certain level—depending on the firm's size and leverage—will precipitously degrade its ability to pay its debts. Therefore, if a highly leveraged firm suffers significant losses because of the conflict with its secondary managers—as happened to many financial institutions in the recent financial crisis—the firm may well default.

The consequences of the conflict can go even further. Increasing leverage not only increases the risk that one firm's failure will systemically trigger failures of other highly leveraged, and thus less financial robust, firms, but of markets themselves. This, too, occurred in the recent financial crisis. In part because of conflicts between financial institutions and their secondary managers, many financial institutions invested in substantial amounts of risky but investment grade–rated mortgage-backed securities. When some of these securities started defaulting or being downgraded because of defaults on underlying subprime mortgage loans, investors started losing confidence in ratings and avoiding debt securities as investments. With fewer investors, the price of debt securities started falling, which in turn required firms using debt securities as collateral to mark them to market and put up cash. Firms had to sell more securities to raise the cash, causing market prices to plummet even further downward in a death spiral. The collapse in market prices meant that banks and other financial institutions holding mortgage-backed securities had to write down their value, causing these highly leveraged institutions to appear even more financially risky, in turn triggering concern over counterparty risk: parties were afraid these institutions might default on their contractual obligations and therefore stopped dealing with them. As a result, the credit markets shut down, severely affecting the real economy.

Finding Solutions

The preceding analysis has shown that conflicts of interest between firms and their secondary managers are no longer harmless. To the contrary, increasing leverage and financial complexity make these conflicts dangerous to both firms and financial markets. This chapter examines possible solutions next.

Limiting conflicts. The most direct way to limit conflicts in our case is by aligning incentives. Because compensation is at the root of the conflict between firms and their secondary managers, the most effective way to align incentives is to tie secondary-manager compensation to long-term interests of the firm. This could be done in various ways.

For example, a firm might retroactively recover (clawback) compensation paid to secondary managers who have structured, sold, or invested in market securities on behalf of the firm if, within some time period, the structure proves inadequate or the securities turn out to be poor investments. Similarly, a firm might pay a portion of a secondary manager's compensation contingently over time or in the form of equity securities with long-term lockdown constraints on selling the securities. The amount of compensation subject to clawback or paid contingently or in equity must be material enough in context to affect secondary management incentives. In determining that amount, a firm will have to take into account, of course, how the deferred, contingent, or equity compensation will affect the firm's ability to compete for the best secondary managers. A firm also should consider timing. Too short a time frame may not sufficiently align long-term incentives, whereas too long a time frame may run into the availability bias: individuals overestimate the importance of events that are imminent, such as receiving a portion of the compensation now, and underestimate events that are remote, such as contingently receiving compensation in the future.

Any such alignment of compensation incentives with long-term interests of the firm would have to also address the compensation of top managers supervising the secondary managers. Although top management should be responsible for monitoring and ensuring that the tasks performed by secondary managers take into account long-term consequences to the firm, top managers themselves may have conflicts that induce them to ignore those long-term consequences. For example, a top manager supervising a secondary manager may get paid based on the firm's (or a business group's) short-term profitability, which is materially driven by the secondary manager's work. In these cases, top management compensation should also be aligned with the firm's long-term interests—at least insofar as top management conflicts could undermine monitoring of secondary management.

Another way a firm can align incentives is to announce a policy to terminate secondary managers who structure market securities that later prove inadequate or who sell or invest in market securities that later turn out to be poor investments. This approach, however, may not be as effective as aligning compensation incentives. Individuals overestimate the importance of imminent events, such as having a job and being paid a bonus, and underestimate events that are remote, such as the possibility of being fired at a future date. Individuals in industries with high job turnover may even expect to be at different jobs before the success of an investment is likely to be known. Furthermore, secondary managers may feel, and in fact be, secure from being fired if many similarly situated secondary managers are acting the same way. In the recent financial crisis, for example, secondary managers often recommended investments in highly complex mortgage-backed securities they did not fully understand, apparently feeling safe in following the herd.

Conflicts can also be limited by better monitoring. This might include better monitoring by top management. It also might include, for example, hiring technically trained control officers who do not have conflicts to supervise relevant aspects of the quality of tasks performed by secondary managers. This could be very expensive, though, because any control officer so hired would face the prospect of losing expertise over time.

Improving the accuracy of signals. Yet another way to help mitigate the conflict of interest between a firm and its secondary managers might be to try to improve the accuracy of signals, such as improving the accuracy of rating-agency ratings or risk models. The viability of this type of approach would be highly fact dependent.

This approach also might have unintended consequences. If the accuracy of a signal is not improved as much as the perception of the signal's accuracy, overreliance may actually increase. For example, if ratings are perceived to be highly accurate and no longer subject to exceptions (like fraud), secondary managers will rely even more on ratings. But if the accuracy of ratings has not increased commensurately to the perception, these managers will be overrelying. Remember that the widespread acceptance of the VaR model for assessing risk contributed to management overreliance.

Should solutions be market-driven or regulatory? It therefore appears that the most effective way to address the conflict between firms and their secondary managers is to align secondary management compensation incentives with the long-term interests of the firm. To what extent should this be left to the market, and to what extent should it be imposed by regulation?

Firms clearly are in a better position than government regulators to determine how best to align secondary management compensation incentives with their long-term interests. Furthermore, firms will want to align those incentives for their own long-term survival. There may, however, be a collective-action problem that individual firms will be unable to solve: any firm that employs a deferred or contingent (or equity) compensation scheme will be disadvantaged in its ability to compete for the best secondary managers. Government action may well be needed to help resolve this collective-action problem.

The question of whether these solutions should be market-driven or regulatory can also be viewed more broadly as a subset of the debate over regulating operational risk. *Operational risk* is the term used to describe, among other things, the risk of loss resulting from inadequate or failed internal processes, people, and systems—and thus it would encompass the secondary management conflicts discussed in this chapter.

Many observers believe that enforced self-regulation is the best way to handle operational risk. But others argue that the answer is more nuanced, contending (for example) that for low frequency, high impact events, enforced self-regulation of operational risk is worse than no regulation at all because it lures parties into a false sense of confidence while costing money.[6]

Although this debate provides an interesting way to frame the regulatory question, it is far from determinative. Risks arising from the conflict between a firm and its secondary managers are difficult to categorize as either low frequency, high impact—for which self-regulation is arguably inappropriate—or high frequency, low impact—for which self-regulation may well be more appropriate.[7]

A final question is whether regulation, if adopted, should apply to all firms, including the large, sophisticated firms that, under the federal securities laws in the United States, are characterized as qualified institutional buyers (QIBs). The securities laws generally assume that QIBs can and will protect their own interests—or at least their own investments. Anomalously, though, QIBs are the very investors who lost the most money in the financial crisis, much of it through bad investing. Any exclusion of QIBs from regulation would first have to explain that anomaly. Furthermore, because QIBs would be as subject to the collective-action problem as any other firms, any regulation addressing that problem should equally apply to them.

CONCLUSIONS

This chapter focuses on rising agency costs associated with increasing complexity of financial markets and the securities traded therein, and the increasing leverage of firms in the modern credit economy. Increasing complexity makes it more likely that secondary managers will act in conflict with interests of their firms. Increasing leverage amplifies returns, but, because it makes firms more susceptible to default, it also heightens the risk for losses from these conflicts. Scholars generally disregarded these conflicts in the traditional noncredit economy because the associated agency costs were relatively small. In a highly leveraged firm, these agency costs can be large. Indeed, in the recent financial crisis, they contributed to the failure of financial institutions and the collapse of financial markets, resulting in massive losses. Conflict of interest oversight of secondary managers thus matters much more today than it did in the past.

The chapter argues that the most effective way to address the conflict is to align secondary management compensation incentives with the long-term interests of the firm. Firms have incentives, and are in a better position than government regulators, to determine how best to achieve this alignment. Regulation may well be needed, though, to help resolve the collective action problem that individual firms that attempt to align incentives will be disadvantaged in their ability to compete for the best secondary managers.

NOTES

1. Steven L. Schwarcz, "Protecting Financial Markets: Lessons from the Subprime Mortgage Meltdown," *Minn. L. Rev.* 93 (2008): 373.

2. For example, if secondary-manager compensation of a large drug company is based on bringing new drugs to market, secondary managers would have an incentive to minimize reporting to senior management about a new drug's possible, latent long-term side effects—a scenario that has certain parallels to secondary managers of a large financial institution not fully reporting to senior management the long-term market risk exposure of a particular financial product.

3. Joe Nocera, "Risk Mismanagement," *New York Times Magazine,* January 4, 2009, 46.

4. For a discussion of rating agencies and their ratings, see Steven L. Schwarcz, "Private Ordering of Public Markets: The Rating Agency Paradox," *U. Ill. L. Rev.* 1 (2002).

5. Steven L. Schwarcz, "Systemic Risk," *Geo. L. J.* 97 (2008):193, 223.

6. See, for example, Kimberly D. Krawiec, "The Return of the Rogue," *Ariz. L. Rev.* 50 (2008): 879–880.

7. Id.

ABOUT THE AUTHOR

Steven L. Schwarcz is the Stanley A. Star professor of law and business at Duke University and founding director of Duke's Global Capital Markets Center. Before joining Duke, he was a partner at two leading international law firms and also taught at the Yale and Columbia Law Schools. Schwarcz has advised the United States Congress and other government bodies on systemic risk and the recent financial crisis. His scholarly works include "Systemic Risk," *Geo. L. J.* 97 (2008): 193; "Protecting Financial Markets: Lessons from the Subprime Mortgage Meltdown," *Minn. L. Rev.* 93 (2008): 373; "Disclosure's Failure in the Subprime Mortgage Crisis," *Utah. L. Rev.* (2008): 1109; "Understanding the Subprime Financial Crisis," *S. C. L. Rev.* 60 (2009): 549; "Conflicts and Financial Collapse: The Problem of Secondary-Management Agency Costs," *Yale J. on Reg.* 26 (Summer 2009); "Too Big To Fail? Recasting the Financial Safety Net," in *The Panic of 2008* (Geo. Wash. Univ. symposium book); "Regulating Complexity in Financial Markets," *Wash. U. L. Rev.* 87 (2010); and *Regulating Financial Systems,* forthcoming from Oxford University Press (co-authored with Kenneth Anderson).

CHAPTER 53

The Financial Crisis
and the Systemic Failure
of Academic Economics

DAVID COLANDER
Department of Economics, Middlebury College

MICHAEL GOLDBERG
Whittemore School of Business and Economics, University of New Hampshire

ARMIN HAAS
Potsdam Institute for Climate Impact Research, Potsdam, Germany

ALAN KIRMAN
GREQAM, Université d'Aix-Marseille lll, EHESS et IUF, Marseille, France

KATARINA JUSELIUS
Department of Economics, University of Copenhagen, Copenhagen, Denmark

BRIGITTE SLOTH
Department of Business and Economics, University of Southern Denmark,
Odense, Denmark

THOMAS LUX
Department of Economics, University of Kiel, Kiel Institute for the World
Economy, Kiel, Germany*

The economics profession appears to have been unaware of the long build-up to the current worldwide financial crisis and to have significantly underestimated its dimensions once it started to unfold. In our view, this lack of understanding is due to a misallocation of research efforts in economics. We trace the deeper roots of this failure to the profession's focus on models that, by design,

*This opinion paper is the condensed version of the Dahlem Report of the working group on "Modeling of Financial Markets" at the 98th Dahlem Workshop, 2008.

disregard key elements driving outcomes in real-world markets. The economics profession has failed in communicating the limitations, weaknesses, and even dangers of its preferred models to the public. This state of affairs makes clear the need for a major reorientation of focus in the research economists undertake, as well as for the establishment of an ethical code that would ask economists to understand and communicate the limitations and potential misuses of their models.

INTRODUCTION

The global financial crisis has revealed the need to rethink fundamentally how financial systems are regulated. It has also made clear a *systemic failure of the economics profession*. Over the past three decades, economists have largely developed and come to rely on models that disregard key factors—including heterogeneity of decision rules, revisions of forecasting strategies, and changes in the social context—that drive outcomes in asset and other markets. It is obvious, even to the casual observer, that these models fail to account for the actual evolution of the real-world economy. Moreover, the current academic agenda has largely crowded out research on the inherent causes of financial crises. There has also been little exploration of early indicators of system crisis and potential ways to prevent this malady from developing. In fact, if one browses through the academic macroeconomics and finance literature, "systemic crisis" appears like an otherworldly event that is absent from economic models. Most models, by design, offer no immediate handle on how to think about or deal with this recurring phenomenon.[1] In our hour of greatest need, societies around the world are left to grope in the dark without a theory. That, to us, is a *systemic failure of the economics profession*.

The implicit view behind standard equilibrium models is that markets and economies are inherently stable and that they only temporarily get off track. The majority of economists thus failed to warn policy makers about the threatening system crisis and ignored the work of those who did. Ironically, as the crisis has unfolded, economists have had no choice but to abandon their standard models and to produce hand-waving common-sense remedies. Common-sense advice, although useful, is a poor substitute for an underlying model that can provide much-needed guidance for developing policy and regulation. It is not enough to put the existing model to one side, observing that one needs, "exceptional measures for exceptional times." What we need are models capable of envisaging such "exceptional times."

The confinement of macroeconomics to models of stable states that are perturbed by limited external shocks and that neglect the intrinsic recurrent boom and bust dynamics of our economic system is remarkable. After all, worldwide financial and economic crises are hardly new, and they have had a tremendous impact beyond the immediate economic consequences of mass unemployment and hyperinflation. It is even more surprising, given the long academic legacy of earlier economists' study of crisis phenomena, which can be found in the work of Walter Bagehot (1873), Axel Leijonhuvfud (2000), Charles Kindleberger (1989), and Hyman Minsky (1986), to name a few prominent examples. This tradition, however, has been neglected and even suppressed.

The most recent literature provides us with examples of blindness against the upcoming storm that seem odd in retrospect. For example, in their analysis of the risk management implications of CDOs, Krahnen (2005) and Krahnen and Wilde (2006) mention the possibility of an increase of systemic risk. But they conclude that this aspect should not be the concern of the banks engaged in the CDO market, because it is the government's responsibility to provide costless insurance against a systemwide crash. We do not share this view. On the more theoretical side, a recent and prominent strand of literature essentially argues that consumers and investors are too risk averse because of their memory of the (improbable) event of the Great Depression (e.g., Cogley and Sargent 2008). Much of the motivation for economics as an academic discipline stems from the desire to explain phenomena like unemployment, boom and bust cycles, and financial crises, but dominant theoretical models exclude many of aspects of the economy that will likely lead to recurrent crises. Confining theoretical models to normal times without consideration of such defects might seem contradictory to the focus that the average taxpayer would expect of the scientists on his payroll.

This failure has deep methodological roots. The often heard definition of economics—that it is concerned with the allocation of scarce resources—is short-sighted and misleading. It reduces economics to the study of optimal decisions in well-specified choice problems. Such research generally loses track of the inherent dynamics of economic systems and the instability that accompanies its complex dynamics. Without an adequate understanding of these processes, one is likely to miss the major factors that influence the economic sphere of our societies. This insufficient definition of economics often leads researchers to disregard questions about the coordination of actors and the possibility of coordination failures. Indeed, analysis of these issues would require a different type of mathematics from that which is generally used now by many prominent economic models.

Many of the financial economists who developed the theoretical models upon which the modern financial structure is built were well aware of the strong and highly unrealistic restrictions imposed on their models to assure stability. Yet, financial economists gave little warning to the public about the fragility of their models,[2] even as they saw individuals and businesses build a financial system based on their work. There are a number of possible explanations for this failure to warn the public. One is a "lack of understanding" explanation—the researchers did not know the models were fragile. We find this explanation highly unlikely; financial engineers are extremely bright, and it is almost inconceivable that such bright individuals did not understand the limitations of their models. A second, more likely explanation, is that they did not consider it their job to warn the public. If that is the cause of their failure, we believe that it involves a misunderstanding of the role of the economist, and involves an ethical breakdown. In our view, economists, as with all scientists, *have an ethical responsibility to communicate the limitations of their models and the potential misuses of their research.* Currently, there is no ethical code for professional economic scientists. There should be one.

Some of the major areas of concern are the following.

Models (or the Use of Models) as a Source of Risk

Models are absolutely necessary to making good decisions and to develop mechanisms that improve the functioning of the economy. But in using models, one must always keep in mind that they are built on assumptions, and if those assumptions are not carefully kept in mind, the use of the models can become a source or risk, and can cause problems. For example, mathematical portfolio and risk management models have been the academic backbone of the tremendous increase of trading volume and diversification of instruments in financial markets. They provide the foundation for pricing and risk management of these products. Portfolio insurance and dynamic hedging are based on derivative pricing models. While useful, these models are far from perfect as a foundation for new financial instruments, because of the limited availability of historical data to base these models on and the analytic computing limitations that led modelers to use simulations with relatively arbitrary assumptions about correlations between risks and default probabilities. These problems made the theoretical foundations of all financial products based on them highly questionable—the equivalent to erecting a building of cement of which you weren't sure of the components.

We agree with many scientists that models are imperfect and that basing them on bold assumptions is how science advances. The problem comes when models are used by nonscientists to design real-world instruments and institutions. In this case, models need to come with strong warnings about their imperfections, and with cautions about their use. In the case of these financial models, those warnings and cautions do not seem to have accompanied the models; the academic financial economics profession did not loudly and publicly warn policy makers about the potential problems of the rapidly expanding credit derivatives market being based on such imperfect models. That, to us, is problematic; in our view, academic researchers should take responsibility for they way in which their models are used; they have an ethical responsibility to point out to the public when the tool that they developed is being misused.

If one can expect that the model one is developing will be used to design real world products and institutions, the nature of the modeling process should change. Much more effort needs to go into the study of robustness and sensitivity analysis to assumptions than currently occurs. For example, in evaluating models, one could rely on probabilistic projections that cover a whole range of specific models (cf., Föllmer 2008). The theory of robust control provides a toolbox of techniques that could be applied for this purpose, and it is an approach that should be considered. Models that explicitly recognize that individuals have imperfect knowledge about the underlying process generating market outcomes (cf., Frydman and Goldberg 2007, 2008), provide another approach worth considering.

Unrealistic Model Assumptions and Unrealistic Outcomes

Many economic models are built upon the twin assumptions of rational expectations and a representative agent. Both assumptions are essentially convenient devices to formulate internally consistent models, but are very questionable as descriptions of real-world phenomena. The representative agent assumes that the whole economy will behave as a single individual, but there are strong theoretical arguments to show that even in very simple settings this will typically not be the case.[3] In the case of rational expectations, we have no explanation as to how all market participants might come to agree on one economist's model, given that academic economists themselves are obviously divided into various camps. Furthermore, neither approach is externally consistent in the sense that they are not compatible with insights from other branches of science on human behavior; nor are they compatible with educated common sense of what aspects of behavior a practical policy-oriented model should reasonably include.[4] Rational expectations and representative agent models do not allow for interactions of their economic actors, and coordination issues are typically missing altogether. As a consequence, any notion of systemic risk or coordination failure is completely absent from these models. In our view macroeconomists need to rethink the concept of microfoundations of macroeconomic models. Since economic activity is of an essentially interactive nature, economists' microfoundations should allow for the interactions of heterogeneous economic agents. The dominance of the extreme form of conceptual reductionism of the representative agent has prevented economists from even attempting to model all such important phenomena.

Robustness and Data-Driven Empirical Research

Currently popular models (in particular: dynamic general equilibrium models) do not only have weak microfoundations, their empirical performance is far from satisfactory (Juselius and Franchi 2007). Indeed, the relevant strand of empirical economics has more and more avoided testing their models and has instead turned to calibration without explicit consideration of goodness-of-fit.[5] In our view, the current approach of using preselected models is problematic, and we recommend a more data-driven methodology. Instead of starting out with an ad hoc specification and questionable *ceteris paribus* assumptions, the key features of the data should be explored with data-analytical tools and specification tests. The general-to-specific approach provides a well-established empirical methodology for such exploratory data analysis (Hendry 1995, 2009) as well as a general theory for model selection (Hendry and Krolzig 2005); clustering techniques such as projection pursuit (e.g., Friedman 1987) might provide alternatives for the identification of key relationships and the reduction of complexity on the way from empirical measurement to theoretical models. Co-integrated VAR models could provide an avenue toward identification of robust structures within a set of data (Juselius 2006). For example, it could help identify the forces that move equilibria (*pushing forces*, which give rise to stochastic trends) and forces that correct deviations from equilibrium (*pulling forces*, which give rise to long-run relations). In our view, these approaches should be given more emphasis.

A RESEARCH AGENDA TO COPE WITH FINANCIAL FRAGILITY

The notion of financial fragility implies that a given system might be more or less susceptible to produce crises. It seems clear that financial innovations have made the system more fragile. Apparently, the existing linkages within the worldwide, highly connected financial markets have generated the spillovers from the U.S. subprime problem to other layers of the financial system. Many financial innovations had the effect of creating links between formerly unconnected players. All in all, the degree of connectivity of the system has probably increased enormously over the last decades. As is well known from network theory in natural sciences, a more highly connected system might be more efficient in coping with certain tasks (maybe distributing risk components), but will often also be more vulnerable to shocks and—systemic failure!

The systematic analysis of network vulnerability has been undertaken in the computer science and operations research literature (see e.g., Criado et al. 2005). Such aspects have, however, been largely absent from discussions in financial economics. The introduction of new derivatives was rather seen through the lens of general equilibrium models: more contingent claims help to achieve higher efficiency. Unfortunately, the claimed efficiency gains through derivatives are merely a theoretical implication of a highly stylized model and, therefore, have to count as a *hypothesis*. Since there is hardly any supporting empirical evidence (or even analysis of this question), the claimed real-world efficiency gains from derivatives are not justified by true science. While the economic argument in favor of ever new derivatives is more one of persuasion rather than evidence, important negative effects have been neglected. The idea that the system was made less risky with the development of more derivatives led to financial actors taking positions with extreme degrees of leverage, and the danger of this has not been emphasized enough. In our view, it should be given much more research emphasis.

CONCLUSIONS

The current crisis might be characterized as an example of the final stage of a well-known boom and bust pattern that has been repeated so many times in the course of economic history. There are, nevertheless, some aspects that make this crisis different from its predecessors: First, the preceding boom had its origin—at least to a large part—in the development of new financial products that opened up new investment possibilities (while most previous crises were the consequence of overinvestment in new physical investment possibilities). Second, the global dimension of the current crisis is due to the increased connectivity of our already highly interconnected financial system. Both aspects have been largely ignored by academic economics. Research on the origin of instabilities, overinvestment, and subsequent slumps has been considered as an exotic sidetrack from the academic research agenda (and the curriculum of most economics programs). This, of course, was because it was incompatible with the premise of the rational representative agent. This paradigm also made economics blind with respect to the role of interactions and connections between actors (such as the changes in the network structure of the financial industry brought about by deregulation and the introduction of new structured products). Indeed, much of the work on contagion and herding behavior (see Banerjee 1992, and Chamley 2002), which is closely connected to the network structure of the economy, has not been incorporated into macroeconomic analysis.

We believe that economics has been trapped in a suboptimal equilibrium in which much of its research efforts are not directed toward the most prevalent needs of society. Paradoxically, self-reinforcing feedback effects within the profession may have led to the dominance of a paradigm that has no solid methodological basis and whose empirical performance is, to say the least, modest. Defining away the most prevalent economic problems of modern economies and failing to communicate the limitations and assumptions of its popular models, the economics profession bears some responsibility for the current crisis. It has failed in its duty to society to provide as much insight as possible into the workings of the economy and in providing warnings about the tools it created. It has also been reluctant to emphasize the limitations of its analysis. We believe that the failure to even envisage the current problems of the worldwide financial system and the inability of standard macro and finance models to provide any insight into ongoing events make a strong case for a major reorientation in these areas and a reconsideration of their basic premises.

NOTES

1. Reinhart and Rogoff (2008) argue that the current financial crisis differs little from a long chain of similar crises in developed and developing countries. We certainly share their view. The problem is that the received body of models in macrofinance to which these authors have prominently contributed provides no room whatsoever for such recurrent boom and bust cycles. The literature has, therefore, been a major source of the illusory "this time it is different" view that the authors themselves criticize.

2. Indeed, few researchers explored the consequences of a breakdown of their assumptions, even though this was rather likely.

3. See Kirman (1992) for details.

4. For a critique of rational expectations models on epistemological grounds, see Frydman and Goldberg (2007, 2008).

5. It is pretty obvious how the currently popular class of dynamic general equilibrium models would have to cope with the current financial crisis. It will be covered either by a dummy or it will have to be interpreted as a very large negative stochastic shock to the economy, that is, as an event equivalent to a large asteroid strike.

REFERENCES

Bagehot, W. 1873. *Lombard street: A description of the money market.* London: Henry S. King and Company.

Banerjee, A. 1992. A simple model of herd behaviour. *Quarterly Journal of Economics* 108: 797–817.

Chamley, C. P. 2002. *Rational herds: Economic models of social learning.* Cambridge: Cambridge University Press.

Cogley, T., and T. Sargent. 2008. The market price of risk and the equity premium: A legacy of the Great Depression? *Journal of Monetary Economics* 55: 454–476.

Criado, R., J. Flores, B. Hernández-Bermejo, J. Pello, and M. Romance. 2005. Effective measurement of network vulnerability under random and intentional attacks. Journal of Mathematical Modelling and Algorithms 4: 307–316.

Friedman, J. 1987. Exploratory projection pursuit. *Journal of the American Statistical Association* 82: 249–266.

Frydman, R., and M. D. Goldberg. 2007. *Imperfect knowledge economics: Exchange rates and risk.* Princeton, NJ: Princeton University Press.

———. 2008. Macroeconomic theory for a world of imperfect knowledge. *Capitalism and Society* 3 (3): Article 1.

Hendry, D. F. 1995. *Dynamic econometrics.* Oxford: Oxford University Press.

Hendry, D. F. 2009. The methodology of empirical econometric modelling: Applied econometrics through the looking-glass. In *The Handbook of Empirical Econometrics*. London: Palgrave, forthcoming.

Hendry, D. F., and H.-M. Krolzig. 2005. The properties of automatic gets modeling. *Economic Journal* 115: C32–C61.

Föllmer, H., 2008. Financial uncertainty, risk measures and robust preferences, in M. Yor, ed *Aspects of Mathematical Finance*. Springer: Berlin.

Kindleberger, C. P. 1989. *Manias, panics, and crashes: A history of financial crises*. London: MacMillan.

Juselius, K. and M. Franchi, 2007. Taking a DSGE Model to the Data Meaningfully. *Economics–The Open-Access, Open-Assessment E-Journal* 4.

Juselius, K. 2006. *The co-integrated VAR model: Econometric methodology and empirical applications*. Oxford: Oxford University Press.

Kirman, A. P. 1992. What or whom does the representative individual represent? *Journal of Economic Perspectives* 6: 117–36.

Krahnen, J.-P. 2005. Der handel von kreditrisiken: Eine neue dimension des kapitalmarktes. *Perspektiven der Wirtschaftspolitik* 6: 499–519.

Krahnen, J.-P., and C. Wilde. 2006. *Risk transfer with CDOs and systemic risk in banking*. Frankfurt: Center for Financial Studies, working paper 2006-04.

Leijonhufvud, A. 2000. *Macroeconomic instability and coordination: Selected essays*. Cheltenham, England: Edward Elgar.

Lo, A., D. V. Repin, and B. N. Steenbarger. 2005. Fear and greed in financial markets: A clinical study of day-traders. *American Economic Review* 95: 352–359.

Minsky, H. P. 1986. *Stabilizing an unstable economy*. New Haven, CT: Yale University Press.

Reinhart, C., and K. Rogoff. 2008. *This time is different: A panoramic view of eight centuries of financial crises*. Cambridge, MA: Harvard University and National Bureau of Economic Research, working paper 13882.

ABOUT THE AUTHORS

David Colander received his Ph.D. from Columbia University and has been the Christian A. Johnson distinguished professor of economics at Middlebury College, Middlebury, Vermont, since 1982. In 2001 and 2002, he was the Kelly professor of distinguished teaching at Princeton University. He has authored, co-authored, or edited more than 40 books and 100 articles on a wide range of topics. His books have been, or are being, translated into a number of different languages, including Chinese, Bulgarian, Polish, Italian, and Spanish. He has been president of both the Eastern Economic Association and History of Economic Thought Society and is, or has been, on the editorial boards of numerous journals, including *Journal of Economic Perspectives* and the *Journal of Economic Education*.

Michael D. Goldberg is the Roland H. O'Neal professor of economics at the University of New Hampshire. He has written extensively in the fields of international finance and macroeconomics, and his columns on asset price fluctuations and policy reform have been published by leading newspapers in more than 50 countries. His bestselling book, *Imperfect Knowledge Economics: Exchange Rates and Risk*, co-authored with Roman Frydman and published by Princeton University Press, proposes a much-needed new approach to economics that places the imperfection of knowledge at the center of analysis.

Armin Haas has a Ph.D. in economics from the University of Karlsruhe (1999). He currently is a senior researcher at the Potsdam Institute for Climate Impact Research (PIK). As a trained economist and modeler, he has worked on cartel dynamics, stochastic economic systems, and agent-based computational economics. His current research interests are the interaction of financial markets and climate change, and innovative approaches for the management of large-scale risks and chances. Haas is speaker of the research activity Integrated Risk Governance of the European Climate Forum (ECF). He also heads the research group Bayesian Risk Management, a joint initiative of PIK, the University of Potsdam, the German Institute for Economic Research (DIW Berlin), and the European Climate Forum (ECF). This group develops and applies Bayesian methods for managing risks.

Alan Kirman has a Ph.D. in economics from Princeton. He is a professor emeritus at the Université Paul Cézanne, and at the Ecole des Hautes Etudes en Sciences Sociales. He is a member of the Institut Universitaire de France. He has held posts at Johns Hopkins University, the Free University of Brussels, the University of Warwick, and at the European University Institute in Florence. He is a fellow of the Econometric Society and was awarded the Humboldt Prize in Germany. His original work was in economic theory, general equilibrium, social choice, and game theory, but more recently he has been interested in the functioning of actual markets and rethinking the economy as a complex adaptive system. He has more than 150 articles in international economics journals, is author and editor of some 12 books, and his latest book on complex economics was published by Routledge at the end of 2009.

Katarina Juselius holds a chair in time-series econometrics and empirical economics at the Department of Economics, University of Copenhagen, Denmark. Her primary research interest has been to develop the co-integrated VAR as a potential research methodology for empirical economics. She has published widely in econometric and empirical economics journals and been on the editorial board of the *Journal of Forecasting, Journal of Business and Economics Statistics,* and the *Journal of Economic Methodology.* She was recently a guest editor for a special issue on "Using Econometrics for Assessing Economic Models" in *Economics: The Open Access, Open Assessment E-Journal.* She has been a member of the Danish Social Sciences Research Council and was the chairperson of the Euro Core and the Forward Look programs of the European Science Foundation. She was ranked eighth among the most-cited economists in the world from 1990 to 2000.

Birgitte Sloth has a Ph.D. in economics from the University of Copenhagen (1994), and is a professor at the Department of Business and Economics at the University of Southern Denmark, Odense. She has contributed research papers in several economic theory journals, mainly within the fields of decision and game theory.

Thomas Lux has a Ph.D. in economics (University of Wuerzburg, 1990). He has been a professor of economics at the University of Bonn before moving to Christian-Albrechts University at Kiel in 2000. Since 2008, he has also been affiliated with the Kiel Institute for the World Economy. Lux's research interests cover various theoretical and empirical aspects of financial economics. He has published widely in economic journals such as the *Economic Journal*, the *Journal of Economic Dynamics and Control*, *Journal of Money, Credit and Banking*, *Journal of Mathematical Economics*, *Macroeconomic Dynamics* and the *Journal of Business and Economic Statistics*. Because of his interests in applying tools from statistical physics in financial economics, some of his recent output also appeared in the journals *Nature, Physica A*, and *Reports on Progress in Physics*, among others. Professor Lux is associate editor of the journals *Quantitative Finance* and *Journal of Economic Behavior and Organization* and is one of the founding editors of the *Journal of Economic Interaction and Coordination*.

CHAPTER 54

Fannie Mae and Freddie Mac: Privatizing Profit and Socializing Loss

DAVID REISS

Professor, Brooklyn Law School*

A s part of its response to the ongoing credit crisis, in the fall of 2008 the federal government placed the Federal National Mortgage Association (typically referred to as Fannie Mae) and the Federal Home Loan Mortgage Association (typically referred to as Freddie Mac) in conservatorship. While they are for-profit, privately owned mortgage finance companies whose shares trade on the New York Stock Exchange, Fannie Mae and Freddie Mac are also two of the few companies directly chartered by Congress, so-called government sponsored enterprises (GSEs). The federal government has given them the mission of providing liquidity and stability to the United States residential mortgage market and achieving certain affordable housing goals.

The privileges attendant to this special relationship with the federal government allowed Fannie and Freddie to pass on certain savings to U.S. homeowners but also to extract monopoly profits in the U.S. residential mortgage market. Meanwhile, their hybrid public-private status enabled them to exert outsized political influence and drive much of the legislative and regulatory agenda regarding their own fates. Thus while Freddie's and Fannie's early successes made the United States's secondary residential mortgage market the envy of other nations for quite some time, the two companies took on monstrously large lives of their own that well surpassed their original purpose. It would take the greatest financial crisis of our lifetime, and a bailout to be measured in the hundreds of billions of dollars,

---

*This article is based in part on earlier articles by the author, including "The Federal Government's Implied Guarantee of Fannie Mae's and Freddie Mac's Obligations: Uncle Sam Will Pick Up the Tab," *Ga. L. Rev.* 42 (2008): 1019; "The Role of the Fannie Mae/Freddie Mac Duopoly in the American Housing Market," *J. of Fin. Reg. & Compliance* 17 (2009), available at: http://works.bepress.com/david_reiss/29; "Fannie Mae and Freddie Mac and the Future of Federal Housing Finance Policy: A Study of Regulatory Privilege," *Ala. L. Rev.* 61 (2009), available at http://works.bepress.com/david_reiss/25. Thanks to Phil Tucker for superb research assistance.

before Fannie's and Freddie's extraordinarily privileged status would be seriously challenged.

Congress has a long history of relying upon GSEs to spur private investment. Indeed, the special privileges accorded a GSE are variants on the longstanding government practice of spurring private investment in various arenas by granting some privilege or monopoly power to a party that could infuse the activity with needed capital or bring focused attention to it. For example, government-granted monopolies can take the form of a charter granting a monopoly on trade, such as the one granted by Queen Elizabeth I to the English East India Company in 1600 for them to increase English trade with Asian nations. They can take the form of a system such as that governing U.S. patents, granting patent holders the sole right to exploit a patent for a certain period in order to encourage innovation. Or they can take the form of a regulated natural monopoly, like a utility company, that is regulated not only to protect consumers from monopoly pricing but also to ensure that the company can make a fair return on its investment.

FANNIE AND FREDDIE CREATE THE MODERN SECONDARY MORTGAGE MARKET

Mortgages have always been bought and sold by investors, but until relatively recently, the secondary mortgage market has been an informal arrangement. The introduction of residential mortgage-backed securities in the 1970s changed that; once mortgages are converted into residential mortgage-backed securities (RMBS), they can be easily traded on the secondary market with comparatively few transaction costs. In the simplest terms, this is how it works:

- Borrowers get mortgages from lenders in the primary market.
- Primary market lenders then sell these mortgages to secondary mortgage market firms and use the proceeds to originate more mortgages in the primary market.
- The secondary mortgage market firms then sell securities backed by the mortgages that they purchased to investors and use the proceeds of the sale to purchase more mortgages from primary market lenders.

In the late 1970s, RMBS securitization took off as traditional lenders could not keep up with the demand for home mortgages. The most important factor in the development of the modern secondary mortgage market has been the creation of Fannie and Freddie. While Fannie Mae had created a secondary market for government guaranteed and insured residential mortgage loans in the 1930s, the broad secondary market began in earnest with the chartering of Freddie Mac in 1970 and the decision to allow both GSEs to purchase and securitize conventional mortgages as well as government-insured or guaranteed mortgages.

Unlike nearly every other financial institution in the 1970s, Fannie's and Freddie's businesses were not geographically restricted, and they could develop a truly national market for mortgages. As the dominant purchasers of residential mortgages, these GSEs have effectively standardized prime residential mortgages by promulgating buying guidelines. Such standardization has led to an increase in the liquidity and attractiveness of mortgages as investments to a broad array of investors.

After Fannie and Freddie established the secondary mortgage market as a profitable enterprise, investment in RMBS exploded again as institutional investors entered the market. Starting sporadically in the late 1970s, nonfederal-related issuers, such as commercial banks and mortgage companies, began to issue RMBS. These private label RMBS are issued without the type of guarantee that Fannie or Freddie would give, and they are typically backed by subprime or jumbo loans.

THE FOUNDATION OF THE FANNIE AND FREDDIE BUSINESS MODEL IS THEIR REGULATORY PRIVILEGE

Fannie and Freddie have two primary lines of business. First, they help mortgage originators package their mortgages into RMBS by providing credit guarantees for those securities in return for a fee paid to the GSE. The credit guarantees help maintain a stable and liquid market for RMBS. Second, the two companies raise capital by issuing debt securities and use those funds to purchase mortgages and related securities. Because of the privileges provided to them as government sponsored enterprises, Fannie and Freddie have been able to profit greatly from this second line of business.

By statute, Fannie's and Freddie's operations are limited to the conforming sector of the mortgage market, which is made up of mortgages that do not exceed an annually adjusted threshold. Loans that exceed the loan amount limit in a given year are known as jumbo loans. Most of the remainder of the RMBS market belongs to private label firms that securitize jumbo mortgages and subprime mortgages that Fannie and Freddie cannot or choose not to guarantee or purchase for their own portfolio. The two companies effectively have no competition in the conforming sector of the residential mortgage market because of advantages granted to them by the federal government in their charters. The most significant of these advantages has been the federal government's implied (and, since their bailout, not-so-implied) guarantee of their debt obligations. The guarantee allowed Fannie and Freddie to borrow funds more cheaply than its fully private competitors. They then can make money on the spread between their low cost of funds and what they must pay for the mortgage-related investments in their portfolios.

FANNIE AND FREDDIE AND THE CREDIT CRISIS

Fannie and Freddie are extraordinarily large companies: together, they own or guarantee more than 40 percent of all the residential mortgages in the United States. As of early 2009, the two companies had a combined $5.36 trillion in mortgage-related obligations, which is of roughly the same magnitude as the $5.81 trillion of federal government debt held by the public at that time.

As the two companies have grown immense, numerous commentators and government officials have called for their reform. However, in combining elements of public instrumentalities and private companies, public-private hybrids like Fannie and Freddie can assert outsized influence in Washington. Fannie and Freddie's powerful lobbying forces have kept these reformers mostly at bay.

As a result, Fannie and Freddie continued to grow at a rapid rate through the early 2000s, until they were each hit by accounting scandals. In response to those scandals, Congress and the two companies' regulators began to take various steps to limit their growth. But once they stabilized in 2007, the current credit crisis commenced, and their market share began to increase once again as other lenders could not raise capital to lend to borrowers. Because of their government guarantee, Fannie and Freddie were thought to be well situated in a landscape in which other lenders began to fail and the secondary market for subprime mortgages dried up. Some prominent financial analysts suggested that Fannie and Freddie could easily ride out the turmoil in the mortgage markets. Even more, some commentators were arguing that Fannie and Freddie would be able to bail out other mortgage market players by buying additional mortgages.

As Fannie's and Freddie's star began to appear ascendant, troubling accounts of possible losses started to emerge: their underwriting models had been too optimistic and had not accounted for the possibility of severe reductions in housing prices across the nation. Furthermore, the two industry giants had much more exposure to the problems in the toxic subprime and Alt-A portions of the mortgage market than they had let on in their public disclosures. These fears were confirmed soon thereafter, as Fannie and Freddie began to report very large losses. These losses meant that Fannie and Freddie did not have the capital to expand their role in the mortgage markets and that their political star began its fall once again.

Because of their poor underwriting, the two companies started posting quarterly losses in 2007 that ran into the billions of dollars, with larger losses on the horizon. As a result, they were having trouble complying with the capital requirements set by their regulator. Their problems began to spiral out of the control along with those of the rest of the financial sector until then-Secretary of the Treasury, Henry M. Paulson Jr. asked that Congress give the Treasury the authority to take over the two companies if they were not able to meet their financial obligations. Congress, with remarkable alacrity, passed the Housing and Economic Recovery Act of 2008, which granted that power to the Treasury.

Within days of the passage of the Housing and Economic Recovery Act, Fannie and Freddie faced demands to raise more capital, pressures that they would not be able to meet. Within a few weeks, the markets were expecting the federal government to bail out the two companies. And within a couple of months, Paulson announced that he was placing the two companies in conservatorship because they were not able to raise the capital they needed to continue operating. Throughout the credit crisis, their reported losses have only continued to increase.

FANNIE AND FREDDIE ARE GENERATING A POOR RETURN ON THE NATION'S INVESTMENT

Fannie and Freddie have attempted to justify their existence by pointing to the benefits they provide to the American public, primarily: offering systemic stability and liquidity to the market, increasing the supply of affordable housing, increasing consumer protection in the residential market, and lowering the overall interest rate for homeowners.

These claims have been contradicted to a great extent, however, by independent research as well as by recent events. First, during the crisis, Fannie and Freddie provided only limited stability and liquidity before full-scale government intervention was required to bail them out. Second, while Fannie and Freddie typically do meet minimal affordable housing goals set forth by the government, a number of studies have indicated that they hit their target by cannibalizing other federal programs and are not particularly effective in this regard when compared to other financial institutions. Third, in the field of consumer protection, Fannie's and Freddie's reputations also took a blow when it became clear that, while refusing to directly securitize mortgages born of predatory lending, they readily bought up suspect subprime and Alt-A RMBS issued by other companies. Finally, Fannie's and Freddie's highly touted impact on the interest rate for homeowners amounts to a modest reduction for the typical borrower. Considering the extraordinary profits received through Fannie's and Freddie's government-granted privileges, this is not an extraordinary benefit to the average homeowner: it can be measured in the tens of dollars a month. This is particularly true when compared to the price tag for the taxpayer bailout of the two companies, which is being measured in the hundreds of billions of dollars. This has turned out to be a disastrous trade-off for the American public.

Budgetary implications of the government's guarantee provide an additional argument against Fannie's and Freddie's special relationship with the federal government. First, the cost of the government's guarantee has been hidden because it has been off-budget—if the government had to quantify and account for this contingent liability in the federal budget, it would trigger debt ceiling limits and materially reduce Congress's ability to increase net spending. Second, the cost of the guarantee is particularly difficult to quantify because it depends on the companies' ever-changing exposure to mortgage obligations. Finally, the cost of the guarantee is not capped by the federal government, given that the federal government has not imposed any meaningful limits on Fannie's or Freddie's growth.

CONCLUSION

The federal government's special treatment of Fannie and Freddie is an extraordinary regulatory privilege in terms of its absolute value, its impact on its competitors, and its cost to taxpayers. The main problem with GSEs is well-documented: they take on a life of their own and can survive well after they have achieved the purposes for which they are created. GSEs should, as a general rule, be created with a sunset clause that would ensure that they would expire once they achieve their congressionally mandated goal. Unfortunately, this is almost never done.

The typical result of poor GSE design is that the GSE ends up driving much of the legislative and regulatory agenda regarding their own fates. Fannie and Freddie reflect what is worst in GSE design. After fulfilling their purpose of creating a national mortgage market, they have taken on monstrously large lives of their own. With Fannie and Freddie, and our nation, at a crossroads, Congress should seize the opportunity to terminate their GSE privileges and convert them to fully private status. Congress should also enact appropriate financial regulation, consumer protection legislation, and affordable housing programs to fill the breach that a fully privatized Fannie and Freddie would leave behind. And Congress should remember the lessons of Fannie and Freddie when it considers using the GSE as a tool of government in the future.

ABOUT THE AUTHOR

David Reiss is a professor of law at Brooklyn Law School and has also taught at Seton Hall Law School. His research focuses on the secondary mortgage market. He was previously an associate at Paul, Weiss, Rifkind, Wharton and Garrison in its real estate department and an associate at Morrison and Foerster in its land use and environmental law group. He was also a law clerk to Judge Timothy Lewis of the United States Court of Appeals for the Third Circuit. He received his B.A. from Williams College and his J.D. from the New York University School of Law. His article, "Subprime Standardization: How Rating Agencies Allow Predatory Lending to Flourish in the Secondary Mortgage Market" in the *Florida State University Law Review*, was granted an award as the best article of 2006 by the American College of Consumer Financial Services Lawyers.

CHAPTER 55

Disclosure's Failure in the Subprime Mortgage Crisis

STEVEN L. SCHWARCZ
Stanley A. Star Professor of Law and Business at Duke University and Founding
Director of Duke's Global Capital Markets Center*

INTRODUCTION

In a separate chapter, I examined financial market anomalies and obvious market
protections that failed, seeking insight into the subprime mortgage crisis. The crisis,
I argued, can be attributed in large part to three causes: conflicts, complacency, and
complexity. This article focuses on the third cause—complexity—and, in particular,
on complexity's undermining of the disclosure paradigm of securities law, causing
investors such as commercial and investment banks to lose many billions of dollars
on securities backed by subprime mortgages.

Most, if not all, of the risks giving rise to the collapse of the market for securities backed by subprime mortgages were disclosed. However the securities were
so complex that the disclosure document, or prospectus, in a typical offering of
these securities was hundreds of pages long. As a result, disclosure failed; many
investors bought the securities substantially based on their ratings, without fully
understanding what they bought.

To understand this failure, one must understand some basic industry
terminology.

---

*This chapter is based on "Disclosure's Failure in the Subprime Mortgage Crisis," *Utah L.
Rev.* (2008): 1109 (symposium issue on the subprime mortgage meltdown), also available at
http://ssrn.com/abstract_id=1113034.

Steven L. Schwarcz is the author of numerous articles and papers on the subprime financial
crisis and systemic risk and has also testified before the Committee on Financial Services of
the U.S. House of Representatives on "Systemic Risk: Examining Regulators' Ability to Respond to Threats to the Financial System," available at www.house.gov/apps/list/hearing/
financialsvcs_dem/ht1002072.shtml.

TERMINOLOGY

The issuance of securities backed by subprime mortgages constitutes a form of securitization. In a securitization transaction, rights to payment from income-producing financial assets—in our case, subprime mortgage loans—are transferred to a special purpose vehicle, or SPV (sometimes called a special purpose entity, or SPE). The SPV, directly or indirectly, issues securities to capital market investors and uses the proceeds to pay for the mortgage loans. The investors, who are repaid from collections of the mortgage loans, buy the securities based on their assessments of the value of those loans.

In the securitizations involving subprime mortgages, the companies originating the mortgage loans were almost always different from the companies that (after purchasing those loans) created, and transferred those loans to, the SPVs. For discussion purposes, this chapter refers to all of these companies collectively as *originators*, in contrast to *investors* who buy the securities issued by the SPVs.

Actual securitization transactions are extremely complex and often rely on multiple SPVs. Furthermore, in order to integrate disparate disciplines such as bankruptcy, tax, securities law, commercial law, accounting, and finance, securitization transactions often appear to be highly convoluted.

The securities issued in securitization transactions add to the complexity. Securities backed directly or indirectly by subprime mortgages are customarily categorized as MBS, CDO, or ABS CDO securities. MBS means mortgage-backed securities, or securities whose payment derives principally or entirely from mortgage loans owned by the SPV. CDO, or collateralized debt obligation, securities are backed by—and thus their payment derives principally or entirely from—a mixed pool of mortgage loans and other income-generating assets owned by an SPV. ABS CDO securities, in contrast, are backed by a mixed pool of MBS and other asset-backed securities owned by the SPV, and thus their payment derives principally or entirely from the underlying mortgage loans and/or other assets ultimately backing those securities.

The classes, or tranches, of MBS, CDO, and ABS CDO securities issued in these securitization transactions are typically ranked by seniority of payment priority. The highest priority class is called senior securities. In MBS transactions, lower priority classes are called subordinated, or junior, securities. In CDO and ABS CDO transactions, lower priority classes are usually called *mezzanine securities*—with the lowest priority class, which has a residual claim against the SPV, being called the *equity*.

The senior and many of the subordinated classes of these securities are more highly rated than the quality of the underlying mortgage loans. For example, senior securities issued in a CDO transaction are usually rated AAA even if the underlying income-generating assets consist of subprime mortgages, and senior securities issued in an ABS CDO transaction are usually rated AAA even if none of the MBS (or other) securities supporting the transaction are rated that high. This is accomplished by allocating cash collections first to pay the senior classes and thereafter to pay more junior classes. In this way, the senior classes are highly overcollateralized to take into account the possibility, indeed likelihood, of delays and losses on collection.

Before engaging in the analysis, below, it is helpful to distinguish the scope of this chapter from that of an earlier chapter examining disclosure's insufficiency in the face of complexity.[1] The earlier chapter examined disclosure's insufficiency from the standpoint of investors in an originator's securities, such as shares of stock. In contrast, this chapter examines disclosure's insufficiency from the standpoint of investors in an SPV's securitized securities. These different focuses lead to different potential solutions. For example, the earlier chapter proposes, as a partial solution to disclosure's insufficiency, that originators should mitigate any material conflicts of interest that create the risk that their management will structure transactions contrary to the interests of investors, at least in those transactions for which disclosure may be insufficient. The reasoning of that chapter is that, absent conflicts, investors should be able to rely on the business judgment of the originator's management, which has a fiduciary duty to those investors, in setting up securitization transactions for the originator's benefit. That solution is inapplicable to this chapter, however, because originators have no such duty to investors in an SPV's securities.

ANALYSIS

Disclosure's Insufficiency

In the subprime mortgage crisis, there has been relatively little dispute that the disclosure documents describing the MBS, CDO, and ABS CDO securities and their risks generally complied with the federal securities laws. The disclosures, however, turned out to be insufficient, cutting into the very heart of federal securities regulation, whose central focus is on full disclosure. The rationale for this focus is that investors are adequately protected if all relevant aspects of the securities being marketed are fully and fairly disclosed. The reasoning is that full disclosure provides investors with sufficient opportunity to evaluate the merits of an investment and to fend for themselves. It is a basic tenet of federal securities regulation that investors' ability to make their own evaluations of available investments obviates any need that some observers may perceive for the more costly and time-consuming governmental merit analysis of the securities being offered.[2]

There are two levels of reasoning that explain the insufficiency of disclosure in the subprime crisis. On an institutional level (most investors in MBS, CDO, and ABS CDO securities being institutional investors), some investors simply may not have the staffing to evaluate complex securitization transactions. This begs the question of whether institutional investors will hire securitization experts as needed to decipher complex deals. The evidence suggests they do not always do so, and theory explains why. Although experts may be hired to the extent that their costs do not exceed the benefits gained from more fully understanding the complexity, at some level of complexity those costs will exceed, *or at least appear to exceed,* any potential gain. This is because the cost of hiring experts is tangible, whereas the benefit gained from fully understanding complex transactions is intangible and harder to quantify. Managers attempting a cost-benefit analysis may well give greater weight to the tangible cost and less credence to any intangible benefit. The more complex the transaction, the higher the costs, and thus the more likely it is that the cost-benefit balance will be out of equilibrium.

The second level of reasoning goes to agency costs stemming from a conflict between the interests of individual employees and the institutions for which they work. In assessing the investment-worthiness of highly complex MBS, CDO, and ABS CDO securities, individuals sometimes take a shortcut, overrelying on the idea that these securities may be rated "investment grade" by rating agencies such as Standard & Poor's and Moody's and not spending the time and effort needed to fully understand the hundreds of pages of disclosure for each investment. Overreliance on ratings appears to have been endemic in the subprime mortgage crisis.[3]

This overreliance is not surprising, particularly when these types of investment securities are generally accepted in the marketplace, as were securities backed by subprime mortgages before the meltdown. Professors Healy and Palepu have found, for example, that investment fund managers who, believing a stock is overvalued, nonetheless follow the crowd, will not be blamed if the stock ultimately crashes.[4] Moreover, the very complexity of securities backed by subprime mortgages makes it difficult to assess their suitability for investment, potentially seducing individuals into seeing what they are already inclined to believe—that these securities are creditworthy.

For these reasons, disclosure of the subprime mortgage securitizations, and by analogy of other complex financing transactions, has inherent limitations.

Addressing Disclosure's Insufficiency
There are at least three ways to respond to disclosure's insufficiency: to tolerate insufficient disclosure, to proscribe transactions for which disclosure is insufficient, and to require supplemental protections to minimize disclosure's insufficiencies. This chapter next examines each of these possible responses.

Tolerating Insufficient Disclosure

Under this response, disclosure would remain the sole paradigm for remedying the information asymmetry between originators and investors. This has been the historical response to complexity since, in an efficient market, it has been believed that stock prices virtually instantaneously reflect all publicly available information relevant to the value of traded stocks. But complex securitization transactions can undermine this result—as the subprime mortgage crisis has well illustrated—because many securitization deals are *sui generis*, obviating creation of a thickly efficient market. Thus, Professors Gilson and Kraakman observe that an innovative investment contract, for example, would take the market more time to understand and reach price equilibration than, say, a change in Federal Reserve Board policy.[5] Furthermore, the efficient market hypothesis might not even apply to debt markets and certainly should not apply to private debt markets. The securities issued in securitization transactions are virtually always debt securities, and many CDO and ABS CDO securities were issued in private placements. It does not even appear that ABS CDO securities always had a secondary market for trading.

The other possible argument for tolerating insufficient disclosure is that—at least after the subprime mortgage crisis—originators engaging in complex transactions may find their share price discounted by investors. This is not, however, a long-term solution because investors have short memories. Once past financial crises recede in memory and investors are making money, investors always "go for the gold." Furthermore, discounting share price based on complexity per se is inefficient since complexity is sometimes justified. When investors do not, or cannot, differentiate between justifiable and fraudulent or excessive complexity, the market will discount in both cases—thereby driving out otherwise beneficial complexity.

For these reasons, it would be inexpedient to continue to tolerate disclosure as the sole paradigm for remedying the information asymmetry between originators and investors. The converse proposition, proscribing transactions for which disclosure would be insufficient, is equally problematic, as discussed next.

Proscribing Transactions for Which Disclosure Would Be Insufficient

If government proscribed or banned transactions for which the information asymmetry exceeds certain bounds, the most immediate consequence potentially would be to eliminate many, if not most, securitization transactions. From a societal standpoint, that result would be unfortunate. Securitization transactions are widely used and accepted in the United States: "Often, these transactions are efficient means of obtaining funding for their participants while simultaneously achieving accounting, tax and regulatory benefits of various types.... [They] reflect the innovation for which the U.S. capital markets are known[,] . . . have many legitimate uses and comprise a significant part of our capital markets."[6]

Indeed, securitization transactions are normally viewed as socially desirable. There is even evidence that, despite the subprime mortgage crisis, securitization has still created overall value in the financial markets.[7]

Another reason that government should not want to proscribe transactions as a means of controlling information asymmetry is that any such proscriptions could create regulatory arbitrage incentives: parties would want to make transactions appear to meet the regulatory requirements. For example, if government were to proscribe transactions for which the information asymmetry exceeded a threshold level, then parties would attempt to structure those transactions in ways that appear to reduce the asymmetry, as measured by the regulatory ban, below that threshold. The end result could be socially undesirable: the regulatory proscription is effectively bypassed, but the overall transaction costs rise because of the expenses of lawyers and other advisers hired for that purpose.

For these reasons, regulators should not want to proscribe securitization transactions as a means of controlling disclosure's limitations.

Requiring Supplemental Protections

The third possible response is to consider whether disclosure can be buttressed by cost-effective, supplemental protections that minimize information asymmetry or mitigate its consequences. Any such supplemental protections would be *in addition to*, not in place of, disclosure since even insufficient disclosure provides value by reducing information asymmetry, and disclosure has other justifications beyond the asymmetric information problem.

In thinking about supplemental protections, it is useful to take into account economic theory on asymmetric information, especially that dealing with the so-called lemons problem. Economists have asked. How do transactions ever occur if the seller has more information than the buyer, and the information disparity cannot be cured (at least at reasonable cost)? Why would a buyer ever be willing to enter into such a transaction? These same questions pertain to the problem of disclosure in the face of complexity.

The lemons problem was introduced and first systematically studied by using the crude but intuitive example of the used-car market.[8] One obvious solution is for the seller to make guarantees, such as warranties on the sale of goods, to shift the risk from the buyer to the seller. Other potential solutions include governmental and private sector certification of quality.

Guarantees. In a securitization context, guarantees would likely take some form of investor recourse to originators, including perhaps a put of securities back to the investment banks structuring the transactions or requiring these investment banks to retain at least a portion of the lowest-ranked tranche of securities being sold. Requiring originators to take a reasonable first-loss position generally makes sense and is typically mandated by investors in securitizations of nonmortgage assets. Subject to the caveat discussed further on, investors should consider extending this mandate to securitizations of mortgage loans.

At least in the subprime mortgage crisis, however, this actually backfired. In ABS CDO transactions, investment bankers customarily purchased some portion of the equity tranches so as to demonstrate their belief in the securities being sold. This induced many investors who otherwise might not have done so to purchase these securities, thereby working against investor caution.

This incongruity raises an important point about complexity, that sometimes things are so complex that the problem is not merely information asymmetry but a mutual information failure—in our case, on the part of originators as well as investors. Thus, "[e]ven the people running Wall Street firms didn't really [always] understand what they were buying and selling."[9]

Certification of Quality. Another approach to protecting a buyer of securities is certification of their quality by either the government or reputable private sector entities. Governmental certification is a form of merit regulation, and can be expensive. In the context of the original enactment of the federal securities laws, it was explicitly rejected as unworkable. There is little current literature on government certification of securities quality because, until recently, disclosure was seen as the complete answer.

Should we now reconsider some form of substantive governmental merit regulation? Such merit regulation would, by definition, rely on government employees to assess the quality of securities. It is doubtful that government employees would do a better job than private sector analysts, who already perform this function for investors. The private sector analysts are likely to be more capable, on average, and also more accountable, because the government generally pays lower salaries than the private sector and government employees are often harder to fire if they perform poorly. Furthermore, the imposition of governmental merit regulation could perversely undermine the market for private securities analysts, thereby eliminating any reduced information asymmetry resulting from their analysis.

Private sector certification of quality, in contrast, already exists in the form of rating agencies (which are private companies notwithstanding the "agency" moniker), which rate debt securities based on their likelihood of timely payment.

Rating agencies, however, have not always proved effective in the face of complexity. It is even being argued that rating agencies contributed to the subprime mortgage meltdown by failing to downgrade, on a timely basis, securities backed by subprime mortgages. Although rating agencies are now attempting to improve their credit rating capabilities, it is too soon to predict the outcome. It is, however, important to strive to improve these capabilities because rating agencies constitute a public good, creating an economy of scale to help individual investors assess the creditworthiness of complex securities.

Certification of the quality of securities, especially by private parties, therefore can help but may not fully solve the asymmetric information problem. And in cases in which there is not merely information asymmetry between originators and investors but also information failure on the part of originators, certification by originators can actually mislead investors.

CONCLUSION

As complexity increases, the disclosure paradigm of securities law has been diminishing in effectiveness. This chapter suggests possible responses. For example, investors could require originators to take a reasonable first-loss position, although this backfired in the subprime mortgage crisis because of information failure by originators. Institutional investors should also try to reduce agency costs stemming from the conflict between the interests of individuals and the institutions for which they work. And rating agencies should try, as they now appear to be doing, to increase the quality of their private certification, through ratings, of securities.

These are, admittedly, only second-best solutions, but there do not appear to be any perfect solutions. Government already takes a somewhat paternalistic stance to mitigate disclosure's inadequacy by mandating minimum investor sophistication for investing in complex securities, yet sophisticated investors and qualified institutional buyers (QIBs) are the very investors who lost the most money in the subprime financial crisis. And any attempt by government to restrict firms from engaging in complex transactions would be highly risky because of the potential of inadvertently banning beneficial transactions.

There is, finally, another way that disclosure failed in the subprime mortgage crisis. Because the motivation of market participants is to protect themselves but not the financial system as a whole, I have argued that disclosure alone will be inadequate to prevent a systemic collapse of the financial system. Investors are simply unlikely to care about disclosure to the extent that it pertains to this systemic risk. The remedy for disclosure's failure, in this case, is to separately deter a systemic collapse.[10]

NOTES

1. That earlier article was Steven L. Schwarcz, "Rethinking the Disclosure Paradigm in a World of Complexity," *Univ. of Ill. L. Rev.* (2004): 1.

2. Thomas Lee Hazen, "The Law of Securities Regulation" §1.2[3][A], 5th ed. (2005): 28.

3. See Steven L. Schwarcz, "Conflicts and Financial Collapse: The Problem of Secondary-Management Agency Costs," *Yale Journal on Regulation* (2009).

4. Paul M. Healy and Krishna Palepu, "Governance and Intermediation Problems in Capital Markets: Evidence from the Fall of Enron," *Journal of Economic Perspectives* 17 (2003).

5. Ronald J. Gilson and Reinier H. Kraakman, "The Mechanisms of Market Efficiency," *Va. L. Rev.* 70 (1984): 549, 568, 585, 615–616.

6. *In re* Enron Corp., No. 01-16034 (AJG) (Bankr. S.D.N.Y. September 21, 2002). First Interim Report of Neal Batson, Court-Appointed Examiner, 22 (noting, for example, that "total outstanding mortgage-backed and asset-backed securities in the United States alone exceed $6 trillion"), available at www.enron.com/corp/por/pdfs/InterimReport1ofExaminer.pdf.

7. Xudong An, Yongheng Deng, and Stuart A. Gabriel, "Value Creation through Securitization: Evidence from the CMBS Market," February 18, 2008, 3 (SSRN working paper 1095645).

8. George A. Akerlof, "The Market for 'Lemons': Quality Uncertainty and the Market Mechanism," *Quarterly Journal of Economics* 84 (1970): 488.

9. Nelson D. Schwartz and Julie Creswell, "What Created This Monster?" *New York Times*, March 23, 2008, BU 1, BU 8 (quoting Byron Wien, chief investment strategist, Pequot Capital).

10. Steven L. Schwarcz, "Systemic Risk," *Geo. L. J.* 97 (Nov. 2008): 193.

ABOUT THE AUTHOR

Steven L. Schwarcz is the Stanley A. Star professor of law and business at Duke University and founding director of Duke's Global Capital Markets Center. Before joining Duke, he was a partner at two leading international law firms and also taught at the Yale and Columbia Law Schools. Schwarcz has advised the United States Congress and other government bodies on systemic risk and the recent financial crisis. His scholarly works include "Systemic Risk," *Geo. L. J.* 97 (2008): 193; "Protecting Financial Markets: Lessons from the Subprime Mortgage Meltdown," *Minn. L. Rev.* 93 (2008): 373; "Disclosure's Failure in the Subprime Mortgage Crisis," *Utah. L. Rev.* (2008): 1109; "Understanding the Subprime Financial Crisis," *S. C. L. Rev.* 60 (2009): 549; "Conflicts and Financial Collapse: The Problem of Secondary-Management Agency Costs," *Yale J. on Reg.* 26 (Summer 2009); "Too Big To Fail? Recasting the Financial Safety Net," in *The Panic of 2008* (Geo. Wash. Univ. symposium book); "Regulating Complexity in Financial Markets," *Wash. U. L. Rev.* 87 (2010); and *Regulating Financial Systems,* forthcoming from Oxford University Press (co-authored with Kenneth Anderson).

PART VIII

The Federal Reserve, Monetary Policy, and the Financial Crisis

CHAPTER 56

Federal Reserve Policy and the Housing Bubble

LAWRENCE H. WHITE
Mercatus Professor of Economics, George Mason University

T he U.S. housing boom of 2002–2007 and the fallout from the bust are not the results of a laissez-faire monetary and financial system. They happened in an unanchored government fiat monetary system with a heavily restricted financial system.

WHAT HAPPENED AND WHY

The seeds of financial turmoil were sewn by unusual monetary policy moves by the Federal Reserve System and novel federal regulatory interventions. Poorly chosen policies distorted interest rates and asset prices, diverted loanable funds into the wrong investments, and twisted normally robust financial institutions into unsustainable positions. There is no doubt that private miscalculation and imprudence have made matters worse for more than a few institutions. Such mistakes help to explain which particular firms have run into the most trouble. But to explain *industrywide* errors, we need to identify price and incentive distortions capable of having industrywide effects.

I focus here on the Federal Reserve policy that provided the means for unsustainable housing prices and unsustainable mortgage financing. I leave it to other contributors to detail the growth in regulatory mandates and subsidies to write riskier mortgages, most importantly HUD's imposition of affordable housing mandates on Fannie Mae and Freddie Mac that accelerated the creation and securitization of subprime mortgages, and the ways in which the Basel II capital requirements rendered bank balance sheets less informative.

THE CREDIT SUPPLY BUBBLE

Some authors, considering the relationship of Federal Reserve policy to asset price bubbles,[1] ask only: Should the Fed actively try to identify and burst growing bubbles? If so, how? As posed, their questions suggest that asset price bubbles arise independent of monetary policy, and that the only Fed role to be discussed is that of bubble-buster. A more important pair of questions is: Does Fed policy as currently conducted tend to *inflate* asset price bubbles? If so, how can we reformulate policy to avoid that tendency? Call our objective a noneffervescent, or flat, monetary policy. The economics profession has not reached a consensus on what the *optimally flat* or nonbubble-prone monetary policy is, but it is now widely agreed that it *isn't* holding interest rates too low for too long. It should also now be clear that a Fed policy of deliberately ignoring feedback from asset prices, as though excessive Fed expansion shows up only in the behavior of consumer prices, is also not the way to avoid asset bubbles.

In the recession of 2001, the Federal Reserve System under Chairman Alan Greenspan began aggressively expanding the U.S. money supply. Year-over-year growth in the M-2 monetary aggregate rose briefly above 10 percent, and remained above 8 percent entering the second half of 2003. The expansion went hand in hand with the Fed's repeatedly lowering its target for the federal funds (interbank overnight) interest rate. The federal funds rate began 2001 at 6.25 percent and ended the year at 1.75 percent. The Greenspan Fed reduced the rate further in 2002 and 2003, pushing it in mid-2003 to a record low of 1 percent, where it stayed for a year. Short-term interest rates were negative—meaning that nominal rates were lower than the contemporary rate of inflation—for an unprecedented two and a half years. In purchasing power terms, a borrower during that period who merely bought and held nonperishable goods with negligible storage costs (like land) whose prices merely rose at the rate of inflation, was profiting in proportion to what he borrowed.

How do we judge whether the Fed expanded more than it should have? One venerable (albeit no longer popular) norm for making fiat central bank policy as neutral as possible toward the financial market is to aim for constancy (zero growth) in the volume of nominal expenditure. In the equation of exchange, $MV = Py$, nominal expenditure is MV. Constancy of MV implies that the Fed should allow consumer goods prices to fall when productivity gains reduce the costs of production.[2] Second-best to constancy of MV would be growth at a low and constant rate. One useful measure of nominal expenditure is the dollar volume of final sales of goods and services (GDP minus change in business inventories). From mid-2003 to mid-2007, the dollar volume of final sales of goods and services grew at an annually compounded rate of 5.9 percent, higher than in most of the Greenspan era.

A widely used norm for Fed policy is the Taylor Rule, a formula devised by economist John Taylor of Stanford University. The Taylor Rule estimates the level of the federal funds rate that would be consistent (conditional on current inflation and real income) with keeping the economy's price inflation rate to a chosen target rate. Exhibit 56.1, from the Federal Reserve Bank of St. Louis, shows that from early 2001 until late 2006 the Fed kept the federal funds rate on a path well below the estimated rate that would have been consistent with targeting a 2 percent inflation rate (the highest rate within the Bernanke Fed's declared "comfort zone").[3] *A fortiori* the Fed held the actual rate even further below the path consistent targeting stability in nominal income. The diagram shows that the Taylor Rule gap was especially large—200 basis point or more—from mid-2003 to mid-2005.

Alan Greenspan has pleaded innocent to the charge of having overexpanded and creating a credit bubble, on the grounds that the housing price bubble was worldwide, meaning the growth of U.S. credit must have reflected a global savings glut, and the monetary base and M2 weren't growing rapidly. There appears to be a

Federal Funds Rate and Inflation Targets

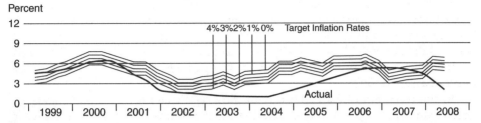

Exhibit 56.1 The Fed Kept Interest Rates Too Low for Too Long
Calculated federal funds rate is based on Taylor's rule.
Source: Federal Reserve Bank of St. Louis *Monetary Trends* (November 2008).

grain of truth to the hypothesis that growth in the global supply of loanable funds to the U.S. market pushed down U.S. real interest rates. Real 30-year mortgage rates in the United States, largely beyond the influence of Federal Reserve policy, did fall. Nominal 30-year rates fell by 113 basis points between 2001 and 2004 while the inflation rate fell only 15 basis points. As noted earlier, however, the Fed lowered the federal funds rate much more, by 525 basis points, indicating a major amplification of cheap credit by Fed policy. M-2 growth, as noted earlier, in fact remained unusually high for at least two years.

The Fed's policy of lowering short-term interest rates not only fueled growth in the dollar volume of mortgage lending, but had unintended consequences for the *type* of mortgages written. By pushing very-short-term interest rates down so dramatically between 2001 and 2004, the Fed lowered short-term rates relative to 30-year rates. Adjustable-rate mortgages (ARMs), typically based on a one-year interest rate, became increasingly cheap relative to 30-year fixed-rate mortgages. Back in 2001, nonteaser ARM rates on average were 113 basis points cheaper than 30-year-fixed mortgage rates (5.84 percent versus 6.97 percent). By 2004, as a result of the ultra-low federal funds rate, the gap had grown to 194 basis points (3.90 percent versus 5.84 percent).[4] Not surprisingly, increasing numbers of new mortgage borrowers were drawn away from mortgages with 30-year fixed rates into one-year ARMs. The share of new mortgages with adjustable rates, only one-fifth in 2001, had more than doubled by 2004. An adjustable-rate mortgage shifts the risk of a rise in interest rates from the lender to the borrower. Many borrowers who took out ARMs implicitly (and imprudently) relied on the Fed to keep short-term rates low for as long as they kept the mortgage. As a group, they began defaulting at an unusually high rate as their monthly payments reset upward in 2006 and 2007. The shift toward ARMs compounded the mortgage-quality problems arising from other sources such as regulatory mandates (see Exhibit 56.2).

Because real estate is an especially long-lived asset, its market value is especially boosted by a lowering of interest rates. This effect, combined with regulatory mandates and subsidies for expanded home ownership, drew the Fed's demand bubble heavily into real estate. As reflected in Exhibit 56.2, real estate loans at commercial banks grew at a 12.26 percent compound annual rate during the period from the midpoint of 2003 to the midpoint of 2007.[5] The Fed-fueled low interest rates and growth of mortgage credit pushed up the demand for and prices of

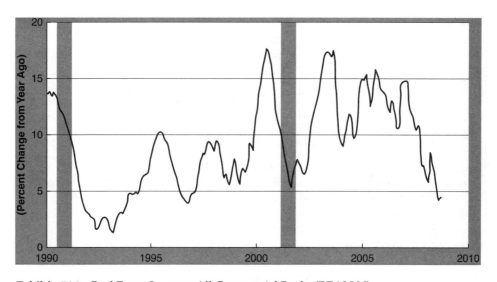

Exhibit 56.2   Real Estate Loans at All Commercial Banks (REALLN)
Shaded areas indicate U.S. recessions as determined by the NBER.
Source: Board of Governors of the Federal Reserve System; 2008 Federal Reserve Bank of St. Louis,
research.stlouisfed.org.

existing houses, and encouraged the construction of new housing on undeveloped land. Housing, land, and other assets, rather than goods in the consumer price index, exhibited the price inflation predicted by the Taylor Rule gap.

Researchers at the International Monetary Fund have provided evidence from simulation studies corroborating the view that the Fed's easy credit policy inflated the housing bubble. As they put in their findings, "The unusually low level of interest rates in the United States between 2001 and 2003 contributed somewhat to the elevated rate of expansion in the housing market, in terms of both housing investment and the run-up in house prices up to mid-2005." After estimating the sensitivity of U.S. house prices and residential investment to interest rates, they find that "the increase in house prices and residential investment in the United States over the past six years would have been much more contained had short-term interest rates remained unchanged."[6] Even Alan Greenspan has acknowledged that "the one percent rate set in mid-2003 . . . lowered interest rates on adjustable-rate mortgages (ARMs) and may have contributed to the rise in U.S. home prices."[7]

The excess investment in new housing has left the United States today with an overbuilt housing stock. Assuming that the federal government does not follow proposals (tongue-in-cheek or otherwise) that it should buy up and then raze excess houses and condos, or proposals to admit a large number of new immigrants, we can expect U.S. house prices and construction activity to remain depressed for several years. The process of adjustment, well underway, requires house prices to fall and resources (labor and capital) to be released from the construction industry to find more appropriate employment elsewhere. Correspondingly, it requires the book value of existing financial assets based directly or indirectly on housing to be written down, and resources to be released from writing and trading mortgage products to find more appropriate employment elsewhere. No matter how painful the adjustment process, delaying it only delays the economy's recovery. Going forward, barring more fundamental reform of the monetary regime, a monetary policy rule that incorporates asset prices in its measure of inflation may offer the best prospects for reduced asset froth.

THE FEDERAL RESERVE'S NEW POST-BUBBLE ROLES

Before 2008, the Federal Reserve System played the traditional central banking roles of conducting monetary policy and (on very rare occasions, like September 12, 2001) acting as a lender of last resort. Monetary policy means controlling the quantity of money in pursuit of economic objectives. Acting as a lender of last resort is an aspect of monetary policy: It means injecting reserves into the commercial banking system to prevent the quantity of money from contracting when there is an internal drain of reserves (bank runs and the hoarding of cash). The lender part of the role's name has long been an anachronism. Central banks in developed financial markets discovered decades ago that they can inject bank reserves without lending, by purchasing government securities in the open market. By purchasing government securities, the central bank supports the money stock while avoiding the dangers of nonmarket credit allocation (and the potential for cronyism) associated with making loans to specific banks on noncompetitive terms or in purchasing private securities.[8]

Federal Reserve policy has traditionally controlled growth in monetary and credit aggregates through such open market operations, varying the federal funds interest rate as an intermediate target for guiding open market operations. Growth in the monetary aggregate that the Fed directly controls, the monetary base, was matched almost exactly by the Fed's accumulation of U.S. Treasury securities, virtually the only financial asset the Fed acquired. Before 2008, the quantity of loans that the Fed made to commercial banks was trivial (less than $300 million on a balance sheet of $800 billion at the end of 2007). Loans to nonbank institutions were out of the question.

In 2008, things changed remarkably—and in a worrisome way. In addition to conducting monetary policy, the Fed took on the new role of *selectively channeling credit in favored directions*. It now makes loans to an array of financial institutions that are not commercial banks.

The Federal Reserve's new interventions into financial markets have proceeded at its own initiative, without precedent, and without congressional oversight. None of the new lending facilities has anything to do with acting as a lender of last resort in the traditional sense. Through all the recent turmoil, there has been no threat of a shrinking money stock. There was only a single run on a commercial bank, the insolvent IndyMac, to which the Fed lending properly did *not* go. Investment banks do not issue checking deposits, are therefore not subject to depositor runs, and are not part of the payment system. Neither are securities dealers. The Fed's expansions of its own activities therefore had nothing to do with protecting the payment system or stabilizing the money supply. The Fed did not need to go beyond open market operations to counteract the money stock reducing effect of higher bank reserve holdings.

The Fed's new activities seem instead to aim at protecting banks and nonbanks from the consequences of holding portfolios overweighted with mortgage-backed securities, or derivatives based on such securities, while keeping levels of capital inadequate for such portfolios. It is a bailout program. Conducting such a bailout is a worrisome role for the Fed to take on, especially at its own initiative, without oversight. That the Fed's bailout program is self-financed does not mean that it provides a free lunch. It is ultimately financed by the Fed's power to levy an implicit tax on dollar holders, putting us all at risk of an inflationary depreciation of the dollar. Because it did not require an appropriation from Congress, the Fed's bailout efforts enjoyed the nearly complete freedom from oversight that Secretary Paulson unsuccessfully sought for the Treasury's bailout. That should change. The claimed threat of a financial meltdown should not be the occasion for a constitutional meltdown. It is time for a public debate on the wisdom of the Fed's remarkable departure from its traditional roles.

NOTES

1. I use the term *bubble* in the popular sense of an unsustainable expansion, not in the technical sense of a path driven by nonfundamentals.

2. George Selgin, *Less Than Zero: The Case for a Falling Price Level in a Growing Economy* (London: Institute of Economic Affairs, 1997).

3. Diagram from Federal Reserve Bank of St. Louis *Monetary Trends* (November 2008), 10. The Taylor Rule formula used in the diagram is spelled out there on page 19. Its inflation measure is the Fed's currently preferred measure, the Personal Consumption Expenditure Deflator. The Fed's deviation from the Taylor Rule has been noted by John Taylor, "Housing and Monetary Policy," in Federal Reserve Bank of Kansas City, *Housing, Housing Finance, and Monetary Policy* (2007 Jackson Hole Symposium), www.kc.frb.org/PUBLICAT/SYMPOS/2007/PDF/Taylor_0415.pdf.

4. As reported by Freddie Mac: www.freddiemac.com/pmms/pmms30.htm.

5. Federal Reserve Bank of St. Louis FRED database, series REALLN. http://research.stlouisfed.org/fred2/series/REALLN?cid=100. My thanks to George Selgin for drawing my attention to this series.

6. Roberto Cardarelli et al., "The Changing Housing Cycle and the Implications for Monetary Policy," in *World Economic Outlook: Housing and the Business Cycle* (April 2008), ch. 3, pp. 19 and 21 (caption to Figure 3.12). John Taylor's paper, cited earlier, arrives at similar findings after running slightly different counterfactual simulations.

7. Alan Greenspan, "The Roots of the Mortgage Crisis," *Wall Street Journal*, December 12, 2007, www.opinionjournal.com/editorial/feature.html?id=110010981.

8. Marvin Goodfriend and Robert G. King, "Financial Deregulation, Monetary Policy, and Central Banking," in *Restructuring Banking and Financial Services in America*, eds. William S. Haraf and Rose Kushmeider (Washington: American Enterprise Institute, 1988).

ABOUT THE AUTHOR

Lawrence H. White is a professor of economics at George Mason University, specializing in the theory and history of monetary regimes. He has previously taught at the University of Missouri in St. Louis, the University of Georgia, and New York University. He is the author of *The Theory of Monetary Institutions* (1999), *Free Banking in Britain* (2nd revised ed., 1995), and *Competition and Currency* (1989), and is the editor of several books. His articles have appeared in the *American Economic Review,* the *Journal of Money, Credit, and Banking,* and other leading professional journals. He is currently writing a book on the great economic policy debates and experiments of the last 100 years.

CHAPTER 57

The Greenspan and Bernanke Federal Reserve Roles in the Financial Crisis

JOHN RYAN

Professor, Center for Economic Policy Analysis, University of Venice, Italy

INTRODUCTION

The terrorist attacks of September 11th, 2001, on New York City and Washington D.C., were immediately detrimental to the U.S. economy. For example, when the New York Stock Exchange reopened on September 17th, the market fell 684.81 points, and by September 21st had fallen to a level of 8,235.81, compared to 9,605.51 a mere 11 days earlier on September 10th.[1] In New York City alone, physical, economic, and psychological damage estimates range into the hundreds of billions. The tragic loss of life left an indelible mark on American society, and the new psychological vulnerability of the nation's financial heart left consumers and producers alike uncertain of both the near- and long-term future. The "[American] economy's success is tied to confidence,"[2] so consequently the Federal Reserve acted to eliminate uncertainty and create a new sense of confidence in the economy's psyche.

In the days following the terrorist attacks, the Federal Reserve injected $45 billion in emergency funds into the economy.[3] The logic behind this was to counteract the natural fear of spending consumers and businesses would exhibit after a destructive shock to the economy. Before the terrorist attacks, the Fed had already cut interest rates seven times during 2001 in response to the earlier bursting of the Internet bubble and various other factors.

The official recession of the American economy had actually begun in March 2001 and lasted only one quarter—the fourth quarter of 2001 (after the terrorist attacks) actually displayed a 1.4 percent growth rate.[4] However, interest rates continued to plummet up through 2004—down to an absolute low of 1 percent. While this is a tactic meant to keep spending up, there are negatives worth mentioning. Savings accounts, especially for retirees and baby boomers, returned very little. Consumers accumulated a high public debt on credit cards and mortgages, and the federal government became more reliant on foreign capital because of a growing trade and budget deficit. Only in late 2004 did the Fed begin to raise interest rates again, up to 2.25 percent by the end of that year.[5] Raising interest rates increases savings returns but also premiums on mortgage, loan, and credit payments.

GREENSPAN'S LEGACY

As the post–September 11th actions of Greenspan's Federal Reserve show, however, excessive low interest can fuel too much spending, high consumer debt, low savings, and now combined with a declining dollar and the subprime crisis, have a serious consequence—namely stagflation.[6]

Overall, the Federal Reserve did a reasonable job of sustaining the U.S. economy after September 11th. Indeed, the purpose of the Federal Reserve is not necessarily to prevent cyclical downturns, but to shield the U.S. economy from sinking too far into the depths of cycles or, conversely, overheating to the point of excessive inflation. The Federal Reserve can also not be blamed for the escalating trade deficit that the federal government accrues by pursuing foreign military operations—it simply must take that into account when fine-tuning the economy. Perhaps more important than measured steps to preserve the U.S. economy would be to end the growing deficits and create a sense of balance in budgetary and trade matters. In the end, the Federal Reserve's actions on interest rates have both positive and negative effects—both micro and macro issues must be included when formulating policy to achieve success in the U.S. economy.

The Fed is one of the most prestigious institutions in the world. In fact, it is not by pure accident that after the terrorist attack on the World Trade Center in September 2001, an institution like the Fed, within a few hours of the attack, can make the following announcement: "The Federal Reserve System is open and operating."[7] This message of the Fed to the financial system as a whole was clear: "We are here," and has been directly translated into real actions. The Fed provided $45 billion to banks through the discount window, 200 times more than the amount provided the week before.

Greenspan's Fed was to hold rates at 1 percent from 2003 to June 2004, long after the dot-com bubble was over. It is clear that monetary policy was too accommodative. Rates of 1 percent were bound to encourage all kinds of risky behavior. Greenspan's book[8] tried to clear his name by blaming the bubble on an Asian savings glut, which purportedly created stimulus beyond the control of the Fed by driving down global bond rates.

The Federal Reserve and Greenspan's[9] leadership of it, however, does bear part of the blame for the subprime collapse and the wider damage to which it has led. As is becoming ever more apparent, many of the lending practices in the mortgage market during these years, especially in the subprime market, involved carelessness, deception, or both. Many people borrowed who had no prospect of servicing the loans they took out; they were hoping either to resell the house at a higher price, or to refinance it and draw on the appreciated value to make their payments. Some borrowers were apparently induced to buy houses they could not afford, or to take out loans they should not have been granted, by irresponsible brokers and other agents keen to make commissions on transactions, despite knowing they were inappropriate.

Many of the banks that packaged these loans into securities also put them into complex investment vehicles they did not understand, and sold them to investors who understood even less about them. The credit rating agencies, on which investors normally rely to inform them of such risks, were at best useless. Today the wreckage, consisting of abandoned houses, defaulted loans, displaced homeowners, banks making good on the billions of dollars of losses they had guaranteed, and uninsured investors marking down their portfolios, can be seen everywhere.

With respect to the housing bubble, the Fed asserts its innocence. It says that monetary policy was appropriate. It also takes the position that while, ex post, it is clear that supervision and regulation were too lax, no one saw the housing and credit bubble forming. Consequently, they cannot be blamed.

The assertion that the stance of monetary policy was appropriate given the measured inflation rate just assumes away the problem. If policy contributed to the bubble, then it was inappropriate regardless of the inflation rate. Contrary to the Fed position, people did see the housing and credit bubbles forming, although they were in the minority. Most importantly, the Fed as the central bank and the principal banking regulator alone had the responsibility of forestalling systemic risks. Even if no one else saw the bubble forming, the Fed should have. Saying no one else saw the crisis brewing is no defense.

BEN BERNANKE'S FEDERAL RESERVE AND THE POWER OF WALL STREET

The United States is now suffering from the aftershock of the irresponsible policies of Alan Greenspan. By keeping rates too low for too long following the terrorist attacks of 2001 and the dot-com crash, Ben Bernanke's iconic predecessor may have pleased his political masters, but he also pumped up America's gigantic real estate bubble.[10]

The Fed now needs to be able to explain why what is good for Wall Street is also good for the economy as a whole. The Fed listened to Wall Street and believed what it heard, or at any rate, acted as if it believed. Wall Street tells the Fed about its pain, what its pain means for the economy at large and what the Fed ought to do about it. Wall Street's pain was indeed great—deservedly so in most cases. Wall Street engaged in special pleading by exaggerating the impact on the wider economy of the rapid de-leveraging that was taking place. Wall Street wanted large rate cuts fast so as to improve its solvency, not its liquidity, and Wall Street wanted the provision of ample liquidity against overvalued collateral. Why did Wall Street get what it wanted?[11]

Throughout the crisis, it is difficult to avoid the impression that the Fed is too close to the financial markets and leading financial institutions, and too responsive to their special pleadings, to make the right decisions for the economy as a whole. Historically, the same behavior has characterized the Greenspan Fed.[12] The Bernanke Fed, like the Greenspan Fed, displays the same excess sensitivity to Wall Street concerns.[13]

There is little room for doubt, that the Federal Reserve under Greenspan treated the stability, well-being, and profitability of the financial sector as an objective in its own right, regardless of whether this contributed to the Fed's legal triple mandate of maximum employment, stable prices, and moderate long-term interest rates. While the Bernanke Federal Reserve has but a short track record, its rather panicky reactions and actions since August 2007 suggest that it too may have a distorted and exaggerated view of the importance of the financial sector for macroeconomic stability.

Ben Bernanke's initial four-year term at the Federal Reserve expired at the end of January 2010. Growing Congressional opposition had been building since President Barack Obama White House reappointed Bernanke for another four year term in August 2009 despite his performance, which has not been impressive. Nevertheless, the Senate Finance committee approved him on December 17 2009.

At the same time there has been a growing criticism in Congress such as from California Senator Barbara Boxer who said "It is time for Main Street to have a champion at the Fed. ... Our next Federal Reserve chairman must represent a clean break from the failed policies of the past."[14]

However at the time of writing the White House campaign to make sure that Bernanke is reappointed had slowly gained traction despite the weakened public support for President Obama and the beleaguered reputation of Ben Bernanke.

The Federal Reserve has been dominated recently by academics who are prisoners of the efficient market hypothesis, which assumes that people act rationally and efficiently in economic matters in ways that can be caught in elegant mathematical models. Ben Bernanke, chairman of the Federal Reserve, shares this view completely, and Alan Greenspan, his predecessor, when it suited him. In such a convenient world, there can be no bubbles and no crashes.

The Fed must show some backbone. If you always take the friendly way out, no bubbles will ever be pricked, and we shall always be reacting to crises in an increasingly speculative world. Paul Volcker, the Fed chairman before Alan Greenspan, had the character to do tough, unpleasant things when necessary. Paul Volcker was replaced for implementing unpleasant but necessary policies. Greenspan and Bernanke, in contrast, have not been able make the hard decisions.

THE UNACCOUNTABLE FEDERAL RESERVE

The Federal Reserve System operates as the central bank for the United States, managing the economy's money supply and overseeing the banking system. Until recently, the Federal Reserve has not picked winners or losers when distributing money, nor has it brought credit risk onto its balance sheet.

It has slowed or stimulated the economy by raising or lowering interest rates. Since March 2008, the Fed has resorted to using its emergency powers to pick winners and losers, and to take massive credit risk onto its books. Since September 2008, the Fed's balance sheet has expanded from around $800 billion to over $2 trillion, not including off-balance-sheet liabilities it has guaranteed for Citigroup, AIG, and the Bank of America, among others. The bank is also monetizing the debt of the U.S. government by purchasing massive amounts of agency and Treasury bonds. An audit is the first step in bringing this unaccountable system under the control of the public, whose money it prints and disseminates at will.

The Federal Reserve is an odd entity, a public-private chimera that controls the U.S. monetary system and supervises the banking system. The system is governed by a board of governors, with 12 regional Reserve Banks that serve a supporting role. While the governors are appointed by the president with confirmation by the Senate, the regional Reserve Banks have boards of directors chosen primarily by private banking institutions. Jamie Dimon, the CEO of JPMorgan when this chapter was written, for example, served on the board of directors of the New York Federal Reserve Bank, as did Goldman Sachs director Stephen Friedman. Appointments such as these create striking conflicts of interest and unseemly appearances in the management of what is ultimately the public's money.

Criticism of banker influence and control of the U.S. monetary system is not new. However, the urgency of the financial crisis and the actions of the Federal Reserve picking investment bank winners and losers have changed the nature of the criticism. The Senate passed a nonbinding resolution in its 2009 session requiring more transparency at the Federal Reserve in its budget resolution. The Federal Reserve has refused multiple inquiries from both the U.S. House of Representatives and the U.S. Senate to disclose who is receiving trillions of dollars from the central banking system. With discussions of allocating even more power to the Federal Reserve as the systemic risk regulator of the credit markets, more oversight over the Federal Reserve operations is clearly necessary.

The net effect of the recent Federal Reserve actions has been to isolate financial policy making entirely from democratic input, and allow the U.S. Treasury department to leverage the Federal Reserve's balance sheet to spend money it cannot get appropriated from Congress. The public does not know where trillions of its dollars are going, and so has no meaningful control over the currency or the federal budget. That has become another negative legacy of the Greenspan and Bernanke Federal Reserve roles in the financial crisis.

NOTES

1. Tom Petruno, "Right Response to September 11th Remains Unclear," *Los Angeles Times*, September 8, 2002.

2. David Eisenberg, "Greenspan's Deficits," *Time*, May 2, 2005, 44.

3. Anonymous. "A Tribute to an Unlikely Hero of 9/11," *Chicago Defender*, April 18, 2002, 9.

4. Richard Stevenson, "Fed Chief Sees Decline Over; House Passes Recovery Bill," *New York Times*, March 8, 2002.

5. Unsigned editorial, "Interest Rates and Deficits," *New York Times*, December 18, 2004.

6. David Eisenberg, "Greenspan's Deficits," *Time*, May 2, 2005, 44.

7. Frederic Mishkin and Stanley Eakins, *Financial Markets & Institutions*, 5th ed. (Upper Saddle River, NJ: Pearson, 2006), 189.

8. Alan Greenspan, *The Age of Turbulence: Adventures in a New World* (New York: Penguin, 2007).

9. Ibid.

10. Ethan S. Harris, *Ben Bernanke's Fed: The Federal Reserve after Greenspan* (Boston: Harvard Business School Press, 2008).

11. Johan Van Overtveldt, *Bernanke's Test: Ben Bernanke, Alan Greenspan and the Drama of the Central Banker* (Evanston, IL: Agate Publishing, 2009).

12. Ibid.

13. Ethan S. Harris, *Ben Bernanke's Fed: The Federal Reserve after Greenspan* (Boston: Harvard Business School Press, 2008).

14. Sewell Chan and David M. Herszenhorn, *Bernanke's Bid for a Second Term at the Fed Hits Resistance*, *New York Times*, January 2010

ABOUT THE AUTHOR

Professor John Ryan is a fellow at the Center for Economic Policy Analysis, University of Venice, Italy. He formerly held senior teaching and administrative positions at the European Business School, New York University, the EDHEC School of Management, in Lille, France, the Cass Business School, the Hult International Business School, and the German Graduate School of Management and Law, Germany. Professor Ryan was a visiting scholar at the Center for European Studies, Bonn, Sciences Po, CRG Ecole Polytechnique, and the Center for European Studies, Bonn. Professor Ryan was educated at Oxford University, Cambridge University, the London School of Economics, the Kiel Institute of World Economics, Germany, and University College, Dublin, Ireland.

CHAPTER 58

The Risk Management Approach to Monetary Policy: Lessons from the Financial Crisis of 2007–2009

MARC D. HAYFORD
Professor and Chair of the Department of Economics at Loyola University Chicago

A. G. MALLIARIS
Department of Economics, Loyola University Chicago

INTRODUCTION

The current financial crisis is the worst since the Great Depression. The U.S. crisis began in the summer of 2007, spread to global financial markets, causing severe declines in numerous national stock markets and has resulted a global recession, with declines in national real GDP averaging about 5 percent.

Capitalist economies are prone to such financial crisis and episodically experience financial booms and busts. During booms, market participants are often euphoric and declare that financial busts are a thing of the past. For example, during the decade of the 1990s, many analysts believed that the United States had entered a new era of stable economic growth, low inflation, and consequently financial stability. This perceived new era, called "The Great Moderation" was thought to be the consequence in part of sound monetary policy. The Great Moderation may have contributed, along with innovations in information technology, to the market euphoria, Keynesian animal spirits or irrational exuberance that drove a stock market boom from the mid- to late 1990s. The boom turned to bust when the stock market crashed in 2000. A mild recession followed.

In this paper we review the monetary policies followed by Fed chairmen Greenspan and Bernanke after 2000 and claim that on several occasions the Fed deviated from what might be considered normal monetary policy by responding to a perceived low probability event, which if it occurred, would impose a high cost to the economy. We argue that this risk management approach to monetary policy had many successes, but it may also have contributed, inadvertently, to the current crisis. We also offer several lessons that may be learned from the current crisis.

MONETARY POLICY IN NORMAL TIMES

In normal times, U.S. monetary policy concentrates on its congressional mandate of maintaining low and stable inflation (around 2 percent) and stable economic growth (around 3 percent). Low, stable inflation is thought to reduce economic uncertainty, encourage investment, and hence eventually contribute to economic growth. This dual mandate is achieved in normal times by the Fed setting a target for the federal funds rate, which is the overnight lending rate banks charge other banks to borrow bank reserves. The setting of the federal funds rate to meet the dual mandate of low inflation and stable economic growth can be characterized by the famous Taylor Rule. According to the Taylor Rule, the federal funds rate should equal the weighted sum of three factors: the deviation of inflation from its desired level (e.g., 2 percent); the output gap, that is, deviations of the growth in real GDP from trend growth (around 3 percent); and the level of short-term federal funds that would be consistent with stable inflation and trend GDP growth. If inflation is above target, then the rules implies a higher federal funds rate, that is, a tighter monetary policy, and when inflation is low and growth is below trend, then the rule implies a lower federal funds rate. Sometimes the goals of price stability and stable economic growth are in conflict, as when the inflation rate is above target and economic growth is below trend or vice versa.

MONETARY POLICY IN DIFFICULT TIMES: RISK MANAGEMENT BY CENTRAL BANKS

The Fed always faces uncertainty when setting monetary policy. Economists distinguish between uncertainty when possible future events can be assigned probabilities and uncertainty when possible events are totally unknowable and it is therefore impossible to assign event probabilities. The first type of uncertainty is usually called *risk*, while the second is called *Knightian uncertainty*. Examples of risks that the Fed faces are how high the price of oil will go and what will be its impact on the economy, will the dollar rise or fall, what will happen to long-term interest rates, and how the stock market will behave. Note that in all of these cases, the Fed has past data and can statistically estimate the probability of events with some degree of confidence. Examples of Knightian uncertainty include the 1998 Russian debt default, the bursting of the Internet bubble of 2000, the terrorist attacks of September 11th, and other similar events that no one can anticipate and no past occurrences allow statistical inferences. These Knightian uncertainty events are often the origin of the financial instabilities that challenge monetary policy and the simple Taylor Rule.

In 2004, then Fed chairman Alan Greenspan (2004) suggested that monetary policy face the challenge of uncertainty by taking a risk management approach: "The conduct of monetary policy in the United States has come to involve, at its core, crucial elements of risk management. This conceptual framework emphasizes understanding as much as possible the many sources of risk and uncertainty that policy makers face, quantifying those risks when possible, and assessing the costs associated with each of the risks."

Risk management has two components: First, the formalization of economic risks (i.e., where uncertainty is captured by some known probability distribution, as opposed to Knightian uncertainty) and second, given the formalization of risk, the tailoring of policy to insure against severe, adverse outcomes. Levine, McAdam, Pearlman, and Pierse (2008) formalize the risk management in the context of central banking by assuming the central bank commits to some policy rule, simple or complex, defining targets, and a welfare function reflecting preferences. The implemented policy then reflects the interplay of shocks, the rule, and the welfare criterion controlling for various forms of risk. The key aspect being that these sources of risk are weighted by their appropriate probabilities in the policy maker's expected welfare function. However, translating these theoretical developments into specific federal funds rates often involves judgment and discretion with their associated risks. Some economists, such as Feldstein (2004), view the risk management paradigm more as a conceptual framework than a practical recipe for policy making. However, two clear-cut points do emerge. First, policy making involves attaching empirically relevant probabilities to different states of the world. Second, it differs from the *minimax* (or worst-case) approach, since a minimax policy completely accommodates a worst scenario irrespective of its likelihood.

Examples of the risk management approach during the Greenspan years include the policy responses to the October 1987 stock market crash, the savings and loan debacle of 1989–1992, the 1997 Asian crisis, the 1998 Russian default and collapse of the Long-Term Capital Management, and the 2000 Internet bubble burst. During these events, the conduct of monetary policy deviated from the Taylor Rule. These events suggested the possibility of a large negative impact on the real economy. Even if the probability of a large negative impact was small, the possibility of the very high cost suggested addressing these events over traditional monetary policy goals. Thus, in response to these events, risk management suggested lowering the federal funds rate and providing liquidity, putting inflation concerns on the back burner for the short term.

RISK MANAGEMENT OF ASSET BUBBLES

At least since Alan Greenspan (1996) gave his how famous "irrational exuberance" speech, economists have debated how central banks should respond to the risk implied by an asset price boom. Bernanke and Gertler (1999, 2001) and more recently Furlaneto (2008) argue that a direct monetary policy response to asset prices has destabilizing effects because it is almost impossible to know whether asset price booms are due to fundamental factors or not. On the other hand, Cecchetti, Genberg, Lipsky, and Wadhawani (2000), Bordo and Jeanne (2002), Akram and Eithreim (2008), and Akram, Bardsen, and Eithreim (2006) argue that monetary policy makers can identify bubbles (i.e., price booms not based on fundamentals and hence are bound to bust) and taking into account the direct effect of bubbles when setting policy interest rates has a stabilizing effect on the economy. These authors argue that a central bank by increasing interest rates during an asset price boom will help stabilize the economy by making the eventual asset price bust smaller. Greenspan (2004), however, is skeptical that monetary policy can successfully dampen asset price bubbles while at the same time maintaining output stability. This sentiment is consistent with Cogley (1999), Bullard and Schaling (2002), and Goodfriend (2002), who all conclude that using monetary policy to attempt to pop asset price bubbles is likely to result in greater economic instability than waiting for bubbles to pop on their own.

Hayford and Malliaris (2001, 2004, 2005a, 2005b, 2006) show that in setting monetary policy, the Fed has not attempted to target asset prices independent of the goals of low inflation and a zero output gap. After an asset price bust, however, the Fed typically eases monetary policy to dampen the negative impact of the bust on economic activity. There are at least three reasons why the Fed has acted in this way: First, academic literature on monetary policy and asset price bubbles gives an ambiguous answer at best to the question of whether or not central banks should try to target asset prices along with inflation and the output gap. Second, the historical episodes of asset price booms and busts (such as in the mid- to late 1920s) suggest that using restrictive monetary policy to dampen bubbles may not work and may in addition destabilize the economy. Third, the political constraints faced by central bankers in setting monetary policy likely exclude the possibility of increasing interest rates solely to deflate an asset price boom. Hence, the Fed has not recently attempted to pop asset price booms using restrictive monetary policy. Instead, once an asset price bubble pops, the federal funds rate is typically cut to offset the impact on the real economy.

THE RISK MANAGEMENT APPROACH TO MONETARY POLICY AND THE CURRENT FINANCIAL CRISIS

The success of the asymmetric approach to managing asset price booms and busts in 1987 and 2000 combined with the risk management approach to central banking may have helped cause the financial crisis of 2007–2009. The Fed responded to the decline in the stock market in 2000–2002 by cutting interest rates to reduce the risk that declines in stock market wealth would cause a large drop in consumption and thus GDP. The federal funds rate target was dramatically cut in January 2001 from 6.5 percent to a low of 1 percent by June 2003. These changes in monetary policy, at least up to 2002, were, given inflation and the output gap, consistent with the Taylor Rule. Then in 2002, a risk management approach dominated monetary policy as concerns of the possibility of deflation and the fear of consequences similar to Japan in the 1990s induced to the Fed to keep the federal funds rate at 1 percent until the end of June 2004. This period of an exceptionally low federal funds rate, rationalized by the Fed as risk management, has since been criticized and cited as at least a contributing factor to the real estate bubble of the mid-2000s.

This argument is made most forcefully by Taylor (2007) who acknowledges that while the Fed had ". . . good reasons stated at the time for the prolonged period of low interest rates, most importantly the risk of deflation following the experience of Japan in the mid-1990s," the Fed could have prevented the housing starts and housing prices boom and bust if instead the Fed had stuck to the Taylor Rule and increased the federal funds rate at the beginning of 2002. Taylor (2009) argues that keeping the federal funds rate so low from 2002 to mid-2004 overstimulated the housing market and thus created the housing prices price bubble with all its various consequences in mortgage markets, subprime mortgages, credit default swaps, and forced de-leveraging in 2007 and 2008.

Taylor's argument seems to ride entirely on whether or not the risk of causing a housing boom and bust was greater than the risk of deflation. The fact that inflation did not accelerate as a consequence of the Fed deviating from the Taylor Rule from 2002 to 2004 provides prima facie evidence that the risk of deflation was real and was dealt with. If the Fed had increased the federal funds rate as Taylor argues, deflation may have occurred along with stopping the boom in housing starts.

Interestingly, when the Fed did start to increase the federal funds rate in 2004, long-term interest rates, such as the 30-day fixed, stayed put. The cause of this bond market conundrum, that is, lack of response of long interest rates to monetary tightening, is still not agreed upon. At least two explanations have been suggested: Ben Bernanke has suggested the cause was a global savings glut, while Smith and Taylor (2007) argue it was due to U.S. monetary policy deviating from the Taylor Rule by not increasing the federal funds rate sooner.

This episode points out the difficulty central bankers face in balancing multiple risks to the economy while having only one monetary policy instrument, as well as the problem that the economy does not always react the same way to changes in the federal funds rate. This episode also suggests that managing one asset bubble may create another bubble. The monetary policy of the 2000s suggests that the effort to keep interest rates low to minimize the economic impact of the 2000 stock market collapse along with the potential of deflation sowed the seeds of the housing bubble of 2006 and 2007.

THE RECENT FINANCIAL CRISIS: LESSONS FOR MONETARY POLICY

We conclude with three lessons for monetary policy suggested by recent events. First, the Great Moderation suggests that monetary policy can be successful in performing its traditional tasks of price stability and stable growth by following the approach of the Taylor Rule.

Second, deviations from the Taylor Rule justified by the risk management approach are sometimes successful, but at other times conditions created to offset one perceived risk may unintentionally create conditions for an unexpected adverse shock to the economy. As argued by Taylor (2007, 2009) this was the case in the current financial crisis. If we think of the risk management approach as insurance, keeping interest rates low from 2002 to mid-2004 was justified by the Fed as an insurance premium against deflation. Sticking with the insurance analogy, the premium turned out to be higher than expected, as the low interest rates may have contributed to the subsequent housing bubble.

A third lesson of this financial crisis is that the Fed's asymmetric approach to asset bubbles must be reviewed. While the Fed was effective during the October 1987 crash and the March 2000 NASDAQ crash, the collapse of the stock market by more than 40 percent during the financial crisis of 2007–2009 demonstrates that rapid decreases of federal funds to essentially .25 percent were totally ineffective in containing the crash. Chairman Bernanke, who was a strong supporter of the asymmetric approach to asset bubbles, has recently revised his position in view of the Fed's ineffectiveness to contain the negative impact on the real economy of the stock market collapse due to the financial chaos, particularly around September 2008. This suggests that in the future the Fed may take a more proactive approach to monetary policy as asset price bubbles begin to develop.

REFERENCES

Akram, Q. F., G. Bardsen, and O. Eithreim. 2006. Monetary policy and asset prices: To respond or not? *Journal of Finance and Economics* 11: 279–292.

Akram, Q. F., and O. Eithreim. 2008. Flexible inflation targeting and financial stability: Is it enough to stabilize inflation and output? *Journal of Banking and Finance* 32 (7): 1242–1254.

Bernanke, B., and M. Gertler. 1999. Monetary policy and asset price volatility. In *New challenges for monetary policy: A symposium sponsored by the Federal Reserve Bank of Kansas City*, Federal Reserve Bank of Kansas City, 77–128.

———. 2001. " Should central banks respond to movements in asset prices?" *The American Economic Review* 91: 253–257.

Bordo, M. D., and O. Jeanne. 2002. *Boom–busts in asset prices, economic instability and monetary policy*. Washington, DC: Center for Economic Policy and Research, Discussion Paper 3398.

Bullard, J. B., and E. Schaling. 2002. Why the Fed should ignore the stock market. *Federal Reserve Bank of St. Louis Review* 84: 35–41.

Cecchetti, S. G., H. Genberg, J. Lipsky, and S. Wadhawani. 2000. *Asset prices and central bank policy*. Washington, DC: Center for Economic Policy and Research, Geneva Reports on the World Economy.

Cogley, T. 1999. Should the Fed take deliberate steps to deflate asset price bubbles? *Federal Reserve Bank of San Francisco Economic Review*, 42–52.

Feldstein, M. 2004. *Risk and uncertainty in monetary policy*. Comments on remarks by Chairman Alan Greenspan, American Economic Association.

Furlaneto, F. 2008. *Does monetary policy react to asset prices? Some international evidence*. New York: Norges Bank, Working Paper 2008/07.

Goodfriend, M. 2002. Interest rate policy should not react directly to asset prices. In *Asset price bubbles: The implications for monetary, regulatory and international policies*, eds. William Hunter, George Kaufman, and Michael Pomerleano, Cambridge, MA and London: MIT Press.

Greenspan, A. 1996. The challenge of central banking in a democratic society. At the annual dinner and Francis Boyer lecture of the American Enterprise Institute for public policy research, December 5, Washington, DC.

———. 2004. Risk and uncertainty in monetary policy. Remarks by Chairman Alan Greenspan at the meetings of the American Economic Association, January 3, San Diego, California.

Hayford, M., and A. G. Malliaris. 2001. Is the Federal Reserve stock market bubble-neutral? In *Asset price bubbles: Implications for monetary and regulatory policy* 13, ed. George Kaufman, 229–243, Amsterdam: Elsevier Science.

———. 2004. Monetary policy and the U.S. stock market. *Economic Inquiry* 42: 387–401.

———. 2005a. How did the Fed react to the 1990s stock market bubble? Evidence from an extended Taylor rule. *European Journal of Operational Research* 163: 20–29.

———. 2005b. Recent monetary policy in the U.S.: Risk management of asset bubbles. *The Journal of Economic Asymmetries* 2: 25–39.

———. 2006. Rethinking monetary stabilization in the presence of an asset bubble: Should the response be symmetric or asymmetric? In *Global divergence in trade, money and policy*, eds. V. Alexander and H.-H. Kotz, 172–191. Cheltenham, England: Edward Elgar.

Levine, P., P. McAdam, J. Pearlman, and R. Pierse. 2008. Risk management in action: Robust monetary policy rules under structure uncertainty. *Working Paper Series*, 870.

Smith, J. M., and J. B. Taylor. 2007. *The link between the long end and the short end of policy rules and the yield curve*. Stanford, CA: Stanford University Press.

Taylor, J. B. 2007. *Housing and monetary policy*. Cambridge, MA: National Bureau of Economic Research, Working Paper 13682.

———. 2009. *The financial crisis and the policy responses: An empirical analysis of what went wrong*. Cambridge, MA: National Bureau of Economic Research Working Paper 14631.

ABOUT THE AUTHORS

Marc D. Hayford is a professor and chair of the Department of Economics at Loyola University Chicago, where he has taught since 1986. His research interests include monetary policy, fiscal policy, and macroeconomics in general. He has published in numerous journals, such as *Economic Inquiry, Applied Economics,* and the *Journal of Money Credit and Banking.* Professor Hayford has a B.A. and M.A. from UCLA and a Ph.D. in economics from Brown University.

A. G. (Tassos) Malliaris is currently professor of economics and finance at Loyola University Chicago, and holds the Walter F. Mullady Sr. Chair in business administration. He has earned two Ph.D.s: one in economics from the University of Oklahoma and a second in mathematics from the University of Chicago. He has authored and co-authored numerous articles in professional journals such as the *Society of Industrial and Applied Mathematics Review, Mathematics of Operations Research, Review of Economic Studies, Journal of Financial and Quantitative Analysis, Review of Quantitative Finance and Accounting, Journal of Futures Markets, Journal of Banking and Finance, Journal of Macroeconomics, Economic Modeling, Journal of Multinational Financial Management, International Review of Financial Analysis, European Journal of Political Economy, European Journal of Operations Research, International Journal of Finance, Multinational Finance Journal, Economic Inquiry, Neural Computing and Applications,* and others. He has also edited and co-edited several books. He is currently interested in financial economics, monetary policy, and the formation of asset bubbles.

CHAPTER 59

Reawakening the Inflationary Monster: U.S. Monetary Policy and the Federal Reserve

KEVIN DOWD
Visiting Professor, Pensions Institute, Cass Business School

MARTIN HUTCHINSON
Financial journalist based in Vienna, Virginia, for BreakingViews.com

I n a series of papers and speeches in the early years of the millennium, Federal Reserve Governor Ben Bernanke outlined what the Fed might do when faced with near-zero interest rates.[1] A distinguished historian of the Great Depression, Dr. Bernanke's main concern was to ensure that "it" never happened again, and the key element of his program was to avert a repeat of the damaging deflation of the early 1930s.

Bernanke was appointed Fed chairman shortly afterward and now finds himself implementing those same policies in the middle of a major financial crisis. The policies themselves boil down to the Fed throwing everything it has into a desperate battle to avert falling prices—an attack on deflation *à outrance*. Their supporters justify such policies by any number of colorful analogies—we need to put out the fire, we need to kick-start the economy, and so forth. With the specter of looming deflation, they also suggest that this is not a time to worry about *in*flation. To quote one eminent authority, using yet another evocative analogy, "Fear of inflation, when viewed in the context of a possible global depression, is like worrying about getting the measles when one is in danger of getting the plague."[2]

A new conventional wisdom has thus evolved, which maintains that the current major threat is deflation rather than inflation, and insists that this threat must be countered by all possible means.

We would argue, on the contrary, that this view and the policies associated with it are fundamentally misconceived; they are also irresponsible and potentially highly dangerous. To start with, as a response to the crisis (and to avert worse to come) they miss the main point. Resolving the crisis does not require stimulus—fiscal or monetary; nor does it require bailouts or near-zero interest rates. Instead, the crisis can only be resolved by an appropriately radical restructuring of the balance sheets of the major financial institutions.[3] Other measures—in fact, most of the policies that have been adopted to deal with the crisis—are no substitute for this, and the failure of policy makers across the world to address this issue has needlessly prolonged the crisis, and done so at a huge longer-term cost.

But leaving aside that they miss the point, we would also take issue with the arguments used to justify recent policies—or rather, the lack thereof. Instead of reasoned analysis, what we have is argument by analogy and the analogies chosen are meant to persuade us that everything possible must be done, immediately, and no time to think. Such analogies, however, only serve to silence informed discussion. The choice of analogy also begs the question at issue. Of course, if we *were* actually dealing with a fire, then we would presumably all agree that we should use all available means to put it out, but we are dealing with a financial crisis, and that is a rather different matter. And if argument-by-analogy is to be the order of the day, then we would suggest that the problem with the economy is that its financial engine is broken, and (the obvious conclusion, given this analogy) the crisis will only be resolved when the engine is fixed. This is all good fun, of course—you give your analogy pointing to the inevitability of your preferred conclusion, and we will give you our analogy pointing to the inevitability of our favorite conclusion.[4] But this doesn't really get us very far: at the end of the day, there is simply no substitute for thinking through the problem the old-fashioned way.

If policy makers' analogies are misguided, there is no reason to believe that their policies are appropriate. Accordingly, in this chapter we attempt to think this issue through from first principles. And our conclusions make disturbing reading: not only is there a very clear and present danger of returning inflation, but there is also a very real danger that the Federal Reserve itself will become insolvent and end up as a victim of its own policy failures.

Let's begin with the monetary basics, the inflation rate and the monetary aggregates. U.S. inflation was 3.2 percent over 2006, 2.9 percent over 2007, and 3.9 percent over 2008. Over this same period, the broader monetary aggregates grew quite rapidly. For example, M2 grew at 5.4 percent, 5.8 percent, and 10 percent over each of these years, and the corresponding growth rates for MZM were 5.7 percent, 12.5 percent, and 12.6 percent. These figures suggest an accommodating monetary policy, and this interpretation is confirmed by strongly negative interest rates since the summer of 2008. This combination of *rising* prices, rapid monetary *expansion*, and *negative* real interest rates make a stark contrast to the *declining* prices, *falling* monetary aggregates, and *very high and positive* real interest rates of the early 1930s.[5]

In the very short term, this monetary growth is likely to have only a limited impact on inflation while the economy remains in deep recession with substantial underuse of resources. However, once credit markets begin to ease and confidence returns, then monetary velocity will return to normal levels, possibly quite rapidly. When this happens, we should expect to see inflation rising again, and possibly rising rapidly.

Once inflation returns, it is also likely that expectations of future inflation will rise with them and then become entrenched. This, in turn, will destroy whatever shreds of inflation credibility the Fed might still have, and would substantially increase the recessionary side effects of the disinflation that the Fed will eventually be forced to implement. But, as in 1979, there will come a point when the existing policies will be seen to have failed and the Fed will reluctantly reverse policy—presumably under a new chairman. The Fed will then raise interest rates sharply and force monetary growth down, and the economy will go into another painful recession. If the Fed then sticks with such a policy—as it did under Volcker—then it will gradually but painfully grind inflationary forces out of the system; if it gives up, as earlier in the 1970s, then inflation will return again, only to need further harsh monetary medicine further down the road. Welcome back stagflation.

Long before all that, higher interest rates would follow naturally from higher inflation expectations and the massive borrowing requirements of the U.S. government. We can also expect higher interest rates for other reasons. The excess liquidity injected into global financial markets in late 2008 led not only to ultra-low short-term interest rates, but also a surge in long-term bond markets, pushing long-term Treasury yields down to historically very low levels. But as risk appetites begin to return, savings flows will flee the negative real returns in the Treasury market, and bond prices will rise. In any case, yields now are so low they can only realistically move in one direction, creating one-way bet scenarios for speculators who go short on bond prices: heads they win, tails they don't lose. Once the selling starts, the flight from bonds is likely to become a stampede, since much of the money that has flowed into Treasuries is short-term and hot in nature. Bond markets are therefore set to crash.

And, of course, we can also expect a major fall in the dollar, and the dollar is already sliding on the foreign exchange markets. In the longer term, the dollar's value is determined by relative inflation rates: if the United States inflates more than its trading partners—as seems likely—then the dollar must eventually fall. But there are also huge speculative dollar holdings. As of May 2009, approximately $3.3 trillion of the $6.9 trillion of Treasury securities outstanding were held by foreigners, of which $2.3 trillion were held by foreign central banks. Foreign private purchases of Treasury bonds and notes were $227 billion in the 12 months to May 2009, a similar figure to the previous year, but official purchases had fallen to a mere $18 billion in the period, in spite of the gigantic amount of securities issued. As the dollar falls, foreign holders of Treasuries are likely to begin selling. These holdings represent a dangerous overhang, the unraveling of which could well cause a sharp decline in the dollar's value once foreign exchange markets start to correct themselves: thus, the ingredients are already in place for a major dollar crisis.

The bleak prognosis just described amounts to a return to the miseries of stagflation. To make matters worse, the current situation is unprecedented in important respects.

There is, first, the extraordinary growth of the monetary base over recent months. After a long period of stability, the monetary base grew from $871 billion in August 2008 to about $2 trillion at the time this chapter was written. The effect of this growth might be relatively muted in the very short run—especially as the collapse in market confidence leads to hoarding cash for the time being—but as market conditions recover, the velocity of all forms of money can be expected to increase back toward historic levels. Unless counteracted, the danger is then that the vastly expanded monetary base would feed through the financial system in textbook fashion and the other monetary aggregates would rise into line with it. This would (considerably!) increase the inflationary pressure already in the system.

In principle, of course, such an outcome can be averted (or at least ameliorated) if the Fed moves quickly to claw back the growth in the base before its inflationary potential is fully unleashed, but in practice this would be very difficult to do. One reason is that the timing and magnitude of the base reversal(s) would be very difficult to judge, given the limited and often conflicting economic signals that policy makers work with in real economic time. Another reason is that such a policy would encounter major opposition from both special interest groups directly affected (e.g., those who would suffer from the Fed's asset sakes) and also from those opposed to such a policy for other reasons (e.g., those who believe that unremitting stimulus is still required). The political pressure against such a policy would therefore be enormous, not least because it would involve reversing a key element of the current stimulus package. Winding back an overexpansionary monetary policy is always unpopular with the markets and the political class, even at the best of times, and winding back recent base growth may in practice be almost impossible.[6]

The second unique feature of the current situation is the remarkable transformation of the Fed's balance sheet over 2008. Traditionally, almost the only assets held by the Fed were U.S. Treasury securities: loans to commercial banks were negligible and the Fed did not lend at all to other institutions. All this has now completely changed. The average quality of the Fed's assets has also declined considerably, and the Fed's equity cushion is now down to just 1.9 percent of its assets, down from 3.9 percent a year before. The Fed's leverage ratio has gone up from just under 25 to about over 50 at the same time as the quality of its assets has markedly deteriorated. As Lawrence H. White put it in a recent paper, "The Fed now looks increasingly like a *very* highly leveraged hedge fund" (White 2008, 11).

Among other problems,[7] this means that the Fed is now in a much riskier financial position itself. The Fed has acquired large amounts of assets, many of which will be have an-as-yet undetermined degree of toxicity: the risk that many of these assets will fall further is therefore very considerable. Also, many of the Fed's assets are interest-sensitive and could fall sharply in value if interest rates were to rise—approximately 20 percent of the Fed's assets now carry a maturity of more than one year and are thus subject to (in some cases substantial) interest rate risk. To make matters worse, the Fed's balance sheet is also seriously exposed to credit risk and the full extent of these risk exposures is unknown, even to the Fed itself.

Of course, even if it suffered such a loss, the Fed would not simply disappear into private bankruptcy like a common hedge fund. However, the Fed could not continue to operate indefinitely while technically insolvent and would therefore need to be recapitalized. There are only three ways this could be done, and all would be unpleasant. The first (and least unpleasant) would be for the Fed to raise new capital by imposing capital charges on Federal Reserve member banks. Charging member banks would, however, seriously impede the ability of the banking system to return to normal, and would run into enormous political opposition. A second (and worse) response would be for Congress to bail the Fed out and authorize its recapitalization financed ultimately by general taxation, but this would put yet another hole in public finances and massively damage the credibility of the whole recovery program—as well as provoke a storm of political opposition. The third and worst but politically most tempting response would be for the Fed to print its way out; that is, it could replace its losses by buying more assets with newly printed money, but this would be an extremely dangerous response that would likely lead to rapid inflation as the newly printed money feeds through the system. Even worse, it could set the Fed on a slippery slope from which the Fed would subsequently find it very difficult to extract itself: if the Fed starts to print money to cover its losses, there is a real danger of a vicious cycle taking off in which in the monetization of the Fed's losses leads to higher inflation, higher interest rates, and thence more losses and even greater inflation.

We hear much these days about the need to learn from the experience of the Great Depression. In this context, we would do well to recall Milton Friedman's assessment, written about 50 years ago:

> *The Great Depression did much to instill and reinforce the now widely held view that inherent instability of a private market economy has been responsible for the major periods of economic distress experienced by the United States. On this view, only a vigilant government, offsetting continuously the vagaries of the private economy, has prevented or can prevent such periods of instability. As I read the historical record, I draw almost the opposite conclusion. In almost every instance, major instability in the United States has been produced or, at the very least, greatly intensified by monetary instability. Monetary instability in its turn has generally arisen either from governmental intervention or from controversy over what governmental monetary policy should be. The failure of government to provide a stable monetary framework has thus been a major if not the major factor accounting for our really severe inflations and depressions. Perhaps the most remarkable feature of the record is the adaptability and flexibility that the private economy has so frequently shown under such extreme provocation.*[8]

More recent U.S. experience is also consistent with Friedman's assessment. A good case in point was the last false deflation scare, when then-Governor Bernanke persuaded Alan Greenspan in 2002 that the United States was (then also) in imminent danger of deflation. The Fed responded by pulling interest rates down to about 1 percent and holding them at that level for a year. The resulting expansionary monetary policy then fed an unprecedented roller coaster of a boom and bust cycle that ended in the collapse of stock and property markets, the specter of renewed inflation, the destruction of much of the financial system and a very sharp economic downturn.[9]

Does the Fed draw the lesson that aggressive monetary policy is ultimately destabilizing? Not at all. Instead, it embarks on an even more activist monetary policy that lays the seeds of an even bigger boom and bust cycle in the future. Former Fed chairman William McChesney Martin once famously said that the role of the Fed was to take away the punchbowl just as the party is getting going. Current Federal Reserve policy would by contrast appear to be just the opposite—as Gerald P. O'Driscoll put it in a recent talk, the Fed's recent policy would appear to be one of "spiking the drinks just as the guests are sobering up."[10] The Fed is thus repeating the same mistakes it made in the mid-1990s and then again in the early years of the new millennium—but on a grander scale. And, in the meantime, there is also that little matter of the inflation in the pipeline to worry about . . .

NOTES

1. See, for example, Bernanke (2002) or Bernanke and Reinhart (2004).
2. Rogoff (2008). Rogoff even goes on to suggest that inflation is actually *needed* to help combat the crisis.

3. For more on how this might be done, see Dowd (2009) or Hutchinson (2008, 2009).

4. The role of argument-by-analogy in discussions of the current crisis is nicely set out by Professor Leczek Balcerowicz in this speech to the Istituto Bruno Leoni Verbania seminar on the financial crisis (Balcerowicz 2009).

5. In the Great Depression of the 1930s, by contrast, nominal rates were significantly higher than they are now in spite of sharply falling prices; the Federal Reserve discount rate fell from 6 percent to 1.5 percent between 1929 and July 1931, then was raised to 3.5 percent in late 1931 and declined to only 2.5 percent during 1932. Based on the GDP deflator for the year, the corresponding *real* interest rates thus rose from roughly 6 percent in 1929 to 11.5 percent in 1931, peaking at the remarkable rate of 14 percent in 1932. The difference between current real interest rates and those of the Depression could hardly be more pronounced.

6. The only alternative would be to sterilize the monetary base growth through reserve requirements. This would, however, choke off the lending that the entire bank recapitalization exercise is intended to revitalize, and, as with selling off the recent Fed acquisitions, this would go seriously counter to the current stimulus measures. Such a measure also has ominous historical overtones: the doubling of reserve requirements by the Fed in 1936 and 1937 is commonly held to have been the principal factor behind the 1937–1938 recession, itself deeper than any since World War II. It is virtually inconceivable that the Bernanke Fed would risk a repeat of that debacle. Thus, sterilization would appear to all intents and purposes to be out of the question.

7. Another serious problem (and one that would have received much more attention but for all the other urgent problems overshadowing it) is that the Fed's acquisitions now make it a key player in selectively channeling commercial credit, as opposed to merely influencing general commercial conditions with selective credit determined by the financial system on old-fashioned commercial terms. This creates the potential for huge inefficiencies, because the Fed has no expertise to take on this role. The Fed's much more activist role in the allocation of credit creates a worrying precedent and means that much of the allocation of credit is now determined by Federal Reserve fiat, that is, is effectively politicized.

8. Friedman, 1960, 9.

9. An additional problem with monetary activism is not just that discretionary monetary policy creates instability, but also that monetary activism entails uncertainty about what future monetary policy might entail, and this uncertainty is also destabilizing. As the Friedman quote in the text aptly suggests, this uncertainty imposes unnecessary risks on private sector parties, and their need to manage these risks is itself a major hindrance to economic recovery.

10. O'Driscoll, 2008.

REFERENCES

Balcerowicz, L. 2009. The causes of the financial crisis and its relevance to the future of capitalism. Speech to the Istituto Leoni Bruno seminar on the financial crisis, June 26, Verbania, Italy.

Bernanke, B. S. 2002. Deflation: Making sure it doesn't happen here. Remarks before the National Economists' Club, November 21, Washington, DC.

Bernanke, B. S., and V. R. Reinhart. 2004. Conducting monetary policy at very low short-term interest rates. International Center for Monetary and Banking Studies Lecture, January 14, Geneva, Switzerland.

Dowd, K. 2009. Lessons from the financial crisis: A libertarian perspective. Expanded version of the Second Chris R. Tame memorial lecture delivered at the National Liberal Club, March 17, Libertarian Alliance, economic notes 111, London.

Friedman, M. 1960. *A framework for monetary stability*. New York: Fordham University Press.

Hutchinson, M. 2008. The bear's lair: The Wall Street of the future. *Prudent Bear*, December 1.

———. 2009a. The financial services rust belt. *Prudent Bear*, January 26.

———. 2009b. The liquidationist alternative. *Prudent Bear*, February 16.

O'Driscoll, G. P. 2008. Money and the present crisis. Remarks to the Cato Institute 26th annual monetary conference, November 19, Washington DC.

Rogoff, K. S. 2008. Embracing inflation. *Guardian*, December 2.

White, L. H. 2008. Federal Reserve policy and the housing bubble. Paper presented at the Cato Institute 26th annual monetary conference, November 19, Washington DC.

ABOUT THE AUTHORS

Kevin Dowd recently retired from Nottingham University Business School. A lifelong libertarian economist, he has written extensively on free banking, central banking, and financial regulation; he also has interests in financial risk management, pensions, macro- and monetary economics, and political economy. His books include *Competition and Finance: A New Interpretation of Financial and Monetary Economics* (Macmillan, 1996) and *Measuring Market Risk* (second edition, Wiley, 2005). He has affiliations with the Cato Institute (Washington), the Institute of Economic Affairs (London), the Open Republic Institute (Dublin), the Taxpayers' Alliance (London), and the Pensions Institute (London).

Martin Hutchinson has an M.A. in mathematics from Trinity College, Cambridge, and an M.B.A. from Harvard Business School. He was a merchant banker in London, New York, and Zagreb for 27 years. He has been a financial journalist since 2000. He is currently a correspondent for BreakingViews.com and Money Morning, editor of the Permanent Wealth Investor web site and writes a weekly column "The Bear's Lair." He wrote a book, *Great Conservatives*, on British history in 2004, and is currently collaborating on another book, on a financial theme, with Professor Kevin Dowd.

CHAPTER 60

The Transformation of the Federal Reserve System Balance Sheet and Its Implications

PETER STELLA
Director, Stellar Consulting LLC, formerly Adviser, Monetary and Capital Markets Department, International Monetary Fund

INTRODUCTION

As a consequence of its active response to the global financial turmoil that erupted in July 2007, the consolidated balance sheet of the combined U.S. Federal Reserve Banks (FRB or Fed) more than doubled during 2008 to $2.2 trillion. By some measures, the Fed is now the largest bank in the United States. Its role in world financial markets has changed fundamentally—from a key, though small, U.S. money market participant into the largest actor and central linchpin of that market and, indirectly, of the world financial system.

Not only has the size of the Fed intervention been truly spectacular, the nature of the intervention has undergone an equally remarkable transformation. In order to comprehend this change, it is necessary to understand the Fed's functioning before the crisis as well as contemplate the change in the nature of the assets it now holds on its balance sheet. This is discussed further on. Following from the analysis of the change in the nature of the Fed's operations and asset holdings, I also discuss the magnitude of the risks to the new Fed balance sheet as well as its ability to cope with those risks. Although risks are considerable in certain unlikely scenarios, FRB capital, earnings capacity, and reserves are more than ample to preserve their financial independence. Nevertheless, the occurrence of losses or a significant drop in FRB profit might lead to an eventual curtailment of Fed operational independence. I also discuss measures that can be taken to minimize the Fed's exposure to losses and preserve its operational independence. The end of this chapter discusses proposals to clearly separate monetary policy from financial stability intervention policy in what might become the new financial architecture once the crisis subsides.

CHANGES IN FED OPERATIONS
AND ASSET HOLDINGS

Although the world's major central banks have somewhat idiosyncratic operating procedures, their basic philosophies are essentially similar and are based on a common financial architectural fact—commercial banks settle their payments among each other with deposits they hold at the central bank. Owing to the vagaries of daily interbank payments, individual banks find themselves on any given day with either a shortage or excess of deposits at the central bank (usually denoted as *reserves*), and an active interbank lending market distributes funds to equilibrate supply and demand for funds at the market interest rate by the end of each settlement day. The central bank, as its name suggests, is both the locus of the settlement of transactions and uniquely positioned to create or withdraw reserves from the system. Monetary operations adjust the supply of reserves so that the interbank market clears at the interest rate set by the monetary policy authority. A focus on the overnight interbank rate allows the monetary authority to provide a clear signal of its policy target while allowing all other interest rates in the economy to be purely market determined. The policy signal is then transmitted to longer-term interest rates, "along the yield curve," allowing the central bank to indirectly influence the amount of credit provided in the economy by influencing its cost. In most countries, the monetary system is designed so that commercial banks as a whole are short of reserves and must rely on small amounts of borrowing from the central bank. Central banks typically lend commercial banks reserves in repo transactions—short-term loans collateralized by high quality securities. When central banks wish to increase reserves in the system, they provide more credit, and when they wish to contract reserves, they lower the amount of credit in the overnight market. In general, although the central bank might be a large provider of funds to the overnight market, the volume of overnight deposits at the central bank before the crisis tended to be a very small proportion of total financial market assets and consequently, the active part of central bank balance sheets was quite small. For example, in the United States, commercial bank balances at the Fed before the crisis were about $20 billion while total commercial banks assets were approximately $10 trillion.

Before 2008, U.S. monetary policy implementation operated as follows. The Federal Open Market Committee (FOMC), the System's monetary policy body, determined the level of the monetary policy operational target, that is, the weighted average brokered interest rate at which banks borrow and lend, overnight and on an unsecured basis (the federal funds rate), deposits they hold at the FRB. The FOMC directed the management of the System Open Market Account (SOMA) at the Federal Reserve Bank of New York to set the supply of reserves so that the market was in equilibrium at the target rate. Over time, the FRBNY also conducted outright purchases of U.S. Treasury securities to accommodate the secular growth in demand for Federal Reserve Notes. Demand for FR Notes was accommodated passively.

In 2006, the average stock of monetary policy instruments—short-term and long-term repos—was $25.3 billion. Until late in 2007, the FRBNY actively managed a small liquid portfolio of repos to target the effective federal funds rate. The operational objective was to minimize volatility in the rate in order to provide a pure monetary policy signal. The FRBNY also used carefully designed risk management and operating procedures to ensure both that its lending operations were virtually risk-free and to minimize price distortions among asset classes it accepted as collateral.

The structure of the Fed balance sheet before the crisis was very simple. About 90 percent of Fed assets consisted of U.S. Treasury securities, and about 90 percent of liabilities were Federal Reserve Notes, that is, U.S. banknotes.[1] The active portion of the balance sheet, that is, the portion adjusted for monetary policy purposes, amounted to about 5 percent.

What happened during the crisis, and how did the Fed respond? The primary fact of relevance for central bank liquidity management is that financial institutions became unwilling to lend to each other—both in the unsecured (without collateral) and secured market, except against the most liquid of collateral, U.S. Treasury securities.[2] The value of most collateral fell, limiting the quantity of financing banks could obtain. Demand for asset-backed securities (ABS) fell sharply, whose sales banks had previously used to obtain fresh funding. To avoid a complete seizure of credit markets, the Fed expanded its lending facilities in terms of to whom it would lend, for how long it would lend, and against what collateral it would lend. In consequence, the Fed became a major credit intermediary. Total bank reserves borrowed from the Federal Reserve rose from only $242 million in July 2007 at the outset of the crisis to $654 billion at the end of 2008.

From the standpoint of monetary policy, it is useful to divide the crisis period into two phases, before and after the insolvency of Lehman Brothers on September 15, 2008. Before the Lehman insolvency, the Fed broadened its lending counterparties, relaxed its collateral requirements, and lengthened maturities but kept the overall money supply and the size of its balance sheet unchanged. It achieved this by absorbing the newly created bank reserves through sales of an equivalent amount of U.S. Treasury securities from its portfolio to the market. The Fed, in essence, replaced in its asset portfolio holdings of U.S. Treasuries with collateralized loans to banks and securities broker-dealers. In so doing, it was able to control the decline in targeted federal funds rate set in successive FOMC meetings.[3]

Although the total size of the balance sheet did not materially change during Phase 1, the composition of Fed assets underwent a large change. The proportion of Fed assets invested in U.S. Treasuries and agency securities fell sharply while loans to financial institutions, including to JPMorgan to assist in the acquisition of Bear Stearns (in March 2008) rose. Consequently, the risk to the Fed increased materially with this degradation of asset composition. The Fed also became much more actively involved in directing the allocation of credit in the economy.

Following the insolvency of Lehman Brothers, the already fragile interbank market suffered a severe shock. Mistrust of even major counterparties rose to historically unprecedented proportions, and the Fed was compelled to provide massive amounts of new financing to replace the lending that was now frozen. The intervention of the U.S. government in the American International Group (AIG) to prevent a meltdown in the credit default swaps market and credit insurance industry in general on September 17 was facilitated by Fed lending. At this point, the Fed no longer attempted to sterilize the liquidity injections from its lending programs, and the size of the balance sheet rose exponentially. Interest rate volatility in the federal funds market rose sharply, and the FRBNY had great difficulty in maintaining the FOMC target.

The massive increase in the level of excess reserves in the fourth quarter of 2008 resulted in the effective federal funds rate trading well below the FOMC target rate until mid-December, when the target was changed to a bank with a ceiling of .5 percent and a floor of zero. In light of deteriorating economic conditions, the FOMC explicitly declared in its December 16, 2008, statement that "The focus of the Committee's policy going forward will be to *support the functioning of financial markets* and stimulate the economy through open market operations and *other measures that sustain the size of the Federal Reserve's balance sheet at a high level.* . . . The Federal Reserve will continue to consider ways of *using its balance sheet to further support credit markets* and economic activity" [emphasis added]. This statement reflected a dramatic departure from previous operational policies, which had been implemented with a small policy-oriented balance sheet aimed at avoiding direct influence over U.S. credit conditions. The Fed is now using its balance sheet to actively intermediate in distressed credit markets, as well as aiming to alter relative prices among asset classes and along the yield curve, placing its capital at risk in the process to compensate for a withdrawal of private risk capital in money and capital market arbitrage.

Although the change in operational policy stemmed the decline in Fed holdings of U.S. Treasuries, it also allowed the Fed to take on a virtually unlimited amount of higher risk claims on the financial system. In particular, the lending to support JPMorgan's takeover of Bear Stearns and the support to AIG, intermediated through corporate structures controlled by the Federal Reserve Bank of New York (named Maiden Lane I, II, and III) rose to over $100 billion. The Fed also announced a high risk lending program called the Term Auction Lending Facility (TALF), which is designed to support the issuance of asset-backed securities collateralized by auto loans, student loans, credit card loans, and loans guaranteed by the U.S. Small Business Administration.[4] Originally capped at $200 billion, this program was subsequently raised to $1 trillion.

FEDERAL RESERVE BALANCE SHEET RISK

Comparing the end-2006 and end-2008 balance sheets, the change in constituent parts is clear. Particularly noticeable is the decline in government securities holdings and the increase in foreign exchange swaps, term auction facility credit, the commercial paper funding facility, "other loans," and the three Maiden Lane LLC holdings.[5] Particularly with the latter interventions, the FRBNY has taken on increased risk. Overall risk is set to increase with the March 18, 2009, announced expansion of the Term Asset-Backed Securities Loan Facility (TALF) although the U.S. Treasury is to take the first 10 percent of any TALF losses. The outer envelope for TALF lending was $1 trillion at the time this chapter was written.

A thorough examination of the risks associated with each Fed program innovation would require an examination of each asset class being supported, their price volatility, projections of future real economy dynamics, and assumptions about recovery rates on collateral.[6] It would also require knowledge of the FRB asset valuations on which "haircuts" are applied. Consideration of any risk-sharing by the U.S. Treasury would also be necessary. The FRB balance sheet is also very much a moving target at the time this chapter was written, with even the outer enve-lope of balance sheet expansion unknown. In a positive development, the FRB and Treasury have announced that as budgetary resources and time permit, Treasury will "seek to remove" the so-called Maiden Lane facilities from the FRB balance sheet. This will reduce the risk to the FRB balance sheet and is consistent with the suggestion here that Treasury use its SFP deposits to purchase those assets.

In light of the aforementioned uncertainties, the strategy adopted here is to take an aggregate approach toward assessing risk and to provide a preliminary discussion of how the FRB might cope with those risks and any eventual losses. The aggregate approach first divides FRB assets on the end-2008 balance sheet into (credit) risk-free and risky assets. A rough calculation is then made to provide a quantitative illustration of possible losses on those risky assets. An important assumption for the projection of the quantitative losses is that the TALF program attains its theoretical maximum of $1 trillion. Approximately half of the projected losses come from losses on TALF assets. The discussion then turns to consider what resources the FRBs have to cope with losses and concludes with several FRB capital projections based on the model developed in Restrepo, Salomó, and Valdés (2009). Those simulations are quite sensitive to the time path of interest rates and the liquidity of the FRB asset portfolio. It is important to note at the outset that no subjective probability is attached to the occurrence of these losses. The intent is to consider a quite severe hypothetical negative outcome and assess the FRB ability to cope with it.

Details on the projection of the losses can be found in Stella (2009). Overall scenario total losses are on the order of $175 to $200 billion. How would the Fed cope with losses on this order of magnitude? In a given year, the FRBs and any commercial bank have the same two primary sources to absorb losses from any one of their business lines—earnings and capital.

Earnings. The FRBs are highly profitable. The FR System has made a profit every year since 1916, including throughout the Great Depression. Average annual profit during the years 2004 through 2008 was $30.7 billion and the average return on capital is close to 100 percent. This compares with an average return on U.S. commercial bank equity of 13.7 percent during the period from 1998 to 2007. Clearly, FRB income generation capacity far exceeds that of any commercial bank owing to the spread between its main conventional financing source, banknotes, and its holdings of Treasury assets. Therefore, while it would take the average U.S. commercial bank approximately seven years to double capital by fully retaining earnings (assuming 1998-to-2007 performance), the FRB could conceivably do so in one. Fed earnings remained strong in 2008. Net income prior to distribution rose from $38.4 billion in 2007 to $38.7 billion in 2008 despite losses of $9.6 billion on the portfolio holdings of the Maiden Lane special purpose vehicles (SPVs).[7]

Capital. With consolidated capital at $42 billion at end-2008, adding one year of average past annual earnings yields a year-ahead buffer of $73 billion.

Banknote issuance. The Fed has one key source of financing that is not available to commercial banks—the ability to issue U.S. banknotes as legal tender. FRBs purchase notes from the Bureau of Engraving and Printing at the cost of produc-tion and issue them in the market at face value. The difference between the cost of production, and the costs of maintaining the banknote supply in good phys-ical condition, which implies replacement at well-defined "soiled" benchmarks, represents seignorage. Net banknote issuance averaged $28 billion during the period from 2004 to 2008.

Adding these three sources provides a first-order ability to cope with losses of about $100 billion.

Stella (2009) shows that coping with a scenario involving one-time losses on the order of $200 billion on a portion of the FRB asset portfolio would entail a decline in FRB capital of approximately $170 billion. To return to positive equity of $45 billion would then require roughly the retention of all profit during the next six years.

The static scenario. The Fed would eventually earn its way out of a deficit position through retention of seignorage and economic growth, but there would be an extended period during which balance sheet capital would be negative and transfers to the Treasury would be suspended.

In none of the several scenarios considered would the FRB suffer catastrophic losses necessitating an abandonment of an aggressive response to rising inflationary expectations. But the FRB would suffer significant losses, and capital would fall below zero. That event and the corresponding loss of Treasury nontax revenue would likely not escape the attention of legislators who might then raise questions as to the legitimacy of the FRB's ability to undertake operations that entail fiscal risk. A belief in financial markets that the Fed will refrain from tightening policy to avoid this political economy risk to operational independence may foster heightened expectations of inflation.

In order to strengthen the Fed's credibility and thereby assuage concerns that the Fed might not respond aggressively to inflationary pressures owing to fears over the impact on its balance sheet, several measures would be of assistance. First, the FRB could begin to retain all of its 2009 profit, building up provisions for future loan losses. If the financial system eventually makes a full recovery, these provisions could be released and the income passed on to Treasury at that time. Second, the Treasury could use $115 billion in its $200 billion in deposits at the Fed (as of July 1, 2009) to purchase the loan to AIG and the Maiden Lane SPVs at their current values. This would move both the risk and return on these loans on to the Treasury balance sheet. Lastly, the Treasury could provide greater insurance coverage on the TALF program, for example, providing 20 percent of first loss insurance compared with the currently agreed 10 percent. The sum of these measures would make it highly unlikely that the Fed would experience negative capital and presumably enhance its inflation-fighting credibility, thereby containing inflationary expectations.

Strong central bank balance sheets are important for credibility, and the Treasury and Congress would be well advised to assure the Fed retains market confidence. Weak balance sheets and lost credibility have been problems for many central banks worldwide, and this has, in general, been associated with poor monetary policy performance.[8]

Whether confidence in the avoidance of negative FRB capital would have a material impact on market participants' expectations in the current U.S. context can only be speculated. As argued in Stella (1997), a central bank need not have positive capital as conventionally defined as long as the underlying strength of its balance sheet (essentially future earnings capacity) is sufficient to allow it to achieve its policy objectives and preserve its financial independence under plausible risk scenarios. Nevertheless, to the extent financial markets may correctly or erroneously believe a strong central bank would deviate from stated policy objectives to avoid losses, a strengthened balance sheet may enhance policy credibility.

As discussed earlier, the Fed has taken increased financial risk in expanding the scope of its operations. Its risk control measures have included: purchasing only highly rated AAA quality paper, applying significant haircuts to unconventional collateral, and requesting indemnity from the Treasury for certain operations or portions thereof. Nevertheless, questions remain as to how the valuation of collateral has been undertaken, the validity of credit ratings agencies' ratings, particularly with regard to asset-backed securities, and the likely magnitude of the current economic turmoil. The FRB also has to be concerned with liquidity risk. Should demand for the current level of excess reserves wane during a period when the monetary stance is being tightened, the FRB will have to reduce liquid interest earning assets or pay an increasingly higher rate of interest on its liabilities.

SEPARATING INSTITUTIONAL RESPONSIBILITIES FOR MONETARY AND FINANCIAL STABILITY POLICIES

A number of writers have made the point that once central banks cut interest rates to zero and embark on unconventional measures, it becomes difficult to separate monetary and fiscal policy. This ambiguity raises politico-economic questions, most importantly those that arise from the notion that monetary and fiscal policies are designed and implemented under quite different governance, accountability, and supervisory structures. One of the significant accomplishments of institutional policy development over the past three decades has been increased independence of monetary policy from political considerations. Perhaps the most prominent discrete example of this worldwide phenomenon was the creation of the European Central Bank, whose design stressed the importance of financial independence.

Increased institutional independence makes the undertaking of what can clearly be perceived as fiscal or at least quasi-fiscal policy by the central bank subject to legitimacy concerns. In particular, legislatures may question the logic of constraining and influencing fiscal policy when conducted within the Treasury or Ministry of Finance while allowing the central bank free rein. They might desire in response to reverse central bank independence, in particular in the area of monetary policy.

The global consensus that emerged over the past two decades stressing the benefits of independent monetary policy is worth preserving. But we would draw a distinction here between *monetary policy* and *central bank* independence. While the case for an independent monetary authority is clear, the case for central bank autonomy in the field of crisis intervention—when fiscal resources are placed at risk—is much less so. In the light of contentious political debates over fiscal policy, it is not evident that the political champions of central bank independence intended to provide central banks fiscal independence.[9] Should political authorities find current central bank activism an affront to their legislative authority, a backlash may ensue whereupon monetary policy independence is curtailed. For this reason, it may be wise to develop an alternative governance structure to handle the banking or, in the modern financial system, market-making roles that had been assigned to central banks in legislation crafted when they were subject to fiscal authority.

The possibility to separate the balance sheet consequences of banking and monetary policy was foreshadowed earlier in this chapter. Until 2007, the FRB and its major central bank counterparts had managed quite successfully through operations of minimal size to steer short-term interest rates to influence economic activity and inflation. Intervention in the crisis, however, required an immense balance sheet expansion and important changes in asset composition. This intervention quickly expanded to include not only conventional monetary operations counterparties but also more distant institutions—including investment banks and insurance companies—and more distant markets such as those for commercial paper and ABS.

Central banks have effectively placed their capital at risk to become market makers to the broader financial system. They have attempted in this role to replace the withdrawn capital of bankrupt or diminished market intermediaries so they could curtail the widening of interest rate spreads. The private traders who are being replaced are not able to create central bank money. Therefore, an entity with an ability to issue high quality securities—backed by government—could undertake this role. It need not be the central bank or monetary authority.

The exact structure of such an entity, which might be named the Market Liquidity Maintenance (MLM) corporation, would need to be spelled out. In concept, the MLM would be intended to be active in capital markets—as the founders expected the Bank of England and Federal Reserve Banks to be in the money market. The capacity to quickly scale up activity, should market conditions dictate, is also important. While in normal times MLM would engage in a modest amount of activity, in a panic it would need to quickly scale up. Its capital structure should therefore allow for scalability—relatively small paid-in capital with legislative preauthorization to expand under certain conditions. The risks and profit from the MLM would be clearly on the fiscal accounts—avoiding potential conflict with monetary operations.

The optimal governance structure for the public body charged with preserving financial sector stability and intervening in stressed financial markets may correspond to neither that of the optimal monetary nor fiscal authority. Therefore, an alternative governance structure could be contemplated, one combining political representation from Treasury with the participation of independent agencies and/or third parties. This would provide political legitimacy to financial market interventions undertaken by the new agency while preserving the political independence of monetary policy that may now be at risk.

NOTES

1. The Fed is the monopoly supplier of U.S. banknotes. Conceptually, when banknotes are purchased from the Fed with reserves held by private commercial banks, the Fed subsequently purchases U.S. Treasury securities from the market, leaving the quantity of money unchanged. Over time, most of the Fed's balance sheet growth has resulted from the growth in currency. The resulting interest revenue is used to pay the operating costs of the Fed, dividends to shareholders, and transfers of residual profit to the Treasury.

2. See Chailloux, Gray, Klueh, Shimizu, and Stella (2008) for a description of how other central banks responded.

3. The FOMC lowered the federal funds target from 5.25 percent in July 2007 to 1.5 percent in October 2008.

4. See FRB press release November 25, 2008.

5. The Fed has recently been providing more detail on the composition of its balance sheet. See Bernanke (2009), Speech at the National Press Club luncheon, Washington, D.C. February 18, 2009. Maiden Lane I relates to the Bear Stearns operation, while II and III pertain to AIG.

6. The Fed provides a web site describing its programs: www.federalreserve.gov/monetarypolicy/bst.htm.

7. The net loss to the Fed from the Maiden Lane SPVs in 2008 amounted to $3.4 billion as the three SPVs registered $1.9 billion in net interest income while $4.4 billion in losses were absorbed by JPMorgan and AIG.

8. See Stella (1997), (2005), and (2008) for country examples and further argumentation. Sims (2003) discusses how central bank balance sheet difficulties can make it impossible to attain an inflation target.

9. See Cukierman (2008) for further discussion of the development of the idea of central bank independence.

REFERENCES

Bernanke, Ben S. 2009. *Federal Reserve Policies to Ease Credit and Their Implications for the Fed's Balance Sheet*. National Press Club Luncheon. Washington, D.C., February.

Cukierman, Alex. 2008. Central bank independence and monetary policymaking institutions—Past, present and future. *European Journal of Political Economy*, December.

Chailloux, Alexandre, Simon Gray, Ulrich Klueh, Seiichi Shimizu, and Peter Stella. 2008. Central Bank Response to the 2007-08 Financial Market Turbulance: Experiences and Lessons Drawn. *IMF Working Paper 08/210* Washington: International Monetary Fund.

Restrepo, Jorge, Salomó, Luis and Rodrigo Valdés. 2009. Macroeconomia, Politica Monetaria y Patrimonio del Banco Central de Chile. *Economia Chilena* 12: 1, 5–38

Sims, Christopher A. 2003. Limits to Inflation Targeting. mimeo. Princeton, New Jersey: Princeton University, March 17.

Stella, Peter, 1997. Do Central Banks Need Capital? *IMF Working Paper 97/83* Washington: International Monetary Fund.

———. 2005. Central Bank Financial Strength, Transparency, and Policy Credibility. IMF Staff Papers 52: 2 Washington: International Monetary Fund.

———. 2008. Central Bank Financial Strength, Policy Constraints and Inflation. *IMF Working Paper 08/49* Washington: International Monetary Fund.

———. 2009. The Federal Reserve System Balance Sheet: What Happened and Why it Matters. *IMF Working Paper 09/120* Washington: International Monetary Fund.

ABOUT THE AUTHOR

Peter Stella received his Ph.D. in economics from Stanford. After a 25-year career at the IMF, he is now an independent consultant. He may be reached at pstellaconsult@gmail.com.

PART IX

Implications of the Crisis for Our Economic Systems

CHAPTER 61

Systemic Risk and Markets

STEVEN L. SCHWARCZ
Stanley A. Star Professor of Law and Business at Duke University School of Law
and Founding Director of Duke's Global Capital Markets Center*

INTRODUCTION

Although banks and other financial institutions (collectively, *institutions*) are important sources of capital, and although a chain of bank failures remains an important symbol of systemic risk, the ongoing trend toward disintermediation—or enabling companies to access the ultimate source of funds, the capital markets, without going through banks or other financial intermediaries—is making these failures less critical than in the past. Companies today are able to obtain most of their financing through the capital markets without the use of intermediaries. As a result, capital markets themselves are increasingly central to any examination of systemic risk. Systemic disturbances can erupt outside the banking system and spread through capital market linkages rather than merely through banking relationships.

This has been dramatically illustrated by the subprime financial crisis. The initial trigger of the cascade of failures that led to this crisis was the historically unanticipated depth of the fall in housing prices. Loans to risky, or subprime, borrowers were often made with the expectation of refinancing through home appreciation. When home prices stopped appreciating, these borrowers could not refinance. In many cases, they defaulted.

These defaults in turn caused substantial amounts of investment grade securities backed by these mortgages to be downgraded and, in some cases, to default. Investors began losing confidence in these securities, and their prices started falling. Mark-to-market accounting rules and the high leverage of many firms exacerbated the fall.

The refusal in mid-September 2008 of the government to save Lehman Brothers, and its resulting bankruptcy, added to this cascade. Securities markets became so panicked that even the commercial paper market virtually shut down, and the

---

*This chapter is based on the author's article, "Systemic Risk," *Geo. L. J.* 97 (2008): 193, also available at www.ssrn.com/abstract_id=1008326.

Steven L. Schwarcz is the author of numerous articles and papers on the subprime financial crisis and systemic risk and has testified before the Committee on Financial Services of the U.S. House of Representatives on "Systemic Risk: Examining Regulators' Ability to Respond to Threats to the Financial System," available at www.house.gov/apps/list/hearing/financialsvcs_dem/ht1002072.shtml.

market prices of mortgage-backed securities collapsed substantially below the intrinsic value of the mortgage assets underlying those securities. Banks and other financial institutions holding mortgage-backed securities had to write down their value, causing these institutions to appear more financially risky, in turn triggering concern over counterparty risk.

Although the federal government has taken numerous steps to address this collapse, including enacting the Emergency Economic Stabilization Act of 2008, most of its steps to date have focused on institutions, not markets. Such a narrow focus worked well when banks and institutions were the primary source of corporate financing. But as the financial crisis reveals, this focus is insufficient now that companies obtain much of their financing directly through capital markets.

Institutional systemic risk and market systemic risk should not be viewed each in isolation. Institutions and markets can be involved in both. This integrated perspective is useful because a chain of failures of critical financial intermediaries, by definition, would significantly affect the availability and cost of capital. These failures, therefore, implicitly become a proxy for market consequences. In contrast, a chain of failures of institutions that are not critical financial intermediaries could only significantly affect the availability or cost of capital when those failures are large enough to jeopardize the viability of capital markets.

As disintermediation increases, therefore, systemic risk should increasingly be viewed by its impact on markets, not institutions, per se.

ANALYSIS

The problem of regulating systemic risk is a subset of the problem of regulating *financial* risk. Scholars argue that the primary, if not sole, justification for regulating financial risk is maximizing economic efficiency. Because systemic risk is a form of financial risk, efficiency should be a central goal in its regulation.

Efficiency has a somewhat unique added dimension in the context of systemic risk. Without regulation, the externalities caused by systemic risk would not be prevented or internalized because systemic risk pertains to risks to the financial system itself. Market participants are motivated to protect themselves but not necessarily to protect the system as a whole. As a result, there is a type of tragedy of the commons, in which the benefits of exploiting finite capital resources accrue to individual market participants, each of whom is motivated to maximize use of the resource, whereas the costs of exploitation, which affect the real economy, are distributed among an even wider class of persons. Any regulation of systemic risk should thus focus not only on traditional efficiency but also on the stability of the financial system.

In examining regulatory approaches to systemic risk, one should also take into account the costs of regulation. These can include direct costs, such as hiring government employees to monitor and enforce the regulations, and indirect costs, such as potential moral hazard. In identifying regulatory approaches, this chapter takes these costs into account, as well as the goals of efficiency and stability.

Historical attempts to regulate systemic risk can be imperfect and messy. Furthermore, the historical focus has been on bank systemic risk and related monetary policy. Modern models of regulating systemic risk should also focus on nonbank and market failures.

To that end, consider the following potential regulatory approaches.

Averting Panics

The ideal regulatory approach would aim to eliminate the risk of systemic collapse, *ab initio.* Theoretically, this goal could be achieved by preventing financial panics, since they are often the triggers that commence a chain of failures. I believe that the subprime financial crisis itself was triggered by financial panic. Any regulation aimed at preventing panics that trigger systemic risk, however, could fail to anticipate all the causes of the panics. Furthermore, even when identified, panics cannot always be averted easily because investors are not always rational.

Requiring Increased Disclosure

Another potential regulatory approach is to require increased disclosure. Disclosing risks traditionally has been viewed, at least under U.S. securities laws, as the primary market regulatory mechanism. It works by reducing, if not eliminating, asymmetric information among market players, making the risks transparent to all.

In the context of systemic risk, however, individual market participants who fully understand that risk takers will be motivated to protect themselves but not the system as a whole. This is because of the tragedy of the commons, mentioned earlier. Imposing additional disclosure requirements may even prove counterproductive, causing market participants to change their behavior. For example, traders may become more cautious, demanding that prices move further before making trades, thereby ultimately reducing market liquidity.

The efficacy of disclosure is further limited by the increasing complexity of transactions and markets. A contributing factor to the recent subprime crisis, for example, is allegedly that many institutional investors bought mortgage-backed securities substantially based on their ratings without fully understanding what they bought.

Requiring increased disclosure would therefore do relatively little to mitigate the potential for systemic risk.

Imposing Financial Exposure Limits

The failure of one or more large institutions could create defaults large enough to destabilize other highly leveraged investors, increasing the likelihood of a systemic market meltdown. This suggests another possible approach to regulation: placing limits on inter-institution financial exposure. Financial exposure limits would facilitate stability by diversifying risk, in effect by reducing the losses of any given contractual counterparty and thus the likelihood that such losses would cause the counterparty to fail. Limits also might reduce the urgency, and hence the panic, that contractual counterparties feel about closing out their positions.

This approach already applies to banks through lending limits, which restrict the amount of bank exposure to any given customer's risk. Its application beyond banks to other financial institutions is potentially appealing, given the increasing blurring of lines between banks and nonbank financial institutions and the high volumes of financial assets circulating among nonbank financial entities.

It is questionable, though, whether the government should impose financial exposure limits on institutions. Large financial institutions already try to protect themselves through risk management and risk mitigation. The subprime financial crisis has raised questions, though, whether conflicts of interest among managers and other failures can undermine institutional risk management.[1]

Requiring Reduced Leverage

Requiring reduced leverage could reduce the risk that an institution fails in the first place. It also could reduce the likelihood of transmitting financial contagion between institutions. But requiring reduced leverage creates significant costs. Some leverage is good, and there is no optimal across-the-board amount of leverage that is right for every institution.

Ensuring Liquidity

Ensuring liquidity could facilitate stability in two ways: by providing liquidity to prevent institutions from defaulting, and by providing liquidity to capital markets as necessary to keep them functioning.

The U.S. Federal Reserve Bank already has the role of providing liquidity to prevent institutions from defaulting, by acting as a lender of last resort. This approach is costly, however. By providing a lifeline to financial institutions, a lender of last resort fosters moral hazard by encouraging these entities—especially those that believe they are too big to fail—to be fiscally reckless. It also can shift costs to taxpayers since loans made to institutions will not be repaid if the institutions eventually fail.

The subprime crisis has shown that, in an era of disintermediation, more attention needs to be focused on providing liquidity to capital markets as necessary to keep them functioning. This approach should also be less costly than lending to institutions. A market liquidity provider of last resort, especially if it acts at the outset of a market panic, can profitably invest in securities at a deep discount from the market price and still provide a floor to how low the market will drop. Buying at a deep discount will mitigate moral hazard and also make it likely that the market liquidity provider will be repaid. The role of a market liquidity provider of last resort might even be able to be privatized.

One might ask why, if a market liquidity provider of last resort can invest at a deep discount to stabilize markets and still make money, private investors won't also do so, thereby eliminating the need for the market liquidity provider. One answer is that individuals at investing firms will not want to jeopardize their reputations (and jobs) by causing their firms to invest at a time when other investors have abandoned the market. Another answer is that private investors usually want to buy and sell securities, not waiting for their maturities, whereas a market liquidity provider of last resort should be able to wait until maturity, if necessary.

Ad Hoc Approaches

The cost and effectiveness of ad hoc, or purely reactive, regulatory responses to systemic risk are, of course, partly dependent on what those responses turn out to be. Ad hoc approaches do not always work. Sometimes they are too late and the harm has been done or can no longer be prevented, and sometimes there is insufficient time to fashion and implement an optimal solution.

Nonetheless, ad hoc approaches should not be dismissed out of hand. They can help minimize the difficulties in measuring, and balancing, costs and benefits, and they can reduce moral hazard cost to the extent an institution cannot know in advance whether, if it faces financial failure, it will be bailed out or allowed to fail.

Market Discipline

Under a market discipline approach, the regulator's job is to ensure that market participants exercise the type of diligence that enables the market to work efficiently. This was the type of approach taken by the U.S. government under the second G. W. Bush administration.

Textbooks claim that perfect markets would never need external regulation, thereby providing support for a market discipline approach. Actual markets, however, including financial markets, are not perfect. Furthermore, because of the aforesaid tragedy of the commons, a firm can lack sufficient incentive to limit its risk taking in order to reduce the danger of systemic contagion for other firms.

The subprime financial crisis dramatically confirms this argument, that preventing systemic risk through market discipline does not always work. Market discipline may nonetheless be attractive as a supplement to other regulatory approaches.

CONCLUSION

Of the regulatory approaches identified, regulation establishing a market liquidity provider of last resort not only should have benefits likely to exceed its costs but is also the approach that would have the best chance of minimizing systemic risk under any number of circumstances. Such a market liquidity provider should be made operational because market collapses can occur rapidly and without warning. Any establishment of a market liquidity provider of last resort should be supplemented by a market-discipline approach. To the extent these approaches fail to deter a systemic meltdown, government should seek to prevent the meltdown or mitigate its impact by implementing whatever ad hoc approaches appear, at the time, to be appropriate.

Because of the difficulty of obtaining reliable empirical data, these recommendations cannot be subjected to a rigorous cost-benefit analysis. Cost-benefit analysis nonetheless provides a useful way of thinking about regulating systemic risk. As the subprime financial crisis has demonstrated, the cost of a systemic meltdown can be catastrophic. Moreover, when regulation deals with health and safety issues—as could arise in the case of systemic risk due to its societal impact—the cost-benefit balancing should go beyond strict econometrics. For example, when addressing the risk of catastrophic events or large, irreversible effects through which the actual level of risk is indeterminate, regulators often apply a precautionary principle under which they may decide to regulate an activity notwithstanding lack of decisive evidence of the activity's harm. This same type of precautionary principle may well apply to a cost-benefit assessment of systemic risk regulation.

Finally, because financial markets and institutions increasingly cross sovereign borders, it is critical to examine how these regulatory approaches might work in an international context. This examination should include the feasibility of internationally regulating systemic risk, the extent to which a market liquidity provider of last resort or other regulatory solutions are universal or should be different for different countries, and the potential for a regulatory race to the bottom if regulation is done only on a national level.

NOTE

1. *Cf.* Steven L. Schwarcz, 2009, "Conflicts and Financial Collapse: The Problem of Secondary-Management Agency Costs," *Yale Journal on Regulations* 26: 2, 457. (Symposium issue on the future of financial regulation), available at http://ssrn.com/abstract_id=1322536.

ABOUT THE AUTHOR

Steven L. Schwarcz is the Stanley A. Star professor of law and business at Duke University and founding director of Duke's Global Capital Markets Center. Before joining Duke, he was a partner at two leading international law firms and also taught at the Yale and Columbia Law Schools. Schwarcz has advised the United States Congress and other government bodies on systemic risk and the recent financial crisis. His scholarly works include "Systemic Risk," *Geo. L. J.* 97 (2008): 193; "Protecting Financial Markets: Lessons from the Subprime Mortgage Meltdown," *Minn. L. Rev.* 93 (2008): 373; "Disclosure's Failure in the Subprime Mortgage Crisis," *Utah. L. Rev.* (2008): 1109; "Understanding the Subprime Financial Crisis," *S. C. L. Rev.* 60 (2009): 549; "Conflicts and Financial Collapse: The Problem of Secondary-Management Agency Costs," *Yale J. on Reg.* 26 (Summer 2009); "Too Big To Fail? Recasting the Financial Safety Net," in *The Panic of 2008* (Geo. Wash. Univ. symposium book); "Regulating Complexity in Financial Markets," *Wash. U. L. Rev.* 87 (2010); and *Regulating Financial Systems,* forthcoming from Oxford University Press (co-authored with Kenneth Anderson).

CHAPTER 62

The Transmission of Liquidity Shocks During the Crisis

Ongoing Research into the Transmission of Liquidity Shock Suggests the Emergence of a Range of New Channels During the Credit Crisis

NATHANIEL FRANK
Researcher at Nuffield College and the Oxford-Man Institute of Quantitative Finance

BRENDA GONZÁLEZ-HERMOSILLO
Deputy Division Chief of Global Financial Stability at the IMF

HEIKO HESSE
Economist in the Middle East and Central Asia Department at the IMF

The rapid transmission of the subprime mortgage crisis in the United States to other domestic and foreign financial markets raises several questions of great importance to central banks and financial regulators. Through which mechanisms were the liquidity shocks transmitted across financial markets during this period? Why did the episode of funding illiquidity in structured investment vehicles (SIVs) and conduits turn into an issue of bank insolvency?

Conceptually, a number of new transmission mechanisms are likely to have been established (or become more important than usual) during periods of turbulence, either through increased market liquidity, funding liquidity, or even default risks. The relative strength of the interaction between these factors during the subprime crisis of 2007 is an empirical question, which we analyze in our research.[1]

GOOD VERSUS BAD TIMES

The mechanisms through which liquidity shocks influence various markets during normal times may operate through different channels to those that appear during times of financial stress. During tranquil periods, market illiquidity shocks are typically short-lived as they create opportunities for traders to profit and, in doing so, provide liquidity and contribute to the price discovery process.

During periods of crisis, however, several mechanisms may amplify liquidity shocks across financial markets, creating systemic risks. These mechanisms can operate through direct linkages between the balance sheets of financial institutions, but also indirectly through asset prices. As the current crisis has demonstrated, price movements are set in motion when financial institutions face mark-to-market losses. As a consequence, positions are de-leveraged, and if the value of the corresponding assets is significantly affected, the creditworthiness of the respective institutions will deteriorate because of increasing default risk. Clearly, then, leverage is procyclical and amplifies the financial cycle.

A STYLIZED ANATOMY OF THE CRISIS

In investigating how the various segments of financial markets in the United States were affected during the subprime crisis, we distinguish between *market liquidity* and *funding liquidity*. Market liquidity is an asset-specific characteristic measuring the ease with which positions can be traded, without significantly affecting their corresponding asset price. In contrast, funding liquidity refers to the availability of funds such that a solvent agent is able to borrow in the market so it can service outstanding obligations.

It is useful to briefly review the chronology of the recent turbulence, starting in the summer of 2007. As is well known, the initial shock came in the form of deteriorating quality of subprime mortgages in the United States. This was essentially a credit, rather than a liquidity event. This shock spread across different asset classes and financial markets because of a high degree of asymmetric information associated with the complexity of the structured mortgage products. This process was subsequently strengthened by a widespread repricing of risk and a general decrease in investors' risk appetite.

The next step in the crisis saw an increase in delinquencies on subprime mortgages leading to greater uncertainty surrounding the value of a number of other structured credit products that had these assets in their underlying portfolios. Consequently, rating agencies downgraded many of these securities and announced changes in their methodologies, first in mid-July but then again in mid-August and in mid-October. Meanwhile, structured credit mortgage–backed instruments measured by the ABS indexes (ABX) saw rapid declines, and the liquidity for initially tradable securities in their respective secondary markets evaporated. The losses, downgrades, and changes in methodologies shattered investor confidence in the rating agencies' abilities to evaluate risks of complex securities. As a result, investors pulled back from structured products en masse.

Spotlight on SIVs

It soon became apparent that a wide range of financial institutions had exposures to many of these mortgage-backed securities, often off-balance-sheet entities such as conduits and structured investment vehicles (SIVs). The SIVs or conduits were funded through the issuance of short-term asset-backed commercial paper (ABCP) for it to take advantage of a yield differential resulting in a maturity mismatch.

This created an inherent maturity mismatch. Because of the increasing uncertainty associated with exposures to the underlying mortgage-backed securities (and their values), investors became unwilling to roll over the corresponding ABCP.

As the problems with SIVs and conduits deepened, banks came under increasing pressure to rescue those that they had sponsored by providing liquidity or by taking their respective assets onto their own balance sheets. As a result, the balance sheets of these banks were particularly strained. A further strain on banks' balance sheets came from warehousing a higher than expected amount of mortgages and leveraged loans, the latter usually passed on to investors so they could fund the highly leveraged debt deals of private equity firms. Both the market for mortgages and leveraged loans dried up because of the collapse of transactions in the mortgage-related securitization market and collaterized loan obligations. Banks also felt obliged to honor liquidity commitments to alternative market participants such as hedge funds and other financial institutions, which were also suffering from the drain of liquidity. Consequently, the level of interbank lending declined for both reasons of liquidity and credit risk. Money markets were affected, as was evident from a widening of the LIBOR and overnight index swap spreads, which in turn led to increased funding costs.

Flight to Transparency

As turbulence related to subprime mortgages heightened, financial markets more generally showed signs of stress, and investor preference moved away from complex structured products in a flight to liquidity. Subsequently, positions were shifted in order to invest in only the safest and most liquid of assets, such as U.S. Treasury bonds.

Hedge funds also felt the sting of reduced liquidity. Those that held asset-backed securities and other structured products were burdened by increased margin requirements, driven in turn by greater market volatility. As a consequence, they attempted to offload the more liquid parts of their portfolios in order to meet these margin calls and also limited possible redemptions by investors.

The Specter of Insolvency

The evident deterioration of market and funding liquidity conditions had implications for the solvency position of banks for several reasons. First, financial institutions saw a decline in the values of the securitized mortgages and structured securities on their balance sheets, resulting in extensive writedowns. Second, funding liquidity pressures forced rapid de-leveraging during this period, further depressing asset prices. Third, funding costs increased because of rising money market spreads, which was amplified by an increasing reliance on funding from wholesale money markets. These pressures resulted in declining capital ratios throughout the banking sector and significant increases in credit default swap spreads across the banking sector.

DATA AND METHODOLOGY

The transmission mechanisms of liquidity shocks across differing U.S. financial markets outlined so far have been described as being unidirectional and sequential. But in periods of financial stress, reinforcing *liquidity spirals* are likely to be set in motion. The likely multidirectionality with which shocks are transmitted during a crisis motivates the use of a Dynamic Conditional Correlation GARCH specification to test these effects.[2] This specification allows us to model the correlation dynamics between asset classes in order to evaluate whether the co-movement between different markets increased during the crisis.

The model uses a system of five corresponding variables to capture key linkages, which act as proxies for overall market liquidity, funding liquidity, default risk, and volatility. First, *funding liquidity* conditions in the *asset-backed commercial paper market* are modeled by the spread between the yield of three-month ABCP and that of three-month U.S. Treasury bills. The second variable examined in the system is the spread between the three-month U.S. interbank Libor rate and the overnight index swap, which measures *bank funding liquidity* pressures. Third, S&P 500 stock market returns are included into the reduced form model, whereby in its second moment, it serves as a proxy for *market volatility.* The spread between the yield on two-year on-the-run (the most recently issued) and off-the-run (previously issued) U.S. Treasuries captures *overall market liquidity* conditions. Finally, the *default risk* of banks is modeled by the credit default swap spreads of 12 large complex financial institutions. Exhibit 62.1 provides a visual representation of the movement in three of the key variables before and during the crisis.

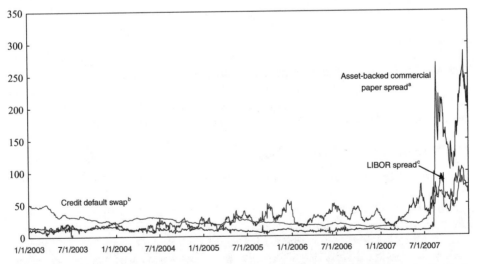

Exhibit 62.1 Aggregate Bank Credit Default Swap Rate and Selected Spreads (in Basis Points).
[a]Spread between yields on 90-day U.S. asset-backed commercial paper and on three-month U.S. Treasury bills.
[b]The unweighted daily average of the five-year credit default swaps for the following institutions: Morgan Stanley, Merrill Lynch, Goldman Sachs, Lehman Brothers, JPMorgan, Deutsche Bank, Bank of America, Citigroup, Barclays, Credit Suisse, UBS, and Bear Stearns.
[c]Spread between yields on three-month U.S. LIBOR and on three-month U.S. overnight index swap.
Sources: Bloomberg L.P.; and IMF staff estimates.

RESULTS

The results from our model indicate a sharply increased interaction between the various proxies for market and funding liquidity. The implied correlations between the ABCP and Libor spreads rise from a precrisis average of approximately 0.3 to above 0.5, a level at which they remain. Furthermore, the linkages between these two funding liquidity measures and the two-year on-the-run–off-the-run spread jump from around zero to 0.2 (see Exhibit 62.2, for example). Stronger interactions between the market liquidity in the bond market and the stock market return volatility are evident with S&P 500 returns and the two-year on-the-run spread becoming more highly correlated with each other and with all other variables.

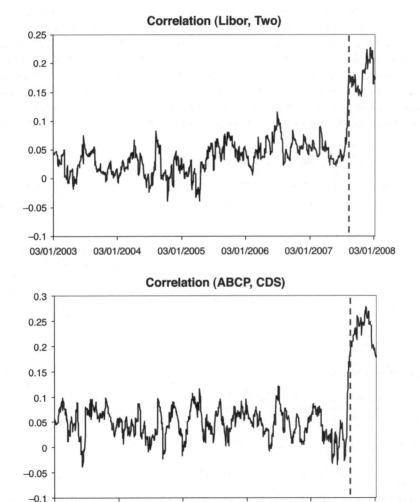

Exhibit 62.2 Selected Conditional Correlations from Dynamic Conditional Correlation GARCH Model

Finally, the co-movement between liquidity and solvency also increases sharply, as again illustrated in Exhibit 62.2. Before the hypothesized structural break at the end of July 2007, changes in the credit default swap spreads remain approximately uncorrelated with all other measures.

In summary, the various proxies for funding and market liquidity, stock market volatility, and bank default risk exhibited extraordinary co-movement during the subprime crisis. As the correlations on these variables were fairly small in the precrisis period, the results suggest that new channels for transmission of liquidity shocks were established during the second half of 2007. The results of a very pronounced interaction between market and funding liquidity are consistent with the emergence of reinforcing liquidity spirals during the crisis. On the one side of this liquidity spiral, financial institutions were exposed to refinancing needs in the form of issuing ABCP, a situation in which market illiquidity in complex structured products led to funding illiquidity. In this regard, the results also show that increased correlations between the ABCP and Libor spreads reduced the possibilities of funding from the interbank money market, thus highlighting systemic risks. Though not shown explicitly in the paper, on the other side of this spiral, many European banks with large exposures to U.S. asset-backed securities had difficulties accessing wholesale funding, leading to subsequent market illiquidity in different market segments.

From Liquidity to Solvency Concerns

In addition to the described period of illiquidity, the subprime crisis increasingly became one of insolvency, as banks such as Northern Rock, IKB, and Bear Stearns had to be rescued. This is captured by the implied correlations between the credit default swaps and other variables in the model, which show clear signs of a structural break during the crisis period. Furthermore, these correlations have remained at elevated levels since then, suggesting that solvency concerns remain an issue.

Finally, it is also shown that seemingly unrelated stock and bond markets were affected during these times of severe stress. These transmission mechanisms were not restricted to the U.S. financial markets, but were also observed across other advanced and key emerging market economies.

NOTES

1. Nathaniel Frank is a researcher at the University of Oxford. Brenda González-Hermosillo and Heiko Hesse are a deputy division chief and an economist, respectively, in the Monetary and Capital Markets department of the International Monetary Fund. The views expressed here are those of the authors and do not necessarily represent those of the IMF or IMF policy.

2. See Frank, González-Hermosillo, and Heiko Hesse (2008) and Chapter 3 in the latest *Global Financial Stability Report* (IMF 2008). We employ the specification developed by Capiello, Engle, and Sheppard (2006). This allows for an evaluation of the time variation in the conditional correlations between variables, in addition to accounting for structural breaks in their respective data generating processes. The multivariate GARCH framework also takes the heteroskedasticity exhibited by the data into account, which is particularly useful for the analysis of crisis periods.

REFERENCES

Cappiello, L., R. Engle, and K. Sheppard. 2006. Asymmetric dynamics in the correlations of global equity and bond returns. *Journal of Econometrics* 4: 537–572.

Frank, N., B. González-Hermosillo, and H. Hesse. 2008. *Transmission of liquidity shocks: Evidence from the 2007 subprime crisis.* Washington, DC: International Monetary Fund.

International Monetary Fund. 2008. *Global financial stability report.* Washington, DC: World Economic and Financial Surveys.

ABOUT THE AUTHORS

Nathaniel Frank holds a Ph.D. from Oxford University and is currently a researcher at Nuffield College and the Oxford-Man Institute of Quantitative Finance. He was previously a visiting scholar at New York University and has also worked for the IMF and the World Bank. Recent research and publications mainly lie in the field of financial econometrics and include modeling the current financial crisis using high frequency data.

Brenda González-Hermosillo is a deputy division chief of global financial stability at the IMF. She has led several analytical chapters of the IMF *Global Financial Stability Report,* including: "Market and Funding Illiquidity: When Private Risk becomes Public"; "Stress in Bank Funding Markets and Implications for Monetary Policy"; and "Detecting Systemic Risk." She has a number of publications on global financial stability, financial crises and early warning indicators, global spillovers and contagion, and international investors' risk appetite, several of which have been published in *Quantitative Finance, Journal of Financial Stability,* and the *North American Journal of Finance and Economics.* She also co-authored a book on *Transmission of Financial Crises and Contagion* (Cambridge University). Before joining the IMF, she held positions at the Bank of Canada, Canada's Department of Finance, several investment banks (Bank of Montreal, Bank of Nova Scotia, Banco Nacional de Mexico), Mexico's Ministry of Finance, and Banco de Mexico. She has taught in the economics department at the University of Western Ontario and obtained her Ph.D. in economics at the University of Tilburg in the Netherlands.

Heiko Hesse is an economist in the Middle East and Central Asia department at the IMF after having worked two years on the IMF's *Global Financial Stability Report.* Before that, he was an economist at the World Bank from 2006 to 2007, working on the Commission on Growth and Development, which brings together 21 leading practitioners from government, business, and the policy-making arenas and is chaired by Nobel laureate Michael Spence. Before that, in 2005 and 2006, he was a visiting scholar at Yale University and a consultant at the World Bank. He also worked at McKinsey, NERA Economic Consulting, and PriceWaterhouseCoopers. Some of his current research involves systemic risk, sovereign wealth funds, Islamic finance and spillovers to EM countries. He has published in refereed academic journals such as the *Journal of Development Economics,* frequently speaks at conferences and central banks and is a regular contributor to the economics blogs VOX and RGE Monitor. Heiko obtained his Ph.D. in economics from Nuffield College, University of Oxford.

CHAPTER 63

Credit Contagion From Counterparty Risk

PHILIPPE JORION
Professor of Finance at the Paul Merage School of Business,
University of California at Irvine

GAIYAN ZHANG
Assistant Professor of Finance, the University of Missouri, St. Louis

PORTFOLIO CREDIT MODELS

Financial institutions have recently developed portfolio credit risk models that focus on potential credit losses at the top level of the institution. These new portfolio credit models are now in widespread use. Notably, they are used to assess economic capital, which is the amount of equity capital the institution should carry to absorb a large loss over a specified horizon with a high level of confidence. These models are also the basis for the recently established Basel II regulatory capital charges for commercial banks. In addition, these models are employed to structure collateralized debt obligations (CDOs), where the junior tranches are sized to absorb most of the losses.

These models are very difficult to calibrate, however. Unlike market risk models, correlations between defaults cannot be observed directly for the borrowers in the portfolio. Instead, default correlations are modeled indirectly, typically using a reduced-form model of default intensity or a structural model of the value of the firm based on a Gaussian copula. Standard models, including the new Basel II capital charges, assume a factor structure in which correlations are induced by a common factor that can be interpreted as the state of the economy. This common feature largely explains why recent comparative studies of industry portfolio models show remarkable similarities in their outputs, or measures of economic capital.[1]

These first-generation models, unfortunately, do not fully capture the clustering in default correlations, sometimes called *credit contagion*. Das et al. (2007) observe some excess clustering in corporate debt default from 1979 to 2004. Unexplained default clustering is a major problem for traditional credit risk models because it generates greater dispersion in the distribution of credit losses. Fatter tails imply a greater likelihood of large losses and an understatement of economic capital. This could lead to a greater number of bank failures in periods of stress, or losses on CDOs that exceed worst estimates. Indeed, unexpectedly large losses on CDOs have been at the heart of the financial crisis that started in 2007. The recent credit crisis demonstrates that credit contagion is a more severe problem than anybody had expected and that traditional credit risk models need reexamination.

CREDIT CONTAGION FROM COMMON FACTORS

Second-generation models attempt to account for this default clustering. They can be classified into two approaches. The first relies on a richer description of the common factor structure. The second relies on counterparty risk and will be described in the next section.

The common factor approach could be made more complex. For instance, Duffie et al. (2009) estimate a frailty model whereby defaults are driven by an unobserved time-varying latent variable, which partially explains the observed default clustering. This could be explained by multiple factor effects, or industry factors. Alternatively, the factor exposures or relationships within common factors need not be linear, as implied by the Gaussian copula model. If so, some common effects would only manifest themselves for large enough shocks.

Exhibit 63.1 describes channels of credit contagion. When Firm A files for bankruptcy, we generally expect negative effects for other firms in the same industry. Contagion effects reflect negative common shocks to the prospects of the industry, and may lead to further failures in Industry A. On the other hand, the failure of a firm could help its competitors gain market share, which is a competitive effect. Generally, the net of these two effects is intra-industry contagion.

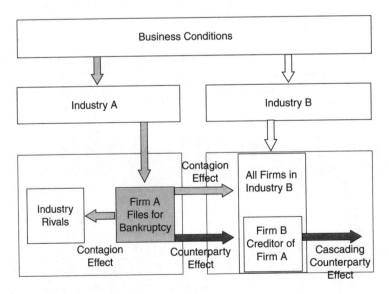

Exhibit 63.1   Channels of Credit Contagion

Common factor-based contagion effects can also arise across industries. Suppose that Industry A is a major client of Industry B. The default of Firm A could reveal negative information about sales prospects for firms in Industry B.

CREDIT CONTAGION FROM COUNTERPARTY RISK

The second approach to credit contagion is through counterparty risk. This effect arises when the default of one firm causes financial distress for its creditors. In Exhibit 63.1, say that Firm B has made a trade credit, or loan, to Firm A. Default by Firm A would cause a direct loss to Firm B, possibly leading to financial distress, even if it is in a different industry. For example, financial distress in the U.S. automobile industry had negative effects on the parts supplier industry. This could cause cascading effects to creditors of Firm B.

Generally, cascading or looping effects are too complex to model analytically because firms may hold each other's debt and also because of the sheer number of networked firms. Jarrow and Yu (2001), for example, provide closed-form solutions but only for a simple case with two firms and no cascading effects. Their model is of limited use, however, because of its simplistic assumptions.

The practice instead is to analyze counterparty contagion effects through simulations, called counterfactual because they focus on what might have happened. Researchers start from the topology of the financial system and examine the cascading effects of one bank defaulting at a time. Upper (2007) summarizes the literature, which suggests that pure counterparty contagion, due to lending in the interbank market, is likely to be rare. However, when it happens, the costs could be very high. In addition, when the default of the first bank is due to common factors that affect other banks, the probability of a systemic crisis increases greatly.

Counterparty risk thus motivates regulatory actions to minimize systemic risk. Chairman Bernanke (2008), for example, justified the rescue of Bear Stearns by explaining that "The company's failure could also have cast doubt on the financial positions of some of Bear Stearns's thousands of counterparties and perhaps of companies with similar businesses."

Similarly, the fear of counterparty defaults among financial institutions could explain the sudden worsening of the credit crisis after the Lehman Brothers bankruptcy in September 2008. Haldane (2009) argues that "The financial system is . . . a network, with . . . links defined by the financial interconnections. . . . When assessing nodal risk, it is not enough to know your counterparty, you need to know your counterparty's counterparty, too. In other words, there are Exhibit 63.1 externalities. There have been many examples of such spillover during this crisis, with Lehman Brothers' failure a particularly painful one. . . . "

This counterparty channel can be distinguished from common factor effects using detailed information about specific counterparty exposures. In Exhibit 63.1, Firm B is distinguished from other firms in the same industry by its counterparty exposure to Firm A. Jorion and Zhang (2009a) provide the first empirical analysis of counterparty credit risk, using an unexplored data source, which consists of the filing documents for 251 public bankruptcies over the period 1999 to 2005. These documents list the top 20 unsecured creditors, their credit amounts, and their credit types.

EVIDENCE ON COUNTERPARTY RISK EXPOSURES

This section examines the creditors' exposures to counterparty default.

Components of Exposures

The total economic effect from a counterparty default can be decomposed into two parts. The first part is the amount of direct exposure, a fraction of which can be lost through the bankruptcy proceedings. This represents assets either on the balance sheet or off the balance sheet, such as credit default swaps (CDS) positions. The second part is the value of the lost business if the counterparty cannot be easily replaced. This is an income effect.

Define EXP as the relative exposure, measured as the dollar amount of unsecured credit exposure scaled by the market value of the equity MVE; REC as the fractional recovery rate; and NPV as the dollar amount of lost future business, also scaled by MVE. The stock price effect for the creditor can be decomposed into a direct expected credit loss (ECL) and NPV:

$$\text{Rate of Return} = -ECL - NPV = -EXP(1 - REC) - NPV$$

For industrial firms, most exposures take the form of trade credit, defined as direct lending in a supplier-customer relationship. In the case of default, the trade creditor will lose part of the unsecured exposure. Also, the ongoing business of the trade creditor can be impaired by the bankruptcy of its borrower because this is often a major customer.

Empirical Evidence

In this bankruptcy sample, the mean exposures are $3 million, $12 million, and $164 million for trade credits, bonds, and loans, respectively. Industrials are exposed to trade credits and bonds only. Financials are exposed to all three categories. When scaled by the market value of the creditor's equity, exposures are generally small. For industrials, the mean is 0.32 percent. Some industrial firms have large and undiversified exposures, however, reaching 37 percent of equity. For financials, the mean exposure is 0.16 percent. Thus, exposures are generally larger in dollar amounts for financial than industrial creditors, but less so in relative terms, when considering the larger balance sheets of financial creditors.

EFFECTS OF COUNTERPARTY RISK

This section now examines the effect of counterparty risk on the creditor's stock prices.

Price Effects of Borrower's Bankruptcy

To investigate the market effects of counterparty risk, Jorion and Zhang (2009a) analyze the reaction of the creditor's stock price and credit spread around the

Exhibit 63.2 Contagion Effects of Chapter 11 Bankruptcy on Creditors' Stock Prices and CDS Spreads

Sample	Observations	Exposure (Percent of MVE)	Stock Return (Percent)	Change in Spreads (Basis Points)
Total	694	0.32	−1.9	5.2
Industrials	583	0.32	−2.3	5.5
Financials	111	0.16	−0.3	2.6

Shown is the average of cumulative abnormal stock returns and credit default swap spread changes for unsecured creditors of the 521 firms filing for Chapter 11 bankruptcy over the period 1999 to 2005. Returns are adjusted for the industry and spread changes for the credit rating. The period covered is 11 days around the announcement date.

announcement of the borrower's bankruptcy. To abstract from common factor-based contagion risk, stock returns are adjusted for general movements in the creditor's industry; credit spreads are adjusted for general movements in spreads with the same credit rating. Hence, these results should reveal pure counterparty risk effects.

Results are summarized in Exhibit 63.2. Creditors experience negative abnormal equity returns and increases in their credit spreads around the announcement of the bankruptcy of the borrower. On average, the creditor's equity falls by 1.9 percent. The size of this effect is greater than the average exposure of around 0.3 percent, which suggests a lost future business effect. As the bottom panel shows, the counterparty effect is indeed more important for industrials than for financials.

The creditor's CDS spread increases by 5.2 basis points, on average. In comparison, the median spread was 59bp for BBB-rated debt. Overall, these effects are relatively small.

Financial Distress Effects

As usual with events studies, this approach can only reveal unanticipated effects in market prices. In practice, bankruptcy is often preceded by other major public announcements about the debtor, such as financial distress, or even some kind of default. If so, the results are biased toward finding no effect. Also, focusing on actual price movements cannot identify the full cascading effects of counterparty risk for large financial institutions, given that regulators regularly bail out important banks.

To investigate this question directly, Jorion and Zhang (2009a) track creditor firms over the following years. Among the 461 industrials that experience a counterparty loss, 12 firms are delisted, and 149 firms are downgraded within two years. These numbers are compared to a control sample of firms in the same industry, with the same credit rating and size. The control sample experienced 3 delisted firms and 60 downgraded firms. These numbers are significantly lower than the sample that suffered credit losses. As a result, we can conclude that counterparty losses have a direct effect on the health of industrial creditors. For financials, differential effects are more tenuous, in line with weaker price effects.

Jorion and Zhang (2009a) also perform simulations of counterparty defaults in a credit portfolio. They find an increase in correlation that fits the value reported by Das et al. (2007). Thus, counterparty risk provides a potential explanation for the observed excess clustering of defaults.

Price Effects from Lehman's Bankruptcy

Thus, in normal times, counterparty risk seems minor for financial firms. The recent upheaval in financial markets, however, provides a relevant environment to evaluate counterparty risk that originates from financial firms. Jorion and Zhang (2009b) examine the stock price reactions of firms that announced the extent of their exposure to Lehman Brothers Holdings after the investment bank declared bankruptcy on September 15, 2008. Out of 81 firms in the sample, 44 had positive exposure, which averaged 7.4 percent of their equity; the other 37 firms reported no exposure.

For firms with exposure, the average abnormal return over the three days surrounding the announcement was –6.4 percent. Firms with no exposure experienced a price increase of 0.1 percent instead. Because these results are adjusted for industry effects, they abstract from common factors and can be solely attributed to counterparty risk. The magnitude of these effects demonstrates that counterparty risk is indeed a channel of credit contagion, which is more severe when the originator is a financial firm and during stress periods.

CONCLUSIONS

By now, it is clear that traditional portfolio credit models have failed badly during the recent credit crisis. The question is how to identify the roots of these failures. One approach is to extend common factor models. Another is to focus on counterparty risk.

This debate has important policy implications. On the one hand, Helwege (2009) argues that if financial defaults are due to common factors, for example, bad investments in mortgage-backed assets, regulators should not prop up the failing institutions. If assistance is required, the best course of action calls for broad intervention, supporting the mortgage market in this example. On the other hand, if counterparty risk is a major channel of credit contagion, there is a rationale for bailing out institutions that could cause a domino effect in the financial system.

In practice, regulatory intervention is predicated on the belief that counterparty risk is a major source of systemic risk. U.S. regulators have responded to fears of cascading defaults by bailing out large troubled financial institutions, including Bear Stearns and American International Group (AIG), and (probably) regret their decision not to bail out Lehman Brothers. In addition, the fear of counterparty risk largely explains movements toward greater disclosure requirements and centralized clearing counterparties (CCPs). A CCP has a better picture of each member's overall risk position than any dealer in a bilateral market, which improves overall transparency in the financial system.

Finding direct empirical evidence of counterparty risk is no easy task, however. Jorion and Zhang (2009a) provide evidence that industrial firms that suffer a counterparty credit loss suffer negative stock price effects and are more likely to experience financial distress later. The effect on financials is harder to trace. Their sample, however, covers a limited period without major disruptions for financial institutions.

The more recent experience of the Lehman bankruptcy, unfortunately, allows us to evaluate counterparty effects directly. Holding common factors constant, financial institutions that had greater exposure to Lehman suffered much larger losses in equity valuations. This confirms the importance of counterparty risk as a direct channel of credit contagion.

NOTE

1. The IACPM and ISDA (2006) study reports similar measures of economic capital across models when adjusted for other parameters.

REFERENCES

Bernanke, B. 2008. *Developments in the Financial Markets.* Testimony before the Senate Banking Committee, April 3, Washington, DC: Board of Governors of the Federal Reserve System.

Das, S., D. Duffie, N. Kapadia, and L. Saita. 2007. Common failings: How corporate defaults are correlated. *Journal of Finance* 62: 93–117.

Duffie, D., A. Eckner, G. Horel, and L. Saita. 2009. Frailty correlated default. *Journal of Finance* 64 (5): 2089–2123.

Haldane, A. 2009. *Why banks failed the stress test.* London: Bank of England.

Helwege, J. 2009. Financial firm bankruptcy and systemic risk. *Regulation* 32.

IACPM and ISDA. 2006. *Convergence of credit capital models,* New York: International Swaps and Derivatives Association.

Jarrow, R., and F. Yu. 2001. Counterparty risk and the pricing of defaultable securities. *Journal of Finance* 56: 1765–1799.

Jorion, P., and G. Zhang. 2009a. Credit contagion from counterparty risk. *Journal of Finance* 64 (5): 2053–2087.

———. 2009b. *Counterparty contagion from the Lehman bankruptcy.* Irvine, CA: University of California, Working Paper.

Upper, C. 2007. *Using counterfactual simulations to assess the danger of contagion in interbank markets.* Basel, Switzerland: Bank for International Settlements, Working Paper.

ABOUT THE AUTHORS

Philippe Jorion is a professor of finance at the School of Business at the University of California at Irvine, where he holds the Chancellor's Professor Chair. He received an M.B.A. and a Ph.D. from the University of Chicago, and a degree in engineering from the Université Libre de Bruxelles. Dr. Jorion has done extensive work in the area of international finance and financial risk management, and has received numerous prizes and awards for his research. He has written a number of books, including *Value at Risk: The New Benchmark for Managing Financial Risk* and the *Financial Risk Manager Handbook.*

Gaiyan Zhang holds a Ph.D. from the University of California at Irvine (finance 2005) and an M.S. degree in finance from Fudan University, China. She is an assistant professor of finance at the University of Missouri at St. Louis. Her research interests include credit risk and credit derivatives, empirical corporate finance, and international finance. Her research has appeared in a number of journals, including *Journal of Finance, Journal of Financial Economics, Journal of Empirical Finance, Journal of Fixed Income, Journal of Alternative Investment, Journal of Management Studies,* and *Chinese Economy.* She wrote book chapters for the book *International Investments: Traditional and Alternative,* and *China's Capital Markets: Challenges from WTO Membership.* Zhang received research awards from the FDIC Center for Financial Research, University of Missouri at St. Louis, University of California at Irvine, and Fudan University. Her papers were presented at conferences including NBER, AFA, WFA, FMA, FDIC, and Bank of Canada.

PART X

International Dimensions of the Financial Crisis

CHAPTER 64

Only in America? When Housing Boom Turns to Bust

LUCI ELLIS
Head of Financial Stability Department, Reserve Bank of Australia*

T he U.S. housing bust has been very painful. Housing prices have fallen more than 30 percent on some measures. Mortgage delinquencies and defaults have risen drastically. Millions of Americans are expected to lose their homes to foreclosure, and millions more will be trapped, unable to move house because they are underwater on their mortgages.

The scale of the bust has been unusual compared to downturns in housing markets in the past or in other countries. Also unusual is that it started before the rest of the economy turned down and before credit availability tightened. In other cases, including the housing busts currently occurring in other countries, housing prices only started to fall, and delinquencies rise, after the economy started to weaken. The scale and timing of the U.S. bust seem hard to explain given the experience in other countries. Housing prices and construction were booming all over the industrialized world, often to a greater extent than in the United States, as shown in Exhibit 64.1. Many observers, from the IMF to the *Economist* magazine, therefore thought that the United States had less of a housing bubble than elsewhere, and hence was less liable to crash.

So why did the U.S. housing market melt down in this way, but not those in other countries? In a paper written for the Bank for International Settlements in 2008,[1] I showed that the United States was in fact especially vulnerable to a housing bust. Compared to other countries, the United States seemed to have built up a larger overhang of excess housing supply, experienced a greater easing in lending standards, and ended up with a household sector that was more sensitive to falling housing prices. Some of these outcomes seem to have been driven by the U.S. tax, legal, and regulatory systems. These systems encouraged households to increase their debt by more than their housing wealth (see Exhibit 64.1), and permitted lenders to facilitate that development.

---

*This chapter draws on work undertaken while the author was seconded to the Bank for International Settlements. While acknowledging the helpful comments and discussions with colleagues from both institutions, this chapter does not reflect the views of either the BIS or the RBA.

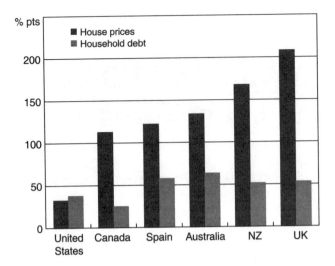

Exhibit 64.1 House Prices and Household Debt—2000 to 2006 (percentage point change in ratios to household income).

Household income is after tax, before interest payments.

Sources: BIS: Standard & Poor;s; national statistical agencies, central banks, Bloomberg, Thomson Reuters, OECD.

Observers who focused on the difference in the increases in housing prices missed the scale of the U.S. housing construction boom, and its implications for the subsequent bust. Unlike in other countries, the U.S. boom created an overhang of excess housing supply. Exhibit 64.2 shows that construction activity peaked in early 2006. The share of vacant, unsold homes was already rising around that time. It soon reached levels well above those seen in the previous 50 years, especially

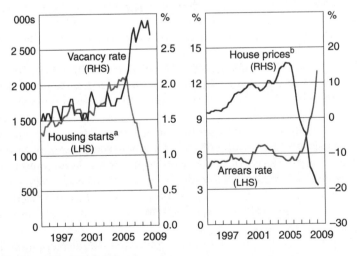

Exhibit 64.2 U.S. Housing Market.

[a]3-month average annualized.

[b]Year-ended percentage change.

Sources: Standard & Poor's; Bureau of the Census, Mortgage Bankers' Association.

for homes built since 2000. This excess of vacant housing began to weigh on prices as well as construction, causing the boom to collapse in on itself without any particular shock forcing that outcome.

Other countries also experienced construction booms over this period, and many seemed bigger than the U.S. boom in regard to their share of economic activity. But unlike in the United States, there doesn't seem to have been as much of a build-up of excess, vacant housing elsewhere. There were many more homes built than new households formed in the United States over this period. In contrast, in countries such as Australia and the United Kingdom, construction barely kept pace with population growth.

In the years since 2000, the United States did not even have a period of unusually strong income growth that might have provided a rationale for the strength in construction and prices. If incomes are growing quickly, the average quality of a new home usually rises to match, and existing homes are more likely to be upgraded. Australia and Canada both enjoyed boosts to income in this period from higher commodity prices; Ireland and Spain had been transitioning to income levels closer to the rest of Europe. No such boost to actual or expected income occurred in the United States, yet the quality of newly built homes increased much faster than in earlier periods when real income growth had been faster.

Exhibit 64.2 also shows that mortgage delinquency rates started to rise rapidly in the third quarter of 2006; this was true even for prime borrowers. The turning point occurred in the same period that the Case-Shiller national house price index recorded its first quarterly fall. Unemployment did not start to rise until a year later.

This sequence of events is exactly the opposite of that seen either in previous U.S. housing busts or in the current downturns in other countries. A sizable increase in unemployment is generally needed to make delinquency rates rise significantly. In the current U.S. bust, falls in housing prices were more important drivers. By contrast, in other countries such as the United Kingdom, the rise has, as in the past, been broadly in line with that in the unemployment rate. The main U.K. mortgage lender industry body even had to revise down its 2009 forecast for home repossessions there.

The U.S. delinquency rate is very high compared with its past or with other countries' experience. If U.S. homebuyers seem to have found it unusually difficult to service their mortgages, one likely reason is that mortgage lending standards eased more there than in other countries. There were many aspects to this easing, beyond the expansion in lending to borrowers with subprime credit scores. An increasing fraction of loans involved low documentation standards, or even none at all. (Low-doc loans exist in other countries, but are less common.) Loan-to-valuation ratios also increased substantially in the U.S. boom. With so many U.S. borrowers having little or no down payment, they were more likely to end up underwater on their mortgage if prices fell, unable to sell or refinance if they got into repayment difficulty.

The exceptional easing in U.S. lending standards was also apparent in a range of practices and products that were not seen anywhere else. Teaser interest rates were very steeply discounted on the reset rate, compared with introductory rate discounts available in other countries. As a result, the payment shock at reset time was often greater. Negative amortization loans (Option ARMs), in which the loan balance could rise, and "silent seconds" (piggyback second mortgages that were not disclosed to the first-mortgage lender) became increasingly common in the U.S. subprime and Alt-A mortgage markets; they are essentially unheard of in other countries. Both products tend to leave borrowers with high loan-to-valuation ratios long after they take out the loan. This raised the number of households liable to end up underwater on their mortgages once prices started to fall. In line with this, total mortgage debt outstanding accounted for a much higher fraction of the value of the U.S. housing stock, even at the peak of the boom, than in other countries, such as Australia.

Two developments seem to have spurred this easing in U.S. standards. First, a range of legislative and policy changes had been made to encourage the development of a nonconforming (subprime and Alt-A), nondepository lending sector. Part of the motivation was to expand home ownership, but the administration also wanted to reduce the dominance of Fannie Mae and Freddie Mac in the market. Second, the flow of new and refinanced loans had fallen following the end of the mortgage refinancing wave of 2003. Rather than allow origination fee income to fall and the industry to shrink, lenders chased new business by easing standards.

What could be causing these differences in experience across countries? One key difference seems to be that new housing supply is more responsive in the United States than in countries such as Australia and the United Kingdom. This is partly because less of the U.S. housing stock is in regions where zoning laws or geographical constraints such as mountains and coastlines restrict supply. Indeed, even more than in the past, the U.S. building boom was concentrated in single-family homes in exurban and new suburban areas, such as Arizona, Nevada, and the Inland Empire region of California, where urban sprawl was possible.

The greater easing of U.S. lending standards reflected a range of underlying causes. For example, the U.S. tax system does more to encourage borrowing against owner-occupied housing. Most of the other countries that had housing price booms in recent years do not allow homeowners' mortgage interest payments to be deducted against tax. The few that do, such as the Netherlands, generally have roughly offsetting taxes on wealth or imputed rent. U.S. property taxes did not have the same effect in the regions that boomed most. Because U.S. households pay mortgage interest out of pre-tax, not post-tax, income, they face greater incentives to take out mortgages with high loan-to-valuation ratios, and to keep that ratio high over time. They were also encouraged to take out (deductible) piggyback second mortgages rather than obtain (until recently nondeductible) mortgage insurance for the whole amount.

On the other side of the transaction, mortgage lenders had stronger incentives to ease lending standards than those in other countries. They were also not adequately constrained from doing so by regulation. Even though mortgages are not nonrecourse in most states (and in California, only purchase mortgages are, not refinancing), in practice lenders have tended to behave as if they were nonrecourse. Foreclosure can start quite quickly after the initial payment default in many states, while it is slower and more expensive for lenders to obtain a court deficiency judgment for any shortfall. So, U.S. lenders have tended to be more concerned with the value of the collateral than with the borrower's ability to repay, compared with their foreign counterparts. This makes them potentially less mindful of the need for prudent underwriting standards.

Regulation simply did not prevent many U.S. lenders from easing lending standards beyond what was prudent. Many important lenders were lightly regulated nondepositories. Consumer protection law did not apply to all lenders, and some markers of fraudulent and predatory lending were only finally banned once the bust was well under way.

Where government intervention has been important in the U.S. mortgage market has been to allow long-term fixed-rate mortgages that can be refinanced cheaply. Such a product is available only in the United States and Denmark. As a result, the U.S. mortgage market is set up to support a higher flow of loan originations (and thus fee income) relative to the total number of loans outstanding. Even when adjustable-rate mortgages became more popular, the products were structured to encourage frequent refinancing. For example, many mortgages with teaser rates were designed to be refinanced around the reset date, assuming credit was still available.

This structure for mortgage products had a number of consequences. Borrowers had more opportunity to refinance with cash out, and thus keep their loan-to-valuation ratios high. More of them were exposed to current credit conditions each time they refinanced. The tightening in credit conditions therefore probably affected proportionately more U.S. households than those in other countries. And more frequent refinancing means more loans are based on appraisals rather than sale prices, implying greater scope for fraud.

Government intervention was also instrumental in creating a large market for securitized mortgages. This market allowed local lenders to avoid concentrating their risk exposures on a single regional housing market. In the boom period, though, it seemed to enable an increase in total risk in the U.S. mortgage market. Lenders can become less concerned about the quality of the loans they write, if other investors will buy those loans. But this effect cannot have been the only reason why U.S. lenders eased their standards so much. Delinquency rates also rose sharply for mortgages on U.S. banks' balance sheets; securitization exists in other countries without having led to large run-ups in delinquency rates. But the dominant position of securitized mortgages relative to balance sheet lending in the United States seems to have been important. Global credit conditions were easy when the boom occurred, and demand for structured finance products was very strong. It was much easier for the large, liquid U.S. market for mortgage-backed securities to absorb that demand than for countries where balance sheet lending was more important. As a result, structured finance products were concentrated in U.S.-domiciled assets. This might also have something to do with those assets' denomination in U.S. dollars, and the availability of inexpensive credit protection from monoline insurers, which had previously serviced the (U.S.-specific) municipal bond market.

Recent events in the U.S. housing market, and the way they contrast with overseas experience, hold a number of lessons for policy makers and other observers. First, the absolute size of the increase in housing prices is not a good guide to a country's susceptibility to a bust. If new housing supply is relatively flexible, prices will rise less than in countries with stickier supply, but a bust becomes more likely. Second, because of the risk of a build-up in excess housing supply, financial regulation probably needs to be tighter, especially around mortgage lending standards, in countries where housing supply is flexible. Third, not all housing price booms need end in a U.S.-style meltdown. Experience in other countries shows that, absent a negative shock to incomes or credit supply, housing price booms can and sometimes do go out with a fizzle rather than a bang. And precisely because housing supply is sluggish, some increase in prices is inevitable in the face of a positive shock to demand. Policies to resist *all* housing booms might therefore be unnecessary and undesirable. The trick is to tell the difference between a bubble and a more benign price boom. Monitoring of lending standards, especially of previously fringe lenders, is an important source of information in this regard. Policy makers also need to be alert to signs of speculative demand for housing, such as a large number of households buying homes with the intention of reselling quickly for a profit.

Finally, more attention needs to be paid to institutional differences across countries when assessing their financial stability. Many of the factors identified here as contributing to the U.S. housing meltdown were longstanding institutional features, and were certainly not secrets. Why, then, did so many observers miss the United States's greater vulnerability? We can probably do no more than speculate on the answer to this question, but the available literature covering the boom suggests that two cognitive biases were present. Much of the commentary on the U.S. boom did not look further afield to notice how singular some U.S. developments and institutions really were. Meanwhile much of the cross-country analysis published by international financial agencies was focused more on drawing out the common factors, and therefore glossed over the differences.

NOTE

1. Luci Ellis (2008), "The Housing Meltdown: Why did it Happen in the United States?" BIS Working Paper 259, available at www.bis.org/publ/work259.pdf?noframes=1 and forthcoming in the *International Real Estate Review.*

ABOUT THE AUTHOR

Luci Ellis has worked at the Reserve Bank of Australia since 1991, mainly in the economic analysis and economic research departments. She spent four years as deputy head of economic analysis department (2003–2006). Before taking up duties as head of the RBA's financial stability department on October 20, 2008, Ellis had spent almost two years seconded to the Bank for International Settlements in Basel, Switzerland, working in their global macroeconomics team. She has a master's degree in economics from the Australian National University and a Ph.D. from the University of New South Wales. She has written on a range of economic and financial topics, including exchange rates, housing prices, mortgage finance, and factor income shares.

CHAPTER 65

The Equity Risk Premium Amid a Global Financial Crisis

JOHN R. GRAHAM
Richard Mead Professor of Finance at the Fuqua School of Business and Co-Director of the Center for Finance Excellence at Duke University

CAMPBELL R. HARVEY
Professor of Finance at Duke University and a Research Associate of the NBER

We analyze the history of the equity risk premium from surveys of U.S. chief financial officers (CFOs) conducted every quarter from June 2000 to March 2009. The risk premium is the expected 10-year S&P 500 return relative to a 10-year U.S. Treasury bond yield. The last two surveys were conducted during the darkest parts of a global financial crisis, and our results show that the equity premium sharply increased during the crisis. The survey also provides measures of cross-sectional disagreement about the risk premium, skewness, and a measure of individual uncertainty. The level of disagreement in late 2008 and early 2009 is 64 percent higher than 2007 levels. We also present evidence on the determinants of the long-run risk premium. Our analysis suggests the level of the risk premium closely tracks both market volatility (reflected in the VIX index) as well as credit spreads.

INTRODUCTION

During any financial crises, risk increases. In the current crisis, we observed market volatility skyrocket and credit spreads explode. Presumably, crises are temporary phenomena. How does the existence of a crisis affect long-term risk premiums. While we can directly observe credit spreads and measures like a volatility index (VIX), the equity risk premium is elusive.

We provide a unique perspective on the risk premium by analyzing the results over the past 10 years of our quarterly survey of chief financial officers (CFOs). The survey is currently conducted by Duke University and *CFO* magazine. The survey closed on February 26, 2009, and measures expectations beginning in the second quarter of 2009. In particular, we poll CFOs about their long-term expected return on the S&P 500. Given the current 10-year T-bond yield, we provide estimates of the equity risk premium and show how the premium changes through time. We also provide information on the disagreement over the risk premium as well as average confidence intervals.

METHOD

Design

The quarterly survey of CFOs was initiated in the third quarter of 1996.[1] Every quarter, Duke University polls financial officers with a short survey on important topical issues (Graham and Harvey 2009). The usual response rate for the quarterly survey is 5 to 8 percent. Starting in June of 2000, a question on expected stock market returns was added to the survey. Exhibit 65.1 summarizes the results from the risk premium question. While the survey asks for both the 1-year and 10-year expected returns, we focus on the 10-year expected returns herein, as a proxy for the market risk premium.

The executives have the job title of CFO, chief accounting officer, treasurer, assistant treasurer, controller, assistant controller, or vice president (VP), senior VP, or executive VP of finance. Given that the overwhelming majority of survey respondents hold the CFO title, for simplicity we refer to the entire group as CFOs. The survey is currently administered over the Internet.

The Premium During the Recent Crisis

The expected market return questions are a subset of a larger set of questions in the quarterly survey of CFOs. The survey usually contains between 8 and 10 questions. Some of the questions are repeated every quarter, and some change over time, depending on economic conditions. The historical surveys can be accessed at www.cfosurvey.org. During the past nine years, we have collected 11,288 responses to the survey. Panel A of Exhibit 65.1 presents the date that the survey window opened, the number of responses for each survey, and the 10-year Treasury bond rate, as well as the average and median expected excess returns. There is relatively little time variation in the risk premium. This is confirmed in Exhibit 65.2, which displays the historical risk premiums contained in Exhibit 65.1. The current premium, 4.74 percent, is the highest reading in the history of the survey. The March 2009 survey shows that the expected annual S&P 500 return is 7.49 percent, and the implied risk premium is 4.74 percent (7.49 – 2.75).[2] The expected annual S&P 500 return is roughly the same level as the year before. A major factor in the increase in the premium is the 10-year bond yield falling by more than 100 basis points.

Panel B of Exhibit 65.1 presents some summary statistics that pool all 11,288 responses. The overall average 10-year risk premium return is 3.46 percent.[3] The standard deviation is 2.67 percent.

The cross-sectional standard deviation across the individual CFO forecasts in a quarter is a measure of the disagreement of the participants in each survey. Disagreement has sharply increased during the global financial crisis. The average disagreement in 2007 averaged 2.5 percent. The most recent observation is 4.11 percent—a two-thirds increase and the highest observation on record.

We also report information on the average of the CFOs' assessments of the 1 in 10 chance that the market will exceed or fall below a certain level. In the most recent survey, the worst-case total return is 1.27 percent, which is a record low. The best-case return is 12.40 percent, which is a record high. This reinforces the recent increase in the degree of uncertainty.

With information on the 10 percent tails, we construct a probability distribution for each respondent. We use Davidson and Cooper's (1976) method to recover each respondent's probability distribution:

$$\text{Variance} = ([x(0.90) - x(0.10)]/2.65)^2$$

where $x(0.90)$ and $x(0.10)$ represent the ninetieth and tenth percentiles of the respondent's distribution. Keefer and Bodily (1983) show that this simple approximation is the preferred method of estimating the variance of a probability distribution of random variables, given information about the tenth and ninetieth percentiles. The average of individual volatilities has also sharply increased. The average in 2007 was 3.21 percent and the current reading is 4.23 percent—another new high.

There is also a natural measure of asymmetry in each respondent's response. We look at the difference between each individual's 90 percent tail and the mean forecast and the mean minus the 10 percent tail. Hence, if the respondent's forecast of the excess return is 6 percent and the tails are –8 percent and +11 percent, then the distribution is negatively skewed with a value of –9 percent (= 5 percent – 14 percent). As with the usual measure of skewness, we cube this quantity and standardize by dividing by the cube of the individual standard deviation. In every quarter's survey, there is, on average, negative skewness in the individual forecasts. The average asymmetry became more negative at –0.47 and is currently at a record low level.

Recessions, the Financial Crisis and Risk Premiums

Our survey now spans two recessions: March 2001 to September 2001 and the recession that began in December 2007. Financial theory would suggest that risk premiums should vary with the business cycle. Premiums should be highest during recessions and lowest during recoveries. Previous research has used a variety of methods, including looking at ex post realized returns to investigate whether there is business cycle–like variation in risk premiums.

While we have only 36 observations and this limits our statistical analysis, we do see important differences. The average risk premium over the entire sample is 3.46 percent. During recessions, the risk premium is 3.97 percent and during nonrecessions, the premium falls to 3.37 percent. We also see variation in disagreement. During recessions, the disagreement among participants is 2.84 percent and during nonrecessions only 2.40 percent.

The recession that began in December 2007 is a much worse than normal recession. For example, the recession of 2001 was relatively mild and lasted only three quarters. The current recession is already double the length and includes some of the highest unemployment since World War II. Nevertheless, the risk premium is not really much different during this recession (so far) than during the 2001 recession. Over the past six quarters, the risk premium has averaged 3.88 percent. The variation in the risk premiums is displated in Exhibit 65.2.

Exhibit 65.1   Summary Statistics Based on the Responses from the 36 CFO Outlook Survey from June 2000 to February 2009

A. By quarter

Survey Date	Survey for	Number of Survey Responses	10-year Bond Yield	Average Risk Premium	Median Risk Premium	Disagreement (standard deviation of risk premium estimates)	Average of Individual Standard Deviations	Individuals' Worst 10% Market Return Scenario	Average of Individuals' Best 10% Market Return Scenario	Skewness of Risk Premium Estimates	Average of Individuals' Asymmetry
June 6, 2000	2000Q3	206	6.10	4.35	3.9	2.99				0.81	
September 7, 2000	2000Q4	184	5.70	4.65	4.3	2.70				0.49	
December 4, 2000	2001Q1	239	5.50	4.20	4.5	2.31				0.37	
March 12, 2001	2001Q2	137	4.90	4.46	4.1	2.59				0.38	
June 7, 2001	2001Q3	204	5.40	3.79	3.6	2.43				0.49	
September 10, 2001	2001Q4	198	4.80	3.77	3.2	2.53				-0.11	
December 4, 2001	2002Q1	275	4.70	3.98	3.3	2.34				0.66	
March 11, 2002	2002Q2	234	5.30	2.88	2.7	2.17	3.21	3.66	12.23	0.30	-0.28
June 4, 2002	2002Q3	321	5.00	3.18	3.0	2.59	3.41	3.11	12.15	1.96	-0.39
September 16, 2002	2002Q4	363	3.90	4.00	4.1	2.27	3.36	3.10	12.01	1.03	-0.25
December 2, 2002	2003Q1	283	4.20	3.71	3.8	2.39	3.19	3.38	11.83	1.31	-0.28
March 19, 2003	2003Q2	180	3.70	3.66	3.3	2.12	3.57	1.92	11.40	0.49	-0.60
June 16, 2003	2003Q3	368	3.60	3.89	4.4	2.34	3.74	2.17	12.07	0.89	-0.33
September 18, 2003	2003Q4	165	4.30	3.21	3.7	1.87	2.80	3.34	10.78	-0.02	-0.42
December 10, 2003	2004Q1	217	4.36	3.83	3.6	2.22	3.24	3.35	11.94	0.74	-0.46
March 24, 2004	2004Q2	202	3.70	4.10	4.3	2.06	3.46	2.84	12.00	-0.03	-0.28
June 16, 2004	2004Q3	177	4.75	3.04	3.3	2.28	3.06	3.11	11.20	0.96	-0.39
September 12, 2004	2004Q4	177	4.25	3.24	3.3	2.32	3.13	2.70	10.98	0.64	-0.47
December 5, 2004	2005Q1	291	4.35	3.20	3.2	2.63	3.00	3.16	11.10	2.01	-0.36
February 28, 2005	2005Q2	275	4.28	3.19	3.2	2.47	2.99	3.23	11.16	1.49	-0.32
May 31, 2005	2005Q3	318	4.07	2.98	2.9	2.21	3.17	2.50	10.88	0.50	-0.25
August 29, 2005	2005Q4	325	4.20	2.93	2.8	2.20	3.23	2.26	10.82	0.96	-0.50

November 21, 2005	2006Q1	342	4.52	2.39	2.5	2.14	3.40	2.35	11.38	0.57	−0.23
March 6, 2006	2006Q2	278	4.61	2.57	2.4	2.37	3.43	2.11	11.18	1.11	−0.36
June 1, 2006	2006Q3	500	5.05	2.69	3.0	2.69	3.26	3.10	11.70	2.00	−0.23
September 11, 2006	2006Q4	465	4.79	2.50	2.2	2.47	3.29	2.57	11.28	1.37	−0.32
November 21, 2006	2007Q1	392	4.58	3.21	3.4	2.92	3.31	2.98	11.75	1.93	−0.29
March 1, 2007	2007Q2	388	4.55	3.13	3.5	2.39	3.31	2.79	11.56	1.83	−0.38
June 1, 2007	2007Q3	419	4.90	2.94	3.1	2.12	3.20	3.10	11.58	0.61	−0.38
September 7, 2007	2007Q4	486	4.48	3.35	3.5	2.81	3.08	3.39	11.54	1.80	−0.33
December 1, 2007	2008Q1	465	4.04	3.78	4.0	2.73	3.25	2.99	11.60	1.47	−0.32
March 7, 2008	2008Q2	388	3.61	3.97	4.4	2.97	3.16	3.11	11.50	2.28	−0.29
June 13, 2008	2008Q3	390	4.15	3.12	2.9	2.72	3.28	2.49	11.20	2.02	−0.41
September 5, 2008	2008Q4	439	3.69	3.53	3.3	2.59	3.22	2.37	10.90	1.05	−0.41
November 28, 2008	2009Q1	545	3.10	4.12	3.9	3.10	3.66	1.77	11.47	1.66	−0.36
February 26, 2009	2009Q2	452	2.75	4.74	4.3	4.11	4.23	1.27	12.40	1.82	−0.47
Average of quarters		11,288	4.44	3.51	3.46	2.51	3.30	2.77	11.50	1.05	−0.36
Standard deviation			0.70	0.61	0.61	0.40	0.27	0.56	0.45	0.67	0.09

B. By individual responses

Survey for

All dates		11,288		3.46	3.30	2.67	3.48	2.49	11.48	1.49	−0.34

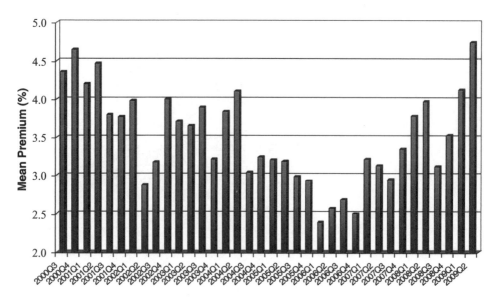

Exhibit 65.2   Ten-Year Forecasted S&P Returns Over and Above the 10-Year Treasury Bond Yield

Explaining Variation in the Risk Premium

While we document the level and a limited time series of the long-run risk premium, statistical inference is complicated by overlapping forecasting horizons. First, we have no way of measuring the accuracy of the risk premiums as forecasts of equity returns. Second, any inference based on regression analysis is confounded by the situation that from one quarter to the next, there are 38 common quarters being forecasted. This naturally induces a moving-average process.

We do, however, try to characterize the time variation in the risk premium without formal statistical tests. Exhibit 65.3 examines the relation between the mean premium and previous one-year returns on the S&P 500.

The evidence suggests that there is a weak negative correlation between past returns and the level of the long-run risk premium. This makes economic sense. When prices are low (after negative returns), expected returns increase.

An alternative to using past returns is to examine a measure of valuation. Exhibit 65.4 examines a scatter of the mean premium versus the price-to-earnings ratio of the S&P 500.

Looking at the data in Exhibit 65.5, it appears that the inference is complicated by a nonlinear relation. At very high levels of valuation, the expected return (the risk premium) was low.

We also examine the real yield on Treasury Inflation-Indexed Notes. The risk premium is like an expected real return on the equity market. It seems reasonable that there could be a correlation between expected real rates of return for stocks and bonds. Exhibit 65.5 examines the 10-year-on-the-run yield on the Treasury Inflation-Indexed Notes.

In this case, there is a weak positive correlation. Lower Treasury Inflation-Protected Securities (TIPS) yields are associated with lower equity risk premiums.

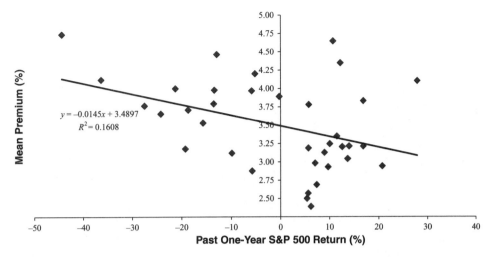

Exhibit 65.3 Equity Risk Premium and Past One-Year Returns on the S&P 500 Index

However, the analysis is only suggestive that the long-run equity premium and real interest rates move together.

Finally, we consider two measures of risk and the risk premium. Exhibit 65.6 shows that over our sample, there is evidence of a strong positive correlation between market volatility and the long-term risk premium. We use a five-day moving average of the implied volatility on the S&P index option (VIX) as our volatility proxy. The correlation between the risk premium and volatility is 0.68. If the closing day of the survey is used, the correlation is roughly the same. Asset pricing theory suggests that there is a positive relation between risk and expected

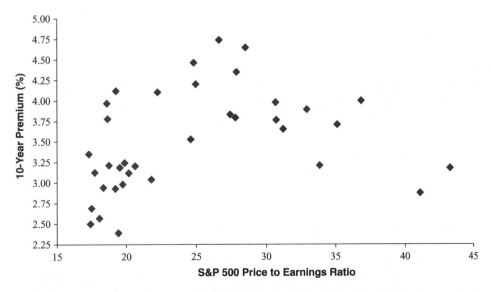

Exhibit 65.4 Equity Risk Premium and the S&P 500 Price-to-Earnings Ratio

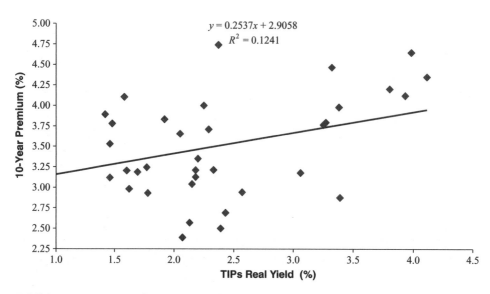

Exhibit 65.5 Equity Risk Premium and the Real Yield on Treasury Inflation Indexed Notes

return. While our volatility proxy doesn't match the horizon of the risk premium, the evidence, nevertheless, is suggestive of a positive relation.

We also consider an alternative risk measure, the credit spread. We look at the correlation between Moody's Baa-rated bond yields less the 10-year Treasury bond yield and the risk premium. Exhibit 65.7 shows a highly significant relation between the time-series with a correlation of 0.61.

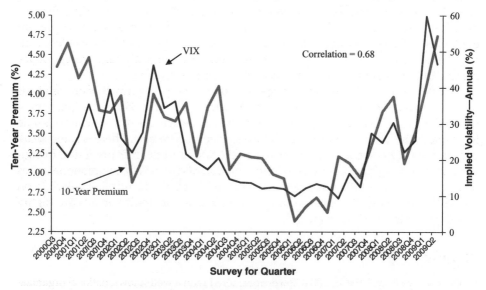

Exhibit 65.6 Equity Risk Premium and the Implied Volatility on the S&P 100 Index Option (VIX)

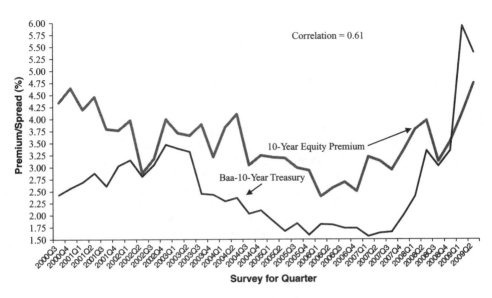

Exhibit 65.7 Equity Risk Premium and Credit Spreads

CONCLUSIONS

During the financial crisis, we study a direct measure of 10-year market returns based on a multiyear survey of chief financial officers. Importantly, we have a measure of expectations. We do not claim it is the true market expectation. Nevertheless, the CFO measure has not been studied before.

While there is relatively little time variation in the risk premium, a number of patterns emerge. We offer evidence that the risk premium is higher during recessions than nonrecessions. Given the current global economic crisis, the risk premium has hit a record high for our nine years of surveys. We also present evidence on disagreement. With higher disagreement, people often have less confidence in their forecasts. We find that disagreement is also higher in recessionary times and the current level of disagreement is at a record level.

While we have 11,288 survey responses over nine years, much of our analysis uses summary statistics for each survey. As such, with only 36 unique quarters of predictions and a variable of interest that has a 10-year horizon, it is impossible to evaluate the accuracy of the market excess return forecasts. There is some weak correlation between past returns, real interest rates and the risk premium. In contrast, there is significant evidence on the relation between two common measures of economic risk and the risk premium. We find that both the implied volatility on the S&P index as well as a commonly used measure of credit spreads are highly correlated with the risk premium.

NOTES

1. The surveys from 1996Q3–2004Q2 were partnered with a well-known national organization of financial executives. The 2004Q3 and 2004Q4 surveys were solely Duke University surveys, which used Duke mailing lists (previous survey respondents who volunteered

their email addresses) and purchased e-mail lists. The surveys from 2005Q1 to present are partnered with *CFO*. The sample includes both the Duke mailing lists and the *CFO* subscribers who meet the criteria for policy-making positions.

2. See, for example, Welch (2000, 2001, 2009), Fraser (2001), Harris and Marston (2001), Pástor and Stambaugh (2001), Fama and French (2002), Goyal and Welch (2003a), Graham and Harvey (2003), and Fernandez (2004, 2006, 2009) for studies of the risk premium.

3. Using the Ibbotson Associates data from January 1926 through March 2009, the arithmetic (geometric) average return on the S&P 500 over and above the 30-day U.S. Treasury bill is 7.20 percent (5.40 percent). Using data from April 1953 to March 2009, the arithmetic (geometric) risk premium is 5.64 percent (4.56 percent). Over the April 1953 to March 2009 period, the arithmetic average return on the S&P 500 over the 10-year U.S. Treasury bond is 4.21 percent. Fama and French (2002) study the risk premium on the S&P 500 from 1872 to 2000 using fundamental data. They argue that the ex ante risk premiums are between 2.55 percent and 4.32 percent for the 1951 to 2000 period. Also see Siegel (1999), Asness (2000), and Jagannathan, McGratten and Scherbina (2001).

REFERENCES

Asness, C. S. 2000. Stocks vs. bonds: Explaining the equity risk premium. *Financial Analysts Journal* 56: 96–113.

Davidson, L. B., and D. O. Cooper. 1976. A simple way of developing a probability distribution of present value. *Journal of Petroleum Technology* September, 1069–1078.

Fama, E. F., and K. R. French. 2002. The equity premium. *Journal of Finance* 57: 637–659.

Fernandez, P. 2004. *Market risk premium: Required, historical, and expected.* University of Navarra, unpublished working paper. Available at SSRN: http://ssrn.com/abstract=601761.

———. 2009. *Market risk premium used in 2008 by professors: A survey with 1,400 answers.* University of Navarra, unpublished working paper. Available at SSRN: http://ssrn.com/abstract=1344209.

Goyal, A., and I. Welch. 2003a. Predicting the risk premium. *Management Science* 49: 639–654.

———. 2003b. *Expectations of equity risk premia, volatility and asymmetry from a corporate finance perspective.* Working paper. Available at SSRN: http://ssrn.com/abstract=292623.

———. 2009. The CFO global business outlook: 1996–2009. www.cfosurvey.org.

Harris, R. S., and F. C. Marston. 2001. The market risk premium: Expectational estimates using analysts' forecasts. *Journal of Applied Finance* 11: 6–16.

Jagannathan, R., E. R. McGrattan, and A. Scherbina. 2001. The declining U.S. equity premium. *Federal Reserve Bank of Mineapolis Quarterly Review.*

Keefer, D. L., and S. E. Bodily. 1983. Three-point approximations for continuous random variables. *Management Science* 29 (5): 595–609.

Pástor, L., and R. Stambaugh. 2001. The equity premium and structural breaks. *Journal of Finance* 56: 1207–1239.

Siegel, J. J. 1999. The shrinking equity premium. *Journal of Portfolio Management* 26 (1): 10–17.

Welch, I. 2000. Views of financial economists on the equity premium and other issues. *Journal of Business* 73: 501–37.

———. 2001. *The equity premium consensus forecast revisited.* New Haven, CT: Yale University, Cowles Foundation for Research in Economics, unpublished working paper. Available at SSRN: http://papers.ssrn.com/sol3/papers.cfm?abstract_id=285169.

———. 2009. Views of economists about the equity premium and policy. Providence, RI: Brown University, unpublished working paper. Available at http://welch.econ.brown.edu/academics/equpdate-results2009.html.

ABOUT THE AUTHORS

Dr. John R. Graham is D. Richard Mead professor of finance at the Fuqua School of Business and co-director of the Center for Finance at Duke University. He is a recipient of the Best Teacher and Outstanding Faculty awards at Duke. His past work experience includes working as a senior economist at Virginia Power, and he is a past or current director of the American Finance Association, the Western Finance Association, and the Financial Management Association. Graham has published more than 30 articles and book chapters on corporate taxes, cost of capital, capital structure, financial reporting, and payout policy, and this research has won a half dozen best paper awards. He is co-editor of the *Journal of Finance* and has been an associate editor of the *Review of Financial Studies* and *Financial Management*. Since 1997, he has been the director of the Global Business Outlook, a quarterly CFO survey that assesses business climate and topical economics issues around the world. Graham is lead author on the textbook *Corporate Finance, Linking Theory to What Firms Do*.

Campbell R. Harvey is a professor of finance at Duke University and a research associate of the National Bureau of Economic Research. He is a graduate of the University of Chicago. Harvey is the editor of the *Journal of Finance*, past president of the Western Finance Association and serves on both the board of directors and the executive committee of the American Finance Association. Harvey has received nine Graham and Dodd Awards, Scrolls, and Roger F. Murray Prizes for excellence in financial writing and has published more than 100 scholarly articles. His 8,000-word hypertextual financial glossary is used by sites such as the *New York Times, Forbes, Bloomberg,* the *Washington Post,* and *Yahoo.* He has recently released an iPhone app for his glossary. Professor Harvey's blog at http://dukeresearchadvantage.com/author/charvey/ includes an entry from 2005 in which he stated "Many banks are operating like hedge funds, taking advantage of internal (cheap) credit lines. The banks' shareholders have no idea what is going on." He warned of an oncoming "contagious systemic" crisis.

CHAPTER 66

Australia's Experience in the Global Financial Crisis

CHRISTINE BROWN
Associate Professor of Finance, University of Melbourne

KEVIN DAVIS
Professor of Finance, University of Melbourne and Director of the Melbourne Center for Financial Studies*

INTRODUCTION

Of developed economies around the world, Australia has emerged as among the least affected by the global financial crisis (GFC). March quarter 2009 GDP growth of 0.4 percent (after two quarters of slightly negative growth), suggested that Australia had largely escaped the worldwide recession. Australia's banking sector was also less adversely affected than elsewhere, with no failures, and profitability remaining strong, although down substantially from previous levels and with increased bad debt levels. However, there have been significant failures of listed financial and investment companies and large investor losses from both domestic- and overseas-created structured products and investment funds, prompting concerns about financial market practices and investor protection. The Australian approach to regulation of securities and investment markets, based on disclosure, education, and advice, did not prevent the marketing of high-risk financial products and levered investment structures to retail and (in hindsight) other unsophisticated wholesale investors (such as local councils) not fully appreciative of the market and counterparty risk involved. As of June 2009, the stock market had fallen by around 41 percent from its high of November 2007, creating significant losses for such investors as well as the large pension fund sector, and prompting concerns about the adequacy of the securities market regulatory structure. This chapter traces the evolution of the impact of the GFC in Australia, explores the reasons for Australia's comparative insulation from its immediate effects, and considers some of the longer-term implications.

*This article draws on and extends earlier work published as "The Sub-Prime Crisis Down Under," *Journal of Applied Finance*, Spring/Summer 2008. Contact details: christine.brown@unimelb.edu.au.

THE EVOLUTION OF THE CRISIS IN AUSTRALIA

The pre-GFC structure of the Australian financial system suggests that Australia had significant potential exposure to the GFC. First, Australia was ranked as the second-largest (outside of the United States) issuer of asset-backed securities.[1] Second, the funds management sector (driven by compulsory private pension contribution arrangements) was the fourth-largest in the world, with $1.2 trillion in funds under management.[2] Third, Australia had the largest hedge fund sector in Asia with no special regulation of hedge funds. Fourth, while the domestic corporate bond and commercial paper markets (excluding securitization) were relatively small, large Australian companies were active issuers in international bond markets. Fifth, the Australian banking sector, where the four biggest banks had a market share of Australian resident assets of 65 percent, had only around 18 percent of assets funded by retail domestic deposits, relying heavily instead on both offshore and domestic wholesale funding. Also, house prices had escalated rapidly over several years with housing affordability at its lowest level ever.

Transmission of the crisis to Australian shores happened quite rapidly through equity market adjustments, but the real economy was buffered for some time by improved terms of trade associated with a resources boom driven by exports to China. Early effects of the crisis were reflected in the collapse of hedge funds Basis Capital and Absolute Capital, which suspended redemptions in July 2007.[3] This was followed by the failure of RAMS Home Loans (a nonbank provider of residential home loans) when in August 2007 it was unable to roll over its extendable commercial paper in the United States because the commercial paper markets had frozen (even though the asset backing was high quality Australian residential mortgages).

In November 2007, the stock market peaked and by the end of January 2008 had dropped 17 percent. The ensuing bear market exposed business models and practices that relied on rising asset prices to be sustainable. A number of large nonbank listed finance and investment companies with highly leveraged structures (including Centro Property, MFS, Allco Finance Group, and City Pacific) suffered catastrophic share price falls of between 50 and 90 percent from August 2007 to February 2008. These entities were highly complex and opaque with intra-conglomerate equity and debt linkages and cross-guarantees. The common theme was a highly leveraged structure financing illiquid real and financial (mortgage) assets that were held both on-balance-sheet and sold into managed fund (unit trust) structures generating profits and a long-term stream of management fees for the parent company.[4]

Short selling, margin lending, securities lending practices, and financial advisory practices all came under scrutiny in the prolonged bear market, and exposed regulatory weaknesses. A number of broking firms had built up substantial margin lending businesses based on a securities lending model (where title was transferred to the provider of cash). Partly as a result of being unable to speedily regain title to stock it had on loan, Tricom Securities caused considerable stock market disruption when it defaulted on a settlement in January 2008. The combination of company insiders having large holdings highly leveraged through margin loans (structured on a securities loan transaction), together with inadequate reporting of short sale transactions, led to major problems for other companies. The most high profile of these was ABC Learning, which collapsed in February 2008 when speculation that margin calls on executives and directors would be triggered unleashed a wave of short selling. Following similar moves around the world, short selling was banned in September 2008 for all stocks. The ban applied only to financial stocks from November 2008 until May 2009.

Problems with margin lending and investor protection arrangements were highlighted by the failure of the broking firm Opes Prime, whose margin loan customers lost title to their investments, and whose failure caused significant reputational damage to the major banks providing its funding. In December 2008, a large financial planning firm, Storm Financial, entered administration and ultimately failed, with many clients suffering major losses from highly leveraged investment portfolios. Major banks again suffered reputation damage because of their funding arrangements with that company. In February 2009, a parliamentary inquiry into corporate collapses, financial services, and products was announced in response to these experiences.

The year 2009 saw a number of further collapses of highly leveraged finance and investment companies. Global investment and advisory firm Babcock and Brown failed in March 2009. Two large companies, Timbercorp and Great Southern, which accounted for around 60 percent of the market in agribusiness-managed investment schemes, failed in April and May 2009, respectively.[5]

The Australian banks had only limited direct exposure to high risk securities such as CDOs. The National Australia Bank, one of the four major banks, reported an exposure to $US1.2 billion of investment vehicles in July 2008. But with the general economic downturn, problem loans were on the rise, and bank profitability, while still high, declined. Following the collapse of Lehman Brothers and the announcement by the Irish government of guarantees on bank deposits, the Australian government announced guarantee arrangements in October 2008 for bank deposits and wholesale funding, despite the strong capital position of the Australian banks. Reflecting their relatively strong performance, each of the four major banks was still rated AA by S&P in mid-2009. There has been some consolidation in the sector with Commonwealth Westpac Banks, two of the four major banks, acquiring BankWest and St. George respectively. Despite having suffered stock price declines on the order of 25 to 50 percent since the November 2007 peak, the four major Australian banks have been able to raise additional equity capital and had jumped significantly in international league tables to be in the top 40 banks worldwide by market capitalization in March 2009.

Another area severely affected by the GFC has been the mortgage and property trust (managed funds) industry. In the wake of the government guarantees on bank deposits, withdrawals from the trusts accelerated in the last quarter of 2008, following large outflows in the first three quarters. Most trusts responded with redemption freezes, with some of the suspended trusts in early 2009 offering withdrawals on a pro rata basis. On another affected front, the Australian government has set up a special purpose funding vehicle to provide finance for car dealers following the withdrawal of GE Money Motor Solutions and GMAC from Australia. The other sector badly hit has been the superannuation (pension fund) sector. Compulsory superannuation saw funds under management reach $1.2 trillion before the crisis. At December 2008, this figure had dropped to $1.05 trillion, reflecting falling asset prices.

Australia's securitization markets froze, paralleling the experience in other countries. Spreads on nongovernment debt widened as risk aversion levels rose in the market. Initially, the Australian currency (AUD/USD) depreciated in August 2007 against the U.S. dollar as speculators becoming increasingly risk averse unwound carry trades on the Australian dollar. The Australian government had notably kept interest rates comparatively high in the lead-up to the crisis (and reduced them later and by less than most other developed nations) because of inflation fears. The currency appreciated against the U.S. dollar,[6] trading in a range of 0.80 to 0.97 from July 2007 to September 2008 depreciating to 0.61 in October 2008 and recovering to around 0.80 in July 2009.

THE "LUCKY" COUNTRY?

Why has Australia been less affected by the crisis than most other developed countries? Luck, good management, and regulation have all had a role to play.[7]

Considering first the banking sector, memories of the problems of the early 1990s (when two state government–owned banks failed) may have limited bank risk taking. But the structure of aggregate financial flows was also relevant in influencing bank behavior. Australian banks were major borrowers in international wholesale financial markets, funding Australia's current account deficit, and therefore more focused on raising funds internationally for lending within Australia than on acquiring complex securities such as CDOs either on-balance-sheet or within special investment vehicles (SIVs) or conduits. High profitability from those domestic loan activities may also have lessened incentives for playing in a different, riskier game, and was reflected in a much lower reliance on trading income than overseas counterparts.

The major banks were also intensively engaged, at great expense, in developing their risk management systems so they could qualify for advanced IRB status for the introduction of the Basel II prudential regulation framework in January 2008. Arguably, this attention to risk quantification and management may have helped them to avoid the excessive risk taking that occurred elsewhere (although the same factor should have been relevant internationally). Probably more relevant in limiting bank risk taking, however, was the role of the prudential regulator, APRA,[8] which had suffered severe embarrassment (and subsequent organizational restructuring) in 2001 when a major insurance company under its supervision failed (with a government decision to provide some $600 million compensation to policy holders, imposing a significant cost on taxpayers).

Within the broader financial sector, the growth of pension funds looking for fixed-interest-style investments, in the absence of a significant local corporate bond market and a small government securities market, had prompted the growth of a significant securitization sector. Subprime-style lending did not evolve, reflecting, on the supply side, potential legal risks for lenders and originators from unconscionable conduct and higher regulatory capital requirements for nonstandard loans. On the demand side, awareness of borrowers to the risk of loss of other assets from defaulting on full-recourse style mortgage loan contracts, and relatively high, by international standards of the time, interest rate levels, were also relevant.

At the real economy level, the strong growth of the Chinese economy and the resources boom (and strengthening terms of trade) during the early part of the crisis period, tended to shield the economy from the worldwide downturn, while also creating inflationary pressures. While a long-standing current account deficit exposed Australia to downturns in international investor confidence, the fact that the accumulated international debt was primarily private, and that the government budget had been in surplus for many years, meant that this did not come to pass. With the eventual slowing of the Chinese economy, ending of the resources boom, and reduced willingness of international speculators to continue the carry trade (speculating that high Australian interest rates would not be offset by exchange rate losses), the consequent fall in the exchange rate after July 2008 helped to moderate the downturn in economic activity.

POLICY RESPONSES AND IMPLICATIONS

Policy responses by the Australian authorities can be grouped into four categories.

The first is Reserve Bank[9] and government actions to unfreeze and restore liquidity to financial markets (see Kearns 2009, for more detail). Relatively early in the crisis, the Reserve Bank expanded the range of securities it would accept as collateral for repurchase agreements to include private sector securities such as residential mortgage-backed securities (RMBS). The term for repurchase agreements was also extended out to as much as one year. In late September 2008, the federal government introduced a RMBS purchase agency within the Australian Office of Financial Management with the objective of government purchases of RMBS restarting the frozen RMBS market. A special purpose vehicle (Ozcar), jointly operated by the government and the four major banks, was established in December 2008 to provide financing for car dealers after the withdrawal from the Australian market of the two largest providers of finance (GE Money and GMAC).

A second type of response has been actions designed to shore up confidence in the strength and stability of the financial system, particularly the banking sector. Most notable here was the government announcement on October 12, 2008, of a blanket guarantee of all bank deposits and debt, following similar announcements by the Irish and, then, other governments, which threatened to undermine the international wholesale market funding of Australian banks. Subsequently, a fee-based, opt-in guarantee scheme (for debt and deposits above $1 million) together with 100 percent guarantee for deposits of less than $1 million was introduced on November 28, 2008, to run for three years.

A third type of response has been the introduction of new regulations aimed at preventing activities in financial markets and institutions from creating further instability. Most important here was the announcement of a ban on short selling on the Australian Securities Exchange (ASX) on September 21, 2008, which applied to all stocks until November 19, and to financial stocks until May 25, 2009. At that time, tougher regulation of margin lending was also foreshadowed. Also, in June 2009, APRA released a consultation paper on proposals for ensuring that executive remuneration practices in financial institutions were consistent with good risk management.

The fourth type of response has been fiscal actions to offset the crisis-induced slowdown in economic activity. In October 2008, a large fiscal stimulus package was announced, and the 2009–2010 budget, announced in May 2009, forecast a very much increased budget deficit. On May 12, the federal government announced a guarantee scheme for borrowings by the state and territory governments to ensure their access to debt capital markets for funding infrastructure.

Notably, a fifth type of response found in many other countries, that of government provision of debt or equity funding to distressed banks, their nationalization, forced mergers with healthier institutions, or bailouts, has not occurred. While there have been a large number of failures of finance companies and high profile financial firms that were using a heavily leveraged business model based on acquiring assets to place in mutual fund vehicles that they managed, stakeholders, including pension fund investors, rather than taxpayers, have borne the losses arising from the failures of these nonprudentially regulated institutions.

CONCLUSION

While Australia had, at mid-2009, withstood the world financial turbulence better than most,[10] the situation was not without risks. Economic slowdown and increasing numbers of company and property developer failures were causing bank loan losses to increase. Housing prices had not fallen significantly (but commercial property prices are down and vacancy rates up), despite their previous boom appearing to be cushioned by higher incomes and lower interest rates, which had improved affordability, together with the effects of ad hoc policy responses such as "first-home buyers" grants. While some analysts pointed to high population growth and a supply shortage as the source of high house prices, the risk of house price deflation remained significant. With household leverage having increased significantly over the past decade, potential risks for bank loan portfolios from the economic downturn and falling asset prices were of concern.

Substantial financial wealth had been destroyed by the stock market collapse, with much of the losses concentrated in both institutional and individual pension funds. But also significant was the extent of losses incurred by both retail and wholesale investors from exposures to high-risk financial products and investment structures, prompting calls for a more proactive regulatory approach rather than *caveat emptor* (and several class action lawsuits).

Within the financial sector, the crisis has seen increased concentration in an already concentrated banking sector, and the decline in mortgage origination and funding outside of the banking sector. Ensuring effective competition and removing government guarantees that enshrine the dominant competitive position of large banks in the financial system are major challenges.

NOTES

1. Securitized products included 78 percent residential mortgage-backed securities and 8 percent asset-backed paper.
2. All dollar amounts are AUD.
3. Australian investors lost over $600 million in the collapses.
4. Davis (2009) provides an outline of this business model, which was popularized by Macquarie Bank and also used by the investment bank Babcock and Brown, which subsequently failed.

5. D'Aloisio (2009) provides more detail on the extent of corporate failures and outlines responses by the securities market regulator (ASIC) to the market failings uncovered by the GFC.

6. Currency is quoted as 1AUD = xUSD.

7. This is the title of an influential book (Horne 1964), which argued that "Australia is a lucky country, run mainly by second-rate people who share its luck."

8. The Australian Prudential Regulatory Authority (APRA) is responsible for the regulation of deposit-taking institutions, insurance companies, and superannuation (pension) funds.

9. The Reserve Bank of Australia (RBA) is Australia's central bank.

10. Stevens (2009) provides an overview and interesting comparison with the experience of Canada. An analysis of the factors that were catalysts for the GFC and arguments as to why Australia was less affected than elsewhere, are provided in Gruen (2009).

REFERENCES

Brown, C., and K. Davis. 2008. The sub-prime crisis down under. *Journal of Applied Finance* Spring/Summer: 16–28.

D'Aloisio, T. 2009. Regulatory issues arising from the financial crisis for ASIC and for market participants. www.asic.gov.au/asic/pdflib.nsf/LookupByFileName/sdia-speech-chairman-May-09.pdf/$file/sdia-speech-chairman-May-09.pdf.

Davis, K. 2009. Listed infrastructure funds: Funding and financial management. *JASSA: The Finsia Journal of Applied Finance* 1: 43–47.

Gruen, D. 2009. *Reflections on the global financial crisis.* Address to the Sydney Institute, June 16. Available at www.treasury.gov.au/documents/1574/PDF/05_Reflections_on_the_Global_Financial_Crisis.pdf.

Horne, D. 1964. *The lucky country: Australia in the sixties.* Melbourne, Australia: Penguin Books.

Kearns, J. 2009. The Australian money market in a global crisis. *Reserve Bank of Australia Bulletin,* June, 15–25. http://www.rba.gov.au/publications/bulletin/2009/jun/pdf/bu-0609-2.pdf

Stevens, G. 2009. Australia and Canada: Comparing notes on recent experience. *Reserve Bank of Australia Bulletin,* June, 36–44. http://www.rba.gov.au/publications/bulletin/2009/jun/pdf/bu-0609-4.

ABOUT THE AUTHORS

Christine Brown holds a B.Sc. (Hons.), M.Sc. and Ph.D. in mathematics and a Dip. Ed. from the University of Melbourne. She joined the Department of Finance at the University of Melbourne in 1991. Christine's research interests include share repurchases, financial engineering, credit unions, risk management, and capital management. She is an associate editor of the *Journal of Applied Finance* and has published extensively in leading international journals. Recent publications include "Keiretsu Affiliation and Stock Market Driven Acquisitions" in the *Journal of Financial Research* and "Capital Management in Mutual Financial Institutions" in the *Journal of Banking and Finance*. She has undertaken consulting assignments for the Australian Treasury and other government and corporate sector clients, most recently for the Board of Taxation on the tax treatment of off-market share repurchases in Australia.

Kevin Davis has been a professor of finance at the University of Melbourne since 1987 and a director of the Melbourne Center for Financial Studies since 2005. He is a graduate of Flinders University and Australian National University. He is co-author or editor of 16 books and numerous journal articles. Primary research interests are financial institutions, financial engineering, financial regulation, and corporate finance. He was appointed by the Australian treasurer in 2003 to prepare a report on financial system guarantees.

CHAPTER 67

Collapse of a Financial System: An Icelandic Saga

TRYGGVI THOR HERBERTSSON
Professor of Economics, Reykjavík University, Member of Parliament in Iceland, and
Special Economic Adviser to the Prime Minister of Iceland during the collapse of the
Icelandic banks*

INTRODUCTION

Many observers of the current financial crisis have concluded that the decision of
the U.S. government to let Lehman Brothers go under on September 15, 2008, was
a grave mistake for financial stability in the world. Some financial experts have
also begun to claim that Europe made a similar mistake with regard to Iceland.
These individuals point out that hard-hit European Union countries like Hungary,
Latvia, and Romania would not be in as dire of an economic shape if Europe had
interfered more aggressively in Iceland and not forced it to go to the IMF.

In the brutal aftermath of Lehman's bankruptcy, almost all the funding lines
of Icelandic banks were cut, and they were left facing severe funding problems.
The usual policy response to a systemic crisis such as this—to use the central bank
as a lender of last resort—was not possible, as the funding needs of the banking
system dwarfed the capabilities of the central bank of Iceland. The central bank's
foreign reserves amounted to about half the country's GDP, while the consolidated
balance sheet of the banking sector was roughly 10 times GDP. The consequent
systemic failure led to the three system banks being taken over by the Icelandic
authorities. The crisis also led to a complete deterioration of the country's capital
account and a fully fledged currency crisis, and later a political crisis.

The direct cost to the Icelandic taxpayer associated with the collapse of the
Icelandic banking system is estimated to be around 85 percent of the country's
GDP. What the cost in terms of lost output will be remains to be seen, but the
current estimate is that GDP could contract by 11 percent in 2009. It is estimated
that as much as 60 percent of the corporate sector in the country is technically
bankrupt.

---

*This chapter is a summary of Eggertsson and Herbertsson (2009) and Herbertsson (2009a,
2009b).

THE ORIGINS

It is useful to start the investigation of what went wrong by summarizing the events of the three years preceding the systemic collapse of the banking system in September and October 2008. In many ways, the origins of the crisis could be traced to late 2005, when a number of analysts' reports by leading financial institutions brought attention to high degree of leverage that characterized the Icelandic financial system and its key institutions. Stories of the shorting of stocks in Icelandic banks and companies—and even the currency—began to surface, and the increase in perceived risk was evident in the widening of spreads on various credit default swaps. In the coming months, Iceland became the talk of the town, with the state of its financial system receiving particularly intense scrutiny in March 2006. The research departments of all major banks paid disproportionate attention to Iceland and issued reports on the country's financial system—the bloodier, the better.

In March 2006, spreads on credit default swaps shot up to 110 basis points, and Iceland came to be viewed as a risky place to invest. In May of the same year, I co-authored a report with Frederick Mishkin of Columbia University (who was appointed to the Board of Governors of the Federal Reserve later the same year) concluding that this was a misconception (Herbertsson and Mishkin 2006). The country's fundamentals, we argued, were in a very good state, and the general outlook was positive. We concluded that if a number of policy recommendations were followed, confidence in the Icelandic economy would be restored. Of course, this prediction could not take into account the depth and severity of the global financial crisis that would eventually topple the Icelandic banking system.

IMPROVEMENT

Following the publication of our report, Morgan Stanley wrote a very positive note on the state of the Icelandic economy, saying they essentially agreed with our position and that there was almost no danger of a financial crisis in Iceland. The authors concluded by recommending investment in the first-tier capital of Icelandic banks. The sense of a return to stability was enhanced by the fact that the Icelandic banks appeared to use this mini-crisis to get their act together. Cross-holdings were reviewed, and some were dissolved, funding structures were changed, transparency increased, and much more emphasis was placed on deposits as a source of funding.

Roughly a year later, however, this positive trend took a turn for the worse in the summer of 2007, especially after Bear Stearns decided to close two of its hedge funds in August. The episode triggered a downward spiral in which wholesale funding became gradually more difficult to obtain. By early 2008, Iceland was more or less entirely closed off from the market for wholesale funding. Icelandic banks ended up spending the first half of 2008 engaged in a scramble to raise funds through new deposits and private placements. By September, however, as the world watched in horror as venerable Wall Street institutions, such as Lehman Brothers and American International Group (AIG), either collapsed or were taken into public ownership, the funding problems of the Icelandic banks became untenable. On September 29, after seeing its credit lines withdrawn in the week following the Lehman collapse, news that Glitnir, the country's third-largest bank, was facing severe funding difficulties and was seeking public help, become known. Glitnir was scheduled to meet a €750m payment on October 15 and saw no other way out of its predicament than to go to the central bank in search of an emergency loan.

CAPITAL INJECTION

The central bank of Iceland, however, rejected Glitnir's request for a loan and insisted that it would inject €600m in equity into the bank in exchange for a 75 percent ownership stake in it. As a consequence, the bank's shareholders were practically wiped out. The following morning, Glitnir's share price fell by 75 percent in a matter of minutes, and the value of Stodir, an unlisted holding company that was its biggest shareholder, fell even more dramatically, forcing it into a moratorium a day later. Also, the majority of Glitnir's stock had been pledged to Kaupthing and Landsbanki, the country's two largest banks. With the fall of Glitnir's share price, stockholders were subject to margin calls that they could not meet, as the collateral used to meet these margin calls became practically worthless. A crippling domino effect was taking hold in which the fall in price of the bank's share price would plunge others into crisis. It became apparent that the authorities would have to resort to something altogether more dramatic to avoid the collapse of the entire Icelandic financial system.

The plan devised in the days that followed detailed how the banks would be taken into public ownership one by one, if needed. It was apparent that the central bank could not come to the rescue of the banking system without taking them over, as the size of the banks was absolutely disproportional to the capabilities of the sovereign. It was decided that a blanket guarantee should be given to depositors in local banks and that depositors should be first in line as claimants on the assets of the banks. Unlike the approach adopted by the Nordic countries during their financial crisis in the 1990s, which provided a blanket guarantee to the creditors as well, Iceland guaranteed only deposits. This meant that the Icelandic banks had now effectively defaulted on their senior debt.

EMERGENCY LAW

The Icelandic parliament rushed through an emergency law giving the Icelandic Financial Supervisory Authority, the financial regulator, the authority to take institutions into public ownership—similar to those of the Federal Deposit Insurance Corporation in the United States. Within one week, all three major banks were nationalized: Glitnir (on October 7, one day after the passing of the emergency law), Landsbanki (on October 9) and, finally, Kaupthing (on October 10, after the British government used antiterrorism legislation to freeze all of Landsbanki's assets in the United Kingdom). The Kaupthing collapse is now ranked as one of the five biggest bankruptcies ever in the world.

The government's plan for the takeover of the banking system included in each case the creation of a new bank, which held all deposits guaranteed directly by the sovereign. A preliminary evaluation of the assets was carried out, and assets amounting to deposits moved to the new banks. The state injected new capital into the banks, targeting a capital adequacy ratio of 10 percent. What remained in the old banks were all assets that had not been moved to the new banks, a note on the new banks, and claims of certain creditors (such as deposits in branches outside of

Iceland and claims of bondholders). The overall size of the assets and liability of the new banking system is about two to three times the country's GDP, compared to almost 10 times GDP before the crisis. Moreover, the new system is almost fully financed in Icelandic krona.

NORDIC TIGER

Thus far, I have described the events that led directly to the collapse of the Icelandic financial system. But it is important to consider some of the more deep-rooted origins of the crisis. Indeed, up to the crisis, it could be said that the first years of the twenty-first century were unusually favorable to Iceland. The liberalization of the economy made the country the fifth-richest member of the OECD. The United Nations ranked Iceland as the number one country in the world according to a number of indicators of living standards. Economically, Iceland appeared to flourish: output, consumption, and investment—both foreign direct and domestic—grew rapidly. Public finances were in great shape, and taxes were lowered. Indeed, at less than 6 percent of GDP, government debt was almost nonexistent at the start of 2008. Moreover, the long-term picture looked rosy: pensions amounted to almost 1.5 times GDP and, unlike many other industrialized countries, the demographic composition of the population was favorable. There was virtually no unemployment. Favorable fundamentals justified optimism: Iceland was the *Nordic tiger*.

Behind this story of success lies an incredible transformation of the country's banking system. At the turn of the century, the Icelandic banking system was more or less government owned. It was a simple depository system with a consolidated balance sheet amounting to approximately one times the country's GDP. The loan portfolio was mostly domestic, fairly low risk, and credit losses were small. The trend toward deregulation and privatization started (with the initial emphasis of deregulation) under Iceland's membership in the European Economic Area and the country's adoption of the European Financial Directive in the early 1990s. After privatization, the banks' flow of foreign credit increased rapidly. Domestic liquidity fueled an investment boom and later an asset-price bubble. International creditors were willing and able to lend what appeared to be limitless amounts to Iceland. House prices rose dramatically with easier access to capital, and the stock market boomed.

PONZI SCHEME

In retrospect, it could be argued that what was happing in Icelandic finance resembled a Ponzi scheme: financiers could start with a certain amount, buy stocks, and pledge the stock in a bank. Then they could buy more of these stocks, thereby increasing its price, and pledge the increase. This would raise funds to start the cycle again, generating and ultimately exacerbating a supposedly virtuous cycle, which pumped up the stock market and created a bubble.

Gradually, the banking and financial system turned from being a fairly simple depository system to fully fledged international financial intermediation. The banking system was, however, not supervised prudently enough. The banks, the regulatory authority, and to some extent, the central bank did not fully understand the systemic risks that had been built up in the system. Too much focus was placed on measures of capital adequacy and other formalities, rather than systemic risk and funding.

There were also problems with the institutional structure of regulation. One of the policy recommendations put forward in the report that Mishkin and I wrote was to consolidate the financial stability mandate of the central bank of Iceland and the banking supervisory functions of the Financial Supervisory Authority in the central bank, which we argued would enable a stronger emphasis on actual risks and financial stability, rather than a narrower emphasis on regulatory requirements. Ultimately, the failure to follow this advice led to the same mistakes—born out of a detachment of lender-of-last-resort and supervision responsibilities—that occurred in the United Kingdom around the time of the collapse of Northern Rock.

MONETARY FRAMEWORK

In addition to issues of finance and banking, the framework for macroeconomic policy was important. In 2001, the framework for monetary policy was changed from a fixed exchange rate regime to one characterized by a floating exchange rate and inflation targeting. This new policy was successful for the first four years. But by the 2005, the carry game being played by both households and firms meant that they were becoming increasingly immune to increases in the policy rate: in fact, the higher the interest rate, the more you gained on the carry trade. Monetary policy, therefore, became almost impotent in preventing the acceleration of the economy, asset prices, and inflation. The sustained strong exchange rate helped to maintain investor confidence and created a perception of low exchange-rate risk related to foreign currency borrowing, increased demand for imports, and an illusionary wealth effect. Both households and firms borrowed heavily in foreign currency, which became a major problem once the currency started to depreciate.

What the Icelandic experience under inflation targeting demonstrated is that the framework can have nonlinear effects, which can be particularly acute for a small, open economy—of which Iceland is a textbook example. When the domestic policy rate is sufficiently close to some average of interest rates in the rest of the world, the domestic monetary transmission mechanism works fine. But as the domestic policy rate moves further away from this global rate, its effects on domestic demand diminish as the carry trade sets in. Consequently, the currency appreciates, and demand increases because of illusionary wealth effects. In the case of Iceland, this led to a sharp increase in inflation (even more so as the target measure included house prices). The current-account deficit rose sharply, and peaked at a monumental 25 percent of GDP.

As mentioned earlier, initial concerns over the Icelandic financial system in 2005 and 2006 did lead to a positive response from the banks. But these efforts would, in retrospect, prove to be a case of too little, too late, as by this time, the banking system had already become far too big for the currency and a country with a population of only 320,000. The banks may possibly have understood their own risks, but they by no means had an adequate understanding of the systemic risks that resulted from their collective action. The early warnings contained in the concerns over the Icelandic banking system in 2005 and 2006 should have been seen as a call for these institutions to de-leverage and de-risk, and they should have been required by the regulatory authorities to do so.

LESSONS

What may the future hold for Iceland, and what lessons can we draw from the crisis? As a starting point, the Icelandic crisis raises fundamental questions about whether a small, open economy can have an independent and freely floating currency in the current global financial system. Although the tipping point in Iceland involved a liquidity crisis, imperfect institutions are primarily to blame for the collapse (and, of course, the bankers, too). The institutions in question are both domestic and international, namely the financial institutions of the European Union, which Iceland acquired through its membership in the European Economic Area, and domestic laws, regulations, systems for monitoring the financial (and business) community, and the monetary framework.

The regulatory failure is partly related to diseconomies of small scale. A country with 320,000 inhabitants is not able to produce a sufficient number of qualified officials required for supervising large financial institutions that operate primarily internationally. The inexperience argument is reinforced by an awareness that free capital movements and sophisticated international banking are new phenomena in Iceland, mostly associated with the twenty-first century.

Interactions between weak institutions and exogenous developments—bad luck—had a central role in the collapse. These factors include reckless lending by foreign private and institutional creditors to Icelandic organizations; the impact of reduced availability of international credit that was felt already in the summer of 2007; the decision to cut Iceland off altogether, once the credit crunch arrived; and the surprising use of antiterrorist laws in the United Kingdom against Icelandic banks.

REFERENCES

Thráinn E., and T. T. Herbertsson. 2009. *System failure in Iceland and the 2008 global financial crisis*. Paper presented at the 13th annual conference of ISNIE, Walter A. Haas School of Business, University of California at Berkeley, June 18–20.

Herbertsson, T. T. 2009a. *The Icelandic banking collapse: A story of broken promises*. Proceedings of the Reinventing Bretton Woods Committee conference, *Building an International Financial System for the 21st Century*, New York, November 24–25, 2008, Mark Uzan, (ed.). www.rbwf.org.

Herbertsson, T. T. 2009b. What the Icelandic collapse taught us. *Central Banker* 19 (3): 51–56.

Herbertsson, T. T., and F. Mishkin. 2006. *Financial stability in Iceland*. Icelandic Chamber of Commerce. www.chamber.is.

ABOUT THE AUTHOR

Tryggvi Thor Herbertsson is a professor of economics at Reykjavík University, a member of Parliament in Iceland, and was special economic adviser to the prime minister of Iceland during the collapse of the Icelandic banks.

CHAPTER 68

Iceland's Banking Sector and the Political Economy of Crisis

JAMES A. H. S. HINE
Senior Lecturer in Organizational Studies and Business Ethics at the
University of Edinburgh's Business School

IAN ASHMAN
Senior Lecturer in Human Resource Management and Leadership,
University of Central Lancashire

WHAT...?

Within one week in early October 2008, Iceland's major banks—Glitnir, Landsbanki, and Kaupthing—collapsed like a house of cards, dragging the economy with them and plunging the society that topped the UN's 2007 league table for social well-being and prosperity into a profound crisis. The situation then has since become well known. Between 2002 and 2008, a nation of 310,000 people produced an international banking system with assets valued at approximately eleven times GDP (CBI 2008) and, at the end, liabilities in excess of US$60 billion. An uncontrolled process of international expansion and imprudent lending to highly geared companies had been funded by cheap credit obtained from the wholesale capital markets. As the US subprime catastrophe spread across the globe, so the supply of credit dried, and illiquidity, hovering above Iceland like the Sword of Damocles, descended.

Despite the credit crunch, the Icelandic banking model was always unsustainable (Buiter and Sibert 2008). Given the possibility of unfavorable economic conditions arising, this small country with its own minor league currency (Krona/ISK), a disproportionately large, internationally exposed banking sector, and a government lacking the fiscal capacity to stand as lender-of-last-resort, was too vulnerable. During the years 2005 and 2006, Iceland was provided with serious storm warnings from the IMF, the rating agencies, and the foreign financial press. In early 2008, accelerating credit default swap (CDS) rates for the three banks were announced. Yet, in October, the crisis appeared to take the people of this socially stable and well-ordered society completely by surprise.

What has happened since October 2008 is not of analytical concern here. The focus of this chapter is twofold. First, an explanation of *how* the crisis came about, reflecting specifically on a banking system that became culturally myopic, imprudent in practices, and grossly overextended as a result. Second, to explore the reasons *why* the banks were permitted, without effective political or institutional constraint, to place their host society in jeopardy.

Despite the integration of its financial services within global markets, the approach adopted here is to treat Iceland as a case, and to permit readers to compare and contrast the Icelandic situation to others with which they may be more familiar. The data supplying the basis for the analysis have been drawn mainly from semi-structured interviews with 16 Icelandic nationals involved at senior levels within the banking sector. The following text represents a condensed version of where their testimonies have concurred. As a new government has set in train an official inquiry into the crisis, which may lead to prosecutions, informant anonymity here has been guaranteed and any *ad hominem* accounts of specific situations discounted.

HOW . . . ?

From the late 1990s, as part of a general process of economic deregulation, the banks were privatized. Hitherto, these organizations had been locally oriented commercial banks. Islandsbanki merged with FBA in 1999 and was rebranded as Glitner in 2006. In 2002, both Landsbanki and Bunarðarbanki were privatized. In May 2003, the latter was acquired in an all-share transaction by Kaupthing Bank, which was previously a stockbroking firm. We will return to the process of privatization further on. It could be noted here, however, that a controlling stake in Landsbanki was acquired by Samson, an investment company owned by father and son Björgolfur Gudmundsson and Thor Björgolfsson, who had no prior experience in banking. Their recent successful sale of a brewing operation in St. Petersburg, Russia, to Heineken led to persistent rumors of collusion in the laundering of Russian money.

From 2003, a rapid process of international expansion was undertaken, as each of the banks acquired financial services organizations in Scandinavia and northern Europe. By the end of 2007, this previously state-owned, locally oriented financial services sector had expanded to include 56 overseas operating units in 21 countries (FME 2007).

The investment capacities of these banks quickly outstripped their traditional commercial banking operations, and corporate banking services entered the Icelandic business scene for the first time. The principal investment targets were private equity companies—Exista, Baugur, FL Group, Samson—all in international expansion mode. These also were, or soon became, substantial owners of the banks they were borrowing from. Indeed, cross-holdings became a primary characteristic of the relationship between lenders and borrowers, with the banks taking equity positions in these corporations and their acquisitions. Thus, the biggest clients of the banks were also their owners, who often pledged only shares as collateral for loans. By raiding the wholesale capital markets for cheap credit, the banks financed the highly leveraged expansion of these organizations while inflating the size of their own balance sheets. But in funding this unceasing, never consolidated drive to expand ever further, the banks were making the cardinal error of forging an imbalance between short-term borrowing and long-term lending.

Meanwhile, within the banks, the apparent success of their own (leveraged) expansion strategies generated dynamic, hard-working cultures. Banking became the career choice for Iceland's best and brightest graduates. Many with science and engineering degrees opted for employment in these institutions, soon characterized by the youthfulness of their middle and upper echelons. By 2004, the CEOs of the three banks were ambitious men in their mid-30s who had known each other since university. Inexperienced in the world of international banking themselves, these leaders surrounded themselves with young executives whose compliance was encouraged with high levels of remuneration. Any dissident, often older, voices were soon shown the door.

The banks generated substantial income from four sources; local retail banking operations, interest and commission on lending, selling equity positions in a rising market, and especially windfall fees from corporate banking services supplied to support mergers and acquisitions (M&As) at home and abroad. As a new component in Icelandic business, benchmark fees for these services were not available. With each deal, hundreds of million of króna were paid for limited work. The purchase of the fishing company Alfresca by Eimskip earned Landsbanki an alleged ISK2 billion in fees; Eimskip being owned by Samson, the controlling shareholder in Landsbanki.

Given the expansionary momentum of their owners, and the income generated by each acquisition, a deal-making culture characterized corporate banking operations. Intelligent, driven young men (yes, men) able to operate complex financial models and provide high impact PowerPoint presentations earned substantial commissions from each deal they brokered. Informants described a narrowly focused dealmaking "addiction" engendered by a combination of the capital requirements of the owners, highly incentivized managers (inexperienced in banking at any level), and intense interbank competition, compounded by the interpersonal rivalries of the three CEOs. Published annual reports on the number of M&As with which each bank had been involved resulted in criticism of the least active bank. To be the biggest bank was the objective. And sitting on their boards were the owners of the companies providing the opportunities for a growth that required lending regulations to be transgressed and Basel Accord capital adequacy ratios (CAD) contravened.

However, with annual returns on equity topping 35 percent, Triple-A ratings, and no end of foreign investors willing to inject fresh capital into the Icelandic banking phenomenon, confidence within the banks had taken on epic proportions. Risk assessment procedures appear to have been downgraded in preference to shoring up the highly geared operations of major shareholders demanding rising share prices from their banks.

But what were the banks using foreign currency borrowings to fund? There was a general consensus that if the subprime liquidity crisis had not delivered the *coup de grâce*, the quality of the banks' balance sheets certainly would have. The growth strategies of the banks' owners were generally assessed as poor, involving ill-considered, overpriced, and sometimes dubious, acquisitions. Why did FL Group buy the loss-making Sterling Airlines, sell it to a business associate, buy it back from him, then sell it to a company owned by both FL Group and this business associate, each time for hugely inflated sums? Why was Baugur investing so heavily in a mature U.K. retail market in which there are far too many financially troubled players? Baugur was a major shareholder in FL Group. And the banks were not in a position to disengage. To call in the burgeoning debts of their owners would have forced default. Better to continue supporting such going concerns. The alternative, the potential bankruptcy of these concerns delivering huge losses and provoking a possible run on the banks, could not be countenanced. The vicious circle was complete.

From late 2005 through 2006, international concerns were expressed about Iceland's overheated economy and macroeconomic imbalances, the current account deficit, foreign debt accumulation, and the possible depreciation of the króna. Specifically, the banking sector was subject to trenchant criticism from various sources (IMF 2008). This focused on the overly rapid process of expansion, excessive level of foreign borrowing, poor deposit ratios, lack of liquidity, dubious risk management, lack of transparency, the concentrated nature of ownership, and the level of cross-holdings.

Fascinatingly, the initial reaction within the upper levels of the banks appears to have been one of irritation at the intervention of meddling foreigners. However, a number of reforms were undertaken. Some effort to reduce cross-holding was made. For example, Kaupthing and Exista disengaged, with the former providing the latter's share as dividends to other shareholders. To increase deposits, both Landsbanki (Icesave) and Kaupthing (Kaupthing Edge) set up overseas Internet banking operations offering attractive interest rates. Together they accumulated, in the United Kingdom alone, more than 8 billion pounds sterling during 2006 and 2007. However, instead of shrinking balance sheets or de-leveraging, the improved liquidity these deposits provided was burned in order to continue supporting the banks' investment operations. In August 2007, Kaupthing announced its intention to acquire the Dutch bank NIBC, thereby widening its CDS rate.

As the storm clouds gathered during 2008, room for maneuver evaporated. For fear of provoking a run on their banks, CEOs were unwilling to provide accurate information to the markets. They resorted instead to irregular activities. To appear to comply with the Basel Accord concerning their capital adequacy ratios, the banks sent each other "love letters," which were same-day loans that would boost each bank's reserves on paper without increasing real capital (EU 2008). Glitnir's Fund 9 became especially infamous because employees phoned the bank's customers to encourage them to deposit money into this fund, which they described as a bulletproof investment. The owners of the three banks, in an attempt to secure liquid funds, used funds in their banks' money market accounts to purchase shares in their own companies just before the collapse. The end had arrived.

WHY...?

Iceland has a tripartite regulatory system: the Central Bank (CBI), the Financial Services Authority (FME), and the government. In regard to the CBI, by 2005, David Oddsson had transferred from the job of prime minister (1991 to 2004) to that of chairman of the Central Bank. The CBI's principal instrument was monetary policy aimed at controlling inflation by manipulating interest rates. This was largely unsuccessful, and interest rates of around 14 percent encouraged the carry trade and hedge fund speculation in the Icelandic economy.

Subsequent to privatization, the CBI's stewardship of the banking sector was characterized by a very light touch. Even as the crisis loomed, a more *dirigiste* effort to manage the banks was not assumed. In November 2006, Standard & Poor's downgraded its outlook for Iceland's sovereign rating from stable to negative because of macroeconomic imbalances exacerbated by banking sector activities. The CBI's position, however, was that the Icelandic banks had performed very well on stress tests carried out by the FME and Central Bank, and that the Icelandic financial system was "fundamentally sound and that it was able to withstand potential shocks to the economy and the financial markets, mediate credit and payments, and redistribute risks appropriately. In other words, the financial system was deemed able to carry out its role effectively and efficiently" (CBI 2007, 8).

The FME, established in 1999, is the agency involved in overseeing the regulatory compliance of the banks. Opinions contrasted. Some negative claims concerning the quality of FME staff were countered by more assessable evidence. Minimal contact and cooperation was achieved between the FME and the CBI, despite a formal cooperation agreement (CBI 2006). The regulatory system established by the government had been designed for the management of retail banking, not a rapidly expanding international banking and investment sector. That it remained underresourced throughout the crucial period during which it had to face new challenges was made clear in its annual reports. The FME also highlighted the problems associated with cross-holdings, noncompliance with Chinese Walls regulations, lack of transparency, and increasing reputational risk (FME 2006, 2007). When the FME attempted actions for serious contraventions of regulations pertaining to the ownership of financial undertakings, these were allegedly stifled or sidelined. *Prima facie*, it appears that the FME, working within a politically managed system of minimal regulation, was always likely to be ineffective. Furthermore, when the FME moved to constrain the banks from bending the rules to the breaking point, they were confronted by teams of corporate lawyers who blocked the regulatory process.

From a different perspective, regulatory failure was attributed by a CBI governor to the adoption of the European Central Bank's less stringent regulatory framework. Apparently, to have maintained Iceland's hitherto stricter format would have put the country's banks at a disadvantage in comparison to their EU counterparts. Also, the Icelandic authorities' hands were tied by the limited legal power provided by EU directives (Fridriksson 2009, 11).

This brings us to the relationship between business and politics. Until the 1990s, Iceland's economy was highly regulated. However, during the Thatcher-Reaganite ascendancy of the early 1980s, a group of young men in Iceland (the Locomotive Group), including David Oddsson, imported the ideas of Milton Friedman and pursued a neoliberal agenda. First elected prime minister in 1991, Mr. Oddsson would go on to lead a series of coalition governments (until 2004), the senior partner of which was his conservative Independence Party (IP), established in 1929. The IP dominated the political landscape following the nation's declaration of full independence from Denmark in 1944. The junior partner was the centrist Progressive Party (PP), established in 1916, with a background mainly in the countryside. These two parties constituted a political duopoly, each representing vested interests. The families behind the IP, colloquially known as the Octopus, dominated fishing, importation, transportation, wholesaling, and insurance. The initially more agrarian elite, the Squid, controlled the PP. Until the mid-1990s, the PP enjoyed disproportionate electoral voting rights, enabling it to negotiate substantial rewards in return for coalition compliance. The IP and PP have shared power on a number of occasions during the postwar years.

One consequence of this political structure has been a widespread system of political patronage. For example, lucrative import licenses and fishing quotas appear to have been disproportionately allocated to IP members. The PP-dominated, demographically small, farming sector has been supported by subsidies worth approximately US$100 million per year, ostensibly to preserve the nation's agrarian heritage. This patronage extends beyond purely business relationships with, also, for example, key civil service posts allocated on a similar basis. Being an office holder in either of the political parties did not disqualify one from assuming a senior civil service role. Furthermore, much of the televisual and press media is run and edited by members of the IP. Indeed, the major daily national, *Morganblaðið*, began as the IP's own organ. In the late 1990s, Oddsson's government passed legislation closing down the National Economic Institute, allegedly for publishing data unsuitable to the IP's political agenda.

Privatization did not sever ties of patronage. In June 2005, the newspaper *Frettablaðið* published details concerning how, in 2002, controlling shares in Landsbanki and Bunaðarbanki had been allocated. In effect, an Executive Committee on Privatization was sidelined by David Oddsson and Halldor Asgrimsson, chairman of the PP, who formed an *ad hoc* privatization committee. The investment company Samson, majority-owned by a long-term member of the IP (Mr. Guðmundsson), acquired a 45.8 percent stake in Landsbanki, despite offering the lowest bid. The same stake in Bunaðarbanki was allocated to the S-Group, formed by the chairman of Samskip, Olafur Olafsson, an affiliate of the PP. In each case, the government's share was sold at near-market prices without the substantial premium that controlling stakes usually attract. In both cases, extensions were added to the payment period. Also in both cases, before having completed the purchase, the new owners appointed directors and assumed operational control of the banks. Additionally, there is evidence that, as part of the bargain, the new owners were instructed that the expansion of the banking sector was an imperative component of Iceland's future development. This press coverage provoked negligible public debate.

Further evidence of the relationship between politics and business was provided in April 2009 as news broke that, in 2006, at the very time that the IP was dealing with a parliamentary bill to limit individual political donations to 300,000 ISK, the party received unusually large, unpublicized, donations from FL Group of 30 million ISK and 25 million ISK from Landsbanki.

When the crisis broke in 2008, both the IP and chairman of the CBI denied any responsibility whatsoever, allocating blame to the banks and their "Viking Raider" owners. Mr. Oddsson refused to resign his post until an interim government forced it by an act of Parliament in February 2009. Ironically, in response to inquiries concerning guarantees for depositors in Icelandic bank branches abroad (e.g., Icesave), Mr. Oddsson announced on Icelandic national television (October 7, 2008) that "the government will not repay debts of people who have not exercised due diligence about where they put their money." As this comment reverberated around the world, the U.K. government invoked the 2001 Anti-Terrorism, Crime and Security Act to freeze the assets of Landsbanki and Kaupthing in the United Kingdom, apparently to stop the transfer of funds to offshore tax havens. The króna collapsed by 65 percent, the Icelandic stock market lost 90 percent of its value overnight, and the country, the UN's prosperity poster child of 2007, was effectively bankrupt.

AND...

Why were Icelanders so shocked at the events of October 2008?

The explanations provided indicate that Icelanders have accepted, more or less uncritically, a status quo structured by political duopoly and organized around clientilistic relationships. If the possibility of personal advantage was too often conditional on patronage, nonetheless the state delivered good public services to an entire population bound together by an insular nationalism based on historical cultural identity and future promise.

For a few years, foreign currency attracted by high interest rates flushed into the Icelandic economy, provoking widespread prosperity. House prices rocketed, construction projects proliferated as numerous shopping malls, offices, and new neighborhoods were added to Reykjavik's (pop. 120,000) already considerable existing stock. The sums didn't add up, but it didn't seem to matter. Aptly put by a locally based British journalist, Robert Jackson, Iceland seemed to have transformed from "ugly pupa to gaudy butterfly." After a millennium of struggle to forge livelihoods in an inhospitable environment, Icelanders believed that, at last, a Golden Age had arrived. The author Hallgrimur Helgasson described how the new capitalists were idolized as titans.... "Awestruck we watched their adventures.... We never had clever businessmen, not for a thousand years, not to mention men who had won battles in other countries."

However, as confidence grew, consumption intensified, and Icelanders took on a level of household debt outstripping even that of the United Kingdom. Mortgages were taken out in lower interest foreign currencies. Loans were index-linked to inflation. The crisis came. The króna collapsed. Inflation increased. Personal indebtedness increased exponentially, businesses failed, and unemployment increased. Public demonstrations brought about the resignation of the government in late January 2009, and the majority of Icelanders were left to pick up the pieces.

This brief account has touched on the political economy underpinning the Icelandic banking phenomenon. On reflection, and in general terms... Is the regulation of the corporate sector a neoliberal political priority? Without constraint, can corporate behavior become excessive? Might there then be more scope for the unbridled self-interest of some in the pursuit of wealth and status? In terms of political structures... Is it possible that democracies might permit the formation of elites that combine to exert their influence to protect and reproduce their political and economic interests? Is Iceland a special case, completely different from any other society? Or, rather, is the difference more one of *degree* than of *species?*

If you wish to ponder these questions, first consider this. Iceland experienced an economic bubble. In the introduction to Charles Mackay's (1995) fascinating analysis of bubbledom, why "the follies of mankind are not unique to the modern world" (written in 1841), Norman Stone notes that the book is "said to be required reading in some of the literate Wall Street financial houses." Clearly, it made the shelves of neither Iceland's bankers and politicians nor their counterparts in other nations in which relatively unrestrained banking sectors have created havoc.

REFERENCES

Buiter, W. H., and A. Sibert. 2008. The Icelandic banking crisis and what to do about it: The lender of last resort theory of optimal currency areas. *Centre for Economic Policy Research*, Policy Insight 26 (October).

Central Bank of Iceland. 2006. *Cooperation agreement between the financial supervisory authority and the central bank of Iceland*. Reykjavik, October 3.

———. 2007. *2006 Annual report*. Reykjavík, ISSN 0559-2712.

———. 2008. *2007 Annual report*. Reykjavík, ISSN 0559-27120.

European Union. 2008. *Delegation of the European commission to Norway and Iceland*. Oslo, Presentation of December 12.

Financial Services Authority 2006. *Annual report*. Reykjavik: Iceland (see www.fme@is).

———. 2007. *Annual report*. Reykjavik: Iceland (see www.fme@is).

Fridriksson, I. 2009. *The banking crisis in Iceland in 2008*. CBI paper, February 6.

International Monetary Fund. 2008. *Iceland: Financial system stability assessment update*. IMF Country Report 08/368.

Mackay, C. 1995. *Extraordinary popular delusion and the madness of crowds*. London: Wordsworth Reference.

ABOUT THE AUTHORS

James A. H. S. Hine is currently a senior lecturer in organizational studies and business ethics at the University of Edinburgh's business school. He has researched and published, funded by U.K. and EU government grants, in the fields of land conflict in the Brazilian Amazon; technological innovation in the U.K. banking sector; institutional change in the St. Petersburg, Russia bakery industry; and the management of strategic change within the United Kingdom's alcoholic beverages industry. From this experience has emerged his current research and publication interests, which concern the occupational ethics of corporate executives and a critical perspective on the theory and practice of corporate social responsibility. Previously a principal and director in a number of companies, Hine holds a Ph.D. from the University of Liverpool, has been an MBA director at his current university. He was chairman of the European Business Ethics Network (U.K. chapter) from 2004 to 2007.

Ian Ashman is a senior lecturer in the Division of HRM and Leadership at the University of Central Lancashire in England. He holds a Ph.D. from Manchester Metropolitan University. He has published widely on the subject of business ethics in such periodicals as the *Journal of Business Ethics*, the *Journal of Mass Media Ethics*, *Business Ethics: A European Review* and *Leadership*. He has a particular interest in the application of existentialism within the discipline and his current research and writing focuses on issues of "ethical leadership."

CHAPTER 69

The Subprime Crisis: Implications for Emerging Markets

WILLIAM B. GWINNER
Principal Finance Specialist, International Finance Corporation

ANTHONY B. SANDERS
Professor of Finance, George Mason University

E merging markets policy makers should take appropriate lessons from the U.S. subprime mortgage crisis. Many observers have blamed the subprime crisis on lending to low-income borrowers. However, evidence shows that weak lending practices were primarily to blame. Before the growth of subprime lending in the 1990s, U.S. mortgage markets already reached low and moderate-income households without taking large risks or suffering large losses. In contrast, in most emerging markets, mortgage finance is a luxury good, restricted to upper-income households. As policy makers in emerging markets seek to extend access to finance, their policies should permit a variety of safe loan products and capital market tools. Ownership should be feasible for those who can afford a mortgage, but policies should not be biased against rental. Securitization is a useful tool when developed in the context of well-aligned incentives and oversight. It is possible to extend mortgage lending downmarket without repeating the mistakes of the subprime boom and bust.

SOFTENED LENDING PRACTICES—BETTING ON THE COLLATERAL RATHER THAN THE BORROWER

Ten years of ballooning property prices in the United States led to excessive optimism by investors and lenders. In the boom, relaxed lending standards led to increased mortgage lending, mortgage lending contributed to rising house prices, and the flood of weak loans drove the subsequent increase in defaults. Average U.S. house prices rose 86 percent between 1995 and 2006, and mortgage originations rose by five times. As this property bubble deflated in 2006 and 2007, rising subprime defaults spurred a reevaluation of credit spreads and credit market conditions that reflected broader and more fundamental issues.

The primary cause of subprime ARM defaults has been weak underwriting, in large part by nonbank lenders. Serious delinquencies for subprime ARMs quadrupled between 2005 and 2008, from 5.15 percent to 22.70 percent. Meanwhile, prime fixed rate delinquencies remained stable at less than 1 percent until the end of 2006, and then rose to 2.10 percent at the end of 2008. About half of subprime loans were made by independent nonbank lenders between 2004 and 2006. Nonbank lenders such as New Century Financial aggressively pursued the originate-to-distribute business model, in which it originated loans for sale to the capital markets. By the end of 2006, New Century was the third-largest subprime lender in the country, with loan production of $51.6 billion. Four months later, rising defaults forced New Century into bankruptcy.

Private and public mortgage insurance (MI) lost market share as a method of credit risk mitigation for lower-income borrowers. MI contributes to financial system stability by indemnifying defaults. Better underwriting and more effective loss mitigation have caused loans with FHA insurance to outperform subprime loans to households with similar incomes. During the subprime boom, loans backed by private MI fell from 17 percent of originations in 1995 to 9 percent in 2006, even as average LTVs rose. The market share for FHA and VA-insured loans fell much further, from 18 percent of originations in 1994 to 3 percent in 2006.

THE SUBPRIME BOOM AND ACCESS TO FINANCE

Before subprime lending grew, U.S. mortgage lenders reached the majority of households, and the overall housing system delivered high quality shelter to 98 percent of households. In the United States, roughly half of all mortgages outstanding were made to households earning less than the median income. Access to a mortgage to buy a home is available to most households that can afford it. By contrast, more than half of subprime loans were made to refinance an existing mortgage rather than to purchase a house. Many subprime borrowers refinanced to pay off riskier subprime ARM loans before they reached the end of their low teaser interest rate period. Each refinancing required the borrower to pay fees to the lender, often the lender's major source of income.

WEAKNESSES IN SECONDARY MARKET PRACTICES

Between 2001 and 2006, between 60 and 80 percent of subprime loans were bundled into mortgage-backed securities and sold to investors in capital markets. This contrasts with the deposit-funded bank lending model followed in most emerging markets. Securitization in the United States is less expensive on a risk-adjusted basis than funding with deposits, and it permits banks more flexibility in managing capital.

Increased Moral Hazard Problems

Securitization comes at the risk of moral hazard. Lenders that sell the loans to another party (investors) have incentives to originate loans that are riskier than they would originate if they had to hold them in their portfolios. For securitization to work properly, there must be a means to control moral hazard.

Market disclosures and contractual constraints failed to prevent weak practices in subprime underwriting. Investors specify standards for the loans that they wish to purchase. Loan originators are required by contract to repurchase or make whole the investor for mortgage loans that were not made according to those agreed standards. So, if investors discover that the loans were inappropriate or that underwriting was weak, the investors can require that the lender repurchase the tainted loans. In practice, lenders may challenge the claims in court, and such cases can take years to adjudicate. More importantly, many lightly capitalized subprime mortgage lenders were bankrupted in 2006 and 2007 because they lacked the capital to pay investor claims to repurchase defaulting loans.

Not Fully Understanding Subprime Lending

The desire for issuance volume and yield caused lenders, securitization conduits, and investors to move downmarket recklessly. In their search to preserve market share and fully use servicing capability, lenders sought borrowers who were previously undetected, underserved, or underqualified. Many originators broadened their market base by developing or expanding not only the subprime credit programs but alternative A-credit borrowers who did not fit either the agency-conforming or standard jumbo underwriting criteria in spite of their income level.

Not Understanding New Mortgage Designs

Investors in the subprime and jumbo markets lacked historical data to evaluate the performance of new, complex mortgage instruments. These newer loan instruments cannot be evaluated with data for other loan designs in rising property markets. It has been suggested that loans with adjustable rates are a big part of the problem, but ARMs have been offered in the United States for many years, and have been the predominant type of mortgage in countries like Canada and the United Kingdom for many decades without major credit problems. What was unknown (because of a heavy reliance on limited historical data) was how a slowdown in the housing market would affect defaults of ARMs with new and complex features because they were extended to a broader population of households, many with limited resources.

Not Fully Recognizing the Adverse Selection Problem

There is evidence that a number of borrowers gave misleading information about their income and operated under the assumption that they could refinance their way out of problems. When housing prices started declining, they discovered that this was more difficult than expected. That so many loans have become delinquent almost immediately after origination suggests that not all borrowers have been victims. In some cases, the borrowers went along with deceptive schemes to fool the underwriter (and loan purchaser).

There is evidence that a number of borrowers took out loans knowing in advance that they could not afford the mortgage payments when an ARM reset took place. These borrowers were effectively speculating on housing prices, hoping for an increase in housing values so that they could sell their properties for a gain before the reset occurred. Once house prices fell, and refinancing became impossible, these borrowers defaulted.

More broadly, there were plenty of incentives for borrowers, lenders, and investors to have protected themselves. While it may be the case that investors in the AAA tranches of subprime structures had little incentive to look closely at risks, the investors in the subordinated tranches certainly had such an incentive. It looks as though they will bear the brunt of losses, and it is unclear so far why they, who were supposed to be the specialists in risk management, were so wrong.

Not Fully Understanding the Shortcomings of Credit Rating Agencies

In addition to being slow to downgrade subprime ABS, the ratings agencies may also suffer from the incentive structure inherent in their business model. Issuing investment banks pay the rating agencies to analyze and rate the collateral underlying credit-sensitive ABS. Given that there are more than two rating agencies, a potential problem surfaces when the issuing investment banks pay for the ratings, in that a ratings agency could give favorable ratings in return for repeat business. However, the incentive for ratings agencies to be overly generous with their ratings is offset to some degree by the reputational effects of being too generous; that is, the ratings agencies must maintain credibility to generate repeat business. Finally, ratings agencies rely on the same type of historical models of default, which sent a false signal about the safety of the mortgage market to investors.

REGULATION OF SUBPRIME LENDING AND SECURITIZATION

Regulation of securitization markets and subprime lending will be geared towards several objectives. The first objective is to reduce exposure to systemic risk and extending regulation to "lightly" or non-regulated financial institutions. The second objective is to increase consumer protection, particularly in the subprime mortgage space. The third objective is increase the credibility of information produced about mortgages and securitizations, such as improving or changing the ratings agencies.

The Importance of Systemic Effects

Most market observers and participants failed to anticipate the threat to system stability that subprime lending posed. Subprime lending has been a relatively small part of overall U.S. mortgage lending, ending up at 12 percent of outstanding mortgages by 2006, and new issuances of subprime loans and securities had evaporated by early 2008. Before the crisis began to materialize in 2007, the regulatory debate in the United States was limited to protecting unwary consumers from exorbitant fees or risky loan products. Until events made it clear, nobody assessed the cumulative risks taken on by foreign investment funds, such as the SIV set up in Ireland by the German Landesbank Sachsen LB, which issued short-term commercial paper to fund investments in medium- and long-term collateralized debt obligations (CDOs) that were in turn backed by high loan-to-value (LTV) subprime mortgages made in places like Ohio, Florida, and California. Nor was there a broad understanding of the exposure of banks to hedge funds that depended on bank lending to leverage their investments and provide strong returns.

Lightly Supervised Nonbank Mortgage Lenders Eased Underwriting Standards

For many years in many countries, it has been thought unnecessary to prudentially supervise nonbank lenders. Since nonbank financial institutions (NBFIs) cannot accept deposits, their activities do not affect the deposit base or the M1 definition of the money supply. When they are a relatively small part of the financial system, NBFIs do not pose a threat to stability. Since NBFIs are funded in the capital markets, policy makers have expected that their debt and equity investors should understand and manage risk. With these factors in mind, U.S. authorities have historically been reluctant to regulate nonbank mortgage lenders. Similarly, the Mexican government in 2005 changed the regulation of nonbank lenders, creating in law a new and more flexible entity that permits a wider range of activities known by its Spanish language acronym as SOFOM. Before the 1998 Asian crisis, NBFIs in East Asia lacked supervision, and their lending for real estate, margin loans for equity, consumer finance, and car purchases became an important source of risk.

Weaker supervision standards for selected institutions produce weaker lending. Lenders tend to choose the corporate structure that permits them to maximize profits in the short term. This was the case for NBFI units of U.S. financial holding companies such as Countrywide Financial. In Asia before 1998, the erosion of the distinction between banks and NBFIs led to compromises in credit underwriting criteria, with the finance company affiliates of banks extending credit that the banks were precluded from extending because of prudential norms.

Consumer Protection Failures in Subprime Lending

Predatory subprime lenders have misled borrowers and persuaded them to take out loans that they did not understand or that carried inappropriate risks. Subprime borrowers are a higher risk than prime borrowers, they pay more for loans, have lower income, are less well financially educated, and less likely to search for the best interest rates and terms for their mortgage loans. In an attempt to comply with underwriting rules, some brokers persuaded borrowers to misstate income or assets, or persuaded them to sign blank application documents that the broker would later fill in with false figures that would be sufficient to have the loan approved.

Penalties for predatory lending are small in comparison to the potential gains for lenders. The penalty that lenders face when found guilty of breaking fair lending laws is to return excessive fees or charges to the affected consumers. There are no punitive damages in law for predatory lending practices.

The Fragmented U.S. Regulatory System Contributed to the Slow Regulatory Response

The U.S. financial regulatory system permits mortgage lenders to move risk to where capital charges are lowest and regulatory scrutiny is lightest. The system has evolved over the years into a complex and fragmented collection of national and state agencies with competing and overlapping mandates. One paradoxical result of the structure of the U.S. regulatory system is that while banks, the largest and safest lenders, are subject to sophisticated and intrusive risk-based supervision, riskier nonbank mortgage lenders are subject to no prudential oversight.

The Role of Auditors

External auditors abetted the boom mentality by underreporting risks and losses. In the case of New Century Financial Corporation, New Century's auditor apparently enabled significant improper and imprudent practices related to loan originations, operations, accounting, and financial reporting processes. Among other actions, the auditor suggested reducing reserves against loan repurchases in 2006 at the same time that early payment defaults rose, and New Century was flooded with repurchase claims from investors.

Basel II Capital Accords Would Have a Limited Effect on the Subprime Boom and Crisis

Basel II was not in effect in the United States during the subprime boom, and it does not apply to nonbank lenders. Basel II Pillar 1 capital standards primarily affect mortgage lending in three respects: lower risk weights for mortgages retained on bank balance sheets in countries where lower losses can be demonstrated, lower risk weights for loans backed by mortgage default insurance, and specific capital requirements for bank investments in mortgage-related securities. Pillar 3 of Basel II requires banks to provide qualitative discussions of securitizations and off-balance-sheet exposures, representing a limited improvement, given the qualitative nature of the requirements. Pillar 2 requires supervisors to review the quality of these disclosures. The more advanced Basel II internal ratings–based standards will be implemented by 2011 by large, internationally active banks in the United States, and so were not in effect during the growth of subprime lending at the beginning of the decade. The Basel II accords do not apply to nonbank lenders, to investment banks, or to credit rating agencies.

OBSERVATIONS AND RECOMMENDATIONS FOR EMERGING MARKETS

Broadly speaking, there has been no subprime mortgage lending in emerging markets. Instead, mortgage lending is typically made on conservative terms to middle and upper income households employed in the formal sector:

- Credit reaches no more than a third of most emerging markets households. Seventy percent of emerging markets households handle their economic lives in cash. Most lack bank accounts, as bank branches are concentrated in wealthier urban areas and their products are targeted at upper income earners.
- Consumer finance markets are relatively small in emerging markets. Consumers who have access to credit tend to carry less debt than do their

developed country counterparts, and they often prepay mortgage debt as rapidly as possible. The household debt-to-GDP ratio ranges between 10 and 30 percent for emerging markets, but between 60 and 100 percent in developed countries.

- Mortgage lending is typically less than 20 percent of GDP in emerging markets, while it ranges between 40 and 100 percent of GDP in developed countries.
- Since the macroeconomic crises of the late 1990s, low interest rates, low inflation, and financial sector reforms have caused mortgage default rates to fall dramatically in emerging markets.
- Many emerging mortgage markets lack long-term funding tools such as covered bonds and securitization that permit lenders to extend the maturity of their loans. In East Asia, the first mortgage-backed securities (MBS) were issued in China, Hong Kong, and Singapore within the past four years. Within Latin America, active large-scale mortgage securitization markets have emerged only in Mexico, Colombia, and Chile, and only Chile has a widespread covered bond market.

Smaller economies have relied on foreign capital to fund growth in domestic financial markets. These countries have suffered in the international credit crunch, as international investors have fled to high quality government bonds from large economies, including Europe and the United States.

Housing policies for low and moderate income groups should not be excessively weighted toward owner-occupied solutions. Households with low and uncertain incomes are often better off renting than owning housing that meets standards for health and safety. If subsidies are provided, they should be available for either ownership (for example with down payment assistance) or rental (for instance with rental vouchers), and in either case for new or used units. There should be balanced protections in law for mortgage lenders and borrowers, and for rental landlords and tenants. Tax treatment should not unduly favor owning or renting.

Primary Market Practices

Maintain standards for risk-based pricing, credit underwriting, and capital and reserve retention during the full real estate market cycle. When a market boom creates disincentives to maintain origination standards, financial regulators need to enforce credit underwriting and risk management requirements for all lenders and for capital market participants. Lenders should avoid excessive reliance on credit scores, but rather use them as a complement to traditional underwriting methods. Basic elements for mortgages include an equity contribution by the borrower, verification and documentation of willingness and ability to pay, and industry standards for appraisal methodology.

Evaluate mortgage credit risk in terms of the borrower's income, not the value of the property. Even though mortgages are secured with a lien on a house, collecting mortgage debt by foreclosing on the house generally results in a loss to the lender, especially when house prices are flat or falling.

The primary means to evaluate the capacity to pay is the borrower's debt-to-income ratio. For prime mortgage loans in the United States, the standard for mortgage debt to gross income is 28 percent for monthly housing payment to gross income and 36 percent for total debt obligations to gross income. For subprime lending, the mortgage payment to income ratio was allowed to rise over 50 percent.

To evaluate the debt-to-income ratio for adjustable rate mortgages (ARMs), the lender should estimate the affordability at a fully adjusted rate of interest. This requires assessing at the time of origination the borrower's ability to pay at the fully indexed rate, ignoring any artificial discounts and taking into account predictable near-term adjustments.

Allow flexibility in sound credit management practices while increasing access for low and moderate income borrowers. Lenders should be required to document borrower income, but be allowed flexibility with respect to the means by which informal income earners establish their ability to pay. This can include structured savings programs, rent and utility receipts, and co-signatures by friends and family members.

Prepayment fees should be limited to the actual financial cost of refinancing incurred by the lender or investor. Yield maintenance fees are common in many countries that feature long-term fixed rate loans. These fees eliminate the financial gain for the consumer from exercising the prepayment option. In some countries, contractual limits on prepayment are the norm. Any such fees or limitations should be clearly disclosed to the borrower. Prepayment fees should not exceed the mark-to-market loss that the lender incurs as a result of prepayment.

Set LTV requirements in terms of the local history of house price movements and prevailing foreclosure costs. Authorities should look at the history of house prices in their markets to see how volatility is likely to affect the equity position of a high LTV loan. Countries with higher volatility will want to set the LTV standard lower than others. Rapidly urbanizing markets, such as China and Mexico, where valuations are based largely on new construction, should require lower LTVs. (In fact, China had recently restricted LTVs to 65 percent in its more overheated cities.) In more mature markets, with a longer history of trading of both new and used housing, higher LTVs may be acceptable. Likewise, longer or more uncertain foreclosure periods or higher costs should drive lower LTV norms.

As property prices rise, discount the appraised value of the collateral property. In rapidly rising markets, authorities should require lenders to discount the appraised valued of properties. Such a discount is embedded in German regulation.

Require lenders to countercyclically adjust loss provisions to reflect changing property prices. As property prices rise, regulators can require lenders to set aside more for expected losses from defaults. Spain has had such a dynamic provisioning rule in effect since 2000.

Create a public database on property prices, mortgage interest rates, mortgage lending volumes, and mortgage loan performance. Confidence increases when investors are aware of price movements and cycles. Regulators and lenders in middle income countries have only recently begun to keep such data.

Prudential Regulation of Nondepository Lenders

Ensure that all lenders have clear incentives to mitigate credit risk. As they grow in importance in any economy, nonbank lenders should be subject to prudential supervision. As Basel II is implemented, banks will have a greater incentive to lay off risk to third parties.

Implementation of Basel II should reflect local market conditions. Risk weights for mortgage lending should reflect local experience with default and foreclosure costs. Preferential weights under either the standardized or internal ratings-based approach should reflect a long history of industrywide data on mortgage performance. If it is not possible to demonstrate that mortgage lending is safer than uncollateralized lending, then it should carry a capital risk weight that reflects that risk.

Provide Robust Links to Capital Markets

Capital market funding can take at least three forms: securitization, covered bonds, and liquidity backstops. Diversity in funding instruments and funding sources provides lenders with choices for managing capital in the context of term matching, credit risk, and operational risk. Several countries have developed securitization and covered bonds along with second-tier liquidity facilities that allow lenders to keep mortgages on balance sheet. Liquidity facilities make markets in portfolios of loans or mortgage-related securities from primary lenders, and fund themselves with bond issues. They may be public or private sector. Spain has developed active markets with covered bonds and securitization as capital market tools.

Dependence by NBFIs on wholesale funding has emerged as a serious weakness in the financial crisis. Major lenders, such as Northern Rock in Great Britain and Countrywide Financial in the United States, suffered serious liquidity shortages and were effectively bankrupted even though neither was primarily a subprime lender. Mexico's SOFOMs lost access to funding when Mexican securitization and commercial paper markets closed to them in the autumn of 2008. The effects of this market failure have extended beyond investors, as SOFOMs are the most significant private mortgage lenders to moderate income households in Mexico. Liquidity facilities and deposit funding are important means to mitigate reliance on capital markets.

Capital market funding can be developed in the context of robust market practices. Authorities should assure that at some stage of the securitization process, at least one participant besides the loan originator reviews the documentation of loans in the collateral pool and assures adherence to a minimum level of credit documentation. This may be the investment bank that arranges the securitization, the rating agency, a mortgage default insurer, or a special auditor. Any third-party reviewer should have a clear mandate, incentive, and accountability that is driven by a long-term perspective to maintain loan quality rather than a focus on production volume.

Financial Reporting

While stronger financial reporting and disclosure standards were not sufficient to prevent the subprime crisis, they remain crucial for improving efficiency in emerging mortgage markets. When lenders securitize portfolios, auditors evaluate whether they meet standards for true sale of the collateral. If issuers retain exposure to the transaction, auditors should evaluate the disclosure of the risk retained, and the adequacy of reserves and capital held against it.

Consumer Protection in Mortgage Lending

Access to finance has to be balanced with appropriate products and consumer protections. Moderate and lower income households are able to pay for appropriately designed mortgages. A house purchase is the largest, most highly leveraged, and most complex financial transaction most consumers will ever undertake. It is unwise to offer mortgage loan products with risky adjustment capacities to households that lack the resources to manage the risk. This is particularly the case for households with limited education and financial training that are more prone to make less rational choices in the face of complexity.

Consumer disclosures are important in emerging markets that issue price level adjusting mortgages, in which the principal amount varies with inflation. Credit risk can rise if mortgages and salaries are not indexed in the same fashion. Clear disclosures and explanations are required to make sure that the borrower understands how the mortgage payment may change over time.

ABOUT THE AUTHORS

William Britt Gwinner is the principal housing finance specialist for Latin America and the Caribbean for the IFC. Before this this position, Mr. Gwinner served as lead housing finance specialist for the World Bank, where he was involved in developing housing finance markets in a number of countries in Latin America, East Europe, and Central and East Asia. Mr. Gwinner was formerly the lead specialist for market risk management for the World Bank, focusing on asset liability and capital management. Before joining the World Bank, he participated in the development of risk-based capital requirements for Fannie Mae, Freddie Mac, and the Federal Home Loan Banks. Mr. Gwinner has worked as a financial consultant for Fortune 500 companies and the U.S. government. Mr. Gwinner is a chartered financial analyst, and he holds an M.B.A. in finance and a master's degree in public policy from the University of Chicago, and a bachelor's degree from George Washington University.

Anthony B. Sanders is a professor of finance in the School of Management at George Mason University where he is the Distinguished Professor of real estate finance. He has previously taught at the University of Chicago Graduate School of Business, the University of Texas at Austin McCombs School of Business, and the Ohio State University Fisher College of Business. He has also served as director and head of asset-backed and mortgage-backed securities research at Deutsche Bank in New York City. His research and teaching focuses on financial institutions and capital markets with a particular emphasis on real estate finance and investment. He has published articles in the *Journal of Finance*, the *Journal of Financial and Quantitative Analysis*, the *Journal of Business*, the *Journal of Financial Services Research*, the *Journal of Housing Economics*, and other journals. Professor Sanders has received six teaching awards and three research awards. He serves as associate editor for several leading journals. He has recently given presentations to the European Central Bank in Frankfurt, Exane BNP Paribas in Paris and Geneva, and the Bank of Japan on the subject of the housing bubble and commercial real estate in the United States and the mortgage market. He has given other presentations in Chile, Japan, China, Poland, England, and Mexico in recent years. Professor Sanders has testified before the U.S. Senate and the U.S. House of Representatives on the U.S. real estate asset and debt markets. He was also an invited speaker to the Federal Trade Commission on the subject of predatory lending.

PART XI

Financial Solutions and Our Economic Future

CHAPTER 70

The Long-Term Cost of the Financial Crisis

MURILLO CAMPELLO
Baltz Professor of Finance at the University of Illinois and a Faculty Research Fellow of the National Bureau of Economic Research

JOHN R. GRAHAM
D. Richard Mead professor of finance at the Fuqua School of Business and co-director of the Center for Finance at Duke University

CAMPBELL R. HARVEY
Professor of Finance at Duke University and a Research Associate of the National Bureau of Economic Research

Most introductory finance courses start by assuming that capital markets are perfect and that companies and banks are able to borrow and lend freely. In this hypothetical setting, corporate executives are free to make decisions that maximize the value of their companies and stock prices.

We are well aware that capital markets are not perfect. There are significant obstructions that prevent companies from making optimal choices and maximizing shareholder value. But, just how severe are these imperfections? And, how big of an obstacle are real-world constraints in regard to limiting opportunities to corporate executives? These are hard questions to answer because unlike in medical science, economic researchers are rarely able to conduct a controlled experiment that treats some companies, while administering a placebo to other firms. Instead, financial economists often study exogenous shocks to the corporate sector, to see how companies with different characteristics are affected, and to get a feel for the magnitudes and effects of real world capital market imperfections.

In the fall of 2008, world financial markets were in the midst of a credit crisis of historic breadth and depth. As devastating as this crisis has been to the livelihood of many, it also represents an enormous shock to the corporate sector that can aid economic research. We study this shock to learn about the ability of the corporate sector to adapt to adverse circumstances, and to better understand how the availability of liquidity affects corporate decision making. Liquidity can be thought of as the oil that lubricates the economic machinery. When liquidity dries up, to what extent does this cause the economic infrastructure to seize up and destroy corporate value?

To better understand how the credit crisis has affected the corporate sector, in a November 2008 joint effort with *CFO* magazine, we surveyed 1,050 chief financial officers (CFOs) in the United States, Europe, and Asia. We asked these corporate financial leaders for detailed information about how their companies are managing the liquidity needs of their firms. We find striking results that financially constrained firms are quickly burning through their cash reserves and are having great difficulty finding new sources of funding. The current lack of liquidity is causing these companies to make drastic cuts to capital spending, hiring, and research and development, and indeed threatens the very survival of many companies.

THE ISSUES

We begin by benchmarking how much cash companies have on their balance sheets in November 2008 versus how much cash they had in November 2007. In the United States, the typical firm had cash and liquid assets equal to about 15 percent of asset value in 2007. The crisis has not affected cash holdings of unconstrained firms, which remain steady at 15 percent of asset value in 2008. In stark contrast, the cash reserves at financially constrained companies have fallen by one-fifth, from 15 percent to about 12 percent of book assets. (We classify a company as being financially constrained if its CFO says the firm has been affected by the cost or availability of external financing.) A similar pattern of cash burn for constrained firms is evident in Europe and Asia. In Europe, constrained firms typically hold less cash than in the United States, while in Asia they hold more. Yet, constrained firms' cash holdings fell around 23 percent in Europe and 11 percent in Asia. All of these patterns are depicted in Exhibit 70.1. This evidence implies that the ongoing credit crisis is affecting some firms greatly, while affecting less the most profitable companies in the economy.

The speed with which constrained companies around the world are burning through cash reserves is alarming. This problem could be severe if these companies have limited access to other untapped sources of liquidity. We therefore investigate corporate access to bank lines of credit. It is generally difficult to gather representative data on line of credit (LC) access. Much of the data available are restricted to public U.S. corporations, so this analysis is novel.

We asked financial executives about the size of the LCs to which they have access. We compare line of credit access now (during the crisis) to their lines of credit in the fall of 2007. The typical firm in the United Stated has a prearranged line of credit of approximately 19 percent (unconstrained firms) to 27 percent (constrained firms) of total book asset value. The differences are more dramatic in Europe and Asia, where constrained firms have committed credit lines greater than 30 percent of asset value. We find no significant changes in the access to lines of credit in the United States (across either constrained or unconstrained firms). In Europe, constrained firms are using 21 percent more LCs than before, while in Asia they are using 10 percent less. Unconstrained firms in those non-U.S. economies have not changed their use of LCs.

We next asked the firms what they do with the proceeds when they draw down lines of credit. About half of CFOs around the world say that they use the funds for daily operations or short-term liquidity needs. Companies that are financially

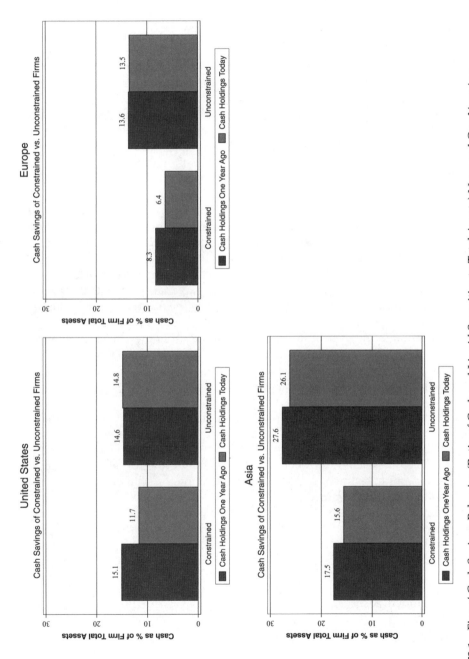

Exhibit 70.1 Firms' Cash Savings Behavior (Ratio of Cash and Liquid Securities to Total Assets) Now and One Year Ago
Responses are averaged across sample partitions based on financial constraints.

constrained use their LCs significantly more than do unconstrained counterparts as a way to fund normal business activities.

More surprisingly, 13 percent of constrained U.S. firms indicate that they have recently drawn on their credit lines so they could have cash for future needs. This purely precautionary use of LCs hints at the following astounding finding. One out of every six constrained U.S. firms has drawn down on its credit line now, just in case its banks might deny a line of credit in the future. That is, there has been a bank run on lines of credit, with many companies drawing on LCs just in case they may not have access in the future. Harvard University professors Victoria Ivashina and David Scharfstein have shown that the amount of this run on LC borrowing has been large enough to offset the overall tightness of available funding pervading the financial sector. Said differently, there has been so much just-in-case use of bank lines of credit by financially constrained companies that it appears to have crowded out normal borrowing opportunities, even though the total volume of borrowing remained high throughout 2008. This effect is slightly stronger in Asia, where 18 percent of surveyed constrained firms report this behavior, while in Europe, that proportion equals 15 percent. By comparison, only about 6 percent of unconstrained firms in the United States, Asia, and Europe say they are drawing on their credit lines for fear that their banks will restrict access to their outstanding lines of credit. These patterns are depicted in Exhibit 70.2.

As robust as credit drawdowns have been, some firms have resisted using their LCs, and we inquire why. The most common explanation is that CFOs want to preserve borrowing capacity in case it is needed in the future. The second most common explanation for not fully drawing on the credit line is to maintain a strong reputation in the eyes of financial institutions. This preserving reputation explanation is significantly stronger among public firms and speculative U.S. firms. In Europe, preserving reputation in the eyes of bankers is significantly stronger among financially constrained companies.

So far, we have documented that around the world, companies that are financially constrained have burned through cash during this past year of financial crisis and have more actively managed lines of credit, including drawing down on them just in case their banks limit future access to credit lines. We next examine the degree to which these credit problems have seeped into the real sector, affecting the operating and investment decisions of corporations, with a close eye on the effects on financially constrained firms.

To study this issue, we examine the pro forma plans of companies conditional on whether they are financially constrained. We find that most companies plan to cut employment, research and development (R&D) spending, capital investment, marketing expenditures, and (on average) dividends in 2009. The results are significantly worse for financially constrained firms. Constrained companies headquartered in the United States planned to dramatically reduce employment (by 11 percent), R&D spending (by 22 percent), capital investment (by 9 percent), marketing expenditures (by 33 percent), and dividends (by 14 percent) in 2009. Constrained firms in Europe are cutting employment by 8 percent, R&D spending by 5 percent, capital investment by 10 percent, and marketing expenditures by 11 percent, while their dividends are being slashed in half. We see similar patterns in Asia as well; except that all firms there (constrained and unconstrained) are not forecasting cuts in employment.

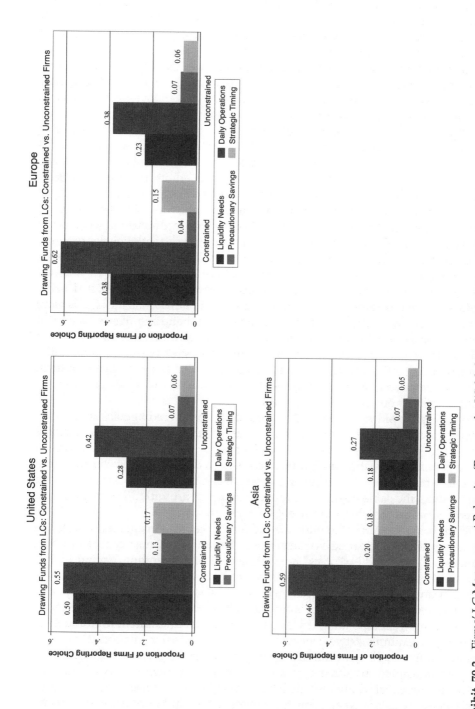

Exhibit 70.2 Firms' LC Management Behavior (Reasons for Widthdrawing Funds from Existing LCs)
Responses are averaged across sample partitions based on financial constraints.

We also study the long-run value implications of slashing corporate invest-ment. Most first-year corporate finance courses demonstrate how a company's managers can maximize stockholder value by choosing positive net present value projects. All this means is that if the returns on an investment outearn the cost of capital required to fund the project, it creates value for the firm. These value-enhancing investments in turn increase shareholder wealth as the stock market capitalizes the increased value into the stock price. Therefore, if the credit crisis is causing companies to cancel value-enhancing projects, this real world constraint is destroying stockholder value.

To investigate this issue, we ask companies about the extent to which credit constraints limit their ability to pursue positive net present value investments. We start by benchmarking how often companies say they have to bypass attractive (NPV > 0) investment projects because of financial constraints. In the United States, in normal credit markets, 46 percent of constrained companies say that they pass up attractive investment opportunities because of financial constraints. Recall that these are firms that declared themselves to be constrained in late fall 2008. Undoubtedly, some of these firms would be constrained and some not constrained in normal times. One interpretation of our result is therefore that 46 percent of these firms are constrained during normal times (which limits their ability to pursue attractive projects in normal times). The 46 percent of self-declared constrained firms that say they pass up attractive investments is significantly greater than the 20 percent of unconstrained firms that say the same. In Europe and Asia, too, more than twice as many constrained firms pass up value-enhancing projects because of credit constraints. In particular, 44 percent of the constrained European firms in our survey say they bypass profitable opportunities because of the cost or availability of credit, compared to only 18 percent of the unconstrained firms in that continent. In Asia, the same comparison is 47 percent for constrained firms versus 20 percent for unconstrained ones.

Because we conducted our analysis during a severe credit crisis, we are able to investigate the effects of financial constraints on investment during extreme circumstances. A surprising 86 percent of constrained U.S. firms say that they bypass attractive investments during the credit crisis because of difficulties in raising external finance, about twice as great as the proportion of unconstrained firms that say the same. Again, these numbers are mirrored in Europe and Asia (80 percent versus 36 percent in Europe, and 69 percent versus 29 percent in Asia).

We next inquire about how firms fund attractive investments when they are unable to borrow in financial markets. About half of U.S. firms say that they rely on internally generated cash flows to fund investment under these circumstances, and about 4 in 10 say that they use cash reserves. Notably, 56 percent of constrained U.S. firms say that they cancel investment projects when they are unable to fund them with external funds, significantly greater than the 31 percent of constrained firms that say the same. Once again, we find these same results in Europe and Asia. In Europe, for example, 69 percent of the constrained firms in our survey say they will cancel their investment plans (compared to 33 percent of unconstrained firms). In Asia, that same comparison suggests a cancellation rate of 41 percent across constrained firms and only 16 percent across their unconstrained counterparts. To our knowledge, this is the first time that constraint-driven project cancellation has been documented in economic research.

These numbers are dramatic and document that real-world constraints are a severe detriment to the ability of companies to pursue value-maximizing policies. We also find evidence of another significant disruption to optimal investment that is imposed by severely disrupted credit markets. Not only do companies cancel investment because of tight credit markets, some sell assets to obtain cash. We find that the vast majority of financially constrained firms have sold assets in order to fund operations in 2008: exactly 70 percent of the constrained respondents in our U.S. survey say that they are selling more assets now in 2008 than previously, compared to 37 percent of the unconstrained respondents in order to obtain funds. We also find evidence of heavy use of asset sales across constrained firms in Europe (61 percent) and Asia (43 percent).

CONCLUSION

The focus of the current credit crisis is on the immediate implications, such as reduced profits and increased unemployment. In contrast, we show that there are worrisome long-term economic consequences of the crisis through its effect on financially constrained firms.

Using a survey of over 1,000 CFOs in the United States, Europe, and Asia, we show that firms are cutting back or canceling projects that they know add to firm value. The elimination of profitable projects is especially acute for firms that face financial constraints.

One of the basic tenets of finance is that projects that enhance firm value should be pursued. Financial constraints potentially prevent the funding of these projects. The current credit crisis is an ideal setting to measure the impact of constraints on value creation.

Turning down or canceling profitable projects is a lesser-known cost of the current financial crisis. In the scramble for short-term cash flow, firms are sacrificing long-term value. This implies lower future growth opportunities and lower future employment growth.

ACKNOWLEDGMENTS

We thank Steve Kaplan, Jeremy Stein, and Luigi Zingales for suggesting questions that we included in the survey instrument. We thank *CFO* magazine for helping us conduct the survey, though we note that our analysis and conclusions do not necessarily reflect those of *CFO*.

ABOUT THE AUTHORS

Murillo Campello is the Baltz professor of finance at the University of Illinois and a faculty research fellow of the National Bureau of Economic Research. Campello's research interests include corporate finance, financial intermediation, financial markets, and applied contract theory. His recent scholarly work has focused on corporate liquidity management and credit markets imperfections. Campello currently serves as an associate editor at the *Review of Financial Studies*, the *Journal of Financial Intermediation*, and the *International Review of Finance*. Campello earned his Ph.D. in finance from the University of Illinois in 2000.

Dr. John R. Graham is the D. Richard Mead professor of finance at the Fuqua School of Business and co-director of the Center for Finance at Duke University. He is a recipient of the Best Teacher and Outstanding Faculty awards at Duke. His past work experience includes working as a senior economist at Virginia Power, and he is a past or current director of the American Finance Association, Western Finance Association, and Financial Management Association. Graham has published more than 30 articles and book chapters on corporate taxes, cost of capital, capital structure, financial reporting, and payout policy, and this research has won a half dozen best paper awards. He is co-editor of the *Journal of Finance* and has been an associate editor of the *Review of Financial Studies* and *Financial Management*. Since 1997, he has been the director of the *Global Business Outlook*, a quarterly CFO survey that assesses business climate and topical economics issues around the world. Graham is lead author on the textbook *Corporate Finance, Linking Theory to What Firms Do.*

Campbell R. Harvey is a professor of finance at Duke University and a research associate of the National Bureau of Economic Research. He is a graduate of the University of Chicago. Harvey is the editor of the *Journal of Finance*, past president of the Western Finance Association and serves on both the board of directors and the executive committee of the American Finance Association. Harvey has received nine Graham and Dodd Awards, Scrolls, and Roger F. Murray Prizes for excellence in financial writing and has published more than 100 scholarly articles. His 8,000-word hypertextual financial glossary is used by sites such as the *New York Times, Forbes, Bloomberg,* the *Washington Post,* and *Yahoo.* Professor Harvey's blog at http://dukeresearchadvantage.com/author/charvey/ includes an entry from 2005 in which he stated "Many banks are operating like hedge funds, taking advantage of internal (cheap) credit lines. The bank's shareholders have no idea what is going on." He warned of an oncoming "contagious systemic" crisis.

CHAPTER 71

Coping with the Financial Crisis

Illiquidity and the Role of Government Intervention

BASTIAN BREITENFELLNER
DekaBank Chair in Finance and Financial Control, Passau University

NIKLAS WAGNER
DekaBank Chair in Finance and Financial Control, Passau University

THE EVOLUTION OF THE CRISIS—WHAT HAS GONE WRONG AND WHY?

The recent financial crisis has been of economic policy concern at least since the spring of 2007, when several low-grade (subprime) lending institutions that were engaged in the U.S. housing market faced severe financial distress. The way the financial crisis spread throughout the worldwide financial system was unprecedented. As of October 2008, the Bank of England (2008) reported the total volume of government support packages set up by governments worldwide to amount to approximately EUR 5.55 trillion. The crisis clearly reveals the vulnerabilities of the financial system in its current form. Therefore, it is of particular importance to understand what triggered the crisis, how it should be dealt with, and how such a collapse might be prevented in the future.

The Tale of Unlimited Risk Transfer—Causes of the Crisis

The market for credit risk is central to the recent financial crisis. The market has grown rapidly since the late 1990s and seemed to be one of the biggest success stories in the history of financial intermediation. The new paradigm was that underwriting and bearing credit risk were perfectly separable. The market for credit risk enables financial institutions to gain exposures in all kinds of credit risk with hardly any constraints. Those institutions willing to limit their exposure in credit risk were able to do so, for instance with securitization transactions.

The instruments to transfer credit risk are numerous, among which residential mortgage-backed securities (RMBSs), credit default swaps (CDSs), and collateralized debt obligations (CDOs) are the most prominent. For a detailed review of credit derivatives products and markets, one can, for example, refer to Batten and Hogan (2002), Scheicher (2003), and Chaplin (2005). The reason behind transferring credit risk is quite obvious. Financial institutions are able to specialize on certain segments of the banking landscape, as originating credit risk and exposures to it are separable. Financial institutions with no expertise in the lending business are able to get exposure to credit risk through the market for credit risk. On the other hand, originators of residential mortgages are able to eliminate the associated credit risk from their books with securitization transactions. The capital relieved through securitization may in turn be used to grant further loans. This development paves the way for new cash flows to credit markets, allowing the economy as a whole to profit from eased funding opportunities.

Welcome to the Fold—The Aftermath of the Crisis

Eased funding opportunities are generally beneficial for the economy. So why do we experience such a devastating crisis? The answer is quite simple. It seems that there has been a lack of risk awareness among overconfident market participants. Still in mid-2007, market participants believed that advances in credit risk transfer and valuation would prevent severe losses on highly rated tranches and credit derivatives (see, e.g., Mills and Kiff 2007).

As described earlier, securitization transactions were widely used to distribute credit risk throughout the financial system. In our opinion, the notion within the market was that loans that are off-balance-sheet do not contribute to the overall risk profile of the respective institution. This opinion proved to be rather myopic. With the increasing number of securitization transactions, further funds could be distributed, for example, through mortgages. As the overall number of high quality borrowers is limited, the average quality of loans, which in turn were securitized, declined. Also, those who invested in the tranches of the securitization transactions were often unaware of the inherent risk and relied on the assessment of external rating agencies. In many cases, these ratings were overly optimistic. After the U.S. housing bubble burst, delinquency rates rose. Consequently, investors in securitization transactions incurred severe losses on their tranches, which put them on the spot to write down their investments. As a consequence, many investors had to liquidate their assets to avoid running into over-indebtedness. Also, the growing uncertainty concerning the actual risk profile of the securitization tranches led to an erosion of liquidity in secondary markets, causing enormous discounts on the tranches' market prices, if they were sellable at all. The collapse of secondary markets absorbed much of the financial system's liquidity. So what happened, although many financial institutions eliminated credit risk from their balance sheets in the first place, was that it finally got there through the back door. As a result of rising illiquidity within the financial system, financial institutions ran into refinancing problems. The fact that many of the institutions were highly leveraged and heavily relied on short-term refinancing further boosted the crisis. What made things even worse was the psychological effect of a loss of trust in the financial system. To avoid over-indebtedness, all kinds of assets were liquidated in fire sale transactions. This created an enormous contagion effect, spreading throughout institutions, markets, and even continents.

DESIGNING A SHEET ANCHOR—GOVERNMENT INTERVENTION IN RESPONSE TO THE CRISIS

In the light of the situation described earlier, several important questions arise. How can one attenuate the consequences of the current crisis? What are the lessons to be learned from the current crisis? What has gone wrong, and how can such events be prevented in the future? Is there a need for stricter regulation within capital markets? In our view, these issues have a short-term and a long-term dimension. In the short run, it is important to cope with the immediate consequences of the crisis, especially illiquidity, to prevent severe consequences for global economic development. In the long run, the financial system itself has to undergo structural changes, which avert the danger of tremendous failures in the future. Our focus is clearly on government intervention in response to the financial crisis. Nevertheless, it is inevitable that the financial system undergo additional changes, besides those induced by governments and regulators.

Immediate Assistance through Rescue Packages

It seems undisputed that immediate action by governments worldwide has helped to dampen the consequences the recent financial crisis has on global economic development and wealth. On top of the agenda is the recovery of liquidity within the financial system. However, the way how this short-term government intervention should be conducted is subject to lively discussion. One important question is whether financial institutions in distress should be rescued by the government and consequently by taxpayers? There does not seem to be a clear answer to this question. On the one hand, rescue measures for single banks seem appropriate in case the bankruptcy costs for the whole economy exceed the costs of the rescue. On the other hand, with the government acting as a lender of last resort, there is little incentive for financial institutions to pursue sophisticated risk management strategies. In the long run, this would lead to an increasing risk appetite at financial institutions, as a lender of last resort equips shareholders of financial institutions with a put option on their firm. In this case, shareholders may call for the government to avoid going bankrupt. In other words, their downside risk is bound.[1] Since their downside risk is limited, shareholders in turn are encouraged to increase the overall risk profile of their institution so as to maximize their expected return at the costs of taxpayers. The result would be an even more unstable financial system, which is clearly not desirable.

Means of Government Intervention

Potential measures of government intervention in the financial system are manifold. In general, they include:

- State-guaranteed lending
- Direct equity injections
- Purchases of distressed assets by the government

The question as to which method is preferable largely depends on the goals of the intervention. Among these are the stabilization of the financial system through recapitalization, protection of taxpayers, separation between good and bad management performance, and providing proper incentives for managers of financial institutions, to name a few. Unfortunately, many of these goals work in opposite directions. For example, recapitalizing the financial system clearly countervails taxpayer protection, at least in the short run. Therefore, there is a need to find a trade-off between the different goals to ensure an optimal outcome for an economy as a whole. This trade-off, however, is difficult to find. When it comes to the decision, whether or not to rescue a certain financial institution, policy makers often debate the systemic relevance of the respective entity. Financial institutions with systemic relevance are those entities for which the bankruptcy costs borne by the overall economy exceed the costs of government intervention. Here, the major problem becomes obvious. How can we measure potential bankruptcy costs for a certain financial institution? The task has become even more complicated in recent years because integration within the financial system has grown so rapidly.

A Possible Design of a Rescue Package

Our focus in this chapter lies in restoring liquidity while separating good and bad management performance. We illustrate how to design a rescue package that allows us to distinguish between solvent but illiquid and insolvent banks. Although this task might not be in the best interest of taxpayers in the short run, it allows us to identify and reward good (pre-crisis) management performance. In the long run, this separation can be helpful for the design of incentive schemes and internal risk management systems, which promote good management performance and help to prevent future misconduct within the financial services industry.

We present a framework for separating illiquid but solvent and insolvent banks in Breitenfellner and Wagner (2009). The mechanism is based on a self-selection approach, through which banks in the same solvency state act homogeneously. This can be achieved by a rescue mechanism based on asset purchase programs initiated by the government (e.g., conducted through the construction of a *Bad Bank*, in which, for example, Went [2009] discusses the implementation of Bad Banks during the Swedish banking crisis in the 1990s). The self-selection mechanism is related to Akerlof (1970) and works in the following way. Suppose the financial system consists of two types of banks, solvent but illiquid banks, and insolvent banks. The different solvency of the two types largely stems from the quality of their assets. Because of the instability of the financial system, both have a liquidity need caused by a shock. There are two possible ways to obtain liquidity, through the capital market, or through a rescue package launched by the government. Further suppose that outside investors cannot distinguish between the two types of banks. Hence, the costs of obtaining external financing is the same for both types of banks. It is obvious that this is clearly to the favor of the insolvent banks, because they can obtain external capital at the same rate as the solvent ones, despite their worse financial health. The opposite holds for the banks of the solvent type. In general, this should lead to a market failure as long as financial institutions are not able to provide a credible signal of the state they are currently in. Given this information, a government rescue package has to fulfill the task of generating a setting in which illiquid but solvent banks can provide a unique signal of being solvent, which cannot be mimicked by a insolvent bank without significant costs.[2]

A possible way allowing a financial institution to signal its current state is through the way it acquires external capital. As long as the government rescue package consists only of state guarantees, this is not achieved. The refinancing problem faced by the two types of financial institutions is identical, regardless of their current sate, because the government, like any outstanding investor, cannot distinguish between the two. Therefore, the costs at which the two types of banks can acquire external financing are equivalent. The same holds for direct equity injections.

Suppose next, that the rescue package includes the possibility to sell distressed assets to a Bad Bank. As the financial system is in distress, that is, there is a liquidity shock affecting secondary market prices, which causes a gap between the economic value and the market value of the assets. For the current financial crisis, according to Bank of England (2008) estimates, about 37 percent of mark-to-market losses on U.S. subprime RMBSs are due to discounts for illiquidity and uncertainty rather than actual credit risk. The price the Bad Bank bids for the distressed assets has a downward boundary as given by the market price and an upward boundary as given by its economic value. Outside investors do not know the quality of the assets, hence they bid a single price. As the different solvency of the two types of financial institutions is due to the quality of their assets, the solvent banks are likely to hold assets of a higher quality. Hence, the situation arises that healthy institutions will find it more rewarding to acquire liquidity with external financing. In contrast, the insolvent institutions will still be willing to sell their assets, because they are of lower quality and therefore less valuable. Therefore, the two types are perfectly distinguishable, as the banks will choose the means of refinancing according to the cohort they are in. Admittedly, the issue of finding the adequate price for the distressed assets is crucial to that problem and far from trivial.

Fostering Long-Term Stability of the Financial System

So far, we have focused on immediate measures to cope with the financial crisis, ensuring that the impact it has on the global economy is as moderate as possible. However, the ongoing financial crisis reveals the vulnerabilities of the financial system in its current form. It is undisputed that there is a need for a redesign. Nevertheless, it is of major importance to act with prudence rather than to draw hasty conclusions.

Regulation of Securitization Markets

In the public discussion, securitization transactions are often blamed as "the root of all evil," triggering the collapse of the financial system. Despite the fact that securitization markets are not the sole cause of the financial crisis, there is broad consensus among experts that securitization transactions significantly contributed to the outbreak of the crisis. In this light, is there still room for securitization transactions? Should securitization markets be subject to stricter regulation?

In our view, the advantages of securitization do warrant the inherent risks. Nevertheless, securitization markets have to undergo certain changes in the future to foster the stability of the financial system as a whole. As argued by the International Monetary Fund (2003) and Franke and Krahnen (2008), securitization markets in their current form are characterized by a misalignment of incentives among the relevant players. This misalignment can be overcome by committing originators to retain a share of the securitization transaction on their own books.

Another issue related to securitization markets is the enormous complexity of its products, which hampers investors' assessment of the inherent risks. Obviously, even rating agencies were not able to quantify the risks inherent with certain transactions. Nevertheless, in our view, it is not the task of regulators to curtail such products. In contrast, it is clearly the task of investors to judge which products provide a risk-adequate return. Hence, a prudent investor would keep one's hands off products one does not fully understand. On the other hand, even the most complex products can be valuable for a prudent investor to optimize her portfolio.

Strengthening the Role of Internal Risk Management

One of the core issues of the financial crisis is the absence of proper risk awareness among market participants, especially within the financial services industry. As outlined earlier, the possibility of transferring or eliminating certain risks by means of securitization or hedging may cause a feeling of spurious safety. What is overseen in many cases is an awareness that there are significant risks besides credit risk, which cannot be that easily transferred or eliminated, such as market risk, liquidity risk, and counterparty risk.

Not accounting for these risks is clearly a failure of internal risk management processes. Given this, the question arises whether stricter regulation regarding internal risk management is needed. A possible solution to the problem may be to require financial institutions to hold an increased equity cushion to better absorb potential losses due to market and liquidity risk. It is undisputed that it is by no means reasonable to require financial institutions to hold equity cushions to absorb all potential losses due to market or liquidity risk. The October 2008 market meltdown is clearly a catastrophic event that cannot be absorbed by regulatory capital. However, it seems doubtful that a crisis of this magnitude would have emerged, if all market participants had at least provided enough capital to absorb moderate losses due to market and liquidity risks. In light of this, a revision of regulatory capital requirements seems inevitable, and the Basel II approach of the Basel Committee on Banking Supervision (2004) will need to be updated.

CONCLUSION

The impact of the first financial crisis in this millennium is unprecedented. It calls for government intervention worldwide for its vast economic impact to be limited. We argue that government intervention has a short-term and a long-term perspective. In the short run, the main focus should be to restore trust and liquidity within the financial system. The means through which this is achieved depend on the goals of government intervention. We present a framework designed to distinguish illiquid but solvent and insolvent banks, which allows us to learn from best practice and to avoid a crisis of such magnitude in the future. In the long run, there is a need for revisions in regulation. Regulatory capital requirements should be adjusted to account for market as well as liquidity risk. Stricter regulation cannot be the sole answer to the crisis. There is also a need for revised management objectives, including a larger focus on long-term stability and profitability instead of short-term profit maximization and cash generation.

NOTES

1. At least as long as they do not lose their share in the institution in case it is rescued by the government.
2. In fact, the costs have to be at least as high as the possible advantage of providing a wrong signal to the public.

REFERENCES

Akerlof, G. A. 1970. The market for lemons: Quality uncertainty and the market mechanism. *The Quarterly Journal of Economics* 84: 488–500.

Bank of England. 2008. *Financial stability report*. London: Bank of England, Financial Stability Reports.

Basel Committee on Banking Supervision. 2004. *International convergence of capital measurement and capital standards: A revised framework*. Basel, Switzerland: Bank for International Settlements, Working Paper.

Batten, J., and W. Hogan. 2002. A perspective on credit derivatives. *International Review of Financial Analysis* 11: 251–278.

Breitenfellner, B., and N. F. Wagner. 2009. Government intervention in response to the subprime financial crisis: The good into the pot, the bad into the crop. Passau, Germany: Passau University, Working Paper.

Chaplin, G. 2005. *Credit derivatives: Risk management, trading and investing*. Chichester, England: John Wiley & Sons.

Franke, G., and J. P. Krahnen. 2008. *The future of securitization*. New York: Center for Financial Studies, Working Paper.

International Monetary Fund. 2003. Financial asset price volatility: A source of instability? In *Global Financial Stability Report*, Washington, DC: International Monetary Fund, 62–88.

Mills, P., and J. Kiff. 2007. Money for nothing and checks for free: Recent developments in U.S. subprime mortgage markets. Washington, DC: International Monetary Fund, Working Paper.

Scheicher, M. 2003. Credit derivatives: Overview and implications for monetary policy and financial stability. In *Financial Stability Report 5*, Vienna, Austria: Oesterreichische Nationalbank, 96–111.

Went, P. 2009. *Lessons from the Swedish bank crisis*. Baltimore, MD: GARP Research Center, Working Paper.

ABOUT THE AUTHORS

Bastian Breitenfellner is a Ph.D. student at Passau University. He holds a diploma degree in business administration and technology from the Technical University at Munich. He also spent a visiting semester at the University of Zurich. He currently works as a research assistant at the DekaBank chair in finance and financial control at Passau University. His research is focused on credit risk valuation, credit derivatives, and risk management.

Niklas Wagner is Professor of Finance at Passau University, Germany. After receiving his Ph.D. in Finance in 1998, Niklas held postdoctoral visiting appointments at the Haas School of Business, U.C. Berkeley, and at Stanford GSB. Academic visits also led him to the Center of Mathematical Sciences at Munich University of Technology and to the Faculty of Economics and Politics, University of Cambridge. Niklas has co-authored various international contributions, including articles in *Economic Notes*, *Quantitative Finance*, the *Journal of Banking and Finance*, and the *Journal of Empirical Finance*. He regularly serves as a referee for well-known academic journals, covering his research interests in the areas of empirical asset pricing, applied financial econometrics, market microstructure as well as banking and risk management.

CHAPTER 72

Fiscal Policy for the Crisis

ANTONIO SPILIMBERGO
International Monetary Fund

STEVEN SYMANSKY
Advisor in the Fiscal Affairs Department, International Monetary Fund

OLIVIER BLANCHARD
Economic Counselor and Director of the Research Department of the International
Monetary Fund

CARLO COTTARELLI
Director of the Fiscal Affairs Department, International Monetary Fund*

The output decline in the current crises could be larger than in any period since the Great Depression. A successful policy package should address both the financial crisis and the fall in aggregate demand. There are obvious interactions and synergies between the two. This chapter focuses on some general features that fiscal stimulus should have in the present context. A fiscal stimulus should be *timely* (as there is an urgent need for action), *large* (because the drop in demand is large), *lasting* (as the recession will likely last for some time), *diversified* (as there is uncertainty regarding which measures will be most effective), *contingent* (to indicate that further action will be taken, if needed), *collective* (all countries that have the fiscal space should use it given the severity and global nature of the downturn), and *sustainable* (to avoid debt explosion in the long run and adverse effects in the short run). The challenge is to provide the right balance between these sometimes competing goals—particularly, large and lasting actions versus fiscal sustainability.

The fall in aggregate demand is due to a large decrease in real and financial wealth, an increase in precautionary saving—a wait-and-see attitude—on the part of both consumers and firms in the face of uncertainty, and increasing difficulties in obtaining credit. A further fall in demand will increase the risk that the perverse

---

*This chapter is a shortened version of a paper by Antonio Spilimbergo, Steven Symansky, Olivier Blanchard, and Carlo Cottarelli that appears as an IMF Staff Position Note, SPN/08/01, December 28, 2008, available at www.imf.org/external/pubs/ft/spn/2008/spn0801.pdf.

dynamics of deflation, rising debt, and associated feedback loops to the financial sector, may materialize. Two macroeconomic policies often used to support aggregate demand are less effective in the current environment. First, while each single country can adopt an export-led recovery strategy, this is clearly not an option open to the world as a whole. Second, the financial nature of the crisis weakens the traditional monetary transmission mechanism, and the room to further lower central bank policy rates is limited.

FISCAL POLICY IN FINANCIAL CRISES—LESSONS FROM HISTORY

A survey of the countries that have experienced severe systemic financial crises shows that these episodes are typically associated with severe economic downturns and that countries have reacted to these downturns quite differently, depending on economic and political constraints.[1] The list of countries that have experienced both financial and economic crises includes some well-known cases: Korea in 1997, Japan in the 1990s, the Nordic countries in the early 1990s, the Great Depression in the 1930s, and the United States during the savings and loan crisis in the 1980s (see Appendix III in SPN/08/01).

Several lessons can be drawn from these case studies. First, successful resolution of the financial crisis is a precondition for achieving sustained growth; delaying action led to a worsening of macroeconomic conditions, resulting in higher fiscal costs later on. Prompt and sizable support to the financial sector by the Korean authorities limited the duration of the macroeconomic consequences, thus limiting the need for other fiscal action. Second, the solution to the financial crisis always precedes the solution to the macroeconomic crisis. Third, a fiscal stimulus is highly useful (almost necessary) when the financial crisis spills over to the corporate and household sectors with a resulting worsening of the balance sheets. Fourth, the fiscal response can have a larger effect on aggregate demand if its composition takes into account the specific features of the crisis. In this regard, some of the tax and transfer policies implemented early in the Nordic crises did little to stimulate output. Fixing the financial system and supporting aggregate demand are, thus, both critical. This contribution focuses only on the fiscal component.

COMPOSITION OF A FISCAL STIMULUS

Two features of the current crisis are particularly relevant in defining the appropriate composition of the fiscal stimulus. First, as the current crisis will last at least for several more quarters, the standard argument that implementation lags for spending are long is less relevant when facing the current risk of a more prolonged downturn. Furthermore, given the highly uncertain response of households and firms to an increase in their income through taxes and transfers, expenditure measures may have an advantage by directly raising aggregate demand.

Second, since the current crisis is characterized by a number of events and conditions not experienced in recent decades, existing estimates of fiscal multipliers are less reliable in informing policy makers about which measures will be relatively effective in supporting demand.[2] This provides a strong argument for policy diversification—not relying on a single tool to support demand.[3]

Public Spending on Goods and Services

In theory, public spending on goods and services has a more direct demand effect than those related to transfers or tax cuts. In practice, the appropriate increase in public spending is constrained by the need to avoid waste. What are the key prescriptions?

First, governments should make sure that existing programs are not cut for lack of resources. Governments facing balanced budget rules may be forced to suspend various spending programs (or to raise revenue). Measures should be taken to counteract the procyclicality built into these rules. For subnational entities, this can be mitigated through transfers from the central government.

Second, spending programs, from repair and maintenance, to investment projects delayed, interrupted or rejected for lack of funding or macroeconomic considerations, can be (re)started quickly. A few high profile programs, with good long-run justification and strong externalities, can also help, directly and through expectations. Given the higher degree of risk facing firms at the current juncture, the state could also take a larger share in private-public partnerships for valuable projects that would otherwise be suspended for lack of private capital.

Public sector wage increases should be avoided because they are not well targeted, difficult to reverse, and similar to transfers in their effectiveness. But a temporary increase in public sector employment associated with some of new programs and policies may be needed.

Fiscal Stimulus Aimed at Consumers

The support of consumer spending also needs to take the present exceptional conditions into account. Three specific factors affect consumption at this juncture: decreases in wealth, tighter credit constraints, and high uncertainty. These three factors have different implications for the marginal propensity to consume out of transitory tax cuts or transfers. The first and the third suggest low marginal propensities to consume, the second a high one. Assessing the relative importance of the three is hard, but suggests two broad recommendations.

The first is to target tax cuts or transfers toward those consumers who are most likely to be credit or liquidity constrained. Measures along these lines include the greater provision of unemployment benefits, increases in earned income tax credits, and the expansion of safety nets in countries where they are limited. Where relevant, support for homeowners facing foreclosures using public resources supports aggregate demand and improves conditions in the financial sector. The second is that clarity of policy, together with a strong commitment by policy makers to take whatever action may be needed to avoid the tail risk of a depression, are likely to reduce uncertainty, and lead consumers to decrease precautionary saving.

Some countries are considering broad-based tax cuts. But the marginal propensity to consume out of such tax cuts may be quite low. Some countries have introduced temporary decreases in the VAT. If the termination date is credible, the intertemporal incentives implied by such a measure are attractive. However, the degree of pass-through to consumers is uncertain, its unwinding can contribute to a further downturn, and it is questionable whether decreases of just a few percentage points are salient enough to lead consumers to shift the timing of their purchases. Possibly, larger, but more focused incentives, such as cash transfers for purchases of specific goods may attract more attention from consumers and have larger effects on demand.

Fiscal Stimulus Aimed at Firms

In this uncertain environment, firms are also taking a wait-and-see attitude with respect to their investment decisions. Subsidies or measures to lower the tax-adjusted user cost of capital (such as reductions in capital gains and corporate tax rates) are unlikely to have much effect. Rather, the key challenge for policy makers is to ensure that firms do not reduce current operations for lack of financing. While this is primarily the job of monetary policy, there is also some scope for governments to support firms that could survive restructuring, but find it difficult to receive the necessary financing from dysfunctional credit markets. In particular, there is an argument for combining restructuring procedures with government guarantees on new credit.

It has been argued that governments should provide support to entire high visibility sectors of the economy because of the potential effect that bankruptcies in these sectors may have on expectations. While there is some validity in this argument, its inherent arbitrariness, and risk of political capture, would make implementation difficult. Direct subsidies to domestic sectors could lead to an uneven playing field with respect to foreign corporations, and result in trade retaliation. An important principle of support should be to minimize interference with operational decisions. Credit guarantee to firms (not sectors) may be needed as long as the credit markets remain dysfunctional.

SUSTAINABILITY CONCERNS

It is essential for governments to indicate from the start that the extent of the fiscal expansion will depend on the state of the economy. While a sizable upfront stimulus is needed, policy makers must commit to doing more, as needed. It is important to announce this at the start, so later increases do not look like acts of desperation.

However, it is also essential that fiscal stimulus not be seen by markets as seriously calling into question medium-term fiscal sustainability. This is key, not only for the medium run, but also for the short run, as questions about debt sustainability would undercut the near-term effectiveness of policy through adverse effects on financial markets, interest rates, and consumer spending.

Although some widening of borrowing costs within the Eurozone may reflect sustainability concerns, financial markets do not seem overly concerned about medium-term sustainability. But markets often react late and abruptly. Thus, a fiscally unsustainable path can eventually lead to sharp adjustments in real interest rates, which in turn can destabilize financial markets and undercut recovery prospects. The following features can help:

- Implementing measures that are reversible or that have clear sunset clauses, or precommitting to identified future corrective measures (e.g., future increases in upper income tax rates as part of the U.K. package)
- Implementing policies that eliminate distortions (e.g., financial transaction taxes)
- Increasing the scope of automatic stabilizers that, by their nature, are countercyclical and temporary
- Providing more robust medium-term fiscal frameworks that should provide confidence that resulting increases in public debt are eventually offset
- Strengthening fiscal governance through independent fiscal councils that could help monitor fiscal developments, and also provide policy advice to reduce the public's perception of possible political biases
- Improving expenditure procedures to ensure that stepped-up public works spending is well directed to raise long-term growth (and tax-raising) potential

Structural reforms to boost potential growth, by removing distortions can also help in strengthening medium-term sustainability. Many countries have succeeded in reducing their public debt burden through growth. A credible commitment to address these long-term issues can go a long way in reassuring markets about fiscal sustainability.

Some Proposals for Discussion

The gravity and singularity of the current crisis may require new solutions, which address specifically the issues of financial disintermediation and loss in confidence. Some proposals that could be considered are:

Greater Role of the Public Sector in Financial Intermediation with the extreme shift in investors' preferences toward liquid T-bills and away from private assets, the state is in a better position than private investors to buy and hold these private assets, and partly replace the private sector in financial intermediation. Although the public sector does not have a comparative advantage in evaluating credit risk, nor in administering a diverse portfolio of assets, the management of the banking activities could be outsourced to a private entity.

Provision of Insurance by the Public Sector Against Large Recessions

In the present environment of extreme uncertainty, the government could provide insurance against extreme recessions by offering contracts, with payment, contingent on GDP growth falling below some threshold level. Banks could condition loan approvals on firms having purchased such insurance from the government. Widespread use of such contracts would provide an additional automatic stabilizer because payments would be made when they are most needed, namely in bad times. An obvious worry about such a scheme is that the government may not be able or willing to honor its obligations.

A COLLECTIVE INTERNATIONAL EFFORT

The international dimension of the crisis calls for a collective approach. There are several spillovers that could limit the effectiveness of actions taken by individual countries, or create adverse externalities across borders:

- Countries with a high degree of trade openness may be discouraged from fiscal stimulus since it will benefit less from a domestic demand expansion. The flipside of these spillovers is that if all countries act, the amount of stimulus needed by each country is reduced (and provides a political economy argument for a collective fiscal effort). At the same time, this collective fiscal effort must be tailored to country circumstances.
- Some interventions currently discussed such as subsidies to troubled industries may be perceived as industrial policy by trading partners. The history of the Great Depression shows that, as the crisis deepens, there is increasing pressure to raise trade barriers. Such a race would bring significant costs in regard to efficiency.

All these factors point to the need for a concerted effort by the international community, and stricter coordination among countries with closer economic and institutional ties. The EU recommendation of a 1.5 percent of GDP stimulus and the decision to finance some of the national expenditures from the EU budget are steps in this direction.

The most recent data are pointing more and more to a worldwide growth slowdown, suggesting that the action should be widespread to maximize its effectiveness. The IMF has called for a sizable fiscal response at the global level. Its precise magnitude should depend on several factors, including the expected decline in private sector demand. Moreover, not all countries have sufficient fiscal space to implement expansionary fiscal policy since it may threaten the sustainability of fiscal finances. In particular, many low income and emerging markets countries, but also some advanced countries, face additional constraints such as volatile capital flows, high public and foreign indebtedness, and large risk premiums. The fact that some countries cannot engage in fiscal stimulus makes it all the more important that others, including some large emerging economies, do their part. Also, the policies should be tailored to those actions that are likely to provide the largest multipliers. In the United States, that is likely to be investment, other spending on goods and services, and some targeted transfers. In Europe, with its relatively large automatic stabilizers, the additional fiscal impulse can probably be somewhat less than in the United States.

CONCLUSION

The solution to the current financial and macroeconomic crisis requires bold initiatives aimed at rescuing the financial sector and increasing demand. The early resolution of financial sector problems is critical. But early, strong, and carefully thought out fiscal responses are also important. Time and action are of the essence.

NOTES

1. See Chapter 4, "World Economic Outlook," October 2008.
2. For a review on fiscal multipliers during the crisis see "Fiscal Multipliers" by Antonio Spilimbergo, Steven Symansky, and Martin Schindler, IMF Policy Note, May 2009, available at www.imf.org/external/pubs/ft/spn/2009/spn0911.pdf.
3. Appendix I of SPN/08/01 provides the pros and cons of some specific spending and revenue measures.

ABOUT THE AUTHORS

Antonio Spilimbergo studied economics at the University Bocconi of Milan. He received his Ph.D. in economics from M.I.T. Since July 1997, he has worked at the IMF. His areas of interest are international trade, development, labor economics, and macroeconomics. His main publications are: "Illegal Immigration, Border Enforcement, and Relative Wages: Evidence from Apprehensions at the US-Mexico Border" (with G. Hanson) in the *American Economic Review;* "Democracy and Foreign Students" in the *American Economic Review;* "Real Effective Exchange Rate and the Constant Elasticity of Substitution Assumption" in the *Journal of International Economics* (with A. Vamvakidis); "Empirical Models of Short-Term Debt and Crises: Do They Test the Multiple Equilibrium Hypothesis?" in the *European Economic Review* (with Enrica Detragiache); The *Carnegie-Rochester Conference Series on Public Policy;* "Income Distribution, Factor Endowments, and Trade Openness" (with J. L. Londoño and M. Székely) in the *Journal of Development Economics;* and "Growth and Trade: The North Can Lose," in the *Journal of Economic Growth.*

Steven Symansky earned his Ph.D. in economics from Wisconsin. He retired from the IMF, where he is currently an adviser in the Fiscal Affairs department. While in the IMF, he has served as the division chief of the Fiscal Surveillance and Policy division, mission chief for Afghanistan for three years, and was in the research department at the IMF for about eight years, where he developed and oversaw the IMF's world econometric model (MULTIMOD). Before that, he spent two years in the research department at the World Bank and eight years in the international division for the board of governors of the Federal Reserve. In addition to his numerous papers on macro modeling, he co-authored a paper with George Kopits on fiscal rules and was a co-author of two recent IMF staff position papers—one on fiscal policy during the crisis and one on multipliers. He has also published papers on debt buybacks, real exchange rates, tax harmonization, and the macroeconomics of drugs. He also led a number of fiscal technical assistance missions to post-conflict countries (i.e., Kosovo, East Timor, Afghanistan, Iraq, and Liberia).

A citizen of France, Olivier Blanchard has spent his professional life in Cambridge, Massachusetts. After obtaining his Ph.D in economics at the Massachusetts Institute of Technology in 1977, he taught at Harvard University, returning to MIT in

1982, where he has been ever since. He is the Class of 1941 professor of economics, and past chair of the economics department. He is currently on leave from MIT, as economic counselor and director of the research department of the International Monetary Fund. He is a macroeconomist who has worked on a wide set of issues, from the role of monetary policy, to the nature of speculative bubbles, to the nature of the labor market and the determinants of unemployment, to transition in former communist countries. In the process, he has worked with numerous countries and international organizations. He is the author of many books and articles, including two textbooks in macroeconomics, one at the graduate level with Stanley Fischer, and one at the undergraduate level. He is a fellow and council member of the Econometric Society, a past vice president of the American Economic Association, and a member of the American Academy of Sciences.

Carlo Cottarelli, a citizen of Italy, has been director of the fiscal affairs department of the IMF since November 2008. After receiving degrees in economics from the University of Siena and the London School of Economics, he joined the research department of the Bank of Italy, where he worked from 1981 to 1987. Mr. Cottarelli joined the IMF in 1988, working for the fiscal affairs department, the European department, the monetary and capital markets department, and the policy development and review department. He was deputy director in both the European department and the policy development and review departments. Mr. Cottarelli has worked on several advanced, emerging markets, and low income countries in the context of surveillance, IMF-supported programs, and technical assistance, including Albania, Croatia, Hungary, Lebanon, Russia, Serbia, Tajikistan, Turkey, Italy, and the United Kingdom. He has written several papers on fiscal and monetary policy and exchange rates.

CHAPTER 73

The Future of Securitization

STEVEN L. SCHWARCZ
Stanley A. Star Professor of Law and Business at Duke University and Founding
Director of Duke's Global Capital Markets Center*

T his chapter examines the future viability of securitization in light of its involvement in the subprime mortgage financial crisis (hereinafter the *subprime crisis*). The article concludes that securitization should, and indeed
likely will, have a viable if not vibrant future. There are many reasons for this.
Securitization efficiently allocates risk with capital. It enables companies to access capital markets directly, in most cases at lower cost than the cost of issuing
direct debt (such as bonds or commercial paper), and it avoids middleman inefficiencies. Moreover, when the securitized assets are loans, securitization helps
to transform the loans into cash from which banks and other lenders can make
new loans.

These positives might be outweighed, however, by securitization's negatives
revealed by the subprime crisis. There are four such potential negatives: subprime
mortgages may be a flawed asset type that should not have been securitized; the
originate-to-distribute model of securitization might create moral hazard; securitization can create servicing conflicts; and securitization can foster overreliance
on mathematical models. This article examines these negatives and the extent to
which they can be remedied in the future.

The subprime crisis also revealed a possible fifth negative: that investors
in securitization transactions—essentially pension funds, mutual funds, hedge
funds, banks, insurance companies, and other institutional investors—may overrely on rating agency ratings. The extent of appropriate reliance on ratings,
and indeed the integrity of the ratings process itself, are questions beyond this
chapter's scope.

*This chapter is based on "The Future of Securitization," *Conn. L. Rev.* 41 (4) (2009 symposium issue on "The Subprime Crisis: Going Forward"), also available at http://ssrn.com/
abstract_id=1300928.

Steven L. Schwarcz is the author of numerous articles and papers on the subprime financial
crisis and systemic risk and has also testified before the Committee on Financial Services of
the U.S. House of Representatives on "Systemic Risk: Examining Regulators' Ability to Respond to Threats to the Financial System," available at www.house.gov/apps/list/hearing/
financialsvcs_dem/ht1002072.shtml.

To follow my analysis, the reader should note the following terminology. Subprime mortgage securitization, the type of securitization whose failure initially triggered the chain of failures that became the subprime crisis, is a subset of mortgage securitization. In the most basic form of mortgage securitization, mortgage-backed securities (MBS) are issued by a special purpose vehicle (SPV), and payment on the securities is derived directly from collections on mortgage loans owned by the SPV. More complex forms of mortgage-backed securities include collateralized debt obligation (CDO) securities in which payment derives directly from a mixed pool of mortgage loans and sometimes, also, other financial assets owned by the SPV; and ABS CDO securities in which payment derives from MBS and CDO securities owned by the SPV (and thus indirectly from the mortgage loans and other financial assets underlying those owned securities). Subprime mortgage securitization can mean any of these types of mortgage securitization in which all or a portion of the underlying financial assets consists of subprime mortgage loans (defined further on).

Before the subprime crisis, most MBS, CDO, and ABS securities were highly rated by rating agencies.

WHAT WENT WRONG, AND WHAT NEEDS TO BE FIXED?

This chapter identifies the following potential negatives of securitization, revealed by the subprime crisis, and examines the extent to which they can be remedied in the future.

Flawed Asset Type

Subprime mortgage securitization failed, initially triggering the chain of failures that became the subprime crisis, because of the particular and almost unique nature of the underlying subprime mortgage loans. These are high-interest-rate home mortgage loans made to risky borrowers. Many of these borrowers relied on refinancing their appreciating home values to repay their loans. This model worked brilliantly as long as home prices appreciated, as they had been doing for decades.

However, when home prices stopped appreciating and began collapsing, those borrowers were unable to refinance. Furthermore, many subprime mortgage loans had adjustable rates, which increased after an initial teaser period. Borrowers who could not afford the rate increases had expected to refinance at lower interest rates. That likewise was stymied by collapsing home prices. As a result, many risky borrowers began defaulting, causing some of the highly rated MBS, CDO, and ABS CDO securities—whose payment depended on collections from the underlying financial assets—to default or to have their credit ratings downgraded. These defaults and downgrades, in turn, caused investors in rated securities to begin losing confidence in the financial markets.

The failure of subprime mortgage securitization was thus caused by its almost absolute dependence on home appreciation. Some believe this type of "particular[] sensitiv[ity] to declines in house prices" was unique.[1] From that perspective, parties structuring securitization transactions can minimize future problems by excluding, or at least limiting and better managing, subprime mortgage loans as an eligible type of underlying financial asset, and also by conservatively assessing the payment prognosis for other types of financial assets underlying securitizations. This is important not only to protect the integrity of securitization transactions but also to avoid the unintended consequence that securitization of a flawed asset type can motivate greater origination of that asset type, in effect magnifying the effect of the creation of the bad asset.

This is not to say these procedures will be fail-safe. Parties to (and investors in) securitization transactions must always be diligent to recognize and try to protect against the possibility that the underlying financial assets might, as in the case of subprime mortgage loans, fail in unexpected ways. What would happen to automobile loan securitizations, for example, if a technological innovation makes cars obsolete, depriving even financially healthy borrowers of the incentive to repay their loans? The invention of a new form of personal transportation is at least as plausible as the idea that home prices—which generally had only risen since the 1930s—would suddenly collapse in value at a rate higher than any seen during the Great Depression, as happened in the subprime crisis.

The subprime crisis also teaches us the danger of mixing politics and finance. Before that crisis, there was political pressure to securitize risky subprime mortgage loans to facilitate financing for the poor. We might see the same type of future political pressure, for example, to securitize risky microfinance loans to facilitate financing for the poor and disadvantaged.

Originate-to-Distribute Moral Hazard

Some argue that securitization facilitated an undisciplined mortgage lending industry. By enabling mortgage lenders to sell off loans as they were made (a concept called, variously, *originate-to-distribute* or *originate-and-distribute*), securitization is said to have created a moral hazard since these lenders did not have to live with the credit consequences of their loans. Mortgage underwriting standards therefore fell, exacerbated by mortgage lenders making money just on the volume of loans originated.

I find the moral hazard argument weak. Mortgage underwriting standards may have fallen, but there are other explanations of why. For example, lower standards may well reflect distortions caused by the liquidity glut of that time, in which lenders competed aggressively for business and allowed otherwise defaulting home borrowers to refinance. They also may reflect conflicts of interest between firms and their employees in charge of setting those standards, such as where employees were paid for booking loans regardless of the loans' long-term performance.[2] Blaming the originate-to-distribute model for lower mortgage underwriting standards also does not explain why standards were not similarly lowered for originating nonmortgage financial assets used in other types of securitization transactions. Nor does it explain why the ultimate owners of the mortgage loans—the investors in the mortgage-backed securities—did not govern their investments by the same strict lending standards that they would observe but for the separation of origination and ownership.

Although I do not believe the originate-to-distribute model was a material cause of the subprime crisis, the model may need fixing to avoid its perception as the cause. There is little question, though, that the model should remain largely intact. It is critical to the underlying funding liquidity of banks and corporations. Furthermore, scholars have at least tentatively concluded that, despite the subprime crisis, it has created value in the financial markets. The goal therefore should be to minimize any potential moral hazard resulting from the originate-to-distribute model without undermining the model's basic utility.

There are various ways this could be done. Potential moral hazard problems could be managed, for example, by requiring mortgage lenders and other originators to retain some realistic risk of loss. In many nonmortgage securitization transactions, for example, it is customary for originators to bear a direct risk of loss by overcollateralizing the receivables sold to the SPV. This was not always done in mortgage securitization because mortgage loans traditionally are overcollateralized by the value of the borrower's equity in the real estate collateral, and thus investors can effectively be overcollateralized even if the originator bears no separate risk of loss.

Moral hazard problems also could be managed by regulating the loan underwriting standards applicable to mortgage lenders. The U.S. government took this type of approach, for example, in response to the margin loan underwriting failures that helped trigger the Great Depression. When stock values began depreciating in 1929, margin loans (that is, loans to purchase publicly listed stock) became undercollateralized, resulting in a high loan default rate which, in turn, caused bank lenders to fail. To protect against a recurrence of this problem, the Federal Reserve promulgated margin regulations G, U, T, and X, requiring margin lenders to maintain two-to-one collateral coverage when securing their loans by margin stock that has been purchased, directly or indirectly, with the loan proceeds.

A similar type of approach, such as imposing a minimum real-estate-value-to-loan collateral coverage ratio on all mortgage loans secured by the real estate financed, would protect against a repeat of the subprime crisis. This protection would come at a high price, however, potentially impeding and increasing the cost of home ownership and imposing an administrative burden on lenders and government monitors. Nor would it protect against different types of financial crises that might arise in the future. Any regulatory approach, to be viable, should have to demonstrate that its benefits are at least likely to exceed its costs.

Servicing Conflicts

There is general agreement that mortgage securitization has made it difficult to work out problems with the underlying mortgage loans because the beneficial owners of the loans are no longer the mortgage lenders but a broad universe of financial market investors in the MBS and other securities. Although, servicers theoretically bridge the gap between investors (as beneficial owners of the loans) and the mortgage lenders, retaining the power to restructure the underlying loans "in the best interests" of those investors, the reality is problematic.

Servicers may be reluctant to engage in restructuring if there is uncertainty that their transactions will generate sufficient excess cash flow to reimburse their costs, whereas all foreclosure costs are reimbursed. Servicers may also sometimes prefer foreclosure over restructuring because the former is more ministerial and thus has lower litigation risk. In many CDO and ABS CDO mortgage securitization transactions, cash flows deriving from principal and interest are separately allocated to different investor tranches. Therefore, a restructuring that, for example, reduces the interest rate would adversely affect investors in the interest-only tranche, leading to what some have called tranche warfare.

These problems—which currently are mostly confined to mortgage securitization—can, and in the future should, be fixed. Parties should write underlying deal documentation that sets clearer and more flexible guidelines and more certain reimbursement procedures for loan restructuring, especially when restructuring appears to be superior to foreclosure. And they should try to minimize allocating cash flows to investors in ways that create conflicts.

Overreliance on Mathematical Models

To some extent the subprime crisis resulted from an abandonment of common sense and an overreliance on complex mathematical models. Models are essential to securitization because of the need to statistically predict what future cash flows will become available from the underlying financial assets to pay the securities issued by the SPV.

Models can bring insight and clarity. If the model is realistic and the inputted data are reliable, models can yield accurate predictions of real events. However, if the model is unrealistic or the inputted data are unreliable, models can be misleading—creating the danger of "garbage in, garbage out."

Subprime mortgage securitization models relied on assumptions and historical data which, in retrospect, turned out to be incorrect and therefore made the valuations incorrect. The models incorrectly assumed, for example, that housing would not depreciate in value to the levels presently seen. Valuation errors were further compounded to the extent subprime mortgage loans increasingly were made with innovative terms, such as adjustable rates, low-to-zero down payment requirements, interest-only payment options, and negative amortization. These terms were so complex that some borrowers did not fully understand the risks they were incurring. As a result, they defaulted at a much higher rate than would be predicted by the historical mortgage-loan default rates relied on by loan originators in extending credit.

Securitization models also have been used, sometimes erroneously, to substitute for real market information. For example, some CDO and ABS CDO securities did not have an active trading market, so investors instead relied on mark-to-model valuation of these securities. When assumptions underlying the models turned out to be wrong, investors panicked because they did not know what the securities were worth.

In theory, this overreliance on mathematical models is self-correcting because the subprime crisis, by its existence, has shaken faith in the market's ability to analyze and measure risk through models. Securitization products are likely to be confined, at least in the near future, to those that can be robustly modeled. The only question will be the longevity of the lesson that future risks cannot always be predicted through mathematical models.

CONCLUSION

Because securitization, properly used, is an efficient financial tool, its future should be assured no matter how investors or politicians might temporarily overreact. Nor should they overreact. As Professor Gorton observes, "[t]here are no such issues [as occurred in the subprime crisis] with securitization generally, or with the use of off-balance-sheet vehicles for the securitization of those [other] asset classes. Other securitizations are not so sensitive to the prices of the underlying assets and so they are not so susceptible to bubbles."[3]

Nonetheless, in the near future at least, it is likely that securitization transactions will need to refocus on basic structures and asset types so they can attract investors. In particular, there will likely be an emphasis on cash flow securitizations in which there are the traditional two ways out. Furthermore, we are not likely to see many highly complex securitization products, like CDO and ABS CDO transactions, which magnify leverage.

In the medium term, securitization's future will be at least marginally influenced by the extent to which the intrinsic values of mortgage-backed securities turn out to be worth more than their market values. I have argued that, as a result of irrational panic, the market prices of mortgage-backed securities collapsed substantially below the intrinsic value of the mortgage loans underlying those securities. A large differential would indicate that the problem was more investor panic than intrinsic lack of worth.

Whether securitization will remain vibrant and inventive in the long term, however, will turn on our ability to better understand the problems of complexity, which was at the root of many of the failures that gave rise to the subprime crisis.

NOTES

1. Gary B. Gorton, "The Panic of 2007," National Bureau of Economic Research, Working Paper 14358 (2008), 67.

2. *Cf.* Steven L. Schwarcz, "Conflicts and Financial Collapse: The Problem of Secondary-Management Agency Costs," *Yale Journal on Regulation* 26 (2) (2009), 457.

3. Gorton, supra note 1, at 67.

ABOUT THE AUTHOR

Steven L. Schwarcz is the Stanley A. Star professor of law and business at Duke University and founding director of Duke's Global Capital Markets Center. Before joining Duke, he was a partner at two leading international law firms and also taught at the Yale and Columbia Law Schools. Schwarcz has advised the United States Congress and other government bodies on systemic risk and the recent financial crisis. His scholarly works include "Systemic Risk," *Geo. L. J.* 97 (2008): 193; "Protecting Financial Markets: Lessons from the Subprime Mortgage Meltdown," *Minn. L. Rev.* 93 (2008): 373; "Disclosure's Failure in the Subprime Mortgage Crisis," *Utah. L. Rev.* (2008): 1109; "Understanding the Subprime Financial Crisis," *S. C. L. Rev.* 60 (2009): 549; "Conflicts and Financial Collapse: The Problem of Secondary-Management Agency Costs," *Yale J. on Reg.* 26 (Summer 2009); "Too Big To Fail? Recasting the Financial Safety Net," in *The Panic of 2008* (Geo. Wash. Univ. symposium book); "Regulating Complexity in Financial Markets," *Wash. U. L. Rev.* 87 (2010); and *Regulating Financial Systems*, forthcoming from Oxford University Press (co-authored with Kenneth Anderson).

CHAPTER 74

Modification of Mortgages in Bankruptcy

ADAM J. LEVITIN
Associate Professor of Law, Georgetown University Law Center*

The United States is in the midst of the most serious home foreclosure crisis since the Great Depression, when Franklin Delano Roosevelt spoke of "one-third of a nation ill-housed, ill-clad, ill-nourished."[1] Over a million homes entered foreclosure in 2007[2] and another 1.2 million foreclosures were started in the first half of 2008.[3] By the end of 2010, another 7 million homes are expected to enter foreclosure.[4] By the time the crisis has run its course, as many as one in five residential borrowers will have entered foreclosure.

Foreclosures create enormous deadweight economic loss. Lenders lose a large percentage of their loan value, families lose their homes, and negative externalities abound. Neighbors see their home values fall; local tax bases are eroded, requiring either higher taxes or reduced services; foreclosed properties become eyesores and loci of crime and fire; and communities' social bonds are ripped apart as families have to relocate.

Yet despite its inefficiency and social harm, there seems to be no sign of foreclosures abating. Voluntary private market solutions to stem foreclosures have failed to keep pace with new foreclosures, and official government programs, based on private market cooperation, have been abject failures.

At first blush, the private market's failure to resolve the foreclosure crisis is puzzling. When a single lender owns a loan, it will modify the loan so it can keep performing as long as the modified loan minus transaction costs performs at a level above what would be realized in net in foreclosure. If lenders lose 50 percent in foreclosure, why aren't they reducing interest rates and writing down principal balances and stretching out amortizations to make the loan perform at 51 percent of current net present value?

A major factor behind the private market's failure to address the foreclosure crisis is that for most mortgages, there are no longer "lenders" of which to speak. Most mortgage loans are no longer owned by a single entity; instead they are securitized, so that thousands of investors have a fractional interest in

---

*A version of this chapter originally appeared in *Harvard Law and Policy Review* 3, online, January 19, 2009.

a pool of loans. The vast majority (over 80 percent) of residential mortgages are securitized.

Securitization creates a variety of obstacles to efficient and socially constructive loan modifications instead of foreclosure. Unless the problems created by securitization are addressed, foreclosures are unlikely to subside until millions of Americans lose their homes. And as long as housing prices continue to slide because of market saturation and foreclosure sale externalities on neighboring properties, financial markets are unlikely to stabilize. This brief chapter argues that permitting modification of mortgages in bankruptcy is the only certain and realistic way to address the impediments to loan modification created by securitization. Bankruptcy modification is an immediately available form of foreclosure relief that has no cost to taxpayers, does not create moral hazard, can address both unaffordable and underwater mortgages, and provides an important future defense against systemic financial system risk.

Securitization is a key reason why the private market has been unable to solve the foreclosure crisis and what the best policy response would be. Although securitization transactions are very technical, complex deals, the core of the transaction is fairly simple. A financial institution owns a pool of loans that it either made itself or purchased. Rather than hold these loans on its books, it sells the pool of loans to a specially created entity, typically a trust. The trust pays for the loans by issuing bonds. Because the bonds are collateralized (backed) by the pool of loans held by the trust, they are called mortgage-backed securities (MBS).

The securitization trust is just a shell to hold the loans. Therefore, a third party, called a servicer, must be brought in to manage the loans. The servicer is supposed to manage the loans for the benefit of the MBS holders.

Securitization is a very effective method of funding lending operations, especially for real estate. It allows the originator of the loans to escape the key problems of real estate lending—lack of liquidity caused by asset-liability maturity mismatch for lenders who fund their lending through bank deposits and other short-term credit and lack of geographic diversification among its mortgages. Securitization also permits lenders to shift the credit risk of the loans' performance to capital market investors and pocket cash and fees now.

An unfortunate consequence of securitization is that it severely complicates loan workouts—the restructuring of defaulted and distressed loans to make them affordable for borrowers.[5] The institutional and contractual infrastructure of securitization that created the problems in the mortgage market by encouraging irresponsible and unsustainable lending is also a major impediment to resolving them.

The problems created by securitization may be reduced to three broad categories: contractual, practical, and economic. First, there are contractual limitations on servicers' ability to modify loans. Sometimes the modification is forbidden outright, sometimes only certain types of modifications are permitted, and sometimes the total number of loans that can be modified is capped. Additionally, servicers are frequently required to purchase any loans they modify at the face value outstanding.

Second, there are a range of practical difficulties. For example, servicers lack sufficient personnel to handle a large volume of customer contacts and the trained loan officers necessary to handle the volume of requested modifications.

Third, there are a number of economic disincentives for servicers to engage in loan modifications. Servicers are sometimes reluctant to engage in modifications for fear of suit by MBS holders who believe that modifications hurt their investments and favor other classes of MBS investors (tranche warfare).[6] And in many cases, foreclosure is often more profitable to servicers than loan modification. Servicers receive fixed rate compensation for a limited duration when a loan is modified, but get unmonitored cost-plus compensation in foreclosure. Servicers, therefore, are incentivized to foreclose rather than modify loans, even if modification is in the best interest of the MBS holders and the homeowners.[7]

Two possible general approaches emerge for dealing with the impediments securitization raises toward efficient loan workouts: carrots and sticks. The carrot approach is to offer lenders and servicers an incentive to engage in more modifications and more meaningful modifications than they otherwise would.

It is not clear, however, whether any positive incentives offered to servicers will be sufficient to change their behavior, in part because we do not know how servicers gauge factors like litigation or redefault risk. Moreover, when servicers are contractually forbidden from loan modification, no positive incentives, short of complete government indemnification, will change their behavior. While a carrot approach might be economically justifiable to overcome collective action problems, it has serious political and moral downsides. It would use taxpayer dollars to benefit a limited subgroup of citizens—defaulted homeowners, some of whom borrowed irresponsibly or even fraudulently; another limited subgroup of citizens—investors who stand to lose more in foreclosure than in a workable loan modification; and loan servicers, who as a fiduciary matter should be doing the modifications anyhow in many cases. It also creates a poor precedent that could encourage moral hazard, if lenders and homeowners alike believe that government will bail them out of the consequences of irresponsible contracts. A carrot approach rewards three groups that do not deserve assistance and does so at taxpayer expense.

On the other hand, the consequences of not offering incentives to encourage loan modifications, regardless of how distasteful the distributional consequences are and any moral hazard it might create, are potentially catastrophic.

Accordingly, it is necessary to also consider a stick approach to motivate loan modifications, as well as methods for simply removing servicers from the loan modification process. The most effective tool for doing so would be to amend the bankruptcy code[8] to permit consumers to modify all mortgage debt in bankruptcy.

Chapter 13 of the bankruptcy code permits qualified debtors to propose a three- or five-year repayment plan, during which time all collection actions against the debtor are stayed.[9] Secured debts and priority must be paid in full,[10] and the debtor's entire statutorily defined disposable income must go to paying unsecured creditors.[11] Upon successful completion of the plan, the consumer's remaining prebankruptcy debts are discharged.[12]

Within these parameters, however, the debtor has significant leeway to restructure or modify almost any type of debt. Interest rates can be reduced, amortization schedules changed, loan tenors increased, and negative equity erased. A consumer debtor can modify car loans, credit card debt, student loans, yacht loans, jet ski loans, snowmobile loans, airplane loans, computer loans, jewelry loans, and appliance loans, as well as investment property mortgages and vacation home mortgages. A consumer debtor can also modify a principal residence mortgage if it is a multifamily property. This means that a consumer who rents out the basement or the attic can modify the mortgage on a house in bankruptcy. The only type of debt that a consumer cannot modify in bankruptcy is debt on a single family principal residence.[13] Currently, single family principal residence mortgages must be repaid according to their original terms or the bankruptcy stay will be lifted and the mortgagee permitted to foreclose.

The policy behind the special protection for single family principal residences is that Congress believed in 1978 that if mortgage lenders were shielded from losses in bankruptcy, competition would ensure that lenders would pass on these gains to consumers in the form of lower mortgage costs, thereby encouraging home ownership.

Unfortunately, the economic assumption behind the special protection for single family principal residence mortgages in bankruptcy is incorrect. Bankruptcy modification risk is not reflected in primary mortgage pricing, secondary mortgage market pricing, or, most crucially, in private mortgage insurance pricing,[14] and there is no discernible effect on home ownership rates from the protection. The markets' indifference to bankruptcy modification risk is because lenders face smaller losses from bankruptcy modification than from foreclosure. They will therefore not price against bankruptcy modification. Indeed, bankruptcy is designed to give lenders at least as much as they would recover in foreclosure,[15] so there is no reason the market would price against bankruptcy modification.

Any attempt to mitigate foreclosures faces the challenges of quickly deciding which homeowners to help, addressing the twin problems of negative equity and affordability, avoiding moral hazard, and determining who will bear the cost of loan modifications. Bankruptcy modification helps solve these very issues and can do so more effectively and cheaper than any other proposed solution. Bankruptcy modification is also the only way to bypass the contractual, legal, practical, and economic problems created by securitization.

Permitting mortgage modification in Chapter 13 would provide an immediate solution to much of the current home foreclosure crisis. Bankruptcy courts are capable of immediately handling a large volume of filings, and the bankruptcy automatic stay[16] would function like a foreclosure moratorium until cases could be sorted through.

Bankruptcy modification would not yield a windfall to housing speculators or second home purchasers and would only help homeowners who could ultimately afford a reasonable mortgage. A mortgage loan modification in bankruptcy can occur only as part of a repayment plan. The automatic stay would likely be lifted on an investment property (or second home) before a plan could be confirmed. Accordingly, speculators and homeowners intent on keeping their second homes are unlikely to file for bankruptcy to seek mortgage modification in the first place.

To qualify for Chapter 13 bankruptcy, in which a loan can be modified, a homeowner must have a regular income,[17] and Chapter 13 plans must be feasible, given the debtor's means.[18] This does not mean that any modification is permissible; federal common law of bankruptcy requires that modified loans reflect a reasonable risk premium for the debtor,[19] and the bankruptcy code requires that a secured creditor receive at least the present value of its collateral.[20] Only a debtor who can afford a loan modified within these limits will be able to keep her home.

Permitting bankruptcy modification of primary home mortgages thus steers a true course between extending the right sort of relief and not extending it too broadly.

Nor would bankruptcy provide a windfall to homeowners in the event that property values appreciate in future years. While the homeowner would benefit from future appreciation, lenders have no reasonable expectation of this appreciation. Bankruptcy is supposed to, at the very least, give lenders what they would get in foreclosure, and when a home is sold in foreclosure, the lender gets cash for the value of the house, and does not receive any benefit from the property's future appreciation.

Bankruptcy modification would also provide a solution for both of the distinct mortgage crises—negative equity and payment shock. Bankruptcy modification would help negative equity homeowners by eliminating their negative equity position (cramdown), which would reduce their incentive to abandon the property.[21] Likewise, homeowners who are unable to afford their mortgage because of a rate reset could modify their loans to make monthly payments at a fixed and affordable level.

Permitting bankruptcy modification would not create moral hazard for lenders or debtors. Lenders will lose loan value. While they will generally do better than in foreclosure, and the loss is not because of bankruptcy *per se*, there is still a high price for lenders that will discourage reckless lending. And for homeowners, Chapter 13 bankruptcy is not a drive-by process. To receive a discharge in Chapter 13, a debtor must live on a court-supervised, means-tested budget for three or five years,[22] and fully repay certain debts, including allowed secured claims, domestic support obligations, and tax liabilities.[23] There are also limitations on how often a debtor may receive a bankruptcy discharge.[24] Nor would bankruptcy modification give homeowners a windfall. At best, a homeowner with negative equity would end up with zero equity, not positive equity. Given the large transaction costs to a sale, debtors are unlikely to sell their properties for anything beyond a *de minimis* profit absent a remarkable recovery of the housing market.

Finally, one of the greatest advantages of bankruptcy modification is that it has no cost for taxpayers. In an age of a trillion dollars in government bailouts, bankruptcy modification is a rare bargain. Bankruptcy courts are overstaffed relative to historical filing levels, and court fees cover the administrative costs of the process. Bankruptcy modification has no effect on the public fisc.

As the foreclosure crisis deepens, bankruptcy modification presents the best and least invasive method of stabilizing the housing market. It could also be combined with a carrot approach for potentially greater effect. Permitting modification of all mortgages in bankruptcy would not have prevented the irresponsible lending leading to the foreclosure crisis. Nor is it a magic bullet solution, but it is a quick, fair, efficient, and administrable response that would help stabilize the housing market and prevent the deadweight social and economic losses of foreclosure. Unlike any other proposed response, bankruptcy modification offers immediate relief, solves the market problems created by securitization, addresses both problems of payment reset shock and negative equity, screens out speculators, spreads burdens between borrowers and lenders, and avoids both the costs and moral hazard of a government bailout. Bankruptcy modification should be at the top of the financial reform and economic stabilization agenda.[25]

NOTES

1. Franklin D. Roosevelt, Second Inaugural Address (January 20, 1937).

2. RealtyTrac, Press Release, "U.S. Foreclosure Activity Increases 75 Percent in 2007," January 29, 2008.

3. Chris Mayer et al., "The Rise in Mortgage Defaults," *Journal of Economic Perspectives* 23 (1) (2009): 27–50.

4. Unsigned Editorial, "Not Much Relief," *New York Times*, July 5, 2009, WK7.

5. See Anna Gelpern and Adam J. Levitin, "Rewriting Frankenstein Contracts: Workout Prohibitions in Residential Mortgage-Backed Securities," 92 *S. Cal. L. Rev.* 1075 (2009).

6. See Kurt Eggert, "Comment on Michael A. Stegman et al.'s 'Preventive Servicing Is Good for Business and Affordable Homeownership Policy': What Prevents Loan Modifications?" 18 *Housing Policy Debate* 243 (2007): 290–291.

7. "Helping Families Save Their Homes: The Role of Bankruptcy Law," Hearing Before the Senate Committee on the Judiciary, 110th Cong. 17 (2008) (testimony of Adam J. Levitin).

8. 11 U.S.C. §§ 101 et seq. (2005).

9. 11 U.S.C. §§ 1301–1328 (Chapter 13 provisions generally); 11 U.S.C. § 109(e) (Chapter 13 eligibility requirements); 11 U.S.C. § 362 (2005) (stay).

10. 11 U.S.C. §§ 1325(a)(5) (secured creditors must receive present value of their collateral or the collateral itself under a plan); 1322(a)(2) (priority creditors must receive deferred cash payments for their full claim). Payment in full does not necessarily mean that cash payment.

11. 11 U.S.C. § 1325(b) (2005).

12. 11 U.S.C. § 1328(a) (2005). There are certain exceptions to discharge. Id.

13. 11 U.S.C. §§ 1123(b)(5); 1322(b)(2) (2005).

14. Adam J. Levitin, "Resolving the Foreclosure Crisis: Modification of Mortgages in Bankruptcy," 2009 *Wisc. L. Rev.* 565 (2009).

15. 11 U.S.C. § 1325(a)(5) (2005).

16. 11 U.S.C. § 362 (2005).

17. 11 U.S.C. § 109(e) (2005).

18. 11 U.S.C. § 1325(a)(6) (2005).

19. Till v. SCS Credit Corp., 541 U.S. 465 (2004).

20. 11 U.S.C. § 1325(a)(5) (2005). See Stan Leibowitz, "New Evidence on the Foreclosure Crisis," *Wall Street Journal*, July 3, 2009; Congressional Oversight Panel, "Foreclosure Crisis: Working Toward a Solution," March 2009 Oversight Report.

21. Chapter 13, *cramdown*, also known as *strip down* or *lien stripping* or *claim bifurcation*, is not to be confused with the unrelated but eponymous Chapter 11 cramdown, the confirmation of a plan of reorganization under 11 U.S.C. § 1129(b) (2005), over the objections of a dissenting class of creditors or interests.

22. 11 U.S.C. § 1325(b) (2005).

23. 11 U.S.C. §§ 1322(a); 1325(a)(5) (2005).

24. 11 U.S.C. §§ 727(a)(7)–(9); 1328(f)(2) (2005).

25. On April 30, 2009, the Senate voted 45–51 against an amendment to the Helping Families Save Their Homes Act of 2009, that would have provided for bankruptcy modification

of mortgages. *Senate Amendment 1014 to S. 896.* Legislation providing for bankruptcy modification of mortgages had previously passed the House of Representatives. On December 11, 2009, another attempt to advance mortgage modification legislation as part of an overall financial regulatory reform package was defeated in the House. *House Amendment 534 to H.R. 4173.* Whether this is the last word on bankruptcy modification remains to be seen as the mortgage crisis deepens and voluntary efforts, including the Obama administration's Making Home Affordable Program have limited success.

ABOUT THE AUTHOR

Adam J. Levitin is an associate professor of law at Georgetown University Law Center and Special Counsel to the Congressional Oversight Panel supervising the Toxic Asset Relief Program. He has previously been the Robert Zinman Resident Scholar at the American Bankruptcy Institute. He holds degrees from Harvard College, Columbia University, and Harvard Law School. Professor Levitin's research and writing focuses on the economics and regulation of consumer finance.

CHAPTER 75

The Shadow Bankruptcy System

JONATHAN C. LIPSON
Peter J. Liacouras Professor of Law at Temple University—James E. Beasley
School of Law*

WHO'S AFRAID OF CHAPTER 11?

Notwithstanding the recent surge in bankruptcy filings, the answer appears to be: lots of people.[1] But this is puzzling. Despite the fact that we face the most significant financial trauma since the Great Depression, Chapter 11 of the bankruptcy code,[2] the principal legal system for addressing business failure in the United States, is surprisingly underused, increasingly misused, or both.

Thus, in the most egregious examples—Bear Stearns, American International Group (AIG) and, until recently, the auto industry—the federal government chose billion-dollar taxpayer subsidies to keep companies out of Chapter 11. Even when it finally capitulated to bankruptcies for Chrysler and GM, the Obama administration exercised extraordinary control over the cases, speeding the companies through the process in record time. In other instances, Chapter 11 has provided cover for what are, in reality, fire sales of firms that could have been made viable.

Chapter 11 was enacted in 1978 to promote the restructuring of a troubled firm's debts through renegotiation, rather than liquidation or litigation, both of which are generally viewed as value-destroying propositions. Although the system certainly has its critics, its overarching goal is to preserve going concerns and jobs, thus (in theory) maximizing recoveries and preventing the collapse of otherwise viable businesses. Why, in the face of such serious financial distress, would we fear the very mechanism Congress created to prevent or remedy the problem of unserviceable debt?

One answer is the rise of the shadow bankruptcy system. *Shadow bankruptcy* describes the largely unregulated, nonbank financial institutions such as hedge funds, private equity funds, and investment banks that increasingly dominate Chapter 11 cases. Shadow bankruptcy adopts and adapts the term *shadow banking*, which has been used to characterize the same players and their questionable activities in the

---

larger financial system. While some may fear Chapter 11, those who operate in its shadows recognize that it can be a lucrative location.

As with shadow banking, shadow bankruptcy thrives in regulatory gaps and ambiguities. Rich and sophisticated private investors exploit interstices within Chapter 11, and between Chapter 11 and other laws that might check their behavior, such as the federal securities laws. Shadow bankruptcy thus promises to do for the Chapter 11 system what shadow banking did for the larger financial system: privatize gains and socialize losses.

SHADOW BANKRUPTCY: THE PROBLEMS

Chapter 11 of the United States bankruptcy code is, like many legal systems, in part an information system. Chapter 11 has often been characterized as a fishbowl because companies that seek to reorganize under it must disclose enormous amounts of information that might not otherwise be public, including about assets, liabilities, and operations. "The key . . . " to successful reorganization under Chapter 11, the U.S. Court of Appeals for the Second Circuit famously observed in the *Lionel* case, "is disclosure."[3]

But the transparency Congress envisioned for Chapter 11 was largely a one-way mirror: it forces debtors, and certain statutorily created entities such as official creditors' committees, to disclose certain information. But it also leaves opaque the identities and intentions of the debtors' many other stakeholders, regardless of their guile or sophistication. This asymmetry makes shadow bankruptcy possible, in three general ways.

Who Goes There?

The first problem presented by shadow bankruptcy is seemingly the simplest: Who are shadow bankruptcy players?

As a general matter, this is not a hard question to answer. As with shadow banking, shadow bankruptcy is dominated by scores, if not hundreds, of private investors such as hedge funds and private equity funds. In specific cases, however, it will often be difficult to know in real time who among many potential private investors has a claim against, or interest in, a particular debtor because these investors, and their investments in distressed firms, can usually remain covert.

It is well known that, unlike commercial banks and other regulated financial actors, hedge funds and private equity funds are subject to little public or governmental scrutiny. While the lack of public accountability may make them more nimble, it also enables them to mask or manipulate their identities so they can gain leverage in negotiations involving distressed firms.

Similarly, their transactions in direct or derivative claims against, or interests in, a debtor are subject to few meaningful disclosure obligations. Rather, a key feature of shadow bankruptcy is the explosive growth in the secondary market for distressed debt that has developed over the last 20 years. Although it is effectively a securities market, it is largely unregulated, requiring neither disclosure nor regulatory supervision in any meaningful sense.

Federal securities laws (in particular, Rule 13d-1) require those who would try to acquire voting control of a firm's equity securities to disclose this to the public in a timely fashion (i.e., so that other market participants can adjust by buying or selling in response to the information).[4] No comparable rule exists with respect to those who acquire control of a firm's debt, before or during bankruptcy.[5]

This is a problem, because once a firm is distressed, debt—not stock—tends to control the company. If a company enters bankruptcy, creditors' votes on a reorganization plan will usually determine the outcome. Even if a troubled firm doesn't enter bankruptcy—and it may not—the general dynamic of prebankruptcy workouts gives lenders far greater control than stockholders. This control tends to reflect their priority in the debtor's assets, which, in conventional terms, will come before that of stockholders.

The claims trading market thus renders unstable the identity of those who really control a debtor's fate. In egregious (albeit unlikely) cases, an investor may indeed remain in the shadows, not revealing his existence and position until late in the game. This investor, in the hope of being bought off, may emerge at the last minute to assert an objection to a plan to which others have agreed.

A more likely problem is simply that one can never be sure who one is dealing with, or that they will remain a stakeholder in a case. The rise of this unregulated secondary market means that private investors can (usually) trade out of a position if they are unhappy with the direction of negotiations. This, in turn, injects an inherent level of uncertainty into the negotiations that were meant to be central to reorganization.

A related problem involves fights over the few disclosure rules that do apply to private investors in this context. Bankruptcy Rule 2019 requires creditors who act in concert (but not through a formal, statutory creditors' committee) to disclose the existence of their ad hoc group.[6] Yet, private investors resist even this modest disclosure. Fights over the application of this rule can be costly, although of little benefit to debtors or their estates.

What Do They Want?

A second, and perhaps more problematic, feature of shadow bankruptcy involves the number and types of direct and derivative claims and interests private investors might hold, and the complex incentives that flow from such multiple holdings.

Historically, there was a tacit assumption that a debtor's stakeholders would generally hold only one type of claim or interest. Thus, a bank might hold senior secured debt, but not also shares of stock. An unsecured trade creditor or bondholder would probably not also hold preferred stock.

New transaction technologies and trading media—in particular hedge funds—have rendered this simple model archaic. Although multitranche holding can take many forms, the most problematic will involve combinations of senior debt and derivative (short) equity positions against the same debtor. A strategic investor holding that combination of rights may actually prefer the debtor's total collapse in a liquidation rather than a reorganization: the secured debt would pay no matter what (assuming sufficient collateral), and the equity short would pay because the shares had no value.

The breadth and depth of this problem are difficult to gauge, chiefly because the market for direct and derivative claims against, and interests in, distressed firms is largely unregulated. Confidential interviews with lawyers, bankers, and other system participants suggest that, at least anecdotally, it is a significant problem in large cases, manifest through distortions in the negotiations that typically accompany reorganization.

When Do They Want It? Timing Issues

A third problem with shadow bankruptcy involves private investors' time horizons, which are opaque and potentially problematic. Under the model Congress envisioned in the bankruptcy code, lenders could be cajoled into long-term investing through a reorganization plan that would satisfy claims with, among other things, new securities in the debtor (e.g., more debt, or equity, or both).

Today's private investors, however, may feel far greater pressure to cash out now, even if this destroys long-term value. Hedge funds, for example, may have obligations to their investors that require them to seek to cash out an investment in a distressed firm, even though the managers of the fund may recognize that there is greater long-term value by holding the position.

Similarly, a short-term investment may have been the strategy all along. Thus, in so-called loan-to-own transactions, a private investor will lend a distressed firm money and take a lien on its assets. Ostensibly, the loan will have been made to help save the firm. In fact, the loan may really have been a way for the lender to obtain control of the company's assets, which it can then strip and sell if the debtor is unable to repay the loan.

Boiled down, shadow bankruptcy creates three classes of costs, none of which appear to benefit reorganizing debtors or the reorganization system generally. First, the ability to mask identity and incentives, through rapid trading and multitranche holding, destabilizes, and therefore increases the cost of, the negotiations that are central to reorganization. Second, fights over identity impose deadweight litigation costs. Third, and most troubling, certain combinations of holdings will give private investors the perverse incentive to cause the debtor to fail disastrously, even if it might otherwise be a viable firm.

SOME SOLUTIONS—POSITIONAL DISCLOSURE

Describing the problems with shadow bankruptcy is easier than developing fair and efficient solutions. Already, the credit crisis has produced scores of proposals for regulatory reform. While many are laudable, and some will doubtless become law, few focus on the specific challenges of shadow bankruptcy.[7] This part briefly considers certain basic approaches available to regulators: forced disclosure and substantive control. Each has strengths and weaknesses in this context.

Positional Disclosure

To call the problem shadow bankruptcy is to imply that disclosure is the solution. Certainly, to the extent that trading distressed debt really creates a securities market, regulating it as such might make sense. Thus, gaps in current securities and bankruptcy laws that permit stealth acquisition of control through debt should be filled by amending, for example, Rule 13d-1 of the federal securities laws, or the bankruptcy code, or both.

The problem is that this is easier said than done. First, there are mechanical and logistical issues: Where would this disclosure occur, and who would pay for it? There are already web sites that track some distressed debt (*Markit*,[8] *Creditex*[9]). Those who use these sites—for example, shadow bankruptcy players—pay to receive the information they sell. These may be prototypes for broader disclosure systems that address problems created by shadow bankruptcy.

Second, and more difficult: when would disclosure obligations be triggered? It cannot simply be at the commencement of a bankruptcy case because, as noted, shadow bankruptcy problems can arise well before bankruptcy. While disclosure should be part of bankruptcy, in appropriate cases, it should begin before a case is commenced.

Third, what should be disclosed? Some features of current bankruptcy law require disclosure of the price paid for securities. It is not clear that this has much value to anyone, although it is easy to see why private investors may want to keep such information confidential. Moreover, while some direct holdings—debt or equity—may have to be disclosed under certain limited circumstances, nothing requires disclosure of derivative positions, for example, equity or debt shorts.

One solution would involve *positional disclosure*. This would require private investors to disclose all material rights against or affecting a distressed firm, whether held directly or derivatively, singly or in concert with others, in real time through online market portals.

Such a proposal embeds too many complex issues to discuss fully here. Some questions (and answers) would include the following:

What are material rights? Material rights would be any claims against or affecting a firm that enable the holder to affect control of the company or its restructuring. While this may be a difficult determination to make in some cases, in many cases it will be easy: any holding of equity or debt sufficient to replace management, foreclose major assets, or the like would be material. Similarly, holding an amount sufficient to block a vote to restructure any important loan agreements or a reorganization plan would be material for this purpose.

What is a distressed company? Shadow bankruptcy occurs before formal bankruptcy, so merely requiring disclosure during bankruptcy is inadequate. But defining *distress* can be difficult; *insolvency* is a notoriously slippery concept. One bright line test would require disclosure following any default under a material lending or similar financial agreement. There is evidence that tripping covenants of this sort tends to lead to secondary market trading in distressed debt. So, connecting disclosure to such events would help to shed light on who obtains control of the company through that market.

Disclose what? In addition to debt and equity, private investors who hold material positions against distressed firms should disclose derivative rights, such as short-sale rights. As discussed further on, disclosure alone may not be enough to correct for all problems with such holdings. But requiring disclosure of the full panoply of rights held by an investor would reveal complex incentives, reduce bluffing, and generally level the informational playing field.

How would this be enforced? A disclosure rule is only as effective as its enforcement mechanism. In the securities context, private investors often act as private attorneys general, suing directors, officers, and insiders for violations of securities laws. The value of these lawsuits is, however, open to question. Perhaps the penalty for failing to make appropriate disclosure in the distress context should be the disallowance of claims held by the nondisclosing private investor.

To be sure, there are many other issues to consider in developing such a regime. But positional disclosure could help to promote informational and market efficiency, which should, in turn, result in more transparent and (one hopes) welfare-maximizing decision making.

Substantive Control

Disclosure is not a perfect solution for many reasons, in particular because it will not solve what may be the most corrosive abuses of shadow bankruptcy, holding multiple positions that include certain types of short sales. As discussed earlier, when a firm is distressed, certain combinations of holdings create incentives to destroy value. Disclosure alone would not prevent the destruction. Indeed, it might have the opposite effect, accelerating the debtor's failure, because the combination would lead other stakeholders to lose faith in the debtor's ability to reorganize.

Thus, substantive limits on certain combinations of holdings may also be appropriate. In particular, senior secured claims and short positions affecting a distressed firm should not be enforceable when held in combination.

As with disclosure, substantive control is a tricky proposition, especially as to timing. While it may be easy enough to define distress (e.g., tripping a covenant under a major lending facility), what do we do about legacy holders? What if, for example, an investor acquired multiple positions while a firm was solvent only to see the firm slide into insolvency? Should that investor face the same penalties as the investor who acquires the same positions when a firm is distressed?

These and many other details would have to be worked out. The important point is to begin to think about concrete solutions to a problem that appears to undermine the reorganization process Congress believed it created when it enacted Chapter 11.

CONCLUSION

The problems presented by shadow bankruptcy are, in many respects, like those presented by shadow banking, only more so: Private actors arbitrage regulatory and market gaps for private gain. Within certain limits, there is nothing wrong with this. It is how people make money.

But, as we have recognized in the larger financial system, transaction technologies—the distressed debt market and hedge funds, for example—have now outrun the regulatory system. Some reregulation will be necessary.

It is difficult at this point to say exactly how to address the unique problems of shadow bankruptcy. This chapter has considered some solutions, and these may well be the best available.

At this point, it is enough to note that almost all proposals contemplating a new financial order fail to recognize the abuses of shadow bankruptcy. If nothing else, this needs to change.

NOTES

1. As Steven Rattner, President Obama's "car czar" said of auto manufacturers: "We were all afraid of bankruptcy." See Micheline Maynard and Michael J. de la Merced, "A Cliffhanger to See if a G.M. Turnaround Succeeds," *New York Times*, July 26, 2009, available at www.nytimes.com/2009/07/26/business/26gm.html?sq=gmbankruptcy&st=cse&scp=12&pagewanted=print, (quoting Steven Rattner, U.S. Department of the Treasury).

2. The current version of the bankruptcy code was originally enacted in 1978 (Bankruptcy Reform Act of 1978, Pub. L. No. 95-598, 92 Stat. 2549) and has been amended several times, including most recently in 2005, the Bankruptcy Abuse Prevention and Consumer Protection Act of 2005 (BAPCPA), Pub. L. No. 109-8, 119 Stat. 23 (to be codified as amended in scattered sections of 11, 18, 28 U.S.C.). Chapter 11 of the Bankruptcy Code appears in 11 U.S.C. §§ 1101–1174 (2006).

3. In re Lionel Corp., 722 F.2d 1063, 1070 (2d Cir. 1983) (citing "Report of the Committee on the Judiciary, House of Representatives, to accompany H.R. 8200," H. R. Rep. No. 95-595, 95th Cong. 1st Sess. (1977) at 226, U.S. Code Cong. and Admin. News, 1978, 5787, reprinted in *Collier on Bankruptcy* 2 (appendix) (15th ed., 1983)).

4. See 17 C.F.R. § 240. 13d-1 (2008). The rule provides as follows: "(a) Any person who, after acquiring directly or indirectly the beneficial ownership of any equity security of a class which is specified in paragraph (i) of this section, is directly or indirectly the beneficial owner of more than five percent of the class shall, within 10 days after the acquisition, file with the Commission, a statement containing the information required by Schedule 13D (§ 240.13d-101); (b)(1) A person who would otherwise be obligated under paragraph (a) of this section to file a statement on Schedule 13D (§ 240.13d-101) may, in lieu thereof, file with the Commission, a short-form statement on Schedule 13G (§ 240.13d-102)."

5. Federal Rule of Bankruptcy Procedure 3001 provides that "[i]f a claim other than one based on a publicly traded note, bond, or debenture has been transferred . . . after the proof of claim has been filed, evidence of the transfer shall be filed by the transferee." *Fed. R. Bankr.*, 3001(e). This rule is of little use in addressing shadow bankruptcy. It applies only if a bar date has been set for the filing of proofs of claim, which may not occur until late in a case. It is designed mainly to aid the process of making distributions on claims. It thus has little to do with disclosing changes of control through claims trading.

6. Fed. R. Bankr, 2019. The rule requires any entity that represents "more than one creditor or equity security holder" to file a statement setting forth, among other things, "the name and address of the creditor or equity security holder . . . the nature and amount of the claim or interest and the time of acquisition . . . the name or names of the entity or entities at whose instances, directly or indirectly, the employment was arranged . . . [and] the amounts of the claims or interests . . . the times when acquired, the amounts paid therefor, and any sales or other dispositions thereof."

7. One of the reports of the Congressional Oversight Panel appointed in connection with the Emergency Economic Stabilization Act (H.R. 1424, 110th Cong. (October 3, 2008) (as signed by the president)) has discussed certain aspects of the shadow bankruptcy system. See Congressional Oversight Panel, "Special Report on Regulatory Reform: Modernizing the American Financial Regulatory System" (2009), 29 (discussing bankruptcy procedures for nonbank financial institutions), available at http://cop.senate.gov/documents/cop-012909-report-regulatoryreform.pdf.

8. www.markit.com/en/products/products.page (accessed October 1, 2009).

9. www.creditex.com/ (accessed October 1, 2009).

ABOUT THE AUTHOR

Jonathan C. Lipson is the Peter J. Liacouras professor of law at Temple University–James E. Beasley School of Law. He teaches contracts, corporations, and commercial law courses, as well as a deal-based simulation. In 2007, he was a visiting professor of law at the University of Pennsylvania. Before that, he was an assistant (1999 to 2002) and associate (2002 to 2004) professor of law at the University of Baltimore. He is a graduate of the University of Wisconsin, where he earned his B.A., with honors (1986) & J.D. (1990) He was a note editor of the law review. Lipson writes, speaks, and blogs frequently on business law subjects, including corporate reorganization and the credit crisis. His work has appeared in, among others, the *UCLA Law Review,* the *Notre Dame Law Review,* the *Business Lawyer,* the *University of Southern California Law Review,* the *Washington University Law Review,* the *Minnesota Law Review,* and the *Wisconsin Law Review.*

CHAPTER 76

Reregulating Fannie Mae and Freddie Mac

DWIGHT M. JAFFEE
Willis Booth Professor of Finance and Real Estate at the Haas School of Business,
University of California, Berkeley*

I n September 2008, the U.S. Treasury and the Federal Housing Finance Agency used their regulatory power to place Fannie Mae and Freddie Mac, the two government-sponsored enterprises (GSEs), into a government-controlled conservatorship. The action was required because the GSEs faced a serious liquidity and solvency crisis as a result of losses on subprime mortgages. The goal of the conservatorship is to return the GSEs to a safe and sound condition, while allowing the firms to continue their mission in support of the U.S. mortgage market. At the same time, the Treasury initiated programs to infuse new capital into the GSEs and to purchase GSE debt and mortgage-backed securities (MBS), which in effect created government guarantees for these GSE obligations. The Federal Reserve also soon contributed additional resources to backstop GSE bonds and MBS.

From year-end 2007, a point at which the GSE subprime losses began to accumulate significantly, through the end of March 2009, the most recent data now available, the two GSEs have lost approximately $156 billion. Given that their combined year-end 2007 capital was about $71 billion, it is clear that without the government's capital infusion of $85 billion, the two GSEs would have been insolvent. It is equally clear that the GSEs will need significantly more government capital support before the subprime crisis ends. In addition, the Treasury and the Federal Reserve have invested a combined $821 billion into GSE bonds and MBS to support the markets for these securities. This already comprises more than 15 percent of the total GSE mortgage holdings and guarantees of about $5.4 trillion as of March 2009. The two GSEs are now, in effect, wards of the state, and this status can be expected to continue at least until losses from the subprime mortgage crisis end and the financial and mortgage markets return to a more normal situation.

Sooner or later, however, the Congress and the Administration will have to determine a new and proper structure for the long-term status and regulation of the two GSEs, and many observers believe it is useful to begin considering the

---

*This chapter is in part an updated and summarized version of material that originally appeared in Jaffee (2009).

possibilities sooner. Federal Reserve chairman Ben Bernanke (2008), speaking in the fall of 2008 at a University of California, Berkeley, subprime mortgage symposium stated:

> *Our task now is to begin thinking about how best to reestablish a link between homebuyers and capital markets in a way that addresses the weaknesses of the old system. In light of the central role that the GSEs played, and still play, any such analysis must pay particular attention to how those institutions should evolve.*

Just recently, the Senate Banking Committee held hearings in June 2009 on the issue, which no doubt will be followed by many such inquiries, with the ultimate goal to determine how to reregulate the GSE.

The goal of this chapter is to provide a framework that the Congress and the Administration can use to help them determine the proper and feasible future role for the GSEs as entities in support of the U.S. mortgage market.

A FRAMEWORK FOR THE REREGULATION OF FANNIE MAE AND FREDDIE MAC

I suggest a three-step process to determine the proper regulatory structure for the GSEs once they are released from their conservatorship:

1. Identify the key mortgage market function the GSE could continue to serve
2. Evaluate the alternative mechanisms, public or private, that may serve this function
3. Determine the best available structure to serve this function

The key GSE mortgage market function is well identified in the mission statement of their charter, namely to promote the stability and liquidity of the secondary market for mortgages. *Secondary market* refers here to transferring mortgage loans from the local lenders who created the loans—"Main Street" for short—to investors in the national or even international financial markets—"Wall Street" for short. This is an important function because local lenders often have insufficient financial resources to hold the loans they create. In earlier periods, before a secondary market system existed, mortgage lending would often come to an abrupt stop when the local banks exhausted their available loanable funds. Today, most observers would agree that the transfer of sound mortgage loans from Main Street to Wall Street remains a critical function that must be served, whether by the GSEs or some other mechanism.

Three primary securitization channels exist for transferring residential mortgage loans from Main Street to Wall street.[1] The oldest channel is a combination of the government's Federal Housing Administration (FHA) mortgage insurance program and the Government National Mortgage Association (GNMA) program for securitizing mortgages. Both these programs reside inside the federal government's Housing and Urban Development (HUD) agency. The FHA was created in 1934 as a government-based mortgage insurance program and has now operated for more than 75 years, with generally sound results. GNMA was created in 1968, as the first entity to create and distribute MBS, with the express goal to securitize—transfer from Main Street to Wall Street—pools of FHA and VA mortgages.[2] GNMA has now reached its fortieth anniversary, and it has operated with systematically outstanding results.

The second channel for transferring residential mortgages from Main Street to Wall Street was created by the GSEs during the 1970s, based on the already successful GNMA MBS structure. The GSE MBS, however, used only so-called conventional mortgages, meaning that, unlike the FHA and VA mortgages that formed the basis for GNMA MBS, the conventional mortgages receive no government guarantee. Instead, the GSEs offered their own corporate guarantee to make timely payment of interest and principal on all their debt and MBS obligations. The market accepted the GSE guarantee with confidence because it presumed that the U.S. Treasury would backstop this guarantee if necessary. This implicit guarantee was indeed tested with the GSE conservatorship in September 2008, at which time the Treasury, as anticipated, in effect created an explicit guarantee for all GSE debt and MBS securities.

The third channel, developed during the 1980s, is described as private label securitization (PLS). PLS followed the lead of GNMA and the GSEs, but the underlying mortgages were generally larger and often riskier than those used by the GSEs. Furthermore, the firms issuing the PLS had no link to the U.S. government and no guarantee, implicit or explicit, from the U.S. Treasury. To induce investors to purchase these admittedly riskier MBS, a structured security was created, in which the overall pool of mortgages was broken into a series of parts or *tranche,* with the most junior tranche taking the first-risk positions with respect to any mortgage defaults. This allowed the most senior tranche to obtain AAA credit ratings, close to the level available on GNMA and GSE MBS. As an additional benefit, all of the PLS provided yields distinctly above those available on the GNMA and GSE MBS. Through the 1990s, the private label MBS performed extremely well. However, with the advent of subprime mortgage lending—most of which were issued as PLS—the PLS performance collapsed. Indeed, PLS MBS can be considered the "ground zero" of the subprime mortgage crisis.

As of this writing in July 2009, the secondary mortgage market is operating as follows:

- The FHA/GNMA channel for government-insured mortgages is strong and active
- The GSE channel for MBS securitization remains active, but this is based entirely on the capital infusions and security purchases by the Treasury and the Fed
- The PLS channel for MBS is almost entirely inactive, as falling house prices have left investors with very little tolerance for the risks that are embedded in these securities

In the short run, the current FHA-GNMA and GSE-Treasury-Fed channels appear adequate to fund the relatively low mortgage market activity level that we are observing. Ultimately, however, the mortgage market will return to a normal state, and it will be necessary to decide how best to reregulate Fannie Mae and Freddie Mac. This is the topic to which I now turn.

THE POLITICS OF REREGULATING OF FANNIE MAE AND FREDDIE MAC

Regulatory reform of Fannie Mae and Freddie Mac has been a continuing quest for most of the firms' history, and with a notable, even remarkable, lack of success. The primary case for regulatory reform has always been based on the systemic risks that the firms pose for the U.S. mortgage and financial markets. But in the absence of an actual crisis, the firms always deterred any serious action; indeed the lobbying power of the two GSEs in this regard is legendary. It is now clear, of course, that the fears of a systemic meltdown were all too accurate and that the GSE model—combining a public mission with an implicit guarantee and a profit-maximizing strategy—is untenable. Indeed, the GSEs failed because, in the search for higher profits and a larger market share, they found a means to purchase PLS just before the subprime mortgage market collapsed. Nevertheless, Fannie and Freddie's mission to support the mortgage market retains strong congressional and public support. It is in this context that I now consider the main existing proposals to reform and reregulate the GSEs.

PROPOSALS FOR THE REREGULATION OF FANNIE MAE AND FREDDIE MAC

Although there are many variations on the themes, there are three basic alternative formats for the reregulation of the GSEs. They range from a completely private market solution at one extreme to a government solution at the opposite extreme, with a rebuilt GSE model in the middle. I describe and evaluate these in turn.

Private Market Mechanisms for the GSE Functions

As discussed earlier, private label securitization (PLS) evolved starting in the 1980s, and by 2005 and 2006, PLS represented more than half of the entire U.S. MBS market. When the U.S. mortgage market returns to a normal state, it is possible the PLS mechanism could once again take on a primary role. Of course, market investors are likely to insist that the underlying mortgages be low risk, with an underwriting quality maintained at the level that was standard before the creation and growth of subprime lending. In this context, Fannie Mae and Freddie Mac themselves could be released from their conservatorship as private market firms, keeping whatever remained of their financial net worth and intellectual capital. It would be essential, however, that both the firms and the federal government explicitly disavow any continuing status for the two firms as government-sponsored enterprises. There is a prototype for such action: by 2004, another GSE, Sallie Mae, specializing in securitizing student loans, successfully gave up its GSE status and became a private sector firm with no continuing links to the federal government.

The primary issue with respect to total privatization is whether the U.S. mortgage market could operate at an acceptable level by combining the traditional FHA-GNMA government-insured sector and a newly rejuvenated PLS sector. One new positive factor is that other regulatory actions may force bank lenders to hold more of their originated mortgages in their own portfolios, thus reducing the role of mortgage-backed securitization.[3] On the other hand, mortgage interest rates would almost surely rise, since financial market investors would have to be compensated for taking on the default risk that necessarily arises in the absence of government mortgage guarantees.

A Public Utility Model for Reformed GSEs

An alternative structure for the mortgage market would recreate the GSEs, but with substantial new regulatory controls. The restrictions could include tougher safety and soundness standards, a maximum rate of return for shareholders, restrictions on executive compensation, and so on. An essential feature would be that the government explicitly guarantees all the new GSE obligations, with the GSEs paying appropriate fees to compensate taxpayers for the risks they are therefore taking. An explicit government guarantee of the new GSE obligations is essential because it is unlikely investors would otherwise accept GSE securities, and as we have learned, an implicit guarantee is actually more costly than an explicit guarantee, since an implicit guarantee delays action to stop or limit the costs of a failure.

The flaw—and I believe the fatal flaw—in applying a public utility model to Fannie Mae and Freddie Mac is that it does not resolve the inherent incompatibility of creating a private firm with a public mission. True public utilities—electric companies, for example—have no such conflict since their private and public responsibilities basically coincide. True public utility regulation is used only to limit the high prices the utility firms might otherwise charge because of their natural monopolies. For the GSEs, in contrast, we have learned from first-hand experience that their private incentives are to expand their size and risk taking as much as possible, and these incentives ultimately dominate any public mission. Of course, it is possible that a draconian regulatory regime of complete safety might be enforced, but what would be the purpose? If all risk taking is to be ruled out in the interests of safety and soundness, then you have eliminated the very benefits that arise with private firms. In this case, you might as well serve the basic functions of insuring and securitizing prime mortgages directly within a government agency. We next turn to this option.

A Government Mortgage Plan for Middle-Income Borrowers

The last possibility is to bring the critical mortgage functions of the GSEs directly into a federal government agency. This is not as extreme as it might sound. For one thing, Fannie Mae spent its first 34 years in this status, and it was transformed into a government-sponsored enterprise only to create the cosmetic appearance of a more balanced federal budget. Since the government has already spent more than $85 billion to bail out the GSEs, and more is on its way, this has turned out to be a very expensive facelift. For another, the government's FHA program for insuring mortgages for lower-income borrowers has worked remarkably well for over 75 years; for further discussion, see Jaffee and Quigley (2008). If the government can carry out a successful mortgage plan for lower-income borrowers, then surely it can do so for middle-income borrowers.[4]

The program I propose would charge borrowers an actuarially based insurance fee in exactly the same manner as the FHA. In fact, with its middle-income clientele, the insurance premiums would be much lower, approaching the same

0.20 percent (20 basis points) annually that Fannie and Freddie have historically charged for their guarantees. This assumes the program would require the same 20 percent down payment loans that have been the core of Fannie and Freddie's conforming loans. The program could be expanded to include lower down payment loans, however—say 10 percent—as long as credit standards are maintained and the proper risk-based insurance premiums are charged. In this regard, it could be efficient to create the new program as a division within the FHA. The FHA could then offer a range of mortgage insurance products depending on the creditworthiness of the borrower and the down payment provided. Furthermore, since these mortgages would carry a government guarantee, they could be included in the same GNMA MBS program that already functions with the highest efficiency for FHA and VA mortgages. Finally, the benefit of access to low-cost capital market funding would be passed back directly and fully to borrowers in the form of the lowest possible mortgage interest rates.

Private sector mortgage originators and mortgage investors would welcome the new government program for the same reason they systematically endorse the FHA and Ginnie Mae programs. Furthermore, private sector firms would continue to originate and private sector investors would continue to hold the mortgages, so private sector activity would be enhanced, not crowded out, by the new program. Similarly, private market securitizers of jumbo mortgages— above the GSE size limits for conforming mortgages—would continue to operate as they do currently. In brief, a new government plan for middle-income borrowers would simply and efficiently replace the existing Fannie and Freddie programs, while avoiding the systemic risks that will unavoidably arise with any recreation of the GSEs.

LOW-INCOME HOUSING INCENTIVES

The last issue of concern is how to replace the support to lower-income borrowers that has been legislatively required of the GSEs. This congressional mandate arose under the mistaken premise that aid to lower-income families from the GSEs was basically available at no cost—it certainly was perceived to be easier to tax the GSEs than to obtain congressional appropriations to increase the budget of the government's Housing and Urban Development (HUD) agency. As the bailout costs have demonstrated, however, the GSEs' support for lower-income borrowers was actually far from free. Furthermore, most academic studies have indicated very modest benefits actually arose from these requirements, Congress should now recognize that specific appropriations to HUD represent a much more effective means to help low-income homebuyers.

NOTES

1. To be clear, there are other less important but still significant channels. The most important of these are the facilities provided through the Federal Home Loan Bank System.

2. Veterans Administration mortgages are a second government insurance plan, with the objective of providing accessible mortgage funding to U.S. military veterans.

3. The recent U.S. Treasury (2009) proposals for regulatory reform would require that banks hold at least 5 percent of any mortgage pools they securitize.

4. James Lockhart (2009), the current director of the Federal Housing Finance Agency, in testifying before Congress on June 3, 2009, argues that the government cannot run an efficient insurance plan. But he fails to mention that the standard FHA mortgage insurance programs have required no government appropriations, whereas the government has already paid out $85 billion and invested close to a $1 trillion to bail out the GSEs under his watch.

REFERENCES

Bernanke, B. 2008. *The future of mortgage finance in the United States.* Speech to the University of California, Berkeley/UCLA Symposium: The mortgage meltdown, the economy, and public policy, October 31.

Jaffee, D. 2009. Reforming Fannie and Freddie. *Regulation* 32 (4): 2–7.

Jaffee, D., and J. Quigley. 2007. *Housing subsidies and homeowners: What role for government-sponsored enterprises?* Washington, DC: Brookings-Wharton Papers on Urban Economics.

Lockhart, J. 2009. *Statement before the Housing Financial Services Committee,* June 3.

U.S. Treasury Department. 2009. *Financial regulatory reform,* June 17.

ABOUT THE AUTHOR

Dwight M. Jaffee is the Willis Booth professor of finance, and real estate at the Haas School of Business, University of California, Berkeley, where he has taught since 1991, and is co-chair of the Fisher Center for Real Estate and Urban Economics. He has served in advisory roles for the World Bank, the Federal Reserve System, the Office of Federal Housing Enterprise Oversight, and the U.S. Department of Housing and Urban Development. His primary areas of research are real estate finance and insurance. Recent research in the real estate field concerns the subprime mortgage crisis, U.S. mortgage market policy, and the role of the government sponsored enterprises. Recent research in the insurance field concerns why private firms do not offer catastrophe insurance, the government's role in catastrophe insurance, and the structure of monoline insurers. Overall, Professor Jaffee has authored six books and more than 100 articles.

CHAPTER 77

Would Greater Regulation of Hedge Funds Reduce Systemic Risk?

MICHAEL R. KING
Senior Economist at the Bank for International Settlements in Basel, Switzerland

PHILIPP MAIER
Bank of Canada, Assistant Chief in the International Department*

T he credit crisis in global financial markets since the summer of 2007 has created a number of casualties, most notably three of the top five U.S. investment banks. At the same time, it is striking how little hedge funds have contributed to the global crisis, despite a widely held view before the crisis that these highly leveraged institutions posed a key systemic risk to the global financial system. This chapter takes a critical look at proposals for greater direct regulation of hedge funds and examines alternatives such as indirect regulation and market discipline.

We argue that direct regulation of hedge funds does not appear feasible and may increase moral hazard. It may also reduce the willingness of hedge funds to act as liquidity providers in times of crisis. Indirect regulation through prime brokers, in combination with market discipline, has led hedge funds to limit their leverage and manage their risk exposures. Institutional investors are demanding greater transparency, while investment by hedge fund managers in their own fund aligns their interests with investors and ensures that managers react quickly to market fluctuations.

---

*The views expressed in this chapter are those of the authors and should not be attributed to either the Bank for International Settlements or the Bank of Canada. All errors and omissions are our own. This article is based on M. King and P. Maier (2009) "Hedge funds and financial stability: Regulating prime brokers will mitigate systemic risks." *Journal of Financial Stability* 5 (3): 283–297.

Michael R. King, senior economist, Monetary and Economic Department, Bank for International Settlements, Centralbahnplatz 2, CH-4002 Basel, Switzerland. Philipp Maier, assistant chief, International Department, Bank of Canada, 234 Wellington, Ottawa, Ontario, Canada K1A 0G9.

STYLIZED FACTS ON HEDGE FUNDS

A typical hedge fund is a private investment company with aggressive trading strategies to earn positive returns in all market environments. It invests the capital of wealthy individuals and institutional investors. Increasingly, the principals that manage the fund invest their own funds alongside investors. A high minimum investment requirement, restrictions on withdrawals, and the limited participation of sophisticated investors allow hedge funds to remain unregistered and leave managers free to pursue proprietary investment strategies that would be imprudent for a more widely held mutual fund.

Global assets under management by the hedge fund sector grew by a compounded 29 percent per year from 1998 to 2007, with over $2.25 trillion in capital managed by an estimated 11,000 hedge funds (Exhibit 77.1). U.S. hedge fund advisers manage about $1.5 trillion of global hedge fund assets. The hedge fund sector is concentrated, however, with the largest 100 hedge funds accounting for 75 percent of total industry assets in 2007. The most recent survey by *Institutional Investor* magazine showed that there were 38 hedge funds managing assets greater than $10 billion at year-end 2007, of which the five largest are shown in Exhibit 77.2. While the hedge fund sector is large, the assets under management are relatively small, compared to funds managed by other institutional investors, or the assets of the 1,000 largest banks (Exhibit 77.2).

Compared to other large financial actors, the rate of hedge fund failures is much higher. Fewer than 15 percent of hedge funds last longer than six years, while 60 percent disappear within three years. According to Hedge Fund Research, 1,471 hedge funds were liquidated in 2008, an increase of over 70 percent from the previous record of 848 liquidations set in 2005. These liquidations have occurred without unduly stressing the global financial system.

Exhibit 77.1   Relative Size of Hedge Funds (US$ trillions)

Year	Hedge Funds[a]	Pension Funds[a]	Mutual Funds[a]	Insurance Comps[a]	Global Assets of the Largest 1000 Banks	Hedge Funds as % of Total[b]
1998	0.22	13.57	9.40	10.40	33.2	0.3%
1999	0.32	17.26	11.40	11.50	35.5	0.4%
2000	0.41	16.07	11.87	10.10	36.7	0.5%
2001	0.56	15.52	11.65	11.50	37.9	0.7%
2002	0.59	14.63	11.32	10.40	39.6	0.8%
2003	0.80	18.34	14.05	13.90	43.9	0.9%
2004	1.00	20.77	16.16	15.00	52.4	0.9%
2005	1.40	22.80	17.77	16.70	60.5	1.2%
2006	1.75	25.97	21.82	17.39	63.8	1.3%
2007[c]	2.25	28.57	26.20	19.13	74.2	1.5%

[a]Global funds under management, estimated at year-end 2007.
[b]This figure does not take account the use of leverage.
[c]Pension fund and insurance assets under management are estimates based on 10% growth versus 2006.
Sources: International Financial Services London; Investment Company Institute.

Exhibit 77.2 Largest Hedge Funds at Year-End 2007

Hedge Fund	Firm Capital (US$ billions)	Strategy
1. JPMorgan Asset Management	44.7	Multi-strategy
2. Bridgewater Associates	36.0	Directional
3. Farallon Capital Management	36.0	Event-driven
4. Renaissance Technologies Corp	33.3	Market neutral
5. Och-Ziff Capital Management	33.2	Multi-strategy

Source: Institutional Investor magazine.

There are two channels through which the hedge fund sector may propagate risk to the financial system. A direct channel occurs when a collapse of one or more hedge funds leads to forced liquidations of their positions at fire sale prices. The impact on asset prices may be amplified through the use of leverage (including derivatives). If hedge fund positions are large relative to the liquidity of the asset, a disorderly unwinding could generate substantial losses to counterparties. This direct channel motivated the 1998 rescue of Long-Term Capital Management. In the indirect channel, forced liquidation of hedge fund positions might exacerbate market volatility and reduce liquidity in other markets. Examples of herding were seen in the 1987 stock market crash and the attacks on European exchange rates in 1992 and Asian exchange rate pegs in 1997.

Rising globalization, financial innovation, and deregulation over the past decade have raised the potential for system risk. Financial globalization implies that shocks are more quickly transmitted across markets (the global credit crisis since summer 2008 provides an example). Financial innovation has increased the complexity of financial assets and information asymmetries, increasing uncertainty. Deregulation has allowed unregulated actors to expand in key markets, with competitive dynamics and poor incentives leading to lower credit standards and weaker monitoring by financial intermediaries.

Currently, the front line of defense against a hedge fund collapse is its prime broker. Prime brokerage refers to a package of services that are sold to hedge funds that include global custody, clearing, margin lending, securities borrowing, financing, execution, portfolio reporting, and operational support. Prime brokers provide a centralized securities clearing facility, handle a hedge fund's collateral, and may provide financing to facilitate trades. As such, they have some knowledge of a hedge fund's positions. The prime brokerage industry is very concentrated, with the top three (10) brokers servicing 58 percent (84 percent) of hedge fund assets under management at year-end 2007. Prime brokers protect themselves against the possibility of a hedge fund collapse through risk management practices such as holding collateral with suitable haircuts.

REGULATION OF HEDGE FUNDS

In what follows, we review the extent to which hedge funds are regulated, and examine the arguments for direct and indirect regulation.

WHO REGULATES HEDGE FUNDS?

The level of regulation and supervision is low for hedge funds. In theory, hedge funds may be subject to securities regulations at three levels—the fund itself, the fund manager, and the distribution of the fund. In practice, hedge funds are often exempt. The primary regulator is based on the hedge fund's legal domicile. In 2006, 55 percent of hedge funds were incorporated offshore, implying minimum regulation and taxation. Fund managers, however, are typically based in financial centers such as London or New York, but are not required to be registered with local supervisors. According to *Institutional Investor* magazine, 78 of the largest 100 hedge funds in 2007 were based in the United States. Distributors of hedge fund products must be registered in Canada and Europe, but can avoid registration in the United States.

U.S.-based hedge funds are not regulated, but U.S. regulators target hedge fund advisers, who must typically be registered as investment advisers. The SEC regulates an estimated 1,991 hedge fund advisers, including 49 of the largest U.S. hedge fund advisers (about one-third of the hedge funds' assets under management in the United States). The SEC, for example, brought 113 cases against hedge funds from October 2001 to June 2007 for misappropriation of funds, insider trading, falsified credentials, and misrepresentation of past returns (GAO 2008).

In practice, many of the largest hedge funds are subject to oversight through their trading activities. Hedge funds trading on U.S.-regulated futures and options markets are supervised by the Commodities Futures Trading Commission (CFTC). In 2008, the CFTC reported that 29 advisers of the 78 largest U.S. hedge funds were registered and are required to report their futures and options positions above a designated threshold. Also, they are required to post margin with futures commission merchants (who themselves must maintain minimum capital requirements). Thus, a significant proportion of hedge funds are registered with the CFTC. The same is true for jurisdictions such as the United Kingdom and Japan.

The Case for More Direct Regulation of Hedge Funds

The case for direct regulation is based on a view of market failure, in which risk management does not prevent excessive risk taking.[1] Proponents of direct regulation make several proposals. A first approach is to require mandatory registration of hedge fund managers, or the distributors of their products. In this view, hedge funds should be held to the same standard as mutual funds, because their investments are increasingly becoming available to lower net worth individuals through a fund of funds.[2] Registration of hedge fund advisers is compulsory in much of Europe and Canada, and efforts are under way in the United States and Japan. Such regulation would increase investor protection, but it does not address systemic issues.

A second approach is to require more disclosure to prime brokers, who are supervised by banking regulators. Increased position transparency would allow prime brokers to limit excessive hedge fund leverage, and mitigate systemic risk through counterparty risk management. But position transparency raises the concern that prime brokers or their proprietary trading desks may use this information to their advantage.

The alternative approach is to provide more transparency on hedge fund positions or credit exposures through the creation of a centralized global registry for all hedge funds. Such a registry could be used to identify concentrations of counterparty credit risk or concentrations in trading strategies (crowded trades) that might lead to herding and contagion. Danielsson et al. (2005) argue that this approach is infeasible, because of time lags to analyze this complex information. Also, it is not clear how supervisors would communicate crowDed trades, if they could be identified. Lastly, to avoid regulation, hedge funds can relocate their trading operations to a less-regulated offshore domicile.

The Case Against Direct Regulation of Hedge Funds

Direct regulation may have unintended consequences, such as moral hazard, that is, a tendency to act less carefully when insulated from risk. In the context of hedge funds, the concern is that increased regulation may lead individual hedge funds to take on more risk, or to invest less in managing risk. Take the proposal for a central registry of positions to detect crowded trades. A hedge fund manager in this situation might trade in the false belief that supervisors will alert them, once strategies become hazardous. Note also that regulation should be designed to mitigate the risk to the financial system, but it should not prevent hedge funds from failing per se. Hedge fund managers and investors need to be concerned about failure to provide incentives to monitor risks, which benefits the system as a whole. Instead, the goal of regulation should be to prevent a hedge fund failure from putting *other* market participants at risk.

A second unintended consequence relates to liquidity provision. By taking contrarian bets, hedge funds provide liquidity on the opposite side of the market, reducing volatility and limiting sharp movements in asset prices. If a hedge fund discloses its positions to its prime broker or supervisors, other trading counterparties may trade to the detriment of the hedge fund. Hence, greater position transparency may make hedge funds unwilling to take contrarian positions, potentially reducing liquidity.

Lastly, the ability of regulation to reduce systemic risk has come under question during the current financial crisis, as supervision of commercial and investment banks did not avoid the build-up of risks and failure of systemically important institutions. In the United States, for example, the SEC established the Consolidated Supervised Entity program in June 2004 to monitor the five independent U.S. investment banks (GAO 2008). Despite regular consultations, three of the five U.S. investment banks have either gone bankrupt or been taken over, while the remaining two converted to bank holding companies to access emergency liquidity provisions. In the United Kingdom, the government had to nationalize Northern Rock and Bradford and Bingley and to recapitalize HBOS, Lloyds TSB, and the Royal Bank of Scotland—some of the largest institutions supervised by the U.K. authorities.

Indirect Regulation of Hedge Funds

The alternative to regulating hedge funds directly are a combination of indirect regulation and effective market discipline. Supervisors regulate hedge funds indirectly by monitoring the collateral and risk management practices of prime brokers, who are the main counterparties of hedge funds. This approach has the advantage of focusing on the institutions and channels through which systemic risk propagates. It is also practical from a regulatory perspective, since these financial institutions are already supervised.

Effective market discipline requires that creditors, counterparties, and investors obtain sufficient information to assess risk profiles and to limit excessive leverage, increase disclosure, and mitigate systemic risk through effective counterparty risk management. The limited impact on financial markets of the liquidation of hedge funds over the past eight years provides some support of this view. If indirect regulation and market discipline are effective in reducing the potential systemic risk from hedge funds, these approaches should result in reduced leverage, improved funding liquidity, increased disclosure, and improved counterparty risk management practices.

Anecdotal reports and surveys suggest that leverage at hedge funds has declined. BIS estimates of effective total leverage—taking into account the embedded leverage in hedge fund positions—show a decline over time (McGuire and Tsatsaronis 2008). Similar surveys from Merrill Lynch report a decline in leverage over the course of 2007 and 2008.

Although hedge fund disclosure and transparency are difficult to measure, there are signs of improvement. Standard & Poor's and Moody's, for example, have announced plans to publish operational risk ratings for hedge funds. In March 2007, the industry association for hedge funds, the Alternative Investment Management Association (AIMA), released recommendations on practices for hedge fund transparency, especially the valuation of portfolios. In sum, as investments in hedge funds have increased, market pressure for more transparency has increased as well.

Evidence for better hedge fund counterparty risk management is anecdotal, but supportive. Amaranth Advisors' $6.6 billion collapse in 2005 did not threaten its counterparties, or the broader financial system, as Amaranth's accounts were fully margined. Its losses on unregulated exchanges did not affect regulated exchanges.

As regards funding liquidity, hedge funds are reducing exposure to illiquidity by seeking more stable funding, such as longer investor lock-in periods, longer redemption notice periods, and debt issues (Garbaravicius and Dierick 2005). Some hedge funds are also negotiating credit lines for liquidity purposes, while others have raised capital through equity or by restricting redemptions. Although these steps may be available only to the largest hedge funds, these are also the most systematically important.

CONCLUSION

Hedge fund failures are relatively frequent, but over the past decade these failures have not posed a risk to the financial system. Counterparty risk management practices such as the use of collateral and haircuts limit the exposure of trading counterparties, notably prime brokers. From a financial stability perspective, hedge fund failures remind investors of the risks they are taking, and limit moral hazard. Indirect regulation by prime brokers and market discipline by creditors, counterparties, and investors appear to have reduced hedge fund leverage, improved funding liquidity, increased disclosure, and improved counterparty risk management practices.

Direct regulation of hedge funds may not be feasible and is not likely to be effective, because of the delays with reporting and processing the information. Also, hedge funds can relocate offshore to avoid regulation. Position reporting may encourage moral hazard, while greater transparency on positions could inadvertently lead to a decline in liquidity, making markets more volatile and increasing financial instability in times of stress.

NOTES

1. Note that proposals concerning regulation of the hedge fund industry are very different from proposals to regulate *markets* in which hedge funds operate. Following the collapse of Amaranth Advisors, for example, there were calls for tighter regulation of OTC energy markets.

2. The SEC attempted to require hedge fund managers with 15 or more individual customers and $25 million or greater under management to register as investment advisers by 2006, but this requirement was overturned by the U.S. Court of Appeals. More than 700 hedge funds deregistered subsequent to this ruling.

REFERENCES

Danielsson, J., A. Taylor, and J.-P. Zigrand. 2005. Highwaymen or heroes: Should hedge funds be regulated? *Journal of Financial Stability* 1: 522–543.

GAO. 2008. *Hedge Funds*. United States Government Accountability Office report to congressional requesters No. GAO-08-200.

Garbaravicius, T., and F. Dierick. 2005. *Hedge funds and their implications for financial stability*. Frankfurt, Germany: European Central Bank, Occasional Paper 34.

McGuire, P., and K. Tsatsaronis. 2008. Estimating hedge fund leverage. Basel, Switzerland: Bank for International Settlements, Working Paper 260.

ABOUT THE AUTHORS

Michael R. King is currently a senior economist at the Bank for International Settlements in Basel, Switzerland, where he works on financial stability issues and foreign exchange markets. He joined the BIS after seven years at the Bank of Canada, where he worked in the financial markets and international departments, providing input to monetary policy. He holds an M.Sc. and a Ph.D. from the London School of Economics, and a bachelor's degree from Queen's University. He also holds the chartered financial analyst designation. Before his Ph.D., King worked in investment banking and trading for six years in New York, London, and Zurich. He also worked for a hedge fund start-up for one year in London. His research has appeared in the *Review of Financial Studies, Journal of Banking and Finance, Journal of Financial Stability, Journal of Applied Corporate Finance, International Finance, Central Banking,* and the *Canadian Investment Review.*

Philipp Maier holds a Ph.D. in economics from the University of Groningen in the Netherlands. He has worked at the Central Bank of the Netherlands and is currently at the Bank of Canada, where he is assistant chief in the international department. He has published in refereed journals, focusing on central bank–related issues. He also wrote *Political Pressure, Rhetoric and Monetary Policy: Lessons for the European Central Bank*, published by Edward Elgar.

CHAPTER 78

Regulating Credit Default Swaps

HOUMAN B. SHADAB
Associate Professor of Law, New York Law School

On June 17, 2009, the United States Treasury Department proposed major changes to the way U.S. financial markets are regulated with the hope of having Congress enact changes by the end of the year. A key component of the regulatory reform proposals are wide-ranging regulation of the over-the-counter (OTC) derivatives markets, including a particular type of OTC derivative known as a credit default swap (CDS). Motivating the reform proposals are the large and unmanageable mortgage-related risks that certain banks and insurance companies took with CDSs. However, given the general role played by CDSs leading up to and throughout the financial crisis, and also the reforms being undertaken by market participants under the supervision of the Federal Reserve Bank of New York, the full extent of the regulatory reform proposals are likely unnecessary to achieve greater transparency and stability in the CDS market.

BACKGROUND

Whenever a lender makes a loan, the lender always runs the risk of not being paid back in whole, in part, or on time. This risk is known as credit risk. A CDS is a contract involving two parties that trade credit risk: a credit protection buyer and a credit protection seller. Each party to a CDS trade is a counterparty to the other. A CDS always references one or more debt obligations, such as a loan made by a bank or the bonds of a public company. Under the terms of a CDS contract, a protection buyer must make periodic payments to the protection seller, and will often do so on a quarterly basis for a period of five years. The protection buyer will typically pay a higher fee in proportion to the degree of credit risk of the debt obligation referenced by the CDS. In return, the protection seller must pay the protection buyer if a credit event takes place. A credit event is a negative development relating to the specified reference obligation, and can include a default or bonds being downgraded by a credit ratings agency. If a referenced loan defaults, the protection seller will pay the protection buyer the amount of the loan the lender is unable to recover. In this sense, a CDS is a type of insurance for credit risk that can help banks and other companies better manage their credit risks. For example, a bank that decides it made too many loans to a specific company or sector of the economy can purchase CDS protection on those loans.

CDS contracts are not traded on centralized exchanges like stocks, but rather between bank-owned dealers and CDS end users. The primary participants in the CDS market are dealers, banks that use CDS in their loan portfolios, hedge funds, and insurance companies. Most CDS trading takes place between dealers. The two most common types of CDS products are single-name and indexes. A single-name CDS references the bonds of a single company or nation. A CDS index is similar in structure to well-known stock indexes such as the Dow Jones Industrial Average and S&P 500. Instead of tracking the price of a group of stocks that make up a stock index, however, a CDS index tracks the prices of a group of component CDSs. A popular CDS index is operated by Markit and comprises 125 underlying CDSs referencing North American investment-grade companies. A payment by the protection seller on the index must be made if any one of the component companies experiences a credit event.

A notable feature of the CDS market was its rapid growth and size after the turn of the century. According to surveys conducted by the International Swaps and Derivatives Association (ISDA) and the Bank for International Settlements (BIS), the notional value of CDS contracts grew from approximately $632 billion in 2001 and reached a high of $57.8 trillion by the end of 2007.[1] The notional value of a CDS contract is the amount of the debt obligation referenced by the contract. For example, a CDS contract that references a $1 million loan has a notional amount of $1 million. Importantly, the notional amount of a CDS is typically far greater than the actual risk created by a CDS transaction. Sellers of CDS protection also often buy CDS protection on the same reference obligation. This has the result of offsetting, or canceling out, their risk exposures. Also, because even loans that are defaulted on will have some value, the payment obligation of protection sellers is reduced by the amount of the debt obligation the lender is able to recover.

As of June 2008, the maximum potential losses to CDS market participants was estimated to be approximately 5.5 percent of the notional value of the CDS market, or $3.2 trillion.[2] CDS market participants also typically post collateral over the course of the CDS contract, which helps to ensure that protection sellers can fulfill their CDS obligations once a credit event takes place. When Lehman Brothers declared bankruptcy in September 2008, sellers of CDS protection on Lehman bonds were only required to pay protection buyers 7.2 percent ($5.2 billion) of the notional value of CDS contracts referencing Lehman because many participants had offsetting trades, and collateral was used to manage the risk from Lehman's CDS payout. Notably, the low payout by CDS sellers took place despite Lehman bonds being worth only about eight cents on the dollar.

CDS REGULATION AND OVERSIGHT

Like other derivatives contracts not traded on centralized and regulated exchanges, CDSs are primarily governed by the contractual relationship between the parties.

Although CDS counterparties are free to tailor the terms of their agreement to their liking, standardized terms for CDS agreements are provided by ISDA. Because of the Commodity Futures Modernization Act of 2000, CDSs are not regulated at the federal level as securities or as futures. CDSs are also not regulated under state law as either insurance products or gambling contracts.

Federal regulation and oversight do apply to the CDS market and its participants, however. CDSs are categorized as *security-based swaps* under federal law. The Securities and Exchange Commission (SEC), the nation's regulator of the securities markets, has jurisdiction to police CDS transactions for fraud, insider trading, and market manipulation. In May of 2009, the SEC brought the first enforcement action for insider trading using CDSs. Bank regulators also have the ability to examine banks' use of CDS for the purpose of assessing the safety and soundness of banks and for broader concerns about the stability of the banking system. The Office of the Comptroller of the Currency publishes a quarterly report on commercial banks' use of derivatives. The Federal Reserve Bank of New York has also helped to coordinate improvements in the CDS market. For example, to decrease operational risks, the New York Fed in 2005 assisted the major derivatives dealers in agreeing to require sellers of CDSs to obtain the consent of their counterparties before transferring the contract to another party.

TREASURY DEPARTMENT DERIVATIVES REFORM PROPOSALS

On June 17, 2009, the U.S. Treasury Department released a comprehensive financial regulatory reform proposal that would affect the way CDSs and other non-exchange-traded derivatives are regulated and used by market participants. Goals sought by the reform proposal are to increase the transparency, integrity, and stability of the market for CDSs and other OTC derivatives.

To achieve these goals, the Treasury Department asked Congress to amend the federal laws for securities and derivatives to require that all standardized CDS trades be cleared by a central counterparty. A central counterparty is an institution that, once a CDS trade is entered into, stands in the middle of the transaction by becoming the buyer to the seller and the seller to buyer. This way, the risk of either party to a CDS trade not fulfilling its obligations is taken on by the central counterparty. Because a central counterparty has its own capital, imposes margin requirements on its members, can distribute losses among its members, and manages risk multilaterally, it has the potential to prevent a domino effect of losses from occurring if a party to a CDS or even a CDS dealer collapses. The proposal seeks to subject CDS central counterparties and others with large exposures to risk from OTC derivatives to prudential supervision by regulators and conservative capital reserve requirements.

A central counterparty would improve transparency in that it would maintain information on the prices and parties to CDS trades and, under the regulations sought by the proposal, disclose that information on an aggregate basis to the public and in a more detailed fashion only to regulators. Nonstandardized CDS trades would be required to be reported to a centralized trade repository, which would make similar disclosures. The proposal also seeks to empower regulators with greater authority to obtain information from OTC derivatives users and police the derivatives markets for fraud, market manipulation, and other abuses.

THE ROLE OF CREDIT DEFAULT SWAPS IN THE FINANCIAL CRISIS

Motivating the Treasury Department's reform proposals is the enormous and un-known level of risk that the misuse of CDSs allowed to be concentrated in the financial system. In particular, CDS referencing mortgage-related debt securities and purchased by banking institutions failed to fully protect the banks against the losses they believed they were protected against. Some municipal bond insurance companies that sold CDS protection on mortgage-related securities were down-graded by credit ratings agencies in June of 2008 for taking too much risk as CDS protection sellers. Banks that had bought protection from the insurers also had to record losses to reflect the insurers' decreased ability to meet their obligations as CDS protection sellers. And by 2005, an American International Group (AIG) sub-sidiary had sold so much CDS protection on mortgage-related securities owned largely by banks that it was unable to meet the nearly $40 billion in collateral obli-gations it was required to post in the fall of 2008 as the value of those securities decreased. The collateral obligations ultimately caused the Federal Reserve of New York and the U.S. Treasury Department to coordinate a series of bailouts for AIG that benefited AIG's CDS counterparties.

CDSs allowed more mortgage-related risks to be spread throughout the econ-omy than otherwise would have been the case. CDSs were often grouped together and repackaged into securities that allowed investors to gain synthetic exposure to mortgage-related securities when they were unable to locate and purchase the actual underlying securities. The use of CDSs by banks also likely led them to un-derwrite more mortgage-related securities because banks believed they were able to reduce risks related to such activities with CDSs. Nonetheless, banks earned substantial fees from underwriting mortgage-related securities. Banks therefore would have sold mortgage-related securities even without being able to purchase CDS protection and often did so by retaining much of the mortgage-related se-curity risks themselves. Overall, the growth of CDS referencing mortgage-related securities was more of an effect rather than a cause of the rapid growth in mortgage-related securitization.

Large and unmanageable losses arising from CDS obligations did not occur throughout the CDS market. Rather, they were limited to the small corner of the CDS market that referenced mortgage-related securities and were sold by the unregulated affiliates or subsidiaries of insurance companies. AIG's entire CDS portfolio, for instance, accounted for less than 1 percent of the CDS market. Large and unmanageable losses from CDSs do not primarily reflect inherent weaknesses in the risk management and infrastructure of the CDS market but were primarily a reflection of the widespread underpricing of the risk of mortgage-related securities—a phenomenon distinct from the growth and use of CDSs. Had it not been for the rapid growth of mortgage-related securitization after the turn of the century, it is unlikely that CDSs would have posed any noticeable problem to the financial system.

Importantly, not all CDS users fundamentally misused the instruments. Relatively less-regulated hedge funds, for example, did not disrupt the financial system with their CDS trades and, unlike AIG, used substantial amounts of collateral to manage CDS risk. Similarly, bank-owned derivatives dealers did not suffer unmanageable losses due to their CDS-trading activities. This is in part because dealers manage risks with collateral and, as part of their business model, buy and sell CDSs to reduce their risk from any particular counterparty.

EVALUATING CDS REGULATORY REFORM

Regulated institutions like banks and insurance companies should be prevented by additional regulation and more effective oversight from taking on too much risk with CDSs, particularly when written on structured debt securities that are difficult to value. Bank regulators already have the authority to limit banks' use of derivatives, including those sold by AIG's subsidiary since AIG was regulated as a bank thrift at the companywide level.

Recent efforts to increase the stability and transparency of derivatives markets by market participants acting under supervision of the Federal Reserve Bank of New York call into question the extent to which regulatory reform is necessary because the efforts meet many of the specific goals sought by reform proposals. In the spring of 2009, CDS market participants agreed to increase the standardization of CDS contracts, which would make them easier to clear through a central counterparty. The ICE Trust clearinghouse began in March of 2009 to centrally clear certain CDS indexes. Other central counterparties will likely also be established, and central clearing will likely spread to other standardized CDSs such as single-name products. On June 2, 2009, the major OTC derivatives dealers, some hedge funds, and other market participants agreed to report customized CDS agreements to a central trade depository, to expand direct access to central counterparties to end users, and take other actions to improve the overall infrastructure of the derivatives market. Transparency in the CDS market has also improved. Since January 2009, the Depository Trust Clearing Corporation has made publicly available aggregate information on CDS trades on a weekly basis. Data provider Markit has also made freely available pricing and other information on CDS transactions.

Any additional regulation should take into account these improvements and also the complexity of the derivatives markets so as not to reduce the benefits of CDSs. During the financial crisis, CDSs helped companies to manage risk. Despite an extremely large number and size of corporate bankruptcies beginning in the fall of 2008, buyers of credit protection were generally able to collect on the protection for which they paid. The prices of CDS contracts also give investors unique information about the credit risks associated with various companies or particular debt instruments. In this way, CDSs make debt markets more transparent and help companies make better investment decisions because they are able to utilize CDS prices as a tool to measure credit risk. CDS prices in particular provided an early warning signal of the problems in the market for mortgage-related securities and led some banks and investors to begin to curtail their exposures to such risk before the market collapsed.

Finally, market participants and regulators should also be aware that the use of central counterparties may not fully address counterparty risk, and could even increase risk. Without sufficient capitalization and strong risk management, a central counterparty could become a new source of overconcentrated CDS risk.

NOTES

1. David Mengle, "Credit Derivatives: An Overview," *Economic Review* 7 (2007); Bank for International Settlements (BIS), "OTC Derivatives Market Activity in the Second Half of 2008," May 2009, 7.

2. Bank for International Settlements, Monetary and Economic Department, "OTC Derivatives Market Activity in the First Half of 2008," November 2008, 4–6, Table 1.

REFERENCES

Duffie, D., and H. Zhu. 2009. *Does a central clearing counterparty reduce counterparty risk?* Stanford, CA: Rock Center for Corporate Governance, Working Paper, 46.

Gibson, M. S. 2007. *Credit derivatives and risk management.* Washington, DC: Federal Reserve Board, Finance and Economics Discussion Series, Divisions of Research and Statistics and Monetary Affairs

Government Accountability Office. 2009. *Systemic risk: Regulatory oversight and recent initiatives to address risk posed by credit default swaps.*

International Monetary Fund. 2006. *Global financial stability report, market developments and issues.* Washington, DC: International Monetary Fund.

Markit. 2009. *The CDS big bang: Understanding the changes to the global CDS contract and North American Conventions.*

Mengle, D. 2007. Credit derivatives: An overview. *Economic Review* 92 (4): 1–24.

Pirrong, C. 2009. *The economics of clearing in derivatives markets: Netting, asymmetric information, and the sharing of default risks through a central counterparty.* Working Paper.

Senior Supervisors Group. 2009. Observations on management of recent credit default swap credit events. Washington, DC: Securities and Exchange Commission, *News Digest,* March 9.

Shadab, H. B. 2009. Guilty by association? Regulating credit default swaps. *Entrepreneurial Business Law Journal* 4 (2).

U.S. Treasury Department. 2009. Financial regulatory reform, a new foundation: Rebuilding financial supervision and regulation. Washington, DC: U.S. Treasury Department.

ABOUT THE AUTHOR

Houman B. Shadab is an associate professor of law at New York Law School whose research focuses on financial law and regulation, and hedge funds and derivatives, in particular. He received his in B.A. from the University of California at Berkeley (economics, 1998) and his J.D. from the University of Southern California School of Law (2002). Shadab is the author of several academic articles and other publications, including *The Law and Economics of Hedge Funds: Financial Innovation and Investor Protection* and *Innovation and Corporate Governance: The Impact of Sarbanes-Oxley*. He is currently working on a chapter on hedge fund lending to be published in a forthcoming book from Oxford University Press.

Index